Bioentrepreneurship and Transferring Technology Into Product Development

Swati Agarwal
Banasthali University, India

Sonu Kumari
Banasthali University, India

Suphiya Khan
Banasthali University, India

A volume in the Advances in Business Strategy and Competitive Advantage (ABSCA) Book Series

IGI Global
PUBLISHER of TIMELY KNOWLEDGE

Published in the United States of America by
IGI Global
Business Science Reference (an imprint of IGI Global)
701 E. Chocolate Avenue
Hershey PA, USA 17033
Tel: 717-533-8845
Fax: 717-533-8661
E-mail: cust@igi-global.com
Web site: http://www.igi-global.com

Library of Congress Cataloging-in-Publication Data

Names: Agarwal, Swati, 1987- editor. | Kumari, Sonu, 1991- editor. | Khan, Suphiya, 1976- editor.
Title: Bioentrepreneurship and transferring technology into product development / Swati Agarwal, Sonu Kumari, and Suphiya Khan, editors.
Description: Hershey : Business Science Reference, 2021. | Includes bibliographical references and index. | Summary: "This book investigates the key role of biological sciences in entrepreneurship (Bioentrepreneurship) that fuels technology transformation into commercial products, focusing on the various factors, including creating business plan, acquiring funding, and adopting a good business model"-- Provided by publisher.
Identifiers: LCCN 2021000722 (print) | LCCN 2021000723 (ebook) | ISBN 9781799874119 (hardcover) | ISBN 9781799874126 (paperback) | ISBN 9781799874133 (ebook)
Subjects: LCSH: Biotechnology industries. | Entrepreneurship. | Technological innovations--Management. | New products.
Classification: LCC HD9999.B442 B5436 2021 (print) | LCC HD9999.B442 (ebook) | DDC 660.6068/5--dc23
LC record available at https://lccn.loc.gov/2021000722
LC ebook record available at https://lccn.loc.gov/2021000723

This book is published in the IGI Global book series Advances in Business Strategy and Competitive Advantage (ABSCA) (ISSN: 2327-3429; eISSN: 2327-3437)

British Cataloguing in Publication Data
A Cataloguing in Publication record for this book is available from the British Library.

For electronic access to this publication, please contact: eresources@igi-global.com.

Advances in Business Strategy and Competitive Advantage (ABSCA) Book Series

Patricia Ordóñez de Pablos
Universidad de Oviedo, Spain

ISSN:2327-3429
EISSN:2327-3437

Mission

Business entities are constantly seeking new ways through which to gain advantage over their competitors and strengthen their position within the business environment. With competition at an all-time high due to technological advancements allowing for competition on a global scale, firms continue to seek new ways through which to improve and strengthen their business processes, procedures, and profitability.

The **Advances in Business Strategy and Competitive Advantage (ABSCA) Book Series** is a timely series responding to the high demand for state-of-the-art research on how business strategies are created, implemented and re-designed to meet the demands of globalized competitive markets. With a focus on local and global challenges, business opportunities and the needs of society, the **ABSCA** encourages scientific discourse on doing business and managing information technologies for the creation of sustainable competitive advantage.

Coverage

- Tacit Knowledge
- Globalization
- Value Chain
- Cost Leadership Strategy
- Business Models
- Innovation Strategy
- Small and Medium Enterprises
- Entrepreneurship & Innovation
- Strategic Management
- Competitive Strategy

IGI Global is currently accepting manuscripts for publication within this series. To submit a proposal for a volume in this series, please contact our Acquisition Editors at Acquisitions@igi-global.com or visit: http://www.igi-global.com/publish/.

The Advances in Business Strategy and Competitive Advantage (ABSCA) Book Series (ISSN 2327-3429) is published by IGI Global, 701 E. Chocolate Avenue, Hershey, PA 17033-1240, USA, www.igi-global.com. This series is composed of titles available for purchase individually; each title is edited to be contextually exclusive from any other title within the series. For pricing and ordering information please visit http://www.igi-global.com/book-series/advances-business-strategy-competitive-advantage/73672. Postmaster: Send all address changes to above address.

Titles in this Series

For a list of additional titles in this series, please visit: www.igi-global.com/book-series

Handbook of Research on Disruptive Innovation and Digital Transformation in Asia
Patricia Ordóñez de Pablos (The University of Oviedo, Spain) Xi Zhang (Tianjin University, China) and Mohammad Nabil Almunawar (School of Business and Economics, University of Brunei Darussalam, Brunei)
Business Science Reference • © 2021 • 661pp • H/C (ISBN: 9781799864776) • US $295.00

Disruptive Technology and Digital Transformation for Business and Government
Kamaljeet Sandhu (University of New England, Australia)
Business Science Reference • © 2021 • 410pp • H/C (ISBN: 9781799885832) • US $225.00

Handbook of Research on Entrepreneurship, Innovation, Sustainability, and ICTs in the Post-COVID-19 Era
Luisa Cagica Carvalho (Polytechnic Institute of Setubal, Portugal & CEFAGE, University of Évora, Portugal) Leonilde Reis (Polytechnic Institute of Setubal, Portugal) and Clara Silveira (Polytechnic Institute of Guarda, Portugal)
Business Science Reference • © 2021 • 451pp • H/C (ISBN: 9781799867760) • US $295.00

Disruptive Technologies and Innovative Strategies for Organizational Success
Nilsa I. Elias (Western Governors University, USA) Terry M. Walker (University of Louisiana, USA) and Robin Walker (Metropolitan State University, USA)
Business Science Reference • © 2021 • 315pp • H/C (ISBN: 9781799837909) • US $225.00

Cases on Digital Strategies and Management Issues in Modern Organizations
José Duarte Santos (Instituto Superior Politecnico, Spain)
Business Science Reference • © 2021 • 300pp • H/C (ISBN: 9781799816300) • US $195.00

Advanced Perspectives on Global Industry Transitions and Business Opportunities
Fanny Saruchera (University of the Witwatersrand, South Africa)
Business Science Reference • © 2021 • 352pp • H/C (ISBN: 9781799843030) • US $225.00

Competitive Drivers for Improving Future Business Performance
Carlos Martins (Lusíada University of Porto, Portugal) and Paula Rodrigues (Lusíada University of Porto, Portugal)
Business Science Reference • © 2021 • 267pp • H/C (ISBN: 9781799818434) • US $225.00

Entrepreneurial Innovation for Securing Long-Term Growth in a Short-Term Economy
Jorge Gamez-Gutierrez (Universidad de la Costa, Colombia) and Jose Manuel Saiz-Alvarez (Universidad Católica de Santiago de Guayaquil, Ecuador & Universidad Autónoma de Manizales, Colombia & CEIEF-Universidad de Santiago de Chile, Chile)
Business Science Reference • © 2021 • 256pp • H/C (ISBN: 9781799835684) • US $215.00

IGI Global
PUBLISHER of TIMELY KNOWLEDGE

701 East Chocolate Avenue, Hershey, PA 17033, USA
Tel: 717-533-8845 x100 • Fax: 717-533-8661
E-Mail: cust@igi-global.com • www.igi-global.com

Editorial Advisory Board

Table of Contents

Detailed Table of Contents

Ever since the onset of civilization, humans have been continuously improvising and innovating on different aspects to make their livelihood more sustainable. This innovation reached a steep uptrend trajectory during the industrial revolution, and with the discovery of DNA and emergence of genetic engineering, our civilization entered a new era of biotechnology where desirable traits can be easily engineered into an organism to obtain a desired product. However, it was soon realized that in order to make the product reachable to the masses, integration of science, biology, and technology with business is of the utmost importance. This resulted in the genesis of the concept of bioentrepreneurship. Presently, it is a rapidly emerging discipline connecting two large domains, namely biotechnology and business. This chapter overviews bioentrepreneurship. It highlights the various requirements and measures implemented to start a bioentrepreneurship programme.

Since the age of civilization, humans have been using products based on biotechnology, and these products have become part of our daily lives. The entrepreneur is the driving force of any organization. Biotechnology entrepreneurship is the alliance of two disciplines, business and science. Biotechnology-related business is aimed to commercialize the bio-products as well as enhance the research to benefit the human race. Firstly, bio-entrepreneurship has the potential to develop new techniques to protect the environment from diseases, fuel production, feed the hungry, and various other product preparations. Hence, these products provide new and better ways with minimum side effects to detect, cure, and prevent harmful diseases. Secondly, these bio-based products including biofuels and renewable chemicals are targeted to grow from approximately $203.3 billion in 2015 to $487 billion by 2024.

The word bioentrepreneurship and entrepreneurship share the similarity in the fact that they must have a great and an innovative idea behind starting a business setup and to raise an investment. Also, they both must have a great idea about marketing of the related products and managing their start-up. If we talk about the difference, the common difference is the sector or field in which a startup is carrying on. In simple words, entrepreneurship is the process of launching any new business based on an innovative idea. On the other hand, bioentrepreneurship is the process that is started in the field of science (i.e., biotechnology). Nowadays, bio-industrialization is the key to being a modern and developed country, and this is the only reason bioentrepreneurs are highly in demand. Thus, this chapter will help you to understand the pillars to setup a startup based on biotechnology that has an excellent future perspective not only for entrepreneurs but also for the nation.

From the beginning of humanity, people have relied on the usage of biotech-based products. Bioentrepreneurship or BioE is the drive of knowledge and innovation, traveling from academic world to industrial platform. In contrast to enterprise, bio-enterprise is the amalgamation of bioscience with business by the application of biological concepts or scientific entities for the benefit and the creation of a corporation. It is a strictly monitored industry because of involved scientific risks, time demands, and ethical clearance, as well as requiring huge capital. Every successful entrepreneur showcases certain traits that they have inculcated or relied on to build their business. These traits are not mere skills, but are the qualities that contribute in becoming an ideal bio-entrepreneur. The chapter deals with striking features of bio-entrepreneurs that have made them a conglomerate of global standard and play an essential role in making them leaders.

Small-scale product development is not for everyone, and it needs a high level of discipline, dedication, persistence, and creativity as well as a lot of work. Before setting up a small-scale business, one needs seed money, physical location of the business venture, construction work, equipment/machinery maintenance, management skills, accounting skills, and last but not least, marketing skills. For the development of any area, the small-scale industry development is very important mainly for the income source of the community and for employment opportunities. On the basis of study, four strategies that are used for the development of small-scale industries were found, and these strategies are 1) promotion and development of institutional, business groups, and cooperatives; 2) determination brands; 3) strategy competition with low cost and product development; 4) to improve final access market orientation strategies. On the basis of analysis of these strategies, they are prioritized, and the first priority is strategy.

Vijay Laxmi, Banasthali University, India
Mary Shobha Rani Inala, Sri Devaraj Urs Academy of Higher Education and Research, India

Intellectual property rights (IPRs) denote distinct types of conceptions of the mind for which property rights are documented. Basic and clinical scientists at research institutions often make ideas that have health benefits if developed and applied to the improvement of human wellbeing. Therefore, learning the basics of intellectual property protection and obtaining professional guidance in its management avoids such losses with a minimal burden of confidentiality on the investigator by using any of the mechanisms (patents, trademarks, copyrights, trade secrets, and know-how agreements). The probability of scientific findings becoming accessible for public benefit is low without suitable intellectual property protection. This reality is particularly true in the life sciences and biotechnology arenas comparative to other areas of science, and hence, it is a prerequisite to know about intellectual property rights and their significance for better development.

Sunita Rao, Dr. B. Lal Institute of Biotechnology, India
Avinash Gupta, ICFAI Business School, The ICFAI University, India
Gajra Garg, Mahatma Jyoti Rao Phoole University, Jaipur, India

The current image of biotechnology in developed countries is practiced at an adequate grade, but the greater part of developing countries is still miserable and far from its future vision. This current gap needs to be filled in some aspects via bioentreprneurship, which is fundamental for the development of the economy, provides a source of welfare with economic growth, promising to bring the social well-being and environment friendliness or all-over sustainable development. As a result, it can generate revenue in a community business, and henceforth, it must be very worthy for biotechnology. Developing nations can indeed turn out to be emerging players in the modern bioeconomy. The advancements in emerging stages towards this issue ought to be an acceptable solution that would be viable in long run. The relevance of bioentrepreneurship to sustainability is conceptualized in the connection with current emerging aspects in developing nations.

Archana Bhaskar, Guru Ghasidas Vishwavidyalaya, Bilaspur, India

Bioentrepreneurship is a biological entity related to sciences that creates, builds, and acquires profit to establish a business. At present, the biggest challenges for bioentrepreneurs is to stand out from their competitors. There are various function that bioentrepreneurs apply to their businesses to be unique, such as marketing. Marketing includes product development, distribution methods, sales, advertising, etc. Despite of all these efforts, entrepreneurs are still facing a problem to sell products as the consumer preference and need is changing day by day. Therefore, to succeed in business today, it is very important to develop new strategies to change the existing products in order to provide good service to the consumers and retain the business. The process taken by the company to develop the existing market is known as market development. This chapter will focus on market development and selling the product according to consumer needs.

Entrepreneurship correlates to the entrepreneur who is creative, has risk taking capability, promotes capital formation, and seeks out investment opportunities in the market. In the National Institute for Transforming India Aayog's 5th Governing Council, the Government of India (GoI) aims to take the Indian economy to USD 5 trillion by 2024. Thus, India needs to significantly increase employment opportunities for which GoI is promoting skill development through biotechnology entrepreneurship and investing appreciably with a special focus on R&D to develop India into a world class bio-manufacturing hub. The DBT in collaboration with BIRAC has implemented flagship schemes such as 'Make in India' and 'Start up India'. The major objectives of this chapter are to lay out (1) the role of GoI to empower startups for growth through innovation and design, (2) a detailed overview of the various schemes offered by GoI for promoting skill development and innovation through bio-entrepreneurship, (3) major challenges faced by the government for implementation of schemes.

Bioentrepreneurship attracts entrepreneurs who can contribute by making scientific methods and products available to the society. Funding, infrastructure, skills, and commercialization capabilities influence the process of bioentrepreneurship. India with its large and highly efficient pool of the scientific community has lot to offer to the global market. Indian research is confined to theoretical research due to a missing link that unites research and commercialization and strict intellectual property regime. To overcome such challenges, the Indian government has taken initiatives to make the working environment friendly, innovative, efficient, and easy for foreign companies and investors by amending existing policies and facilities India's biotechnology industry. Foreign investment in India's biotechnology industry has led to an exponential increase from US$530 million in 2003 to US$4.3 billion in 2013. Foreign investment has played a big role in helping India's flourishing biotechnology industry.

The agricultural biotechnology sector shares a common scientific foundation with the therapeutic biotechnology sector, including similar characteristics of a lengthy time to market for emerging products.

But the challenges, goals, and opportunities for agricultural applications of biotechnology provide a very different context for innovation and entrepreneurs. Innovation means something novel, which can be a process or a way of doing something novel. Biotechnology entrepreneurship is summing all integrated activities that can create, develop, and finally, commercialize a biotechnology product. These sectors offer new business opportunities that, like agricultural biotechnology trait creation, enable entrepreneurs to think about creating disruptive businesses, not just disruptive technologies for today's business models. In this chapter, the authors conclude the unique aspects of entrepreneurship in the industry of biotechnology in contract with other industries and also discuss the importance of biotechnology entrepreneurs in agriculture.

Chapter 12
Bioentrepreneurship in Medical Biotechnology: Starting, Managing, and Leading Innovative Technologies 201
Neeti Sharma, Banasthali University, India

Being a developing sector, biotechnology combines both medical science and various facets of a sustainable environment. Scientific innovations from academics and industry contribute towards the rise of bioentrepreneurship across the world. Medical biotechnology helps the treatment and prevention of human diseases by using living cells and cell materials to research and produce pharmaceutical and diagnostic products. It requires incubation of research, product, and its yield for the improvement of humans to transform medical research into an entrepreneurial industry. Biotechnology provides an opportunity for entrepreneurs to harness the power of genomics for the development and marketing of new therapeutics. These opportunities allow entrepreneurs to visualize the creation of both disruptive business and disruptive technologies for today's business models. This chapter will summarize multiple features of entrepreneurship in the biotechnology industry in combination with other industries and will explain the significance of bio-entrepreneurship in the field of medical biotechnology.

Chapter 13
Entrepreneurship in Industrial Biotechnology: Biotech Entrepreneurship 229
Shaili Yadav, Janta College, Chhatrapati Shahu Ji Maharaj University, Kanpur, India
Jyoti Mathur, Banasthali University, India

In the 20th century, biotechnology has been growing quickly on industrial platforms with a vast scope for innovation and the entrepreneurial market. Entrepreneurship in biotechnology including its various sub-disciplines focuses on biotech commercial components and possible fundamental strategies combined with laboratory practical analysis and productive outcome of working biotech entrepreneurs, professionals, researchers, and scientists. Likewise, biotechnology in India has risen with the various pharma-biotechnology-based industries leading the charge. Across India, more than 350 well-capitalized companies are working in various related fields of biotechnology including biopharmaceuticals, nanotechnology, bio-services, agriculture computational biotechnology, and bioinformatics.

Chapter 14
Bioentrepreneurship in Environmental Biotechnology 254
Shalini Verma, Banasthali University, India
Mohd. Bilal Khan, Bhagat Phool Singh Government Medical College, India

Preface

The book named *Bioentrepreneurship and Transferring Technology Into Product Development* presents basic as well as application aspects of bioentrepreneurship as a practice and a discipline. While genetically engineered foods and biopharmaceuticals have made biotechnology part of our everyday lives, launching a bioventure is among the most complex and risky entrepreneurial undertakings, given long development cycles, high levels of technological and market uncertainty, and extraordinary capital requirements. The work thus differs, in both intention and execution, from many of the books on entrepreneurship that are being published today. There are not much articles and books are available on bioentrepreneurship. Bioentrepreneurship is neither a science nor a business management. It is a practice. It has a knowledge base, of course, which this book attempts to present in organized fashion. The opening chapters of this book discussed briefly the basic and fundamental concepts of bioentrepreneurship, its significance and its essential characteristics. The fundamental knowledge of entrepreneurship and its relation with biotechnology is necessary. It summarizes the crucial features of bioentrepreneurship, how it relates and differs from general entrepreneurship. For being a bioentrepreneur, a scientific as well as marketing knowledge is necessary. As we move the next chapters describes the scientific part of bioentrepreneurship, which is small scale product development or as we can called it the laboratory part. With the development of lab scale product the next step is its commercialization. For product commercialization the knowledge of funding agencies, large scale product development, patents, property rights and which market we should target is mandatory. There are several schemes of Indian Government available, which provide funds for young entrepreneurs for their innovation and small scale product development. Detailed information of Indian as well as foreign investors for product marketing was described carefully. Next part of the book covers the most important aspect of bioentrepreneurship, which was the comprehensive description of different biotechnology fields for entrepreneurs. It includes all the possible applied fields of biotechnology which is being now used for commercial product formation like, agriculture, medicine, environmental, biofuel, bioenergy etc. The last section of this book concludes with a discussion of individual entrepreneurs, their roles and their decisions with detailed description of biotech companies of India as well as globally. This section motivates the young entrepreneurs to make their research commercial and fruitful.

Only in the last few years have writers on management begun to pay much attention to innovation and entrepreneurship involved science and technology. Yet this is the first work that attempts to present the subject in its entirety and in systematic form. This is surely a first book on a major topic rather than the last word—but I do hope it will be accepted as a seminal work.

Swati Agarwal
Sonu Kumari
Suphiya Khan
2021

Introduction

The present book entitled *Bioentrepreneurship and Transferring Technology Into Product Development* is written for a range of undergraduate, postgraduate and doctorate courses, with the aim of developing an understanding the role of science in entrepreneurship as well as developing the entrepreneurial skills with scientific aptitude. Generally the science student have a mind set for research purpose, they don't know how to commercialize their research in the productive form. This book encourages the science students towards product commercialization and make their research are more useful for the society.

The book blends the practical and the theoretical aspects of bioentrepreneurship with up-to-date research. It covers the process of bioentrepreneurship from small scale product development, understanding the property rights to marketing the product. Detailed description of different government policies with top bioentrepreneurs and bioentrepreneur companies worldwide are included in this book. Entrepreneurship especially in the field of biotechnology is very risky and anything you can do to reduce the risk of failure must be good. So, students can learn from the successes and mistakes of other bioentrepreneurs. This book contains not only the success story of famous bioentrepreneurs but also their struggle and their journey throughout their innovative ideas, product development and its marketing.

This book encompasses the basic knowledge of bioentrepreneurship as well as current concepts and research ongoing in the field of science and technology. This book contains 15 detailed chapters on bioentrepreneurship. The opening chapters of this book discussed briefly the basic and fundamental concepts of bioentrepreneurship, its significance and its essential characteristics. It summarizes the crucial features of bioentrepreneurship, how it relates and differs from general entrepreneurship. As we move the next chapters describes the scientific part of bioentrepreneurship, which is small scale product development or as we can called it the laboratory part. With the development of lab scale product the next step is its commercialization. Detailed information of Indian as well as foreign investors for product marketing was described carefully. Next part of the book covers the most important aspect of bioentrepreneurship, which was the comprehensive description of different biotechnology fields for entrepreneurs. It includes all the possible applied fields of biotechnology which is being now used for commercial product formation like, agriculture, medicine, environmental, biofuel, bioenergy etc. The last section of this book concludes with a discussion of individual entrepreneurs, their roles and their decisions with detailed description of biotech companies of India as well as globally.

The major challenge facing scientific community today is how to encourage and develop the entrepreneurial skills of science students. This book is designed to address this issue. It is written to motivate science students to become more entrepreneurial at the same time as providing frameworks to nurture these precious skills in a systematic way. At its core is creativity and innovation – invaluable skills in today's competitive markets. Its holistic nature crosses artificial subject boundaries and integrates traditional disciplines. Its practical focus means that skills have to be applied.

We hope students and the research community will continue to make use of this book for making their research commercialize. View and suggestions from readers and users are welcome for improvement of this book in future editions.

Chapter 1
Introduction to Bioentrepreneurship

Dwaipayan Sinha
https://orcid.org/0000-0001-7870-8998
Government General Degree College, Mohanpur, India

Anjana Singh
Department of Botany, Deshbandhu College, University of Delhi, India

Pawan Kumar
Department of Botany, Kalindi College, University of Delhi, India

ABSTRACT

Ever since the onset of civilization, humans have been continuously improvising and innovating on different aspects to make their livelihood more sustainable. This innovation reached a steep uptrend trajectory during the industrial revolution, and with the discovery of DNA and emergence of genetic engineering, our civilization entered a new era of biotechnology where desirable traits can be easily engineered into an organism to obtain a desired product. However, it was soon realized that in order to make the product reachable to the masses, integration of science, biology, and technology with business is of the utmost importance. This resulted in the genesis of the concept of bioentrepreneurship. Presently, it is a rapidly emerging discipline connecting two large domains, namely biotechnology and business. This chapter overviews bioentrepreneurship. It highlights the various requirements and measures implemented to start a bioentrepreneurship programme.

INTRODUCTION

Entrepreneurs are euphoric people with persistence even in the presence of any controversy. Effective utilization of resources, increase in per capita income, employment, conservation of resources, improved quality of life & infrastructure, promotion of technology and export are some of the key roles played by an entrepreneur. Burhanuddin et al., in 2013 described an entrepreneur as an aggressive catalyst which

DOI: 10.4018/978-1-7998-7411-9.ch001

can hasten the economic growth. They are the instigators of jobs, wealth through hard work and innovation (Bygrave & Zacharakis, 2010). Salgado-Banda (2007) researched on 22 countries on the impact of entrepreneurship on economic growth and found positive relationship between economic growth and innovation, also stated that growth of economy will be higher with the increase in the number of entrepreneurs. Biotechnology being the fastest growing and knowledge-based sector in the world has enormous potential where direct or indirect use of living organisms or parts of organisms in their natural or modified forms can be utilized in an innovative manner for industrial production. It is the application of all sciences and engineering to achieve an aim by modifying course when required, to undertake the never been done venture by taking risks, as both entrepreneurs and science are the acts of trial and error. Steve Jobs once said that just like the digital one, 21st century will be at the intersection of biology and technology which will be marked by the beginning of a new era. So, the integration of science (bio) and entrepreneurship is defined as bioentrepreneurship, wherein a business can be established by using biological entities or any idea, related to sciences to earn the profit. It can be voiced by several different names such as bioscience enterprise, biotechnology enterprise, life science entrepreneurship, BioE or simply as science entrepreneurship. Therefore, bioentrepreneurship encloses an understanding of an idea, invents something, brings about the sum of all activities to create an environment and infrastructure for well-trained professionals to build research-based projects and their commercialization. Bioentrepreneurship is manifested as the key driver of the new bioeconomy (Christopher & Kaur 2011). For a person to be a bioentrepreneur, few skills are prerequisite like positive energy, leadership qualities, appropriate track record, technical knowledge of the field, articulating and managerial skills (Walton, 1998).

The whole world economy is changing its face by transforming sectors related to health, agriculture, energy and environment with bioentrepreneurship. Science education particularly biology focused education at the school level needs to be linked to “real-world” situations to have an applicability to the social issues (Teng, 2012). U.S Department of Agriculture (USDA) in 2018 published a report according to which the worth of bio-economy together with polymers, industrial biotechnology, biofuels, renewable chemicals, biomaterials and enzymes is $355.28 billion, which by 2024, is expected to increase to approximately $487 billion. Although the field is new, but there are bioentrepreneurship based biotech companies like Cambrian Genomics, MaterializeX, AntiverseAbbVie Biotech Company, Abbott Diagnostics Division, Amgen Inc., Genentech Inc., Gilead Biotech Company, Neurotech Inc., XBiotech, Novozymes North America Inc., Lonza Biologics Inc., Syros Pharmaceuticals, Amyris Inc., Canon U.S. Life Sciences, Inc., Santa Cruz Biotechnology Inc. etc. that are helping scientists in bridging a gap between the science of biotechnology and the commercialization of knowledge. Technology, money, scientific and managerial talent are the essential foundations of bioentrepreneurship. It is suggested that bioentrepreneurship programmes should clearly define its learning objectives, some of which include: protection of ideas, understanding of intellectual property rights, knowledge of the legal implications, consumer analysis, validation of marketing assumptions and identifying important market segments, recognizing regulatory and reimbursement environment in international markets, understanding FDA approval for their product or service, knowledge about stages of new product development; understanding management of R & D Portfolio, innovation and business plan development writing, to learn about the manufacturing of products, to develop and interpret capitalization table, interpretation of basic financial statements; to demonstrate managerial skills, understand potential legal and ethical risks involved in clinical trials, ability to present innovative plans to stakeholders, recognize technology transfer in the industrial, academic and government laboratory setting, illustrate emotional and social intelligence skills. Bioentrepreneurs must realize how technologies can be made available for underdeveloped countries. To carry out this, hands-on sessions need to be offered in bioentrepreneurship programmes, to the students to handle the practical problems arising, by providing them a chance to interact with mentors and supervisors for the feedback which can enhance their skills. It should also assimilate international business by incorporating business models and funding (Meyers & Hurley, 2008). Throughout the world, bioentrepreneurship is heterogenously practiced, mostly occuring in the United States and Canada, with Europe and Japan, other countries such as Hong Kong, Australia, Singapore, Korea, China and India. These countries are also utilizing the technique for their economic growth (Persidis, 1998; Littlejohn, 2002) and in healthcare technology areas such as medical devices, diagnostic kits, pharmaceuticals etc. (Audretsch & Stephan, 1996; Fetterhoff & Voelkel, 2006). For example, such bioenterprises are proving to be fruitful for the production of vaccines against Coronavirus pandemic in 2020. The whole idea lies in choosing an issue with the solution which is prevalent and is in high demand in the society exactly like the principle of demand and supply in business. The prime purpose of this chapter is to develop the concept of bioentrepreneurship, categorize its main dimensions, pillars, challenges in India and world and its relevance in future.

ORIGIN OF BIOENTREPRENEURSHIP

Bioentrepreneurship is an emerging field of biology that involves the integration of biotechnology with entrepreneurship. It aims to foster the goals of biotechnology with the help of academia-industry collaboration. The present day use of the term bioentrepreneurship refers to the use of any idea from biology that can be utilized to serve humanity, and acquire profit by establishing a business. It involves building an enterprise that can develop and commercialize the products of biotechnology (Afandi, 2018). French word '*entreprendre*' has led to the origin of the word entrepreneurship which means 'to pursue opportunities or to undertake' (Hayes, 2020). The first appearance of this word in the French dictionary dates back to 1723 (Hayes, 2020). In 1971, Ben David, a sociologist of science by profession, explored the impacts of reforms in the academic system of American universities that encouraged the "professionalization" of scientists leading to early development of the concept of scientific entrepreneurships (Ben-David, 1971; Oliver, 2004). Literature suggests that the professional training of University students to pursue research and applying it to the best possible standards seeded the need of having scientific entrepreneurship. During that time, American Universities started upgrading their research laboratories so that they could train their graduate students and professors' in the best possible ways keeping them up-to-date with the technology (Ben-David, 1971; Oliver, 2004). The idea of autonomy in research in American Universities acted as a catalyst to fasten growth of the scientific community on professional backgrounds ultimately forming the roots of bioentrepreneurship and its formal conceptualization. Thereafter, the concept of "entrepreneurial scientists'' became popular where Scientists started showing their vested interests in establishing knowledge firms (Oliver, 2004). The work of Zucker et al., 2002 was among the pioneers to label such distinguished scientists as "Star- Scientists" based upon the success of their firms and their scientific publications. It was found that there was a direct positive correlation between the scientific publications and the success of their forms that contributed to increase in the citation rates and numbers of patents (Ben-David, 1971; Oliver, 2004). In the European context, the major advancements in the bioenterprise sector occurred after 1980. In the United Kingdom, (UK), remarkable increase in the funding of basic research by boosting the grants released to the National Research Council led to development of British bioenterprises (Gurau, 2006). This was further augmented with an increase in the capital investments that could encourage scientific discoveries (Walsh & Green, 1993). The launch of 'biotechnology means business' programme in 1995 and other crucial changes in the regulatory bodies had a greater impact on innovation and entrepreneurship (Gurau, 2006).

RELATIONSHIP BETWEEN BIOTECHNOLOGY AND BIOENTREPRENEURSHIP

Bioentrepreneurship is a syngenesis of two large domains namely biological science and entrepreneurship with the former largely encompassing on the biotechnological process. Its main motive is utilization of biological entities or any innovative idea related to biological science to set up a business and gain profit through production and sale of products for the benefit of human beings. It is a holistic term which includes all activities required for building an enterprise for production of biotechnology related products (Afandi, 2018). Biotechnology on the other hand is a diverse technological field which involves working with living cells or use of molecules derived from a cell in order to apply for the human welfare through the use of various tools or technologies largely conceptualised from the biological processes (Gupta et al., 2016). Though unknowingly discovered centuries ago through selective breeding of plants and animals along with preparation of fermented products such as cheese (Verma et al., 2011), its foundation was laid down after the discovery of DNA in 1950s (Gupta et al., 2016). As the secret of DNA and its molecular structures gradually began to unveil through rigorous research of the scientists, this paved the way for the development of altogether a new discipline in the name of genetic engineering in which a segment of DNA carrying a desired gene is made to integrate into the DNA of an organism or a microbe to get a desired product or phenotype. Gradually as an elaboration of biotechnology, it was also applied in the plant world especially in agriculture domain to obtain desired variety of crops. In early 1980s, the first transgenic tissue and plants were generated by means of *Agrobacterium tumefaciens* strains (Lijsebettens & Angenon, 2013). The first genetically modified crop was developed in 1983 which was resistant to antibiotics and in 1996, the first genetically altered crop was produced which was a tomato plant with delayed ripening and was released commercially (Zeljezić et al., 2004). Now with the proliferation of research in biotechnology, a number of desirable results were obtained which required to be disbursed to the general population for their benefit. This resulted in the requirement for establishment of companies which would deal exclusively with biotechnology and its products. Thus, the first biotechnology company, Genetech was established in 1976 to study and utilize the products of recombinant DNA technology (Pisano, 2006). This led to a connection between science and business and since then there was no looking back. A classic example is the case of Europe in which France has set up more than 2000 biotechnology firms followed by Spain housing more than 1000 firms (Mikulic, 2020). In the year 2019, the private biotechnology sector in Europe raised a whopping 3.3 billion dollars which was 35% more than that of previous year (Senior, 2020). Thus, with the rise in demand of desired biotechnological products for the welfare of mankind, pure academic research related to biotechnology which flourished somewhere in 1950s paved the way to business which is in a booming mode at present. Various measures are being currently undertaken by governments of different countries to promote biotechnology with an effort to connect with entrepreneurship programme thereby linking both the domains. The measures taken to promote biotechnology programme and its integration with entrepreneurship would be discussed in detail with an Indian perspective.

PILLARS OF BIOENTREPRENEURSHIP

In order to establish a company under bioentrepreneurship programme, some of the parameters should be considered as a foundation stone. They can also be considered as pillars above which the entire programme would be spread. All the pillars need to act synergistically for a period of over at least ten years in order to make a company well functional. Functioning of all these pillars are very important and any weakness in one of the pillars during the first decade becomes the determining factor of future of the bioentrepreneural programme and consequently affects the biotechnology company housing the same (Schoemaker & Schoemaker, 1998). The following are the pillars above which any bioentrepreneural programme is based upon (Figure 1):

Figure 1. The pillars of bioentrepreneurship

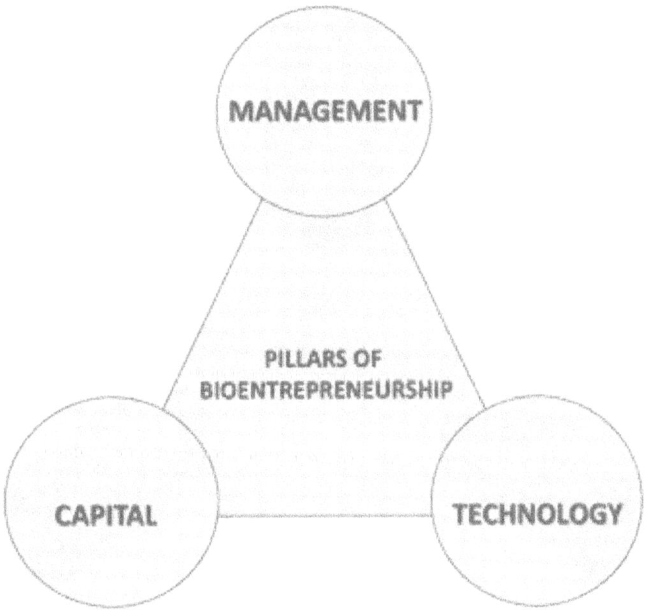

Management

The management forms the first pillar which a biotechnology company needs to secure and establish. Management is largely responsible for getting the work done in a systematic way and is the architect of transformation of scientific innovation into products for sales. The activities of management can further be classified into five groups (Figure 2):

- **Planning**: A pre-determined course of action in order to achieve a predetermined goal.
- **Organizing**: It is an act of bringing the human resource or the work power together for implementing the plan and achieving a desired goal in the form of products.
- **Staffing**: This is also an important activity which is performed by the management. It consists of total activity involving the human resources and appointing them in appropriate places. In addi-

tion to it, involves equipping the human resource of the company with required training to produce the desired product.

- **Directing**: It is the function through which an entrepreneur guides and stimulates its employees for better functioning and in order to achieve a goal. It is considered to be the final action taken by the entrepreneur after completion of all preparatory tasks.
- **Controlling**: It is the last component of the managerial functioning and is basically involves a cross checking to determine whether the actions of the company is in parity with the plans made or not. If any variation is observed, then corrective steps are performed in order to accomplish the desired target (Sinha, 2020).

Figure 2. Various activities of management in entrepreneurship programme

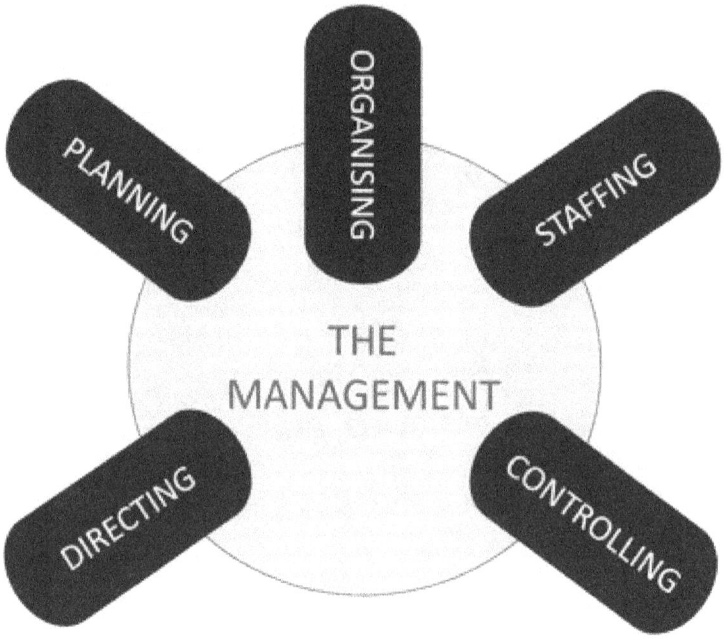

Capital

Capital forms the second pillar of a bioentrepreneural programme. Infact all types of organisations or companies need capital for proper functioning. A capital is generally a mix of assets that a company can depend for financing its business. It comprises of cash and other assets owned by the company. The monetary assets in the company are generally stored in the form of shares, equity and debt funds. From the time of inception, the company is required to focus on how much capital it is having and how much it is getting generated during its functioning years. Lack of capital or restricted access of capital may result in constrained growth of the company (Alper, 2002).

Technology

This forms the third pillar of a bioentrepreneurship programme on which the entire programme will be implemented. Since it is intricately related to biotechnology, the basic aspects of the subject are taken into consideration for generation of a desired product.

CONTRIBUTIONS OF BIOENTREPRENEURSHIP

There three pillars are required for setting up a biotechnology enterprise such as management, threshold capital, and technology inspired by innovation (Schoemaker & Schoemaker, 1998). Biotech-industries that are built around the concept of bio-entrepreneurship consist of sectors such as Biopharma, Agri-biotech, Bioinformatics, and Bio-services (Indian Biotechnology Industry report, 2020). Each of these sectors has made significant contributions in the following arenas of our day-to-day life (Figure 3):

Figure 3. Contributions of bioentrepreneurship

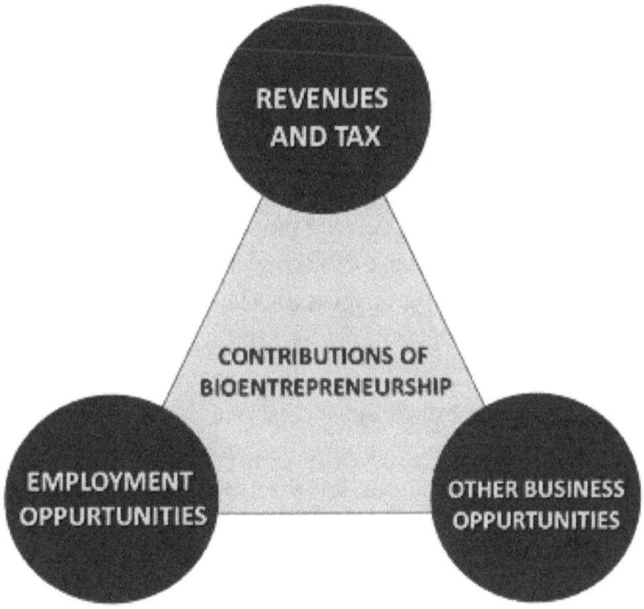

Generation of Revenues and Tax

According to a report published by the Economic Contributions of the Biotechnology Industry (retrieve on Jan, 2021), the size of the industries dealing with bioentrepreneurship have doubled i during 1993-1999. Such industries could generate revenues of $20 billion and $10 billion of tax revenues in total. In the European counterparts, Germany has one the fastest-growing bioenterprises globally accounting for 525 German biotech companies that generate total revenue of more than €3 billion (EuropaBio, 2006).

Creation of Employment Opportunities

According to a report by the Economic Contributions of the Biotechnology Industry (retrieved on Jan, 2021) biotechnology industries in the US played significant roles in economy by generating at least 437,400 jobs of which 150,800 jobs were solely from biotechnology companies and others were from companies depending upon the primary biotech industries. While in the European context, Germany alone has a capacity of generating 17,277 jobs (EuropaBio, 2006). These are jobs that are directly related to the bioenterprises. Industries that are major suppliers of raw material and other services are the major contributors of employment generation (Persidis, 1998). Furthermore, the jobs created by bioenterprise industries are clean and high paying as compared to the other sectors of industries.

Fosters the Growth of Other Businesses and Services that Rely upon Primary Bioenterprise

Some of such businesses include setting up industries that supply consumables, raw materials and other equipments. It also generates a large pool of professionals in the corporate sector and other public sectors (Shimasaki, 2014).

ESSENTIAL BIOENTREPRENEURIAL SKILLS

Entrepreneurship may be considered as the capacity of an individual to convert biological concepts generated in the mind into action resulting in a fruitful outcome which is beneficial for living beings. Entrepreneurship is largely associated with industrial innovations. Entrepreneurship is a broad domain and includes creativity, innovation and capacity of taking risk by an individual or an organization at a whole. It is very important in promoting the growth of economy through promotion of industry (EU Skills Panorama, 2014). Bioentrepreneurship is a subset of the entrepreneurship and can be defined as the process of creation of values from innovations in life science (Meyers, 2008). It is a very sophisticated domain and includes two different disciplines, first one is 'biology' which is grossly knowledge and science of life and the second one being 'entrepreneurship' which is the process of conversions of thoughts into action to generate a valuable output. It is the use of biological components or an idea which is having its genesis in the biological domain and turning into action in order to obtain profit through establishment of industry and setting up of business (Afandi, 2018). Certain skills are required to develop a successful entrepreneurship programme. Figure 4 depicts the skills required for bioentrepreneurship. The skills required for a bioentrepreneurship programme are discussed below:

Curiosity

'Curiosity' is the key factor which determines the success of a bioentrepreneurship programme. It is most important element that helps to narrow down the key problem and find out the potential and the opportunity of solving the problem. It is the curiosity that is the driving force for innovation which results in finding a probable solution.

Figure 4. Skills required for bioentrepreneurship

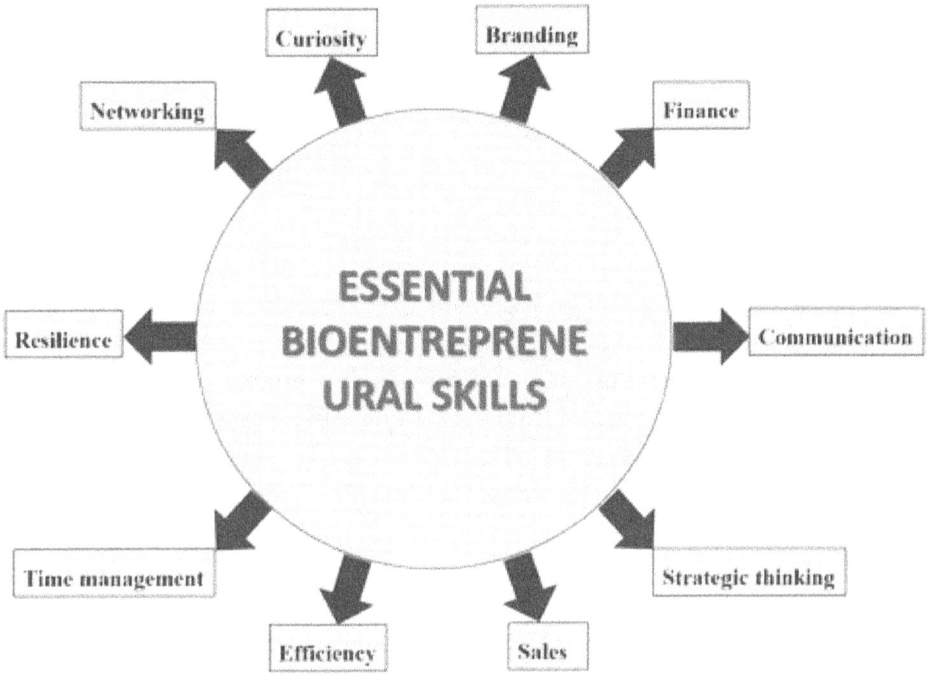

Time Management

'Time management' is another important aspect of bioentrepreneurship. Since it needs to be associated with biological entity, a constructive approach of time management should be taken into consideration within the time-span required for completion of a biological process and any scope to enhance the knowledge through biotechnological approaches must be emphasized. Once the time-frame is standardized, milestones require to be set which psychologically and strategically boost the programme towards maturity and enable the entrepreneur to deliver the outcome in proper time.

Strategic Thinking

Bioentrepreneurship is closely associated with research (Meyers & Hurley, 2008). Research is closely associated with thinking of the scientists. It is the thinking process that leads to development of new ideas in order to jot down creative solutions. Strategic thinking also implies to the immediate tactics which is required to raise money from the bioentrepreneurship programme in order to sustain the research and development process. Thus, it can be said that research, strategic thinking and bioentrepreneurship programme are closely woven to one another (Carsrud et al., 2008).

Efficiency

'Efficiency' is required in order to solve a problem successfully and in optimal time. As the name suggests, the entire system is closely associated with biological system and thus efficiency is not only required in the machinery domain for production but also very important in biological domain too. For example, an efficient microbial inoculant is required for development of a manure or biofertilizer through biotechnological approach (Alori & Babalola, 2018; Atieno et al., 2020). Without these criteria, it would become very difficult to ascertain the potential of the developed fertilizer and its consequent percolation in the market. In addition to it, efficiency in mechanical terms is very vital for enhancing the production of the products.

Resilience

'Resiliency' can be put into the psychological domain and can be defined as the capability to recover from difficulties and constraints. It indicates the psychological elasticity of an individual. A resilient researcher is likely to have more success in bioentrepreneurship programme as he shifts his focus towards new opportunity by shifting himself from a zone of contrivance to a zone of enhancement. He also optimizes himself according to the demand and milieu of the research and thus is able to squeeze out the best from any situation thereby, delivering a sustainable output.

Communication

'Communication' is of paramount importance in any bioentrepreneurship programme. As the programme is a syngenesis between biology, industry and business and thus communication stands out to be a major factor. Communication with a proper mode of representation of the products to the client stands out as a determining factor towards any successful business programme and at the same time, listening to the grievances or any after sales issue also requires to be solved. In every aspect communication acts like a medium through which such issues can be floated. An effective communication leads to overall success in business. In addition to it, communication is also vital for in house efficiency in the industry. Effective communication helps to build a strong bond between entrepreneurs and their employees. In addition to it, effective communication strategies also help to implement strategic decision by an entrepreneur in an organisation thereby, speeding up any constructive process. Communications also helps to promote creativity in an organisation thus, increasing the chances of success. All these ultimately result in business development (Gupta, 2019).

Networking

Engaging in network activities leads to overall success in career and overall business (Jacobs et al., 2019). Networking provides flow of information which enables effective distribution of knowledge and information, labour and capital (Stam & de Ven, 2019). Networking provides better opportunities, partnership deals and finding potent employees which can lead to betterment of industry and hence steady inflow of capital through profit. It also expands the horizon and provides an efficient path of flow of information to a wider domain (Peshev, 2017).

Finance

'Finance' refers to a monetary transaction or any exchange or measurement related to money. It is largely the skill of money handling and capital management (Alhabeeb, 2014). Success in entrepreneurship programme depends on managing and handling the finances properly and carefully assessing the investment and the risks involved.

Branding

'Branding' is the practice through which a company generates its own identity by making unique registered symbol or design. This is very important as it not only makes an impression of the company in the mind of the client or consumer but also enables the customers about their expectations from the company. Branding is very important as it impacts the customers and subsequently influences the market (Smithson, 2015).

Sales

'Sales' form the ultimate skill in any entrepreneurship programme. Sales form the key role in building loyalty between customer and the company. The loyalty in turn forms the base upon which a customer prefers or recommends one company. Loyalty is achieved by a successful interaction between the sales representative and the customer and in this case also communication forms an important platform (Oxford College of Marketing). By successfully channelizing the sales, the revenue earning capacity of the company can be increased and hence it can bring success to the entrepreneur with concomitant increase in business growth.

BIOENTREPRENEURSHIP ON A GLOBAL LEVEL

The United States (US), Europe and Japan are among the top leaders where the most bioenterprises are clustered. Countries in these locations generally document higher rates of scientific discoveries coupled with innovating ideas creating a vast pool of new knowledge that can be tested. Creation of new knowledge and innovations has been linked to increase in the sales of laboratory hardwares and reagents required for bioenterprise research such as enzymes and antibodies through academia-industry collaborations (Persidis, 1998). A report of EuropaBio (1997) has shown that about 60% of hardwares in the laboratory such as automated nucleic acid sequencers are sold in the markets of North America whereas 40% are sold in other countries (Persidis, 1998). Interestingly, the shares of reagent sold in North America accounted for 55%, whereas 30% in Europe, and 10% in Japan, and the remaining 5% in the rest of the world (EuropaBio, 1997; Ernst and Young, 1997). Similar trends were discernable for the percentage share of total drugs produced by these countries where North America ranked on the top followed by European clusters and Japan respectively (EuropaBio, 1997). In the European context, the European universities have played a crucial role in accelerating the venture of bioenterprises globally (Witholt, 1999). Based upon the existing research facilities, universities such as Heriot Watt University in Edinburgh, UK, developed the concept of 'research parks' during the early 1970s offering employment to a large number of people from the university. Furthermore, more than 50 such parks were developed that enrolled around 1,400 companies and 25,000 employees (Witholt, 1999). Another University in Goteborg, Sweden had set a trend of creating at least 15 such companies since 1979 offering employment to around 3,000 people (Witholt, 1999). Some of the other universities that have played a pivotal role in fostering bioentrepreneurship include Federal Institutes of Technology located in Zürich and Lausanne,

Switzerland. These universities have led to flourishing of bioenterprise clusters in and around the university campuses where most of the academia-industry collaborations have seeded into mature projects (Witholt, 1999). For example, many of such new bioenterprise clusters are seen in the UK, between Oxford and Cambridge located in the M4 corridor and, and several others are more prominent near the German urban centres (Witholt, 1999). Another factor that fuels the growth of bioenterprise industries is the capital investment policies that are implemented by a country's government bodies. The US federal government has better vested capital investment policies than their European counterparts for their early-stage research projects providing bioentrepreneurs a better scope for realizing higher success rates. For example, the total capital invested by the US is three fold than in Europe (Witholt, 1999). Such smart investment policies have greatly supported budding bioenterprise industries. The entire bioenterprise can be grouped into four kinds of industries as large, medium, small and startup industries based upon the size of the enterprise. Furthermore, based upon the types of products and services involved, these bioenterprise industries fall into multiple domains. Biopharma deals with drugs, vaccines and diagnostics; Bioindustrial enterprise deals with biofuels and enzymes based products; Bioagri industries cater to hybrid crops, biopesticides and biofertilizers. Other biotech industries such as Bioservice enterprise cater to synthesis, manufacturing and development of contract research, while bioinformatics deals with data analysis and database services (Bio Entrepreneurship Development, 2018). As per a 2019 report, the Biopharma industry has shown significant growth accounting for a total revenue of 1.25 trillion USD worldwide where Pfizer has ranked on top of the charts in world's leading pharmaceutical companies. Pfizer, having its global headquarters located in New York City, has alone generated total revenue of approximately 51.7 billion USD. Other Biopharma industries from the United States include Johnson & Johnson, AbbVie, and Merck & Co. The market size of the global bioagri industries was estimated at around 89.89 USD billion in 2018 (Agricultural Biotechnology Market Size, Industry Report, 2019) while the Bioinformatics enterprise was projected to value between 4000-5000 million USD in 2020 (Bioinformatics Market Size Research, Industry Outlook Report, 2015).

BIOENTREPRENEURSHIP IN INDIA AND ITS CHALLENGES

Bioentrepreneurship is a syngenesis of biology, industry and market. When application of biology comes into the picture, it is the biotechnology that dominates the application arena. India is among the 12 destinations of biotechnology in the world and comprise of greater than 2700 biotechnology start-ups and greater than 2500 biotechnology companies throughout the country. The biotechnology industry in India amounted to 63 billion US dollars in the year 2019 and is projected to reach 150 billion US dollars by 2025 with a compound annual growth rate of 16.4% (India Brand Equity Foundation). Inspite of a considerable boom in the biotechnology industry which promotes the bioentrepreneurship programme, it also faces some issues and challenges which pose hindrance towards a smooth growth. The focal point of the issue is the booming population of India which primarily requires an affordable and trustworthy healthcare solution. This is required to save the lives of millions of poor people which make the Indian population. This is one of the foremost challenge a bioentrepreneur faces, as the entire process requires a perfect streamlining and meticulous planning so that the products every Indian citizen (Kumar, 2020). In addition to it, in India, there is a lack of encouragement for innovation. Though a lot of discussion is made on academic and theoretical level but 'made in India' concept is hardly discussed, assimilated and celebrated. Infact, it is still not on a triumphant figure possibly due to a lack of strong policy making or may be due to lack of general awareness which has overall slowed down its progress (Babu, 2020). In addition to it, lack of proper funding compels the innovators to house their intellectual property rights to other countries (Mazumdar-Shaw, 2020). This results in lagging of our country in the global innovation index. Our country ranked 48 in the indexed in comparison to China which ranked 14th in 2020 (Wipo website, 2020).The sad part in any innovative programme in India is that it has not recognized in its own soil and thus most of the talents migrate to other countries specially towards the western part of the world to nuture their innovative dreams. Reports say that around 6% of the United States residents who are in the process of invention or innovation and listed in European Patent Office possess an Indian name or surname which is almost same as that of China and greater than Germany, France and Italy combined (Breschi et al., 2019). This is reflected by the fact that India allocates less than 1% of its GDP on research and development which is way low in comparison to its global counterparts (Das, 2019). Thus, the major challenge of India is creation of economy which is knowledge driven. The country requires using knowledge prudently for increasing productivity in the field of agriculture, industry, healthcare in order to render a state of art service to its booming population majority of which is either village centric or hovering around the poverty level mark (Dahlman & Anuja, 2005). For flourishing of innovation, ideas need to be equipped with an efficient funding system. This can be achieved by incorporation of innovation ecosystem in the financial cycle which would certainly unleash a series of potent innovators delivering state of art technologies for the benefit of Indian population (Mazumdar-Shaw, 2020).

MEASURES TO PROMOTE BIOENTREPRENEURSHIP IN INDIA

In India, the government has taken a number of innovative approaches to promote bioentrepreneurship. Presently, India is gradually moving towards a start-up ecosystem. A start-up business is basically a nascent company, established by one or a group of entrepreneurs for development of a product or service and percolating the same to the market for consumer. The Government has started this start up initiative in 16th January, 2016 and consists of 19 action points which guide the initiative. Since its inception, 19,351 start-ups have been recognised by Department for Promotion of Industry and Internal Trade till June, 2019. In addition to it, the Government of India has established 'Funds for Fund of Start-ups (FFS)' with a core value of Rupees 10,000 crores in order to meet various funding requirements of start-up companies with Small Industries Development Bank of India as the operating agency (Press information Bureau, Government of India). The following are some of the start-up programmes initiated by the government to promote entrepreneurial programme:

Aspire

It is an initiative by the Indian government, launched to set up network of technology centres and incubation centres in order to promote start-ups for innovative approaches in industry related to agriculture. The objective of this scheme is to create new jobs thereby reducing unemployment. It is also aimed to promote entrepreneurship culture in the country and for overall development at grass-root level. Aspire scheme is also aimed to facilitate innovative business solution and to strengthen the competition in MSME sectors (Startup India website).

Pradhan Mantri Mudra Yojana

'Pradhan Mantri MUDRA Yojana' is a scheme which is launched by honourable Prime Minister of India on 8th April, 2015 in order to provide loans with a maximum capping of Rupees 10 Lakhs to non-corporate and non-farm small micro enterprises. The loans are disbursed by banks, non-banking financial organisations, small finance banks, and micro finance institutions. As on Jan 01, 2021, Rs 159837.84 crores have been sanctioned and Rs 132954.73 crores have been disbursed (Mudra website).

Atal Innovation Mission

It is a government of India flagship initiative for promoting a culture of innovation and entrepreneurship throughout the country. Its main objective is developing new policies and programmes for harbouring innovation in different economic sectors. It also aims to provide platforms and opportunity of collaboration for different stakeholders and creating an umbrella structure to visualise and monitor entrepreneurship environment. It helped to increase the ranking of India in Global innovation index from 81 in 2015 to 48 in 2020 (Atal Innovation Mission, Niti Ayog website).

eBIZ Portal

This is another initiative of the Indian government and is developed by Infosys Technologies Limited under the supervision of Department of Industrial Policy and Promotion, Government of India. Its motive is to promote business development in the country through an online portal which will connect government with business services. This is anticipated to reduce the processing time and unnecessary delays which is required for business start-ups (Digital India website).

Dairy Processing and Infrastructure Development Fund (DIDF)

It is an initiative by Government of India and was created in December, 2017 with a total scheme outlay of Rs 10.881 crores. Under this scheme, an amount of Rs 8004 crores has been allocated for creation of infrastructure related to dairy processing between the period 2017-2018 and 2019-2020. Out of the remaining, Rs 2001 crores will be the contribution of end borrowers and Rs 12 crores will be the share from National Dairy Development Board / National Cooperative Dairy Corporation and Rs 864 crores will be given by Department of Animal husbandry and dairying. At present the funding period is extended upto 2022-2023. The main aim of the initiative is modernization of milk processing plants. It also aims to create additional capacity for milk processing. Another motive of this scheme is to enable optimum value of milk to farmers and supply of milk of good quality in the market (National Dairy Development Board).

Focussing on the domain of bioentrepreneurship, the Government of India has put the biotechnology sector on a strong and uptrending trajectory. The Department of Biotechnology plans to increase the number of biotechnology start-ups by establishing 300-500 start-ups each year in order to reach a figure of 2000 start ups by the year 2020. The following are the measures which are adopted by the Department of Biotechnology in association with Biotechnology Research Assistance Council (BIRAC):

- Setting up of five new Bio-clusters, fifty new Bio-Incubators, one hundred and fifty technology transfer offices and twenty Bio-Connect offices in various research institutes and Universities across India.
- Setting up of Biotech Equity Fund to provide financial assistance to young biotech start-ups.
- Encouraging global partnership- Bengaluru-Boston Biotech Gateway is established with a motive of sharing ideas and guide the entrepreneurs in various fields of biological sciences including computational biology, genomics, drug discovery and development of vaccines in collaboration of Institutes of Boston.
- Diversification and amplification of bioentrepreneurship through BIRAC regional entrepreneurship centres (BREC). The main objective is to train bioentrepreneurs with necessary skills and equipping them with necessary knowledge which is required to convert their innovation into successful business leading to development of unique products. The Department of Biotechnology aims to set up five regional mini-BIRACs in coming five years (Government of India, Ministry of Commerce and Industry, 2020).

Moreover, in order to promote research and innovative aptitude among new generation students, the government has come up with a number of measures. One of such is the setting up of an 'Innovation Core programme. The programme is initiated for school children with a target of ten lakh innovations obtained from 5 lakh schools among which one lakh innovation would be targeted and top 10,000 would attract the prototyping support. Finally the best 100 would be shortlisted and displayed in the Annual festivals of innovation in '*Rashtrapati Bhavan*' (Government of India, Ministry of Commerce and Industry, 2020). Another programme is "National Initiative for Developing and Harnessing Innovations" (NIDHI) promoted by department of science and technology. It is an umbrella programme for promoting ideas and innovations in both technology guided and knowledge based form. One such programme under NIDHI is the entrepreneur in residence (EIR) which is launched in order to inspire potential talents for being entrepreneurs and also minimizing risk associated in pursuing start up process and partially setting off the opportunity cost (DST website). Another scheme is the '*Uchchatar Avishkar Yojana*' initiated jointly by MHRD and DST. This scheme was introduced in order to promote innovation of higher capacity which is required for industries thereby improving the competitiveness of Indian manufacturing units. The main objectives of the scheme are as follows:

- Promoting innovation in domains which are directly of relevance to the manufacturing and design industry.
- To unleash innovative mindset amongst the students and faculty members in top technological institutes.
- To set a coordination in action between academics and industry.
- To strengthen the infrastructure of laboratories in research organizations.
- To set up outcome based research funding (Government of India, S/2015-TS.II/TC, dated 22.12.2015).

FUTURE PROSPECTS AND CONCLUSIVE REMARKS

In developing countries, bioentrepreneurship can only be ingrained with the initiation of business and strong base for research. Also, economic growth can be achieved by the aid of research scientists and entrepreneurs in the field of biotechnology for successful start-ups. Presently, developing nations and policy makers should start focusing on financial budget allocation for biotechnology companies for the survival and maintenance of biotechnology enterprises. It is suggested that coexistence of technology and scientific proficiency play a determining role in the growth of any nation. Bioentrepreneurship conferences should be a regular event every year to provide a platform for students, start-ups, life science entrepreneurs, investors, scientists and industry leaders to learn and expand their matrix in an encouraging environment (Poon and Liyanage, 2004).

In view of growth of agriculture sector of any nation, science centres play a significant role to widen education so as to ensure the continuous support from rural base that feeds the entire nation. To expedite the selection of new seed technology and agronomy practices in a rural area of any country, adult education programs must be implemented and designed with utmost simplicity (Teng, 2012). In recent years major developments in the biotechnology companies have occurred in India due to favorable policies, persistent government funding, availability of venture capital and great entrepreneurial skilled taskforce but despite that analytic gap remain as hindrance for the development. Innovative research is the only key solution to achieve sustainable growth that would last for long, but problem is the lack of experience to manage funds, involvement of huge investments to successfully float new molecules. In addition to this, other problematic areas lies in miscalculation of risks, insufficient patent protection and lack of regulatory framework because of which many pharmaceutical firms avoid India because their drugs can be transformed by the Indian scientists into domestic generic equivalents without legal consequences. Shortage of skilled labour resulting due to 'brain drain' also encounters poor rating. Scientists leave for Europe and United States in order to get higher perks and salaries, to avoid this, India must take dynamic steps to streamline and strengthen its biotech regulatory apparatus; support the commercialization of biotech products and to build greater public knowledge about biotechnologyy by providing basic facilities and well-furnished labs, thereby helping India to emerge as a distinguished voice on an international platform about biotechnology related affairs.

To facilitate necessary knowledge, training and skills to bio-entrepreneurs, BIRAC has partnered with C-CAMP to set up BIRAC Regional Entrepreneurship Centre (BREC) transforming innovative biotech ideas into successful & sustainable ventures, hence, creating national and global impact. Centre for Cellular and Molecular Platforms (C-CAMP) which is Department of Biotechnology, Ministry of Science and Technology, Government of India supported initiative, organizes National Bio Entrepreneurship Competition (NBEC) every year to identify, nurture and attract bio-entrepreneurs having novel business ideas with significant social impact. Developing countries despite of many efforts and potential, face few challenges like political instability, lack of technical experts, dearth of interest by the governments, policy flaws and poor research facilities. This can be overcome by starting new degree courses which can generate graduates completely dedicated to entrepreneurship programmes to facilitate the involvement of science in the global market to meet its goal (Collet and Wyatt, 2005). Many universities are there which have strong reputations in entrepreneurship, they either do not address it or only the biotechnology field is addressed in a hasty way. There is vast scope of improvement as bioentrepreneurship educational programmes have a lot of potential to address market needs contributing to the economic spirit of a community and helping to gain expertise in the industry worldwide (Meyers & Hurley, 2008).

Generally, the aim of universities is not to initiate products into the market, which is why technological innovation is not so common. However, to bring about this, universities should promote basic research and should also develop business oriented entrepreneurial mind set among the trainees (Kunert et al., 2012).A synergistic approach of academic and research institutions, industries, governmental planning and overall awareness of the common people would lead to success in the bioentrepreneurship programme ultimately paving the way of economic prosperity.

REFERENCES

Afandi, M. H. (2018). What is Bioentrepreneurship? *Nculineers website*. Retrieved December 1, 2020, from https://nuclineers.com/whats-bioentrepreneurship/

Agricultural Biotechnology Market Size, Share & Trends Analysis Report By Application (Vaccine, Flower Culturing, Biofuels), Organism (Plants, Animals, Microbes), By Region And Segment Forecasts, 2019 - 2025. (2019). Report ID: GVR-3-68038-839-8. Retrieved December 10, 2020, from https://www.grandviewresearch.com/industry-analysis/agricultural-biotechnology-market

Alhabeeb, M. J. (2014). *Entrepreneurial finance: fundamentals of financial planning and management for small business*. John Wiley & Sons.

Alori, E. T., & Babalola, O. O. (2018). Microbial Inoculants for Improving Crop Quality and Human Health in Africa. *Frontiers in Microbiology*, *9*, 2213. doi:10.3389/fmicb.2018.02213 PMID:30283427

Alper, J. (2002). The rise of the European bioentrepreneur. *Nature Biotechnology*, *20*(6), BE3–BE5. doi:10.1038/nbt0602supp-BE3 PMID:12089569

Atieno, M., Herrmann, L., Nguyen, H. T., Phan, H. T., Nguyen, N. K., Srean, P., Than, M. M., Zhiyong, R., Tittabutr, P., Shutsrirung, A., Bräu, L., & Lesueur, D. (2020). Assessment of biofertilizer use for sustainable agriculture in the Great Mekong Region. *Journal of Environmental Management*, *275*, 111300. doi:10.1016/j.jenvman.2020.111300 PMID:32871522

Audretsch, D. B., & Stephan, P. E. (1996). Company-scientist locational links: The case of biotechnology. *The American Economic Review*, *86*(3), 641–652.

Babu, S. M. (2020). *Why 'Make in India' has failed*. Retrieved December 12, 2020, from https://www.thehindu.com/opinion/op-ed/why-make-in-india-has-failed/article30601269.ece

Ben-David, J. (1971). *The Scientist's Role in Society: A Comparative Study*. Prentice-Hall, Inc.

Biotech Consortium India Limited (BCIL). (2018). *Bio entrepreneurship development*. Retrieved December 14, 2020, from https://www.biotech.co.in/sites/default/files/2020-01/Bioentrepreneurship-Development.pdf

Biotechnology Innovation Organization Website. (n.d.). *The Economic Contributions of the Biotechnology Industry*. Retrieved January 1, 2021, from https://archive.bio.org/articles/economic-contributions-biotechnology-industry

Breschi, S., Lissoni, F., & Miguelez, E. (2019). *Does India gain from high-skilled migration to the US?* Ideas for India Website. Retrieved December 12, 2020, from https://www.ideasforindia.in/topics/productivity-innovation/does-india-gain-from-high-skilled-migration-to-the-us.html

Burhanuddin, H., Nurmalina, R., & Pambudy, R. (2013). Entrepreneurial Activity and Economic Growth: Learning from Indonesian Broiler Farmers. *Asia Pacific Journal of Innovation and Entrepreneurship*, *7*(3), 25–51.

Bygrave, W. D., & Zacharakis, A. (2010). *The portable MBA in entrepreneurship* (4th ed.). John Wiley & Sons Inc.

Carsrud, A. L., Brännback, M., & Renko, M. (2008) Strategy and Strategic Thinking in Biotechnology Entrepreneurship. In Handbook of Bioentrepreneurship. Springer. doi:10.1007/978-0-387-48345-0_5

Christopher, D., & Kaur, S. (2011). Entrepreneurship in Biotechnology Sector. *IUP Journal of Entrepreneurship Development*, *8*(3), 40–59.

Collet, C., & Wyatt, D. (2005). "Bioneering"–teaching biotechnology entrepreneurship at the undergraduate level. *Education + Training*, *47*(6), 408–421. doi:10.1108/00400910510617033

Dahlman, C. J., & Utz, A. (2005). *India and the knowledge economy: leveraging strengths and opportunities*. World Bank Publications. doi:10.1596/0-8213-6207-0

Das, G. (2019). *At 0.7% of GDP, India's R&D expenditure in science is less than BRIC nations*. Retrieved December 12, 2020, from https://www.businesstoday.in/current/world/india-gdp-randd-expenditure-in-science-is-less-than-bric-nations/story/390874.html

Digital India. (n.d.). *Ebiz*. Retrieved December 12, 2020, from https://digitalindia.gov.in/content/ebiz

DST website. (n.d.). *NIDHI Entreprenuer-in-residence program. Nurturing budding entreprenuer*. Retrieved December 14, 2020, from http://www.nidhi-eir.in/about.php

Ernst & Young. (1997). *European Biotech 97—A New Economy*. Ernst & Young.

EU Skills Panorama. (2014). *Entrepreneurial skills Analytical Highlight*. Retrieved December 01, 2020, from https://skillspanorama.cedefop.europa.eu/sites/default/files/EUSP_AH_Entrepreneurial_0.pdf

EuropaBio. (1997). *Benchmarking the Competitive–ness of Biotechnology in Europe. EuropaBio Independent Report, 1997*. EuropaBio.

EuropaBio. (2006). *The European association of bioindustries. Biotechnology in Europe: 2006 Comparative Study*. Retrieved December 28, 2020, from https://anibalcavacosilva.arquivo.presidencia.pt/archive/doc/Critical2006.pdf

Fetterhoff, T. J., & Voelkel, D. (2006). Managing open innovation in biotechnology. *Research Technology Management*, *49*(3), 14–18.

Government of India, Ministry of Commerce & Industry, Department for promotion of Industry and Internal Trade. (n.d.). *Problems being faced by Indian Startups*. Retrieved December 28, 2020, from https://dipp.gov.in/sites/default/files/lu2115_0.pdf

Government of India, order number F.NO. 21-10S/201S-TS.lI/TC, dated 22.12.2015. Retrieved December 24, 2020, from https://www.iitrpr.ac.in/sites/default/files/uay_guidelines.pdf

Grand View Research Website. (2015). *Bioinformatics Market Analysis By Product (Sequence Analysis, Manipulation, Alignment, Structural & Functional Analysis Platforms, Data Management, Sequencing, Data Analysis Service, Generalized, Specialized Biocontent), By Application (Genomics, Molecular Phylogenetics, Metabolomics, Proteomics, Transcriptomics, Chemoinformatics & Drug Designing) And Segment Forecasts To 2020*. Report ID: 978-1-68038-008-8. Retrieved December 14, 2020, from https://www.grandviewresearch.com/industry-analysis/bioinformatics-industry

Gupta, S. (2019). *The Role of Effective Communication in Entrepreneurial Success*. Retrieved December 10, 2020, from https://www.entrepreneur.com/article/336347

Gupta, V., Sengupta, M., Prakash, J., & Tripathy, B. C. (2016). An Introduction to Biotechnology. *Basic and Applied Aspects of Biotechnology*, 1–21.

Gurau, C. (2006). Bio-entrepreneurship in different economic systems: A comparative analysis of bio-entrepreneurs' profile in UK, France and Germany. *International Journal of Biotechnology*, *8*(3-4), 169–186.

Hayes, A. (2020, July). *Entrepreneur*. Retrieved https://www.investopedia.com/terms/e/entrepreneur.asp

India Brand equity foundation website. (2020). *Biotechnology Industry in India*. Retrieved December 12, 2020, from https://www.ibef.org/industry/biotechnologyindia.aspx#:~:text=The%20Indian%20biotechnology%20industry%20amounted,%25%20from%203%25%20in%202017

Jacobs, S., De Vos, A., Stuer, D., & Van der Heijden, B. (2019). "Knowing Me, Knowing You" the Importance of Networking for Freelancers' Careers: Examining the Mediating Role of Need for Relatedness Fulfillment and Employability-Enhancing Competencies. *Frontiers in Psychology*, *10*, 2019.

Kumar, A. (2020) IILM College of engineering and Technology website. *Biotechnology entrepreneurship: An Indian perspective*. Retrieved December 14, 2020, from https://iilmcet.ac.in/blog/biotechnology-entrepreneurship-an-indian-perspective/

Kunert, K. J., Okole, B., Vorster, B. J., Brewin, N. J., & Cullis, C. A. (2012). A general model for training the next generation of biotechnology entrepreneurs based on recent experience of USA-UK-South Africa collaborations. *Journal of Commercial Biotechnology*, *18*(4), 63–66.

Littlejohn, T. (2002). Sunbaked biotechnology in Australia. *Nature Biotechnology*, *20*(9), 873–877.

Mazumdar-Shaw, K. (2020). *The challenges and opportunities of innovating in India.Observer* Retrieved December 12, 2020, from https://www.orfonline.org/expert-speak/challenges-opportunities-innovating-india/

Meyers, A. (2008). Enterprise for Life Scientists: Developing Innovation and Entrepreneurship in the Biosciences. *Journal of Commercial Biotechnology, 14*, 355–356.

Meyers, A. D., & Hurley, P. (2008). Bioentrepreneurship education programmes in the United States. *Journal of Commercial Biotechnology*, *14*(1), 2–12.

Mikulic, M. (2020). *Number of biotechnology firms in selected European countries in 2017*. Retrieved December 25, 2020, from https://www.statista.com/statistics/439960/number-of-biotechnology-companies-europe-eu/

Mudra Website. (n.d.). Retrieved December 14 2020 from https://www.mudra.org.in/

National Dairy Development Board. (2017). *DIDF - Dairy Processing & Infrastructure Development Fund*. Retrieved December 12, 2020, from https://www.nddb.coop/didf/didf-in-brief

Nitiayog. (n.d.). *Atal Innovation Mission*. Retrieved December 14, 2020, from https://niti.gov.in/aim

Oliver, A. L. (2004). Biotechnology entrepreneurial scientists and their collaborations. *Research Policy*, *33*(4), 583–597.

Persidis, A. (1998). Bioentrepreneurship around the world. *Nature Biotechnology*, *16*(1), 3–4.

Peshev, M. (2017). *What Are The Most Important Skills Entrepreneurs Need?* Retrieved December 10, 2020, from https://www.forbes.com/sites/quora/2017/09/11/what-are-the-most-important-skills-entrepreneurs-need/?sh=4c867954106c

Pisano, G. P. (2006). Can science be a business? Lessons from biotech. *Harvard Business Review*, *84*(10), 114–150.

Poon, P., & Liyanage, S. (2004). Commercialisation of biotechnology in newly industrialised economies. *International Journal of Biotechnology*, *6*(2-3), 243–259.

Press Information Bureau Government of India Ministry of Commerce & Industry. (n.d.). *Start-up India Scheme*. Retrieved December 12, 2020, from https://pib.gov.in/newsite/PrintRelease.aspx?relid=190914

Salgado–Banda, H. (2005). *Entrepreneurship and economic growth: An empirical analysis*. Research Paper. Banco de Mexico.

Schoemaker, H. J., & Schoemaker, A. F. (1998). The three pillars of bioentrepreneurship. *Nature Biotechnology*, *16*(1), 13–15.

Senior, M. (2020). Europe's biotech renaissance. *Nature Biotechnology*, *38*(4), 408–415.

Shimasaki, C. (2014). Five Essential Elements for Growing Biotechnology Clusters. In Biotechnology Entrepreneurship (pp. 57-72). Academic Press.

Sinha, D. K. (2020). *Main Functions of an Entrepreneur (Explained With Examples)*. Retrieved December 16, 2020, from https://www.yourarticlelibrary.com/entrepreneur/4-main-functions-of-an-entrepreneur-explained-with-examples/40646

Smithson, E. (2015). *What Is Branding And Why Is It Important For Your Business?* Retrieved December 12, 2020, from https://www.brandingmag.com/2015/10/14/what-is-branding-and-whyisitimportantforyourbusiness/#:~:text=Branding%2C%20by%20definition%2C%20is%20a,from%20other%20products%20and%20services

Stam, E., & van de Ven, A. (2019). Entrepreneurial ecosystem elements. *Small Business Economics*, 1–24.

StartupIndia website. (n.d.). *Aspire-A Scheme for Promotion of Innovation, Rural Industries and Entrepreneurship*. Retrieved December 12, 2020, from https://www.startupindia.gov.in/content/sih/en/government-schemes/aspire-scheme-promotion-innovation-entrepreneurship-and-agro-industry.html

Teng, P. P. (2012). Linking education to socially-relevant bioentrepreneurship for Sustainable Development. In *Biology Education for Social and Sustainable Development* (pp. 5–18). Brill Sense.

Van Lijsebettens, M., & Angenon, G. (2013). Thirty years of transgenic research in plants. *The International Journal of Developmental Biology*, *57*(6-8), 447.

Verma, A. S., Agrahari, S., Rastogi, S., & Singh, A. (2011). Biotechnology in the realm of history. *Journal of Pharmacy & Bioallied Sciences*, *3*(3), 321–323.

Walsh, V., & Green, K. (1993). Walsh, V. and Green, K. (1993) 'Demand, the public sector and innovation in biotechnology. In E. J. Blakely & K. W. Willoughby (Eds.), *The Management and Economic Potential of Biotechnology* (pp. 28–46). Special Publication of the International Journal of Technology Management.

Walton, A. (1998). Some thoughts on bioentrepreneurship. *Nature Biotechnology*, *16*(1), 7–8.

WIPO website. (2020). *Global Innovation Index 2020.* Retrieved December 12, 2020, from https://www.wipo.int/global_innovation_index/en/2020/

Witholt, B. (1999). The European university as a startup generator. *Nature Biotechnology*, *17*(1), BE7–BE8.

Zeljezić, D. (2004). Geneticki preinaceni organizmi u hrani—proizvodnja, detekcija i moguće opasnosti [Genetically modified organisms in food--production, detection and risks]. *Arhiv za Higijenu Rada i Toksikologiju*, *55*(4), 301–312.

Zucker, L. G., Darby, M., & Armstrong, J. (2002). Commercializing knowledge: University science, knowledge capture, and firm performance in biotechnology. *Management Science*, *48*(1), 138–153.

Chapter 2
Significance of Bioentrepreneurship

Diksha Kumari
Banasthali University, India

ABSTRACT

Since the age of civilization, humans have been using products based on biotechnology, and these products have become part of our daily lives. The entrepreneur is the driving force of any organization. Biotechnology entrepreneurship is the alliance of two disciplines, business and science. Biotechnology-related business is aimed to commercialize the bio-products as well as enhance the research to benefit the human race. Firstly, bio-entrepreneurship has the potential to develop new techniques to protect the environment from diseases, fuel production, feed the hungry, and various other product preparations. Hence, these products provide new and better ways with minimum side effects to detect, cure, and prevent harmful diseases. Secondly, these bio-based products including biofuels and renewable chemicals are targeted to grow from approximately $203.3 billion in 2015 to $487 billion by 2024.

INTRODUCTION

Now we are living in the "biotech century" (Rifkin, 1999). As the products, which we consume in our routine works are manufactured with the help of biotechnological processes. Biotechnology is currently one of the hot zones driving the stock markets and outskirts of information as well as work creation. Although, human society is not new to biological products such as beverages, food and feed but new biological knowledge has expanded the application of science (Teng, 2008). For example, the pest resistant crops and fruits are biotechnologically engineered foods; wine is manufactured from gene-manipulated vines and beer is formed through genetically engineered yeast. The kitchen plates and cups are produced through modern biotechnological processes that are biodegradable plastics. As well as the medicines, drugs and diagnostic tests are also developed through biotechnological processes and methods. But on the other side, the media society continuously warn us the danger of "bioterrorism" that is, the terrorists will exploit the new technology and engineer toxic bacteria and viruses to use as vicious weapons ever known.

DOI: 10.4018/978-1-7998-7411-9.ch002

In India, One of the fastest growing industries is Biotechnology which plays an important role in nation's economy. The present image of biotechnology as a science proposes its potential for practical turn of events, if to think about its ecological similarity, financial reasonability and social duty. However, biotechnology serves a major element in the transition from an agricultural based science to knowledgeable economic world in which biotech has a major impact in industrial sectors. Business in the form of new product creation, productivity enhancement, technology improvement and good services are the agents of progression (Malhotra et al., 2012). Still, a biotechnological application in agricultural field and its diffusion to farmers is a time taking process that requires investment. But due to this biotechnology related business, the products which were imported in the developing countries are now manufactured using the biotech technology (Tonukari, 2004).

The first biotechnology firm was established in the late 1970s in India. Since then, the modern bioentrepreneurial projects are described as good technological practices with market uncertainty and long product development periods. The most complex entrepreneurial task is the establishment of biotechnology firm, as the failure rate of firms is high and because of their specific characteristics in market field, the success factors which are crucial for the other industries context are moderately applicable for young biotech firms. So, innovative strategies like vital alliances between firms and co-operations between different firms have developed. Due to the novelty and less understanding of this industrial founding, limited biotechnology firms are authorized. This chapter focuses on significance of bioentrepreneurship and research in science field of the bio-based company.

STEPS OF BIOENTREPRENEURSHIP DEVELOPMENT

Biotechnology entrepreneurship is the alliance of two disciplines, business and science both (Ahmed, 2017). Effective development of bio-based endeavours at the territorial or national level necessities further deliberate research. A biotechnology based venture can be developed by following various steps as represented in Figure 1. It can also be described as 'use of bio-based products or any motivational idea to attain profit through commercialisation'. It is relatively new integrative field which sometimes referred to as bioscience enterprise, life science entrepreneurship or bioscience entrepreneurship (David and John, 2008). It joins biomedicine, sociologies, common sciences and innovation with development measures. Business venture in these areas requires explicit kinds of ability that join various regulation and societies, just as a perspective that encourages the rise and improvement of mechanical advancement on economic models that frequently require reexamining or rethinking (Bello et al., 2020).

However, bioentrepreneurship study is a learning cycle that affirms learning through utilizing the enclosing surroundings and preparing understudies to make important products sell and do financial examination so learning is more significant and pleasant. Bio-entrepreneurship shows the normal understudy reaction poll all in all including great standards. This demonstrates that the use of learning bio-entrepreneurship got a positive reaction (Prihatiningrum et al., 2020). According to Uctu and Jafia (2013), bio-entrepreneurship is like a bridge between biotechnology and knowledge commercialization in industrial level. Thus, it shifts biotechnological studies from academic field to commercial market (Lynn, 2014). It is summaries by (a) it accomplishes the research commercialization in industrial field, (b) time consuming and valuable research which is burdened with market risks and (c) it also connected with value addition in market (David & John, 2008).

Figure 1. Steps of bioentrepreneurship development

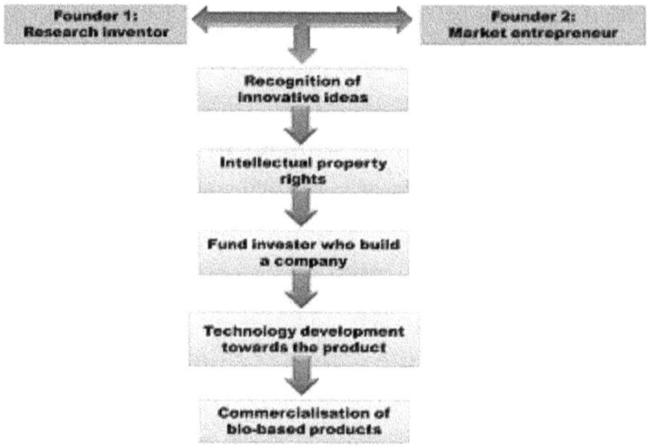

Successful dispatching of a bio-based product needs very much ideal advertising plans. Advancement of the Indian biotechnology area is high on the policy agenda of the Government of India. Biotechnology has been perceived as one of the key need areas under the 'Make in India', Expertise India' and Start-up India' activity of the Government of India, being one of only a handful few areas on solid development direction to drive supportable economic development direction to drive supportable and create huge scope work openings. Indeed, even the potential success may end up being a finished disappointment in the market if the worth of the product, its preferences and best highlights are not appropriately passed onto the general population. The plans should keep in mind how to promote it to applicable groups of purchasers/clients, how to build up a brand name that would pull in the audience and how to monitor other biotechnological organizations in rivalry to dominate over their product standard, cost and so on.

Biotechnology products have faced obstacles in their acknowledgment in all market just as in the hearts of society (Stone, 2012). The explanation behind this can be followed down to be multifactorial, not many of which possibly wasteful marketing strategies to pass on to the shoppers/ public/ purchasers the significance of the product, its viability, or preferences over contemporary products or the disappointment in research study on the part of bio-based businesses to meet the needs/ requests of the market (Kinch, 2014). Entrepreneurship depend on development has extensive production potential. Given this empowering, unique situation and advancing independent work as a profession choice for youngsters will be of most noteworthy significance. Most policymakers and academics admit that entrepreneurship is basic to the turn of events and prosperity of society. Business person drive and shape advancement, in this way accelerating primary changes in the economy. Entrepreneurship is in this way work as adjuvant for economic growth and national competitiveness.

Nonetheless, numerous biotechnology companies never offer a product for sale to the public and neglect to effectively market their innovation. One purpose behind these successive disappointments is that the bio-based company's current circumstance is exceptionally unique and serious (Fildes, 1990; Greis et al., 1995), and that offering biotechnological products for sale to the public is consequently quite possibly the most perplexing administrative. Besides, new product advancement expenses and product disappointment rates are significant (DiMasi et al., 2003; Evans and Varaiya, 2003), representing that biotechnology can be portrayed as a high hazard industry. Understanding the components that add to the achievement of biotechnology adventures has been a significant exploration road for analysts from the field of technique and business venture. In addition, just one out of 5000 starting medication up-and-comers arrives at market dispatch (Evans and Varaiya, 2003). The bio-entrepreneur is a risk manager to evaluate the future risks and potential of any company that passionately working to solve the future challenges of a growing global population. A good bio-entrepreneur does not obscured by business challenges but scientific challenges haunting him. The entrepreneur is the strength of any organization that works as driving force. A man should have both innovation and industrial knowledge including intellectual property rights. A successful entrepreneur should have a good leadership quality with holder of higher science degrees like MBAs, PhDs and other master degrees (Suryana, 2013; Janeitz, 2003).

Bio-entrepreneurship begins with an imaginative thought, which is formed into administration or a product, which when received in the commercial centre turns into an innovation (Teng, 2008). Innovation is a cycle of transforming opportunity into groundbreaking thoughts and putting these into broadly utilized practice (Tidd and Bessant, 2011). Innovation is in excess of a revelation or an invention, the two of which result from inventiveness. An inventive thought or a novel item is not a development until it has been broadly acknowledged. This definition likewise proposes that advancement requires an efficient cycle which incorporates building up the thought or product into a structure that is wanted by the customer. This is particularly the situation with bio-based products such as seeds or microorganisms, some of which may have impacts (positive or negative) on their surrounding environment and on purchasers.

As per Adams and Sparrow (2008) bio-entrepreneurship has built up a science that manages living life forms through new developments into something that can be marketed. The bio-based entrepreneurship does not depend on one single business person in biotechnology. It is a dispersed cycle as in it is a blend of abilities appropriated over a wide scope of people and associations. Dispersed entrepreneurship is a promising methodology where business emerges with an aggregate organization of heterogeneous entertainers, who are indivisible from one another (Swain, 2019). Bio-entrepreneurship is studied as far as people/ society recognizing and following up on circumstances in bio-based business sectors. The business related to biotechnology is aimed to commercialize the bio products and also enhance the research to benefit the human race. Firstly, bio entrepreneurship has the potential to develop new techniques to protect the environment from diseases, fuel production, feed the hungry and various other product preparations. Biotechnological tools and techniques help in reducing health risks of individual human beings by providing targeted treatments. Hence, these products provide new and better ways with minimum side effects to detect, cure and prevent harmful diseases. Secondly, these bio-based products including polymers, bio fuels and renewable chemicals- are targeted from 2015 to 2024. Biotechnology field have boosted up the wealth of researchers or scientists over the past few years. Most of the activities include-

1. Commercialization of research or international products. For example, improved seeds multiplication for sale to farmers
2. Establishment of biotechnology companies which enhance biotech applications in developing countries like genetically modified crops or medicinal plants.
3. Some other biotech companies and institutes like research centre, training centre and firms for consulting
4. Application of genetic engineering and DNA fingerprinting biology for identification of parents or solving the criminal case.

The response of bioentrepreneurship on creative learning has resulted positive. The study related to bioentrepreneurship is now activity involve in learning activities that can develop students learning potential (Kristani et al., 2012). According to Fitriah (2012), bioentrepreneurship study can develop entrepreneurial interests in scientific research and also better the life skills (Fitriah, 2016). The contextual teaching and learning (CTL) can make students enthusiastically strong who explain their business after development in this era (Adlim et al., 2014). Each action of bioentrepreneur's based on intellectual properties and rights and can be source of any biotech companies advantage (Schneider, 2002). According to Oyovwi (2016), entrepreneurial education in scientific research is better way of mitigating scarcity. The study declared that biology teachers and students, both retained the competence for entrepreneurial skills but entrepreneurial teaching facilities have inadequate provision.

Effective growth of a biotechnology product is as significant as finding the correct approaches to advertise it to target crowd, interested organizations or firms that may put resources into its deal. These might be drug organizations, research labs, instructive foundations, specialized labs or scholars and so on (Lamertz, 2005). Innovation and entrepreneurship are two main components in all phases in the improvement of any organizations; nonetheless it has been perceived that the bio-based organization worldwide is inadequate in entrepreneurs and biologists with suitable enterprising and business abilities. The rule of marketing can be valuable in drawing a practical and inventive advancement design for a specific biotechnology organization or its relevant product (Meckenna, 2001). In the 21st century, utilize web-based media approaches lead ahead different choices in publicity (Lovejoy, 2012). They have, without a doubt, become the absolute most significant advertising apparatus (Lawrence, 2000). Bioentrepreneurship enhances the opportunities for students of entrepreneurship based on entrepreneurial values in research field (Anwar et al., 2012). Bioentrepreneurship with project based learning model develop unique and new ideas in students. According to Titu (2016), project based learning activity is strongly related with creative thinking of students. Jonhnson (2007) stated that the creative learning is mental activity that encourages new visions and original ideas. Entrepreneurship based learning can promote the quality of education by managing learning system (Saputra, 2015).

CATEGORIES OF BIOTECH FIRMS

Nowadays, different industries employ different biotechnological processes and products. Distilleries, for instance, utilize genetically modified yeast to prepare beer. Although usage of a life form adjusted by modern biotechnological strategies, in any case, it would rarely sees distilleries as bio-based companies. Therefore, it is very significant to describe the categories which arrange the firms according to the biotechnology sector. The regional distribution of different bio-based industries is represented in Figure 2. The literature by Ernst and Young (2000) is most commonly used to distinguish the biotech firm categories-

Figure 2. Regional distribution of Indian bio-based industries (a) Regional revenue (crore rupees) generated in 2009-2010. (b) Regional contribution of bio-based companies.

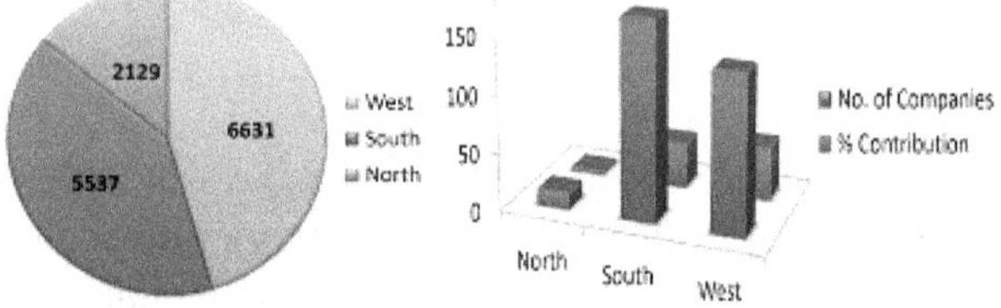

Category I– These small and medium sized companies are known as "Entrepreneurial Life Sciences Companies (ELISCOs)". The main business objective of these companies is to commercialize the modern biotechnology (Ernst & Young, 2000), which frame the prototype of biotech companies in the Anglo-Saxonian sectors. These firms are managed by co-interaction of scientists and entrepreneurs and financed by venture centre.

Category II these firms are known as "Extended Core Companies" (Ernst & Young 2002). These are small and medium-sized firms with less than 500 employees. The object of these companies is not exclusively commercializing modern biotechnology but these firms generate their 50% of earning through biotech processes and products.

Category III these are large sized firms with more than 500 employees which generate most of their revenues through biotechnology products and these products are developed by biotechnogical processes and research (Ernst & Young, 2000). Such as pharmaceutical companies like food manufacturer plants which draw more than 10 million of their annual earning through biotechnogical products and methods (Ernst & Young, 2000).

Some bio-based firms use their restrictive innovation for their own product improvement other than marketing it. These 'cross breed organizations' have the preferred position to create incomes not long after their commencement. Those incomes are put resources into in-house product improvement. In this manner, the organizations are not productive at an early improvement stage, but rather do not solely rely upon outer financial specialists for example, investors. Biological science incorporates all the sciences that relates to an understanding of life, while a bio-venture is business action which includes the utilization of science and the comprehension of life measures, and makes financial incentive for its proprietor. The applications of biotechnology have a wide range from agriculture to industries and many more. The biotcchnology industries can be divided under different categories-biopharmaceuticals, bioservices and bioinformatics, bioagriculture, and bioindustrial (Figure 3).

Bioagricultural Sector

Bioagriculture is one of the most important economic safe areas in biological science. In India, this sector is more standardized than other bio-based inputs in market. Biofertilizer production has increased speedy in India from 1992 that was around 2005 tonnes to 24,455 tinnes in 2008. The successfully introduced biofertilizers are *Rhizobium*, Blue Green Algae, Phosphate Solubilizer, *Azotobacter* and *Azospirillium* (Malhotra et al., 2012). Worldwide acceptance rate of genetically modified crops is quite impressive and India has become the fourth biggest adopter country in the world, uprooting Canada in 2008 (Jagannathan, 2009). Transgenic innovation, including a huge range of insecticidal genes from the bacterium, *Bacillus thuringiensis* (BT) have rules the bio-agricultural market.

Apart from these innovations and victories, agri-biotechnology is lingering a long ways behind health biotechnology, as Indian populations have unfair attitude towards the bio-agricultural products. Major part of the population does not comprehend the significance of health biotechnology products than bioagriculture products.

Bioinformatics Sector

Bioinformatics, which is generally a help based section, caters basically the homegrown requirements. It is the littlest fragment of Indian bio-based industry as of now, however it will accept essentialness with enhancing several clinical preliminaries and entire genome sequencing endeavors. India can possibly turn into a pioneer in bio-based contract research benefits because of enormous patient pool and higher speed of patient enlistment, a huge and generally economical, logical and specialized workforce that talks English, skill in programming innovations, and an all around created public R&D foundation (McNally, 2009). Numerous Indian firms are accepting the outsourcing to accelerate the product advancement. Simultaneously, bioservices firms get double advantage of attaining financial asset and admittance to innovation and ability to progress further towards advancement in own product revelation.

Biopharmaceutical Sector

Since the modest beginning, biopharmaceuticals area has been the focal point of India's bio-based industry and India has gotten one of the worldwide producers of genetic medications. In India, biopharmaceuticals involve around 200 organizations with a big contribution of Rs. 8,829 crore incomes in 2009–10. Furthermore, 62% of market shares with Indian biotechnology industry (Anonymous, 2010; Chakraborty and Agoramoorthy, 2010). As large scale manufacturing of pharmaceutical products by Indian organizations, the expense of these medications has brought down impressively in Indian market. Regardless of the development and accomplishments, health biotechnology faces challenges to smooth out the administrative environment. Commercialization of bio-based pharmaceutical products into domestic markets requires endorsement from few legal bodies that causes postponement and raises vulnerability. This requires more smoothed out the guidelines that give single window administrative approval for commercialization of bio-pharmaceutical products.

The biopharmaceutical industries cover a wide scope of products such as hormones, vaccines, interferon and tissue plasmogen activator and so on. The vaccine industry drove the market with Rs. 2,180 crore income representing 50-60% of biopharmaceuticals market. India is probably the biggest manufacturer of traditional vaccines, furthermore, considered the 'immunization capital' of the world. One of the first greatest examples of overcoming adversity for health biotechnology of India is the commercialization of hepatitis B vaccine identified 'Shanvac-B', by Hyderabad-based Shantha Biotechnics. As of now, this organization supplies almost 40% of UN Children's

Asset's worldwide hepatitis B prerequisite. Essentially, Panacea Biotech supplies oral polio immunization to the Indian government furthermore, UNICEF (Sarah et al., 2007). In 2010, Cipla in a joint effort with UNICEF, built up a kit containing a scope of anti-retroviral medications and anti-infection agents called Mother-Baby Pack, to lessen possibility of HIV transmission from infected mother to new conceived child (Som, 2011).

Bioindustrial Sector

Different enzymes such as protease, amylase, pectinase, glucoamylase, catalase, papains etc., are used in pharma industries for various applications. Detergents, material preparing, leather, food-feed and paper are the predominant items of bioindustrial area (Chandel et al., 2007). Detergent market is the significant purchaser of industrial enzymes (40%) trailed by the starch business (25%). Expanded utilization of enzymes is additionally expected in food preparing, particularly in beer and brew industry for esteem option. Novozymes had the biggest market share (50%) in this portion with a turnover of Rs. 268 crore in 2009–10 followed by Advanced Enzymes Technologies that created Rs. 121 crore incomes.

In India, a bio fuel is an appealing field both for agri-biotech and bioindustrial. Ministry for New and Renewable Energy has declared the 'Public Biofuels Policy' in December 2009, which centers on multisphere improvement at public and state both levels by advancing bio fuels estate and preparing. India has set a characteristic objective of 20% mixing of bio fuels, both for bio-diesel and bio-ethanol by 2017. It has been acknowledged universally that algae can be a possible wellspring of bio-fills as it does not rival food and consumable oils and can be filled in waste and saline water. Praj Industries, an expanded biofuels and distillery innovation arrangement supplier, has teamed up with Novozymes for upgrading the enzymatic hydrolysis measures engaged with creation of bio-fuels. It will empower critical decrease in the expense of enzymes for cellulosic ethanol production (Anonymous, 2010).

Figure 3. Different biotechnology based industries in India

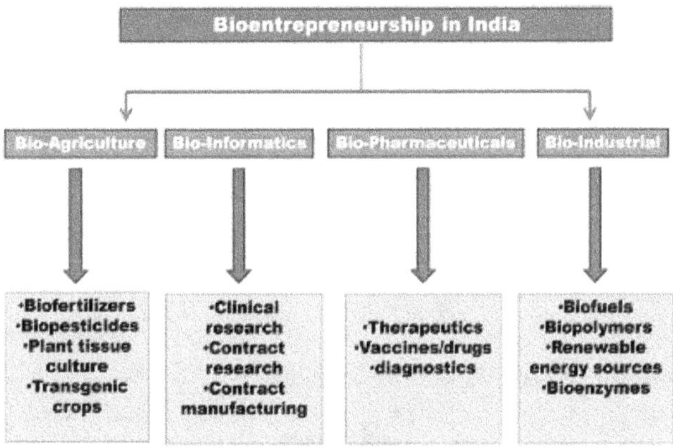

IMPORTANCE OF BIO-BASED ENTREPRENEURSHIP

The term 'Entrepreneurship' has different definitions with specific application to health, medical science and engineering science. Bio entrepreneurship can be defined as opportunity stalk in the life science field by using limited resources. Biotechnological firms develop many life saving devices and medical treatments (swain, 2019). According to Chesbrough and Rosenbloom (2002), the business model portrays how the firm programs to arrange money and determines the position of the firm in the worth chain. The main aim of bio entrepreneurship is to construct human/customer specific values through innovation, research and commercialization of healthcare/ bio products and it also bears the industrial risks to accomplish the set goals (Ojone, 2017). Inventiveness and proactiveness are crucial for the making of a biotechnology adventure while reliability remains the foundation of the bio entrepreneur's character. The bio entrepreneur is a risk manager to evaluate the future risks and potential of any company that passionately working to solve the future challenges of a growing global population. A researcher builds up a thought, develop something and afterward share it with whole universe, a for-benefit consequently. Along with these, not just the nature and society getting advantage from that development. Yet additionally, the creator itself gets a prize for his/her diligent effort. It envelops the acknowledgement of thoughts and ideas that emerge from science and other science fields. Also, further implementing them into prospective business plans and startups. That was the reason behind the creation of bio entrepreneurship. As new innovative ideas are tentative but results may not be positive always. So, entrepreneurs have the patience to see the success of work. Ojone (2017) studied the student's response of bio entrepreneurial events in scientific research. Aside from significances, this field is hampered by different challenges such as low awareness of bio entrepreneurship, poor funding and class shortage (Ejilibe, 2012).

Moreover, it is demonstrable that all new firms are information based since biotechnology is generally recognized as a science based and even a science driven area (Cohen et al., 2002). Another attractive element of biotechnology is that new firms are quite often real instances of business venture, as in they are new innovation based firms. Companies are based upon the utilization of another innovation or the creation of another bio-based product. They generally do not utilize nonexclusive innovations as of now broadly grew somewhere else. The project based scientific study with bio entrepreneurship skills aims to: 1) develop entrepreneurship skill by conventional biotechnology study, 2) enhancing students interest in biotechnology study, 3) encouraging students abilities to associate the convention biotechnology, entrepreneurship skills, technology science and society, and 4) also employing them to solve problems. The products based out of biotechnology are the miracles for our ancestors. These products are generated by their great knowledge and our research work.

As we have seen the role of different biotechnology based industrial products in our daily life involvement. This examination underlines innovation driven business which is fundamental to more cost effective assembling, innovation and tasks type work openings. The biotechnology based products have a vast majorly of significances. As shown in Figure 4.

Figure 4. Several functional activities of bioentrepreneur

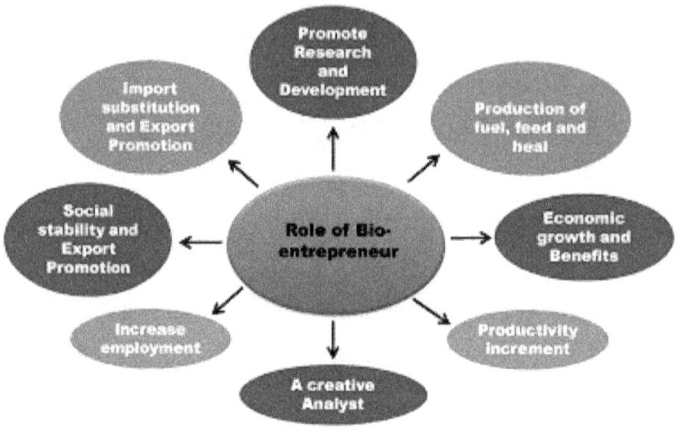

Production of Fuel, Feed and Heal

The bio-entrepreneurship is a dynamic force that promotes the application of bio-based products to support the research and development. The biotechnology based products and technologies protect the environment by fighting with different diseases, production of various useful products such as fuel and feed the hunger.

Environmental Protection

One of the most growing new significant approaches in scientific research is industrial biotechnology which effectively involve in conserving natural resources and energy, controlling pollution and for sustainable processing. As the industrial biotech applications are growing, the bio based economy is also growing that meets the global population needs at early stages.

Industrial biotechnology generates useful products through the use of natural processes like fermentation and harnessing of microbes, yeasts and enzymes as microscopic manufacturing. All the products being made through industrial biotechnology are renewable chemicals, biodegradable plastics, multi vitamins, detergents with low temperature-energy saving, bio fuels and pollution-saving bacteria. Bio entrepreneurs targeted to commercialize these natural industrial products.

Health Biotechnology: Helping to Save and Extend Lives

Biotechnology based products provide better and new ways to detect, cure and prevent disease to save the life's. As biotechnological tools and techniques access new scientific outlet for devising how healthy bodies function and in unhealthy body what goes wrong. These biotechnology based products provides targeted treatment with minimum side effects and low health risks and bioentrepreneur play a significant role in generating innovative ideas towards the social development of the country. Biotechnological tools and techniques help in reducing health risks of individual human beings by providing targeted treatments. In other words, biotechnology entrepreneurship is a continuous process for optimum performance in any organization.

Feed the Hunger

To address the demand of growing population, biotechnologist and bio entrepreneurs are working to solve this dilemma. As today, the total population is more than 7 billion on our planet, which is expected to reach 9 billion by 2050. According to the United Nations Food and Agriculture Organization (UN-FAO), the food production will be double to feed the upcoming generation. However, present arable world's land is in production but we will need to make current production land to be more productive and biotechnological research is working in this progressive area.

The biotechnological generated crops are grown on more than 420 million acres area by 17.3 million farmers in 28 countries. The government approval of biotechnological generated crops was started in the 1990s with commercialization of corn, cotton, soya beans, papaya and canola. As biotechnological crops have enormous production advantages, so these crops have become most speedily accepted technology in agriculture field.

Economic Growth and Benefits

Bio entrepreneurship is the world's second largest economy. The economic growth and prosperity of the country increases through bio entrepreneurship as it generates employment options, wealth and capital creation opportunities, improving life standard, rising per capita income and GDP, betterment of backward facilities, connection between forward and backward society as well as the economic independence. It ensures the optimum utilization of limited resources. Bio entrepreneurship leads to bio economy as it modernize the potential of biotechnology science which favor the economic growth in agricultural, medical and environmental fields. So it's a backbone of the capitalist system and bio entrepreneurs are enhancing the production and services of goods resulting growth and development of the society.

The funding in bio entrepreneurship business came from various sources, such as government and private equity. But around 57% of the investment came from venture capital in renewable chemicals and bio-based polymers. The worldwide production of biotechnology based products- bio fuels, biopolymers and renewable sources- are estimated to grow from $400 billion in 2020 to $487 billion by 2024. In recent years, bio-based business have deposit largest share. Although, bio-based industries require millions of dollar for the establishment.

It is always a difficult task to find a big investor with good fortune in research and development. That is why biotech companies use to prefer join with other commercial industries and big investors for commercialization. For better future of biotech industries, a bio-entrepreneur must have a good estimation of total capital required to remain stable and profitable. Otherwise the funding gaps cause termination of company. A full advantage cost examination of innovation needs to think about the expense to society of bringing regarding new technologies.

Employment Options

Bioentrepreneur develop better way in generating the employment options through constituting new units in trading, manufacturing, services, small scale industries, employing surplus workers in different firms or service centre and encourage self employment as basic object. The bioentrepreneur organizes technologies and resources into productive business experiments and generates job opportunities not only in urban areas but in backward areas also.

Productivity Increment with Modern Production System

The most significant role of bio entrepreneurship is to increase productivity. A good productivity is chiefly attain through improve production techniques. There are two keys to increase the productivity and that are research and development. Investment in new industries and plant is a risky task but R & D and investment programmes are closely linked with good entrepreneurial input in both. Entrepreneurs are the opportunity planner, market makers as well as technology manufacturer. Also, they are the creator of employment and development.

Biotechnological industries endeavors a big control over the production processes of various bio-based products that own a significant decrease the risks of pathogenic contamination. Before commercialization, the bio based product goes through several rounds of trails and safety check through government authorities. Also after commercialization, the products are analyzed by regulatory authorities. The requirements of different regulatory authorities vary with agricultural products, laboratory/medical tests and therapeutic devices.

Import Substitution and Export Promotion

Entrepreneurs play a center role in substitution of import and in promotion of export. Legalization, provocation and globalization (LPG) are main course which increase promotion of export and import substitution to entrepreneurs through establishing the firms producing import substitution goods, new industries beginning exclusively for export, foreign exchange reserves earning, utilizing the available productive resources and exploration of new global markets.

Social Stability and Balanced Regional Development

Bio entrepreneurs have a significant role in establishing social stability and balanced regional development through improving education facilities, employing local workers at new industries, establishing fair competition, remove poverty, empowering weak sections of nation and women, equal salary distribution as well as developing social infrastructures. The bio entrepreneurs supply qualitative good products and services at local demands with satisfactorily.

Commercialization of bio-based products for example, vaccine or drug requires more than IT-based products. Bioentrepreneurial startups take more time for completion and approval from government in comparison to other startups. Because creation of software programs are much easier than biological molecules with bio-safety. In recent years, social networking for the transmission of any information regarding the biotech company or its benefits has picked up a lot of significance. Related organizations are additionally utilizing promoting packs and advertising agencies to aid design a polite procedure for fruitful presentation of the product into the market.

Bioentrepreneur is a Creative Analyst

According to Joseph Schumpeter, entrepreneurs are the creative destructor as they destroy to creat new inventions. Bio entrepreneurs search changes and enhance the product value. The biggest significance of an entrepreneur lies in the fact that in identifying the problems and search its alternatives, chooses the best alternative by comparing the cost and advantages. So, bioentrepreneurship is a better way to develop technology skills and resources of nation.

There are some characteristics that must be required for the bio entrepreneurship. These characteristics are more than the entrepreneurial skills. According to Walton (1998), the bioentrepreneur should have following characteristics-

1. Awareness of Known-Unknown

A bioentrepreneur faces mainly two types of problems- Known and Unknown. A bioentrepreneur is usually an expert in specific science field such as bioscience, biology, chemistry or biotechnology. But whenever there are some problems related to the finance or accounting. Then he must have to connect with commerce related exports to resolve the problem. Because the entrepreneurs do not have the awareness about rational decisions. It is a safe resolving decision to connect with expertise to the relative filed.

2. Master of technical languages

A leader bioentrepreneur are trained to be technical and they need to understand the languages of science and business both. They are great researcher as they are suspicious about the experimental work until reproductive results are documented. Most of the bioentrepreneurs can quickly spot the inconsistencies and errors within the scientific work. That makes their discoveries more productive but they have no interest of marketing and finance. A good product but no market values make investors doubtful. So, a bioentrepreneur must know the marketing of bio-based products for the commercialization.

3. A good leadership skill

A bioentrepreneur should have a good leadership quality to motivate people to achieve their goals. A leader should know about factors to encourage the person which depends on the desires and capabilities of that particular person. A leader bioentrepreneur listen carefully in order to understand the communicated thoughts and ideas.

4. Resiliency

A bioentrepreneur should be resilient towards the challenges and failures of any organization. In any entreprenueurial startup failure is the most common thing at the starting. So, a strategic approach is essential to achieve the targets in bioentrepreneurship. A resilient bioentrepreneur manage the work with patience and motivate the followers to always target at their goals. The struggles during the setup make people more wisdom and a good decision maker.

5. Creativity

For a successful bioentrepreneurship, a bioentrepreneur must have creative and innovative mind other than technical knowledge and business strategies. New concepts build better companies establishment that is essential for every biobased entrepreneur. Creative and imaginative bioentrepreneur can achieve great things when united with business minded person.

This practice helps in sharpening the decision making skills of a bioentrepreneur. Besides, these capabilities are used by bioentrepreneurs in generating new technologies in place of old technologies that results grater performance.

Bioentrepreneurship Promotes Research and Development

Innovation is seen both as an imaginative cycle and as a basic component of a successful administration structure and procedure for accomplishing development in a bio-based organization. On the inventory side of innovations, industrial and experimental abilities are significant in figuring out what is appropriate, yet that relies upon interests into fundamental and applied innovative work (R&D). Entrepreneurship promotes invention of new and ideal products but also impact the existing business. Along with new business ideas, bioentrepreneurs encourage innovative research and development which flow from academia to industry. The research work and industrial innovation is accelerated by the action of many entrepreneurs as they share innovative ideas, motivate each other for social development of the nation. The biotechnology based business started by a researcher, so a bioentrepreneur has more knowledge about the research product than any other entrepreneur. The entrepreneurs also change the industrial climate with opening the suggestion box for others.

Therefore, we see the importance of bioentrepreneurship as multifunctional firm which promote social changes and development of the nation.

CONCLUSION

Development in the biotechnology market is required to quicken in the near future because of appeal for bio-based products and economic growth of India as well as at the worldwide level. The general bio-based market will stay light in spite of the new economic downturn. The biggest test for the nation is to streamline the utilization of biotechnology related to conventional technologies to protect supportable development with fewer assets. India is getting dynamic in creating assorted, community oriented connections to enlarge the biotechnology market. India's developing accentuation on adjusting Indian norm with worldwide norm in assembling and research centre practices will help preceded with infiltration of unfamiliar business sectors also, upgrade of the business worldwide and nearby standing. Nonetheless, India requires solid public, political and monetary uphold for the turn of events and transformation of biotechnological products that add security in future. With a liberal mechanical approach combined with enormous pool of scientific talent, a-list IT industry, a active pharmaceutical area, astounding development in farming area, extending bio-based markets, broad clinical explores, scientific product patent system, India is seen as a expected region for producing excercises and elevated level bio-based research programs.

ACKNOWLEDGMENT

Authors gratefully acknowledge Prof. Aditya Shastri for providing us research facilities and the Bioinformatics Centre, Banasthali University, Rajasthan (India) for extensive use of computational facilities.

REFERENCES

Adam, D. J., & Sparrow, J. C. (2008). Enterprise for Life Scientists: Developing Innovation and Entrepreneurship in the Biosciences. *Journal of Commercial Biotechnology*, *14*(4), 355–356. doi:10.1057/jcb.2008.21

Adlim, M., Samingan, & Rossy, A. H. (2014). Integrating entrepreneurial practice in contextual learning of biotechnology for senior high school student. *Journal of Turkish Science Education*, *11*(2), 111–122.

Ahmad, H. (2017). *Bioentrepreneurship: Beginner's guide*. Retrieved from https://techooid.com>Money

Anonymous. (2010a). BioPharma to grow over 10% for next 5 years. *BioSpectrum*, *8*, 36–38.

Anonymous. (2010b). Enzyme market leader. *BioSpectrum*, *8*, 70.

Anwar, M., Supriyadi, & Sugiharto. (2012). Pengembangan Perangkat Pembelajaran Biologi Dengan Pendekatan Bioenterpreneurship Untuk Meningkatkan Keterampilan Proses Ilmiah dan Minat Berwirausaha Siswa. *Innovative Journal of Curriculum and Educational Technology*, *1*(1), 38–44.

Bello, G., Alabi, H. I., Ahmed, A. R., Sulaiman, M. M., Bello, Z. A., & Bello, A. A. (2020). Biology education and bioentrepreneur opportunities in Nigeria. *Nigerian Online Journal of Education Sciences and Technology*, *1*(2), 1–17.

Chakraborty, C., & Agoramoorthy, G. (2010). A special report on India's biotech scenario: Advancement in biopharmaceutical and health care sectors. *Biotechnology Advances*, *28*(1), 1–6. doi:10.1016/j.biotechadv.2009.10.007 PMID:19931371

Chandel, A. K., Rudravaram, R., Rao, L. V., Ravindra, P., & Narasu, M. L. (2007). Industrial enzymes in bioindustrial sector development: An India perspective. *Journal of Commercial Biotechnology*, *13*(4), 283–291. doi:10.1057/palgrave.jcb.3050065

Chesbrough, H., & Rosenbloom, R. S. (2002). The Role of the Business Model in Capturing Value from Innovation: Evidence from Xerox Corporation's Technology Spin-Off Companies. *Industrial and Corporate Change*, *11*(3), 529–555. doi:10.1093/icc/11.3.529

Cohen, W. M., Nelson, R. R., & Walsh, J. P. (2002). Links and Impacts: The influence of Public Research on Industrial R&D. *Management Science*, *48*(1), 1–23. doi:10.1287/mnsc.48.1.1.14273

David, A., & John, S. (2008). Enterprise for life scientists: Developing innovation and entrepreneurship in the biosciences. *Journal of Commercial Biotechnology*, *14*(4), 355–356. doi:10.1057/jcb.2008.21

DiMasi, J. A., Hansen, R. W., & Grabowski, H. G. (2003). The price of innovation: New estimates of drug development costs. *Journal of Health Economics*, *22*(2), 151–185. doi:10.1016/S0167-6296(02)00126-1 PMID:12606142

Ejilibe, O. C. (2012). Entrepreneurship in biology education as a means for employment. *Knowledge Review*, *26*(3), 96–100.

Ernst & Young. (2000). *Gründerzeit - Deutscher Biotechnologie-Report*. Ernst & Young.

Ernst & Young. (2002). *Neue Chancen - Deutscher Biotechnologiereport*. Ernst & Young.

Evans, A. G., & Varaiya, N. P. (2003). Assessment of a biotech market opportunity. *Entrepreneurship Theory and Practice*, *28*(1), 87–105. doi:10.1111/1540-8520.00033

Fildes, R. A. (1990). Strategic challenges in commercializing biotechnology. *California Management Review*, *32*(3), 63–72. doi:10.2307/41166618

Fitriah, E. (2012). Pengembangan perangkat pembelajaran bioteknologi berorientasi bioentrepreneurship untuk meningkatkan keterampilan proses sains, minat wirausaha dan hasil belajar siswa. *Scientiae Educatia: Jurnal Pendidikan Sains*, *1*(1), 1–14.

Fitriah, E. (2016). Implementasi bioentrepreneurship pada pembelajaran biologi untuk meningkatkan life skills dan minat wirausaha siswa madrasah aliyah berbasis pesantren di Cirebon. *Scientiae Educatia: Jurnal Pendidikan Sains*, *2*(1), 1–19.

Greis, N. P., Dibner, M. D., & Bean, A. S. (1995). External partnering as a response to innovation barriers and global competition in biotechnology. *Research Policy*, *24*(4), 609–630. doi:10.1016/S0048-7333(94)00789-6

Jagannathan, P. (2009). India fourth largest adopter of biotech crop in world. *ET Bureau*. http://www.biotechnitaly.com/pdfuffici/RubriaIndia.pdf

Janeitz, E. (2003). 'Biotech + medicine'. *Technology Review*, *106*(8), 72–79.

Johnson, E. B. (2007). Contextual Teaching and Learning: Menjadikan Kegiatan Belajar-Mengajar Mengasyikkan dan Bermakna. In Contextual Teaching and Learning: What It Is and Why It's Here To Stay. Bandung: Penerbit MLC.

Kinch, M. (2014). The Rise and Decline of Biotechnology. *Drug Discovery Today*, *19*(11), 1686–1690. doi:10.1016/j.drudis.2014.04.006 PMID:24747562

Kristanti, E. A., Bintari, S. H., & Ridlo, S. (2012). Pengembangan perangkat pembelajaran bioentrepreneurship pembuatan makanan dari limbah cair pengolahan kedelai. *Journal of Innovative Science Education*, *1*(2), 112–118.

Lamertz, K. P., Heugens, P. M. A. R., & Calmet, L. (2005). The configuration of organizational images among firms in the Canadian beer brewing industry. *Journal of Management Studies*, *42*(4), 817–843. doi:10.1111/j.1467-6486.2005.00520.x

Lawrence, N. W. (2000). *Social Research Methods: Qualitative and Quantitative approaches* (International Edition). Pearson New.

Lovejoy, K. (2012). *Information, community, and action: How nonprofit organizations use social media*. Wiley Online Library.

Lynn, J. L. (2014). Building a curriculum for bioentrepreneurs. *Nature Biotechnology*, *32*(9), 863–865. doi:10.1038/nbt.3012 PMID:25203028

Malhotra, B., Huddone, S., Verma, A., Chamil, A., Sanju, S., Thakur, A., Sindhu, R., Singh, Y., Patil, V. U., Siddappa, S., Gupta, R., & Pattanayak, D. (2012). Indian entrepreneurship in biotechnology comes of age. *Journal of Plant Biochemistry and Biotechnology*, *21*(1), 90–99. doi:10.100713562-012-0145-y

McNally, J. (2009). Indian CROs can stay competitive. *BioSpectrum*, *7*, 90–92.

Meckenna, R. (1991). Marketing is everything. *Harvard Business Review*, *69*(1), 65–79. PMID:10109473

Ojone, A. S. (2017). Effects of students' awareness of bio entrepreneurship opportunities in biology education in biology education on combating economic recession in Nigeria. *International Journal of Education and Evaluation*, *3*(10), 22–29.

Oyovwi, E. O. (2016). Developing entrepreneurial skills in biology education: A necessary tool for poverty alleviation. *Ibadan Journal of Educational Studies*, *16*(2), 31–42.

Prihatiningrum, P., Susilowati, S. M. E., & Prasetyo, A. P. B. (2020). Effect of Bioentrepreneurship on Biology Learning Achievement, Creativity, and Entrepreneurial Interest. *Journal of Innovative Science Education*, *9*(3), 250–259.

Rifkin, J. (1999). *The biotech century*. New York, NY: Penguin Putnam. *Journal of Technology Education*, *10*(2), 272.

Saputra, K. (2015). *Entrepreneurship Based Education*. Yogyakarta: Diva Press.

Sarah, E. F., Rahim, R., Stephen, M. S., Monali, R., Abdullah, S. D., & Peter, A. S. (2007). India's health biotech sector at a crossroads. *Nature Biotechnology*, *25*(4), 403–417. doi:10.1038/nbt0407-403 PMID:17420744

Schneider, J. (2002). Intellectual property: The driving force for growth and funding. *Journal of Commercial Biotechnology*, *8*(4), 320–324.

Som, N. (2011). Cipla at the forefront of HIV battle. *BioSpectrum*, *9*, 12–14.

Stone, B. (2012). *The Flavr Savr Arrives*. Academic Press.

Suryana. (2013). *Enterpreneurship: Kiat dan Proses Menuju Sukses*. Jakarta: Salemba Empat.

Swain, T. (2019). Biotechnopreneurship: A Resource for the Developing Countries. *Thirteenth Biennial Conference on Entrepreneursh*, *120*, 1133-1141.

Teng, P. S. (2008). Bioscience entrepreneurship in Asia: Creating value with biology. National Institute of Education Singapore.

Tidd, J., & Bessant, J. (2011). *Managing innovation: Integrating technological, market and organizational change*. John Wiley & Sons.

Titu, M. A. (2015). Penerapan Model Pembelajaran Project Based Learning (Pjbl) Untuk Meningkatkan Kreativitas Siswa Pada Materi Konsep Masalah Ekonomi. *Prosiding Seminar Nasional Pendidikan Ekonomi FE UNY: Profesionalisme Pendidik dalam Dinamika Kurikulum Pendidikan di Indonesia pada Era MEA. Fakultas Ekonomi UNY*, *13*(7), 176–186.

Tonukari, N. J. (2004). Fostering biotechnology entrepreneurship in developing countries. *African Journal of Biotechnology*, *3*(6), 299–301. doi:10.5897/AJB2004.000-2055

Uctu, R., & Jafia, R. C. C. (2013). Bio-entrepreneurship as a bridge between science and business in a regional cluster: South Africa's first attempts. *Science & Public Policy*, *41*(2), 219–233. doi:10.1093cipolct049

Walton, A. (1998). Some thoughts on bioentrepreneurship. *Nature Biotechnology*, *16*(S1), 7–8. doi:10.1038/5396 PMID:9591250

Chapter 3 Entrepreneurship vs. Bioentrepreneurship

Sneha Upreti
Banasthali University, India

ABSTRACT

The word bioentrepreneurship and entrepreneurship share the similarity in the fact that they must have a great and an innovative idea behind starting a business setup and to raise an investment. Also, they both must have a great idea about marketing of the related products and managing their start-up. If we talk about the difference, the common difference is the sector or field in which a startup is carrying on. In simple words, entrepreneurship is the process of launching any new business based on an innovative idea. On the other hand, bioentrepreneurship is the process that is started in the field of science (i.e., biotechnology). Nowadays, bio-industrialization is the key to being a modern and developed country, and this is the only reason bioentrepreneurs are highly in demand. Thus, this chapter will help you to understand the pillars to setup a startup based on biotechnology that has an excellent future perspective not only for entrepreneurs but also for the nation.

INTRODUCTION TO ENTREPRENEURSHIP

With the advance and rapid developments in technology and rapid globalization process, the world has come across as a global village with a rapid growth in terms of commerce and its competition. Being a part of the advanced universal economy, it's important to develop certain ability and readiness to run a business or organization throughout the world. Terms like entrepreneurial initiative, entrepreneurial function,entrepreneurial behaviour, entrepreneurial factor which are coined frequently in the present era have a close association with the word "Entrepreneurship".Usually, the entrepreneurship is termed as the entrepreneurial "spirit". A novel factor that differs from the known streamlines ideas is called the entrepreneurial factor. Miller, 1983 defined the term "entrepreneurial factor" as finding and management of the opportunities for the construction of projects or enterprise.

DOI: 10.4018/978-1-7998-7411-9.ch003

In simple words, entrepreneurship is the activity of establishing a trade or business, organisation or businesses, taking on financial risk to foresee profit. This refers to the concept of mounting and managing a business endeavour in order to look on for profit by taking risks. In developing new business, entrepreneurial behaviour plays an important role or you can say this behaviour is the key of setting a new business. Entrepreneurial behaviour is defined as the potentiality that manages to unite alteration, innovation and risk taking audacities. It includes goal oriented acts or decisions of an entrepreneur (Knight, 1921).

According to Reynolds in 2005, entrepreneurship described as the discovery of new opportunities which is followed by the fabricating of the new economic campaign with the development of new organization. He conceptualized it as an entrepreneurial function. He also suggested that developing new capabilities to obtain resources and create new opportunities is the basic motive of entrepreneurship.

The entrepreneurial occupation helps to discover, invent and assess new prospects of developing services, products etc. It also implies the advance tactics and organizational forms for the results that are not exist prior (Shane & Venkataraman, 2000).

The individuals often have a different mechanism for turning the input assets into particular outputs. Also, there is always a difference while evaluating the intrinsic worth of an asset, due to the different perceptions of the individuals which is the leading cause for the continuation of entrepreneurial opportunities. The hypothesis of the entrepreneur, basically emphasizes on the heterogeneity of viewpoint about the worth of assets and resources (Alvarez & Busenitz, 2001).

A proactive and innovative approach, combined with risk taking behaviour is generally called as the entrepreneurial behaviour (Miller, 1983). Additionally, it unites the classic theories of Schumpeter's innovative entrepreneur (1934, 1942) (According to Schumpeter, the manufacturing process is marked by a blend of material and immaterial productive forces).It is important here to highlight the fact that a risk-taking entrepreneur with a high-quality inventive imagination as proposed by Knight (1921) creates a lot of new opportunities.

The entrepreneurial activity is illustrated through three essential pillars. The first pillar focuses on the personage.The entrepreneurial move is envisioned as a soul trait. What makes the entrepreneurs different from the rest of society is their keenness to face indecision (Kihlstrom & Laffont, 1979), challenging risks, and the need for accomplishment (McClelland, 1961).

The economic and environmental factors like the dimension, structure (Acs & Audretsch, 1990) and demographic of the market, the technical changes (Tushman & Anderson, 1986), and the factors like industrial dynamics are elementary factors that facilitate entrepreneurial activity. The second pillar focuses on these key aspects.

The third and last pillar is associated with the working of organizations, societal and culture values. These approaches are not elite (Eckhardt & Shane, 2003), primary entrepreneurial action is also defined as a human activity and remains unconstrained exclusively due to the monetary surroundings or technical,normative or demographic changes.

Eckhardt and Shane (2003) described entrepreneurship in unusual ways. The business progression embraces the recognition and appraisal of new chances, the pronouncement to utilize them oneself or sell them, efforts to get more assets or funds and advancement of the tactics and organization of the new setup project.According to Stevenson and Jarillo, 1990, Entrepreneurialism is an activity by folks – either by their own or by joining with any organisationpuruse opportunities to get profit or to make an aura in the world.Entrepreneurship affects all groups/organisations/industries despite of age, size or kinds of association i.e. private or public body. Its significance for the financial system is reflected in its noticeable expansion, aiming interest for the monetary press and in intellectual literature. And as a result, it is a subject of concentration to business, governments and academics the world over.

Entrepreneurship study works with the principal that directs us to stab to respond a succession of doubts, i.e. What happens on initiating up a new business? What is an entrepreneur? What work does an entrepreneur do? When and why an entrepreneurs act? It is also helpful to get an idea about opportunities that Why, when and how do they are useful for the production of goods and their services coming into existence? And lastly, when, why and how are different forms of action used to utilize entrepreneurial opportunities (Shane & Venkataraman, 2000)?

Origin of the Term "Entrepreneurship"

The term "entrepreneur" originated from the starting of 13th century. It was originated from the French verb, entreprendre, which mean "to do something" or "to undertake." The noun form, entrepreneur was being used from 16thcentury and referred to the individuals undertakes a business venture (Gupta & Khanka, 2003).

An economist Richard Cantillon used this term at first in the year 1730 and he also acknowledged the eagerness to go through the personal financial risk of a business venture as the features mark of an entrepreneur. Mill used the term "entrepreneur" in his popular 1848 book, **Principles of Political Economy**, mentioning a person who assumes both the risk and the management of a business (Ely & Hess, 1937).

In the commencing of 1800's, economists Jean-Baptiste Say and John Stuart Mill, 1827 further signified the scholastic use of the word "entrepreneur." Say stressed the role of the entrepreneur in creating value by shuffling possessions out of less productive areas and into more productive ones.

How the Concept of Entrepreneurship Came into the Market?

The term entrepreneur has been used since the 13th century. It is obtained from the French word that means "go-between". A primal illustration of the entrepreneur as go-between is Marco Polo, who endeavoured to launch trade routes to far faster. As a go between/ entrepreneur Marco Polo would accept the indenture with a capitalist to sell his stuffs, which endowed him with a great fund including insurance. At the centre point, the domination of feudal system led to the hampering development and entrepreneurship.

In the earliest of 17th century, Entrepreneur word was basically used for an individual who signs a treaty or bond with the administration so as to execute a go over since the contract has a fixed price, and the entrepreneur's approach defined the profits and losses which were precisely referred to as his belongings, as a result on supposing the risk as a outcome of his expedition. As observed by a French economist, he distincted an entrepreneur as a businessman "who buys stuffs at a certain price and sells at an uncertain price, and bears the operating risk" (Ely & Hess,1937).

The foremost economist who focused on the character of entrepreneurship in the middle of the 20th century was Schumpeter, 1972. According to him, the entrepreneur's responsibility is to transform the drumming or pulsating production by the application of new inventions. In other words, Entrepreneurship often called 'new product' that allows businessmen to upgrade to a newer version of business organization and business activities serving the diversify essentials of the society. The generosity of cultural inflexibility is primarily a result of this new product 'entrepreneurship'.

WHO IS AN ENTREPRENEUR?

In French, The term entrepreneur is referred as "go-between" and has been in use since the introduction of 12th Century. Marco Polo is one of the ancient most examples of an entrepreneur or as go-between. He endeavoured to ascertain trade directions to the Far East. As an entrepreneur, Marco Polo would mark a regular contract with a capitalist to trade, as a result of which he endowed a credit to the merchant–adventurer at a rate of elevated interest, inclusive indemnity. The consumerist, being the unreceptive risk holder, and the merchant, carrying the substantial and poignant risk used to trade the goods (Ronstadt, 1984).

The word entrepreneur derived from a French word "entreprendre", which means "to undertake." The term was used for the people occupied in military expeditions during the early stage 16th century. With the approaching of 17th century, it was unmitigated to wrap up the construction or creation and civil engineering works. In the 18th century, the term was famous in perspective of business and monetary activities. Richard Cantillon, a French Banker, is endorsed for the exploit of the word 'Entrepreneur' for the first time that means a person who bears uncertainty and risk.

An entrepreneur is an individual who participates in risk taking and running an enterprise by paying a certain price for holding and using resources to manufacture a product and reselling the product for an uncertain price.According to Joseph Schumpeter (1952) an entrepreneur is "an innovator playing the role of a dynamic businessman adding material growth to economic development".

Zimmerer and Scarborough (2002) described the word entrepreneur as "one who creates a new business in the face of risk and uncertainty for the purpose of achieving profit and growth by identifying significant opportunities and assembling the necessary resources to capitalize on them".

One must know the personality traits and characters of an entrepreneur. People often confuse in term entrepreneur, manager and capitalist .But as a business point of view. The practitioner must have knowledge of the differences among them,nonetheless in many cases, an individual may perform all three. Table 1 shows the differences among them (Zimmerer & Scarborough, 2002).

ROLE OF AN ENTREPRENEUR

In accordance with Schumpeter (1934), innovation and ingenuity is the core of the functions of an entrepreneur. He explained that innovation entails doing innovative things or practicing existing things in a fresh manner. Figure 1 shows the various functions of entrepreneurships.

Palmer (1971) explained the main characteristics of an entrepreneur i.e. risk management. The perils are not solitary in respect to an ambiguity to the accomplishment of the latest trade endeavour, but also on the professional and personal aspects such as career openings foregone for the sake of initiating the fresh project family relation and clairvoyant wellbeing .

An entrepreneur has to be hunger opportunities, he needs to analyse already present opportunities in his surroundings. He also needs to catch the most appealing opportunity for himself (Naidu & Rao, 2008).

An entrepreneur should have his business plans in drafting manner. Also, he should have detailed knowledge about what he is going to do. Last but not the least, he should have knowledge about supervision. This includes monitoring, reporting and more sophisticated methods of control (Gupta & Khanka, 2003).

Table 1. Entrepreneurs, managers and capitalists

ENTREPRENEUR	MANAGER	CAPITALIST
ascertain and develops new opening. An originator who motivates and initiates the route of change.	manages and administrates resources, A supervisor	Controlling shareholder Capital owner, Passive shareholder, Shareholder
Uses his second sight, is alert, explores new business Accepts risks. Identifies business opportunities Leadership, begins new ways of acting Formation and development of new Enterprise	Generates and maintains competitive advantage A version to risktaking “Rational” decision-maker. Exploits business Supervision of the administrative process Creates trust to enhance Cooperation	A version to risktaking Choice of venture assets Works on alternatives

Figure 1. Tasks of an entrepreneur

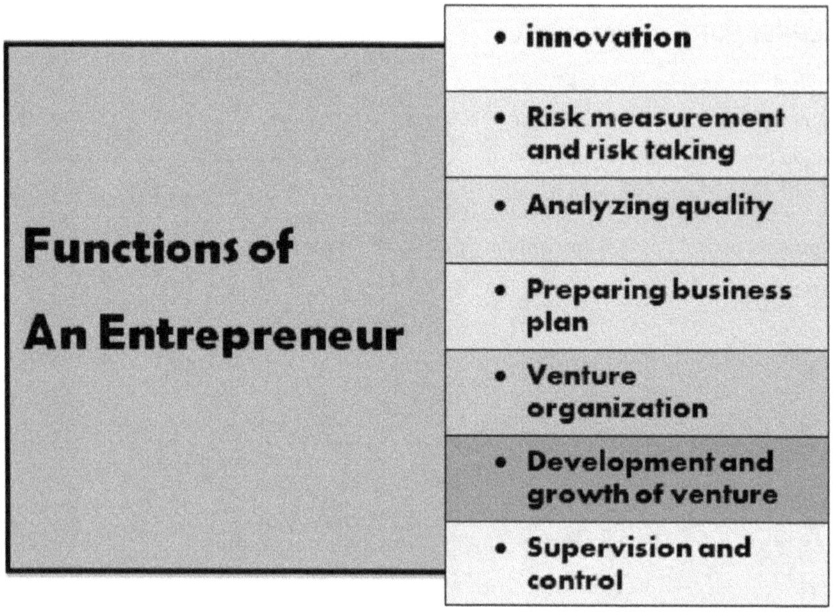

ONGOING PICTURE OF ENTERPRISE IN INDIA

The augmentation, success and growth of entrepreneurship denote the collection of ideas, innovation, facility and encouraging surrounding. The success of entrepreneurship is directly proportional to the economy of the country. The idea of entrepreneurship helps to fulfil the aspiration of individuals and achieving their objectives, gaining financial stability and social recognition (Jacobs,1969).

Expansion of entrepreneurship indicates the collection of ideas, innovations and possibilities. These factors indicate the growth of entrepreneurship. The growth of entrepreneurship based on the aiding, facilitating and cheering atmosphere. The accomplishment of entrepreneurial events gives a positive imprint on the country's economy. It is also helpful in achieving the aspirations of an individual and attaining goals, i.e. social identification, financial gains and self-fulfilment (Onuoha, 2007).

The ongoing entrepreneurship expansion in India has greatly intensified, priorly with an ascend in knowledge-intensive services. There is a budding count of young entrepreneurs, who do not have prior entrepreneurial experience. In this matter, Easy access to funding and other institutional support to 'techno-preneurs' have helped perk up the climate for entrepreneurship in India. As per few investigations, carried out by Price Waterhouse Coopers (PWC) and Goldman Sachs, it is predicted that India has the looming talent to be among the world's foremost financial system by the year 2050.

In India, this is the era of advancement of entrepreneurial, where the enterprenual skill is being endorsed by the government in the education system, society and other corporate organisations. With the mount of the knowledge of demanding services, the scenario of endorsement and development of entrepreneurship in India has been intensified. Now days, the promising number of young entrepreneurs has risen constantly. 'Techno-Preneurs' have uplifted and boosted the atmosphere for entrepreneurship in India in terms of accessing finance and industrial support (Naidu *et. al.,* 2008).

In India, developmental actions of entrepreneurship are restricted to MSME (Micro, Small and Medium Enterprises) sector, preferably called as the 'growth engine'. It is measured as lively and dynamic area of Indian financial system as it endow a huge count of employment to both rural and urban areas. MSME report (2012) defines that this sector devotes 37.54% to countrywide GDP, 45% to entire manufacturing and 40% to entire exports. MSMEs also donate to 30.50% of total services. The Indian MSMEs are being termed as the frame for the "Make in India" vision.

Indian states have been graded on the basis of three constraints, i.e. a development leaning economy, enabling surroundings and forward-looking governance. It is reported that the majority of the financially established states are at the pinnacle of the catalog on the basis of providing an permitting growth and an environment oriented economy, stated in table 2. Chhattisgarh and Himachal Pradesh along with Delhi and Gujarat, are at the top of the list in terms of futuristic supremacy. On the other hand, States like, Jharkhand, Odisha, Bihar, Assam, Chhattisgarh, along with Uttar Pradesh and Uttarakhand are outlined at the bottom of the list (India Entrepreneurship Report, 2014).

If we talk about the current year, the outburst of the pandemic"COVID-19" has haggard an exponential attention towards entrepreneurship. This pandemic has totally changed the commerce landscape appreciably. It has led an increase for a career in entrepreneurship. Opportunities reappeared during pandemic includes Dairy (Milk, Value-added products), Yoga (Training and consulting), Ayurveda (Manufacturing, Trading and Consulting), Agriculture (Organic & Medicinal), proficiency development (training for workers, unorganized zone self-employed, farmers, youth), local Craft (Production and Trade), Bio-technology (R&D and Production of hsealthcare goods) etc.

A composite index, i.e. **National Entrepreneurship Context Index (NECI),** represents in one form the average state of the Entrepreneurship scaffold situation in a specific state / country. To visualize which countries achieve highest and lowest on the NECI, Figure 2 presents the 2019 NECI (thus pre-COVID-19) for 54 economies.

INTRODUCTION TO BIO-ENTREPRENEURSHIP

Bio-entrepreneurship, as the word defines itself:bio and entrepreneurship. It is an amalgamation of two different disciplines, i.e. science and business. It is the gush of innovation from academic circles to the industry. Bio-entrepreneurship, a broad concept is d trending nowadays as it has set an awful elevation for research and innovation in the country. In simple terms, Bio-entrepreneurship can be defined as an entrepreneurial activity in biotechnology or biology sphere (Persidis,1996).

In the configuration of biotechnology, Persidis (1996, cited in Hine and Kapeleris 2006) stated bio-entrepreneurship as a privileged conception that arises from the core of biology (life science) findings in the laboratory scale and then are practices in the viable marketplace. In the year 2008, Meyers depicted bio-entrepreneurship as a progression of producing goods and value from innovations of life science. For our function, we illustrate bio-entrepreneurship as the type of entrepreneurship that includes a bio-entrepreneur, who recognizes a business thought from the life science areas i.e. biotechnology, that seeks to commercialize the idea by establishing a new business.

In other words, it is merely defined as the formation of biotechnology ventures. Bio-entrepreneurs lean to have diverse characteristics than those needed in the conventional context.

Table 2. Upcoming entrepreneurial readiness index source: India Entrepreneurship Report, 2014

State	Indices of Sub-Parameters			Future Entrepreneurial Readiness Index
	Facilitating Background and environment	Growth-based Economy	futuristic Governance	
Gujrat	1	1	3	1
Punjab	4	6	8	3
Delhi	2	2	2	2
Himanchal Pradesh	3	7	1	4
Kerla	6	5	10	6
Karnataka	5	3	7	5
Tamilnadu	8	8	6	8
Andhra Pradesh	10	12	12	9
Maharashtra	7	4	4	7
Madhya Pradesh	9	16	18	11
Rajasthan	15	9	11	10
Haryana	12	13	13	13
West Bengal	13	10	9	12
Jharkhand	11	18	15	14
Uttarakhand	16	14	16	16
Uttar Pradesh	14	17	17	15
Chhattisgarh	18	15	5	18
Bihar	17	11	14	17
Assam	19	20	20	19
Odisha	20	19	19	20

Biotechnology is considered as a chief augmentation commerce and a considerable donor for financial growth in several countries. Consequently, national governments across the universe take it gravely (Hine & Kapeleris, 2006) as indicated by the fact that they have endowed billions of dollars into strategies to improve biotechnology research, development and commercialization (Collet & Wyatt, 2005).

Figure 2. National Entrepreneurship Context Index (NECI) for 54 economies source: GEM Adult Population Survey, 2019

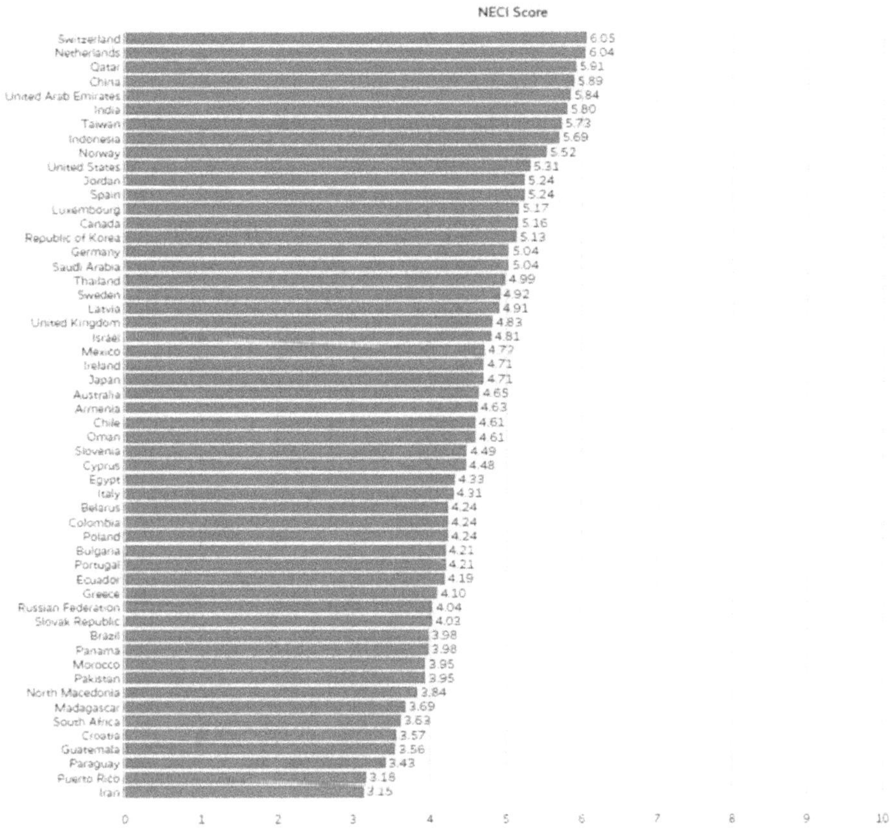

Table 3. Difference between bio-entrepreneurs and traditional entrepreneurs

Criteria of differentiation	Bio-entrepreneurs	Traditional entrepreneurs
Educational background	Technical and scientific biotech, microbiology (MBA, masters or PhD)	MBA, commerce and business
Age objectives	Relatively older Depth knowledge about products	Younger Involved with marketing of products only

Meyers, Uctu, and Jafta (2014) defined bio-entrepreneurship as a progression of developing value from life science innovations. According to Poon and Liyange, 2004, bio-entrepreneurship is the form of entrepreneurship in which ideas related to science, i.e. biology and biotechnology are being utilized to set up a new business and an individual doing the same is referred as a bio-entrepreneur. In simplest terms, bio-entrepreneurship is the conception of biotechnology ventures. Bio-entrepreneurs tend to possess diverse inimitability than those required in the conventional context (table 3) (BioBusiness, 2004).

Several countries activate the training programmes related to the bio-entrepreneurship to establish appropriately capable and expert people to expand the industralisation of biotechnology (Meyers & Hurley, 2008), and thus to generate 'bio-entrepreneurs' in their nation. This is a promising trend in the globe and the bio-entrepreneurship training area is still at the runny phase in which many troupes are in the process of mounting programmes, and no overriding design or accomplishment account has yet emerged.

Biotechnology is a rising and rapidly increasing that has the Potential to transform the civilization and society in the next coming decade. It assures to grant enhanced health care and cure of ailment, new therapeutics, improved diagnostics, improved yield in food production and better environmental supervision (Woiceshyn & Hartel, 1996).

"Biotechnology" is quoted as "The relevance of engineering and scientific principles to the dispensation of resources by organic agents to offer goods and services". Hence, it open numerous opportunities for the development of bio-industrialization (Ramachandran, 1992).

Nowadays, people are also toggling to sustainability and new methods of farming which is in favor of establishing Bioentrepreneurship strongly. As the whole world at present is so much echo up with the buzz word "Biotechnology" with the belief that this field has a lot of opportunities and solutions of their problems, that is why Biotechnology variously depicted as "the preceding revolution of the current century.

Biotechnology gives an outline and proportions to agri-business and industries concerned in same in the modest century due to its potentials.

The potential of biotechnology is described below:

- It is a boon to the mankind as it provide products which were never available before
- It can facilitate stuffs that are currently in short supply.
- It can provide cost effective techniques for the production of needed products.
- It can give safer, better, cheaper, quality product.
- It is helpful to give smart materials for several applications.

AN OUTLINE OF BIOTECHNOLOGY TRADES

'Biotechnology industry' is actually a misnomer. It is a branch of science that plays an important role to allow a vast numeral of diverse industries. The biotechnology industry clutches a huge series of relationships and companies. However,drug discovery companies (DDC's) are the hub of the biotechnology industry. These enterprises, called as miniature companies (sometimes also known as miniature molecule groups) are those entrepreneurial firms which operate on the strategy based on a particular scientific content. Many other firms, offer assistance, support and exit openings to these DDC's. These surrounded companies are called as large molecule companies which include mainly pharmaceuticals (Garnier, 2008).

Another cluster of corporations is known as contract research sectors. The work of these corporations is to grant a wide range of services to the DDC's counting research and carrying out the field trials. They are usually comparatively small and entrepreneurial. There are other companies too that are associated with biotech enterprises and are termed as tool box corporations. The work of these companies is to manufacture several apparatus and tackles that the DDC's can exercise during drug detection. This sector displays speedy transformation. While, the biotechnology enterprise does not display frequent amend as the drug industry is deeply synchronized and the regulations change only gradually. Residing close to the heart of the industry, there is a final group of companies known as diagnostic companies. The job of these companies is to design and construct the products which are utilized to detect an assortment of diseases (Brush, *et. al.,* 1999).

Model Plan For Biotechnology Business

According to Chaturvedi and Chataway (2006) an ultimate biotechnology trade tends to clinch the following given factors:

1. An efficient and cost effective product
2. Sturdy logical asset situation
3. Fits along with the product line of a developed pharmaceutical business
4. An analytic manufactured product to grant cash flow to support research and development.

Important Triumph Factors

Important triumph factors also called as critical success factors are designed to create a vital success of an enterprise in the market. The indulged aspects in the drug advancement segment of the biotechnology trade are as follows:

1. The symphony and quality of the management squad
2. Suppleness and flexibility
3. Subsidy/financial support which is imperative and progressively more tricky to gain.

The administration or management squad in an enterprise needs to comprise folks with diverse abilities and the panorama of these skills will diverge over the period of time. Triumphant biotechnology industries move through numeral of stages. The initial phase of development relies upon the medical and experimental study with experiments on animals. If a product is recognized as a potentially effective, the company may apply to the food and drug administration (FDA) for acquiescence to pierce into a trial phase i.e. Phase I trial (IND). In the stated stage, the product is dosed to a moderately small number of vigorous humans to assure that it is non-toxic. 70% of the products going towards the stage I trials are triumphant. If no destructive effects are observed, the succeeding procedure begins, i.e. Phase II trial, where the manufactured goods is worn on a diminutive scale to treat tangible diseases in human welfare. Typically, placebos are known to half of model inhabitants to observe if the product is valuable in treating a disease. Only 33% of the goods entering this stage are triumphant. In Phase III, which is a last stage, bulky ranged model samples are utilised to establish the safety and efficiency of the product. 70-90% of the goods entering this stage are successful. This denotes the success of an enterprise (Haeussler, 2007).

Biotechnology Fields For Setting Up An Enterprise

As an accepted definition, 'Biotechnology' engrosses the use of existing organisms or their parts with the help of biological dispensations to produce fresh and novel products to develop new production methods.

The budding biotechnology trade has become a major locomotive for economic growth.

Biotechnology has been known worldwide as a significant sector to national economies. This industry is recognized as high-cost and scientific advances.

A lot of biotechnology industries specialize in core competency activities related to their expertise. For instance, according to the Woicheshyn and Hartel an organization may involve in drug detection for the detection of drug targets. However, they may not have an essential capital familiarity to take a specific drug sprinter to market. It can get at least US$100 million to do this. A biotechnology corporation thus will require a tactical association with a huge pharmaceutical companionship to take their product to market. The process from target identification to final market launch may take up a long time (George et. al., 2001). Hence, there is a need of alliance and detailed knowledge of the market (Mazzarol, 1999)

Biotechnology industry involves a vast list of technology areas such as pharma, cell culture, cloning technology etc. to start a small setup as Bioentrepreneurship (table 4) (Mazzarol, 1999).

There are some essential elements that are important for setting up entrepreneurship in biotechnology industry, which include (Schoemaker & Schoemaker, 1998).

- Market awareness
- Opportunity acknowledgment
- Product acquaintance
- A tendency for intended risk-taking which is the most familiar of all elements amongst entrepreneurs
- The desire and capacity to innovate
- The ability to gather
- The ability to utilize resources

The advanced and grooming technology is the result of thinking of certain fields in biotechnology for setting up an organisation. Therefore, it can be said that the opportunities fashioned in science and for business are opportunities created by technology.

PILLARS THAT ARE REQUIRED FOR SETTING UP AN BIOTECHNOLOGY ENTERPRISE

The three chief and structural rudiments are required for the success of biotechnology, that is known as "three pillars of bioentrepreneurship" i.e. a quality administration team, ample finance and of course admitting to modern and new technology that leads the production of products.

Let us talk about each element briefly:

1. Management

Management is the first pillar that is needed to be protected in any fresh bio-pharmaceutical company. It is impossible to transform any new technical opportunity into the product auction without any consideration of expertise or skilled management capability.

Management is considered as the weakest element in most of the biotechnology ventures. This is due to the gamut of supervisory skills required to navigate the organization from root i.e. startup to its commercialization.

Table 4. Chief technology regions and their appliances in biotechnology

Technology areas	**Applications**
Cell and tissue culture technology	• Tissue substitution therapies and embryonic stem cells • Reinstate animal testing for assessing safety and efficacy of medicines • In-vitro promulgation of microorganisms
Monoclonal Antibody skill	• Helps in diagnosis of infectious diseases in humans, animals and plants • Locate ecological pollutants and xenobiotics • Distinguish between cancer cells and normal cells
Recombinant DNA/Genetic alteration Technology	• Include novel medications and vaccines • Locate and treat genetic disorders • Enhance bio-control agents in agriculture • Increase agriculture yields
Protein Engineering/ Proteomics	• Growth of latest and improved Proteins • Expansion of new biocatalysts (enzymes) • Cleaner more competent production using biocatalysts instead of chemical catalysts

If a company gets success in its initial phase and thinks to begin its commercial action, the s there is a need of next et of management skills either internally or externally. At the same moment, managerial spotlight should also be heading towards collaboration with the other organizations as the company positions itself for development and augmentation (Mehta, 2004).

2. Capital

Capital or fund is considered as the succeeding support of every biotechnology enterprise. It is unambiguously fact that, in the untimely stages, no biotechnology company can get a good resource. Feeble CEO and under capitalization and are the main roots of the majority biotechnology company collapse. Being opportunistic in the souk when economic windows are unwrap is advice that cannot be taken too profusely. Hences, bioentrepreneurs must expend significant energies on cultivating financial resources for their juvenile companies (Meyers & Hurley, 2008).

3. Technology

The mid-1970s surfacing technologies were relied upon the genetic engineering, monoclonal antibody and recombinant DNA techniques, which emerged from the inventory work of technical and methodological partnerships of i.e. Cohen and Boyer, and Kohler and Milstein, recognized the fundamentals for the biotechnology trade. This is the third pillar on which each corporation must be built. At present, most biotechnology corporations still seem first to academia for sources of new technology. Academia provides a mainly productive ground for yielding such discoveries, the importance of which cannot be minimized. The Bayh–Dole Act, legislation that persuades educational institutions to license discoveries that originate from federally funded research, will most likely continue to fuel the biotechnology revolution (Mehta, 2004).

The immense confront for any bioentrepreneurs in this time is of astonishing opening is to maintain a meticulous spotlight on the preferred product and its basic technology.

MEASURING SUCCESS IN BIOTECHNOLOGY

Biotechnology companies provide a huge employment opportunities and even larger economic returns. Alone in the United States around 130,000 people work in these type of 2000 companies (Reynolds, 2005). A major fraction of these, around 1,700 are private companies and rest 300 companies are publicly apprehended. The net worth of all companies is near around $110 billion.

Product auctions, market values and profitability of these companies can be used to approximate the success rate of these groups, based on these lesser than a dozen have been recognized as truly glorious. Out of these dozen corporations, the investment community has categorized some of these companies with market assessments in excess of $1 billion as first-tier companies.

The most inquisitive fact about biotechnology without marketing product is that many corporations have resulted in enough investor returns. The low success rate of these companies can be tempered by the understanding that for these industries the terminal financial transactions play a major role in determining of the company's succession to the product sales and profitability.

CURRENT STATE OF INDIAN BIOTECHNOLOGY SECTOR

The Indian government's augmented focus on the country's biotechnology industry is the result that it is growing at a gross yearly growth rate (CAGR) of about 20% over the past decade. The biotechnology areas in India has reached an anticipated size of Rs 20,441 crore (US$ 3.8 billion) in value over FY125, and is forecasted to reach Rs 55,300 crore (US$ 10.4 billion) by 20156. This exceptional growth has been facilitated by the biotechnology industries, i.e. pharmaceuticals, bio-services, bio-industries, agri-biotech and bio-informatics. Figure 3, shows that bio-pharmaceuticals is the principal sub-sector of the biotech industry, whereas agri-biotech is the fastest growing (ABLE annual survey).

Figure 3. Market size of biotechnology sector

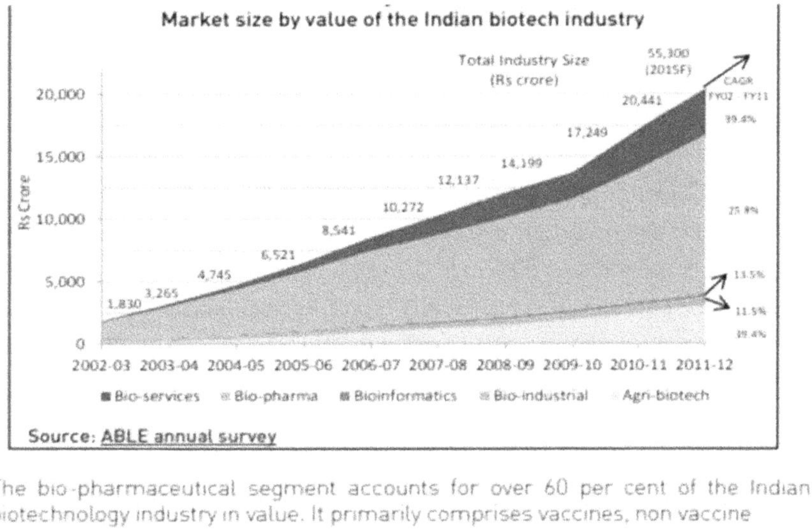

At present, biotech commerce in India is at the verge of remarkable growth. For instance, in the animal and human products segment of the industry alone, the vaccines marketplace wholly is valued at US$ 230 million and is growing at 20% (Alok, 2011). India thrived in deciphering the genome information of rice chromosome 11 and filed six patents related to the mass construction of bio control agents, also called as bio pesticides. Further, the total culture depository at the National Centre for Cell Science reached 1,161 samples after the addition of 34 new cell lines.

Other than that biotechnology playing an excellent role in cosmetic sector by producing the product for skin hygiene. For example, oligomers of glucuronic acid (i.e. Hyaluronic acid) are accompanied with the aging of human skin by penetrating through skin and rejuvenate the acidic content. A viscoelastic film has been developed after applying these oligomers to the skin surface which maintain the skin moisture by inhibiting the penetration of foreign substance to skin dermal layer (Saranraj & Naidu, 2013).

With increasing demand of enzymes, biotechnology is now doing great in leather, textiles sectors too. For example, fats and oil are main ingredients of the food. Modification of oil and fat is critical area in food processing industry and it has great demand in green technologies. Lipases are capable to improve the position of fatty acid chains in the glyceride and restore them into new one. In biotechnology, there are assorted industrial applications that result in production of different biotech products that we are using in daily life at home. Lipase has vast application in food industries like in flavor development, EMC technology and cheese ripening. It is also used in flavor and fragrance compounds which are addition in food to adjust flavor by synthesis of ester (fatty acids and alcohols) (Thakur, 2012).

Biotechnology has a great future in biofuels production too, i.e. biodiesels orbio fuels are the mono-alkyl ester of extended chain of fatty acids and small chain of alcohols. Through direct transesterification reaction of triglycerides with an alcohol group of short chain (i.e., ethanol and methanol) in the existence of proper catalyst synthesis of biodiesels molecules take place (Srivastava & Prasad, 2000,). Transesterification is a procedure similar to breaksdown of water but here instead of water, alcohol is employed. In this reaction, displacement of alcohol from an ester to alcohol takes place (Jegannathan *et. al.,* 2010).

Enzymes or microbial cells posses towering specificity and monetarylead without any environmental collision, hence they are used as an effectual biocatalyst. This is because enzymes work better at moderate temperatures and other environmental conditions.

FUTURE OF BIOTECHNOLOGY INDUSTRIES

Presently in India, the biotech industry is at the verge of remarkable intensification. For instance, in the animal and human products section of the industry unaided, the vaccines market solely is costed at US$ 230 million and is mounted at 20%. The triumph of industries like Bharat Biotech and Shanta Biotech emphasized the fact. India's first genetically modified vaccine, Shanta Biotech's Shanvac against Hepatitis B, costs $4, less than half the cost of comparable vaccines generated by multinational companies. If India is to become a global-player in the field of biotechnology it should tie up with first-rate biotechnological labs. Biotechnology is an enormous vicinity consisting multi-dimensional promising and it doesn't possible excel in all areas. Therefore, it is very important to create a specific and expand core competence. Much also depends on political stability and willingness to take risks. Most important is the contribution of the private sector. Some States, particularly Karnataka and Andhra Pradesh, have taken the lead in establishing biotechnology parks (Kermani & Bonacossa, 2003).

The society we are living in, needs a ravenous requirement for gradually sophisticated health care that must cost effective and useful. New technologies and products are required now days for quick recovery and hence, modification in the healthcare liberation system is altered too. Biotechnology corporations are outstandingly proficient of countering to the pharmaco economic essentials of today's healthcare market.

The product growth and advancement efforts of upcoming biotechnology companies will be science-driven and intended at disease prevention, early diagnosis, and improved therapeutics.

By means of the biotechnology tackles, treatments can now be produced at the genetic and molecular altitudes that will be helpful in providing enhanced, improved, more precise, and less expensive products. The appearance of genomics, the procedure by which genes are associated to particular ailment, is one major example of new and modified technology in biotechnology.

Bioentrepreneurs, who can construct a company grounded on the three pillars of management, capital, and technology, will provide the next cohort of "successes" in biotechnology's rapidly evolving history.

CONCLUSION

"Biotechnology" is the appliances of engineering and scientific principles that can be used as processing of equipments/ materials by the means .of biological agents to provide goods and services to the society. This is the main reason for the high demand of bio-industrialization now days.

Biotechnology comprises the application of biological organisms and processes. Moreover, agriculture is also on high demand and people are looking for new and sustainable methods of farming. This is also a reason of trending Bioentrepreneurship.

Biotechnology is the only field that gives new proportions and dimensions to industries and agribusiness involved in 21st century due to its potentials. Today, the entire planet is so much reflects up with the buzz word "Biotechnology" with strong belief that this is the field which will give lot of new opportunities and resolution to the problem that's why Biotechnology variously termed as "the last revolution of the current century."

The rapid increase in number of biotechnology compounds is the proof that there is a great future of biotechnology companies. Recombinant DNA technology has been recognized as a key tool in biotechnology over the past 20 years. It is used to build up a number of beneficialand therapeutic proteins, including cytokines, antibodies, hormones and vaccines for diagnosing a range of disorders.

As with nearly all the sectors were affected by the present state of the world economy, the biotechnology industry is facing funding difficulties. Capital to finance. However, all along with eminent risks, biotechnology corporations can attain high rewards. For those drugs that do make it via the final trial phase and authoritariansanction, the impending demand is enormous. After all, remedial need does not rely on the economy and there linger disease areas where the current therapies are less than ideal. Although the biotechnology industry has suffered several hunch over its 20-year history, the overall inclination have been positive by many important measures i.e. number of companies, number of accepted products, market capitalisation and revenues. These positive factors are the keys to strategies the commercial companies to prosper in the future.

Thus, this article will help you to differentiate between the two terms entrepreneurship and Bioentrepreneurship. Other than that it will make you understand that what is the basic requirement for setting up a future in biotechnology industry and what are the fields in which you can get a chance to start your own enterprise.

REFERENCES

Acs, Z. J., & Audretsch, D. B. (1990). *Innovation and Small Firms*. MIT Press. doi:10.1007/978-94-015-7854-7

Ahn, M. J., & Meeks, M. (2008). Building a conducive environment for life science-based entrepreneurship and industry clusters. *Journal of Commercial Biotechnology*, *14*(1), 20–30. doi:10.1057/palgrave.jcb.3050076

Alok, K. S. (2011). Biotechnology: The New Horizon for Indian Leadership. *VSRD Technical and Non Technical Journal*, *2*(3), 144–159.

Alvarez, S. A., & Busenitz, L. W. (2001). The entrepreneurship of resource-based theory. *Journal of Management*, *27*(6), 755–775. doi:10.1177/014920630102700609

Beltramino, N. S., Lema, D. G. P. D., & Juarez, L. E. V. (2020). Impact of the human capital on the performance of micro-enterprise: An empirical study in Argentina. *International Journal of Entrepreneurship and Small Business*, *40*(4), 439–464. doi:10.1504/IJESB.2020.109009

BioBusiness. (2004). Landmark discoveries in biotechnology. Academic Press.

BioCentury. (2005). *The Bernstein Report on BioBusiness*. Academic Press.

Brown, T. E., Davidsson, P., & Wiklund, J. (2001). An operationalization of Stevenson's conceptualization of *entrepreneurship* as opportunity-based firm behaviour. *Strategic Management Journal, 22*(10), 953–968. doi:10.1002mj.190

Brush, T. H., Bromiley, P., & Hendrickx, M. (1999). The relative influence of industry and corporation on business segment performance: An alternative estimate. *Strategic Management Journal, 20*(6), 519–547. doi:10.1002/(SICI)1097-0266(199906)20:6<519::AID-SMJ32>3.0.CO;2-8

Bruyat, C., & Julien, P. A. (2000). Defining the field of research in *entrepreneurship. Journal of Business Venturing, 16*(2), 165–180. doi:10.1016/S0883-9026(99)00043-9

Chaturvedi, K., & Chataway, J. (2006). Strategic integration of knowledge in Indian pharmaceutical firms: Creating competencies for innovation. *International Journal of Business Innovation and Research, 1*(1–2), 27–50. doi:10.1504/IJBIR.2006.011087

Collet, C., & Wyatt, D. (2005). "Bioneering"–teaching biotechnology entrepreneurship at the undergraduate level. *Education + Training, 47*(6), 408–421. doi:10.1108/00400910510617033

Eckhardt, J. T., & Shane, S. A. (2003). Opportunities and entrepreneurship. *Journal of Management, 29*(3), 333–349. doi:10.1177/014920630302900304

Garnier, J. P. (2008). Rebuilding the R&D engine in big pharma. *Harvard Business Review, 86*(5), 68–70. PMID:18543809

George, G., Zahra, S. A., Wheatley, K. K., & Khan, R. (2001). The effects of alliance portfolio characteristics and absorptive capacity on performance: A study of biotechnology firms. *The Journal of High Technology Management Research, 12*(2), 205–226. doi:10.1016/S1047-8310(01)00037-2

Gupta, C. B., & Khanka, S. S. (2003). *Entrepreneurship and small business.* Academic Press.

Haeussler, C. (2007). 'Proactive versus reactive m&a activities in the biotechnology industry. *The Journal of High Technology Management Research, 17*(2), 109–123.

Jegannathan, K. R., Jun-Yee, L., Chan, E. S., & Ravindra, P. (2010). Production of biodiesel from palm oil using liquid core lipase encapsulated in κ-carrageenan. *Fuel, 89*(9), 2272–2277. doi:10.1016/j.fuel.2010.03.016

Kermani, F., & Bonacossa, P. (2003). Current and future prospects for the global biotechnology industry. *Journal of Commercial Biotechnology, 10*(2), 154–161. doi:10.1057/palgrave.jcb.3040069

Kihlstrom, R., & Laffont, J. J. (2002). Entrepreneurial theory of firm formation based on risk aversion. *Entrepreneurship: Critical Perspectives on Business and Management, 1*(4), 29.

Kihlstrom, R. E., & Laffont, J. J. (1979). General equilibrium entrepreneurial theory of firm formation based on risk aversion. *Journal of Political Economy, 87*(4), 719–748. doi:10.1086/260790

Mazzarol, T., Volery, T., Doss, N., & Thein, V. (1999). Factors influencing small business startups. *International Journal of Entrepreneurial Behaviour & Research, 5*(2), 48–60. doi:10.1108/13552559910274499

Meyers, A. D. (2008). 'Book reviews (Enterprise for life scientists: Developing innovation and entrepreneurship in the biosciences)'. *Journal of Commercial Biotechnology*, *14*(4), 355–356. doi:10.1057/jcb.2008.21

Miller, D. (1983). The correlates of entrepreneurship in three types of firms. *Management Science*, *29*(7), 770–791. doi:10.1287/mnsc.29.7.770

Naidu, N. V. R., & Rao, T. K. (2008). *Management and Entrepreneurship*. International Publishing House.

Onuoha, G. (2007). Entrepreneurship. *AIST International Journal*, *10*, 20–32.

Palmer, M. (1971). The application of psychological testing to entrepreneurial potential. *California Management Review*, *13*(3), 32–38. doi:10.2307/41164291

Persidis, A. (1996). Building molecular value. *The Journal of Business Strategy*, *17*(2), 18–21. doi:10.1108/eb039765

Poon, P., & Shantha, L. (2004). 'Commercialisation of biotechnology in newly industrialized economies'. *International Journal of Biotechnology*, *6*(2-3), 243–259. doi:10.1504/IJBT.2004.004812

Ramachandran, S. (1992). Agricultural research under conditions of biotic and abiotic stress and scarce resources. *Biotechnology and Crop Improvement in Asia*, 9-15.

Reynolds, P. D. (2005). Understanding business creation: Serendipity and scope in two decades of business creation studies. *Small Business Economics*, *24*(4), 359–364. doi:10.100711187-005-0692-x

Ronstadt, R. C. (1984). *Entrepreneurship*. Lord Publishing Corportaion.

Saranraj, P., & Naidu, M. A. (2013). Hyaluronic Acid Production and its Applications: A Review. *International Journal of Pharmaceutical and Biological Archives*, *4*(5), 853–859.

Say, J. B. (1827). *Production, Distribution and Consumption of Wealth, John Gragg No.* North Forth Sheet.

Schoemaker, H. J., & Schoemaker, A. F. (1998). The three pillars of bioentrepreneurship. *Nature Biotechnology*, *16*(1), 13–15. doi:10.1038/5399 PMID:9591253

Schumpeter, J. (1952). *Can Capitalism survive*. Harper and Row.

Schumpeter, J. A., & Nichol, A. J. (1934). Robinson's economics of imperfect competition. *Journal of Political Economy*, *42*(2), 249–259. doi:10.1086/254595

Shane, S., & Venkataraman, S. (2000). The promise of entrepreneurship as a field of research. *Academy of Management Review*, *25*(1), 217–226. doi:10.5465/amr.2000.2791611

Shoemaker, H., & Shoemaker, A. (1998). The three pillars of bioentrepreneurship. *Nature Biotechnology*, *16*(S1), 13–15. doi:10.1038/5399 PMID:9591253

Srivastava, A., & Prasad, R. (2000). Triglycerides-based diesel fuels. *Renewable & Sustainable Energy Reviews*, *4*(2), 111–133. doi:10.1016/S1364-0321(99)00013-1

Stevenson, H. H., & Jarillo, J. C. (1990). A Paradigm of Entrepreneurship: Entrepreneurial Management. *Strategic Management Journal*, *11*, 17–27.

Stevenson, H. H., & Jarillo, J. C. (2007). A paradigm of entrepreneurship: Entrepreneurial management. In *Entrepreneurship* (pp. 155–170). Springer.

Thakur, S. (2012). Lipases, its sources, properties and applications: A Review. *International Journal of Scientific and Enginewering, 3*(7), 1–29.

Tushman, M. L., & Anderson, P. (1986). Technological discontinuities and organizational environments. *Administrative Science Quarterly, 31*(3), 439–465. doi:10.2307/2392832

Uctu, R., & Jafta, R. C. (2014). Bio-entrepreneurship as a bridge between science and business in a regional cluster: South Africa's first attempts. *Science & Public Policy, 41*(2), 219–233. doi:10.1093cipolct049

Woiceshyn, J., & Hartel, D. (1996). Predicting value-added progress of biotechnology firms: An exploratory study. *Journal of Engineering and Technology Management, 13*(2), 163–187. doi:10.1016/S0923-4748(96)01002-8

Chapter 4
Essential Bioentrepreneurial Characteristics:
A Walk Down the Lane Learning the Attributes of a Successful Bioentrepreneur

Vaishali Nitin Paul
LCIT College of Commerce and Science, India

Arundhati Mehta
Guru Ghasidas Vishwavidyalaya, Bilaspur, India

Shivangi Mudaliar
LCIT College of Commerce and Science, India

ABSTRACT

From the beginning of humanity, people have relied on the usage of biotech-based products. Bioentrepreneurship or BioE is the drive of knowledge and innovation, traveling from academic world to industrial platform. In contrast to enterprise, bio-enterprise is the amalgamation of bioscience with business by the application of biological concepts or scientific entities for the benefit and the creation of a corporation. It is a strictly monitored industry because of involved scientific risks, time demands, and ethical clearance, as well as requiring huge capital. Every successful entrepreneur showcases certain traits that they have inculcated or relied on to build their business. These traits are not mere skills, but are the qualities that contribute in becoming an ideal bio-entrepreneur. The chapter deals with striking features of bio-entrepreneurs that have made them a conglomerate of global standard and play an essential role in making them leaders.

DOI: 10.4018/978-1-7998-7411-9.ch004

INTRODUCTION

Biotechnology can be defined as an interdisciplinary branch of biology involving the use of living organisms to develop or make products intended for the use of humans and its interest (Amarakoon et al., 2017; Steiner, 2020). To a layman, biotechnology is the amalgamation of biology with the modern technologies aimed at making our lives easier. Biotechnology is correlated to the field of medicine, agriculture, diagnostics, food and beverage industry etc. where it facilitates the production of biotechnologically significant products (Singh et al., 2016). Many of these applications related to these fields have posed as a perfect opportunity for commercialization of the technique or the end product. Biotechnology is the process of industrialization of living organisms, using any of the following techniques such as Genetic engineering, enzyme engineering, etc. (Gupta et al., 2016). Due to its potential for creation of new products via different processes, biotechnology has emerged as a key tool for the acceleration of economic development of any developing nation.

An individual who creates a new business opportunity by investing into an idea and executing it all the way to a commercial product, bearing most of the risks is called an entrepreneur. According to Joseph Schumpeter's vision, "the function of the entrepreneur is to reform or revolutionise the pattern of production by exploiting an invention or, more generally, an untried technological method of producing a new commodity or producing an old one in new way, opening a new source of supply of materials or a new outlet for products, by organizing a new industry" (Bull & Willard, 1993). Due to the initiatives of the government, entrepreneurs are also moving towards Biotechnology for a sustainable business. According to Segen's Medical Dictionary, Bioentrepreneur is a person who is the driving force behind a start-up biotechnology company holding key patents or has performed the fundamental scientific work which underpins the company. (Tajonar, 2014). According to Global Market Insights, Inc., biotechnology market value would be worth $729 billion by 2025 (Global Market Insights, 2021).

Many researchers and investors have metamorphosized into becoming a bio entrepreneur with a small idea and have made it successful with a workplan. The enthusiasm showed by the governments have been one of the major factors that have been a crucial push amongst entrepreneurs to establish a start-up venture in this field and put an economic footprint on a country's growth rate (Table 1). Every successful bioentrepreneur displays a set of values that put them on a pedestal of success. This chapter deals with all those characteristics that an individual should possess for becoming a successful bio entrepreneur. This chapter will also trace the journey of success for few such bio entrepreneurs who displayed all these qualities.

WHAT DOES IT TAKE TO BE A SUCCESSFUL BIOENTREPRENEUR?

Many studies and research have been conducted to investigate various traits that has been considered to promote an individual to choose entrepreneurship as career choice and become successful. Various studies found that the effectiveness of an entrepreneur's action relies on accompanying mental qualities such as establishment, inspiration, perseverance, endurance, behaviour at the time of failure, intensity etc. (Bagodi, 2021). These qualities decide if an individual has innovative capacities later on or not. These examinations recommend that simple financial fitness isn't sufficient to portray the wonder of business, distinguished and mental models for a successful business (Brady & Saranga, 2013).

Table 1. Detailed list of biotechnology companies along with their founders and/or CEO's

Name of the company	Founder / CEO's	Originated in (Country)	Product manufactured
Oncoqr	Christof Langer & Geert C Mudde	Austria	Adjustable cancer immunotherapy
Biomay	Hans Huber & Angela Neubauer	Austria	Recombinant allergens
Nabriva Therapeutics	Ted Schroeder	Austria	Pleuromutilins against multi-drug resistant pathogens
Tissuegnostics	Rupert Ecker	Austria	Quantitative analysis of tissue images
Haplogen	Dr Georg Casari	Austria	Haploid genetics tool
Austrianova Biotechnology	Dr. Brian Salmons	Austria	Bioinert polymer encapsulation
Horizon Discovery	Terry Pizzie	Austria	Genetically-defined cell lines
Valneva	Thomas Lingelbach	Austria	Innovative vaccines against infectious diseases
Biocrates	Dr. Nicolas Schaue	Austria	Metabolic phenotyping solutions
Manetco	Tanguy Van Regemorter	Belgium	Management and new technologies development and implementation
Immunxperts	Sofie Pattijn	Belgium	Immunogenicity assessment
Oncurious	Patrick De Haes	Belgium	Treating medulloblastoma
Biocartis	Herman Verrelst	Belgium	Molecular diagnostics solutions
Amplycell	Geoffrey Holsbeek	Belgium	Optimizing monoclonal antibody production
Oncodna	Jean -Pol Detiffe	Belgium	Deep sequencing of tumor DNA
Integrated Dna Technologies	Trey Martin	Belgium	Custom oligonucleotides
Oxyrane	WouterVervecken	Belgium	Enzyme replacement therapies
Active Motif	Joe Fernandes	Belgium	Epigenetic research
Diagenode	Didier Allaer	Belgium	Epigenetics solutions
Switchgear Genomics	Nathan Trinklein	Belgium	Genomic regulation
Ebioscience	Todd R Nelson	Belgium	Immunology reagents
Biogazelle	Jan Hellemans	Belgium	Transcriptome sequencing services
Syngene	Jonathan Hunt	Cyprus	Gel imaging and analysis systems
Lentikat	LudekKarasek	Czech Republic	Biocatalyst: encapsulation of enzymes or microorganisms
Bavarian Nordic	Paul Chaplin	Denmark	Poxviral-based vaccine
Clc Bio	Thomas Knudsen, Founder & Ex-Ceo, Bjarne Knudsen, Founder	Denmark	Sequence analysis software
Taconic Biosciences	Robert Phelan	Denmark	Research model provider
Expres2ion Biotechnologies	Bent U. Frandsen	Denmark	Production in drosophila s2 cells
Barentzymes	Jan Buch Andersen, Sigurd Aase	Denmark	Enzyme based solution
Immunodiagnostic Systems	Jaap Stuut	Denmark	Vitamin d determination
Chemometec	Steen Søndergaard	Denmark	High-speed cell counting
Agilebio	Pierre Rodrigues	France	Collaborative tools that enhance research productivity
IddBiotec	Hélène Rouquette	France	Differentiated therapeutic mabs
Poietis	Fabien Guillemot	France	4d Bioprinting
Synthelis	Bruno Tillier	France	Cell-free system
Antabio	Marc Lemonnier	France	Next generation of antibacterial drugs

continues on following page

Table 1. Continued

Name of the company	Founder / CEO's	Originated in (Country)	Product manufactured
Novaptech	Marine Faussillon-Laville	France	Development of aptamers
GEG-Tech	Nicolas Grandchamp	France	Vectorization systems
Pep Therapy –	Antoine Prestat	France	Innovative peptides as targeted therapies for oncology
Neurosys	Yann Jaudouin	France	Drug discovery for neurodegenerative diseases
Oncodesign	Philippe Genne	France	Preclinical evaluation of anticancer therapies
Invectys	Pierre LangladeDemoyen	France	Therapeutic cancer vaccine
Proteogenix	Philippe Funfrock	France	Services in molecular biology and immunology
Cellectis –	André Choulika	France	Gene-editing
Valneva	Thomas Lingelbach	France	Innovative vaccines against infectious diseases
3d Matrix	Keiji Nagano	France	Synthetic extracellular matrix
Biotek	Dr Norman Alpert	France	Microplate instrumentation and software
Biolife	Mike Rice	France	Enzymatic extraction
Nvh Medicinal	David Vandroux	France	New generation of collagen-based products
Cytena	Jonas Schöndube	Germany	Single cells on demand
Bavarian Nordic	Paul Chaplin	Germany	Poxviral-based vaccine
GnaBiosolutions	Lars Ullerich	Germany	Ultra-fast laser heating of nanoparticles
Insphero	Dr. Jan Lichtenber	Germany	Organotypic 3D cell culture models
Herolab	Nick Etemadipour	Germany	Universal benchtop centrifuges
Lophius Biosciences	Bernd Merkl	Germany	Early diagnosis and immunomonitoring
Probiogen	Lutz Hilbrich	Germany	Intelligent biopharma solutions
Chromotek	Marion Jung	Germany	Single domain camel antibodie
Cytena	Jonas Schöndube	Germany	Single cell separation
Abnova	Wilber Huang	Germany	Innovation through integrated solutions
Isarna Therapeutics	Philippe Calais	Germany	Selective TGF-β inhibitor
Schrodinger	Ramy Farid	Germany	Advanced molecular simulations
Synaptic Systems	Henrik Martens	Germany	Antibodies for neuroscience and cell biology
Artes Biotechnology	Michael Piontek	Germany	Expression platform
Biogenes	Alexander Knoll	Germany	Host cell protein assay development
Ebioscience	Todd R. Nelson	Germany	Immunology reagents
Genetalk	Prof. Dr. Peter Krawitz, Dr. Tom Kamphans	Germany	Expert knowledge portal for human sequence variants
Cristal Therapeutics	Axel Mescheder	Netherland	Next generation nanomedicines
Pharmacell	Alexander Vos	Netherland	Cell therapy and regenerative medicine cmo
Cimaas	Gerard Bos	Netherland	Cellular immunotherapy
Amarna	Steen Klysner	Netherland	Next-generation viral vector platform
Agendia	René Bernards	Netherland	Decoding cancer
Applikon Biotechnology	Arthur Oudshoorn	Netherland	Advanced bioreactor systems
Selvita	BoguslawSieczkowski	Poland	Accelerating drug discovery
Cebiotex	Joan Bertran	Spain	Drug delivery with electrospun nanofiber technology
Mint Labs	Paulo Rodrigues	Spain	Neuroimaging in the cloud

continues on following page

Table 1. Continued

Name of the company	Founder / CEO's	Originated in (Country)	Product manufactured
Chemotargets	Dr. Scott Boyer	Spain	Predicting the target and safety profile of small molecules
Amarna	Steen Klysner	Spain	Next-generation viral vector platform
Ysios Capital	Joël Jean-Mairet	Spain	Private equity for biotech and biopharma companies
Sygnis	Pilar De La Huerta	Spain	Innovative polymerases
TIB Molbiol	Olfert Landt	Spain	Custom synthesis of oligonucleotides
Readycell	Josep Oriol Nicolás I Pallejà	Spain	Easing your screening
Merozyne	EskilSöderlind	Sweden	Muscular dystrophy
Biotage	Tomas Blomquist	Sweden	Instruments for analytical, organic and peptide chemistry
Bioinvent	Martin Welschof	Sweden	Antibody drug discovery
Saromics	Björn Walse	Sweden	Structure-based drug design
Gyros	Dan Calvo	Sweden	Miniaturized immunoassays
Denator	Ulf Järnberg	Sweden	Stabilizing the proteome
Biothema	Karsten Pedersen	Sweden	Luminescent assays
Newron Pharmaceuticals	Luca Benatti	Switzerland	Innovative therapies for central nervous system
Biognosys	Oliver Rinner	Switzerland	Next-generation proteomics
Insphero –	Jan Lichtenberg	Switzerland	Organotypic 3d cell culture models
Mymetics	Ronald Kempers	Switzerland	Virosomes based vaccines
Crispr Therapeutics –	Samarth Kulkarni	Switzerland	Crispr-cas9 genome-editing
Calypso Biotech	Alain Vicari	Switzerland	Auto-immune diseases
Amsbio	Alex Sim	Switzerland	Tissue products
Capital Cell	Daniel Oliver	UK	Life science equity crowdfunding platform
Scancell	Cliff Holloway	UK	Innovative immunobody
Inivata	Clive Morris	UK	Non-invasive tumour analysis from circulating dna
Cupid Peptides	Jonny Ryves	UK	Cell permeable peptides
Crownbio	Dr. Armin Spura	UK	Cancer immunotherapy and xenograft models
Applikon Biotechnology	Arthur Oudshoorn	UK	Advanced bioreactor systems
Motif Bio	Graham George Lumsden	UK	Antibiotics against multi-drug resistant bacteria
Twistdx	Ruth Powell	UK	Isothermal dna and rna amplification technology
Adaptimmune	Adrian (Ad) Rawcliffe	UK	Engineered, increased affinity t cell receptors
Immunodiagnostic Systems	Jaap Stuut	UK	Vitamin d determination
Syngene	Jonathan Hunt	UK	Gel imaging and analysis systems
Biorbyt	Qun Yang	UK	Custom peptide synthesis
Roslin Cells	Aiden Courtney	UK	Pluripotent stem cells
Lumora	Laurence Tisi	UK	Innovative molecular diagnostics
Biomarin	Jean-Jacques Bienaimé	UK	Therapies for rare genetic diseases
Valneva	Thomas Lingelbach	UK	Innovative vaccines against infectious diseases
Fortebio	Joe Keegan	UK	Analytical systems for biomolecular interactions
Bmg Labtech	Robert Mount	UK	Microplate readers
Oxyrane	WouterVervecken	UK	Enzyme replacement therapies

continues on following page

Table 1. Continued

Name of the company	Founder / CEO's	Originated in (Country)	Product manufactured
Asterand	Martyn Coombs	UK	Human tissue and biofluids
Gentronix	John Nicholson	UK	Genotoxicity assays
Immunocore	BahijaJallal	UK	T cell receptor-based drugs
Clc Bio	David Leangen	Japan	Sequence analysis software
Prior Scientific	Thomas Freda	Japan	Microscope automation
Valneva	Thomas Lingelbach	Japan	Innovative vaccines against infectious diseases
Bmg Labtech	Thomas Räbiger	Japan	Microplate readers
Active Motif	Ted Defrank	Japan	Epigenetic research
Clontech	Kazuki Yamamoto	Japan	Cloning tools
Protein Simple	Tim Harkness	Japan	Powering protein research
3d Matrix	Keiji Nagano	Japan	Synthetic extracellular matrix
Activx	Shigeru Ogihara	Japan	*In-situ* kinase profiling
Origene	Wei-Wu	China	Gene company
Switchgear Genomics	Nathan Trinklein	China	Genomic regulation
Protein Simple	Tim Harkness	China	Powering protein research
Hytest	JuhanaRauramo	China	Antibody development for cardiac markers
Ascletis	Jinzi Jason Wu	China	Rnai therapeutic
Xcelris Genomics	Dushyant Singh Baghel	India	Nucleic acid purification kits
Syngene	Jonathan Hunt	India	Gel imaging and analysis systems
Biogenex	Krishan L. Kalra	India	Cell and tissue staining
Biocon	Kiran Majumdar Shaw	India	Delivering affordable innovation
Toolgen	Jongmoon Kim	Korea	Genome engineering
Panagene	Sung Kee Kim	Korea	Pna technologies
Aptsci	Sung Ho Ryu	Korea	Aptamer solutions
Nanoentek	Sung Ho Ryu	Korea	Live cell imaging systems
Kapa Biosystems	Paul Mcewan	Africa	Enzyme solutions
Synexa Life Sciences	Paul O'riordan	Africa	Biomarker expertise
Biotech Africa	Dr AlexioCapovilla	Africa	Eradicating disease through early and innovative diagnostics

Entrepreneurs under the conditions of uncertainty make use of their knowledge, skills and identifies the opportunity to have a socio-economic value (Sucharitha & Venkateswarlu, 2012). Even though the financial worth shows in new items or administrations, new causes of provisions, techniques for creation, business sectors, or potentially news associations, can cumulatively contribute in the yield of the business cycle.

An entrepreneur is the one having multiple dimensions in his or her characters that can make a distinction. Here we are listing some of these attributes commonly found:

1. *Passion*: For a successful bioentrepreneur, passion is one of the most important traits. Being passionate means he or she has a strong belief in their respective ideas and vision. This belief gives

them the energy to drive their work consistently and making them optimistic with a clear vision for their goals ultimately resulting in success.

2. *Creative mind (out of the box thinking):* A creative mind or a creative way of presenting their ideas is also an imperative quality in a bioentrepreneur. The ability to enhance revenue, a bioentrepreneur must-have skills and innovative ideas which could be different, cost-effective, and eco-friendly. For being a bioentrepreneur one should think out of the box because this innovation only will lead to their success (Horoszowski, 2021).
3. *Risk Taker:* Every idea rises from an innovation and an ability to look at that potential with pros and cons can be termed as risk factor analysis. The business visionary should be set up to survey the danger that undermines its business exercises and take it for themselves (Jessica Leitch, 2021). Facing challenge likewise affirms the reality to begin another movement leading to the prize i.e., generation of revenue.
4. *Achiever:* The requirement for accomplishment alludes to a person's craving for critical achievement, dominating of aptitudes, and achieving testing objectives. Specialists estimate that entrepreneurs may hold a serious requirement for accomplishment, as building a business without any preparation shows one's capacities in manners that are regularly difficult to coordinate when working inside a framework in which duty is diffused (Phạm, 2021).
5. *Challenge themselves:* The ability of an individual to set apart from the hostile environment and setting the hostilities into the path of success by moving out of their comfort zone. The attitude of pushing themselves physically, mentally, and socially is what makes them strong. It makes them better able to deal with the issues that we all face in life with an active mind and positive attitude.
6. *Opportunistic:* A good entrepreneur has those "opportunistic glasses" from which they can identify opportunities in every situation. They look at the things and circumstances with an entrepreneurial mindset they can identify opportunities in just about every situation around them. This opportunity tends to be in the niches, and as the old saying goes, the riches are in the niches. Once they find a niche, they are even better at solving problems for people in that niche. They generally scan the environment which leads to more generalized business opportunities.
7. *Familiar with technology:* A bioentrepreneur needs to have proper knowledge of the technology and the source from where they can have it. Interestingly enough, many of these incredible entrepreneurs are techno Neanderthals, but that never stopped them from believing in the importance of it (Örnek & Danyal, 2015). Nor does it stop them from investing vast sums of money into technology to do what they do better. It is that belief that is more important than their skills. As new technology becomes available, they will try it, invest in it, and see how it can make their business and their life more on par with what they want to achieve.
8. *Innovator:* According to Schumpeter, the one who brings a new combination to the market is the entrepreneur, this newness can be introduced in the market by producing new goods or by creating new production methods that are new to the market. An entrepreneur is probably going to be pulled in to continually changing conditions and the oddity of new difficulties. People who flourish with difficulties and novel conditions are the individuals who present inventive arrangements. The introduction of new ideas, products, or services, the management process to be developed in business models and introduced on the market. In the questionable and high climate of latest pursuit creation, numerous specialists speculate that business visionaries flourish with a solid feeling of individual self-viability to execute their dreams and a pointy eye for development to acknowledge new items

and markets. Self-viability portrays a person's conviction that he/she can perform undertakings and satisfy jobs, and is straightforwardly identified with desires, objectives, and inspiration.

9. *Management skill:* it is the basic pillar for any company to stand on. Without any managerial capabilities, the transformation of a technological opportunity into a selling product can't occur. One with good management skills will possess an optimistic attitude towards authorities, they have the quality that helps them to represent their units higher. A manager must be a great competitor, he or she must compete for themselves as well as for their company and this will help them to perform better in the pyramidal nature of the hierarchic organization. Along with this, they will be good at supervising others in their work, all these activities will help one to do various tasks responsibly and a good manager has the zeal to do what the job requires.
10. *Capital:* Initially a biotech company can't have much of the resources so they have to have a good knowledge of different sources that could help them in their company set-up. Many biotechnology companies have faced failures because of undercapitalization. It is the need for an entrepreneur to strategize their energies and spend it wisely in cultivating financial resources for their startups. Running a biotech company needs a huge number of technical assets and assets to cost a huge amount. That's why Elmar Maler, CEO of GPC Biotech said "Raising money when it is available, not when needed". So, a bio entrepreneur must have an eagle's eye on the opportunities available regarding capital and should grab it early.

ISSUES FACED BY A BIOENTREPRENEUR

Biotechnology is said to be one of the fastest growing sectors due to its vast scope for incubation, innovation and entrepreneurship. The indigenous biotechnology sector of India has transformed and metamorphosized, making the country a hub for biopharmaceuticals industry (Sibanda, 2021). Despite the biotechnology industry's rapid emergence in India, critical gaps remain as obstacles for development. There are a few hurdles that a bioentrepreneur must come through to establish an enterprise with long term growth and sustainability.

1. Unskilled labour

Entrepreneurs find it difficult to get skilled manpower as there lies a huge gap between the industrial requirements and the training received during university level education.

2. Regulatory restrictions

In India, the regulatory framework and various hierarchy in bureaucratic organizations and processes hinders the process where biological molecules can be transformed into domestic generic equivalents without significant legal repercussions.

3. Under-Estimation of risk factors

Even though each new wave of start-ups appears to improve on the past, biotech companies consistently overestimate their projected revenues and underestimate the time to breakeven. However, given increasing private investment in R&D and impetus by recent policy reforms, there is an immense potential for growth, especially in segments such as biopharmaceuticals, bio services, and agriculture.

4. Gap between revenue investment and time frames

Long development cycles and underestimation of risk have resulted in the destruction of capital and assets for a biotech firm. Most companies focused on achieving milestones specific to product development, financing and strategic alliances whilst losing the sight of what could be the end goal of a business venture: profit.

5. Intellectual property hassles

The issues of intellectual property have constituted the main deterrent for the growth of the Indian biotechnology industry. After the Patent Amendments Act in 2005, Indian patent laws have a few obscure issues such as the patentability of new use of a known substance remains to be fully settled. The major implementation of foreign ventures investing in the Indian Biotechnology sector also remains in disdain. Foreign venture capitalists are wary of insufficient patent protection and access to patent litigation in India.

6. Brain drains

In pursuit of a better standard of living and quality of life, higher incomes, access to modern technologies and more secure political conditions in various places around the world, brain drain is characterized as the movement of skilled workers.

7. Lack of awareness and mentorship

The lack of awareness and mentorship starting from the fundamental step, pose as a crucial hindrance in setting forth an entrepreneurial culture in India.

BIOENTREPRENEURSHIP SCENARIO IN INDIA

While the biotechnology sector has attracted many investors and entrepreneurs alike but as creating self-sustaining profitable companies, the old models of the biotechnology have not been very successful. Long development cycles and underestimation of risk have resulted in the destruction of capital and assets for a biotech firm. Most companies focused on achieving milestones specific to product development, financing and strategic alliances whilst losing the sight of what could be the end goal of a business venture: profit.

Despite India's more advanced research base, significant advances have occurred in biotechnology companies in developed countries due to strong and persistent government support, favorable policies, venture capital availability and an ambitious workforce. In India, the expertise necessary for the implementation of biological innovation in the Indian bio-pharmaceutical industry is vastly different and not yet available (Cauchon, Oghamian, Hassanpour, & Abernathy, 2021). Knowing and executing the criteria, minimizing the go-to-market time for goods and gaining a sustainable competitive edge internationally is the most interesting challenge ahead.

In order to keep a biotech start-up ahead of all these crises, the policy structure and the right module lie in a basic business model covering the following bases:

- The business must produce viable goods effectively.
- The intellectual rights of the company must be defensible and any patents should not obstruct the product commercialization route of your company.
- To make a substantial profit, there must be a simple and visionary business plan or approach.
- In order to target a huge and fast expanding global market, the business should be smart enough.
- To execute the business strategy, the management should be reasonably competent and have shrewd skills.

In turn, a stable regulatory climate and a vibrant domestic biotech sector will help India create a base to appear in international discussions on biotech-related issues as a more influential voice. In order to improve and streamline its biotech regulatory contraption, India must take constructive steps; facilitate the commercialization of biotech advances; and encourage inclusive domestic dialogue to create greater public awareness of biotechnology, relevant standards and baseline practices. Also, owing to the brain drain from the finest colleges, professional work gets a low ranking. Many of India's best-educated scientists are leaving for even higher wages in the United States and Europe than are required in India.

In addition to the Start-up India umbrella program, which supports the generation of start-ups in all sectors, a wide variety of experimental programmes and services is launched by the ministries of the Government of India and Departments to promote a creativity and entrepreneurship community. Those programs include the financing of schemes such as proof-of-concept, validation, contract analysis, infrastructure, support, mentoring, intellectual property rights support etc. Recognizing the role of women's entrepreneurship and economic participation in facilitating the development and development of the country, by providing access to credit, networks, markets and training, the government also seeks to bring women to the forefront of India's business ecosystem.

Because of its inherent strengths, such as the abundance of rich bio-resources, technological skills, trained labour, ambitious government policies and rapidly expanding access to foreign markets, India is in an advantageous position to exploit the potential of biotechnology (Cvele, 2021). Promotion of the Indian biotechnology industry is high on the Government of India's policy agenda. Biotechnology has been recognised as one of the main priority sectors within the context of 'Make in India' is one of the Government of India's 'Skill India' and 'Start-up India' initiatives. Sustainable economic development and the generation of large-scale job opportunities are among the only industries on a strong growth trajectory. There is a critical need to improve the current biotech industries as well as build new biotech industries in order to meet the $100 billion target of the Indian biotech industry. Innovation-based entrepreneurship has tremendous potential for innovation. Given this context, it would be of utmost importance to facilitate and support self-employment as a career choice for young people.

There are government funding sources that have been set up to expressly promote and finance innovative innovations from the concept validation stage to the full-scale commercialization stage, in order to emphasize innovative R&D and support indigenous technologies by accelerated marketing. The national agencies such as Department of Biotechnology (DBT), the Department of Science and Technology (DST), the Department of Scientific and Industrial Research (DSIR), the Council of Scientific and Industrial Research (CSIR), Defence Research & Development Organization (DRDO), Technology Information, Forecasting and Assessment Council (TIFAC), the Ministry of Micro Small Medium Enterprises (MSME), etc., have funded biotech companies and academia in various fields with a view to improving advanced research and development and technology.

CASE STUDIES

The above-mentioned traits/attributes can be better explained with the following case studies which shows the presence of more than one of such traits in these following bioentrepreneurs who have personified the phrase Rags to Riches:

Biocon Limited

Founder: Kiran Mazumdar-Shaw
CEO/ Chairperson: Siddharth Mittal
Founded: 1978 (43 year ago)
Industry: Biopharmaceutical

"I managed to do things with a lot of common sense, a lot of determination, and a lot of foolish courage". Kiran Mazumdar Shaw, Women in Chemistry, Science History Institute.

Biocon Ltd. is an India based multinational biopharmaceutical firm founded by Kiran Mazumdar-Shaw, headquartered in Bangalore, that develops generic APIs (Active Pharmaceutical Ingredients), novel biotechnology and biosimilar products including insulins as well as antibodies (BBC, 2011; Biocon, 2010). Biocon is one of those prescient corporations that have conscious of change, shows adaptability and insightful in terms of growth opportunities, all under the eminent hands of its founder.

As one of India's forefront leaders in international circles, Shaw's entrepreneurial trajectory embarks the tale of courage and perseverance (Kathuria, 2020). She has facilitated Biocon's transformation from the production of industrial enzymes, to a highly integrated bio-pharmaceutical organization, with a rational product market portfolio and an emphasis on research analysis on diabetes, autoimmune diseases like rheumatoid arthritis, psoriasis and oncology (BloombergTV; Forbes, 2021; Levy, 2012; PTI, 2013). Shaw's perception of "affordable innovation" invariably contributed to Biocon's progress. Driven by the need for affordable/generic medicines, she has searched for ways to build cost efficient strategies and economical alternatives within the least wealthy countries (Estudio; Mazumdar-Shaw, 2014).

Shaw, believes in the fixation of underlying root cause, favouring the concept of "compassionate capitalist" because she asserts that well implemented business models or marketing strategies would be a durable framework for sustainable revolutionary reform (Levy, 2012; Read et al., 2012). Apart from actively engaging in different biopharmaceutical sectors, Mazumdar- Shaw is involved in several education and health outreach programs like Arogya Raksha Yojna, public health campaigns (Queen of Heart) etc. (Desai, 2013; Pharmabiz.com, 2013; Pota, 2010). She addresses the significance of strengthening Indian infrastructure by highlighting the necessity to tackle issue such as efficient democratic accountability, malnutrition, health deprivation and job development (Pota, 2010)

Shaw holds true essence of hard work, loyalty, integrity and endurance. She often highlights to learn the art of endurance as it boosts research stamina helping scaling up and make us less reluctant. She underlined that the genetic makeup of women is entrepreneurial in nature. they just have to find desire and confidence to do so. She acknowledges strongly that women have the capability to double the GDP in the country if they eventuate their entrepreneurial aspirations (Kathuria, 2020).

Novartis International AG

Founders: Johann Rudolf and Alexander Clavel
CEO: Dr. Vasant Kalathur Narsimhan
Founded: 1996 (24 years ago)
Industry: Pharmaceuticals

"One thing we know about human motivation is that people feel their best when they have a sense of purpose and a sense of autonomy". Dr. Vasant Kalathur Narsimhan

Novartis AG was founded as an autonomous venture from the merger of Ciba-Geigy and Sandoz (Novartis.in, 2021). It is a multinational Swiss pharmaceutical corporation headquartered in Basel, Switzerland (Novartis.in, 2021; The Seattle Times, 2018). The tale of Novartis is written on the unified fate of 3 enterprises of Basel: the chemicals and dyes business Geigy, built in the 1800s; the dyes industry, Ciba, established in 1859 and the chemical firm Sandoz, founded in 1886 (Novartis.in, 2021). These organizations conveyed a mutual hallmark on Novartis: a desire for the creation and commercialization of novel products which make a significant contribution to human development via scientific and health breakthroughs. Based on this legacy, Novartis' technical expertise are now focused on combating the unfulfilled necessities of patients globally.

Dr. Vas Narasimhan, a McKinsey alumni and successor of Joseph Jiminez stepped up to took the lead of Novartis, emerging as one of the Fortune 500's youngest CEOs. He leads his business through a strategic and cultural transition driven by innovative therapy and information science platforms (Dandekar & Sukumar, 2018; Phadnis, 2017). He believes that to be a successful leader, one must have an inspiration with a profound sense of intent and an intellectual curiosity. Jimenez used traditional business metrics progressively in Novartis for pharmaceutical cash flow, acquisitions and competitive bidding, trusting that its expertise in consumer commodities would improve the operations of Novartis. His cost-cutting efforts, which primarily concentrated on marketing and management, were consistently reduced by over one billion in 2010, and much higher than in 2011 (Staton, 2012).

Since taking over as CEO in 2018, the company has executed strategic significant transactions worth over $70 billion (Mathew & Jayakumar, 2020). Vas leans on his student philosophical intellect when it refers to its approach of leadership and being an avid reader, he revealed that two paperbacks (books) namely, The classic 6th Century BC Chinese text (Tao Te Ching) and Drive: The Surprising Truth About What Motivates Us (Daniel Pink, 2009) have especially influenced him in his voice (Smale, 2020).

Monsanto Company

Founders: John Francis Queeny
CEO: Hugh Grant
Founded: 1901 (119 years ago) ~ Reformed in 2000
Defunct: 2018 (2 years ago)
Industry: Agribusiness

"I put a lot of value and focus on getting management directly involved with people at all levels in the organization." ~ Hugh Grant

The Monsanto Company was an American agricultural biotechnology and agrochemical corporation which was recently procured by Bayer becoming a part of its crop science department in 2018. It had it premises in Creve Coeur, Missouri, U.S. Monsanto launched crackdown, a glyphosate-based herbicide, and became a major producer of genetically modified crops. Also, this was one of the pioneer firms to use the innovations devised by biotechnology pharmaceutical industries and to adopt biotech business model/ prototype for agriculture sector (Leonard-Barton & Pisano, 1990). The archetypes of Monsanto in farming reforms, biotech products, the coalition of federal agencies and its backbone as a chemical business contribute to a variety of disputes (Paull, 2018).

Until the acquisition by Bayer, Hugh Grant served as the last business executive of the Monsanto and has been ranked to the top 30 most prestigious CEOs on the annual Barron list of around the globe (St. Louis Business Journal, 2009) as well as titled CEO of the Year, 2010 by Chief Executive magazine (Donlon, 2010). Community culture have a central role when it comes to the nature of leadership and stance to diversity of Hugh Grant. The effort for teamwork, transparency and advocacy over the time had affected his management strategy (DiversityInc Staff, 2013; Grant, 2011).

The administrative framework for the company and its associated leadership team was updated with an emphasis on biotech dependency. The new structure was aimed at increasing the organizational influence on the three main principles involved: promoting viable, productive development of capital on the part of Monsanto chemical undertakings; improving the revenue rate of seed and traits firms; and renewing endorsement of the adoption of biotechnology (AgBiotechNet, 2003) He added executive pay to diversity statistics, consistently worked with the 13 resource groups of the organization and had been a leading developer in the industry (DiversityInc Staff, 2013; Grant, 2011). Grant left the Chairman and CEO position, after the attainment of Monsanto by Bayer in an all-cash deal (Brennan, 2018).

AstraZeneca Plc

Predecessors: Merger of Astra AB & Zeneca Group plc
CEO: Pascal Claude Roland Soriot
Founded: 1999 (21 years ago)
Industry: Pharmaceutical and Biotechnology

"We can help choose some of those investments but we can also help along the way the startup companies, develop products and find their way around the world". ~ Pascal Soriot

AstraZeneca (AZN) is a public limited research based biopharmaceutical corporation which offers a catalogue of therapeutic products and services in key areas of ailments such as GI disease, Cancer etc. (AstraZeneca, 2015; Legal500, 2019). AZN emerged after the amalgam of the Swedish firm- Astra AB and British enterprise- Zeneca Group (AstraZeneca, 2019; Fortune, 2009) and it's been among the world's premier pharmaceutical entities since the alliance with a headquarter situated in Cambridge, England (Carroll, 2013).

AstraZeneca has announced vet Pascal Soriot of its Swedish rival Roche as its chief executive, stepping over David Brennan (Kollewe, 2012). New president of AstraZeneca, Leif Johansson welcomed ascension of Soriot as a "pivotal selection for AstraZeneca at an essential milestone" (Kollewe, 2012). Pascal has both a devotion to science and medicine and a comprehensive background in developing and evolving markets, a clear strategic vision, an excellent track record of transition and to tactically implement change and a capacity to manage a complex corporation (AstraZeneca, 2012). Soriot describes his entire leadership personality as 'casual strength'. For his tenure in Genentech, a California-based biotech, Soriot was able to assign this characteristic aspect to the CEO. In that business, he took up the pattern of governance where the community was highly relaxed but firmly assisted by a hard work ethic. He just attempts to not take himself very earnestly (Lee, 2020).

Pascal would like to be stable and understandable, but be competitive at the same point (Lee, 2020). He is a risk taker and work on a rule to recruit an individual who can be his supervisor or boss (Soriot, 2016). Soriot's simple rearing taught him that leaders are built and not born. He is leading by example and constantly attempt to do the appropriate thing. He assumes that it is possible to accommodate greatest achievement by only taking action to enhance every day. Soriot suggests that people ought to loop around others who hold believe close to others. Indeed, he's the lowest paying CEO in the sector (Lee, 2020). AstraZeneca has been an active supporter of international health agencies in combating the COVID- 19 outbreak by donating face masks and PPE kits (Brackley, 2020) and announced the success of COVID- 19 vaccine created in collaboration with the University of Oxford as a "winning formula" with 70% efficiency (Entrepreneur, 2020; Gallagher, 2020).

CONCLUSION

In biotechnology, new discoveries are changing life as we know it. Biology and technology converge in this area and continue to lead the production and commercialization of new technologies intended to enrich lives. Biotechnology is everywhere, from vaccine production to the manufacture of biologics, from plant and animal research to medical equipment; Hence there are immense opportunities available. The bioentrepreneur has to pick the correct area with his own wit. The Indian government is also contributing through "Make in India" to create possibilities for budding talent. The founders should catch these opportunities to create stories that exemplify the potential of one's determination.

ACKNOWLEDGMENT

This research received no specific grant from any funding agency in the public, commercial, or not-for-profit sectors.

REFERENCES

AgBiotechNet. (2003). *Grant Changes Monsanto Management Team.* AgBiotechNet.

Amarakoon, I. I., Hamilton, C.-L., Mitchell, S. A., Tennant, P. F., & Roye, M. E. (2017). Biotechnology. *Pharmacognosy*, 549–563. doi:10.1016/b978-0-12-802104-0.00028-7

AstraZeneca. (2012). *AstraZeneca: Our Leadership Team.* Author.

AstraZeneca. (2015). *AstraZeneca to present comprehensive data from its diabetes portfolio and pre-clinical research at EASD 2015.* Author.

AstraZeneca. (2019). *Key Facts: AstraZeneca.* Author.

Bagodi, V. (2021). *Unit -1: Entrepreneurship: An Introduction.* Retrieved 12 January 2021, from https://www.academia.edu/27130605/Unit_1_Entrepreneurship_An_Introduction

BBC. (2011). *Start-up Stories: Kiran Mazumdar-Shaw.* BBC News.

Biocon. (2010). *Biocon Annual Report, 2010.* Author.

BloombergTV. (n.d.). *Need To Change Mindset: Kiran Mazumdar Shaw.* Bloomberg TV.

Brackley, P. (2020). *Coronavirus: AstraZeneca donates nine million face masks and steps up Covid-19 drugs research.* Cambridge Independent.

Brady, M., & Saranga, H. (2013). Innovative Business Models in Healthcare: A Comparison Between India and Ireland. *Strategic Change, 22*(5-6), 339–353. doi:10.1002/jsc.1944

Brennan, V. (2018). *Grant, other executives to leave Monsanto after Bayer acquisition closes.* St. Louis Business Journal.

Bull, U., & Willard, G. E. (1993). Towards a theory of Entrepreneurship. *Journal of Business Venturing, 8*, 183-195. doi: 10.1.1.458.709

Carroll, J. (2013). *UPDATED: AstraZeneca to ax 1,600, relocate thousands in global R&D reshuffle.* FierceBiotech.

Cauchon, N., Oghamian, S., Hassanpour, S., & Abernathy, M. (2021). Innovation in Chemistry, Manufacturing, and Controls—A Regulatory Perspective From Industry. Academic Press.

Cvele, S. (2021). *Strategic alliances, mergers and acquisitions - the influence of culture on successful cooperation.* Academic Press.

Dandekar, V., & Sukumar, C. (2018). There's an explosion of data & digital opportunities in Indian healthcare: Vasant Narasimhan, CEO, Novartis. *The Economic Times.*

Desai, R. (2013). *Biocon Foundation – Social impact through sustainable community development.* Academic Press.

DiversityInc Staff. (2013). *Diversity Leadership: Hugh Grant, Monsanto.* DiversityInc.

Donlon, J. P. (2010). *Monsanto's Hugh Grant, CEO of the Year 2010.* Chief Executive Magazine.

Entrepreneur. (2020). *AstraZeneca Claims to Have the 'Winning Formula' for Its Vaccine.* Author.

Estudio. (n.d.). *India: Biocon.* Estudio AGML.

Forbes. (2021). Power Women #68 Kiran Mazumdar-Shaw. *Forbes.*

Fortune. (2009). *Global 500 – Pharmaceuticals.* Author.

Gallagher, J. (2020). *Covid-19: Oxford University vaccine is highly effective.* BBC News.

Global Market Insights. (2021). *Biotechnology Market Value Worth $729 Billion by 2025*. Global Market Insights, Inc. Retrieved 12 January 2021, from https://www.prnewswire.com/news-releases/biotechnology-market-value-worth-729-billion-by-2025-global-market-insights-inc-300969541.html

Grant, H. (2011). *Improving Lives/Interviewer* . Leaders Magazine.

Gupta, V., Sengupta, M., Prakash, J., & Tripathy, B. C. (2016). An Introduction to Biotechnology. *Basic and Applied Aspects of Biotechnology*, 1–21. doi:10.1007/978-981-10-0875-7_1

Horoszowski, M. (2021). *5 Reasons Your Business Should Be Socially Responsible*. Retrieved 12 January 2021, from https://blog.movingworlds.org/5-reasons-your-business-should-be-socially-responsible/

Kathuria, C. (2020). *Entrepreneurship Lessons From Kiran Mazumdar Shaw*. SheThePeople.TV.

Kollewe, J. (2012). AstraZeneca appoints new chief executive. *The Guardian*.

Lee, A. (2020). *10 Things You Didn't Know About Pascal Soriot*. Academic Press.

Legal500. (2019). *GC Powerlist: Sweden Teams 2019- AstraZeneca*. Author.

Leitch, J. A. (2021). *10 principles of strategic leadership*. Retrieved 12 January 2021, from https://www.strategy-business.com/article/10-Principles-of-Strategic-Leadership

Leonard-Barton, D., & Pisano, G. P. (1990). Monsanto's March into Biotechnology (A). *Harvard Business Review*, 17.

Levy, A. (2012). Drug Test Can one self-made woman reform health care for India, and the world? *The New Yorker*.

Mathew, J. C., & Jayakumar, P. (2020). *We need short-term launches to keep driving growth: Novartis CEO*. Business Today.

Mazumdar-Shaw, D. K. (2014). *Healthcare Innovation: An Interview with Dr. Kiran Mazumdar-Shaw/ Interviewer: D. B. Weidmann*. Nature Education, Sitable.

Novartis.in. (2021). *Company History*. Author.

Örnek, A. S., & Danyal, Y. (2015). Increased Importance of Entrepreneurship from Entrepreneurship to Techno-Entrepreneurship (Startup): Provided Supports and Conveniences to Techno-Entrepreneurs in Turkey. *Procedia: Social and Behavioral Sciences*, *195*, 1146–1155. https://doi.org/10.1016/j.sbspro.2015.06.164

Paull, J. (2018). Genetically Modified Organisms (GMOs) as Invasive Species. *Journal of Environment Protection and Sustainable Development*, *4*(3), 31–37.

Phadnis, A. (2017). *Indian-origin Vasant Narasimhan to head $48 billion pharma giant Novartis*. Buisness Standard.

Phạm, L. (2021). *Unit-1: Introduction to Human Resource Management Structure of Unit*. Retrieved 12 January 2021, from https://www.academia.edu/11542314/Unit_1_Introduction_to_Human_Resource_Management_Structure_of_Unit

Pharmabiz.com. (2013). *Biocon puts the spotlight on heart disease in women via 'Queen of Heart' campaign*. Pharmabiz.com

Pota, V. (2010). *India Inc.: How India's Top Ten Entrepreneurs are Winning Globally*. Academic Press.

PTI. (2013). *Biocon to launch psoriasis drug novel biologic in July*. The Indian Express.

Read, J. S., & Wiltbank, R. (2012). *How one social entrepreneur creates progress and profits*. Academic Press.

Sibanda, M. (2021). Enabling Intellectual Property And Innovation Systems For South Africa's Development and Competitiveness. Academic Press.

Singh, R., Kumar, M., & Mittal, A. (2016). Microbial enzymes: industrial progress in 21st century. *Biotech, 3*(6), 174 doi:10.100713205-016-0485-8

Smale, W. (2020). *It was never my plan to be the boss of a huge company*. BBC News.

Soriot, P. (2016). *The magic of leadership: one man's leap into the unknown*. Academic Press.

St. Louis Business Journal. (2009). *Monsanto's Grant named among world's best CEOs. St. Louis Business Journal.*

Staton, T. (2012). *Joseph Jimenez - The 25 most influential people in biopharma today*. Fierce Biotech.

Steiner, U. (2020). Biotechnology. *FachenglischfürBioTAs und BTAs*, 1–80. doi:10.1007/978-3-662-60666-7_1

Sucharitha, P., & Venkateswarlu, D. (2012). Socio-Economic Conditions of Women Micro Entrepreneurs - A Case Study of SPSR Nellore District. *Paripex - Indian Journal of Research, 3*(3), 17-19. doi:10.15373/22501991/mar2014/5

Tajonar, A. (2014). How to start a biotech company. *Molecular Biology of the Cell, 25*(21), 3280–3283. https://doi.org/10.1091/mbc.E14-06-1162

The Seattle Times. (2018). Novartis 1Q profit jumps 12 percent as heart drug sales soar. *The Seattle Times*.

KEY TERMS AND DEFINITIONS

Bio-Pharmaceutical: Any prescription drug product produced from, derived from, or semi-synthesized from biological sources is a biopharmaceutical product, also known as a biologic(al) medicinal product, or biologic.

Bioentrepreneurship (BioE): The process of generating value from the advancement of life sciences is bioentrepreneurship. Multiple terms, like bioscience entrepreneurship, life science entrepreneurship or bioscience corporation, apply to it.

Biotechnology-Based Products: The term bio-based product refers to biomass-derived products, wholly or in part, such as seeds, trees or animals (the biomass can have undergone physical, chemical or biological treatment).

Business Plan: A business plan is a structured text that explains in depth how a business determines its priorities and how to accomplish its goals, typically a start-up. A strategic strategy sets out a written vision from marketing, financial, and organizational backgrounds for the organization.

Intellectual Property Rights: Intellectual property is a property concept that encompasses the human intellect's intangible inventions.

Make in India: Make in India is the Government of India's main national initiative aimed at encouraging investment, fostering creativity, enhancing skills growth, securing intellectual property, and developing the country's best in class manufacturing infrastructure.

Chapter 5
Small-Scale Development of Product

Jyoti Yadav
Banasthali University, India

Swati Agarwal
Banasthali University, India

Suphiya Khan
Banasthali University, India

ABSTRACT

Small-scale product development is not for everyone, and it needs a high level of discipline, dedication, persistence, and creativity as well as a lot of work. Before setting up a small-scale business, one needs seed money, physical location of the business venture, construction work, equipment/machinery maintenance, management skills, accounting skills, and last but not least, marketing skills. For the development of any area, the small-scale industry development is very important mainly for the income source of the community and for employment opportunities. On the basis of study, four strategies that are used for the development of small-scale industries were found, and these strategies are 1) promotion and development of institutional, business groups, and cooperatives; 2) determination brands; 3) strategy competition with low cost and product development; 4) to improve final access market orientation strategies. On the basis of analysis of these strategies, they are prioritized, and the first priority is strategy.

INTRODUCTION

For the feasible growth and sustainability, all organizations require innovations and new products development. In 21st century people have begun to recognize the value of innovation. Although innovation is highly complicated but it's the core of every business strategy. Major complications in between the path of any innovation are- intense competition, the lack of clearness in market and short utility period of any product (Calantone et al., 2010). Besides all of these complications' implantation of innovation

DOI: 10.4018/978-1-7998-7411-9.ch005

in organization and its all processes and products are very necessary (Acs & Audretsch, 1988; DiBella, 1997). In every small or large businesses; innovation networks, market environment and product formation characteristics play a very important role in innovation of products (Karlsson & Olsson, 1998). In current period non innovative firms are growing very hardly as compare to small innovative firms. According to a case study of Germany, output growth of businesses was increased by different innovative strategies but it put a very negative impact on employment because of this step employment reduces very rapidly. As compare to Germany, UK and Irish were focused on more balanced development of small firms which includes increment in employment and productivity both by different innovation strategies (Roper, 1997). Variation in small firm's innovation strategies is a very important aspect but it is still under research because of lack of data (De Jong & Vermeulen, 2006). Irrespective of all these aspects small firms are faces many barriers like shortage of technically qualified workers/expertise, low budget due to difficulty in attracting sponsors and high cost of regulatory consent (Freel, 2000).

Opening of new opportunities for market, initiative in marketing and new products development, all of these can only possible through innovation (Armstrong & Foley, 2003; Ulrich & Eppinger, 2011). Innovation can hold a firm's control on the whole industry. New technology, unique products and new resource all of these can be an innovation. Achievement of new position which are unoccupied by opposition is also considered as an innovative exposure. New resource development is highly challenging subject for manager. Bringing beneficial value to any creativity and unique technology is the complete course of innovation management (Teece, 2000). Establishment of an effective idea from different new generating ideas is very challenging process because it requires results from different parts these parts are customers, suppliers, employees and rival companies. The chances of success for any innovation, depends on effective ideas and multiple point of views which are required in the process of development of products (Boyer & Verma, 2009). The whole innovation process is categorized into three parts: the effective idea for innovation, development of new products and its marketing. Thus, innovation has become an important part of business strategies because of some reasons which are advancement in productive manufacturing techniques, good marketing, develops loyalty in customers and maintain a positive brand image.

Table 1. Different dimensions of innovation

S.No.	Categories	Opportunities for Innovation
1.	Products and services	Designs Feature Technology Quality Price
2.	Manufacturing processes	Equipment Technology
3.	Materials	Composition Properties
4.	Business practices	Management practices Business design

Invention and Innovation

In business world, invention and innovation are two different aspects (Baregheh et al., 2009; Dewenter & Malatesta, 2001; Kirner et al., 2009). Both of these are different definitions in different areas. They can be untouched or completely new and may be acquired from previous processes with some different qualities or new technical features which are untried by others, that an institute or company can patent these ideas or imprint designs which are involved in the process (Table 1). Development of new processes is invention (Lettice et al., 2006; Motohashi, 2013; krans et al., 2012). Invention discovers new opportunities, with good results that are both undefined and untouched (Wagner et al., 2002; Kannebley et al., 2005; Albaladejo & Romijn, 2000). That's why in inventions we face more failures as compare to successes. In the whole scenario, invention is very challenging because there are only some points or ideas which are not taking under consideration by others before this. Still possibilities of inventions are increasing day by day (Nybakk & Jenssen, 2012; Rogers, 2000).

One of the central features of every business is the successful conversion of invention into innovation or we can also say that formation of a new commercialized product. Every innovation doesn't give a significatory benefit, there is a great difference in invention and innovation which have good possibility to outweigh the implementation cost (Khilji et al., 2006). A technological innovation includes direction and effective arrangement of human and capital resources which includes many steps like: (1) New knowledge creation (2) new ideas which can enhanced capability of any previous product or can generate new product and can increase effective manufacturing and services (3) conversion of ideas into working product (4) manufacturing of that product at a larger scale in firm (5) distribution into market and their use (Roberts, 2007).

Innovation is always a requirement for human being along with that it is also a controversial subject. It is undoubtful and clear according to academic literature and always implicit in political terms. If we see innovation from political point of view of any developing politics, direction and speed of innovation is a desirable factor atevery level either it is at industrial scale or at the level of national economy. These innovation imporatance are more likely assumed so in the absence of any evidence we can also assume or can say that innovation carried two different aspects which are supply side facors and demand side factors. Supply side factors is some type of driving force for scientific discoveries or technical innovations and the result or outcome of market is considered as demand side factors (Walsh,1984). Inspite of all these optimistic results, biotech companies or firms becomes matured because of growth management and attentive innovations (Zucker & Darby, 1996).

In contrast to invention, innovation is a gradual process where a previously considered idea or products are explored further (Björk & Magnusson, 2009). Products or ideas are technically improved further for achieving good market shares (Figure 1).

Innovation Strategies

Companies for gaining competitive advantages should focus on their innovation strategies. For development and modification of goods or services, innovation strategies are to be planned by applying new creative ideas (Mumford, 2000). If any company wants to increase the value of their product or want to generate something brand new that gains the attention of consumers for this, they have to add some unique effective strategies in their product development.

Figure 1. 6 steps for idea to innovation

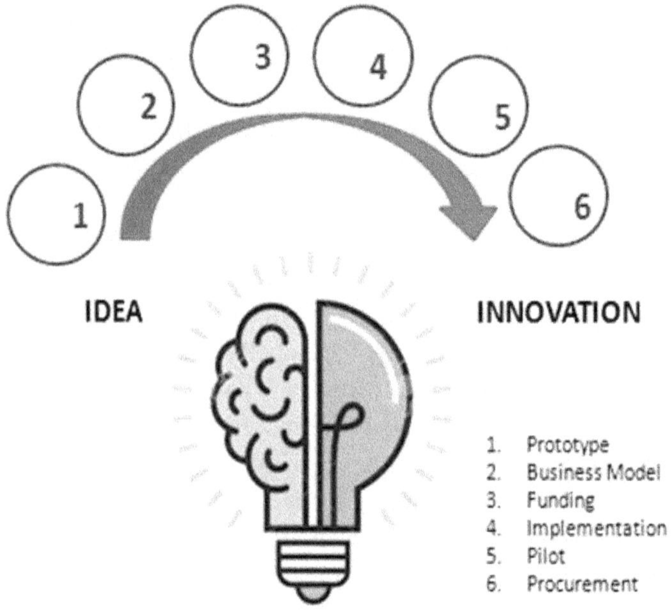

Categorization of innovation strategies can be done in four different ways i.e., proactive, active, reactive and passive innovation strategies (Dodgson et al., 2008). In **proactive innovation** strategies, companies work under high-risk exposure and they approach knowledge from broad range of sources (Von Krogh et al., 2001). These invention strategies are having strong research orientation and they are mainly market leader in technology. Companies in **active innovation** strategies, hedge their bets due to which they are exposed to medium or low risk and similar to proactive innovation strategies they also access broad source of knowledge (Carneiro, 2000). Rather than using unapproved technologies they believe in once proven technology or we can say that these companies are using defending existing markets or technologies. Companies with **reactive innovation** strategies are followers and they approach to low risk opportunities for that they take a wait-and-see approach or focus on their operations (Kettinger et al., 2011). While in **passive innovation** strategies, companies do any change in their product or service after their customer demand (Stamboulis & Skayannis, 2003).

Different data sources are used as input in different types of technological innovation. In recent time, collection and analyzation of current situation evidences is the required need of current users in any product and services designs (Muller & Thoring, 2012). Some new perspective of product growth is smart growth, innovation-based development and knowledge depended development. These all aspects describe, that technological innovation in advance economy is mainly depend on knowledge and high skills and increases need of business and public sectors (Komninos, 2016). Competing firms of global markets faces many challenges and opportunities of technologies and market changes. In long term strategies of any company or firm, innovation is the main focus with increased international competition (Veugelers & Cassiman, 1999).

Before the development of any new product a considerable research should be done for getting a required amount speed and level of technologies in various industrialized Asian countries. Before

1980s, some countries or we can say mainly developing countries like Taiwan, Singapore, South Korea or Asian firms largely depends on foreign firms for borrowing technologies. After that significant shift comes in Asian firms' strategies for technologies development has come and it is more focused towards models which are knowledge based and it further apply this knowledge and technology in advantageous rent-generation (Poon & MacPherson, 2005). Those innovation which actually do not introduce new technologies to society are considered under non-technological innovations according to 1997 Oslo manual but these technologies by using new processes can make some significant changes in goods and services. On the basis of various factors like models, methodologies, strategies, inherent concepts, focused subject and analysis or measurements perspective of innovation can vary (Souitaris, 2002). Our recent research is mainly focusing on these factors during innovation (Ferreria et al., 2009). Because of demand of new and uncertain technologies, in today's market innovation seems very critical and risky in this uncertain or dynamic market. Under all these circumstances, success of any new product with greater probabilities is depend on variety of tools and techniques which assist any scientist to effective innovation. According to new literature of any product development, innovation requires many tools for help and these innovation tools are based on a process of six different strategies which are speed processing, hands on training, marketing, technologies and quantitative (Lynn et al., 1998).

PROCESS DEVELOPMENT

In this entire globally-linked economy, for competing successfully the product development is the base line (Yusuf & Nabeshima, 2005). Organization of development process, reducing waste and providing products to meet customer needs these all are fundamental approaches of successful product development and all these are required for competition in our own market as well as on global basis it also compete effectively.

Process development is helpful in selecting in new valuable developing process for manufacturing of products and along with this make sure the quality of product as well its reproducible manner by implementing process control (Davenport, 1993). They also include the optimization of manufacturing system performance. For the final product development, it includes several steps and these steps are:

1. For optimization of the manufacturing process, they refine the existing process and devising new ones.
2. In laboratories, factories or pilot plants they plan, carrying out and supervising their process trials.
3. To ensure the quality of product during large-scale production and scaling up their production process they use new materials or make changes to components.
4. For improving efficiency and quality in bottle neck areas they investigate new machinery or alternative materials and improving yields by reducing cost.
5. To assess the production process, they have to devise test methods.
6. For showing the improvement they have to validate new processes.
7. At various stages of development, they have to work with product pipelines.
8. For ensuring compliance with specification of finished products they have to develop formulae, specify them and labelled declarations.
9. For new product development they advise on equipment modification to enable changes in process.
10. Reading and writing technical reports.

11. Specify and maintain appropriate records.
12. Based on reading and research they initiate and generate ideas.

PRODUCT DEVELOPMENT

The product concept is transformed into actual tangible product after the approval of all strategies (Kaplan et al., 2004). A prototype or limited production model is built up by the different development stages of new product development. All previous strategies and branding are applied and tested in this stage.

The actual product development goes through the process of product development (Ragatz et al., 2002) (Figure 2). At this point only a drawing, a word description or a rough prototype may exist for many new product concepts. The product concept must be developed into a physical product after passing the business test and it ensure the turning of product concept into a workable market offering (Kotler & Armstrong, 2010). In this whole scenario the problem is that after all these processes comes a huge increase in investment because of Research & Development (R&D) and engineering costs.

One or more product concept in their physical form is developed by R&D department. Development of a successful prototype depends on the product and prototype method on the basis of basis of prototype the product development can take days, weeks, months or even years in its completion. Also, after completion the product must goes under testing to make sure that it performs effectively or and this can be done by outsourced or firm itself (Brown & Wilson, 2007).

Experiences of consumers may be helpful in product development stage and for this in many cases actual customers are involved by marketers in product testing (Veryzer Jr, 1998). They work with their pre-release product and evaluate its prototype.

Figure 2. Complete process of new product development

Idea Generation

Idea generation is the first step in the development process of any new product. It refers to organized research for new ideas of product. To find a best idea in the end a company have to generates hundreds or even thousands of ideas.

After review on various marketing literatures on new product idea generation tools or technique we clearly identified two important points of idea generation which is somewhat different from each other, one is traditionally used and another is LU idea generation method they divided into two type on the basis of the type of information is collected and from whom we collected that information (Rangaswamy & Lilien, 1997). Two main identifying points of traditional idea generation technique are very common. One noticeable point is that they collect information from their nearby markets which are near to the centre of target market (Lonsdale et al., 1996) and another or second important point in traditional idea generation technique is that they only obtain their information and to make it easy they assign these tasks at various levels (Shah, 2000).

Information collection or we can say feedback collection from set of customers or randomly is the traditional idea generation technique which is totally depend on customers. But opposite to this "lead user process" some what different approach as compare to traditional technique. In this they collect information from two different type of users i.e., users at the leading edge of the target market or from others which faces similar problems but at much extreme level (Lilien et al., 2002). Today's products are mainly customer focused so for the better results and effectful product or generation they collect information from potential users and process this information across various companies of that related product (Eliashberg et al., 1997). Inspite of this idea generation strategies of new effective product development, many companies or firms don not get that much of success at market level in this whole competitive development (McDonough et al., 2001). The main failure behind any product or companies is that, they all developed idea at their level but for the successful idea development they need a new or breakthrough ideas which should be different from all ordinary idea and it mainly comes screening of idea, that's why next step in product development which is idea screening is very important (Haman, 1996).

Various idea generation techniques are available in today's markets to assist engineer in this whole process (VanGundy,1998). For this purpose, mainly more than 100 idea generation techniques are available which are based on different aspects like psychology, engineering and business (Fogler & LeBlanc, 2014). These idea generation are always being used in engineering and development of different product to create, invent and innovate (Römer et al., 2001). All these idea generation or design phases put a direct impact on product cost which is significantly based on conceptual designs (Plucker & Beghetto, 2000).

Idea Screening

Further the next step in the development process of new products is idea screening. Idea screening refers to filtration of generated ideas to pick out good ones (Cooper & Edgett, 2009). More simply, we can also say that all generated ideas are screened to drop poor ones as soon as possible or to spot good ones. The main purpose of idea screening is to reduce the number of ideas in the succeeding stages which are generated in large number in previous stage (Alam & Perry, 2002). The reason of idea screening is that the cost of product development rises greatly in later stages. Therefore, the company would like to go with those ideas which can be turn into profitable products. As soon as dropping the poor ideas is, consequently, of crucial importance.

Concept Development and Testing

For the development process of any new product, an attractive idea must be converted into a product concept (Durmuşoğlu & Barczak, 2011). Detailed version of any idea is a product concept. You have to distinguish:

- Idea for a possible product or product idea.
- A product concept is nothing more than a detailed version of any idea with meaningful consumer terms.
- Consumable potential product is a product image.

MARKETING STRATEGIES

After the product development stage, the next step in production of new product is development of marketing strategy (Hart, 2003; Morris, 2009; Jeannet & Hennessey, 2005). For introducing new product to the market, a promising product has been developed or tested and this is the time to develop initial marketing strategy.

The fundamental aim of every business is marketing which involves its survival, profit and growth rate (Homburg et al., 2009; Smith, 1995). Mutual satisfactory exchange between two parties can be facilitated by different marketing activities and it is the ultimate aim of every small or large businesses marketing strategy (Saxena, 2005; Hooley et al., 1992; Noble & Mokwa, 1999). The whole marketing process focuses on every aspect of a product success rate in market i.e., setting goals of marketing, development of marketing strategy by selecting a target achievement of that product, environment scanning, calculating market performance of that product after a certain period, evaluation of marketing efforts and make changes if required (Cant et al., 2009).

Business Analysis

Evaluation of proposed product business attractiveness by management is also a main step in product development (Cooper, 1990). To find out that these products are satisfying company objectives or not, for this company apply costs, a review of the sales and profit projections in the development process (Palepu et al., 2020). If the product fulfills the company's objective than the particular product can pass on further development stage (Marshall, 2020).

By conducting market surveys or comparing the sales history of similar products company can estimate sales (Gomez et al., 2004). They can assess the range of risk by estimating the minimum and maximum sales. By involving the R&D operations and marketing company can estimate the expected profit or cost of any product before sale forecast is ready (Vernon, 2005). For analysis of the financial attractiveness of the new products firms have to use all the sales and costs figure together.

Test Marketing

Before commercialization of new product, the last stage in the product development is test marketing (Cooper, 1988). In realistic market the product and its proposed marketing program are tested in this stage. Before introduction of new product to the market company can use marketer experience by test marketing of their product (Segal & Johar, 1992). Before the full investment this test marketing, stage allows the company to test the product and its complete marketing program i.e. packaging, advertising, distributions, targeting and positioning strategy etc. with each new product different amount of test marketing is necessary (Deepak & Jeyakumar, 2019). A lot of test marketing is required when the company is not sure for their product or its marketing strategy or when the firm taking a high risk by introducing the large investment in new product.

LAUNCHING AND COMMERCIALIZATION

New product should be launched or not this final decision is taken out on the basis of the information given to the management by test marketing. Commercialization is the final stage in the product development process of new product (Akgün et al., 2007). At this stage the company may need to build or rent a manufacturing space by incurred the large amount of cost. In the first year of launching the product, the company may need to spend a very large amount on sales promotions, advertising and in other marketing efforts. For the assurance of their product into market a company or firm need to mobilize its resources into their network. For the successful transformation of an invention into innovation needs successful commercialization of their product (Schumpeter, 1934). Some companies can't get a breakthrough attention to their product because they do not put much focus on their commercialisation networks (Heikkinen et al., 2007; Millson & Wilemon, 2008; Partanen et al., 2008). Some research studied the contribution of users and stakeholders for an innovative diffusion (Troshani & Doolin, 2007) and launch (Biemans, 1991; Harrison & Waluszewski, 2008).

Commercialization Strategy

- **What's the Offering?**

An aggregated overview of the product benefits of using the products by consumer point of view what your product is and what it does these are the offering of product and it is clearly states by commercialization strategies. It also involves the pricing strategy for distributions channels as well as for end-user.

- **How does the Product Align with your Core Business?**

Determination of strategic directions which is required for the commercialization plans it clears the how closely the product launching is aligned to the business core. A lot of infrastructure is reusable and only some new strategies are required for product development and it is also close to the core business (Grudin & Pruitt, 2002). Diversity of work determined its closeness, more diverse more strategies are required in product development.

- **Identifying the Target Markets/Customers**

After the test marketing which is carried out in previous phase, company should plan an initial target market and also plan a customer profile initially. It is the final time to capitalize all the hard work which carrying new product to this stage.

- **Business Plan and Forecast**
  Forecast is also the main part of business and commercialization and in this stage, company looking three years ahead. The forecast elements are following:
  - Sales quantities
  - Gross margin and gross margin as a percentage of sales
  - Operating income and operating income as a percentage of sales
  - CAPEX- Capital Expenditure
  - RONA- Return on Net Assets

Commercialization Process

This stage of product development includes several steps:

- Develop a direct marketing campaign: Social media is best platform of marketing any product through this they can directly connect with customers in target markets (Mangold & Faulds, 2009). These marketing campaigns are such as direct mail, social sites etc.
- Create your advertising plan: Companies have to plan their advertising target market where consumers can get product information. It can be done by planning advertising well and print advertises in book or online publications.
- Create communications materials: For commercialization companies also use brochure or poster before launching and draw attention of customer towards their new product.
- Develop public relations and new media strategy: Companies use their public relations for commercialization of their new product or them also targeting interested industries journalists. Media also advertises innovation stories.
- Develop a sales plan: By comparing previous similar products firms can strategies their sales plan of new product and set a realistic, healthy sales target.
- Develop a pricing strategy: By strategizing pricing list of product company can identify premium price, minimum sale price and entry-to-market price.
- Contact your distributors: By contacting with local distributors before launching of new products and also gives them advertising banner of product. Through forecast firms can also calculate their products numbers.
- Get professional advice: Various organizations provide support to startup and also help in commercialization.

Commercialization Risk and Issues

In this stage firstly firm have to identify risks and potential issues through risk analyzation process which can also affect the commercialization of the new product (Luoma et al., 2008; Kim & Wilemon, 2002). After analyzing all issues, order them high to low and ensure that company have other plans to overcome the risk (Smith & Tushman, 2005; Bannerman, 2008; Bannerman, 2015). For risk analysis one of the best methods is given below:

- Risk description: - Complete detail of risk.
- Rank the likelihood of the risk occurring: - How much chances of risk to occur?
- Rank the impact of the risk occurring: - If in any case risk occur than what will be its impact?
- Calculate risk value: - By calculating minimum and maximum possibility of risk, firm can get risk value.
- Assess risk values: - For assessing the risk value of any product before launching, pareto chart is a best method (Diadrago, 2013).
- Generate action plan for all critical risk: - A backup plan needs to be generated if in any case product may face risk (Teller & Kock, 2013; Odzely et al., 2009).
- Re-evaluate risk after action are-in place: - For calculating how successfully the action will be implemented company have to re-evaluate the risk factor.

SELLING OF PRODUCT

Before launching of any new product company have to take all legal measures to protect the intellectual rights of product and these legal measures are such as patents, trademark registrations etc. company can precede their plans to bring new products to the market after once property rights are secured (Poltorak & Lerner, 2011). Internally or third parties both can manufacture the product. Promotion efforts should be done when the product is ready for the open market and these efforts bring awareness of the product to the target market. Once the company creates distribution channels or contacts with retailers than, product completes its commercialization process (Chesbrough, 2007). A product which is sells in houses directly gives the most significant profit because it doesn't share with intermediates.

CONCLUSION

Conclusively, the phenomenal growth of small scale companies is mainly due to the people's quest to be self employed and not because it is easy to establish or manage. Small scale product development requires several stages from idea generation to product selling. All the above mentioned stages are highly connected to each other. Each step requires expertise peoples in that field, proper environment and infrastructure. And the last important thing for any successful product marketing is the demand of consumers for that product. he increasing demand for consumer products creates a large market for small scale companies and this added to improving business environment and government commitment to promoting small business provided bright future prospects for small enterprise.

REFERENCES

Acs, Z. J., & Audretsch, D. B. (1988). Innovation in large and small firms: An empirical analysis. *The American Economic Review*, 678–690.

Akgün, A. E., Byrne, J. C., Lynn, G. S., & Keskin, H. (2007). Team stressors, management support, and project and process outcomes in new product development projects. *Technovation*, *27*(10), 628–639. doi:10.1016/j.technovation.2007.02.008

Alam, I., & Perry, C. (2002). A customer-oriented new service development process. *Journal of Services Marketing*, *16*(6), 515–534. doi:10.1108/08876040210443391

Albaladejo, M., & Romijn, H. (2000). *Determinants of innovation capability in small UK firms: an empirical analysis*. Eindhoven Centre for Innovation Studies.

Armstrong, A., & Foley, P. (2003). Foundations for a learning organization: Organization learning mechanisms. *The Learning Organization*, *10*(2), 74–82. doi:10.1108/09696470910462085

Bannerman, P. L. (2008). Risk and risk management in software projects: A reassessment. *Journal of Systems and Software*, *81*(12), 2118–2133. doi:10.1016/j.jss.2008.03.059

Bannerman, P. L. (2015). A reassessment of risk management in software projects. In *Handbook on Project Management and Scheduling* (Vol. 2, pp. 1119–1134). Springer. doi:10.1007/978-3-319-05915-0_20

Baregheh, A., Rowley, J., & Sambrook, S. (2009). Towards a multidisciplinary definition of innovation. *Management Decision*, *47*(8), 1323–1339. doi:10.1108/00251740910984578

Biemans, W. G. (1991). User and third-party involvement in developing medical equipment innovations. *Technovation*, *11*(3), 163–182. doi:10.1016/0166-4972(91)90032-Y

Björk, J., & Magnusson, M. (2009). Where do good innovation ideas come from? Exploring the influence of network connectivity on innovation idea quality. *Journal of Product Innovation Management*, *26*(6), 662–670. doi:10.1111/j.1540-5885.2009.00691.x

Boyer, K., & Verma, R. (2009). *Operations and supply chain management for the 21st century*. Nelson Education.

Brown, D., & Wilson, S. (2007). *The black books of outsourcing: how to manage the changes, challenges, and opportunities*. John Wiley & Sons.

Calantone, R. J., Harmancioglu, N., & Droge, C. (2010). Inconclusive innovation "returns": A meta-analysis of research on innovation in new product development. *Journal of Product Innovation Management*, *27*(7), 1065–1081. doi:10.1111/j.1540-5885.2010.00771.x

Cant, M. C., Strydom, J. W., Jooste, C. J., & du Plessis, P. J. (Eds.). (2009). *Marketing management*. Juta and Company Ltd.

Carneiro, A. (2000). How does knowledge management influence innovation and competitiveness? *Journal of Knowledge Management*, *4*(2), 87–98. doi:10.1108/13673270010372242

Chandy, R., Hopstaken, B., Narasimhan, O., & Prabhu, J. (2006). From invention to innovation: Conversion ability in product development. *JMR, Journal of Marketing Research*, *43*(3), 494–508. doi:10.1509/jmkr.43.3.494

Chesbrough, H. (2007). Business model innovation: It's not just about technology anymore. *Strategy and Leadership*, *35*(6), 12–17. doi:10.1108/10878570710833714

Cooper, R. G. (1988). The new product process: A decision guide for management. *Journal of Marketing Management, 3*(3), 238–255. doi:10.1080/0267257X.1988.9964044

Cooper, R. G. (1990). Stage-gate systems: A new tool for managing new products. *Business Horizons, 33*(3), 44–54. doi:10.1016/0007-6813(90)90040-I

Cooper, R. G., & Edgett, S. J. (2009). *Generating breakthrough new product ideas: Feeding the innovation funnel*. Product Development Institute.

Davenport, T. H. (1993). *Process innovation: reengineering work through information technology*. Harvard Business Press.

De Jong, J. P., & Vermeulen, P. A. (2006). Determinants of product innovation in small firms: A comparison across industries. *International Small Business Journal, 24*(6), 587–609. doi:10.1177/0266242606069268

Deepak, R. K. A., & Jeyakumar, S. (2019). *Marketing management*. Educreation Publishing.

Dewenter, K. L., & Malatesta, P. H. (2001). State-owned and privately owned firms: An empirical analysis of profitability, leverage, and labor intensity. *The American Economic Review, 91*(1), 320–334. doi:10.1257/aer.91.1.320

DiBella, A. J. (1997). Gearing up to become a learning organization. *Journal for Quality and Participation, 20*(3), 12.

Didraga, O. (2013). The role and the effects of risk management in IT projects success. *Informatica Economica, 17*(1).

Dodgson, M., Gann, D. M., & Salter, A. (2008). *The management of technological innovation: strategy and practice*. Oxford University Press.

Durmuşoğlu, S. S., & Barczak, G. (2011). The use of information technology tools in new product development phases: Analysis of effects on new product innovativeness, quality, and market performance. *Industrial Marketing Management, 40*(2), 321–330. doi:10.1016/j.indmarman.2010.08.009

Eliashberg, J., Lilien, G. L., & Rao, V. R. (1997). 12 Minimizing technological oversights: A marketing research perspective. *Technological innovation: Oversights and foresights, 214*.

Ferreira, J. J., Fernandes, C. I., Alves, H., & Raposo, M. L. (2015). Drivers of innovation strategies: Testing the Tidd and Bessant (2009) model. *Journal of Business Research, 68*(7), 1395–1403. doi:10.1016/j.jbusres.2015.01.021

Fogler, H. S., & LeBlanc, S. E. (2014). *Strategies for creative problem solving*. Prentice Hall.

Freel, M. S. (2000). Barriers to product innovation in small manufacturing firms. *International Small Business Journal, 18*(2), 60–80. doi:10.1177/0266242600182003

Gomez, M. I., McLaughlin, E. W., & Wittink, D. R. (2004). Customer satisfaction and retail sales performance: An empirical investigation. *Journal of Retailing, 80*(4), 265–278. doi:10.1016/j.jretai.2004.10.003

Grudin, J., & Pruitt, J. (2002). Personas, participatory design and product development: An infrastructure for engagement. In *Proc. PDC* (*Vol. 2*). Academic Press.

Haman, G. (1996). Techniques and tools to generate breakthrough products. In PDMA Handbook of New Product Development. John Wiley and Sons.

Harrison, D., & Waluszewski, A. (2008). The development of a user network as a way to re-launch an unwanted product. *Research Policy*, *37*(1), 115–130. doi:10.1016/j.respol.2007.10.001

Hart, S., Jan Hultink, E., Tzokas, N., & Commandeur, H. R. (2003). Industrial companies' evaluation criteria in new product development gates. *Journal of Product Innovation Management*, *20*(1), 22–36. doi:10.1111/1540-5885.201003

Heikkinen, M. T., Mainela, T., Still, J., & Tähtinen, J. (2007). Roles for managing in mobile service development nets. *Industrial Marketing Management*, *36*(7), 909–925. doi:10.1016/j.indmarman.2007.05.014

Homburg, C., Kuester, S., & Krohmer, H. (2009). *Marketing management*. McGraw-Hill Higher Education.

Hooley, G. J., Lynch, J. E., & Jobber, D. (1992). Generic marketing strategies. *International Journal of Research in Marketing*, *9*(1), 75–89. doi:10.1016/0167-8116(92)90030-O

Jeannet, J. P., & Hennessey, H. D. (2005). *Global marketing strategies*. Dreamtech Press.

Kannebley, S. Jr, Porto, G. S., & Pazello, E. T. (2005). Characteristics of Brazilian innovative firms: An empirical analysis based on PINTEC—industrial research on technological innovation. *Research Policy*, *34*(6), 872–893. doi:10.1016/j.respol.2005.04.003

Kaplan, R. S., Kaplan, R. E., Norton, D. P., Davenport, T. H., & Norton, D. P. (2004). *Strategy maps: Converting intangible assets into tangible outcomes*. Harvard Business Press.

Karlsson, C., & Olsson, O. (1998). Product innovation in small and large enterprises. *Small Business Economics*, *10*(1), 31–46. doi:10.1023/A:1007970416484

Kettinger, W. J., Zhang, C., & Marchand, D. A. (2011). CIO and Business Executive Leadership Approaches to Establishing Company-Wide Information Orientation. *MIS Quarterly Executive*, *10*(4).

Khilji, S. E., Mroczkowski, T., & Bernstein, B. (2006). From invention to innovation: Toward developing an integrated innovation model for biotech firms. *Journal of Product Innovation Management*, *23*(6), 528–540. doi:10.1111/j.1540-5885.2006.00222.x

Kim, J., & Wilemon, D. (2002). Strategic issues in managing innovation's fuzzy front-end. *European Journal of Innovation Management*, *5*(1), 27–39. doi:10.1108/14601060210415153

Kirner, E., Kinkel, S., & Jaeger, A. (2009). Innovation paths and the innovation performance of low-technology firms—An empirical analysis of German industry. *Research Policy*, *38*(3), 447–458. doi:10.1016/j.respol.2008.10.011

Kotler, P., & Armstrong, G. (2010). *Principles of marketing*. Pearson education.

Kraus, S., Pohjola, M., & Koponen, A. (2012). Innovation in family firms: An empirical analysis linking organizational and managerial innovation to corporate success. *Review of Managerial Science*, *6*(3), 265–286. doi:10.100711846-011-0065-6

Lettice, F., Roth, N., & Forstenlechner, I. (2006). Measuring knowledge in the new product development process. *International Journal of Productivity and Performance Management*, *55*(3/4), 217–241. doi:10.1108/17410400610653200

Lilien, G. L., Morrison, P. D., Searls, K., Sonnack, M., & Hippel, E. V. (2002). Performance assessment of the lead user idea-generation process for new product development. *Management Science*, *48*(8), 1042–1059. doi:10.1287/mnsc.48.8.1042.171

Lonsdale, R. T., Noel, N. M., & Stasch, S. F. (1996). *Classification of sources of new product ideas*. Wiley.

Luoma, T., Paasi, J., & Nordlund, H. (2008, June). Managing commercialisation risks in innovation development: Linking front end and commercialisation. In *Proceedings of the XIX ISPIM Annual Conference. Open Innovation: Creating Products and Services through Collaboration. Tours, France* (Vol. *18*). Academic Press.

Lynn, G. S., & Akgün, A. E. (1998). Innovation strategies under uncertainty: A contingency approach for new product development. *Engineering Management Journal*, *10*(3), 11–18. doi:10.1080/10429247.1998.11414991

Mangold, W. G., & Faulds, D. J. (2009). Social media: The new hybrid element of the promotion mix. *Business Horizons*, *52*(4), 357–365. doi:10.1016/j.bushor.2009.03.002

Marshall, C. (2000). *Enterprise modeling with UML: designing successful software through business analysis*. Addison-Wesley Professional.

McDonough III, E. F., Kahnb, K. B., & Barczaka, G. (2001). An investigation of the use of global, virtual, and colocated new product development teams. *Journal of Product Innovation Management, 18*(2), 110-120.

Millson, M. R., & Wilemon, D. (2008). Designing strategic innovation networks to facilitate global NPD performance. *Journal of General Management*, *34*(2), 39–56. doi:10.1177/030630700803400203

Morris, N. (2009). *Understanding digital marketing: marketing strategies for engaging the digital generation*. Academic Press.

Motohashi, K. (2013). The role of the science park in innovation performance of start-up firms: An empirical analysis of Tsinghua Science Park in Beijing. *Asia Pacific Business Review*, *19*(4), 578–599. doi:10.1080/13602381.2012.673841

Müller, R. M., & Thoring, K. (2012). Design thinking vs. lean startup: A comparison of two user-driven innovation strategies. *Leading Through Design, 151*, 91-106.

Mumford, M. D. (2000). Managing creative people: Strategies and tactics for innovation. *Human Resource Management Review*, *10*(3), 313–351. doi:10.1016/S1053-4822(99)00043-1

Noble, C. H., & Mokwa, M. P. (1999). Implementing marketing strategies: Developing and testing a managerial theory. *Journal of Marketing*, *63*(4), 57–73. doi:10.1177/002224299906300406

Nybakk, E., & Jenssen, J. I. (2012). Innovation strategy, working climate, and financial performance in traditional manufacturing firms: An empirical analysis. *International Journal of Innovation Management, 16*(02), 1250008. doi:10.1142/S1363919611003374

Odzaly, E. E., Greer, D., & Sage, P. (2009, October). Software risk management barriers: An empirical study. In *2009 3rd International Symposium on Empirical Software Engineering and Measurement* (pp. 418-421). IEEE.

Palepu, K. G., Healy, P. M., Wright, S., Bradbury, M., & Coulton, J. (2020). *Business analysis and valuation: Using financial statements*. Cengage AU.

Partanen, J., Möller, K., Westerlund, M., Rajala, R., & Rajala, A. (2008). Social capital in the growth of science-and-technology-based SMEs. *Industrial Marketing Management, 37*(5), 513–522. doi:10.1016/j.indmarman.2007.09.012

Plucker, J. A., & Beghetto, R. A. (2000). Book review: Conceptual blockbusting, Creative teachers, creative students, Fundamentals of creative thinking, Creativity is forever, Serious creativity: Using the power of lateral thinking to create new ideas, The mind's best work, Understanding those who create, Creativity in the classroom: Schools of curious delight, A whack on the side of the head (Rev. ed.). Gifted Child Quarterly, 44(2), 135-138.

Poltorak, A. I., & Lerner, P. J. (2011). *Essentials of intellectual property: law, economics, and strategy*. John Wiley & Sons. doi:10.1002/9781118983805

Poon, J. P., & MacPherson, A. (2005). Innovation strategies of Asian firms in the United States. *Journal of Engineering and Technology Management, 22*(4), 255–273. doi:10.1016/j.jengtecman.2005.09.001

Ragatz, G. L., Handfield, R. B., & Petersen, K. J. (2002). Benefits associated with supplier integration into new product development under conditions of technology uncertainty. *Journal of Business Research, 55*(5), 389–400. doi:10.1016/S0148-2963(00)00158-2

Rangaswamy, A., & Lilien, G. L. (1997). Software tools for new product development. *JMR, Journal of Marketing Research, 34*(1), 177–184. doi:10.1177/002224379703400115

Roberts, E. B. (2007). Managing invention and innovation. *Research Technology Management, 50*(1), 35–54. doi:10.1080/08956308.2007.11657418

Rogers, M. (2000). *Understanding innovative firms: An empirical analysis of the GAPS*. Academic Press.

Römer, A., Pache, M., Weißhahn, G., Lindemann, U., & Hacker, W. (2001). Effort-saving product representations in design—Results of a questionnaire survey. *Design Studies, 22*(6), 473–491. doi:10.1016/S0142-694X(01)00003-5

Roper, S. (1997). Product innovation and small business growth: A comparison of the strategies of German, UK and Irish companies. *Small Business Economics, 9*(6), 523–537. doi:10.1023/A:1007963604397

Saxena, R. (2005). *Marketing management*. Tata McGraw-Hill Education.

Schumpeter, J. A. (1982). *The theory of economic development: An inquiry into profits, capital, credit, interest, and the business cycle (1912/1934)*. Transaction Publishers.

Segal, M. N., & Johar, J. S. (1992). On improving the effectiveness of test marketing decisions. *European Journal of Marketing*, *26*(4), 21–33. doi:10.1108/03090569210012390

Shah, S. (2000). *Sources and patterns of innovation in a consumer products field: Innovations in sporting equipment* (Vol. 4105). Cambridge: Sloan Working Paper.

Smith, N. C. (1995). Marketing strategies for the ethics era. *Sloan Management Review*, *36*, 85–85.

Smith, W. K., & Tushman, M. L. (2005). Managing strategic contradictions: A top management model for managing innovation streams. *Organization Science*, *16*(5), 522–536. doi:10.1287/orsc.1050.0134

Stamboulis, Y., & Skayannis, P. (2003). Innovation strategies and technology for experience-based tourism. *Tourism Management*, *24*(1), 35–43. doi:10.1016/S0261-5177(02)00047-X

Teece, D. J. (2000). Strategies for managing knowledge assets: The role of firm structure and industrial context. *Long Range Planning*, *33*(1), 35–54. doi:10.1016/S0024-6301(99)00117-X

Teller, J., & Kock, A. (2013). An empirical investigation on how portfolio risk management influences project portfolio success. *International Journal of Project Management*, *31*(6), 817–829. doi:10.1016/j.ijproman.2012.11.012

Troshani, I., & Doolin, B. (2007). Innovation diffusion: A stakeholder and social network view. *European Journal of Innovation Management*, *10*(2), 176–200. doi:10.1108/14601060710745242

Ulrich, K. T., & Eppinger, S. D. (2011). *Product design and development*. McGraw-Hill/Irwin.

VanGundy, A. B. (1988). Techniques of Structured Problem Solving, Van Norstrand Reinhold. *Techniques, 4*(6), 4-57.

Vernon, J. A. (2005). Examining the link between price regulation and pharmaceutical R&D investment. *Health Economics*, *14*(1), 1–16. doi:10.1002/hec.897 PMID:15386673

Veryzer Jr, R. W. (1998). Key factors affecting customer evaluation of discontinuous new products. *Journal of Product Innovation Management, 15*(2), 136-150.

Veugelers, R., & Cassiman, B. (1999). Make and buy in innovation strategies: Evidence from Belgian manufacturing firms. *Research Policy*, *28*(1), 63–80. doi:10.1016/S0048-7333(98)00106-1

Von Krogh, G., Nonaka, I., & Aben, M. (2001). Making the most of your company's knowledge: A strategic framework. *Long Range Planning*, *34*(4), 421–439. doi:10.1016/S0024-6301(01)00059-0

Wagner, M., Van Phu, N., Azomahou, T., & Wehrmeyer, W. (2002). The relationship between the environmental and economic performance of firms: An empirical analysis of the European paper industry. *Corporate Social Responsibility and Environmental Management*, *9*(3), 133–146. doi:10.1002/csr.22

Walsh, V. (1984). Invention and Innovation in the Chemical Industry: Demand-pull or Discovery-push? *Research Policy*, *13*(4), 211–234. doi:10.1016/0048-7333(84)90015-5

Wind, Y., Douglas, S. P., & Perlmutter, H. V. (1973). Guidelines for developing international marketing strategies. *Journal of Marketing*, *37*(2), 14–23. doi:10.1177/002224297303700205

Yusuf, S., & Nabeshima, K. (2005). Creative industries in east Asia. *Cities (London, England)*, *22*(2), 109–122. doi:10.1016/j.cities.2005.01.001

Zucker, L. G., & Darby, M. R. (1996). Star scientists and institutional transformation: Patterns of invention and innovation in the formation of the biotechnology industry. *Proceedings of the National Academy of Sciences of the United States of America*, *93*(23), 12709–12716. doi:10.1073/pnas.93.23.12709 PMID:8917483

Chapter 6
Intellectual Property Rights

Vijay Laxmi
Banasthali University, India

Mary Shobha Rani Inala
Sri Devaraj Urs Academy of Higher Education and Research, India

ABSTRACT

Intellectual property rights (IPRs) denote distinct types of conceptions of the mind for which property rights are documented. Basic and clinical scientists at research institutions often make ideas that have health benefits if developed and applied to the improvement of human wellbeing. Therefore, learning the basics of intellectual property protection and obtaining professional guidance in its management avoids such losses with a minimal burden of confidentiality on the investigator by using any of the mechanisms (patents, trademarks, copyrights, trade secrets, and know-how agreements). The probability of scientific findings becoming accessible for public benefit is low without suitable intellectual property protection. This reality is particularly true in the life sciences and biotechnology arenas comparative to other areas of science, and hence, it is a prerequisite to know about intellectual property rights and their significance for better development.

INTRODUCTION

Intellectual property rights (IPR) includes, ideas of human mind in various forms like brands, creations, designs, innovations and trade secrets. It demonstrates the right to use them in a hasty manner. As the ideas are easy, and cheap to copy by various means, they have to be protected. The non-protected ideas are the basics for creating new IPR (Shukla, 2020). Though there are similar IPs like rules from pre existing laws like a first national patent law, copyright, and World Intellectual Property Organization (WIPO), the ideas are not being protected in a hastily way. Hence, some important features are necessary for developing an established Intellectual Property system (Watal, 2001). Those rules are to be established and enforced by national laws and should be territorial; transferable; diverse and registered. The set of rules will enable people to earn recognition; financial benefits for their distinct designs, artistic works, inventions and other designs (El-Said, & El-Said, 2007).

DOI: 10.4018/978-1-7998-7411-9.ch006

Patents, copyrights, trademarks are some important types of IPR. There by incorporating any one of these rights seems to be good for better documentation, and planning that helps in protection of invention. For any successful industrial organization, maintaining their IPR policies is important for growth (Bogers et al., 2012). Hence, pharmaceutical industries are currently focussing on evolving individual IPR policies for a better approach in the coming era.

It is also established that the intellectual labour associated with the innovation should be given due to priority for providing good emanates from it. There was a jump in research and development costs with an associated jump in investments required for putting new technology in the market (Hall et al., 2014). The stake of the designers of technology have been very high and there upon the need to protect the knowledge from unlawful use has become expedient at least for a period that would ensure recovery of R&D and other connected costs and satisfactory profits for continuous funds in R&D (Saha & Bhattacharya 2011). IPR is a resilient instrument for defending investments, phase memory, and power expended by an IP inventor, since it gives the inventor a finite amount of time to use his invention (Horner, 2014). As a result, IPR aids a country's economic development by encouraging fair competitiveness and facilitating manufacturing and financial development.

BACKGROUND

The intellectual property scheme is believed to be built on the principle of IPR. The first laid foundation to protect inventions by patent form was made by Venetian Lea in 1474. At the end of the nineteenth century, the rapid development of cities, the discovery of railway linkages, the share of wealth, and increasing transoceanic trade raised popular interest in protecting ideas. International Intellectual Property scheme was born with the Paris convention for the protection of industrial property in 1883 and the Berne convention for the protection of literary and creative Works in 1886. As days passed by, concepts and knowledge became major parts of the trade. Several high skills products and novel medications depend on the extent of invention, research, design, and testing models. Books, recordings, electronic applications, songs, and other internet resources are embraced and traded because of the knowledge and imagination they provide, not because they are made into products, i.e. by plastic or metal, and paper. Several low-technology products or services have a higher proportion of demand based on discovery and nature (example include branded clothes or new plant varieties). As a result, content owners have complete control of who will use their work. All these rights are together called intellectual property rights. World Intellectual Property Organization (1967) established a convention for the succeeding list of topics protected by intellectual property rights. Those are technical discoveries, creations in fields of human endeavour, literacy, artistic and precise works, industrial designs and trademarks. The importance and role of intellectual property rights has been maintained in the Trade-Related Intellectual Property Systems Agreement since the establishment of the World Trade Organization (Prabu et al., 2017).

NATURE OF IPR

The intangible, indispensible essence of intellectual property provides access to information, wisdom, and insight that benefits all, for example, innovation (Tiwari et al., 2006). There are monopoly privileges granted by the state, which means that no one can use them without the permission of the owner.

It is necessary to note that, with the exception of copyright and trade secrets, these protections must be renewed on a regular basis in order to remain in effect. IPR set a limit, except for trademarks and geographical signs, which may have an unlimited life if extended after a given time period by paying official fees. IPR, like any other domain, may be reserved, gifted, sold, and approved. Unlike other movable and immovable goods, these rights can be used in other several countries at the same time. Only licensed individuals, i.e. those with the lawful right to sell and purchase goods, can possess IPR. Copyrights, architectural inventions, Patents, design, integrated circuit layout and trade secrets, in particular, are synonymous with the new or unique. However, geographical indications could be used to cover such agricultural and traditional goods (Correa, 2006).

IPR IMPORTANCE IN DEVELOPING COUNTRIES

The relative scale of their technical operation determines the possible importance of IPR in developed countries. Developing countries agreed to the TRIPS deal for a number of reasons, ranging from the promise of increased access to rich countries' food and fashion markets to the belief that better intellectual property rights will promote further technological transfer and innovation. However, in many countries, especially in the poorest, the long-term benefits are unpredictable and expensive to obtain. There are reasons to think that enforcing intellectual property rights has a positive effect on development opportunities. Domestically, higher levels of innovation stimulate productivity, but this effect is usually minor before countries reach middle income status. Stronger IPRs undoubtedly have short-term consequences for developing countries, such as higher premiums for technology and safe goods (Pawar, 2020).

INDIA'S INTELLECTUAL PROPERTY SYSTEM

As previously stated, the Monopolies act in England in 1623 tracked the growth of the primary system of intellectual property defence established by the Venetian Ordinance (1485), which added Patent rights for knowledge inventions. Between 1880 and 1889, the United States pushed for patent rules, which were monitored by European countries. Whereas the Indian Patent Act was enacted in 1856 and remained in force for 50 years until being revised as "The Indian Patents and Designs Act 1911," and after independence, a comprehensive bill on patent rights was enacted in 1970 and dubbed "The Patents Act, 1970."

In India, the following four types of rights patents (Patents Act, 1970), copyright (Copyright Act, 1957), designs (Designs Act, 1911), and Trademark (Trade and Merchandise Marks Act, 1958) (Pawar, 2020).

EXPANSION OF TRIPS COMPLIED REGIME IN INDIA

TRIPS agreement defined nominal morals for the defence of IPR rights, as well as a time frame for different countries to make changes in their legislation to reach the terms of the requisite level of protection (Malik & Zafar, 2005). Due to this, India has an engaged work plan to change and numerous IP Act (Patent Act, 1970; Trade Marks Act, 1999; Copyright Act, 1957; Design Act, 2000; Geographical Indication of Goods, 1999 and Plant Variety and Farmers Right Protection Act, 2001) in the last five years (Gargate & Momaya, 2018).

Patents Act, 1970

Since India signed the TRIPS agreement as a counter-signatory, the Patents Act of 1970 was revised in different ways between 1995 and 2005 to satisfy India's TRIPS obligations. The objectives were largely focused on improving India's technical competence as well as the need to align the IP climate with regimes and foreign norms. The modification make the act more new, coordinated, and open in order to protect community interests while also fulfilling India's international obligations under the TRIPS agreement (Priapantja, 2000). Consequently, the guidelines of Patent Act have become operative from May 2003. The formed rules are further revised by Patent rules 2005 with effect from 01. January, 2005 was fully in force and operative (Watal, 2014).

Trade Mark Act, 1999

The trademarks act was rationalized under trademarks act of 1999. It is a sign for unique goods accessible for sale or put on the market by one or other trade. This act has been covered in India for four decades under the provisions of the Trade and Merchandise Mark (TMM) Act of 1958. This act upon modernization had taken up targets for rising developments in trading and commercial practices. It is also amended to meet the investment flows and transfer of technology, and simplify the trademark management system. To accomplish these commitments, the Trademarks Bill act was modified and introduced in 1994 (Correa, 1999).

The primarily concentrated on the reforms that the Indian government is contemplating and considering, but it lapsed in 1994. As a result, the proposed legislation was carefully evaluated. Later that year, a bill was passed that repealed the Trade and Merchandise Mark Act of 1958 and was signed into law on December 30, 1999 as the Trade Marks Act, 1999 (Correa, 1997). The following are some of the attributes of the Act. It expands the definition of a registered trademark to cover not just the products and services that are covered by registration, but also those that are supposed to be available. Second, the new law strengthens the recourse for trademark violations by granting the police the authority to seize unauthorised publications without a warrant (Herz & Mejer, 2019).

Copyright

It is regulated in India by the Copyright Act of 1957, which has been updated several times in order to keep up with the times. It also covers authors for up to 60 years after their death, as well as rights to cultural goods and services produced through author or collective creativity. All novel intellectual creations that are represented in a reproducible manner may be grouped together as works that are protected by copyright. Literacy, artistic, musical works, sound effects, and cinematography films are examples. These works are preserved regardless of their literary or artistic merit or approved type (Kerry & Lee, 2007). Novel and changing copyright rights include the freedom to assert authorship of a work and the right to challenge modifications to it that could jeopardise the creator's identity. The owner of the copyright will exercise his right administratively and in court by inspecting pages for signs of unlawfully produced pirated merchandise relevant to preserve works. A computer industry is the important field of copyright protection act. The copyright Act 1957 was rewritten in 1984, and computer programming was comprised with the definition of literacy work (Mane & Khot, 2019).

Design Act, 2000

Design Act 2000 was passed in response to a perceived need for a more robust regulatory structure for the protection of industrial designs and to promote the use of design in product development. As a result, in order to balance changing desires and have an appropriate impetus for design development, the Designs Act of 2000 was enacted, removing barriers to the unrestricted use of existing designs. This act complies with TRIPS conditions, making it crucial for international trade. The beauty or initial design of an industrial object is the subject of industrial design law. A modern industrial product combines elements of architecture and craftsmanship. A tea cup with a hollow container for storing tea and a handle for handling the cup, for example, has unknown characteristics. A form or ornamentation, on the other hand, may be registrant. The design act has provisions for increasing the space for prior disclosure, identifying non-registrant designs, and revoking a licenced design's two-year term of confidentiality (Heikkilä, J. 2019).

Act on Geographical Indications of Goods, 1999

Geographical signs in India are yet to be registered, and in the absence of regulatory protection, these designations are being misappropriated by people outside of India to designate goods that do not originate in the designated Indian location. Some cases, such as the patenting of turmeric, neem, and basmati rice, have drawn a lot of attention to intellectual property rights. It's worth remembering that under the Agreement on Trade-Related Aspects of Intellectual Property Rights (TRIPS), no government is obliged to have widespread mutual protection unless a geographical indication is threatened in the country of origin. Our country lacks a clear legislation governing commodity geographical signs that would protect the producer's interest in such commodities (Ginarte & Park, 1997). To resolve such cases, the parliament passed the Geographical Indication of Goods (Registration and Security) Act, 1999, which establishes broad-reaching rules for the registration and adequate protection of geographical indications. The geographical signal registry is in charge of enforcing this law, and is regulated by the controller general of patents, crafts, and trademarks (Yang & Maskus, 2001).

THE SILENT FEATURES OF LEGISLATION

Setting up of the definition of numerous chief terms like goods, packages, producers, geographical signal, registered proprietor, and legal user. Development of register into two parts to conservation of geographical clues and also used computers devices to conserve it. Part one will contain all recorded geographical clues, while Part second will contain information about registered official users. Required advertisement for all accepted geographical indication requests and for inviting protests. Necessities for a higher level of security for reported goods and provisions relating to offenses and penalties (Eaton & Kortum, 1996).

PLANT VARIETIES PROTECTION ACT AND FARMER RIGHTS OF 2001

Plant breeders' rights was developed from the ground up to provide incentives for plant breeders engaged in groundbreaking work that prioritises agricultural productivity over study savings, and to persuade researchers to put society's needs ahead of their own. The debate over enacting a law in India relating to plant variety safety and farmer rights has gained momentum, particularly in light of the WTO's TRIPS agreement, which aims to encourage successful intellectual property rights enforcement in all fields of technology (Malik & Zafar, 2005). Article 27 of the TRIPS Agreements specifies patentable subject matter and allows participants to protect plant varieties by patenting, sui generis schemes, or hybrids. Conservation of Plant Varieties and Farmers Rights (CPVFR) Act, 2001, were passed by the government.

The aim of the CPVFR is to provide an authority that will provide an effective scheme of protection for plant breeders' and farmers' interests, as well as promote the creation of new flora varieties and provide a consequence to the TRIPS agreement agreement supplies (Singh, 2016). Purpose of this Act is to promote both public and private sector participation in R&D. Formation of new plant species is aided by adequate returns on such investments. It purposes have to encourage domestic and foreign investment in the country's seed industry in order to ensure that Indian farmers have access to high-quality seeds and planting materials. It also identifies farmers' roles as cultivators and preservers. It contributes to the country's agriculture biodiversity by rewarding traditional, rural, and tribal communities for their influence through assistance and defending farmers' traditional rights.

This Act also creates the Protection of Plant Varieties and Farmers Rights Authority, which is charged with fostering and advancing new plant varieties as well as safeguarding farmers' and breeders' rights (Yang & Maskus, 2001). Plants are covered in India in two ways: genetically engineered characteristics are protected under the Patents Act 1970, and plant species are protected under the Protection of Plant Varieties and Farmer's Rights Act 2001, which is a sui generis law (Singh, 2016).

NEED OF INTELLECTUAL PROPERTY RIGHTS IN AGRICULTURE

The introduction of GM seeds using GM technology drew widespread condemnation from environmental groups, NGOs, farmer's groups, and others. These organisations argued that in the agricultural sector, monopolies in the form of intellectual property rights should be avoided. Despite this desire, IP protection has become increasingly important due to the shifting global economic environment and the necessity to foster innovation and economic development in the relevant industry. As the human population has risen, so has the diversity of crops available, both edible and for commercial uses (Figueiredo et al., 2019). As a result, plant varieties have been experimented with, and a demand for plant variety protection as well as the rights of farmers and plant breeders to support the development of new plant kinds has arisen. Transgenic crop development is a lengthy process that necessitates a favourable ecology and governmental approval, as well as a significant commitment of time and money. It must pass a significantly affecting procedure and can only succeed if the public accepts it. IPR protection is essential for investors who want to invest in R&D and gain the benefits (Singh, 2016).

Proponents of IPRs said that they would create incentives for investment in technological development, particularly private R&D, resulting in the rise of the seed business, which would give farmers with additional seed options. Furthermore, without invention protection, high-yielding varieties and hybrids created in technologically sophisticated nations would be unavailable to underdeveloped nations, as any rival could readily duplicate and sell them. The inability of emerging nations to get high-yielding cultivars will limit their ability to increase crop output (Prasanna et al., 2020).

INTERNATIONAL INSTRUMENTS CONCERNING IPR

A set of fixed rules were made by International Property System. Several International Treaties or conventions address issues of IP and industrial property rights, which are governed by the World Intellectual Property Organization, also known as WIPO.

World Intellectual Property Organization (WIPO)

The World Intellectual Property Organization (WIPO) is a United Nations based organisation. It aspires to be a well-organized and accessible international intellectual property structure that rewards originality and contributes to economic development. WIPO was founded in 1967 by the WIPO Convention, with a mandate from its Member States to foster intellectual property rights around the world through state cooperation and partnership with other international organisations. Its headquarters are located in Switzerland. Agreement with the World Trade Organization in 1996, WIPO expanded its position and increased the importance of intellectual property rights in the organisation of globalised trade (WTO) (Abbott et al., 2012). It allows for collaboration in the execution of the TRIPS Agreement, such as the publication of laws and regulations, as well as legal-economic aid and technological cooperation in the interests of developed countries. A joint venture to assist developing countries in meeting their TRIPS commitments was thrown out in July 1998 (Gargate & Momaya, 2018). It should be remembered that WIPO administers 24 treaties and has a diverse and rich programme of operation. WIPO member of a secretariat associated with coordinating national intellectual property laws and procedures. IR information exchange, offer technical legal and assistance to developing and developed countries, and assist remote intellectual property dispute resolution (Birkbeck & Carolyn Deere, 2016). India is currently widely regarded as a centre for industrial R&D, notably in industries such as information technology, medicine and pharmaceuticals, space research, biotechnology, entertainment, and a variety of other growing industries. India's TRIPs-compliant IP laws, along with a robust enforcement mechanism and a thriving court system, have produced the strongest investment prospects and a favourable climate for preserving IP rights, allowing the industrial community to broaden its commercial operations (Gargate & Momaya, 2018).

Significance of Intellectual Property Law in India

Several large and small intellectual property law societies in India, the United States, Chicago, United Kingdom and other countries provide high-quality assistance to product inventors and manufacturers. In India, the intellectual property rights are securely sheltered and organized by a well-established statutory and judicial framework. Various states of India also had various attorneys and laws governed by Intellectual Property Rights. It comprises two distinct forms in which Literary and Artistic works belong to industrial property whereas Books, paintings, musical compositions, plays, movies, radio/TV programs, and performances belong to copyright. Patented products, architectural designs, trade secrets, concept designs, and geographical indications shield industrial property, which is a tangible matter that is the result of an invention or commercial uses.

The major classes of IP are as follows (Figure 1).

Figure 1. The major classes of IP

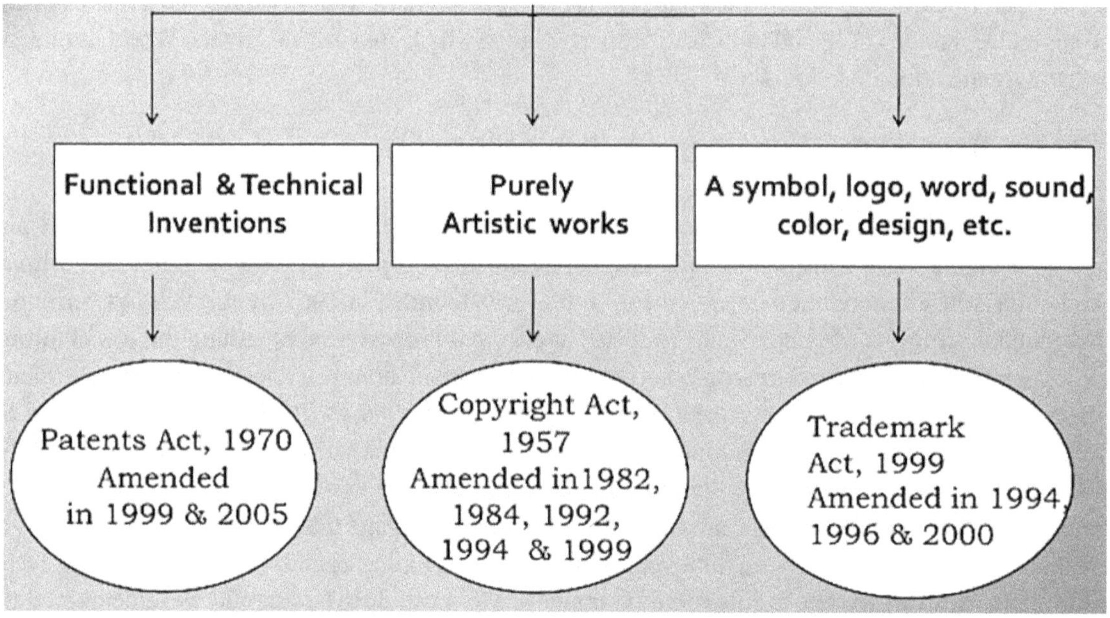

Patent Act, 1970 and its Regulations

The word patent originated from the Latin word *Pater* that means to "lay open" (i.e., to make available for public inspection) which was a royal decree granting exclusive rights to a person, predating the modern patent system. It is also defined as intellectual property right, provided by the government to the patentee, in exchange for full disclosure of his invention for a limited period. India has four patent offices at Chennai, Delhi, Kolkata and Mumbai (Deb & Kaushik, 2013).

Salient Features of Patents

An innovation must be new and have never been made public in any manner, anytime prior to the date the application is filed. It requires innovation steps and must be non-obvious to a person trained in that particular art, i.e., it cannot be deduced simply or objectively from prior knowledge. A technology must have Industrial Use and be usable in industry. As a division from solely abstract or artistic practise, it can involve any useful, functional activity. An innovation could not be ruled out (Teixeira & Ferreira, 2019).

Non-Patentable Matters

Any technology that is detrimental to public order or morality, as well as too human, plants and animals health or the environment is banned. Other technologies relating to atomic energy must not be copyrighted since the production of atomic energy is solely the responsibility of the federal government. Copyright cannot be applied to any living being, non-living things, or object discovered in nature. Patents cannot be granted for the simple arrangement, rearrangement, or replication of known instruments. Patents will not be granted for chemical, surgical, diagnostic, clinical, or human or animal processes (Prabu et al., 2017).

Stages to Obtain a Patent

The following stages are to be followed for filing a patent. The first stage includes, filling an application according to the territorial limits where the applicant or the first-mentioned applicant in case of joint applicants for a patent normally resides or where the invention originated. The second stage requires an early appeal for examination; no claim for a patent will be reviewed if the claimant does not make a request form with a charge of 2,500/- or Rs. 10,000/. To secure a patent, you must do so within 48 months of the date of precedent of the application or the date of registration of the application whether you are owner or not. The first inspection report containing the objections/requirements is normally transmitted to the claimant via the address of service within six months of the date of the order for examination or the date of publishing, whichever is later. The third stage entails withdrawing an application at least three months before its initial release (Bhattacharya et al., 2006). The application that was rejected after the date of publication cannot be refilled because it has already been made available for public review. The fourth stage involves the approval of a patent six months from the date of publication under Section 11(A). The fifth stage involves pre-grant and post-grant resistance, and the final stage includes the patent's terms and date. Each patent would have a 20-year term beginning on the filing date of the patent application (Haakonsson & Richey, 2007). The patent date is the date on which the patent application is filed. Patent limitations include expense, time, knowledge loss, infringements, and the inventor's use of the invention (Arundel & Kabla, 1998).

Utility of Patents

Utility patents are intellectual property rights issued by a state to patent owner(s) inside its jurisdiction, preventing others from commercialising a technology that is recognised as innovative and innovative as stated in the issued patent for a specific period of time (With rare court exceptions, up to 20 years is possible). The commercial use, offer to use, sale, offer of sale, production, or distribution of a patented technology or its products is referred to as commercialization (Wyse & Luria, 2021).

COPYRIGHT ACT, 1957 AND ITS REGULATIONS

The system of copyrights governs Indian copyright act 1957, which is amended in 1999. It is a right that grants protection to the unique expression of ideas. The term copyright means the work 'originated' with the author. This requires no newness or distinctiveness like patent law and protects the expression of an idea. Literacy, films, dramatic, musical, artistic, and sound recordings are roofed by copyright act. Copyright act does not cover other actions like ideas, recipes, works lacking originality and names, titles, or short phrases (Khidzir & Ahmed, 2018).

Essential qualities for filing a copyright in India should satisfy the following conditions. Predominantly, the work should be first published in India; secondly, the author at the date of publication must be a citizen of India. If the publication was made after the authors' death, the author must be citizen of India at the time of death. In the case of unpublished work, the author must be an Indian citizen or resident at the time the work is created. (Selvadurai & Matulionyte, 2020).

Copyright is a package of economic rights and moral rights

Economic rights: include, literacy, dramatic or musical work and has the following characteristics. Firstly, to reproduce the work in any material form and by electronic mean. Secondly, to issue copies of work to the public and to make any translation and adaption of the work.

In the case of the computer program, the right consists of the following features. Foremost, to do any of the acts specified in article above mentioned and to sell or give a hire, or offer for sale or hire any copy of the computer program regardless of whether such copy has been sold or given on hire on earlier occasions

In the case of creative works, the right includes the ability to express the work in public, use it in every cinematographic video, and adapt the work. Whereas in case of cinematographic film, the rights have to make a copy of the film or a photograph of any image forming part; to sell or give on hire or offer for sale or hire any copy of the film; to communicate the film to the public (Kariyawasam, & Paliyaarachchi, 2020).

In the case of sound recording, right is defined as the ability to produce any other sound recording including it, as well as the ability to sell, give on hire, or offer for sale or hire any copy of the sound recording, regardless of whether such copy has already been sold or given on hire (Dureja, 2016).

Moral rights include the ability to choose whether or not to write. It also requires the ability to assert authorship of a work that has been written or exhibited, as well as the right to prohibit modification and any acts that may harm the writer image. The following criteria are part of the registration procedure: first, one must apply by filling out a simple application form and paying the application fee; Second, one may not be required to submit a copy of their work, and the work may be published under the same subject, but each activity will have its own copyright rights because it was developed independently.

Copyright protection normally lasts for the author's lifetime up to 50 years from the end of the calendar year in which the author dies; 50 years for films and sound recordings; 25 years for typographical arrangements in a printed edition; and copyright protection normally lasts until December 31 of the calendar year in which the author dies.

TRADEMARK ACT, 1999 AND ITS REGULATIONS

The Trade Marks Act 1999 regulates the effect on September 15, 2003, and replaced the Trade and Merchandise Marks Act, 1958, which applied in India. It is defined as any sign or combination of signs, capable of distinguishing the goods or services of one undertaking from those of other undertakings, and be capable of constituting a trademark (Schmoch, 2003). Such signs, in particular personal names, letter, numerals, figurative elements, and combinations of colours as well as any combination of such signs, are eligible for registration as trademarks (Nitu, 2014).

Signs That May Serve as Trademarks

Words: name of the company, surnames, forenames, geographical names, and any other words or sets of words invented and slogans

Letters and Numerals: any combination of one or more letters/numbers. Apps involve fancy devices, images, and objects, as well as two-dimensional models of products or containers.

Colored Marks: This category includes terms, instruments, and any colour variations. For example, the Mercedes star can serve as a trademark.

Audible Signs: Two typical categories of sound marks can be distinguished namely those that can be transcribed in musical notes or other symbols. For example, the cry of an animal.

Olfactory Marks: For example, a company sells its goods with a certain fragrance and the consumer becomes accustomed to recognize the goods by the smell.

Trademark Registration

The following steps make up the trademark approval process: To begin, trademark registration applications must be filed with the appropriate government agency, such as the trademark or patent office and industrial property office (Blind, 2006). Second, the application form must include the applicant's name and address, as well as the sign submitted for registration, which must be included in the application form or attached as a figure. Third, the applicant must identify the things for which the trademark will be registered, as well as pay trademark registration costs. Finally, once the application is approved, the owner receives a certificate from the office (Gotsch & Hipp, 2012).

Duration and Renewal

There is no reason to restrict the value of trademarks and they do not guarantee an exclusive right to be exploited. In trademark legislation, a time limit is usually specified for procedural reasons, though registrations can be renewed after the time restriction has passed.

Remove Trademark from the Register

For the licensee, the cancellation of a trademark registration is important because it results in the loss of the registration's protection. Nonetheless, there are several grounds for a trademark's exclusion from the register.

TRADE SECRETS

A trade secret is a method, template, tool, or design that is kept hidden in order for a firm or trade to gain a competitive edge and profit. A trade secret can be a reagent, a production methodology, building or preservation items, or even a list of clients or firms. It's also known as "secret information" or "confidential information." To be protected by trade secrets, the matter must be "classified." Although the definition of a trade secret differs depending on who you ask, factors listed below are regarded to be consistent (Nealey et al., 2015).

- Its owner benefits financially in some way.
- The importance of data or information to him or his rivals.
- The general population is unaware of this.

Every organisation or entity can secure its sensitive data or facts by engaging into a non-disclosure agreement with its workers. A law like this that safeguards secret information and records gives the government dominion over all sensitive data and information. For an indefinite period of time, trade secrets give limitless security. Unlike a copyright, this one does not expire. Any company invests time and money into studying how to better its various practises and processes. If other organisations utilise the same data, the first company's prospects of surviving and dominating the industrial arena are little to none. If trade secrets are discovered, the technology's originator has the legal right to treat it as intellectual property (Henry & Ponce, 2011).

Trade secrets are kept confidential and not shared with the general public. Parallel efforts are taken by the owner or developer to guarantee that his expertise does not slip into the hands of a rival. A worker would be willing to sign a form ensuring not to disclose any critical facts or data about his boss in order to be recruited by a trade secret holder. If there is any carelessness or violation of the regulations, financial penalties will be enforced. Other business partners or businesses with which the developer works are frequently requested to sign similar agreements and failing to do so might result in penalties or fines (Rao et al., 2018).

Protection of Trade Secrets

Any electronic files or data that include trade secrets that you want to keep private should be marked with a notice or some other mark. Allow access to the content to those who have a valid need to know about trade secrets. The explanation for your request should be reasonable and useful to your business (Defrancesco, 2019). Anyone who uses trade secrets should have to sign a legal agreement. It should include any valuable information about the trade secret, such as how the person can use it, what would happen if he breaks the agreement, and so on. All employees should consider the trade secret as sensitive data or information, even if they are unaware of it. Always keep your trade secret in a secure and secluded location (Bruns & Brittany, 2017).

CONCLUSION

To succeed in any social, technological, and economic advancement, IPR stands as a main stream for the protection of ideas and aid in growth of technology. Since various kinds of IPR are available to help in protecting the ideas; the technology transfer can be lice sensed in any of the ventures and succeed. The major purpose of IPR stands in protection of their investments as incentives and to encourage in their research. Among various IPR systems generated, patent are rights connected to an invention set by government in exchange for full discovery of their invention by the patentee. Each type of IP protection is different varying in subject and expenditure and hence it is important to consider many factors before choosing the best protection strategy. Some techniques require strong IP protection to commercialize, and therefore, IP departments weigh these considerations and perform necessary IP protection functions. Considering the above facts, one has to know that IP has important role in the advancing world.

REFERENCES

Abbott, R. B., Bader, R., Bajjali, L., ElSamen, T. A., Obeidat, T., Sboul, H., & Alabbadi, I. (2012). The price of medicines in Jordan: The cost of trade-based intellectual property. *Journal of Generic Medicines*, *9*(2), 75–85. doi:10.1177/1741134312447499

Arundel, A., & Kabla, I. (1998). What percentage of innovations are patented? Empirical estimates for European firms. *Research Policy*, *27*(2), 127–141. doi:10.1016/S0048-7333(98)00033-X

Asha, C. N., & Bhattacharya, S. (2011). Intellectual property rights: An overview and implications in pharmaceutical industry. *Journal of Advanced Pharmaceutical Technology & Research*, *2*(2), 88–93. doi:10.4103/2231-4040.82952 PMID:22171299

Bhattacharya, S., & Guriev, S. (2006). Patents vs. trade secrets: Knowledge licensing and spillover. *Journal of the European Economic Association*, *4*(6), 1112–1147. doi:10.1162/JEEA.2006.4.6.1112

Birkbeck, C. D. (2016). *The World Intellectual Property Organization (WIPO): A Reference Guide*. Edward Elgar Publishing. doi:10.4337/9781785364785

Blind, K. (2006). A taxonomy of standards in the service sector: Theoretical discussion and empirical test. *Service Industries Journal*, *26*(4), 397–420. doi:10.1080/02642060600621597

Bogers, M., Bekkers, R., & Granstrand, O. (2012). Intellectual property and licensing strategies in open collaborative innovation. In Open innovation in firms and public administrations: Technologies for Value Creation (pp. 37-58). IGI Global. doi:10.4018/978-1-61350-341-6.ch003

Bruns, B. S. (2017). Criticism of the Defend Trade Secrets Act of 2016: Failure to Preempt. *Berkeley Technology Law Journal*, *32*, 469–502.

Coombs, R., & Miles, I. (2000). Innovation, measurement and services: the new problematique. In *Innovation systems in the service economy* (pp. 85–103). Springer. doi:10.1007/978-1-4615-4425-8_5

Correa, C. M. (1997). New intellectual standards for intellectual property: Impact on technology flows and innovation in developing countries. *Science & Public Policy*, *24*(2), 79–92.

Correa, C. M. (1999). Review of the TRIPs Agreement: Fostering the transfer of technology to developing countries. *The Journal of World Intellectual Property*, *2*(6), 9–39. doi:10.1111/j.1747-1796.1999.tb00100.x

Correa, C. M. (2006). Implications of bilateral free trade agreements on access to medicines. *Bulletin of the World Health Organization*, *84*(5), 399–404. doi:10.2471/BLT.05.023432 PMID:16710551

Deb, R., & Kaushik, V. (2013). Management of Intellectual Property Rights: A Focus on Biotechnology. *Global Journal of Management and Business Studies*, *3*(9), 1029–1034.

Defrancesco, L. (2019). Genentech trade secrets theft highlights risk for biotechs. *Nature Biotechnology*, *37*(1), 9. doi:10.1038/nbt0119-9b PMID:30605145

Dureja, C. (2016). Economic rights of broadcasting organisation under copyright law 1957. *International Journal of Advanced Research in Management and Social Sciences*, *5*(5), 37–51.

Eaton, J., & Kortum, S. (1996). Trade in ideas Patenting and productivity in the OECD. *Journal of International Economics*, *40*(3-4), 251–278. doi:10.1016/0022-1996(95)01407-1

El-Said, H., & El-Said, M. (2007). TRIPS-Plus implications for access to medicines in developing countries: Lessons from Jordan–United States Free Trade Agreement. *The Journal of World Intellectual Property*, *10*(6), 438–475. doi:10.1111/j.1747-1796.2007.00330.x

Figueiredo, L. H. M., Vasconcellos, A. G., Prado, G. S., & Grossi-de-Sa, M. F. (2019). An overview of intellectual property within agricultural biotechnology in Brazil. *Biotechnology Research and Innovation*, *3*(1), 69–79. doi:10.1016/j.biori.2019.04.003

Gargate, G., & Momaya, K. S. (2018). Intellectual property management system: Develop and self-assess using IPM model. *World Patent Information*, *52*, 29–41. doi:10.1016/j.wpi.2018.01.005

Ginarte, J. C., & Park, W. G. (1997). Determinants of patent rights: A cross-national study. *Research Policy*, *26*(3), 283–301. doi:10.1016/S0048-7333(97)00022-X

Gotsch, M., & Hipp, C. (2012). Measurement of innovation activities in the knowledge-intensive services industry: A trademark approach. *Service Industries Journal*, *32*(13), 2167–2184. doi:10.1080/02642069.2011.574275

Haakonsson, S. J., & Richey, L. A. (2007). TRIPs and public health: The Doha Declaration and Africa. *Development Policy Review*, *25*(1), 71–90. doi:10.1111/j.1467-7679.2007.00360.x

Hall, B., Helmers, C., Rogers, M., & Sena, V. (2014). The choice between formal and informal intellectual property: A review. *Journal of Economic Literature*, *52*(2), 375–423. doi:10.1257/jel.52.2.375

Heikkilä, J. (2019). IPR gender gaps: A first look at utility model, design right and trademark filings. *Scientometrics*, *118*(3), 869–883. doi:10.100711192-018-2979-0

Henry, E., & Ponce, C. J. (2011). Waiting to imitate: On the dynamic pricing of knowledge. *Journal of Political Economy*, *119*(5), 959–981. doi:10.1086/662721

Herz, B., & Mejer, M. (2019). Effects of the European Union trademark: Lessons for the harmonization of intellectual property systems. *Research Policy*, *48*(7), 1841–1854. doi:10.1016/j.respol.2019.04.010

Hombal, S. G., & Prasad, K. N. (2012). Digital copyright protection: Issues in the digital library environment. *DESIDOC Journal of Library and Information Technology*, *32*(3), 233–239. doi:10.14429/djlit.32.3.2380

Horner, R. (2014). The impact of patents on innovation, technology transfer and health: A pre-and post-TRIPs analysis of India's pharmaceutical industry. *New Political Economy*, *19*(3), 384–406. doi:10.1080/13563467.2013.796446

Kariyawasam, K., & Palliyaarachchi, R. (2020). The song would be nothing without someone to sing it: Copyright and performers' rights in music. *International Review of Law Computers & Technology*, 1–24. doi:10.1080/13600869.2020.1820684

Kerry, V. B., & Lee, K. (2007). TRIPS, the Doha declaration and paragraph 6 decision: What are the remaining steps for protecting access to medicines? *Globalization and Health*, *3*(1), 1–12. doi:10.1186/1744-8603-3-3 PMID:17524147

Khidzir, N. Z., & Ahmed, S. A. A. M. (2018). Legal Protection of Intellectual Property Rights (IPR) in Bangladesh. *International Journal of Law, Government and Communication*, *3*(12), 71–89.

Kumar, V., & Sinha, K. (2015). Status and challenges of intellectual property rights in agriculture innovation in India. *Journal of Intellectual Property Rights, 20*, 288-296.

Malik, K. A., & Zafar, Y. (2005). Intellectual Property Rights in Plant Biotechnology: A Contribution to Crop Biosecurity. *Asian Biotechnology and Development Review*, *8*(1), 7–43.

Nealey, T., Daignault, R. M., & Cai, Y. (2015). Trade secrets in life science and pharmaceutical companies. *Cold Spring Harbor Perspectives in Medicine*, *5*(4), a020982. doi:10.1101/cshperspect.a020982 PMID:25414378

Nitu, V. I. (2014). Comparative Analysis of the Community Trademark Registration Activity of Germany, the United States and China. *Procedia Economics and Finance*, *15*, 603–608. doi:10.1016/S2212-5671(14)00528-0

Pawar, R. K. (2020). Article. *International Journal of Rudiments in Pharmaceutical Sciences and Clinical Research.*, *1*(1), 14–18.

Prabu, S. L., Timmadonu, N. K. S., & Thirumurugan, R. (2017). *Introductory Chapter: Intellectual Property Rights, Intellectual Property Rights*. Intech Open.

Prasanna, P. L., Rao, L. S., Prasad, A. H., Waris, A., Meera, S. N., Nirmala, B., & Syamaladevi, D. P. (2020). Intellectual property rights protection for plant varieties in India: status, emerging issues, and challenges. *Agricultural Economics Research Review, 32*.

Priapantja, P. (2000). Trade secret: how does this apply to drug registration data. In *ASEAN Workshop on the TRIPS Agreement and its Impact on Pharmaceuticals. Department of Health and World Health Organization*.

Rao, Y. V., & Srirekha, G. (2018). Intellectual property rights in business organizations. *International Journal of Engineering and Management Research*, *8*(1), 118–124.

Schmoch, U. (2003). Service marks as novel innovation indicator. *Research Evaluation*, *12*(2), 149–156. doi:10.3152/147154403781776708

Selvadurai, N., & Matulionyte, R. (2020). Reconsidering creativity: Copyright protection for works generated using artificial intelligence. *Journal of Intellectual Property Law & Practice*, *15*(7), 536–543. doi:10.1093/jiplp/jpaa062

Shukla, A. C. (2020). IPR: An Overview. In *Advances in Pharmaceutical Biotechnology* (pp. 439–447). Springer. doi:10.1007/978-981-15-2195-9_28

Singh, K. K. (2016). Intellectual property rights in agricultural biotechnology and access to technology: A critical appraisal. *Asian Biotechnology and Development Review*, *18*(3).

Teixeira, A. A., & Ferreira, C. (2019). Intellectual property rights and the competitiveness of academic spin-offs. *Journal of Innovation & Knowledge*, *4*(3), 154–161. doi:10.1016/j.jik.2018.12.002

Tiwari, R., Tiwari, G., Rai, A. K., & Srivastawa, B. (2011). Management of intellectual property rights in India: An updated review. *Journal of Natural Science, Biology, and Medicine*, *2*(1), 2. doi:10.4103/0976-9668.82307 PMID:22470229

Vishwasra, S., Mane, & Khot, N. (2020). Copyright Act, (1957): A Study with reference to selected cases in India. *Journal of Advancements in Library Science*, *6*(1), 336–341.

Watal, J. (2014). Is TRIPS a Balanced Agreement from the Perspective of Recent Free Trade Agreements? In *EU Bilateral Trade Agreements and Intellectual Property: For Better or Worse?* (pp. 41–57). Springer. doi:10.1007/978-3-642-39097-5_3

Wyse, J., & Luria, G. (2021). Trends in intellectual property rights protection for medical cannabis and related products. *Journal of Cannabis Research*, *3*(1), 1–22. doi:10.118642238-020-00057-7 PMID:33526141

Yang, G., & Maskus, K. E. (2001). Intellectual property rights and licensing: An econometric investigation. *Weltwirtschaftliches Archiv*, *137*(1), 58–79. doi:10.1007/BF02707600

KEY TERMS AND DEFINITIONS

Copyrights: It is right to give owner to make copies of creative work

Design: It is the plan for creating an object for the implementation of an activity, or process.

Intellectual Property Rights: Rights that are aimed at protecting creations of intellectual.

Invention: The process of inventing something.

License: Official permission to use.

Patents: It is form of intellectual property that gives its owner the right to exclude others from making use of his ideas.

Trademarks: It is a type of intellectual property that consists of sign, design, or expression.

Chapter 7
Bioentrepreneurship:
Emerging Stages

Sunita Rao
Dr. B. Lal Institute of Biotechnology, India

Avinash Gupta
ICFAI Business School, The ICFAI University, India

Gajra Garg
Mahatma Jyoti Rao Phoole University, Jaipur, India

ABSTRACT

The current image of biotechnology in developed countries is practiced at an adequate grade, but the greater part of developing countries is still miserable and far from its future vision. This current gap needs to be filled in some aspects via bioentreprneurship, which is fundamental for the development of the economy, provides a source of welfare with economic growth, promising to bring the social well-being and environment friendliness or all-over sustainable development. As a result, it can generate revenue in a community business, and henceforth, it must be very worthy for biotechnology. Developing nations can indeed turn out to be emerging players in the modern bioeconomy. The advancements in emerging stages towards this issue ought to be an acceptable solution that would be viable in long run. The relevance of bioentrepreneurship to sustainability is conceptualized in the connection with current emerging aspects in developing nations.

INTRODUCTION

Bioentrepreneurship is the combination of both science and business. This incorporation may be new to a few, yet both include experimentation, accomplishment of an objective, settling on high-risk choices and endeavoring something novel. Bioentrepreneurship takes care of worldwide issues by transforming essential logical information into creative and manageable answers for the society. A good model for utilization of the biotechnology to find out the solution to feed every human in the economic way is still

DOI: 10.4018/978-1-7998-7411-9.ch007

a challenge (Muller et al., 2004). According to the prediction of World Bankthat by 2050 we should find out the way to bring upmore food sources to feed the population considering the environmental changes for the yieldfor decrease in the profitability. As time passes, there are more noteworthy moves to interface industry and the scholarly world which are major mainstays of this field (Shahid & Azim, 2019)

Biotechnology empowers the creation of genetically modified organisms (GMOs) in crop harvest with the minimal or no utilization of the harmful pesticides.Biotechnology has been involved in many fragments of our life style, frequently in different manners. They had empowered the formation of advanceditems and innovations to battle illness, ensure the climate, feed the ravenous, production, and to make other valuable items. We can see biotechnology has taken a part in different works every day in our homes and in work environments. Biotechnology empowers and improves the creation of the food we eat, the garments we wear, the different items we use along with the medications we take. People have utilized some type of biotechnology since the beginning of human advancement (Mendoza & Escamilla, 2018). The biotech results of today may seem like marvels to our precursors, yet they are created on an establishment of hard-won logical information found by innumerable ages of scientists and visionaries. As a biotech business person or speculator, we will expand on this establishment and be important for the most extraordinary industry of the twenty-first century (Li & Halal, 2002).

This work will help save lives and improve the personal satisfaction for conceivably billions of individuals around the globe. The cutting-edge biotechnology industry arose during the 1970s, in light of on another recombinant DNA technique distributed in 1973 by Stanley Cohen of Stanford University and Herbert Boyer of the University of California. Recombinant DNA and resulting disclosures have improved and quickened our capacity to create reasonable biotechnology items to help us carry on with longer and better lives, have a more bountiful and feasible food supply, use cleaner and more effective cycles for modern assembling (Ahmann & Dorgan, 2007).

One of the biggest challenges that biotech scientists and business visionaries are endeavoring to handle is the manner in which we address the necessities of absolute people. Today, there are approximately 7 billion people living on our planet. Regardless, by 2050, the overall population will reach a remarkable number of 9 billion indicating growth indicating the greater number of people to deal with requirement of food. For sure, as shown by the United Nations Food and Agriculture Organization (UN-FAO), we should twofold world food creation to do it. With a huge part of the world's arable land successfully in progress we'll need to make existing grounds essentially more beneficial. Biotechnology is helping us with unique characteristics and have distinct role instead of other technology-based industries (Meyers & Hurley, 2007).The hour of biotechnology-redesigned agribusiness began during the 1990s with government support for business sending of modified soybeans, corn, cotton, canola, and papaya. Because of their enormous creation inclinations, biotech crops have become the most immediately grasped development all through the whole presence of cultivation and, in 2013, biotech crops were used by more than 17.3 million farmers on more than 420 million segments of place that is known for farmland in 28 countries (ISAAA, 2012).

Biotech crops are continuously capturing the crop market, in this manner improving the food security and empowering the critical natural, financial, and wholesome advantages. Biotechnology likewise contributes for expanding the advantages for animals. Genetically modified crops can help for increment in yields, which is basic in the event that we are to take care of the developing total populace. Today more than 90 percent of corn, 90 percent of cotton, and 93 percent of soybeans of the total crops in the United States are genetically modified crops (USDA, 2013). Farmers have expanded the corn yield by in excess of 33 percent and soybean yield by 22 percent in the United States since the presentation of biotech crops.

Through 2010, biotech crops have helped produce an extra 300 million tons of canola, cotton, corn, and soybean. Biotech crops additionally have huge ecological advantages. The appropriation of HT crops has expanded no-till horticulture by 69 percent (Conservation Technology Information Center), which diminishes soil disintegration and improves the water quality. Through 2013, biotech crops have helped to drive a 1.05-billion-pound decrease in pesticide applications. Decreased plowing and pesticide usage likewise implies the less energy use and diminished ozone degrading substance those are discharges. In 2011, biotech crops forestalled the arrival of 23 billion kilograms of CO_2, Genetic designing for bug safe plants found to increase the yield by 10.2 million. Biotech crops additionally increment rancher salaries. In 2011, biotech crops made a net monetary advantage of $19.8 billion at the ranch level. The greater part of these homesteadspay gains went to ranchers in non-industrial nations (Economics, 2013). Of the 17.3 million farmers growing hybrid crops, is an asset for 90%, helpless farmers from non-industrial nations. The extra pay created by the utilization of biotech crops have a huge effect in the personal satisfaction of farmers and capacity to take care of their families. So, plant biotechnology helps to feed the world, develop the agrarian economy, for improving human wellbeing and sustenance for a cleaner climate. However, we are as yet in the beginning of this innovation, with a lot more likely advantages available (ISAAA, 2017).

ENTREPRENEURSHIP IN BIOTECH

A Brief Comparative Analysis Based on the extension of globalization, powered by the more extensive utilization of new IT and programming advances, all financial action has seen huge changes in the direct of business (Shoemaker & Shoemaker, 1998). The more created and incredible the economy is, the simpler it adjusts to change, and this is an energizing variable for quickening and broadening change (Chaganti & Greene, 2002). Accordingly, it should not be astounded that the US economy has adjusted rapidly to the new business climate (Acs et al., 2009), making it generally simple to progress from the traditional administrative economy to the better approach for working together, in view of animating and creating business. Europe additionally puts forth supported attempts to create and reinforce the business-based economy, however the cycle is harder for in any event two reasons. From one perspective, there are huge contrasts in monetary advancement both between European nations and at a local level inside every public economy (Lerner & Merges, 1998).

The plant biotechnology market is tremendous. In 2015, the market for horticultural biotechnology, which is just a single area inside the entire plant biotechnology business, represented in excess of 20 US $, and is developing by around 10% every year; it is normal that it will arrive at 39.5 $ by 2022 (Wise Guy Reports, 2017). The business is drawing in much consideration, and the number and measure of interests in plant biotechnology organizations are quickly developing. Along these lines, this is a proper second for business visionaries with foundation information on plant organic chemistry, atomic science, plant hereditary qualities and genomics, or related logical territories, to go into business by making items and administrations that convey an incentive to organizations or customers. This part expects to move future business people, by introducing various models and genuine uses of plant biotechnology instruments and methods. The part is coordinated into various segments, portraying explicit innovations that can be utilized to give business items and administrations. These strategies incorporate sub-atomic markers, mutagenesis, *in-vitro* culture procedures, transgenesis, 'omics' innovations and furthermore natural agribusiness and phytochemistry; toward the finish of the part, there is a segment on viewpoints and how the fate of plant biotechnology is being molded. Hence, this fast-growing sector have numerous opportunities to convert into a business (Israel-Roming & Ghidurus, 2019).

ROLE OF BIOTECHNOLOGY CLUSTER FOR ENTREPRENEURSHIP

A biotechnology cluster comprises of various contributors such as interlinked companies, institutions, product suppliers, service providers in business sectors those cooperate and compete with each other (Chiesa & Chiaroni, 2005). Su and Hung, 2008 demonstrated biotechnology as a fast-growing industry and also proved that clustering is the utmost characteristic of it. They figured-out a life cycle of an industrial cluster (Figure 1).

Figure 1.

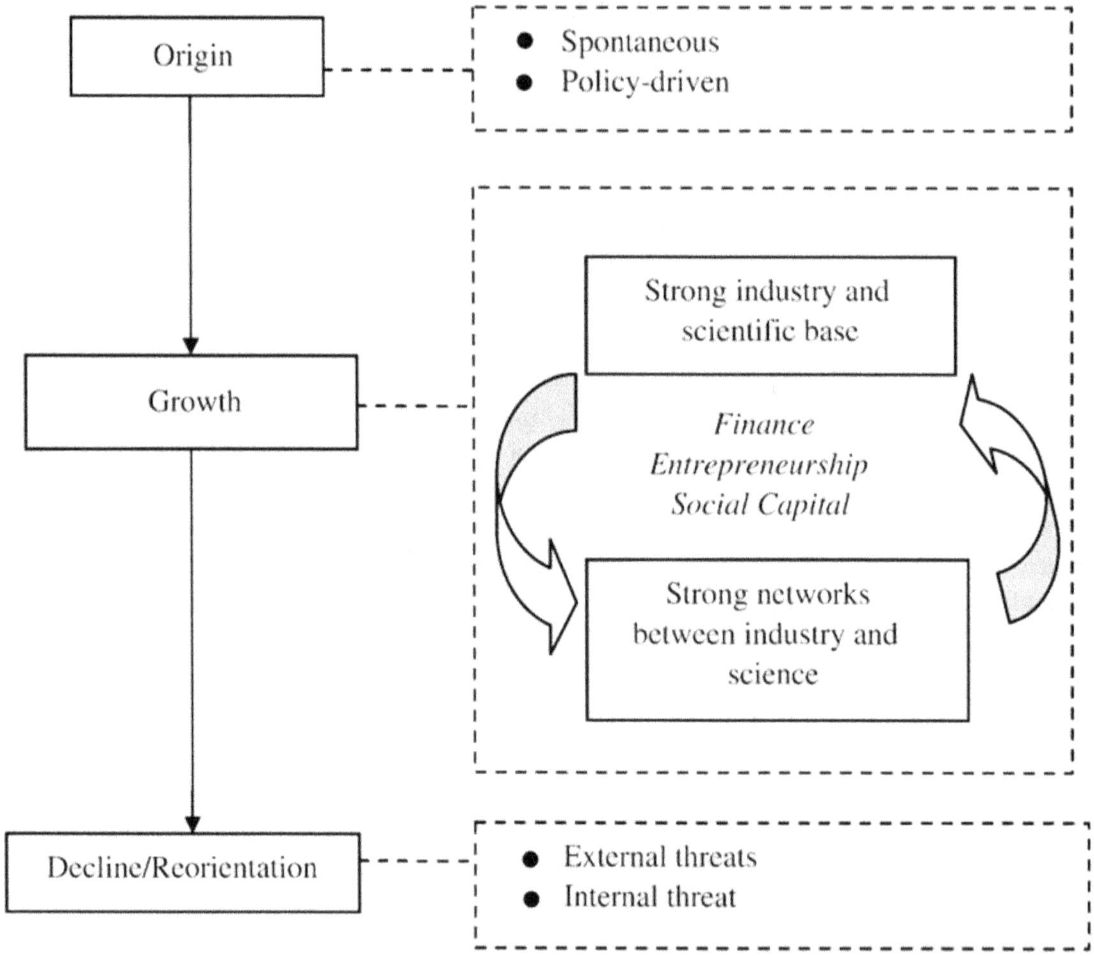

In 2012, the U.S. government delivered the National Bioeconomy Blueprint taking note of that bioscience businesses are "an enormous and quickly developing section of the world economy that gives significant public advantage" (National Bioeconomy Blueprint, 2012). The financial advantage and personal satisfaction effect of a develop biotechnology group in its region and neighborhood government is huge. All districts uphold different financial advancement programs that are focused to improve the personal satisfaction and monetary security of their area. Beside the widespread advantages of biotechnology items for wellbeing, farming, fills, and energy, biotechnology groups have significantly more to bring to the table neighborhood areas and governments, with a portion of the advantages recorded underneath:

1. The biotechnology business makes clean and high technology occupations: Regional regions and governments are looking for approaches to draw in and hold high-innovation occupations which will in general be perfect ventures that create fewer natural issues when contrasted and other significant information-based enterprises basic for propelling excellent positions (State Bioscience Industry Development Report, 2012). This was notwithstanding a cross country decrease in most of the work classes. An essential purpose behind the strength of the bioscience business is the different arrangement of business sectors it serves. These business sectors length biomedical medications, diagnostics and gadgets, agrarian items from creature wellbeing, to seeds and harvest assurance, and bio-based mechanical items, for example, compounds for industry synthetic cycles and bioremediation, biofuels, and bioplastics. The biotechnology business has additionally fared obviously superior to the general economy through the new U.S. downturn and recuperation (Meyers, 2012).
2. The biotechnology business makes lucrative positions: The normal wages paid to bioscience industry laborers came to $82,697 in 2010, more than $36,000 or 79 percent more noteworthy than the normal paid in the general public private area (State Bioscience Industry Development Report, 2012). Bioscience wage development outperformed that of the private area, expanding by 13.1 percent in expansion changed terms since 2001 contrasted and a 4.4 percent increase in salary among any remaining enterprises.
3. The biotechnology business makes lucrative positions: The normal wages paid to bioscience industry laborers came to $82,697 in 2010, more than $36,000 or 79 percent more noteworthy than the normal paid in the general public private area. Bioscience wage development outperformed that of the private area, expanding by 13.1 percent in expansion changed terms since 2001 contrasted and a 4.4 percent increase in salary among any remaining enterprises (State Bioscience Industry Development Report, 2012).
4. New openings and lucrative positions create individual and deals charges for nearby governments: Because biotechnology representatives will in general have altogether more significant compensations than the public midpoints, these workers on normal buy more products and ventures, creating more expense income to the neighborhood economy. All nearby governments require charge income to work and support their framework administrations for their locale. As these courtesies and administrations improve and increment, this thusly can pull in different ventures to the area with more occupation movements.
5. Biotechnology organizations bring an inventive and gifted labor force: Biotechnology organizations require differently talented workers that are knowledgeable about different controls, including innovative work, drug plan, clinical gadgets, mechanical and biomedical designing, clinical issues, science, sub-atomic science, administrative undertakings, clinical preliminaries, and a large group of other expert orders. Frequently industry experts can contribute a bit of their time and assets to

the nearby economy by partaking in different neighborhood uphold and humanitarian exercises in their locale (Newman & Cragg, 2016).

POLICIES AND ACTS RELATED TO DRUG DISCOVERY

Various milestone laws and fundamental public arrangements empowered the development of a strong biotechnology industry in world. It includes:

1. **National Institutes of Health (NIH):** The NIH finances a significant part of the essential clinical examination in the United States, spending about $31 billion yearly lately. In excess of 50,000 serious awards from the NIH uphold in excess of 325,000 specialists at in excess of 3000 colleges, clinical schools, and exploration establishments, notwithstanding research, the NIH conducts at its own offices (https://www.nih.gov/about-nih/what-we-do/financial plan). The NIH has put many billions of dollars openly subsidizing more than seventy years. This monstrous venture was the main consideration in putting the United States at the cutting edge of biomedical advancement. NIH subsidizing has assisted researchers with unraveling the hereditary code, succession the human genome, and get synapses and protein-collapsing, among numerous different essentials of biology.
2. **Bayh-Dole Act:** This law awards colleges and not-for-profit foundations select rights to the protected innovation they produce through governmental subsidized examination. Since Bayh-Dole was received in 1980, in excess of 6000 U.S. organizations have been established to popularize college research. NIH-subsidized exploration and innovation move under Bayh-Dole prodded the ascent of examination colleges as the center points of biotechnology industry bunches (Ferguson & Kaundinya, 2014).
3. **Hatch-Waxman Act:** This law finds some kind of harmony between the public advantages of acquainting minimal effort conventional medications with the market with the need to keep up the impetuses for interest in new biopharmaceutical development. On account of the extensive item advancement, testing, and survey measure, most medications don't arrive at the market until a critical bit of their term-of-patent insurance has just passed. Incubate Waxman reestablishes a portion of this successful patent life, while likewise making a pathway for the possible endorsement of nonexclusive medications (Holman, 2020).
4. **Orphan Drug Act:** This law, passed in 1983, gives monetary motivations to urge organizations to create medicines for little patient populaces. It gives designers the restrictive option to advertise a vagrant medication—a medication or biologic that treats an uncommon illness or condition—for that sign for a long time from the date of FDA endorsement. As indicated by the National Organization for Rare Disorders (NORD), in excess of 400 new medications have been endorsed for the treatment of vagrant illnesses since the marking of the Orphan Drug Act. In the 10 years going before the endorsement of the Orphan Drug Act, just 10 new treatments had been created (Padula, 2020).
5. **Patent Protection:** Since most biotech organizations are independent companies without any items available, they should depend on external private speculation, frequently raised from investment firms, to finance their innovative work. Biotechnology drug improvement is a protracted and costly cycle. Solid licenses give the required motivators to draw in private financing from speculators important to support biomedical exploration (Suzuki, 2019).

6. **Drug Reimbursement:** All in all, this doesn't restrict or confine professionally prescribed medication costs however permits the unrestricted economy to work. With sound repayment approaches set up, patients have more prominent and quicker entry to advanced treatments and prescriptions. Market-based medication valuing furnishes financial specialists in new medication advancement with more prominent certainty they will have the option to procure an adequate profit for their speculation. Then again, government value controls diminish motivations for interest in new medication improvement. As the biggest buyer of professionally prescribed medications through Medicare, Medicaid, and other freely subsidized wellbeing programs, the United States government's valuing and repayment approaches can hugely affect biomedical advancement (Czech et al., 2020).
7. **FDA:** The mission of the FDA is to authorize laws instituted by the U.S. Congress and guidelines set up by the Agency to secure the customer's wellbeing, security, and wallet. The Federal Food, Drug, and Cosmetic Act is the essential food and medication law of the U.S. With various alterations, it is the broadest law of its sort on the planet. The law is planned to guarantee the customer that nourishments are unadulterated and healthy, protected to eat, and created under clean conditions; that medications and gadgets are protected and powerful for their expected uses; that beautifying agents are protected and produced using fitting fixings; and that all marking and bundling is honest, instructive, and not tricky (Shweta et al., 2012).

THE CHALLENGE FOR LIFE SCIENCES COMPANIES

It is a world focused on potential and driven by innovation. The essentiality for life sciences enterprise are vision, optimism and exuberance. Such an international attitude offers to look cost differently. However, these days, companies feel compression to do additional with less improvements in their research & development output. They need to seek few conducts to replace revenue losses and to reconceive in more advanced ways (Mehta, 2004). In this regard, companies must evaluate their pipeline tasks and need to improve their expiring patents. On the other hand, the prerequisites for drug plans have expanded essentially in recent years, while simultaneously the market circumstances have become progressively testing such as for biopharmaceutical firms (Grossmann, 2003). The pressure is also on value-based healthcare where intense pricing led to the drug manufacturers to capture value through the products they generate. Organizations that can ponder their resources, the worth they can make through utilizing internal expertise, and innovative ways to deal with serving the medical care needs of patients, will discover better approaches to catch an incentive outside of their items (Wang et al. 2018). As a result, it is also an outlook that "Innovation can bridge the gap between need and affordability". There are many serious problems our world is facing from feeding and fueling a growing population, Thus, whenever addressing any worldwide epidemic of chronic diseases, the biotechnology business stands prepared with arrangements (Ashammakhi et al., 2017). As it is known that the mysteries of numerous genomes are being solved and by that means biotechnology is emerging as an era for modified medicine development. It has been additionally revolutionized in conversion of industrial productions into organic processes. This industry has depended on the drive of business visionaries who have creative mind, vision, and backbone to defeat the monetary, logical, and administrative snags to change our reality.

FUTURE PROSPECTIVE

The European enactment is clearly restricting the improvement of business applications in the field of plant biotechnology, and it is damaging the European farming area for different locales where the guideline is more merciful. Leaving aside this reality, there is a need of setting up an obvious administrative structure with a drawn-out vision, to offer security to business people, speculators, and partners who are eager to make organizations dependent on plant biotechnology. Plant biotechnology-based new businesses for the most part require a lot of cash to carry another item or administration to the market, and entrepreneurs, who get this capital, need steady and clear guidelines since vulnerability implies danger and it is the thing that all financial specialists need to limit (Blind, 2012; McKinsey, 2015). Hence, business people should know about administrative systems and how they are being created, as this is one of the principal drivers that will shape the eventual fate of plant biotechnology. Aside from enactment, there is a reality that business visionaries should mull over when beginning their own plant biotechnology business, there are more open doors for progress when various individuals, with various practicalities, information, and experience, cooperate. Consequently, the remainder of this part will be positioned on how the blend of plant biotechnology devices with different innovations and subject matters can possibly disturb numerous enterprises, for certain instances of new businesses growing new items and administrations. Energy creation from plants has not been incorporated unequivocally in this section since this theme is necessary to enhance the business creation of biofuels. Here, we will make reference to some new advancements around there, utilizing a totally sole methodology. Plants are our essential wellspring of energy, as their rot has shaped a large portion of the fuel products we use today. These should be supplanted by reasonable wellsprings of energy. Though numerous organizations are attempting to utilize wind, water, or the sun to create energy, explicitly power, there are a couple of activities attempting to deliver power straightforwardly from plants. For instance, Plant-e (www.plant-e.com) and Bioo (www.biootech.com) are the two dynamic companies utilizing the decay of natural material delivered by plants to generate power. These two companies are utilizing, by implication, the aftereffect of photosynthesis to collect energy that isn't utilized by the plant. Plant photosynthesis is the most effective approach to create energy from daylight; as the consequence of millions of long periods of development, it has reached almost 100% of quantum productivity, implying that through photosynthesis plants can change over pretty much every photon of daylight that they catch into an electron. This effectiveness is, by a wide margin, path higher than current sun powered boards, which by and large work at the 15%–17% territory, arriving at a limit of 22% (Energysage, 2018). The hole between the counterfeit sun powered boards and photosynthesis is colossal, which implies that there is an incredible open door for business people with information in plant biotechnology, yet in addition in nanotechnology, photonics, and different fields, to create advancements that could fill this gap (even just incompletely) and change the entire energy industry. Plant-e and Biooare industries, instances of what driven business people in the field of plant biotechnology can accomplish. Regardless of whether this probably won't appear glaringly evident, the apparel, or design, the business is perhaps the most encouraging zones for plant biotechnology. This industry is tremendous, estimated at around 31012 US $ and with assumptions to develop somewhere in the range of 3.5 and 4.5% in 2019 (McKinsey, 2018). One of the major difficulties the business is confronting is the utilization of common crude materials. Engineered filaments have been to a great extent utilized in the business for a long time, yet now mindfulness is rising with respect to the issues presented by these materials on account of the arrival of microplastics, which end up in the seas and enter into the food chain. Microplastics have become a major ecological issue, and engineered materials are the fundamental wellspring of these particles, representing around 35% of the aggregate (Boucher &Friot, 2017). Then again, the utilization of normal filaments additionally conveys a few issues as the cultivating of these strands is substance, water, and land broad; for instance, 20,000 L of water are needed to create 1 kg of cotton, the amount expected to deliver one shirt and some pants (Wu & Li, 2019). Besides, handling the filaments to produce the ideal material is a cycle that includes the utilization of perilous and defiling synthetics, for example, various colors. Plant biotechnology will assume a focal job in the competition to discover elective textures and ecologically neighborly preparing techniques, a race that has just begun. This will incorporate the improvement of less asset requesting plants, the utilization of hereditary designing to acquire adjusted common filaments with properties that these days must be accomplished by utilizing engineered materials or even to build the yield of characteristic colors creation to fulfill the current need of the business. Biotechnology devices are as of now being utilized to manage these issues, and there are organizations, for example, Pili Inc. (www.pili.bio), which is utilizing microorganisms to deliver colors and dyes, or Bolt Threads Inc. (www.boltthreads.com), which is creating new textures along with more sustainable materials through biomaterials. Comparative methodologies can be utilized to create similar items from plants, and business visionaries who effectively enter the design business will approach capital and assets to drive the new arrival of development in the garments business.

CONCLUSION

The emerging sector of biotechnology with entrepreneurship comprises all biotechnology products from basic to high level research. A brilliantbioentrepreneur is the one who start and lead thecompany with ultimate enthusiasm and deliver innovative products to the marketplace. However, the challenges are much but handful opportunities are also available. Industrial clusters deliver profits to local community by creating high paying jobs for the wellbeing. Being a company builder, a bioentrepreneur must be a potential communicator, risk taker and must be comprehended with the business language.At last, there are likewise opportunities for financial experts to add to the comprehension of cycles in the pioneering biotechnology industry. Thus, bioentrepreneurship research is as yet an underexplored field with a lot of chances for scientists.

REFERENCES

Acs, Z., Braunerhjelm, P., Audretsch, D. B., & Carlsson, B. (2009). The knowledge spillover theory of entrepreneurship. *Small Business Economics*, *32*(1), 15–30. doi:10.100711187-008-9157-3

Ahmann, D., & Dorgan, J. R. (2007). Bioengineering for Pollution Prevention through Development of Biobased Energy and Materials State of the Science Report. Washington, DC: U.S. Environmental Protection Agency. EPA/600/R-07/028. doi:10.1089/ind.2007.3.218

Ashammakhi, N., Elkhammas, E. A., & Hasan, A. (2017). Glomerulus-on-a-chip life up. *Transplantation*, *101*(11), e343–e344. doi:10.1097/TP.0000000000001896 PMID:28737605

Battelle/BIO. (2012). *State Bioscience Industry Development Report*. Author.

Blind, K. (2012). *The impact of regulation on innovation*. Nesta Working Paper 12/02.

Boucher, J., & Friot, D. (2017). *Primary microplastics in the oceans: a global evaluation of sources*. IUCN. doi:10.2305/IUCN.CH.2017.01.en

Chaganti, R., & Greene, P. G. (2002). Who Are Ethnic Entrepreneurs? A Study of Entrepreneurs' Ethnic Involvement and Business Characteristics. *Journal of Small Business Management*, *40*(2), 126–143. doi:10.1111/1540-627X.00045

Chiesa, V., & Chiaroni, D. (2005). *Industrial Clusters in Biotechnology—Driving Forces, Development Processes and Management Practices*. Imperial College Press.

Czech, M., Kooiker, A. B., Atikeler, K., Demirtshyan, M., Gaitova, K., Voloskova, M. H., Stiolica, A. D., Kooiker, C., Piniazhko, O., Konstandyan, N., Zalis'ka, O., & Cegielska, J. S. (2020). A Review of Rare Disease Policies and Orphan Drug Reimbursement Systems in 12 Eurasian Countries. *Frontiers of Public Health*.

Energysage. (2018). *What are the most efficient solar panels on the market? Solar panel cell efficiency explained*. Academic Press.

Ferguson, S. M., & Kaundinya, U. S. (2014). Licensing the Technology: BiotechnologyCommercialization Strategies UsingUniversity and Federal Labs. In C. Shimasaki (Ed.), *Biotechnology Entrepreneurship: Starting, Managing, and Leading Biotech Companies*. Elsevier Inc. doi:10.1016/B978-0-12-404730-3.00014-2

Grossmann, M. (2003). *Entrepreneurship in Biotechnology: Managing for Growth from Start-Up to Initial Public Offering*. Springer-Verlag Berlin Heidelberg. doi:10.1007/978-3-642-57432-0

Handoo, S., Arora, V., Khera, D., Nandi, P. K., & Sahu, S. K. (2012). A comprehensive study on regulatory requirements for development and filing of generic drugs globally. *International Journal of Pharmaceutical Investigation*, *2*(3), 99–105. doi:10.4103/2230-973X.104392 PMID:23373001

Higgins, M. C. (2005). *Career Imprints: Creating Leaders Across an Industry*. Harvard Business School.

Holman, C. M. (2020). GlaxoSmithKline v. Teva: Holding a Generic Liable for an artificial Act of Inducement. *Biotechnology Law Report*, *39*(6), 425–439. doi:10.1089/blr.2020.29209.cmh

ISAAA. (2012). *Global Status of Commercialized Biotech GM Crops*. ISAAA.

ISAAA. (2017). *Global status of commercialized biotech GM crops in 2017: biotech crop adoption surges as economic benefits accumulate in 22 years. ISAAA brief no. 53*. ISAAA.

Israel-Roming, F., & Ghidurus, M. (2019). The potential of Biotechnology to generate prosperity. In F. Matei & D. Zirra (Eds.), *Introduction to Biotech Entrepreneurship: From Idea to Business. Springer Nature Switzerland AG 2019*. doi:10.1007/978-3-030-22141-6_1

Jones Lang LaSalle. (2012). *Life Sciences Cluster Report Global*. Author.

Lerner, J., & Merges, R. P. (1998). The control of technology alliances: An empirical analysis of the biotechnology industry. *The Journal of Industrial Economics*, *46*(2), 125–156. doi:10.1111/1467-6451.00066

Li, J., & Halal, W. (2002). Reinventing the biotech manager. *Nature Biotechnology*, *20*(S6), BE61–BE63. doi:10.1038/nbt0602supp-BE61 PMID:12089592

McKinsey. (2015). *The impact of regulation*. Author.

McKinsey. (2018). *The state of fashion 2019: An 'Urgent Awakening' for the Industry*. Author.

Mehta, S. (2004). Paths to entrepreneurship in thelife sciences. *Nature Biotechnology*, *22*, 1609–1612. PMID:15605429

Mendoza, N., & Escamilla Silva, E. M. (2018). Introduction to phytochemicals: Secondary metabolites from plants with active principles for pharmacological importance. In T. Asao & M. Asaduzzaman (Eds.), *Phytochemicals. Source of antioxidants and role in disease prevention*. IntechOpen. doi:10.5772/intechopen.78226

Meyers, A. (2012). The birth of a discipline: Bioentrepreneurship. *Journal of Commercial Biotechnology*, *18*(4), 3–4. doi:10.5912/jcb567

Meyers, A. D., & Hurley, P. (2008). Bioentrepreneurship education programmes in the United States. *Journal of Commercial Biotechnology*, *14*(1), 2–12. doi:10.1057/palgrave.jcb.3050078

Monsanto. (n.d.). *Omega-3-Enhanced Soybean Oil*. Author.

Muller, C., Fujiwara, T., & Herstatt, C. (2004). Sources of bioentrepreneurship: Thecase of Germany and Japan. *Journal of Small Business Management*, *42*(1), 93–101. doi:10.1111/j.1540-627X.2004.00099.x

Newman, D. J., & Cragg, G. M. (2016). Natural products as sources of new drugs from 1981 to 2014. *Journal of Natural Products*, *79*(3), 629–661. doi:10.1021/acs.jnatprod.5b01055 PMID:26852623

Obama Administration. (2012). *National Bioeconomy Blueprint*. Author.

Padula, W. V., Parasrampuria, S., Socal, M. P., Conti, R. M., & Anderson, G. F. (2020). Market exclusivity for drugs with multiple orphan approvals (1983–2017) and associated budget impact in the US. *PharmacoEconomics*, *38*(10), 1115–1121. doi:10.100740273-020-00934-2 PMID:32533523

Shahid, M. F., & Azim, M. K. (2019). Bio-entrepreneurship: Scenario and opportunities for developing countries. *Pakistan Journal of Biochemistry and Molecular Biology.*, *52*(2), 27–33.

Shoemaker, H., & Shoemaker, A. (1998). The threepillars of bioentrepreneurship. *Nature Biotechnology*, *16*(S1), 13–15. doi:10.1038/5399

Su, Y. S., & Hung, L. C. (2008). Spontaneous vs. policy-driven: The origin and evolution of the biotechnology cluster. *Technological Forecasting and Social Change*, *76*(5), 608–619. doi:10.1016/j.techfore.2008.08.008

Suzuki, K. (2019). Competition, patent protection, and innovation with heterogeneous firms in an endogenous market structure. *Journal of Public Economic Theory*, *22*(3), 729–750. doi:10.1111/jpet.12415

USDA. (2013). *Adoption of Genetically Engineered Crops in the U.S.* USDA.

Wang, R., Cao, Q., Zhao, Q., & Li, Y. (2018). Bioindustry in China: An overview and perspective. *New Biotechnology*, *40*, 46–51. doi:10.1016/j.nbt.2017.08.002 PMID:28827157

Wise Guy Reports. (2017). *Agricultural biotechnology – global market outlook (2016–2022).* Author.

Wu, J. X., & Li, L. (2019). Sustainability Initiatives in the Fashion Industry. In R. Beltramo, A. Romani, & P. Cantore (Eds.), *Fashion Industry - An Itinerary Between Feelings and Technology*. IntechOpen London.

KEY TERMS AND DEFINITIONS

Enactment: (British legal term) the term enactment may refer to the whole or part of a piece of legislation or to the whole or part of a legal instrument made under a piece of legislation.

Endorsement: It is a statement or action which shows that you support or approve of something or someone.

Industrial Cluster: A business cluster is a geographic concentration of interconnected businesses, suppliers, and associated institutions in a particular field. Clusters are considered to increase the productivity with which companies can compete, nationally and globally.

Innovation: Innovation is the practical implementation of ideas that result in the introduction of new goods or services or improvement in offering goods or services.

Reimbursement: It defines as a negotiation of a price between manufacturer and payer that allows the manufacturer access to that market.

Chapter 8
Bioentrepreneurship Market Development:
Bioentrepreneurship and Marketing

Archana Bhaskar
Guru Ghasidas Vishwavidyalaya, Bilaspur, India

ABSTRACT

Bioentrepreneurship is a biological entity related to sciences that creates, builds, and acquires profit to establish a business. At present, the biggest challenges for bioentrepreneurs is to stand out from their competitors. There are various function that bioentrepreneurs apply to their businesses to be unique, such as marketing. Marketing includes product development, distribution methods, sales, advertising, etc. Despite of all these efforts, entrepreneurs are still facing a problem to sell products as the consumer preference and need is changing day by day. Therefore, to succeed in business today, it is very important to develop new strategies to change the existing products in order to provide good service to the consumers and retain the business. The process taken by the company to develop the existing market is known as market development. This chapter will focus on market development and selling the product according to consumer needs.

INTRODUCTION

Nature has provided with several biological resources and the business that sells and marketed by means of product that was created from these biological materials are known as bioenterprise. The person, who organizes, operates and assumes the risk of a business venture to bring together manpower material and capital required to meet that human needs are referred as bioentrepreuner. The process by which bioentrepreuner creates its business is known as bioentrepreneurship. Simply it can be defined as creation of wealth derived from the application of the biosciences to the business context (Garau, 2021; Joseph, 2010).

Bioentrepreneurship consist of two words bio and entrepreneurship thus we can say that it is the integration of two different disciplines science (bio) and entrepreneurship. Bioentrepreneurship can be defined as sum of all the biological entities or activities or any idea that has been created from life science

DOI: 10.4018/978-1-7998-7411-9.ch008

innovation. It is also referred as bioscience entrepreneurship, life science entrepreneurship or bioscience enterprise or entrepreneurship in biotechnology or biotechnology enterprise (Adams & Sparrow, 2008). It creates or builds the enterprises that are involved in the commercialization of the biotech products. As Steve Jobs once said, "I think the biggest innovations of the 21st century will be at the intersection of biology and technology. A new era is beginning, just like the digital one."

Scientists and technologists are constantly working to merge the biotech companies and natural resources to produce new innovations or discovery that fulfill the human needs. Thus bioentrepreneurship can be regarded as "a condition that creates new business in terms of risk taking expected profit". In other words we can say bioentrpreneurship is an ideas and concepts that arise from biology and other science field for the benefit of society (Joseph, 2010; Tyagi, 2018). There are many factors which are motivating the young generation to start their own business or become entrepreneur. Some factors are:

- The bio entrepreneur is independent to choose their own life and have to spend with their family and friends.
- The bioentrepreneurs may be considered as role model for others especially because of achievements and the status they get in real life.
- Young generations have lot of innovative idea and it is good platform to explore their own ideas and development of new technology.
- They can increase the share of services in total gross domestic productivity.
- No age limit is there anyone can start their business at any stage of their life
- Bioentrepreneur can globalize or develop their business worldwide and can significantly obtain the additional profits.

Bioentrepreneurship is very much similar to entrepreneurship as both are concerned with innovative ideas and to raise the investment of the companies. But still there is difference between the two. Entrepreneurship is simply related to start of new business in any field whereas bioentrepreneurship is starting a new business which is based on various fields of science, like biotechnology etc. Further the biotech-based startups take more time for the development of products, for example making vaccines or drugs or antibodies as compared to normal startup companies. Biology based product market is time consuming as the owner has to get approval from ethical committees in the institutes or the concerned institutes in which they are working and even it requires huge investment i.e. in millions of dollars to convert their innovative ideas in product for human welfare (Bixia, 2009). Bioentrepreneurship is concerned with introducing new approaches and revolutionizing the world. The author Craig Shismasaki in his book biotechnology entrepreneurship writes "decisions made in one field immediately impact the other, meaning successful biotech business requires effective integration between business and scientific issues (Shismasaki, 2014). Drucker says, "Until entrepreneurial act, every plant is a seed and every mineral just another rock".

The characteristics of bioentrepreneurship are as follows:

- It involves the economic activity as it is basically concerned with the production, creation and distribution of goods and services in such a way that it utilizes the resource towards productive use.
- Innovation is the key of bioentrepreneurship. It involves the production or marketing of new product or using a new raw material recourses or new method of production which was not used by other companies or exploring the product in new market.

- Bioentrepreneurship is a goal oriented activity. It is not just an imaginary decision making in a paper but it is concerned with processes by which work must be completed in order to earn profits through satisfaction of consumers' needs.
- Bioentrepreneurship emphasizes on results, achievements and targets achieved.
- Biontrepreneurship is about growing a business and pursuing opportunities as they arise.
- It is the process of creating value in terms of new products, services, transactions, approaches, resources, technologies, and markets.
- Bioentrepreneurship is a creative response that requires innovation or introduction of something new or improved which changes the environment of entreprise.
- The next characteristic of bioentrepreneurship is growth of bioentreprise.
- Bioentrepreneurship should have managerial skill and leadership skills to run its companies.
- Bioentrepreneurship should have a vision and a willingness to work with a variety of people or making a good team to achieve their goal.
- Bioentrepreneurship has the ability to coordinates and control the efforts of all the persons engaged in his enterprises means they are organization builder.
- Bioentrepreneurship also brings the productive resources of society.
- Bioentrepreneurship should have an open mindset, honest and realistic self-assessment. The company must have the ability to accept failures.
- For development of business the bioentrepreneur should be flexible to accommodate a change in order to achieve the best results or to satisfy the consumers need.
- The successful bioentrepreneurship not only writes a good business plan but also implement, and execute it properly due to which they success in their field.
- Last but not the least bioentrepreneurship should be learner, in every step of success or failure the company or the organizer should learn that will prepare them to be more professional for the next challenge.

Some characteristics which make the bio entrepreneurship different from other entrepreneurs are:

- The life science or the biotechnology company not only take the risk of business but also takes the scientific risk.
- The bioentrepreneur should have knowledge of business as well as science both.
- The person who wants to start bioentrepreneurship should have full knowledge and unique ideas related to science. They should also have information about different skills including marketing, raising investments, building a skilled team and solution for specific problems.
- During startup the bioentrepreneur requires more investment with no financial returns at early starts.
- Strict regulatory requirements for discovery as well as for clinical trials.
- Long development timelines of products.

Bioentrepreneurship is all about biotechnology business and its different fields. In developed as well as in developing countries the biotechnology is an emerging field. Whether it's simple production of cheese or fermented foods to the more advanced technology such as gene therapy or development of drugs and vaccines or genetic elaboration of biopharmaceuticals or industrial production of antibiotics or production of novel crops and genetically modified crops or environmental services have illustrated the need of biotechnology and to practice it worldwide. Biotechnology business also provides the economical, efficient, pollution-free biological technologies which contribute to sustainable development of industries and also has significant contribution to health care of mankind (Figure 1).

Figure 1. Different sectors of bioentrepreneurship

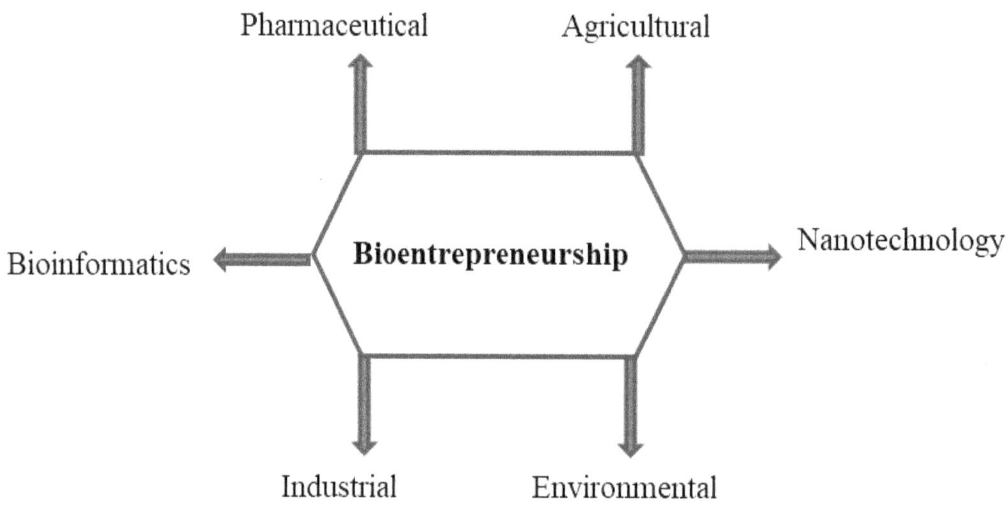

Broadly bioentrepreneurship or biotechnology business has been classified in following sectors:

Pharmaceutical Companies

This sector includes with the preparation or discovery of vaccines or drugs for various life threading diseases such as tuberculosis, hepatitis, malaria, respiratory infections, chronic diseases and many more. This firm also involved in testing the drugs in different phases of clinical trials. After the successful testing of the product it is commercialized in the market for human needs. Further the excessive use of gene therapy in the treatment of cancer and other infectious diseases has widely increased the genetic engineering technology. The products of genetic engineering technology such as recombinant proteins and recombinant antibodies are driving the global genetic engineering market in medical organization. But still the techniques required lots of investment, dearth of trained professionals and the wrong public perception has hampered the growth of the market (Reddy & Anbalagan, 2011; Acres et al., 2007).

Agricultural Companies

This includes the production of crops which are insect resistant, virus resistant and herbicide tolerant. Genetically modified crops and the improved composition of crops with vitamins and minerals is also the product of this sector. Further the novel hybridization systems and the plant tissue culture including the *invitro* rooting, organogenesis, micro propagation, embryogenesis, artificial or synthetic seed production and somaclonal variation has increased the production of food crops and thus brings revolution in the world. Many medicinal products are also developed by using the latest technology of plant tissue culture. Some scientists believes that the agriculture biotechnology as an effective means to combating hunger, malnutrition and poverty by increasing the production rate of crops in many developing countries (Reddy & Anbalagan, 2011; Matthew & Renkoski, 1997).

Environmental Companies

The products of this sector include many products which are developed from biotechnological interventions and are helpful in the pollution free environment or are ecofriendly. Some of them are production of biopesticides, biocatalyst, bio-fuels, and conversion of toxic chemicals into harmless byproducts, bioremediation of wastes and biomass of value-added foods. This is a cost effective method that controls the algal boom and biological invasion of the environment. It also cleans the environment and is helpful in risk assessment and monitoring of environment (Reddy & Anbalagan, 2011; Sadique, 2018).

Industrial Companies

In developing countries like India rising demand for new technologies such as recombinant technology, DNA sequencing, fermentation, bioprocess technology and tissue engineering has driven the popularity of industrial biotechnology. The industrial biotechnology is revolving around study of three field's i.e. genomics, proteomics, and bioinformatics. The detailed knowledge of this helps the scientist to work with nature in such a way that can maximize or optimize existing biochemical pathways used for manufacturing of products or will help in the resource conservation, pollution prevention, and cost reduction of product. The bioprocess technology product includes the commercial proteins, enzymes from (plants, animals, and microbes), fermentation products, milk products, soft drinks, biofuels and essential fatty acids etc. The genetic engineering products include recombinant vaccines, transgenic plants, transgenic cell lines, different therapeutic products, and transgenic animal's etc. Today there is expansion in the biotechnology-centered incubators and economic development centers that will increase the number of industrial biotechnology companies and products present in the market in coming year. So it would not wrong to say that the industrial biotechnology is the third wave in the healthcare industry (Zaur Rzakhanov, 2004; de Lorenzo et al., 2018).

Bioinformatics and Nanotechnology

Bioinformatics is the mathematical representation of the database in the bioinformatics tools which helps scientists for the prediction of diseases and production of new drugs. The nanotechnology has produced the biosensors, nano materials and nano robots that is applicable to target the smart drugs for advanced diagnostics. Recent advancements in both the technology or by integrating nano-technology with bioinformatics also known as bio-nano-informatics has accelerated the discovery of novel biomarkers in the emerging field of personalized or predictive medicine. Biomarkers or the predictive medicine uses genetic or molecular information to predict disease development, progression, and clinical outcome to know the molecular profile of each individual (Reddy & Anbalagan, 2011; Anandaram, 2017; John et al., 2009).

BACKGROUND

Life science business is facing many challenges as the demand of consumer need is changing day by day as in daily life. It is very necessary for the firms to develop new strategies to change the products or markets timely in order to provide a good service to the consumers and retain the business. The companies that fail to consistently launch new products timely will fail to maintain their business in the long run and will lose with their competitors. But the launching of new products alone is not enough for success of any business. Numerous studies have shown that the failure of company or firm or organizer is not only dependent on the innovation of new ideas and creation of new products. The failure can occur due to many reasons like:

- The product is poorly designed or manufactured.
- Ineffective marketing.
- The launching of product to market may be too early or too late.
- Lack of understanding of customers need.

In 21st century the bioentrepreneurship will get success only when they are standing out from their competitors. As the consumers or the young generation's preference is changing the bioentrepreneur should be flexible to develop their business in many aspects to be unique and fulfill the consumer need and think of human welfare. The development of business in terms of ideas, initiatives and activities are very important to survive in market and make the business better. Further the growth of business also includes business expansion globally, increasing revenues, building strategic partnerships, increasing profit and sales growth. For the successful development of business all the departments are equally involved like sales, marketing, manufacturing, human resources, finance, product development, management team and the market development (W.H & Cunningham, 1981; Sandy & Pfister, 2007; Perju-Mitran, 2019).

Before starting a bioentreneurship or any biotechnology (life science) related field the bioentrepreneur should have good knowledge of business in terms of strengths, weaknesses, opportunities, and threats collectively called as SWOT analysis. Bioentrepreneur should also know the competitor developments, sources of sales, overall industry of business, growth projections, consumer profile, cost areas and the possible options for cost-savings, new and unexplored market opportunities, new products and new sectors for expansion of their existing business (Namugenyi et al., 2019; Boaz, et al., 2010).

Bioentrepreneurship is the fundamental process of bringing life science discovery or invention from the research phase through development to a commercial market. The start-up of new business was not an easy task. The growth of bioentrepreneurship doesn't depends on the character, looks of the bioentrepreneur but it requires skills, patience and perseverance. Besides all these the biggest challenge for bioentrepreneurship is to get success. Basically there are three structural elements or the three pillars which is necessary for development of bioentrepreneurship.

Three pillars of bioentrepreneurship are

Management Team

The skilled managerial capability is very important in the success of any bioenterprise or startup of any biotech firms. Without the management team it would not be possible to any company or research and development to bring a single product for commercialization in the market.

Capital

Adequate financing is another pillar of the bioentrepreneurship as at the early stages, the biotechnology business doesn't have too much of this resource. Many biopharmaceutical companies are launched through private investments and even venture capital leading to the initial public offering is the more common route by which emerging companies acquire growth financing.

Market Development

This is the last element of bioentrepreneurship. Access of new technology to create new products from the existing product increases the revenue of the business.

All this three pillar or elements work in synergetic way at least up to 10 years, then only the company will get profit. The weakness in any one of the pillar can cause a decline of the company. The focus of the chapter is the market development, so we will discuss this in detail.

MARKET DEVELOPMENT

Bioentrepreneur apply various functions or different ways like increase in advertising budget, expanding their sales team, changing their distribution methods and investing heavily in product development etc. to their business in order to increase the revenue of companies. One such strategy which strengthens the business and helps in the growth of business is market development.

To succeed in business today it is very important to develop new strategies to change the existing products timely in order to provide a good service to the consumers this strategy is known as market development. Market development is defined as the expansion of total addressable market or the existing market rather than looking for a new market. The expansion of market can be done by entering new segments of the market, converting non-users into users or developing a new product and selling to new users or to the existing consumers or selling an existing products to a new demographic area. All this strategy of expansion will effectively increase the growth of business (Adams, et al., 2006; Costa, 2004; Pacifico & Polacek, 1981).

MARKET DEVELOPMENT EXPANSION

A market development is a small strategic plan designed by the companies to expand their business worldwide. Every organization or the business revolves around geography, customer base, and the products for the market expansion (Pacifico & Polacek, 1981; Perju-Mitran, 2019).

The three spheres which influence the market development expansion most are as follows.

Geographical

If the business is succeeded in any one country then the existing product can be expanded to the new geographical area means promoting the product expansion not only in the different parts of the country but also in the other countries or into the new markets where the product currently doesn't exist.

Consumers Base

In this step the bioentrepreneur focus on demographic expansion in which the firm targets the non-user to become their customers. If the product is manufactured for young people only or to a particular age group the company can change the existing product to be used by all the age groups (middle aged adults, or seniors, or kids, or teenagers). The existing product should be modified in such a way that it must be useful for different genders also. In other words we can say that the company must not be constraining to any one age group or gender. Simply this is a selling to different types of consumers.

Products

This includes both new and existing products. The goal of this strategy is to expand or to reach their products into a different segment or unexplored market. This can be achieved through a variety of methods, including offering free trials, advertising, giving discount or incentives, changing the packaging and trying different pricing of existing product. This step attracts the consumers from their competitors and also new customers. After doing lots of research the firm can know the need of consumers and can change or modify the products accordingly. In this the market can be divided into different segments based on consumers' personality traits, values, or interests and their lifestyles. Bioentrepreneur should have good relationship with their existing consumers so that they could believe in the quality and price of product. This will help the business to get benefits by introducing the new product in the existing market.

Market development is not an easy task. Before implementing market development strategy to any business organization the bioentrepreneur should considers various factors which determines that the company is ready to develop a new market development strategy for the product. The key factor for development of market strategy is the understanding of the current baseline performance and to know how this strategy will affect their business. Only after analyzing the entire factor the bioentrepreneur should move for market development.

The factors required for the market development strategy include:

- Whether the strategy is profitable for the consumers.
- Whether there is need to introduce the new or modified product in market.
- Whether the company has unexplored market place.
- Whether the company has done market research for the consumers need.
- Whether the company has already reached or sells their goal in particular market area.
- Whether the companies can effort the investment required for developing new market development.
- Whether the new strategy will compete with the competitors in terms of price, features or quality of the product.

There are many strategies which are required by the bioentrepreneur to upgrade their company or business in terms of revenue, customer base, international coverage and profits. The mathematician and business manager, H. Igor Ansoff, has summarized these potential growth strategies into four strategies known as Ansoff Matrix which helped many bioentrepreneur to better understand the market development and risk associated with them (Ansoff, 1957).

ANSOFF MATRIX

In 1957 Igor Ansoff has published an article in Harvard Business Review titled "Strategies for Diversification." This article explains the four strategies of market development and is applicable for all type of business. It is 2x2 matrix shown in quadrant made up of new and existing products on one axis, and new and existing markets on the other (Ansoff, 1957; Loredana, 2017; Kotler & Armstrong, 2015). It is also known as product/market expansion grid (Table 1).

The four strategies of the Ansoff matrix are:

Market penetration: This strategy focus on the increasing sales of existing product to an existing market.
Product development: This includes introducing new products to an existing market.
Market development: This includes using an existing product to totally new market.
Diversification: This includes introducing a new product to new market.

Ansoff matrix also discusses the risk associated with each one of quadrant. As the firm moves into a new quadrant (horizontally or vertically), risk increases. Of all the four strategies market penetration is the least risky and diversification is the most risky. We will discuss this matrix in detail and how to apply them.

Market Penetration or Existing Products into Existing Markets

This is the first quadrant of the Ansoff matrix and it is concerned with selling or expanding the existing product in known market. This strategy is adopted by the organization when there is need of growth within the market or the competition is intense for the particular product. This is the safest of all the four strategy as the firm is already familiar with the existing products and the existing consumers. There is a strong relationship between the existing firm and the consumers and because of the existing product knowledge this strategy pays back more quickly as compared to other strategy. Market penetration rate can be calculated by dividing the number of consumers by the size of the target market and then multiply the result by 100. The higher the percentage the penetration rate of that firm is good. For example: Previously orange was taken only during breakfast but by advertising the use of orange juices, its nutritive value has expanded its usage in consumers.

The market penetration can be executed in number of ways to increase the growth of company or business firm like:

- Play with prices of the product.
- Improving distribution network or channels.
- Investing more in marketing and advertising.
- Increase production capacity of product.
- Giving attractive offers.
- Attracting competitor consumers.
- Increasing the loyalty of existing customers.
- Increasing the uses of the same product.

Product Development or New Products in Existing Markets

This is the strategy in which the firm modified or changes the existing product according to the consumers need and launches it in the same known market. This strategy is needed when the business organization has already reached the saturation with the existing product and where the market penetration is no longer fruitful. Further, when the company has good market share, strong understanding of their current market, good consumer base and the bioentrepreneur has innovative ideas to meet the needs of an existing market then this strategy is applied. For the expansion of any business organization it is necessary to introduce new products timely to attract the consumers. The process requires extensive research and development and expansion of the company's product range. It is slightly more risky as compared to market penetration. Research and development activities play a dominant role in this strategy. This strategy is risky than market penetration strategy because developing, testing a new products and then creating awareness, interest, and availability for the consumers takes a time. Further the developed product may not meet the needs of consumers. For example: In 2020 for corona virus pandemic which is spread worldwide many pharmaceutical industry such as Pfizer, Merck and many more are involved in research and development in order to come up with new and innovative drugs or vaccines for welfare of human mankind.

The product development strategy can be executed in number of ways:

- Doing an extensive research on competitor's product which are on demand by the consumers and merging with other resources to generate a new product which fulfill the needs of consumers.
- Doing some innovative things in existing product that can attracts the non-users.
- Investing in business organization without thinking of profit at early stage of product development.
- Establishing a partnership with other firms.

Market Development or Existing Products in New Markets

In this strategy the company expands its existing product into totally new market. The expansion may be reaching new geographical area or making new consumers or new demographic expansion. This strategy should be implemented only when the firm was able to predict the profit and loss, has capability to earn profit from it and the behavior or the needs of consumers was same as that was in existing market. In this strategy the return on marketing investments is longer than market penetration strategy because it takes longer time to build awareness, distribution, and product trial of existing product. For small firms this strategy may found to be of great use, if they got success in doing so. For example, the fast food restaurants such as Macdonald have moved into international markets, they have often changed their menus according to the food preferences of consumers in local markets.

The market development strategy can be implemented by any one of the following approaches:

- By expanding the product regionally or globally, but the bioentrepreneur should know how to enter foreign or new markets.
- By advertising new use of the same product.
- Creating awareness about the products.
- Developing distribution channels.
- By finding some new features or new benefits for the existing product.
- By catering to a new consumers

- There was no competitor or no such product was available in that new market.

Diversification or New Products in New Markets

This strategy is the most risky as it was concerned with entering the new or unproven or unfamiliar product into a totally new or unfamiliar market which the firm may not have been understood completely. In other words we can say that this is really the creation of a completely new business. This strategy also requires patience for the bioentrepreneur to get return of investment. The risk can be diminished by offering somewhat related product.

Diversification strategies can be classified into three types:

1. Related Diversification

This is also known as concentric or horizontal diversification. In this diversification the new product launched is similar to the existing product that has already saturated the market or new product was entered the market which is related to the existing market. In other words we can say that there is synergy between the existing product or the market. In this the bioentrepreneurship focus only in a particular field for example Gilead sciences works only on infectious disease similarly OSI pharmaceutical company only works on oncology.

2. Unrelated Diversification

This is also known as conglomerate or lateral diversification. In this diversification the company is offering a new product in a completely new market which is not related to the existing product or existing market. In other words we can say that there is no synergy between the existing product and the market. For example: Pharmacogenomics the fusion of therapy and diagnostics is completely new area that is of great importance in near future.

3. Vertical Diversification

This is also known as vertical integration. In this diversification the firm may move forward or backward for the expansion of firms. This strategy refers to the integration of further steps apart from the drug discovery or the drug development. In this the bioentrepreneurship integrated all the activities from target validation to the launching of product in the market. The steps involved target validation, screening, lead organization, pre-clinic, clinical trials phase I, II, III and if got success in all steps finally enters the market. For example-In 2020 corona virus vaccine named covaxin was developed by Bharat Biotech in collaboration with the Indian Council of Medical Research goes through all the steps and trial and now available in the market for use.

Life science business is the fastest growing and knowledge-training based sector in India and the world. Bioentrepreneurship in unique business as it is the application or sum of all the initiatives and activities required to process the materials by biological agents to provide goods and services. This has open several opportunities for bio-industrialization and hence developed the economy of that nation. It would not be wrong to say that the gross domestic productivity of any country increases because of this biotechnology revolution known as bioentrepreneurship that has open several doors for industries and to start small bio-business companies. Bioentrepreneurship has become the world second largest economy that remodels the potential of biotechnology to endorse economic growth by transforming health, nanotechnology, agriculture, environment, bioinformatics, genetic engineering and many more (Sadique, 2018).

In the past 50 years the business of life sciences industry in India was increased rapidly from the era of dependency on other country to become a self-sufficient country. In this journey, the firm or business organization has passed through lots of up and down. At present the life science business or the bio entrepreneurship has achieved several successes and contributed significantly not only in India but abroad also. This includes:

- India has become the third largest contributor in reducing the merchandise trade deficit by contributing through life science business. This also generates a significant number of jobs for India.
- In pharmaceuticals, India is now the eighth largest country. It has built a strong position in market globally and involved in number of clinical trials conducted by health care organization.
- India life science organization has contributed in selling many drugs and vaccines in affordable price as compared to markets globally.
- India is the primary supplier of essential medicines for numerous diseases, helping save millions of lives globally.
- In research and development also India built world class capabilities and in manufacturing, it has highest number of FDA-approved formulation plant.

Till 21st century India has registered over 5.0 billion USD in revenue by biotechnology sectors. Today more than 500 companies in India are engaged in biotech-industry including biopharmaceuticals, bio-agriculture and other services with having a share of 3% in the global biotechnology market. Bioentrepreneurship has considered to be broadly involved in a bundle of technologies that operates the natural idle things into modified outcomes with its increased potential and sustainable return of products. It has a broad domain which are being practiced in various fields such as food, chemical, industrial, medical, marine, pharmaceutical, nano-science, biomedical, genetic engineering etc (Stefanec, 2011; OPPI Annual Report, 2013-14; Coasta, 2004). It has been working for the benefit of humans and environment with corresponding development in scientific research and technological development. Despite of this endless goal of the life science industry or the boom of these industries, they are still facing challenging opportunities globally (Gurau, 2021; Tiago & Verissimo, 2014).

The challenges that bioentrepreneurship facing are:

Developing a New Product

It is the most challenging process to make new product or altering the existing product in laboratory and then converting it in into industrial framework.

Time Consuming

On an average the pharmaceutical company needs 10 to 15 years to develop novel drug from the basic concepts which goes through different clinical trials and then commercializing it in the market.

Marketing a New Product

The major obstacle the companies have to face after product development is bringing the invention from labs to the market users. There are multiple competitors are already present in the market. The novel product should satisfy the consumers and current needs of human mankind's as this is the key of success.

Expertise Requirement

For development of any product skilled people are in high demand for their knowledge and hands-on expertise.

High Levels of Risk

It is just hide and trial process in research and development to develop a new product. It requires lots of investment, lengthy period and with only hope to get back the invested money. The product launched may get success or may not.

Policy Challenges

The biosciences firms have to get approval from the FDA for their invented drugs so that they can sell it in the market, which is again a lengthy process. Also the FDA keeps a close watch at every clinical trial; the product may even fail at any stage which is again a great loss to the bioentrepreneur. It was estimated that, around 36% of drugs fail in preliminary stage of drug development, another 68% fails at intermediate stage and only 40% are able to be knocked out in the final stage. Till this point, a lot of money and time has been invested in research and development or in any bioscience organization.

Affordability

The new products developed are so costly that the layman is not able to afford it. This is again another challenge to manage the investment and get benefit from it.

Privacy

Patients are having confidential issues, so they are not easily ready for the most advance technologies like gene therapy etc.

Genetically Modified Food Adoption

Genetically modified crops are produced by isolating a gene from a plant, organism or animal and splice it into others to make resistance to pesticides and herbicides, increases crop yields, and resistance to drought tolerance or any other diseases. Still this is not adopted by the farmers or the bioentrepreneur of lesser developed countries because it was concerned about adverse effects on human health, the environment, and ethical considerations.

Society Concerns

As this field is rapidly changing and new technologies developed are adapted by the human may considered to have direct impact on human lives in term of lifestyle, health issues and decreasing the life span. There is also a loss of cultural activities and the natural biodiversity of the world.

Production/Laboratory Safety

While working on it the technician should have all the protected condition in the laboratory otherwise in may great loss to humankind.

For example: pandemic of corona virus in 2020.

Bioterrorism

Another concern is that the heavy number of biological toxins and infectious organisms could be used to attack animals, humans and plants. Example: Plague, Anthrax, Botulin etc.

Ethical Issues

While working on the new drug development, stem cell research, gene therapy, genetic engineering requires an ethical clearance from their respective institutes, which is again a slow process.

Lack of Digital Marketing

Most of the companies are involved in traditional marketing and exploring their market digital which hinders their discoveries.

Funding Agency

This plays a crucial role in development of products in institutes. There is constrained or limit of funds given by organization which again determines the timeline of the product.

Lack of Collaboration

Lack of collaboration between Indian and overseas companies and between private and government sectors

Other Issues

Some other issues may be loss of patents, high research and development cost with less productivity and hence the return on investment is less.

The bioentrepreneurship discover, develop, manufacture, and then sell their products to their consumers. The companies may have a great innovative idea, may have hired an expertise persons to develop an experienced team in order to develop the product. They may also have raised money from funding agencies for development of product, testing and may have got a regulatory approval to work. As the company navigates through these obstacles and overcomes these hurdles still it is not necessary that there is commercial success of the product unless the company has accomplished a powerful market development strategy. In other words we can say that just developing a product would not be able to earn economy or sell the products in markets. The process requires an identification of the target market consumers and a strong market development strategy. The good marketing strategy before commercialization of the product will help the business organization to earn profitable money. The bio entrepreneurs should have think of plans or an idea of a market development strategy during the early stage of the firm or before developing new products (Kearney, 2018; Kotler, et al., 2010; Porter, 1998).

MARKET DEVELOPMENT TOOLS AND CONCEPTS

There are many market development tools that are essential for developing a sound market strategy, but here we will discuss only the strategies which are related to and useful in the process of bioentrepreneurship (Perju-Mitran, 2019; PAREXEL Biopharmaceutical, 2014; Persidis, 1997). This strategy includes:

Market Segmentation

It would not be possible by any business organization to market their product to every individual; therefore the large population/area should be divided into smaller consumers groups on basis of similar needs, desires, location, demographics, and purchasing habits. For example it would be better to focus on some clinical and make new drugs that was not available in the market.

Targeting Consumers

It is the next step after market segmentation and it is the process in which the firm focuses to the best consumer segments.

Product Positioning

Positioning means the efforts taken by any firm to introduce their products to the target consumer segments. In this the companies differentiate their product position from their competitors' products, so that the consumer can easily identify their products. For example: Biosciences products are positioned to benefit the human's inspite of just gaining status, image and money from the consumers.

Product Brand

It is a logo that a company achieves after working for many years andgaining a profit from that product. Brand is a product trade names that consumers can recognize it easily. It is the perception of the person's mind, once the consumers start using any brand product then they will restrict to that only. For example: Patanjali has started with some small house hold products but now they are in market with so many products even medicine. Another example is the colgate, they have launched a food products in the market but unable to succeed. This may be due to imagination of consumers mind of food taste.

Analysis of Competitors Market

Porter has given a conceptual model known as five forces model of Industry structure. It consists of the threat of new entrants or substitute product or services and bargaining power of consumers or suppliers.

Marketing Plan

It depends on the four P's that are uniqueness of the product, price, place of distribution and promotion.

Selecting Product and Screening

The product developed has to go through three stages: prescreening, screening for degree of fit and detailed business analysis. For new drug development this process shows inverse triangle means if sixty new product ideas entered the screening process only five were able to reach the final screening and only one drug will get success.

New Market Development

Two extreme situations has encountered in field of biosciences business which has made many discoveries. The situations are technology-driven development, and market-driven development. For example: Human growth hormone, insulin, tissue plasminogen activator, recombinant hepatitis B vaccine all are market-driven and much needed drugs of that time.

Pricing

Playing with price structure of the product is another tool of market development strategy.

Promotion and Advertising

This is the process of communicating with their consumers either physically or through media to make aware of the product and the brand.

Distribution Channel

It is a process of developing a wide distribution channel via direct or digital or drip marketing to reach their target segmented consumers.

PMT Matrix

The PMT matrix was considered as milestone to achieve the goal of market development of any organization, where P stands for uniqueness and superiority of the product, M is for strategy used for marketing that may be consumer, sales, product or society oriented and T is for new technologies used to develop the product.

Apart from the above market development strategies, there is need of developing a marketing strategy plans in every field of life sciences business. Government is also encouraging the young generation to get more and more involved in field of bioentrepreneurship. Government is also making a lot of strategies to overcome from the challenges that the bioentrepreneur is facing now a days (DBT website, Goretti. et al., 2020; Muller, 2002; Tyebjee & Hardin, 2004). Some of the strategies are:

- For research emphasis in medical field both basic and applied research would be supported at molecular, cellular level, genomics, proteomics, system biology, stem cell biology, RNA interference, host response and new platform technologies.
- Research to improve production and manufacturing process of product should mainly be focused on vaccines, diagnostics, new therapies based on cell and tissue replacement, therapeutic antibodies, herbal medicine, plant based medicine, nucleic acids, therapeutics, drug and vaccine delivery systems and new anti-microbial agents
- Improvements in infrastructure and networks should be done for the interdisciplinary translational research having a pool of scientists, physicians, engineers, and public health persons.
- Several stem cell research centers/banks and umbilical cord stem cell bank was established by the government.
- Streamline guidelines and procedures for the approval of recombinant pharmaceutical products was developed.
- Funding agencies like Indian council of medical research, department of biotechnology, and department of science and technology are ready to give funds for translational biology, clinical trials, molecular epidemiology and product development.
- Regenerative medicine is an emerging field that has formulated a comprehensive human tissue act.
- A clear law for animal testing has been made in the country.
- Encouraging the researchers, clinical practice and pharmacokinetics expertise to work simultaneously to get clinical application/utility in focus of the product in same time.
- Providing incentives for this group of clinician-researchers to bring these scientific advances to the patient bedside
- The bioengineering research emphasis will be on development of tissue engineered skin, cartilage, cornea, acute liver support, large segment bone repair and small diameter artery
- Regenerative therapy for the failing myocardium through drug therapy, stem cell technology and advanced dressing of burn and wound dressings
- Biosensors were developed for detecting and monitoring metabolites and identifying specific genetic materials and for home monitoring of critical parameters like creatinine, cholesterol and triglycerides.
- Good clinical trial practice manual has developed taking into account international guidelines and disseminate these widely and also strengthen the clinical trial capacity in medical schools and hospitals to create centers of excellence.
- Public awareness was created in order to allay fears through education programs, industry conferences and seminars.
- Emphasize on intellectual property rights, confidentiality and feedback was given to trained the scientists and the researches.
- Collaboration of public-private with government sector has been done to improve the product quality and to reduce the time frame needed to develop a new product and also there is urgent need

to promote and improve the levels of horizontal integration between public-public and public-private laboratories.

- In a long term perspective for development of crops agriculture research was promoted for international treaty and protocol was made for biosafety, germplasm exchange, production of transgenic plants, engineering of metabolic pathways etc has been encouraged strictly for research and development using modern technologies for feasibility, socio-economic considerations and promotion of trade.
- Broadening of alliances of small companies with large agricultural companies globally in order to reduce developmental costs has been done.
- For environmental development there should be promotion of horizontal networking between remote sensing experts, field biologist, computer specialists and between biotechnologists, foresters, oceanographers and field biologists for inventorisation of bioresources based both on primary and secondary sources of information.
- More efforts were given to industrial biotechnology that will develop eco-friendly green technologies in coming future.
- For procurement of medicinal plants regulatory norms were prescribed by drugs controller general of India, they will evaluate the efficacy, safety, and quality of herbal products.

Some examples are

- Microbial type culture collection (MTCC) at IMTECH, Chandigarh was developed for preservation cell lines.
- Inter-ministerial agriculture biotechnology board was developed for cross cutting issues such as: duplication of research development and promotion of horizontal partnerships
- A board was developed including Indian council of agriculture research, department of biotechnology, regulatory authority, expert scientists, industry, and the farming community they will access, release and efficient system for biosafety assessment of genetically modified crops.
- Review committee on genetic manipulation was developed for monitoring test and recombinant technology to give approval for large scale testing on preclinical animal toxicity test and recommend to drugs controller general of India.
- Drugs controller general of India will permit human clinical trials, and after reviewing the data grant permission for manufacturing and marketing the product.
- Central drugs standard control organization of the government of India was developed that is responsible for approval of licenses of specified categories of drugs after the success of human clinical trial.
- The genetic engineering appraisal committee was developed for approval of living modified organism.
- Genetech and Amgen were collaborated with theestablished pharmaceutical companies known as Big Pharma.
- Mayo clinic of Mexico is a worldwide health centers for cancer specially multiple myeloma that provides services for patients, family and referring physicians.
- Recently the private sector Bharat Biotech has developed a COVID-19 vaccine in collaboration with government institute ICMR.

- Some successful biotech companies areNovo Nordisk A/S (NVO), Alexion pharmaceuticals (ALXN), Vertex pharmaceuticals (VRTX), Jazz pharmaceuticals PLC (JAZZ), Biomarin pharmaceutical.

Bioentrepreneurship is a field that merges four different disciplines of life sciences which is indicated by colours: red for medical process, white for industrial processes, blue for marine processes and green for agricultural processes respectively. But all they have only one objective that is to provide or fulfill the basic needs of human by production and improvement of products which are required for health, shelter, clothing, food and environment. Every cloud has a silver lining" or "A coin has two sides" means irrespective of having many advantages of market development there are some disadvantages also (Ramazan et al., 2014).

Advantages of Market Development Strategies

- It will keep pace with the changing times.
- Consumers will not get bored by seeing the same offering and products, so they will restrict to that brand or firm only.
- The firm is able to compete with their competitors and the company will be in sparking position and earning profit.
- If the firm has new and strong developmental strategy than the media, reports and bloggers will be eager to expand the business by advertising.
- Building a strong team will put the firm in top listed companies
- It also helps wonderful planning and immediate decision making process.
- It is a source of generating new ideas and provides goods to consumers according to their need.
- In also has benefited society by improving the living standard and providing employment to may peoples.
- It helps in earning and increasing profit and thus improving the economic condition of the country.
- Removes unemployment as lot of people are working on a company.
- Improves health issues and offers medical advancement opportunities.
- It also reduces the rate of many dreadful diseases such as cancer or infectious diseases.
- Improves the quality of food crops by adding of nutritive values.
- It produces the product in surplus quantity means in under developed countries it also removes the poverty and hunger.
- It helps us to minimize or eliminate waste products and make eco-friendly environment.

Disadvantages of Market Development Strategies

- It is risky to introduce the new products in the market as it may not get benefit or disliked from the consumers.
- It is time consuming and even getting success is not sure.
- It requires lots of investment and after launching the product may fail to attract the new or the existing consumers.
- Advertising of new product may again require lots of expenditure and the company may not get the return of investment.

- If the firm is launching some new product it may possible at the same the competitor is also launching same product at more reasonable price which may affect the sale of product.

CONCLUSION AND FUTURE DIRECTIONS

Bioentrepreneurship is the most challenging and exciting of all the business. It requires energy, enthusiasm, investment and innovative ideas of the individual. Market development is key to success of any business. Market development strategy is concerned with market survey, gathering data, choosing the right price, launching the product at right time and understanding the consumer needs. This provides direction and rationale to manage time, money and human resources in developing the business to to achieve success in market.

Bioentrepreneurship and market development strategy also increases the national income of country, removes unemployment, allows us to preserve resources, improves health, offers medical advancement opportunities, reduces the rate of many dreadful diseases such as cancer or infectious diseases, improves the quality of food crops, adding of nutritive values, surplus production, helps us to minimize or eliminate waste products and make eco-friendly environment.

In short we can say that bioentrepreneurship whether it is small or medium or in early stage or in mature stage entails market development for their growth and has excellent future perspectives and hope for future expansion.

Table 1. Ansoff matrix quadrant

	Existing markets	**New markets**
Existing products	**Market penetration** Increasing sale to the existing market	**Market development** Finding new market for existing product
New products	**Product development** Creating new products for existing consumers	**Diversification** Creating new products for new markets

ACKNOWLEDGMENT

I would like to thank my family member; my husband Mr. Vinay Miri for moral support and my daughters miss Anshika and Advika who supported me and gave time to write this chapter. I would also like to thank my friend Dr. Vaishali Paul for encouraging me to write this chapter.

CONFLICT OF INTEREST

There is no conflict of interest.

REFERENCES

Acres, B., Limacher, J. M., & Bonnefoy, J. (2007). Discovery and development of therapeutic cancer vaccines. *Current Opinion in Drug Discovery & Development, 10*(2), 185–192. PMID:17436554

Adams, D., & Sparrow, J. (2008). Enterprise for Life Scientists: Developing Innovation and Entrepreneurship in the Biosciences. *Journal of Commercial Biotechnology, 14*(4), 355–356. doi:10.1057/jcb.2008.21

Adams, R., Bessant, J., & Phelps, R. (2006). Innovation Management Measurement: A Review. *International Journal of Management Reviews, 8*(1), 21–47. doi:10.1111/j.1468-2370.2006.00119.x

Anandaram, H. (2017). A Review on Application Of Biomarkers In The Field Of Bioinformatics & Nanotechnology For Individualized Cancer Treatment. *MOJ Proteomics & Bioinformatics, 5*(6), 00179. doi:10.15406/mojpb.2017.05.00179

Ansoff, I. (1957). Strategies for Diversification. *Harvard Business Review, 35*(5), 113–124v.

Bell, J. (2010). Handbook of bioentrepreneurship. New England Journal of Entrepreneurship, 13, 79-80. doi:10.1108/NEJE-13-01-2010-B007

Boaz, N., Murnane, J., & Nuffer, K. (2010). The basics of Business-to-business sales success. *The McKinsey Quarterly.*

Cabaleiro-Cerviño, G., & Burcharth, A. (2020). Licensing agreements as signals of innovation: When do they impact market value? *Technovation, 98*, 102175. doi:10.1016/j.technovation.2020.102175

Campart, S., & Pfister, E. (2007). Technology, cooperation and stock market value: An event study of new partnership announcements in the biotechnology and pharmaceutical industries. *Economics of Innovation and New Technology, 16*(1), 31–49. doi:10.1080/10438590600661764

Costa, C. (2004). *A methodological approach to the marketing process in the biotechnology based companies.* Academic Press.

de Lorenzo, V., Prather, K. L., Chen, G.-Q., O'Day, E., von Kameke, C., Oyarzún, D. A., Hosta-Rigau, L., Alsafar, H., Cao, C., Ji, W., Okano, H., Roberts, R. J., Ronaghi, M., Yeung, K., Zhang, F., & Lee, S. Y. (2018). The power of synthetic biology for bioproduction, remediation and pollution control. *EMBO Reports, 19*(4), e45658. doi:10.15252/embr.201745658 PMID:29581172

Department of Biotechnology, Ministry of Science and Technology. (n.d). http://www.dbtindia.nic.in/#

Gurău, C. (2021). Entrepreneurship in biotechnology. In *World Encyclopedia of Entrepreneurship.* Edward Elgar Publishing. doi:10.4337/9781839104145.00031

Kearney, C. (2018). Regulation and market influences on innovation in biotechnology. *Journal of Commercial Biotechnology, 24*(3), 57–62.

Kotler, P., & Armstrong, G. (2015). *Principles of marketing-global edition.* Pearson.

Kotler, P., Kartajaya, H., & Setiawan, I. (2010). *Marketing 3.0.* John Wiley & Sons, Inc. doi:10.1002/9781118257883

Loredana, E. M. (2017). The use of Ansoff matrix in the field of business. *Annals-Economy Series, 2*, 141–149.

Müller, C. (2002). Strategic Management: A Tool for Growth in the Biotechnology Sector. *Journal of Commercial Biotechnology*, *8*(3), 226–234. doi:10.5912/jcb436

Namugenyi, C. (2019). *Shastri L Nimmagadda*. Torsten Reiners.

Namugenyi, C., Nimmagadda, S. L., & Reiners, T. (2019). Design of a SWOT Analysis Model and its Evaluation in Diverse Digital Business Ecosystem Contexts. *Procedia Computer Science*, *159*, 1145–1154. doi:10.1016/j.procs.2019.09.283

Pacifico, C., & Polacek, R. (1981). *New Product Development. ACS Audio Course*. American Chemical Society.

Perju-Mitran, A. (2019). Key Elements of the Biotech Market. In F. Matei & D. Zirra (Eds.), *Introduction to Biotech Entrepreneurship: From Idea to Business*. Springer. doi:10.1007/978-3-030-22141-6_11

Persidis, A. (1997). Bioentrepreneurship around the world; Bioentrepreneur II. *Nature Biotechnology*, 16.

Phan, Moffitt, Stokes, Liu, Young, Nie, & Wang. (2009). Convergence of biomarkers, bioinformatics and nanotechnology for individualized cancer treatment. *Trends in Biotechnology, 27*(6), 350-358. doi:10.1016/j.tibtech.2009.02.010

Porter M. (1998). *Competitive strategy: Techniques for analyzing competitors*. Free Press.

Reddy, A. C., & Anbalagan, C. (2011). Application and Analysis of Marketing and Management on Biotechnology. *International Journal of Research in Management, Science and Technology*, *1*, 61–65.

Renkoski, M. A. (1997). Marketing Strategies of Biotechnology Firms: Implications for U.S. Agriculture. *Journal of Agricultural and Applied Economics*, *29*(1), 123–128. doi:10.1017/S1074070800029175

Sadique, S. (2018). Bio Entrepreneurship for Future Sustainable Small Business Perspective. *International Journal of Family Business Management*, *2*(2), 1–3.

Shimasaki, C. (2014). *Biotechnology Entrepreneurship*. Academic Press. doi:10.1016/B978-0-12-404730-3.00004-X

Stefanec, N. P. (2011). The impact of firm strategies on stock market value in the biotechnology industry. *Applied Financial Economics*, *21*(5), 343–352. doi:10.1080/09603107.2010.530214

Tiago, M. T. P. M. B., & Veríssimo, J. M. C. (2014). Digital marketing and social media: Why bother? *Business Horizons*, *57*(6), 703–708. doi:10.1016/j.bushor.2014.07.002

Tyagi, P., Kumar, A., & Sengar, R. S. (2018). The opportunities to develop a successful entrepreneurship and business model in biotechnology: An overview. *Journal of Commercial Biotechnology*, *24*(3), 63–68.

Uctu, R., & Jafta, R. C. C. (2014). Bioentrepreneurship as a bridge between science and business in a regional cluster: South Africa's first attempts. *Science & Public Policy*, *41*(2), 219–233. doi:10.1093cipolct049

Xu, B. (2009). *R&D innovation and the value of cash in the biotech industry*. Academic Press.

Chapter 9
The Role of the Indian Government in Bioentrepreneurship:
A Journey Towards "Aatm Nirbhar Bharat"

Shubhita Mathur
Jaipur National University, India

ABSTRACT

Entrepreneurship correlates to the entrepreneur who is creative, has risk taking capability, promotes capital formation, and seeks out investment opportunities in the market. In the National Institute for Transforming India Aayog's 5th Governing Council, the Government of India (GoI) aims to take the Indian economy to USD 5 trillion by 2024. Thus, India needs to significantly increase employment opportunities for which GoI is promoting skill development through biotechnology entrepreneurship and investing appreciably with a special focus on R&D to develop India into a world class bio-manufacturing hub. The DBT in collaboration with BIRAC has implemented flagship schemes such as 'Make in India' and 'Start up India'. The major objectives of this chapter are to lay out (1) the role of GoI to empower startups for growth through innovation and design, (2) a detailed overview of the various schemes offered by GoI for promoting skill development and innovation through bio-entrepreneurship, (3) major challenges faced by the government for implementation of schemes.

INTRODUCTION

Bio-Entrepreneurship

Entrepreneurship correlates to the entrepreneur, his vision, his ability to address the problem, innovate and its implementation (Marcati et al., 2008). A potential entrepreneur must be creative, promote capital formation, have risk taking capability and should seek out investment opportunities in the market. In addition to create new firms, entrepreneurs must aim to create new job opportunities in their respective

DOI: 10.4018/978-1-7998-7411-9.ch009

field. Bio-entrepreneurship is rightly explained as generation of fortune resulting from the application of biosciences to the business framework (Lepeley et al., 2019). Entrepreneurs are the driving force of economic growth and social development.

Bio-entrepreneurs are individuals involved in the business (Bonnafous-Boucher & Lamy, 2010). They may be research scientist who are willing to start their own company using the seed fund provided by government for the commercialization of the product based on their research or an expert, trained and experienced professional manager hired by a private equity investor that provides capital to companies exhibiting high growth potential for product commercialization or bio-entrepreneursmay be people who leads their company into research and development (R&D) at clinical trialstagefor the successful launch of the products like vaccines and drugs.

The concept of "bio entrepreneurship" is rightly novel in India (Ullah & Zohra, 2018). Scientist in India still follow the traditional research culture, they do not take risks associated with market like launch of new technology and therefore consider playing safe by following old traditional methodologies. Every bio entrepreneur should try to innovate while working on basic research in order to increase the commercial value of product. The top biotech companies in India includes, Biocon, Serum Institute of India, Panacea Biotec, Rasi Seeds, Aventis Pharma, Bharat Serums, etc. (Mueller, 2007).

Outline of Indian Start-Up Ecosystem

The Government of India has shown great dynamism to encourage innovation and entrepreneurship to boost Indian economy at global level. In the NITI Aayog's 5th Governing Council, the honorable prime minister Narendra Modi led government aims to take the Indian economy to USD 5 trillion by 2024. To achieve this goal, India needs to significantly increase employment opportunities. This ambition cannot be fulfilled by the existing large ventures alone. Therefore, Indian government is promoting skill development through biotechnology entrepreneurship.

India's startups will empower the Indian economy by fetching innovative and rational thinking, dynamism, and creating jobs in the Indian market. However, approximately 90% Startups in India fail within a span of first 5 years (Kerr & Kerr, 2020). In recent years, the Indian startup ecosystem has taken off and acquired greater visibility.

However the success of the SSI and the growing Start Up sectors has been unsatisfactory- high failure rate – estimated (Subrahmanya, 2015). Driven by factors such as, availability of funding, foreign investors, evolving technology space and a burgeoning demand within the domestic market. Other factors: growing unemployment, declining jobs in organized sector, global trends, largely oppressive / exploitative rather than nurturing government machinery, few tie ups with established industrial enterprises / large & medium enterprises.

BACKGROUND

The Indian startup ecosystem is the 2nd largest in the world, anticipating a year-over-year growth of 10-12% (Braun & Schreiber, 2017). At present there are approximately 20,000 startups in India (Dossani & Kenney, 2009). On an average there are three to four tech startups born every day in India. Start-up India enterprise is headed by Ministry of Commerce and Industry, Government of India. India has drawn attention from the global investors and unicorns at a quick pace because of world-class technology startups owned by Indian entrepreneurs. The Biotechnology sector is one of the expanding sectors in India. The Indian government is investing appreciably with a special focus on R&D to develop India into a world class bio manufacturing hub. The Department of Biotechnology (DBT), since its inception in 1986, under the Ministry of Science has laid emphasis on promotion of excellence and innovation for discovery, early and late stage translational research in the areas of agriculture, affordable healthcare & medical technology, food & nutritional security, animal biotechnology, environmental safety, clean energy & bio-fuel, bio-manufacturing, etc. (Vijayaraghavan & Dutz, 2012). Innovation driven research in Biotechnology and modern biology is being facilitated and supported by the Department through its various schemes across the country. Through its various initiatives in connection to promote innovative research, the major thrust of the Department includes developing right kind of infrastructure, building new national and international partnerships, supporting public-private partnership, development of products and their commercialization for a robust bio-economy.

The Indian biotechnology industry is burgeoning with a wealth of investment and an eager graduate workforce with strong emphasis on translational research. In 1986, with the stimulation of then-prime minister late Rajiv Gandhi, India became one of the first countries in the world to have a government unit devoted exclusively to biotechnology (Nogrady, 2018). The government of India is continuously striving hard to encourage investment in the field of biotechnology which is evident from the fact that the Department of Biotechnology (DBT) has received the highest hike in the Union Budget (2020-2021).

The major initiative in the form of various schemes includes "Innovate in India", "Startup India", "Make in India", "Atal Innovative Mission", "Skill India", etc. The funding schemes initiated by DBT, Department of Science and Technology (DST) and Department of Scientific and Industrial Research (DSIR), several public-private collaborative incubation centers encourages Bio-entrepreneurship amongst scientists and research fellows to promote innovation that has potential for commercialization. A public limited company, Biotech Consortium India Limited (BCIL), New Delhi was set up by All India Financial Institutions and fostered by DBT, Ministry of Science and Technology, Government of India. BCIL acts as a junction for commercialization of biotech products or processes (Agathangelou, 2014).

CURRENT SCENARIO OF INDIAN BIO-ENTREPRENEURSHIP

Radical innovation transforms the market through startups and propels mammoth capital not only for individuals or firms but also for nations. Within a fleeting span, few startups extend their valuation to billion dollars and earn the title of Unicorns. Unicorn is an expression employed in investment industry which delineates a privately held startup company with a value of over $1 billion (Hogarth, 2017). A report by Gerard J. Tellis, Director of the Center for Global Innovation, at the USC Marshall School of Business, ranks the countries according to shares of Unicorn Population (van Tulder & Lucht, 2019). Globally, India stands at third position in generating billion dollar startups with 4% share in comparison to US (65%) and China (14%). In the year 2018, around 50,000 startups were reported and in 2019, 1300 new tech start-ups were initiated. The share of women entrepreneurs increased to 14%. The start-up initiative schemes crafted a niche for approximately 40,000 new professions (Quy Loan Duong-Saarits, 2012). One of the world-leading innovation policy advisory and research firm known as "The Startup Genome" listed Delhi as runners-up of top global ecosystem. In India, more than 26 states have startup policies and financial support is offered to micro, small and medium enterprise (MSME) sector by the financial institution "Small Industries Development Bank of India (SIDBI)" (Bisman & Goela, 2010).

The major challenges confronted by Indian bio-entrepreneur are:

Funding of R&D

R&D attracts little national funding. India's Gross expenditure on R&D (GERD) nearly tripled from 39,437 crore in 2007-08 to an estimated 1,23,847 crore ($17.7 b) in 2018-19. Private sector need to collaborate with industry-academia for promoting research and innovation ecosystem in the country.

Ardous and Lengthy Funding Procedures

The system for accessing such funding are frequently complicated, cumbersome, bureaucratic, and lengthy, i.e, non- conducive to innovation and entrepreneurship.

Fragmented Policy and Policy Implementation

So far, the mechanisms to operate existing, fragmented policies were not uniform, which resulted in failure to achieve the desired effects of such policies.

Angel, Venture Capital, and Seed Funding

There are low levels of early-stage venture capital investment: Indian angels are constrained by regulations that make investment and exit cumbersome.

Weak Connectivity between Stakeholders

The feeble connection exists between medium and small-scale enterprises and academic institutions or R&D. Industry necessitates verified technologies, but the institutions can only offer technologies mostly at a laboratory or pilot scale, implying that bringing the technologies to market requires arduous amount of work. Furthermore, private sector does not supply sufficient funding and mentorship which limits their capacity for mutual understanding and technology transfer.

Non-Conducive Education System

The current education system is focused on grades instead of supporting innovation projects. The educated manpower is often ill suited to either innovative industries or entrepreneurship.

Risk Aversion Among Entrepreneurs

Indian entrepreneurs often seek established technology as a basis for starting their business. They lack innovative ideas because of the risks involved, such as stumpy availability and elevated cost of funds. As a result, these bio-entrepreneurs look for minimum risk and quick returns.

Inadequate Protection of Intellectual Property Rights

In India, the intellectual property regime is weak. Innovators do not generally seek protection for their intellectual property unless forced to. This is because of low rate of Patent literacy, even among educated innovators. Except in the medicine and pharmaceutical industry, there is a lack of expert help available.

INITIATIVES BY INDIAN GOVERNMENT

With an aim to encourage innovation and Startups in the country, the Government of India launched a Startup India Action Plan that offers support to recognized supports through Handholding, Funding/ Incentives and Incubation (Gaurav et al., 2019). More than 4000+ Startups have been profited through several schemes of the Central Government (Manshani & Dubey, 2017). along with the sanctioning of 828 Cr for infrastructures.

- **Tax Exemptions:** IT exemptions for 3 years, Capital gains exemption to people investing such capital gains in the Govt. Recognized Fund of Funds, Tax exemption on investments above Fair Market Value.
- **Legal Support in Patent Filing:** Fast track of Startup Patent applications, Panel of facilitators to assist in filing applications, govt. bears facilitation costs: 423 facilitators for patent & design, 596 for trademark applications, 80% rebate in filing of patents: 377 startups benefitted.
- **Easy Compliance**: Self-certification and compliance of 9 environments and labour laws through Startup India web portal/mobile app. online self-certification for Labour, Laws enabled through 'ShramSuvidha' portal.
- **Relaxed Norms for Public Procurement**: By easing the requirement of prior experience and prior turnover in tenders for application by start-ups.
- **Credit Guarantee Scheme for Start-Ups:** Corpus of 2,000 Cr across 3 years, Collateral Free, Fund & Non-Fund Based Credit Support, Loans of up to 5 Cr. per Startup to be covered.

TRANSLATIONAL AND INDUSTRIAL DEVELOPMENT PROGRAMES

Biotech parks, special economic zones, and technology incubators have been set up in India which provides infrastructure support for promoting technology incubation, manufacturing and scaling up of products.

Biotech Parks

The Biotechnology Parks have been established by DBT in collaboration with State/Central Government Organizations across the country to provide infrastructure support for research, innovation and commercialization of research results and new technologies (Figure 1) (Mitra, 2007). The scientists and Small and Medium sized Enterprises (SMEs) avail the facility at these Biotechnology Parks for authentication of their technology and pilot plant studies for fast-track commercialization of their product. So far, DBT has supported following nine Biotechnology Parks in several states. The Department so far, has supported 9 Biotechnology Parks in various States (Patra, 2014). These are:

- Biotech Park Technology Incubation Centre, Guwahati, Assam
- Industrial Biotechnology Parks (IBTPs), Jammu & Kashmir UT
- Biotechnology Incubation Centre, Hyderabad, Telangana
- Chhattisgarh Biotech Park, Naya Raipur, Chhattisgarh
- Biotech Park, Lucknow, Uttar Pradesh
- Biotechnology Park, Bangalore, Karnataka
- The Golden Jubilee Biotech Park For Women, Chennai, Tamil Nadu
- Biotechnology Incubation Centre, Cochin, Kerala
- Tidco Centre For Life Sciences (TICEL) Biotech Park, Chennai, Tamil Nadu

Figure 1. The concept of research parks. The biotech parks help biotechnologists in facilitating commercialization of products

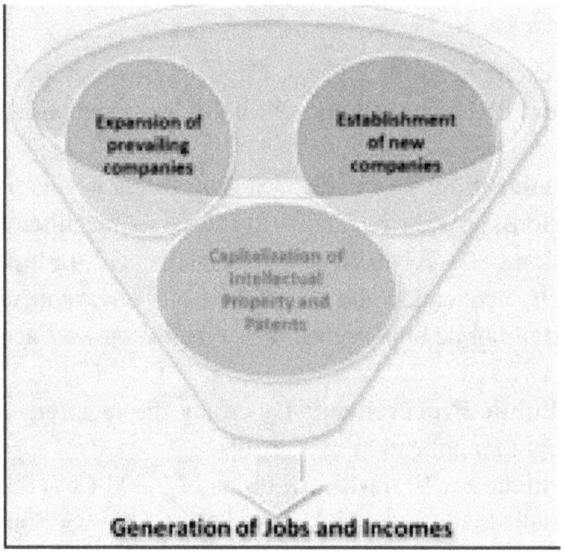

DBT further strengthened the above Parks by creating an ecosystem to absorb the start-ups which have graduated from incubators. 'National Biotechnology Parks Scheme' was established by DBT to provide a platform for scaling up R&D activities in partnership with the state government and industry. The major objectives of the 'National Biotechnology Parks Scheme' are as follows:

1. To empower the biotechnology segment across the country by strengthening the prevailing infrastructure facilities.
2. To make Indian biotech industry an international leader by nurturing innovation and entrepreneurship.
3. To establish amiable environment for superior infrastructure, high end central equipment amenities to foster R&D, product development, piloting and validation by scientists, Biotech industries and technically competent SMEs.

INCUBATION CENTRES

GoI has set up incubation centres across the country in collaboration with private public enterprise under the Start-Up India action plan announced by Honourable Prime Minister on 16th January 2016 to scale up biotech start up ecosystem (Garg & Gupta, 2021). NITI Aayog provides funding for the establishment of the incubators as a part of Atal Innovation Mission

Technology Incubation centres consists of:

- Well-equipped instrumentation facility including physical infrastructure.
- Mentorship support
- Laboratory modules
- Access to networks
- Access to markets

Under conventional funding schemes there is limited financial assistance for R & D projects, thus, this facility permits scientists and SME with restricted capital to commercialize their research ideas and improve existing technologies. Establishment of physical infrastructure requires huge funds which is provided by the government. SMEs can use this facility for small scale manufacturing or pilot studies of the biotech products.

Following departments and agencies along with private sector have signed MoU for building academia-industry tie-ups which will nurture innovation in academic institutions:

- Department of Science and Technology,
- Department of Industrial Policy and Promotion,
- NITI Aayog
- Ministry of Micro, Small and Medium Enterprises,
- Department of Higher Education,
- Department of Biotechnology and
- Department of Electronics and Information Technology.

DBT, GoI has established a Public Sector Enterprise, an Interface Agency known as Biotechnology Industry Research Assistance Council (BIRAC) which provides incubation space to entrepreneurs and Start-ups (Figure 2) (Surana et al., 2020). BIRAC links industry and academia besides providing a common equipment facility, mentorship for IP and mobilization of resources through networking platform. There are following 20 Bio-incubation centres across India supported by BIRAC in Table 1

Make-In India (MII)

The GoI and DBT comprehends the requirement for entrepreneurship development among Indian youth and has therefore taken initiative to promote Indian biotech system in various sectors (healthcare, industrial and agriculture biotechnology) in collaboration with BIRAC (Ratna, B., & Kalam, 2016). The MII was launched on 25th September, 2014 by the GoI for extensive propagation of the Government schemes, for the development of SMEs and startups and companies (Gauba & Dhingra, 2018). DBT and BIRAC are working in collaboration to achieve $100 Billion Bioeconomy of India by 2025 and have

Figure 2. The figure depicts the various schemes initiated by Indian central government departments for the establishment of incubators.

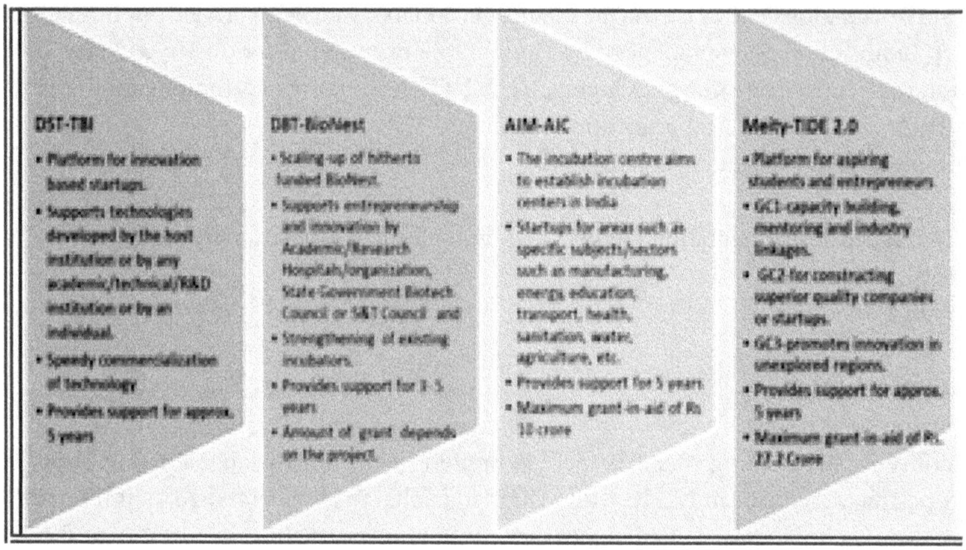

Table 1. List of bio-incubation centres across India supported by BIRAC.

S.No.	Bioincubation centre	References
1.	FIIT, IIT Delhi	http://fitt-iitd.in/
2.	Zonal Technology Management - Business Planning and Development Unit" - ZTM-BPD, IARI	http://ztmbpd.iari.res.in/
3.	BITS Pilani K K Birla Goa campus	www.bits-goa.ac.in
4.	Entrepreneurship Development Centre, Venue Centre, NCL, Pune	www.venturecenter.co.in
5.	Ahmedabad University	https://ahduni.edu.in
6.	KSIDC, Trivendrum	www.ksidc.org
7.	SIDBI Innovation & Incubation Centre (SIIC) at IIT Kanpur	www.iitk.ac.in
8.	RCB, Faridabad	www.rcb.res.in
9.	HTIC, Chennai	https://htic.iitm.ac.in
10.	IKP Knowledge Park, Hyderabad	www.ikpknowledgepark.com
11.	a-IDEA, NAARM-TBI, Hyderabad	www.aidea.naarm.org.in
12.	SBTIC, Hyderabad	www.sbtic.org
13.	Society for Innovation and Entrepreneurship (SINE)	www.sineiitb.org
14.	Bangalore Bioinnovation Centre (BBC)	www.bioinnovationcentre.com
15.	IT Madras Research Park, IIT Madras	www.iitm.ac.in
16.	Gujarat State Biotechnology Mission (GSBTM)	https://btm.gujarat.gov.in
17.	Women Bio Park,Chennai	www.biotechpark.co.in
18.	B. V. PATEL PERD Centre	www.perdcentre.com
19.	KIIT-TBI, Bhuwneswer	www.kiitincubator.in
20.	C-CAMP, Bangalore	www.ccamp.res.in

focussed on commercialization of products from Agriculture, Food processing and Health sector. Under MII initiative following schemes was introduced:

- In 2018, BIRAC, DBT provided financial support for the establishment of Secondary Agriculture Entrepreneurial Network (SEAN) (Bagchi et al., 2017). SEAN was instituted in Punjab by Department of Science, Technology and Environment through Punjab State Biotech Corporation. The goal of this project is to address the unmet needs of agriculture and food industry through short-term industry oriented programs for which Punjab Agriculture University (PAU), Centre for Innovative and Applied Bioprocessing (CIAB), National Agri-Food Biotechnology Institute (NABI) and Guru Nanak Dev University (GNDU) have been provided with a funding of approx. 85 lakhs. The advantage of this project is that the research institutes work in collaboration with industry. The latter provides their units for illustration and execution of the research outcomes, thus capping the fissures for the commercialization of products.
- The objective of BIRAC in alliance with Kalam Institute of Health Technology (KIHT) is to expedite the testing and standardization of medical devices by supporting researchers, start-ups, entrepreneurs, incubation centres, and SMEs.

Start-Up India

"Startup India" is a distinguished program initiated by the Government of India on January 16, 2016 with an aim to foster innovation and startups in the country for creating employment opportunities (Singh, 2020). Under this enterprise, following activities were covered:

- DBT and BIRAC established "Clean Energy International Incubator Centre (CEIIC)" (Bagchi & Chatterjee, 2017). CEIIC is the first international incubator in India under Mission Innovation where startups from EU countries can come and incubate in India and similarly startups from this incubator can move to the partnering countries thus, supporting innovations globally in the energy space.
- DBT has established 35 Bio-incubators for the commercialization of research into products.
- BIRAC has set up a Facilitation Unit known as "Facilitation of Innovation and Regulations for Start-ups and Innovators (FIRST HUB)" which provides a single platform for Start-ups, SMEs, Researchers, Entrepreneurs, Incubator centers, Academicians to address queries related to Mentorship, Regulatory pathways and Regulation, Intellectual property, funding opportunities, market access, investment opportunities and Industry Academia collaborations. These queries are addressed by officers from DBT, BIRAC, NIB (National Institute of Biologicals), CDSCO (Central Drugs Standard Control Organization), ICMR (Indian Council of Medical Research), BIS (Bureau of Indian Standards), and other relevant government organization.
- BIRAC's initiative- "Sustainable Entrepreneurship and Enterprise Development Fund" (SEED Fund) and "Accelerating Entrepreneurs Fund" (AcE Fund) aims to provide financial assistance to Start-ups. Under SEED Fund, elected BIRAC funded incubators will be provided a grant-in-aid assistance up to INR 200 Lakh. On the other hand, the AcE Fund which is an equity fund solely for Biotech Start-ups caters to a capital assistance of up to INR 7 crores against equity to Start-ups. Start-ups can utilize this fund for the purpose of innovation, research and product development.

START UP INDIA SEED FUND SCHEME (SISFS)

The Startup India Seed Fund Scheme (SISFS) would become effective from 1st April 2021. The scheme has been approved for the period of next four years starting from 2021-22 which will be implemented with effect from 1st April 2021. The major objective of the scheme is to provide financial assistance to startups for proof of concept, prototype development, product trials, market entry and commercialization. The scheme is expected to support about 3600 startups.

Patent Facilitation

The "Biotechnology Patent Facilitation Cell (BPFC)" established in July 1999 by the Department of Biotechnology provides a facilitation platform for the scientists and researchers to create awareness and understanding about Intellectual Property Rights (IPR) (Ninawe & Indulkar, 2017). The major objectives of IPR cell are:

- To provide facility for patenting to the Biotechnologists, researchers, academicians and biologists for filing Indian and foreign patent applications on a persistent basis.
- Continuous surveillance on new developments in the IPR sector for highlighting critical issues among scientists, policy makers, biotech industries, academicians etc.

Biotechnology Ignition Grant (BIG)

Biotechnology Industry Research Assistance Council (BIRAC)

BIRAC provide funding and mentorship to innovative ideas through a funding scheme known as Biotechnology Ignition Grant (BIG) (Surana et al., 2020). This grant is available to scientist entrepreneurs in research institutes, academia and start-ups which help in commercialization of research discoveries. Further it links the cavity between discovery and invention.

The major objectives of the scheme are as follows:

- Developing ideas among the scientific community to move its product from concept to market place i.e commercialization of products.
- Authenticate proof of concept and scale up from research and development (R&D) to pilot-scale and full production.
- Encourage establishment of start-up business.

MAJOR SCHEMES INITIATED BY GOI FOR PROMOTING BIO-ENTREPRENEURSHIP

Venture Capital Assistance Scheme

The farming sector is colossally expanding because of the ever-increasing requirement for high value processed food products. However, restraints such as access to information and access to credit limit the growth of new agribusiness projects.

Venture capital assistance scheme for agribusiness development is financial funding in the form of an interest free loan financed by Small Farmer's Agri Business consortium (SFAC) to qualifying projects (Hanumappa & Bhinde, 1995). This is done to encounter the gap in the funds required for implementation of thc project. The objectives of the scheme are as follows:

- To provide assistance to Agripreneurs for investing via financial involvement in order to set up agribusiness projects (Agriculture/ allied sector, Poultry and dairy projects).
- Agripreneurs, Units in Agri-Export Zones, Farmers, Producer groups, Agripreneurs and Agriculture graduates are provided with a financial support to prepare bankable Detailed Project Reports (DPRs) through empanelled institutions under Project Development Facility (PDF).

Capital Investment Subsidy Scheme under National Bamboo Mission

In India, the worth of bamboo and rattan industry is Rs. 28,000 crores. The National Bamboo Mission (NBM) was initiated in 2006-07 with an aim to resuscitate the under developed bamboo industry in India, to propagate and cultivate bamboo and to release funds for the maintcnance of bamboo plantations (Gupta, 2008). The major objectives of NBM are as follows:

- To encourage bamboo plantations in farmer's land, non-forest Government land, farmhouses, private lands, arable wastelands, community lands, irrigation canals, etc., for augmentation of farm income.
- To elevate product development by nurturing entrepreneurship at micro, small and medium levels through research and development.
- In order to increase the income of the primary producers, efforts have to be re-oriented for decreasing the reliance on import of bamboo products. This can be achieved by improving productivity and sustainability of domestic raw materials.
- To establish primary processing units, primary treatment plants, market infrastructure and preservation technologies close to the production site which will help in improving post-harvest management.

High Risk-High Reward Research Scheme (SERB under DST)

High Risk-High Reward Research scheme provides funding for the revolutionary or transforming ideas that challenge the usual approach of a methodology by a novel and distinctive way in the form of new hypothesis formulation or establishment of new technology. The objective of the scheme is to provide funding for conceptually new and risky proposals.

There are more than 100 schemes under Start-up India Initiative. The table 2 and table 3 lists some of the schemes under Start-up India initiative implemented by various Indian Government departments and ministry to promote Bio-entrepreneurship.

Table 2. The table depicts brief overview of the various schemes initiated by GoI.

S.No.	Scheme	Ministry and Department	Major objective	Funding*	Duration*
1.	High risk –High reward research	Ministry of science and Technology, Department of Science & Technology	Proposals that are conceptually new and risky, expected to have a paradigm shifting influence on the S&T.	No budget limit	5 years
2.	Promoting Innovations in Individuals, Start-ups and MSMEs (PRISM)	Department Of Science & Industrial Research	To support individual innovators ,Institutions or organizations for expanding state of art new technology solutions for helping MSME clusters. (inclusive development)	50.00 lakh for R&D proposals *(Terms and conditions)	-
3.	Biotechnology Ignition Grant (BIG)	Ministry of science and Technology, Biotechnology Industry Research Assistance Council (BIRAC)	support the ideas which require funding and mentorship for commercialization by traversing the aperture between discovery and invention.	50 Lakhs	18 months
4.	ExtraMural Research or Core Research Grant	Science and Engineering Research Board (SERB) under Ministry of Science & Technology (Renamed as Core Research Grant)	Provides fund to eminent scientist for basic research in all frontier areas of Science and Engineering	Approx. INR 80 laks.	3 years
5.	Sustainable Finance Scheme	Ministry of Finance, Small Industries Development Bank of India (SIDBI)	Provides financial assistance to new/ existing MSME unit for renewable energy projects such as wind energy generators, power plants, mini hydel power projects, solar power plants, etc.	Scheme covers up to 90% of the project cost as submitted by the MSME. Maximum loan amount INR 150 lakh.	Either 36 months or 60 months depending upon the amount of loan sanctioned.
6.	Research & Development in Processed Food Sector	Ministry of Food Processing Industries	Provides capital assistance for R&D involving food processing industry with respect to the development and commercialization of product and process, improved packaging, standardization chemical contaminants, microbiological contaminants, colouring agents, preservatives, pesticide residues, additives, etc.	For General areas-50% of equipment cost and for North East States and difficult areas 70% of equipment cost.	3 years

Table 3. The table depicts brief overview of the various schemes initiated by GoI.

S.No.	Scheme	Ministry and Department	Major objective	Funding*	Duration*
7.	Dairy Entrepreneurship Development Scheme (DEDS)	The department of Animal Husbandry, dairying and fisheries , National Bank for Agriculture and Rural Development (NABARD)	To generate self employment and create infrastructure by promoting dairy farms for clean milk production, promote heifer calf rearing etc.	Back ended capital subsidy @25% or @33% of the project cost.	Depend on the nature of activity and cash flow, varies between 3- 7 years.
8.	Small Business Innovation Research Initiative (SBIRI)	Biotechnology Industry Research Assistance Council (BIRAC), Department of Biotechnology, Ministry of Science & Technology.	To support proof-of-concept research/indigenous prototype development/optimization of process in biotechnology by industry (projects with TRL upto 6)	No limit on funding	The Company shall shell out royalty to BIRAC @5% on yearly Net Sales of the product(s) industrialized with aid from BIRAC
9.	Ayurvedic Biology Programme	Science and Engineering Research Board (SERB), Ministry of Science & Technology	To improve health care with the help of scientists and Ayurvedic experts in India. Thrust areas includes amalgam of traditional medicine with Molecular Biology, immunology and chemistry.	No limit on funding	Normally 3 years, may vary depending upon the project work proposed.
10.	Raw Material Assistance Scheme	National Small Industries Corporation (Ministry of Micro, Small and Medium Enterprises)	Grants support to MSMEs by providing capital for the procuring of Raw Material (both indigenous & imported).	For a single unit-Rs. 5 crore and For group of units -Rs. 15 crore.	One year. Thereafter, the limit can be renewed for one year provided conduct of the account was satisfactory during last year.
11.	The Women Entrepreneurship Platform (WEP)	Niti Aayog	Provides support services like incubation, marketing, training, mentorship, etc. for nascent and existing women entrepreneurs.	-	-
12.	Drugs & Pharmaceutical Research	Department of Science and Technology	Provides supports for both human and veterinary drug in the areas like Clinical studies, Chiral synthesis of drugs, development of new formulations, testing of traditional formulations etc.	Pharma industrial R&D Projects - 70% of the project cost. Grant-in-aid for Clinical trials to industry for creating drugs for neglected diseases.	-

CONCLUSION

Bio-entrepreneurs seek commercial value in every facet of technology that they aim to exploit for addressing social issues. Innovation is the crux of a biotechnology venture whereas integrity defines the backbone of the bio-entrepreneur's character. A bio-entrepreneur faces copious challenges in a rapidly evolving marketplace like ambiguous IPR laws, risks associated with the qualms of research and development and venture capital finance. India was the first country in the world to establish a department exclusively dedicated to biotechnology in the year 1986. The Indian biotechnology industry is ranked among the top twelve biotechnology destinations in the world and third in Asia Pacific. The biotech industry is one of the sunrise sectors of India which has the potential to be $ 100 billion (Rs. 6 lakh crore) industry in the next decade as anticipated by the Association of Biotechnology Led Enterprise (ABLE). The contemporary Indian market bestows various opportunities for Bio-entrepreneurs to establish their start-ups which creates an environment for employment through research and innovation. The last decade has witnessed more start-ups in India due to multidimensional support from the government in form of capital assistance for initiating their business and commercialization of biotech products, mentoring and networking, strengthening infrastructure facilities and providing laboratory equipment facilities.

Thus, there is no scarcity of support for the empowerment of start-ups in India by Indian Government. Moreover, GoI in partnership with private players is fostering research and Innovation. For example, in 2005, the Small Business Innovation Research Initiative (SBIRI) scheme of the DBT, MST aims to enhance Public-Private-Partnership (PPP) efforts in the country. SBIRI promotes risk innovative research and commercialization of products under an umbrella by SMEs thus bringing together the government, public institutions and private industry. Furthermore, there are more than 200 schemes implemented by GoI for nurturing start-up ecosystem in India.The industrious initiatives by Indian Government are complemented by startups such asMake in India, The Skill India programme, Standup India, Digital Indiaand Atal Innovation Mission (AIM).

The success of a start-up is not judged with its initiation within a span of 2-3 years, rather, a successful start-up is one that is be able to sustain itself within the changing market ecosystem. Start-ups do not endure on one's jack, but are part of the economic dynamism by sparking innovation and inoculating competition among the stalwarts in market. In order to address the stigma concomitant with insolvency of Start-up enterprises and to boost experimentation among start-up organization through disruptive business models, fiscal policy reforms were taken by GoI like Credit Guarantee Funds for Startups, Income Tax exemption to Startups for 3 years, Tax exemption on Capital Gains and Tax Exemption on Investments above Fair Market Value (FMV) besides easy registration and regulation, legal support etc. To empower entrepreneurs, GoI has established Bio-incubators across the country with an aim to turn leading-edge research into marketable biotech products. Many Indian Universities (such as ASPIRE-BioNEST at University of Hyderabad, IIT Madras Bioincubator at Chennai, Tamil Nadu, IIT Delhi's Biotechnology Business Incubation Facility (BBIF) etc.) have also established bio-incubators for entrepreneurs for commercialization of innovative research into products.

The following elements deter the entrepreneurial ecosystem in India:

- The entrepreneur is encumbered with regulatory hurdles and financial blocks in moving the start-up ahead, thus a firm grip is required at the initial stage.
- Restricted availability of risk capital from venture capital companies or banks.
- Poor infrastructure accessibility surges the operational budget for the startups.

- Entrepreneurial culture is also missing as the institutions of learning train students for wage employment rather than in becoming entrepreneurs.
- Adverse social attitudes towards risk and failure prevail

The Bio-entrepreneurship attained momentum from 2014 onwards which led to the formulation of active Government policies to patronage start-up ecosystem in India. One of the imperative initiative by the GoI was the Start-up India and Make in India flagship programs. These schemes have demystified the complete funding, procurement, and the incubation processes and aim to make India a global manufacturing hub creating a positive impact for commercialization of biotech products through research and innovation.

The Road Ahead

In spite of meticulous support from GoI, Indian startups encounter noteworthy challenges. Surmounting such challenges require efforts not only from governmental authorities but also from start-up themselves and from all stakeholders. This will encourage individuals for risk taking and developing impactful and scientific solutions according to the societal needs. However, the dispersal of assistance provided by government to bio-entrepreneurs varies. The authentic ground level execution of these schemes is an apprehension for the start-up ecosystem in India.

Though the Indian government is trying its best for the implementation of policies in place, lack of a practical attitude and novel idea among burgeoning bio-entrepreneurs may dampen the outcome of these schemes and initiatives. Many of the Indian start-ups fail not only due to lack of funds, but owing to lack of innovation, dearth of new technologies for scaling their products at affordable price or absence of unique business models. Most entrepreneurs prefer conventional business rather than thinking out of the box. Hence, non-conventional business startups must be recognized by GoI to encourage a milieu of innovation which would result in increased number of patents.

Lack of skilled workforce, low business ethics, inadequate formal mentoring and lack of experienced leadership, reducing documentation and paperwork, setting up standardized operating procedures, are some of the other issues that need to address by policy makers for making India a global leader in bio-entrepreneurship. Moreover, entrepreneurship courses with small projects or hands-on training must be integrated in college and university curriculum in order to make students more skilful. Indian startup ecosystem is losing energy as major startups are concentrated in cities like NCR, Mumbai, Chennai, Pune, Jaipur and Bangalore.

The start-up ecosystem consisting of bio-incubators or biotech parks with world class equipment facilities for Bio-entrepreneurs are geographically heaped in major Indian metro cities. Contrarily, lack of proper infrastructure and high-tech equipment restricts the budding Bio-entrepreneurs of non-metro cities in implementing their technology-oriented research ideas, thus, pushing them to conventional start-ups with low return value. Thus, along with better infrastructure facilities and extensive filed research, a Bio-entrepreneurship project will go far in solving societal issues, thereby leading to a whole new world of opportunities.

REFERENCES

Agathangelou, A. M. (2014). Wither Anarchy? Harvesting the 'Global' Bio-tech Body, Indian Markets and Biomedical Technologies. In *The Global Politics of Science and Technology-Vol. 2* (pp. 179–204). Springer.

Bagchi, N., & Chatterjee, K. (2017). Identification of gaps in performance of services provided to start-ups in high technology, low technology and social & agri-business incubation centers in India: Constraints to growth. *ASCI Journal of Management, 46*.

Bagchi, N., Roy, K., Roychowdhury, A., Subrahmanya, M. B., Chatterjee, K., Gulati, M., ... Chakravarthy, S. (2017). Science, Technology and Innovation. *Journal of Management*, *46*(1).

Bisman, J., & Goela, N. (2010). The Small Industries Development Bank of India: A retrospective on SME financing. *Indian Journal of Economics and Business*, *9*(4), 803.

Bonnafous-Boucher, M., & Lamy, E. (2010). Hybridisation of the profiles of entrepreneurs and intrapreneurs: The case of French biotechnology SMEs. *International Journal of Entrepreneurship and Small Business*, *10*(3), 410–427. doi:10.1504/IJESB.2010.033575

Braun, A., & Schreiber, F. (2017). *The current InsurTech landscape: business models and disruptive potential* (No. 62). I. VW HSG Schriftenreihe.

Dossani, R., & Kenney, M. (2009). Service provision for the global economy: The evolving Indian experience. *The Review of Policy Research*, *26*(1-2), 77–104. doi:10.1111/j.1541-1338.2008.00370.x

Garg, M., & Gupta, S. (2021). *Startups and the Growing Entrepreneurial Ecosystem*. Academic Press.

Gauba, R., & Dhingra, R. (2018). *Make in India-An Initiative to Change the Economic Landscape of the Country*. Academic Press.

Gaurav, J. K., Rathi, V., Burnwal, K., & Chaturvedi, A. (2019). Green startups in India: Challenges and opportunities. *Special Issue on Environment*, *235*, 234.

Gupta, A. K. (2008). National Bamboo Mission: A holistic scheme for development of bamboo sector in Tripura. *Indian Forester*, *134*(3), 305.

Hanumappa, H. G., & Bhinde, M. J. (1995). Towards operationalizing Small Farmers' Agri-Business Consortium: A case of dharwad district in Karnataka. *Agricultural Economics Research Review, 8*, 59-77.

Hogarth, S. (2017). Valley of the unicorns: Consumer genomics, venture capital and digital disruption. *New Genetics & Society*, *36*(3), 250–272. doi:10.1080/14636778.2017.1352469

Kerr, S. P., & Kerr, W. R. (2020). *Immigration policy levers for us innovation and startups.* National Bureau of Economic Research Working Paper Series, (w27040).

Lepeley, M. T., Kuschel, K., Beutell, N., Pouw, N., & Eijdenberg, E. L. (2019). *The Wellbeing of Women in Entrepreneurship. A Global Perspective*. Routdlege. doi:10.4324/9780429279836

Manshani, S., & Dubey, A. (2017). Startup Women in Startup India: A Study Of Women Entrepreneurs in India. *International Journal of Business and Management*, 91–100.

Marcati, A., Guido, G., & Peluso, A. M. (2008). The role of SME entrepreneurs' innovativeness and personality in the adoption of innovations. *Research Policy*, *37*(9), 1579–1590. doi:10.1016/j.respol.2008.06.004

Mitra, R. M. (2007). *India's emergence as a global R&D center. An overview of the Indian R&D system and potential.* ITPS WorNing paper, 12.

Mueller, J. M. (2007). Biotechnology patenting in India: will bio-generics lead a sunrise industry to bio-innovation. *UMkC l. reV.*, *76*, 437.

Ninawe, A. S., & Indulkar, S. T. (2017). Intellectual Property Rights and Innovation in Marine Biotechnology. *Asian Biotechnology and Development Review*, *19*(1).

Nogrady, B. (2018). How Indian biotech is driving innovation. *Nature*, *564*(7735), S53–S53. doi:10.1038/d41586-018-07671-9 PMID:30542184

Patra, S. K. (2014). Knowledge Production by Indian Biotechnology Parks. *Asian Biotechnology and Development Review*, *16*(1).

Quy Loan Duong-Saarits, D. (2012). *Establishing an oriental business in Finland: case: start-up Vietnamese handmade home-textiles company*. Academic Press.

Singh, V. K. (2020). *Policy and Regulatory Changes for a Successful Startup Revolution: Experiences from the Startup Action Plan in India*. Academic Press.

Subrahmanya, M. B. (2015). New generation start-ups in India: What lessons can we learn from the past? *Economic and Political Weekly*, 56–63.

Surana, K., Singh, A., & Sagar, A. D. (2020). Strengthening science, technology, and innovation-based incubators to help achieve Sustainable Development Goals: Lessons from India. *Technological Forecasting and Social Change*, *157*, 120057. doi:10.1016/j.techfore.2020.120057

Ullah, R., & Zohra, R. R. (2018). *The Entrepreneurial Scientists Serving Science and Society*. SATHA.

van Tulder, R., & Lucht, L. (2019). Reversing Materiality: From a Reactive Matrix to a Proactive SDG Agenda. In Innovation for Sustainability (pp. 271-289). Palgrave Macmillan.

Vijayaraghavan, K., & Dutz, M. A. (2012). *Biotechnology innovation for inclusive growth: a study of Indian policies to foster accelerated technology adaptation for affordable development*. The World Bank.

KEY TERMS AND DEFINITIONS

Bio-Entrepreneurship: Bio-entrepreneurship is rightly explained as generation of fortune resulting from the application of biosciences to the business framework.

Biotechnology Parks: The Biotechnology Parks provide infrastructure support for research, innovation and commercialization of research results and new technologies.

BIRAC: Biotechnology Industry Research Assistance Council (BIRAC) - An Interface which provides incubation space to entrepreneurs and start-ups.

Entrepreneurship: Entrepreneurship correlates to the entrepreneur, his vision, his ability to address the problem, innovate and its implementation.

Unicorn: Unicorn is an expression employed in investment industry which delineates a privately held startup company with a value of over $1 billion.

Chapter 10
Foreign Investors in Bioentrepreneurship in India

Sonia Sharma
Guru Nanak Dev University, India

Swati Sihag
Panjab University, India

Ritu Saxena
Guru Nanak Dev University, India

ABSTRACT

Bioentrepreneurship attracts entrepreneurs who can contribute by making scientific methods and products available to the society. Funding, infrastructure, skills, and commercialization capabilities influence the process of bioentrepreneurship. India with its large and highly efficient pool of the scientific community has lot to offer to the global market. Indian research is confined to theoretical research due to a missing link that unites research and commercialization and strict intellectual property regime. To overcome such challenges, the Indian government has taken initiatives to make the working environment friendly, innovative, efficient, and easy for foreign companies and investors by amending existing policies and facilities India's biotechnology industry. Foreign investment in India's biotechnology industry has led to an exponential increase from US$530 million in 2003 to US$4.3 billion in 2013. Foreign investment has played a big role in helping India's flourishing biotechnology industry.

INTRODUCTION

Bioentrepreneurship is basically integration of two disciplines, science and business, whereby it creates opportunity to produce, develops and ultimately commercializes a product (Prihatiningrum et al., 2020). There are three basic pillars that are structural components, essential for any bioentrepreneurs to be successful, i.e. innovative ideas, adequate financial inflow and a high-quality managing team (Schoemaker and Schoemaker, 1998). Some very important drugs, industrially important enzymes, medical devices,

DOI: 10.4018/978-1-7998-7411-9.ch010

advanced fuels, and efficient crops have been the result of commercialization of product of number of scientific endeavours. Bioentrepreneurship offers a large scope and attracts entrepreneurs, who can contribute by making scientific methods and products available to the society. Funding, infrastructure, skills and commercialization capabilities are few factors that influence process of bioentrepreneurship in developing as well as developed countries. Biotech industry in India has predominantly five sectors, *viz.*, pharmaceutical, agriculture, bioservices, industrial and bioinformatics (Tang et al., 2003; Parmar, 2005; Konde, 2008).

India with its large and highly efficient pool of scientific community has lot to offer to national as well as global market. Even having strong technical talent and scientific pool, Indian research is confined to theoretical research instead of industrialization, due to a missing link that unites research and commercialization (Langer, 2014). Another issue in Indian scenario is strict intellectual property regime and low patent protection, which limits products that can be patented and affects small foreign biotechnology companies to sell their products. To overcome such challenges, Indian government has taken some initiatives to make working environment friendly, innovative, efficient, and easy for foreign companies and investors, by amending existing policies and improving India's intellectual property regime, research priorities, resources and facilities to make India's Biotechnology industry, a better suited market for a bioentrepreneur. Some of the amendment in policies include area of Stem cell research, Pharma, agriculture wherein, Special Economic Zone (SEZ) Act and Foreign Trade Policy, are among important plans which aims at loosen some controls and interference and thereby creating transparency and atmosphere of trust. This has become possible by simplifying procedures and offering attractive incentives (Duhera, 2007; Ramanaiah, 2002). To boost exports, attract investments, SEZ's concept was introduced by GOI in 2000, which came into force in India on 10th February, 2006 to develop infrastructure and generate employment (Duhera, 2007; Ramanaiah, 2002; Konde, 2007). In this chapter, we are going to get insight about the biotech industry in India with emphasis role of foreign direct investment (FDI),determinants of FDI, policies to attract foreign investment and thereby increasing opportunities in Indian Biotech Industry.

BIOTECHNOLOGY

Science which involves living organisms directly or indirectly along with advancing technology to get insight into cellular and molecular processes, to develop products benefiting humans is known as Biotechnology (Bio, 2001; Evans and Furlong, 2011; Ravi et al., 2014). Biotechnology is further categorised into five major branches based on the area under investigation (Fig 1).

Agricultural Biotechnology

Agricultural biotechnology is a science that gives handle to plant breeders to develop plants with beneficial traits such as insect and pest resistance, disease resistance, abiotic stress resistance and herbicide toleranceby making precise genetic changes in plants (Altman, 1997; National Research Council, 2002). Agricultural Biotechnology sector is flourishing after the introduction of biotechnology improved commercial crop in 1996 on acres of land at lower cost with disease resistant variety along with eco-friendly impact (Herdt, 2006).

Figure 1. Branches of biotechnology

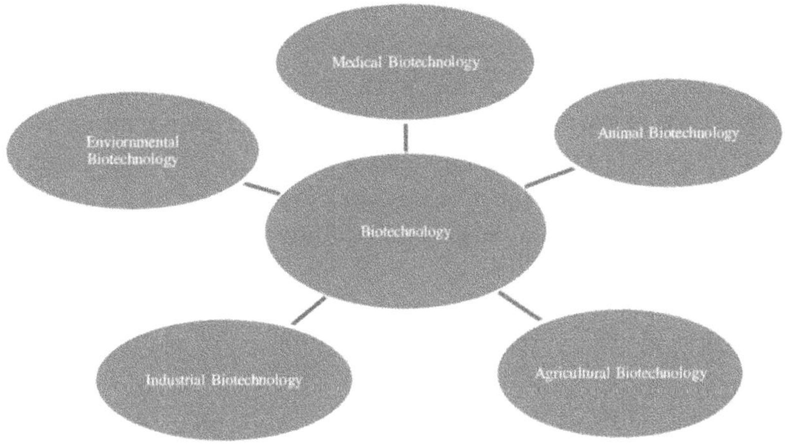

Medical Biotechnology

Medical biotechnology is defined as the technology driven field where living organisms are in use for the diagnosis or treatment of a disease. This serves purpose by the application of biotechnology tools for developing methods for diagnosis, prevention, and treatment of diseases using living cells or organism (Mahboudi, Hamedifar & Aghajani, 2012; Pham, 2018). Modern Biotechnology or Molecular biotechnology came up in early 1970 with an interesting means of heterologous cloning (Mahboudi, Hamedifar & Aghajani, 2012), which led to the first biopharmaceutical products, recombinant insulin and recombinant human growth hormone, the first gifts of modern biotechnology (Rader, 2008). Medical biotechnology has provided few very promising products and have been adding to the list, thus medical biotechnology is honoured by describing it as "technology of hope" (Mahboudi, Hamedifar & Aghajani, 2012). With advances in biotechnology techniques medical products were generated using recombinant DNA technology, gene manipulation, cell culture, stem cell therapy and tissue engineering.

Environmental Biotechnology

Environmental biotechnology is integration of natural sciences and technology in order to use organisms, cells and molecular knowledge for better product and services. It deals with developing and using the processes that would protect and help in maintaining quality of the environment. This area of research is constantly evolving to develop methods to detect, prevent and repair the damage caused by emission of pollutants into the environment. The research in this field is aimed to modify wastes either by recycling into a new product, or by purifying to a less harmful product. Other major initiatives of this field are replacing chemical materials and processes to 'Green technology' to reduce environmental damage.

Industrial Biotechnology

Industrial biotechnology also known as white biotechnology involves the use of microorganisms and enzymes to produce goods for sustainable production of chemicals, materials, and fuels from renewable

(Tang & Zhao, 2009; Erickson et al., 2011). Industrial biotechnology exploits the fact that countless metabolic processes take place in a single cell which break down and convert nutrients into new products. These processes have been in use for a long time using either microbes or enzyme. The production of bread, yoghurt and vinegar using microorganisms and the use of enzymes in detergents are few examples of contribution of industrial biotechnology. This field is regarded as the third wave of biotechnology, after medical (red biotechnology) and agricultural (green biotechnology). Increasing interest in this field is due to reduced energy consumption, greenhouse gas emissions, and waste generation. It also seems to have potential to enable the paradigm shift from fossil fuel-based to bio-based, green production of value-added chemicals (Tang & Zhao, 2009).

Animal Biotechnology

This branch of biotechnology deals with genetically modified animals in order to improve their suitability for various agricultural, industrial, or pharmaceutical applications. Animal biotechnology is a science of producing genetically engineered animals with useful and novel properties for improved dairy, meat production and for the production of therapeutically important proteins (National Research Council, 2002; Singh, 2018). The major objective is to develop a commercially potential technology, process or product (Madan, 2005).

BIOENTREPRENEURSHIP

A single man army might be enough to explore any of these branches of biotechnology to complete research project and develop any process and product for social benefit but it requires a company to scale up the process and thereby making it possible for general public use. Developing any enterprise requires skilled entrepreneur, a leader that could make scientific endeavour commercially viable. Thus, the integration of science and entrepreneurship to commercialize the transformative products of amazing human benefits viz., life-saving medicines and devices, instruments, fuels, industrial important enzymes and efficient crops, is defined as bioentrepreneurship (Shimasaki, 2020).

Biotechnology industry globally, has several challenges in way to cross through such as high research and development costs, constrains imposed by regulatory bodies and need of continues innovative product pipelines. Thus, there is an increasing look for, by pharmaceutical and biotechnology companies to attain low-cost and suitable alternatives (Parmar, 2005). India has strong hold, particularly in clinical data management, novel bioactives for drug discovery and low-cost manufacturing, which give an advantage to foreign investors and Indian market too (Palnitkar, 2004). According to Association of Biotechnology Led Enterprises (ABLE), the Indian biotechnology industry sector has the potential to become $ 100 billion industry in the next decade.

FASTEST GROWING BIOTECHNOLOGY INDUSTRY: INDIA

For a developing economy like India, biotechnology industry promises to be a powerful and enabling technology that has potential to revolutionize various sectors *viz.*, agriculture, healthcare, industrial biotechnology and environmental sustainability. India is one the fastest growing biotechnology industries, ranking 3rd largest in Asian countries with advantage of diverse flora and fauna. This bio-diversity along with largest agricultural land, varied climate proves advantageous to the country in conducting field research with large and diverse sample. Also it is helpful in conducting research and development for developing different Agri-biotech based products available world-wide (Kumar and Shrivastva, 2012). Indian biotech industry has emerged as a leader globally in the sector of drugs and vaccines production like DPT, BCG and measles. It contributes about 70% WHO vaccines and ranks 48th on Global Innovation Index. The Indian biotechnology industry has been broadly classified into five categories namely pharmaceutical, agriculture, bioservices, industrial and bioinformatics (Fig 2).

Figure 2. Sectors of Indian biotechnology industry

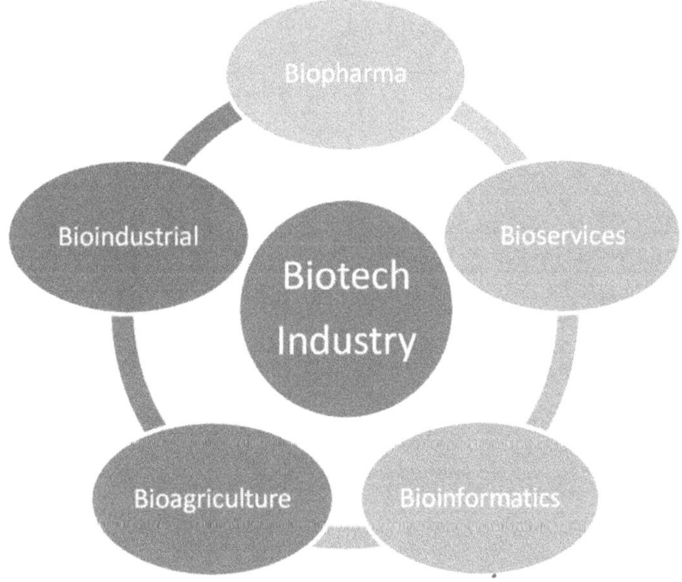

Biopharma

India is emerging as the largest generic drugs, vaccines, diagnostics provider globally. Indian Biopharma Industry for the year 2018-19 has crossed Rs 22,124 crore as compared to previous year's revenue (Rs 18,290 core) with exports growth comprising of Rs 14,423 crore from last year recorded export 13,925 crore (BioSpectrum, 2021). Pharmaceutical sector of India fulfils over 50% of global demand for various vaccines (40% US and 25% UK). About 80% of the global requirement of antiretroviral drugs, to combat AIDS (Acquired Immune Deficiency Syndrome) are produced and exported by Indian pharmaceutical firms. India's large pool of scientists and engineers has made this growing industry to attain greater heights with Rs 1.4 lakh crore (US$ 20.03 billion) turnover in domestic pharmaceutical market in 2019 (IBEF, 2020), accounting for about 60% of the Indian biotechnology industry. This sector comprises of biologics viz., therapeutics, vaccines, biosimilars, regenerative medicines, medical technology and diagnostics methods. Vaccines and bio-similars account as the major component of the Indian bio-pharma sector and constantly creating manufacturing and development opportunities in India to make it hub for global biologics. Addition to medication from generic and biosimilar, in-vitro diagnostic market has also been getting boon. Healthcare industry requirement for invitro diagnostic kit becomes important to detect underlying prevalence of diseases and also increasing demand of health insurance companies has contributed to spur the demand of diagnostic services. India has already been recognised as a largest manufacturer of high-quality drugs and formulations at economical cost but the future of biopharma lies in biologics, especially protein and antibody production, vaccine manufacturing, biosimilars, developing diagnostic protein chips, stem cell research and cell-based therapeutics which also create foreign investment attraction of the world in India. Bio-Pharma industry of India constituting of around 300 companies has observed growth at 12% (2018-2019) with 20 companies contributing 89%of total pharma industry. Top ten Indian companies contributing in Bio-Pharma with their revenue and growth rate is listed in Table 1.

Table 1. Top 10 bio-pharma companies of India.

S. No.	Indian Bio Pharma companies	Revenue in Crores (2018-2019)	% growth
1	Serum Institute of India Ltd	4984	25
2	Biocon Ltd	3946	37
3	Reliance Life Science Pvt Ltd	850	20
4	Bharat Biotech International Ltd	774	10
5	Intas Pharmaceuticals Ltd	33	60
6	Biological E Ltd	672	33
7	Bharat Serums & Vaccines Ltd	600	11
8	Indian Immunologicals Ltd	538	17
9	Macleods Pharmaceuticals Pvt Ltd	406	20
10	Lupin Ltd	381	10

Bioagriculture

Agriculture accounts for the primary source of livelihood and income for about 58% of India's population and in addition to this India is the leading exporters of agricultural products worldwide. Bio agricultural industry is the third largest sector of biotech industry in India which has reached INR 53,125 Million in 2020. Gross Value Added (GVA) by Bio agricultural industry (agriculture, forestry and fishing) was estimated to be around Rs. 19.48 lakh crore (US$ 276.37 billion) in 2020 (IBEF, 2020). Bio-agriculture not only deals with genetically modified (GM) crops, bio-fertilizers bio-pesticides and bio-fuels but also emerged as a sector dealing with breeding nutritious, high-yielding and less resource demanding crops. India holds fourth position in growing genetically modified (GM) crops with respect to production of Bt cotton and in addition to these, bio-fertilizers, bio-fuels and bio-pesticides are also contributing to the growth of the Indian agri-biotech market. With India's growing population, the need for food is also growing directly making this sector increasingly important for the country to explore. Future opportunities in this sector lies in developing medicinal and aromatic plants, biofuels,animal biotechnology, marine biotechnology and biopesticides.

Bioindustrial

Bioindustrial sector comprises of area which include harnessing of microorganisms which are useful for production of enzymes and bioactives that have multiple industrial uses and application in bio-energy from biomass and bio-fuels (Chandel et al., 2007). Enzymes have diverse application in industrial processes viz., food and nutrition, biopharmaceutical, textile, leather and green chemicals (i.e. polymers derived using bio-based enzymes). Bioindustry plays a very important role in flourishing Indian Biotech industry (Chandel et al., 2007). Novozymes, is rapidly flourishing in India by developing the enzymes applicable in various sector of food, beverages and leather industries (Binod et al., 2013). Futuristic potential lies in exploring technologies associated with bioremediation, bioenergy and algae research (Raheem et al., 2018; Nie et al., 2020).

Bioservices

It is the second largest sector with about 33% market share of the biotechnology industry.Indian Bio-Suppliers market has registered growth of 9% in 2019-20 (Rs 8666 crore) over the revenue of Rs 7950 crore in 2018-19 (6% growth). The increased growth rate has become possible with government's aid of Rs 1,900 crore for research in the Union Budget 2019-20 along with Rs 62,659 crore support for the Ministry of Health and Family Welfare, has helped the biosuppliers (BioSpectrum 2021). Bioservices has further divisions into contract and clinical research organizations (CROs), as well as contract manufacturer organisation (CMOs) and is often referred to as Contract Research and Manufacturing Services (CRAMS), few listed in Table 2. The CRAMS industry, especially biotechnological contract services has grown today to be an important contributor to India's bio-economy.

Table 2. Some leading companies in bioservices

CRO's	CMO's	CRAM's
Parexel	Innovexia Life sciences Pvt. Ltd.	Biocon
IQVIA	Medlock Healthcare	Dishman Pharmaceuticals and Chemicals
ACM Global Laboratories	Biophar Lifesciences Pvt. Ltd.	Divis Laboratories
AXIS clinical	Sunwin Healthcare Pvt. Ltd.	Jubilant Life Sciences
BioAxis	Arlak Biotech Pvt. Ltd.	Piramal Healthcare
CliniRx	Healthcare Pvt. Ltd.	Dr. Reddy's Laboratories
Eurofin Advinus	Saffron Medicare Pvt. Ltd.	Sun Pharmaceuticals

Looking into the future, the entry of a number of small CROs into the market is estimated to be looking at BA/BE studies. Mandatory registration of all clinical trials has added transparency into the system in India and this in turn has also lead to a rise in the number of global companies outsourcing clinical trials to India. India because of its diverse gene pools offers a suitable population for clinical trials which cover a large number of diseases. Also cost effectiveness, skill sets and increased confidence on capabilities have propelled many global pharmaceutical companies to start their own clinical research investment in India.

Bioinformatics

Bio-informatics and systems biology serves an important inter-disciplinary tool for deeper biotechnology studies in health and medicine. The bio-informatics segment, is the smallest sector among all biotech industry sectors, constituting barely 2% of the market share. This sector is creating and providing opportunities in areas like Next generation sequencing, Data mining and in-silico analysis, bio-banking, molecular marker studies, disease and organ models analysis, pathway analysis and software tool development. India having skilled and enthusiastic IT professionals, scientists, engineers, is also growing and becoming attraction for foreign investment. Infosys, Cognizant Technologies, HCL, Mphasis, and TCS are few companies that have made significant strides in bioinformatic sector.

RAPIDLY GROWING INDIAN BIOTECHNOLOGY INDUSTRY

India's Biotechnology industry is flourishing with the advantage of havingunique strengths such as abundance bio-resources, availability of strong pool of scientists and technical expertise, skilled manpower that makes India a strong technical base (Kumar et al., 2004; Malhotra et al., 2012). Moreover, progressive government policies and foreign investments have led to rapid expansion of access to international markets. Foreign investment has contributed greatly to the Indian biotechnology industry. India's low-cost manufacturing has led to large production of vaccines viz., Hepatitis B vaccine and Rotavirus vaccine. India's first indigenously produced hepatitis B vaccine through recombinant expression of hepatitis B surface antigen in Pichia pastoris host was manufactured and commercialized under name Shanvac-B. Shanvac-B vaccine uses novel expression technology and is an important success story Indian biotechnology sector (Kumar et al., 2004). Biotechnology has been given importance as one of the highest priority sectors under the Government of India initiatives; 'Make in India', 'Skill India' and 'Startup India' to attain sustainable economic growth and generate large scale employment opportunities which has led to a steep growth due to the betterment agenda of the Government of India in this sector. Make in India aimed to enhance investment, encourage innovation and skill development, protection of intellectual property and developing best manufacturing infrastructure (Singh & Jaiswal, 2018). Skill India aimed to develop skill in youth and making them ready for implementing their constructive ideas into reality and thus have a paying occupation through their skills (Gaur & Padiya, 2015). Startup India gives an initiative platform to eligible companies to get recognized as Startups by Department for Promotion of Industry and Internal Trade (DPIIT), in order to access tax benefits, easier compliances, IPR fast- tracking etc (Rani, 2017).

FOREIGN INVESTMENT

FDI, according to the international monetary fund is defined as "Investment that is made to acquire lasting interest in an enterprise operating in an economy other than that of investor. The investor's purpose is being to have an effective voice in the management of enterprise" (Singh, Chadha and Sharma, 2012). Foreign investment in the form of capital comprises of private foreign capital and public foreign capital, but it can also include managerial power, technical knowledge, technical personnel, excogitations in products and production techniques from one enterprise residing in country to enterprise of another country to develop product using host country resources and manpower. The foreign investment specifically is categorised into two types as depicted in Fig 3 (Wu. Li & Selovar, 2012).

Figure 3. Types of foreign investment

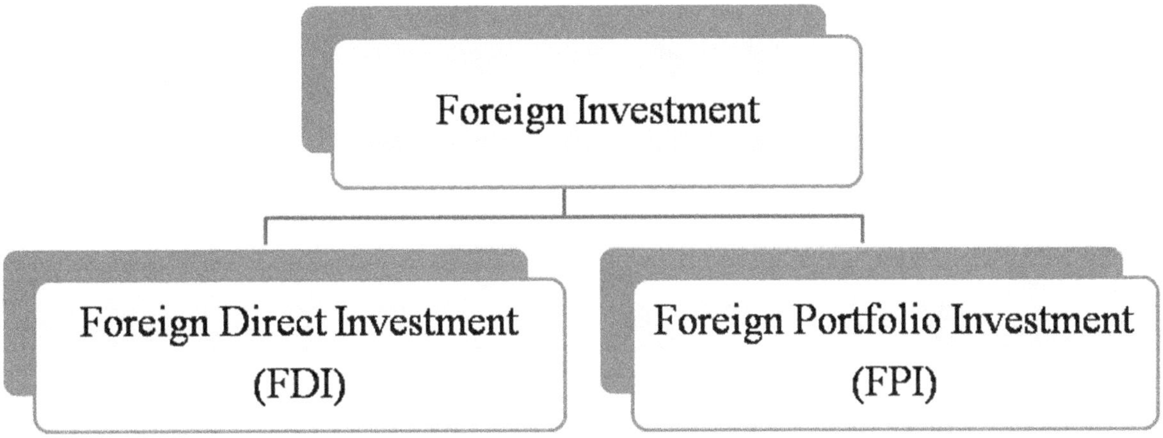

Foreign investment in form of capital, managerial power, technical knowledge, technical personnel, excogitations in products and production techniques from one enterprise residing in one country to enterprise of another country to develop product using host country resources, manpower. Broadly, foreign investment is categorised into Foreign Direct Investment (FDI) and foreign portfolio investment (FPI).

Foreign investors can help by supporting scientific expertise and seed funding used to develop ideas on innovation. India's biotechnology industry has experienced an exponential increase from US$530 million in 2003 to US$4.3 billion till 2013, which makes India the third largest biotech industry in the Asia-Pacific region. Foreign investment has played a big role in the flourishing Indian biotechnology industry. Recently, Singapore and Mauritius are among the few foreign investors that invested in Indian biotech industry. In 2019, Government of India formulated new policies for investment with respect to FDI. According to these new policies, different sectors in biotech were brought under the automatic route, i.e., no prior regulatory permission is required to invest and there is direct route investment allowed in those sectors. Gujarat and Maharashtra have attracted huge foreign investments whereas there are few states that have lagged in receiving foreign investment. The reasons for this uneven inflow are many; some are related to state administration decisions and eye-catching opportunities, but with change in policies it is expected that other states in India that are still behind in the race would get enough considerations.

Foreign Direct Investment (FDI)

According to the Organisation for Economic Co-operation and Development (OECD) (1996), FDI is a long-term relationship that gets established when a corporation or a resident entity in one country establishes a business operation with significant influence in another economy, through setting up a new enterprise, or acquiring a local enterprise, or forming a joint venture with the existing company in the host economy. FDI investment in developing economies takes in at least four different forms: FDI in extractive industries; FDI in infrastructure; FDI in manufacturing and assembly; and FDI in services

(Moran, 2012). OECD (1996) defined direct investment enterprise as an incorporated or unincorporated enterprise in which a foreign investor owns at least 10%or more of the ordinary shares and thus voting power in an enterprise. However, the ownership of 10% of the ordinary shares or voting power in some cases, may not necessarily lead to the benefits of any significant influence. While, on the other hand, in some cases a direct investor owning even less than 10% may have substantial influence over the management. Major contributors of FDI inflow in India are listed in Table 3.

Table 3. Major investors in India from April 2019 to September 2020.

S.No.	Investor Country	Amount of FDI (in Rs Crore)	% inflow
1	Mauritius	810,960.08	28.94
2	Singapore	671,645.60	21.19
3	USA	229,487.83	7.38
4	Netherland	219,628.30	7.07
5	Japan	201,037.14	6.83
6	United Kingdom	160,565.71	5.91
7	Germany	70,442.24	2.48
8	Cyprus	58,348.30	2.16
9	France	59,005.44	1.93
10	Cayman Island	65,520.18	1.93

Foreign Portfolio Investment (FPI)

Foreign Portfolio Investment is another form of foreign investment that has an amount of securities and some form of regulation. It does not involve any management control, but is motivated by profit only. Portfolio investment, wherein individual investors invest, mostly through stockbrokers in stocks of foreign companies in foreign land for the sole purpose of profit opportunities (Singh, Chadha & Sharma, 2012). Foreign portfolio investment (FPI) investment across the countries is an investment in order to achieve higher returns by diversifying the risk of their portfolio. There are several reports wherein, FPI has importance across countries has been recorded that include Grubel (1968), Levy and Sarnat (1970), Grauer and Hakansson (1987), Harvey (1991), and De Santis and Gerard (1997). Being the developing country, portfolio flows in India can play a pivotal role in bridging the saving–investment gap. It can provide the foreign exchange to support finance and thus developing countries across the globe have been interested in and therefore making conscious efforts to attract foreign financial capital which is helpful in providing an acceleration to any economy in terms of economic growth and financial market development in the host country.

Route of Foreign Investment

Route of FDI by an individual or a company from outside the country is regulated by automatic route and approval route.

1. The Automatic Route

This is less restricted route wherein investment norms and regulations are liberalized and thus overseas investors or Indian company does not require any prior permission or approval for investment from Reverse bank of India (RBI) or GOI for making an investment.

2. **Approval/Government Route**

This route is restricted wherein the investor has to take a prior approval of investment from the Reserve Bank of India (RBI) or the GOI before making an investment.

Attraction of Foreign Investment in India

India is the 2nd largest populated country, hosts an ever-growing consumer base thus making it one of the world's largest markets with high demand for manufactured goods and services. Manpower is economic with advantage of well educated, good communication, hard-working and skilled workers (engineers, management staff, accountants and lawyers). India has a great advantage of proximity to key manufacturing sites, resource, suppliers and low development costs. 'Transparency International 'gave Indian companies the top ranking among the emerging market multinationals in terms of transparency and compliance. A well-established administration, judiciary and calm and stable political environment in India makes the country an effective base from which multi-national companies can export to other high-growth emerging markets. Moreover opening up of economy since 1991 has improved Foreign investment climate in India. This has become possible largely due to ease in FDI norms across different sectors of Indian economy. This led to increased FDI inflow in last 20 years in India (April 2000- September 2020) i.e., 729.8 bn US dollar, which was 319 USD from 2014 to 2019, accounting for 50% of total inflow in last 20 years (Biospectrum).

Government Initiatives to Attract Foreign Investors

GOI In 2019 has formulated new policies to attract investment with respect to FDI. These new policies led to inclusion of different sectors like biotechnology under the automatic route wherein, no regulatory permission or approval is required prior to invest which in turn allow direct route invest in various sectors. The policies of GOI includes, tax and non-tax investment incentives in sectors and regions like Northeast region, Jammu & Kashmir, Himachal Pradesh and Uttarakhand. GOI has also created alluring incentives for manufacturing companies to set up their plants in Special Economic Zones (SEZ) (Mukherjee et al., 2016; Aggarwal, 2019), National Investment & Manufacturing Zones (NIMZ) (Casey, 2013) and Export Oriented Units (EOUs). In addition GOI has plans for providing additional investment incentives which includes subsidised land prices, attractive interest rates on loans for the set up (offer medium to long-term loans), reduced tariffs on electric power supply, tax concessions, etc (Shapiro & Mathur, 2014). GOI has recently raised FDI limit to relax FDI policy and to attract FDI in a variety of sectors and has also introduced 'automatic route' in addition to including many sectors in its ambit thus easing conditions for investment. Foreign investment in Biotechnology is allowed to 100% under automatic route for Green-field pharma, agriculture and up to 100% in manufacturing medical devices whereas FDI limit has been increased in brownfield from 74% to 100% under approval/government route.

Moreover, government has taken steps to reduce fiscal deficit and public debt. Most landmark change Government of India has introduced is GST (Good and Services Tax), that is to boost tax revenues to make the economy more competitive. All the initiatives and amendment in policies has been for the only motive to strengthen Indian economy and also the Biotech industry.

Protection of Foreign Investment

India has provided transparency and has ensured protection to foreign investors that gives the sense of security to the investors attract them and make them consider India among the secure and favoured countries to invest in. Few steps that have been taken in India in this direction are mentioned below:

1. Bilateral Investment Conventions Signed by India

BIT between two countries is to encourage, promote and provide protection of investments in other's territories. These conventions typically cover scope and definition of investment, admission to establishment of investment, nation treatment, fair and equitable treatment, compensation in the event of expropriation or damage to the investment, guarantees of free transfers of funds and dispute settlement mechanisms. India has bilateral investment treaties with the United Kingdom, France, Kazakhstan, Nepal, South Korea, Sri Lanka, Thailand, Germany, Canada, Malaysia, and Mauritius.

2. International Controversies Registered By UNCTAD

The Investment Dispute Settlement (ISDS) Navigator contains information about known international cases initiated by investors against States pursuant to international investment agreements, which provides transparency to investors.

3. Multilateral Investment Guarantee Agency

The Multilateral Investment Guarantee Agency (MIGA) is an international institution aiming to promote investment in developing countries with the framework of offering political and economic risk insurance. The agency aims to support economic growth, reduce poverty, and improve people's lives all through encouraging foreign direct investment into developing countries. India is member of MIGA that provide sense of security and assurance to investor to invest in India.

Recent Foreign Investment

1. Indo- Sweden has signed a joint call for "Artificial intelligence for advancing healthcare across both the countries". They have agreed on 26 proposals which were evaluated by a technical advisory committee.
2. The Department of Biotechnology partnered European Commission for collaborative research about the 'Green Deal: Building a low-carbon, climate-resilient future program'. This program will generate essential knowledge of Sustainable Development Goals.

3. In November 2020, Serum Institute of India, Bangladesh-based pharmaceutical company Beximco Pharmaceuticals Ltd. and the Government of Bangladesh has signed a tripartite MoU for procurement of the Oxford/Astrazeneca COVID-19 vaccine.
4. Bharat Biotech has plans to invest a total of Rs. 300 crores (US$ 40.54 million) to produce different types of vaccines including malaria and COVID-19 with its upcoming unit in Bhubaneswar, Odisha.
5. In September 2020, Sree Chitra Tirunal Institute for Medical Sciences and Technology, a Thiruvananthapuram-based organisation has announced an upcoming collaboration with the Kerala government to set up a Rs. 260 crore (US$ 35.44 million) medical devices park in Thonnakkal (Thiruvanthapuram).
6. In September 2019, Biocon Ltd. acquired the Chennai-based research and development facility from Pfizer Healthcare India Ltd. This was aimed to help Biocon accelerate its development in field of biosimilars from lab to pilot scale. Some other major investing partners are listed in Table 4.

State Wise FDI Inflow in India

The highest FDI inflow attracting state in Indian from October 2019 to September 2020 was Gujarat with inflow of 138530.40 crore rupees that accounts for total 35% FDI inflow in India. Maharashtra (20%), Karnataka (14.60%), Delhi (12%) attracted considerable FDI inflow but rest of the states were less than one percent successful to attract inflow. The reason for Gujarat, Maharashtra, Karnataka and Delhi to be ahead of other states in attracting FDI inflow is because of good infrastructure facilities, resources, rich heritage of entrepreneurship, favourable government responses and quick bureaucracy. It is pertinent to indicate here that states like Punjab have locational disadvantage resulting in poor FDI. Moreover, in big state like Bihar lags far behind in FDI due to poor infrastructure (Wellington & Jammu, 2014).

Impact of Foreign Investment on Host Country

Foreign Direct Investment in India has increased after the liberalization policy and the structural changes made in foreign trade policy. As far as FDI inflow in India with respect to biotechnology are, 100% Foreign Direct Investment (FDI) is allowed under the automatic route for greenfield pharma, 100% Foreign Direct Investment (FDI) is allowed under the government route for brownfield pharma in up to 74% FDI is under automatic route and beyond 74% is under government approval route and FDI up to 100% is allowed under the automatic route for the manufacturing of medical devices.

India has recognized the importance of biotechnology as a tool for upgrading the economic system. In continuation with this, India initiated the first Export Processing Zone in Kantla. The Indian biotechnology sector has inherent power of low operational costs for running the unit, low cost for the technology, availability of skilled human resource, IT enhanced network of life science research laboratories along with abundance of raw material inputs such as plant, animal and human genetic diversity. The enormous flow of Foreign Direct Investment has resulted in the transformation of Indian Biotechnology sector from the share of just two percent global biotech product supply in 1999 to the position among top twelve largest destinations of Biotechnology product supply.

Table 4. Key investors in biotech industry in India.

Year of investment	Investor	Investment
May 2020	Gilead Sciences Inc	Jubilant Generics Ltd in a non-exclusive licencing agreement with US-based Gilead Sciences Inc to produce and sell the potential COVID-19 drug Remdesivir in 127 countries, including India.
September 2020	Auro vaccines (Aurobindo Pharma) US	Aurobindo Pharma collaborated with BIRAC to develop the COVID-19 vaccine.
October 2020	Netherlands	India and Netherlands collaborated with an aim to provide digital health facilities and security to all citizens
November 2019	Advent International (Boston, US)	Advent International, invested to acquire a majority interest in Bharat Serums and Vaccines Limited.
September 2019	Bayer AG (German chemical and pharma major)	Bayer AG (German chemical and pharma major), completed the integration of Monsanto's India business to form Bayer CorpScience Ltd.
September 2018	PE investment	PE investment deal worth USD $ 217mn through 39 investments
June 2018	Tyumen (Russia)	Tyumen, a keen player to host pharmaceutical venture of Indian firms
July 2016	Singapore	Helix investment holding Pte Ltd., Singapore invested $12 mn in Concord Biotech Ltd.
January 2016	Venaxis Inc.	Invested in standard life sciences
October 2015	Recipharm	Invested 109.92 USD million in Nitin Lifesciences
August 2015	Mauritius	Tano India Pvt., Mauritius invested $7.4 mn in Windlas Biotech Ltd
December 2014	Leaders Group Asia Ltd.	Invested in Mumbai-based drug ingredients and formulations maker Dr Datsons Labs Ltd.
October 2014	B Braun Singapore Pte Ltd.	7.89 (USD million) invested in Ahlcon Parenterals Ltd.
May 2014	Amglo Gulf Ltd.	7 (USD million) invested in SciGen Biopharma Pvt Ltd.
May 2013	Bio Harvest Pte Ltd.	51.06 (USD million) invested in Camson Biotechnologies Ltd.
October 2012	GE Equity International	302.13 (USD million) invested in Syngene International Ltd.
March 2012	Origio A/S	Investment of 8.6 (USD million) in Trivector Scientific Pvt Ltd.
	Amgen Inc. (US)	Syngene International Ltd, the contract research services arm of Biocon Ltd, is setting up a drug discovery and development center in Bengaluru for Amgen Inc., a biotechnology company based in the US.
	Boston Scientific Corp. (US)	US-based medical devices maker Boston Scientific Corp. Investment plans to make India its biggest research and development (R&D) hub outside the US, for developing devices such as stents, catheters and pacemakers at its Gurgaon facility for the Asia Pacific, Middle East and African markets.
	Frost and Sullivan (US)	Frost & Sullivan has signed a memorandum of understanding (MoU) with The Neotia University (TNU) to set up biotechnology parks in India.
	Monsanto	Biotechnology giant Monsanto has planned to set up a seed plant in Buldhana district of Maharashtra.
	CCAB (Canada)	Canada's Centre for Commercialisation of Antibodies and Biologics (CCAB) has partnered with ZydusCadila to manufacture antibody-based cancer treatments.

CURRICULUM TO ENCOURAGE BIOENTREPRENEURSHIP

A successful biotechnology industry depends on its trained professional team who not only understand science integrity but are also have skilled in the complexities of commercialization. Thus every bioentrepreneur must understand the basics, research, collaboration, infrastructure, and technology and capital. Biotechnologist out of academia and into industry remains a mystery to many scientists, moreover lack of knowledge of commercial sector in academic circles can lead to a lag of many years in present business practice, in the era where industry models are constantly evolving (Langer, 2014). Life science researchers and technicians are simply not ready to take up the innovation to commercial scale as they are not trained in the complexities of commercialization. Proper education to budding researchers to understand entrepreneurship and developing the skill are needed to succeed in the commercial world thus to translate discoveries into products, building companies and also providing the knowledgeable recruits that industry wants to hire.

MAJOR OPPORTUNITIES IN THE BIOTECHNOLOGY SECTOR

Drug discovery and clinical trials, medical devices manufacturing, biosimilars and secondary agriculture are few ventures that are gaining attraction and are new investment opportunity in India. Of all, biosimilars are gaining more attention as biosimilar is a biologic medical product highly similar to the already approved biological medicine. Biosimilar is getting attention because of the expected outcome low-cost medicine from innovative ideas (Bigoniya, 2017). In addition to biopharma India provide suitable population for clinical trials because of its diverse gene pools, skilled professionals propel expansion of biopharma and bioservices sector in India, which in turn is a great opportunity for Biotech industry of India to cash in. Biotechnology is expected to offer investment opportunities and the growth is expected in the areas as listed below (Parmar, 2005; Kumar and Srivastva, 2012).

1. Vaccines: Vaccines and recombinant therapeutics is a promising and leading sector growing rapidly in the biotechnology industry in India. This area is expected to witness introduction of newer vaccines, therapies, and in this direction, major emphasis would be on the monoclonal antibodies, regenerative medicine or stem cell therapies, growth factors etc.
2. Bioactive Therapeutic Proteins: Proteins and antibodies production and fabrication of diagnostic chips would be an area in demand and promising for investment, which is expected to show up to 25% growth in near future. Stem cell research, regenerative medicine, cell engineering-based therapeutics is another area getting attention due to high expertise pool of scientist in India, where India could cash in its expertise.
3. Agriculture sector: India is among the major producer of transgenic rice and several genetically modified (GM) or engineered vegetables. Increased use of molecular markers in crop breeding has led to bright future in the productivity and quality of crops such as rice, wheat, eggplant (brinjal), tomato and lady's finger. Hybrid seeds, using genetically modified seeds has been come up as a new business opportunity in India.
4. Contract Research: The research and development sector potential has led to number of foreign companies stepping in India. Biotech sector is constantly working in direction to develop of new

products. Indian pharma companies with the advantage of having competitive skills in chemical synthesis and process engineering, have the potential to develop new chemical entities.

Clinical Trials and outsourcing: India has a great diversity with respect to genetic pools that is covering a large number of diseases, this makes India a suitable population for clinical trials. Due to high costs of R&D in abroad, global companies especially US and European based companies are looking for contract research in India. Contract research with support from IT, has led to promising collaboration for outsourcing business in various segments like clinical trial data management, statistical analysis, and electronic data capture.

5. Bioinformatics: Indian bioinformatics companies are playing a significant role in critical areas such as data mining, mapping and DNA sequencing, besides functional genomics, proteomics and molecule design simulation in world market for bioinformatics services. The IT skill of Indian manpower also offers services in bioinformatics and data mining.

Besides these, tremendous scope for investment in the Biotechnology sector include medicinal and aromatic plants, aquaculture and marine Biotechnology, Seri biotechnology, stem cell biology, animal biotechnology, genome Analysis, Agriculture and Plant Biotechnology, Bio-Fuels, Bio Pesticides, Healthcare, Bio-Informatics, Environmental Biotechnology, Microbial and Industrial Biotechnology (Kumar and Srivastva, 2012).

CONCLUSION

Science which involves living organisms directly or indirectly along with advancing technology to get insight into the cellular and molecular processes to develop products of human utility is known as Biotechnology. Integration of two disciplines, science and business, whereby it creates opportunity to produce, develop and ultimately commercialize a product is known as bioentrepreneurship. Bioentrepreneurship offers a large scope and attracts entrepreneurs, who can contribute by making scientific methods and products available to the society. India with its large and highly efficient pool of scientific community has lot to offer to national as well as global market. India is particularly strong in clinical data management, drug discovery and low-cost manufacturing, which give an advantage to foreign investors and Indian market too. According to the Association of Biotechnology Led Enterprises (ABLE), the Indian biotechnology industry sector has the potential to become $ 100 billion industry in the next decade. Foreign investment in form of capital, managerial power, technical knowledge, technical personnel, excogitations in products and production techniques from one enterprise residing in one country to enterprise of another country to develop product using host country resources, manpower. Broadly foreign investment specifically is categorised into Foreign Direct Investment (FDI) and Foreign portfolio investment (FPI). Foreign investors can help by supporting scientific expertise and seed funding used to develop ideas on innovation. India's biotechnology industry has experienced an exponential increase from US$530 million in 2003 to US$4.3 billion till 2013, which makes India, the third largest biotech industry in the Asia-Pacific region. Foreign investment has played a big role in flourishing Indian's biotechnology industry. Recently, Singapore and Mauritius invested 810960.08 crore and 671,645.60 Crore Rupees respectively in Indian biotech industry. In 2019, Government of India formulated new policies for investment with respect to

FDI, which has attracted foreign investment. According to these new policies, different sectors in Biotech was brought under the automatic route, i.e., no prior regulatory permission is required to invest and there is direct route invest allowed in those sectors.

ACKNOWLEDGMENT

The authors are grateful to Dr. Ramandeep Kaur, Associate Professor, Panjab University, Chandigarh for the valuable suggestions and ideas.

REFERENCES

Aggarwal, A. (2019). Promoting Special Economic Zones as a Strategy of Industrialization and Lessons Learned. In *A Concise Handbook of the Indian Economy in the 21st Century* (pp. 276–320). Oxford University Press. doi:10.1093/oso/9780199496464.003.0010

Altman, A. (1997). *Agricultural biotechnology*. CRC Press. doi:10.1201/9781420049275

Associate of Biotechnology led Enterprises. (n.d.). https://www.ableindia.in

Bigoniya, P. (2017). Biosimilar: Opportunity Thrusted over Indian Pharmaceutical Market. *Annals of Pharmacology and Pharmaceutics*, *2*(14), 1073.

Binod, P., Palkhiwala, P., Gaikaiwari, R., Nampoothiri, K. M., Duggal, A., Dey, K., & Pandey, A. (2013). *Industrial enzymes-present status and future perspectives for India*. Academic Press.

Biotech Consortium India Limited (BCIL). (n.d.). https://www.biotech.co.in/en

Business Opportunity in India: Investment Ideas. (n.d.). Industry Research, Reports IBEF. Https://www.bio.org

Casey Jr, W. L. (2013). National investment promotion policies and foreign direct investment flows. *International Journal of Business and Economics Perspectives, 8*(1), 14-29.

Chandel, A. K., Rudravaram, R., Rao, L. V., Ravindra, P., & Narasu, M. L. (2007). Industrial enzymes in bioindustrial sector development: An Indian perspective. *Journal of Commercial Biotechnology*, *13*(4), 283–291. doi:10.1057/palgrave.jcb.3050065

De Vita, G., & Kyaw, K. S. (2009). Growth effects of FDI and portfolio investment flows to developing countries: A disaggregated analysis by income levels. *Applied Economics Letters*, *16*(3), 277–283. doi:10.1080/13504850601018437

Duhera, R. (2007). Destination India: Favorable policies. *Biospectrum India*, (April issue), 32–36.

Erickson, B., & Winters, P. (2012). Perspective on opportunities in industrial biotechnology in renewable chemicals. *Biotechnology Journal*, *7*(2), 176–185. doi:10.1002/biot.201100069 PMID:21932250

Evans, G. G., & Furlong, J. (2011). *Environmental biotechnology: theory and application*. John Wiley & Sons.

Garg, R., & Dua, P. (2014). Foreign portfolio investment flows to India: Determinants and analysis. *World Development*, *59*, 16–28. doi:10.1016/j.worlddev.2014.01.030

Gaur, A. D., & Padiya, J. (2015). A Conceptual Study of "Skill India" Mission Bridge to "Make in India" Program. Editorial Advisory Board, 52.

Grubel, H. G. (1968). Internationally diversified portfolios: Welfare gains and capital flows. *The American Economic Review*, 1299–1314.

Herdt, R. W. (2006). Biotechnology in agriculture. *Annual Review of Environment and Resources*, 31.

Konde, V. (2008). Biotechnology in India: Public–private partnerships. *Journal of Commercial Biotechnology*, *14*(1), 43–55. doi:10.1057/palgrave.jcb.3050079

Kumar, A., & Srivastava, L. (2012). Biotechnology industry in India: Opportunities or challenges. *African Journal of Business Management*, *6*(44), 10834–10839. doi:10.5897/AJBM10.1236

Kumar, N. K., Quach, U., Thorsteinsdóttir, H., Somsekhar, H., Daar, A. S., & Singer, P. A. (2004). Indian biotechnology—Rapidly evolving and industry led. *Nature Biotechnology*, *22*(12), DC31–DC36. doi:10.1038/nbt1204supp-DC31 PMID:15583682

Langer, L. (2014). Building a curriculum for bioentrepreneurs. *Nature Biotechnology*, *32*(9), 863–865. doi:10.1038/nbt.3012 PMID:25203028

Lewis, K. K. (1999). Trying to explain home bias in equities and consumption. *Journal of Economic Literature*, *37*(2), 571–608. doi:10.1257/jel.37.2.571

Mahboudi, F., Hamedifar, H., & Aghajani, H. (2012). Medical biotechnology trends and achievements in Iran. *Avicenna Journal of Medical Biotechnology*, *4*(4), 200. PMID:23407888

Malhotra, B., Huddone, S., Verma, A., Chamail, A., Sanju, S., Thakur, A., & Pattanayak, D. (2012). Indian entrepreneurship in biotechnology comes of age. *Journal of Plant Biochemistry and Biotechnology*, *21*(1), 90–99. doi:10.100713562-012-0145-y

Moran, T. H. (2012). *Foreign direct investment and development*. The Wiley-Blackwell Encyclopedia of Globalization. doi:10.1002/9780470670590.wbeog217

Mukherjee, A., Pal, P., Deb, S., Ray, S., & Goyal, T. M. (2016). Special SEZs for Services: India's Experiences and the Way Forward. In *Special Economic Zones in India* (pp. 117–152). Springer. doi:10.1007/978-81-322-2806-6_6

National Research Council. (2002). *Animal biotechnology: science-based concerns*. Author.

National Research Council. (2002). *Environmental effects of transgenic plants: the scope and adequacy of regulation*. Author.

National Research Council of Canada. (n.d.). https://nrc.canada.ca/en

Nie, J., Sun, Y., Zhou, Y., Kumar, M., Usman, M., Li, J., & Tsang, D. C. (2020). Bioremediation of water containing pesticides by microalgae: Mechanisms, methods, and prospects for future research. *The Science of the Total Environment*, *707*, 136080. doi:10.1016/j.scitotenv.2019.136080 PMID:31869621

Parmar, H. (2005). Biotechnology in India: Emerging opportunities. *Journal of Commercial Biotechnology*, *12*(1), 61–66. doi:10.1057/palgrave.jcb.3040150

Pham, P. V. (2018). Medical biotechnology: techniques and applications. In *Omics Technologies and Bio-Engineering* (pp. 449–469). Academic Press. doi:10.1016/B978-0-12-804659-3.00019-1

Press Information Bureau (PIB), Media Reports and Press Releases, Department of Industrial Policy and Promotion (DIPP), Department of Biotechnology. (n.d.). http://globalbusinessventures.in/biotechnology-report/

Prihatiningrum, P., Susilowati, S. M. E., & Prasetyo, A. P. B. (2020). Effect of Bioentrepreneurship on Biology Learning Achievement, Creativity, and Entrepreneurial Interest. *Journal of Innovative Science Education*, *9*(3), 250–259.

Rader, R. A. (2008). *Paucity of biopharma approvals raises alarm*. Academic Press.

Raheem, A., Prinsen, P., Vuppaladadiyam, A. K., Zhao, M., & Luque, R. (2018). A review on sustainable microalgae based biofuel and bioenergy production: Recent developments. *Journal of Cleaner Production*, *181*, 42–59. doi:10.1016/j.jclepro.2018.01.125

Ramanaiah, T. V. (2002). Indian Acts, Rules, Regulations and Procedures for Handling Genetically Modified Organisms and r-DNA Products. *International Conference on Biotechnology and Development: Challenges and Opportunities for the Asian Region*.

Rani, M. A. (2017). Startup India: Opportunities & challenges "Start up India stand up India". *ACADEMICIA: An International Multidisciplinary Research Journal*, *7*(1), 104–113. doi:10.5958/2249-7137.2017.00008.8

Ravi, I., Baunthiyal, M., & Saxena, J. (Eds.). (2014). *Advances in biotechnology*. Springer India. doi:10.1007/978-81-322-1554-7

Schoemaker, H. J., & Schoemaker, A. F. (1998). The three pillars of bioentrepreneurship. *Nature Biotechnology*, *16*(1), 13–15. doi:10.1038/5399 PMID:9591253

Shapiro, R. J., & Mathur, A. (2014). *How India can attract more foreign direct investment, create jobs and increase GDP: the benefits of respecting the intellectual property rights of foreign pharmaceutical producers*. Georgetown McDonough School of Business Research Paper, (2540591).

Shimasaki, C. (2020). What is Biotechnology Entrepreneurship. In *Biotechnology Entrepreneurship* (pp. 3–16). Academic Press. doi:10.1016/B978-0-12-815585-1.00001-2

Singh, A., & Jaiswal, K. K. (2018). Ease of doing business in India: A vision of make in India. *Economic Affairs*, *63*(1), 129–135. doi:10.30954/0424-2513.2018.00150.16

Singh, R. K. (2018). *Animal biotechnology*. Oxford and IBH Publishing.

Tang, C. M., Mahmud, M. A., Foo, F. K., Chu, S. Y., Chiu, R. I., Tanticharoen, M., Zhang, L., & Chang, T. W. (2003). Realizing potential: The state of Asian bioentrepreneurship. *Bioentrepreneur*, 1–10. doi:10.1038/bioent731 PMID:12874972

Tang, W. L., & Zhao, H. (2009). Industrial biotechnology: Tools and applications. *Biotechnology Journal: Healthcare Nutrition Technology*, *4*(12), 1725–1739. doi:10.1002/biot.200900127 PMID:19844915

Wellington, S., & Jammu, S. (2014). Foreign direct investment in India. *International Journal Of Econometrics And Financial Management*, *2*(3), 95–101.

Wu, J., Li, S., & Selover, D. D. (2012). Foreign direct investment vs. foreign portfolio investment. *Management International Review*, *52*(5), 643–670. doi:10.100711575-011-0121-0

Chapter 11
Bioentrepreneurship in Agricultural Biotechnology

Avni Jain
Banasthali University, India

Neha Singh
Banasthali University, India

Sonu Kumari
Banasthali University, India

Suphiya Khan
Banasthali University, India

ABSTRACT

The agricultural biotechnology sector shares a common scientific foundation with the therapeutic biotechnology sector, including similar characteristics of a lengthy time to market for emerging products. But the challenges, goals, and opportunities for agricultural applications of biotechnology provide a very different context for innovation and entrepreneurs. Innovation means something novel, which can be a process or a way of doing something novel. Biotechnology entrepreneurship is summing all integrated activities that can create, develop, and finally, commercialize a biotechnology product. These sectors offer new business opportunities that, like agricultural biotechnology trait creation, enable entrepreneurs to think about creating disruptive businesses, not just disruptive technologies for today's business models. In this chapter, the authors conclude the unique aspects of entrepreneurship in the industry of biotechnology in contract with other industries and also discuss the importance of biotechnology entrepreneurs in agriculture.

DOI: 10.4018/978-1-7998-7411-9.ch011

INTRODUCTION

Biotechnology entrepreneurship is the addition of all the activities required to build an enterprise through the melting of both scientific and business disciplines. An enterprise can create, develop and ultimately commercialize a biotechnology product through these integrated activities (Shimasaki, 2014). The term entrepreneur means "one who organizes, manages, and assumes the risks of a business or enterprise". The most of the medical and life-saving devices, efficient crops, and advanced aircraft fuels, have been developed and commercialized through biotechnology enterprises. Biotechnology entrepreneurship is primarily based on two distinctly different disciplines- Science and Business (Collins, 2009).

Innovation means something novel, which can be a process or a way of doing something novel not means physical invention and is not same as "invention". An invention is something physical, but does not possess any commercial value whereas innovation can be successfully commercialized (Carsrud et al., 2008). The intellectual property is of great concern in case of biotechnology entrepreneur and plays different role in respect to an innovation and an invention on the basis of business. Emergence of genetically modified (GM) crops technique and use of GM crops has also led to a major development and growth in croplands. To fulfil the needs and scarcity of food in various countries, this technique has proved to be a boom for everyone (Conner et al., 2003). Farmers are also highly benefitted with this technique and it is always made sure that they have proper accessibility towards it. However, intellectual property rights have been a hurdle for them to access it. All the countries in the world are facing and will face a great challenge in fulfilling the needs of food for about 6 to 9 billion people (Bakshi, 2003). Genetic modifications like Insects resistant crops, drought resistant crops and biofortification have led to a major growth in agricultural biotechnology industry and several crops like maize, rice and cotton have been grown with enhanced properties. Plant based herbal medicines and various other drugs and vaccines have shown a great success over artificial medicines and vaccines. As plants are an infinite source of novel chemotypes, pharmacophores and drug development for curing multiple diseases (Vreesham, 2012). Biotechnological approaches such as tissue culture and micropropagation techniques, polyploidyinduction, mutation breeding and genetic manipulation and engineering techniques are being used to develop ornamental plants. Plant with new characteristics like floral architecture, colour, fragrance, resistance toabiotic stress and post-harvest life can be produced through biotechnology (Miri and Roughani, 2018). In this chapter, we will outline the unique and efficient aspects of entrepreneurship in the biotechnology industry contrasted with other industries and also the ways like GM crops and plant- Nano interactions to overcome such serious issues.

MODERN AGRICULTURAL BIOTECHNOLOGY PRODUCTS FOR ENTREPRENEURSHIP

Globally, agricultural biotechnology has capacity to advance crop productivity, improve food security and production enhancement. Based on the studies of DNA, several scientific techniques are used for crop and livestock improvement in agricultural biotechnology which is otherwise not possible with only conventional breeding. An another feature of agricultural biotechnology implies modern molecular plant breeding techniques like marker-assisted selection (MAS) and use of recombinant DNA. However, recombinant DNA technology results in new traits unlike molecular plant breeding and cannot be achieved through conventional breeding.

Large Scale Production of Plants

For the diverse agricultural production and for reducing the loss of crop plants during cultivation, storage and transport, employment of modern techniques is necessarily required, as the population is increasing rapidly and so it needs higher food stocks (Sahayaraj, 2014). For instance, such as plant derived bioactive compounds are widely used to fulfil such requirements. Many valuable as well as endemic species of plants are being extinct because of continuous and rapid demolition of natural habitats for a number of plants. However, cultural techniques like callus and cell suspension are being used for large-scale production of plant metabolites since mid-1950s (Yesil-Celiktas et al., 2010).

The secondary metabolites such as enzymes, hormones, proteins, natural pesticides and food additives was obtained with the use of various culture techniques from cultured cells or tissue harvest. Many countries initiated large scale cultivation of tobacco and various vegetable cells which in-turn initiated studies of plant cell culture on the industrial application during late 1950's and early 1960's. In 1956, first patent was received for the cultivation of plant tissue. Soon afterwards, plant cell & tissue culture techniques started getting support from the National Aeronautics and Space Administration (NASA) for more research in this field for regenerative life support systems (Sajc et al., 2000).

Many alternative and attractive approaches have been implied in the field of plant cell culture techniques covering multiple sub-fields under certain circumstances, such as,

- The source plant is hard to be cultivated.
- The source plant requires a long period for cultivation.
- A commercially important compound is produced by the source plant but it cannot be chemically synthesized on large scale.
- Plant source has a low metabolite of the required compound.

A much strong and rapid continuous growth has been seen in the micropropagation industry as the *in vitro* technique of plant propagation has flourished and the transplants by tissue culture have been adopted commercially (Prakash, 1989). Almost five million plants per year are being produced in countries like USA, UK & Netherland and it is expected to be above 20 million per year in the upcoming future.

One such *in vitro* method of production of large amount of disease-free, genetically uniform plants is Micropropagation. The micro propagation from cells can be done either by direct organogenesis from hairy roots or regeneration via somatic tissue. Plant micropropagation is a well-favoured technique and is mostly preferred over conventional propagation cuttings and seeds because it offers better advantages (Murashige, 1974). The direct organogenesis by shoots or somatic embryogenesis can be used for cell micropropagation. Out of these, the best considered and widely adopted commercial regeneration technique is Organogenesis via shoots. The possibility for micropropagation through somatic embryogenesis provides a valuable alternative to the above propagation system (Chen et al., 1987). Since large number of somatic embryos can be produced within less time, limited medium and with low cost requirement, somatic embryogenesis technique is much promising and susceptible for large-scale plant micropropagation. The embryos develop through callus or directly from explants describe the diverse potential functions of somatic embryogenesis. In addition, the use of *Agrobacterium rhizogenes* offers the opportunity to introduce foreign genes into plant genomes when a hairy root is reduced, enabling the alteration of plant's properties by gene manipulation (Hamill et al., 1987).

GM Crops

The global construction and commercialization of genetically modified (GM) crops has increased and developed rapidly all over the world with the application of Transgenic Biotechnology (Nap et al., 2003). Global agricultural and seed market have flourished enormously and experienced some important changes with the introduction of GM crops technology. Private sector has started investing more in crop improvement because of the higher economic returns and more intense Intellectual Property Rights (IPR) and thus, extend business to market (Qaim and De Janvry., 2003). The application of GM Crops has proven to be boom for poverty alleviation and also to solve malnutrition problems all over the world. These alterations take place using various predesigned genetic engineering techniques. Generally, the main aim of GM crops is to propose a completely new and different trait to a plant which is not naturally present in that particular species (Conner et al., 2003). The most studied GM crops are cotton, maize and soybean (Fischer et al., 2015). Traits which are infused in the GM crops involve resistance towards pests, also some climatic conditions and ability to survive in worst climatic conditions and also resistance to some diseases. It also provides resistance to the use of chemical treatments like herbicides etc. Many herbicide tolerant soybeans, cotton and other plants have been made enable to use herbicides with lower risk and break down rapidly and easily. It is also responsible for the enhancement of nutritional value and content of a particular crop or species. This technique has been willingly adopted by farmers and has led to huge increase in the global croplands (Bakshi, 2003).

Figure 1. Few GM crops approved by USDA

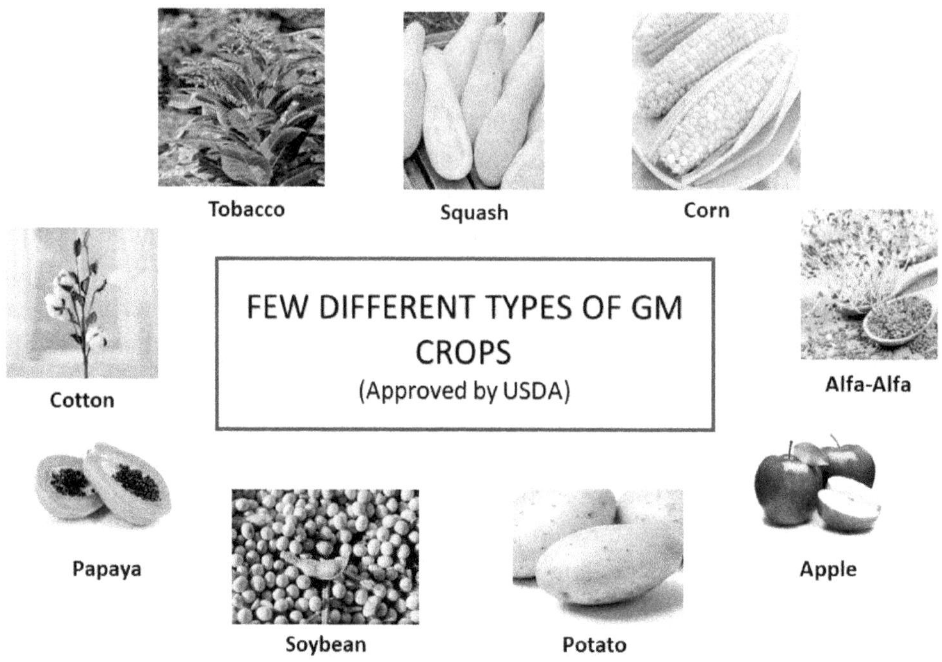

There are various examples of GM crops which include vegetables, fruits, Pulses, oilseeds and many commercial crops which have been targeted to improve several traits prominently disease and pest resistance, abiotic stress tolerance including drought resistance, Insects resistance (Figure 1). There are biosafety regulatory systems which are different in every country for the development and implementation of GM organisms so that it ensures safe trade and use. Mainly the four GM crops are traded even internationally, cotton, soybean, maize and canola (Bakshi, 2003).

Bacillus thuringiensis, a soil bacterium, is transferred to cotton crop plant making it *Bt* cotton turning it defiant to major insect pests. Monsanto developed this technology for the first time. This technology was developed and widespread adopted rapidly for one specific reason as it resulted much profitable to farmers. Bt cotton is improvised to be resistant to cotton bollworm complex (*Helicover pagelotopoeon* and *Heliothis virescens*), leaf worm (*Alabama argillacea*), and the pink bollworm (*Pectinophoragossipiella*), and almost all primary insects and pests. Bt cotton production has reduced the use of pesticides in various countries to a great extent in countries like India (39%) (Wang et al., 2008), Argentina (44%) (Qaim and Dejanvry, 2003). One such crop is mushroom. Mushroom crop is not only nuitritious and eco-friendly but it also has various medicinal benefits. With the rapid increase in population, there is extreme pressure on environment. Mushroom cultivation has provided a much relief in this situation. Although, in comparison to other crop plants, mushroom's breeding and production is quite limited.

Mushroom breeding is also done to introduce various improved growing qualities into the crop such as short growth cycle and reduced or no spore formation. Many mushroom cultivars are available to breeders which are also efficiently disease resistant. *Agaricus bisporus*and *A. bitorquis*are valuable horticultural crops cultivated throughout the world with numerous strains andhybrids (Chakravarty, 2011). Hybrid breeding, transgenic breeding, agrobacterium based transformation are some techniques used in mushroom breeding.

Another example is Eggplant or (*Solanum melongena* L.). In various countries all over the world, eggplant is considered to be very important economically although it has low efficiency to bear several biological and other related stress. Studies have been done on its Genetic resources to assess it resistance against many severe pests and diseases (bacterial and fungal wilts, nematodes and shoot and fruit borer) (Kashyap et al., 2002). It is a crop in a very long-time duration and grows using hybrid varieties or open-pollinated varieties (OPVs, for which seeds can be saved and used later). With the help of somatic hybridisation, cultivated eggplants have been introduced with traits like bacterial and fungal resistance. However, when the parental lines were distantly related, most somatic hybrids were sterile (Colloneir et al., 2001). Insect resistant transgenic eggplant has been made to produce partheno-carpic fruits. It has also been made abiotic stress tolerant.

There are various applications of GM crops. These GM crops can be best used for the production of recombinant vaccines. Various oral vaccines in fruits and vegetables can be directly consumed. Thus, becoming a better solution for disease spread in various under developed countries (Qaim and Zilberman, 2003).

Although being an improved and important technique, GM crops have been reported to have various controversies for direct gene transfer techniques like consumers, biotechnological companies, non-governmental organisations and infact scientists (Qaim and Zilberman, 2003). There is also lot of objections on GM crops on criteria like environmental impacts, food safety, fulfilment of food needs and accessibility to farms. Genetic modifications can be done for various needs, few of which are describe in figure 2.

Insects Resistance

The most successful transgenic technique is the development of insect-resistant GM crops. Almost 15% of the total World's GM crops cultivation area is inherited by insect-resistant GM crops. It has somehow, convinced to be the most effective tool to control insects by modifying the crops with genes that confer protection from insects. These are used on a very high-level agricultural scale. Cry proteins from *Bacillus thuringiensis* (*Bt*) are the only available genes which are expressed by the current commercially available GM crops. Many other proteins like VIP proteins from *Bt* lectins and protease inhibitors also encode insecticide resistance tested in plants and crops and will be soon be commercially feasible in the upcoming future (Malone et al., 2008). Some other lepidopteran-active *Bt* toxins, Cry1F and Cry2Ab2, are almost commercialised, and are represented as single variety pyramid genes (Malone et al., 2008). Maize, cotton, potato and rice have been transformed with *cry* genes that code for proteins which are highly effective against the most important insects and pests (Heinrichs, 1986).

Rice is the staple food crop in India, China and for more than half of the globe's population. Genetically modified insects resistant rice, *Oryza sativa* was only produced and commercialized in China at first because of the markable insects' pest's status of stem borers and leaf folders in rice germplasm (Chen et al., 2010). The major and most commercially profitable advantage of transgenic crops is reduced use of synthetic insecticides (Malone et al., 2008). Insect resistant maize plant has also been developed and commercialized (Hellmich et al., 2008). Various seed companies have commercialized new transgenic *Zea Mays* OR *Bt* Maize (Maize) hybrid resistant to European Corn Borer (ECB).

Figure 2. Systematic diagram showing genetic modifications in several plant species

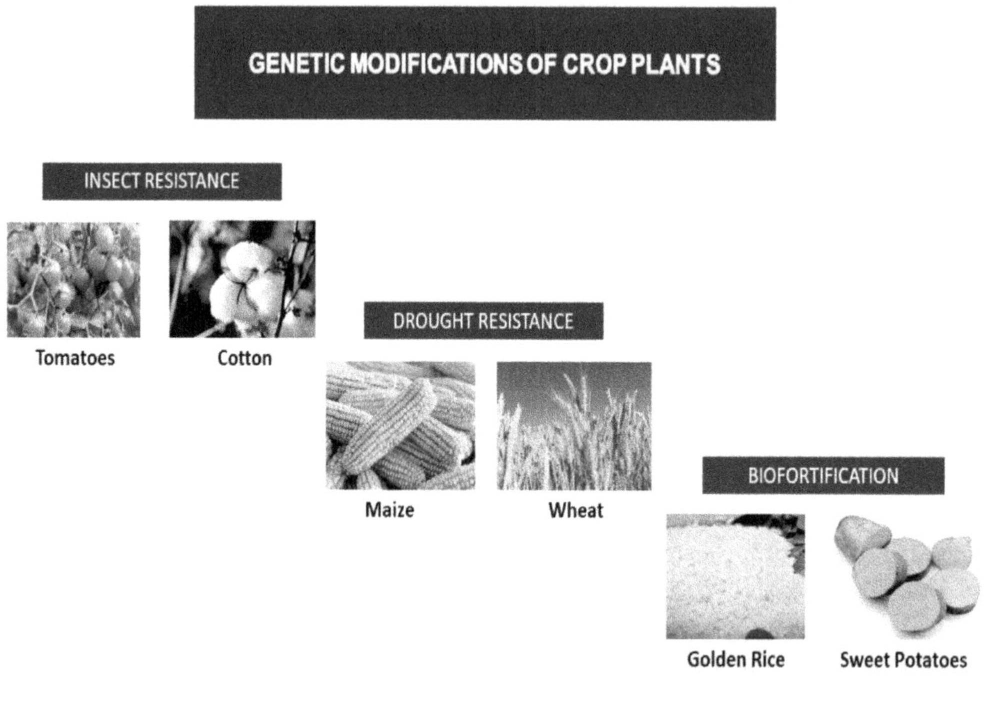

Drought Resistance

Drought resistance is an important trait in crops because drought is the most common yield limiting factor almost wherever the crop is grown. Unavailability or less water available for crop yield destroys the majority of farmed regions all over the world. Evaluation for drought tolerance is difficult and requires a large investment in testing over locations and years (Teran and Singh, 2002). In growing plant, drought condition can appear at any life stage and can remarkably lower the plant's productivity to a great extent depending on the time and intensity of drought condition. If it occurs at reproductive stage, crop yield is almost 50% reduced. Drought resistance are generally related to leaf like leaf rolling, stomatal density or physiological traits like Abscisic Acid content (ABA), relative water content and various root traits as well. Genetic material is an important consideration in breeding for drought tolerance. A very exciting progress has been made by the breeders for the development of drought tolerant crops (Hu and Xiong, 2013).

Techniques to transform gene required identification of the target gene responsible for drought resistance and their transfer. Although many efforts have been made for developing drought resistant crops, the success rate of this is extremely low because of lack of efforts, lack of screening methods, lack of knowledge and negative impacts on crop plants (Mitra, 2001). One such crop plant is maize. Grain yield depends on various factors including adequate water supply, nutrient supply, vigorous growth etc. Maize is seen to be readily affected by drought stress. Accumulation of abscisic acid may increase the rate of survival for the plant but decreases its productivity (Leung and Giraudat, 1998).

Biofortification

More than half of the world's population suffers from micronutrient malnutrition. It is a major health problem, especially in growing countries. A technique has been introduced for improvising the micronutrient content of staple foods through crop breeding. This technique is called biofortification. It might be considered to be a pro-poor, pro-rural, agriculture-based intervention to lessen the health burden of micronutrient malnutrition (Steur et al., 2010). For other micronutrient interventions like supplementing, diversifying diet, biofortification is treated as tremendous alternative (Steur et al., 2012). Three things must be accurately fulfilled for the success of Biofortification method and they are First, high nutrient content must be combined with high yields and high profitability to make the breeding successful. Second, efficacy must be demonstrated—the status of micronutrients in humans much improve and increase after consuming biofortified crops or products normally.

Some advantages of biofortification technique are (Bouis et al., 2011) –

- Reaching the malnourished in rural areas.
- Once a crop is biofortified and made stable it is highly sustainable.
- It is much low in cost and is thus, very cost effective.
- Biofortification helps us to reach out to under-nourished and malnourished people, who have less or no access to commercialized fortified food in market in rural areas and provide them with fortified foods.
- It provides surety that the daily intake of a consistent and large amount of food staples by all members of the family has increased.

The best and most concrete example of biofortification is the rice. It has been fortified with more iron, zinc, provitamin A and folate (Bouis et al., 2011). Iron deficiency anaemia, is a severe matter of concern globally. Reproductive age of women is mostly the age when they are highly deficient with iron, with anaemia prevalence estimates of 44% in developing countries. A study was conducted, 32% of women between 15 and 49 y of age are anaemic and as many as 75% may be iron deficient. Introduction of multi-biofortified rice or Golden rice has lowered the burden almost 46% (Steur et al., 2012).

Although, it has a few disadvantages too as varying impact throughout the lifecycle and a lot of time is required to develop a fortified crop, almost a decade and more to build up storage bodies (Bouis et al., 2011).

HYBRID SEED PRODUCTION

In hybrid seed technology, hybrid seed is produced that show the inferior traits then parents via cross pollination of diversely related two pure lines showing desire traits. Many methods can be used during hybrid seed production to prevent self-pollination of the female line: mechanical removal of anthers or male flowers, application of male-specific gametocides, or use of genetic cytoplasmic or nuclear-encoded male sterility. In Cytoplasmic male-sterile (CMS) lines, the male sterility is inherited as a dominant whereas maternally has transmitted trait as a result of mutation in their mitochondrial genome. "The CMS can be used for hybrid seed production as shown in Figure 3, only if (1) CMS mutants are available in a given crop; (2) (nuclear) restorer genes are available to restore the fertility of the CMS lines when the seed is the harvested product; and (3) the CMS mutation is not associated with a yield penalty (Perez-Prat & Van Lookeren Campagne, 2002)". CMS mutants are widely used for hybrid seed production despite of all limitations in important broad-acreage crops such as rice, sorghum and sunflower.

Hybrid seed are produced by crossing between two genetically dissimilar parents. In "crossing, pollen from male parent (Pollen parent) will pollinate, fertilize and set seeds in female (seed parent) to produce F1 hybrid seeds". For hybrid production, process of crossing between two parents is vital which leads to heterosis. In process of crossing self pollinated it's difficult to cross whereas it's easier just in case of cross pollinated crops. The characteristics of the resulting plants, such as better yield, greater uniformity, improved colour, disease resistance are often advance via hybrid seed production.

New hybrid breeding techniques allow greater genetic diversity to be introduced to varieties leading to enhanced levels of success in producing desirable agronomic characteristics such as oil yield, hybrid vigour, wider sowing window, yield advantage, reduced seed rates etc. In hybrid seed production the breeders have different responsibilities such as:

- To develop inbred lines
- Identification of specific parental lines
- To develop system for pollen control

As well as breeders and producers faces some problems as:

- Maintenance of parental lines
- Separation of male and female reproductive organs
- Pollination

Figure 3. Different crops produced by using hybrid seed technology.

Biotechnology has added new possibilities to obtain male-sterile plants, broadening the potential to produce hybrid seeds for different crops as shown in Fig. 4. Biotechnology has enabled the development of several new pollination control systems that could be useful for hybrid seed production. However, for most of them, their potential application for the commercial production of hybrids is limited by the inability to propagate the male-sterile female parent line in an efficient and cost-effective way. On-going and future research should take into consideration the importance of developing strategies to propagate the male-sterile lines generated because female parent propagation is, for many crops, the limiting factor for the production of hybrids on a large scale.

BIOFERTILIZERS AND BIOPESTICIDES

The rise in global population, increases demand for food supply that has motivated scientists and engineers to design and construct new technology to boost agricultural production (Mastronardi et al., 2015). With restricted availability of land resources and water supply, increased in agricultural growth can be achieved through good agronomy and effective utilization of modern technology. Advancement in agronomical method lays down the stress of farmers to meet up the demand of market through use of more effective biofertilizers and biopesticides (Table 1). In last few decades, the role of biofertilizers and biopesticides in crop protection has gained momentum as alternatives to synthetic pesticides and fertilizers. However, biofertilizers and biopesticides have not attended their desired level of application because of several problems in terms of high solubility, effectiveness, stability, enhanced target activity with effective concentration, delivery systems and field applications.

In the last few decades, nano-biopesticides have been one such promising field of research and development exploring diverse means for targeted pest detection, treatment, and control. From its point of conceptualization, the knowledge landscape in nanotechnology has rapidly metamorphosed and penetrated almost every aspect of our lives. In living system, they should possess a great ability in targeted delivery of nutrients. In order, to achieve their target of loading by desired nutrients in living system, they must follow the respective ways:

- adsorption on nanoparticles of desired biopesticides and biofertilizers;
- attachment on the nanoparticles;
- encapsulation in nanoparticulate;
- entrapment in nanoparticles

In recent times, nano-biopesticides have attracted the attention of researchers in academics and industry alike. "It is to be appreciated that the "innovation value chain" is integrally linked with comprehensive management of "Intellectual Property Rights" (IPR), as the system of IPR provides a structured and balanced framework for responsible governance of knowledge, including knowledge ownership, equitable knowledge sharing, owned-knowledge transactions with fair benefit sharing, and productive commercialization of innovations for societal progress (Ganguli, 2019).

Table 1. Types of biofertilizers commonly used (Pathak and Kumar, 2016)

S. No.	Biofertilizers	Character specification requirement
1.	*Rhizobium*	All species listed on the packet must show efficient nodulation
2.	*Azotobacter*	Atleast the strain should be capable of fixing 10 mg of nitrogen per g of sucrose consumed
3.	*Azospirillum*	Formation of white pellicle in semisolid N-free bromothymol blue media
4.	PSB	The strain should have phosphate-solubilizing capacity in the range of minimum 30%, when tested spectrophotometrically. In terms of zone formation, minimum 5 mm solubilization zone in prescribed media having at least 3 mm thickness

BIO-FEED FOR LIVESTOCK INDUSTRY

In agricultural production, agricultural and food-industry remains comprise a foremost proportion (almost 30%) worldwide (Figure 4, Table 2). These remain wastes of agricultural and food-industry comprise mainly of sugar-industry wastes, fruit and vegetable wastes, lignocellulosic materials, as well as animal and fisheries refuse and by-products (Ajila et al., 2012). Major and valuable waste of agro residues present potential solutions to problems of animal nutrition worldwide and supply protein and calories, if suitable technologies can be used for their valorisation by nutrient enrichment. In traditional as well as modern ways demand for food supply increased. Therefore, modern science research techniques must emphasize on the management of wastes, its processing technology, and subsequent feeding value for livestock.

The nonconventional food resources mainly include feed stuff such as single-cell proteins, feed materials derived from agro-industrial by-products of plant origin, palm press fibre (oil palm by-products), poor-quality cellulosic roughages from farm residues, such as slaughter house by-products and by-products from processing of sugar, cereal grains, citrus fruits and vegetables from the processing of food for human consumption (Devendra, 1987).

Figure 4. Systematic diagram represents general animal feed system in live-stock farms

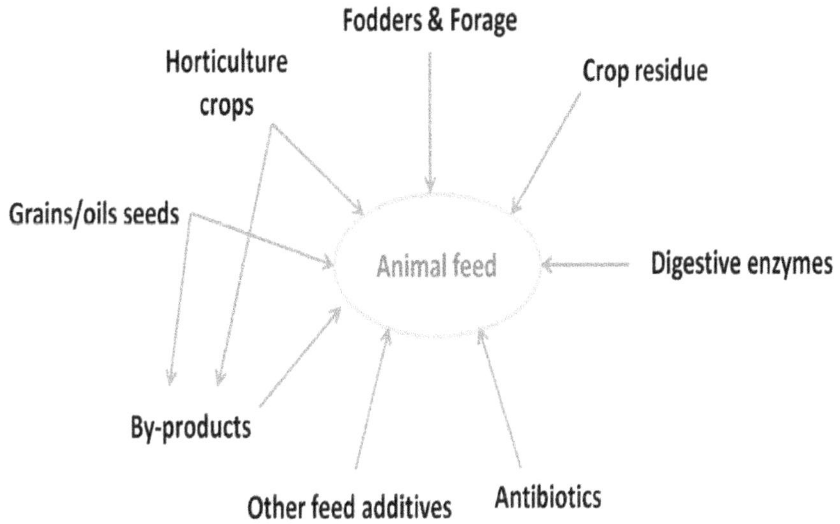

Table 2. Utilization of agro-industrial and nonconventional feed resources as animal feed

S.No.	Feed Source	Characteristics	Animals
1.	Energy and protein concentrates (e.g. rice bran, coconut cake, soybean meal, poultry litter)	Increase energy and increase protein	Poultry, pigs, ducks, cattle
2.	Good-quality crop residues (cassava peels, cereal-grain waste, animal waste etc)	Increase protein and increase energy	Pigs, ducks, cattle
3.	Medium-quality crop remains	Average proteins	Pigs, ruminants
4.	Low-quality crop remains	Little protein and increase fiber	Ruminants

PLANT BASED DRUGS AND MEDICINES

The most important and efficient source of drugs and their new leads is Plant. Many anti-cancer and anti-infectious drugs and agents have been developed from plants and they sure contribute more to new clinical trials (Saklani and Kutty, 2008). For pharmacological research, plants have always been the preferable choice. Plants can be used for therapeutic agents from their bioactive phytocompounds as well as contribute to the synthesis of drugs or models (Ahmad et al., 2014). Although, all the focus of pharmaceutical industries shifted to synthetic drugs as the plant or nature-based drugs developing method showed some difficulties. But eventually, unwanted side-effects, Toxic effects, inefficiency and several other problems were monitored in synthetic drugs. They did not meet the expected results. This became the reason for the decline in number of new drugs reaching the market (Saklani and Kutty, 2008).

There are various plant-derived products being used in various therapeutic categories as drugs. Plant-based drugs and many herbal preparations possess different alternating effects on immune system and have much beneficial immune-modulatory effects (Patwardhan and Gautam, 2005).

Table 3. Different plant sources and drugs inherited from them

Plant Source	Drug/Medicine	Clinical/Medical Use
Digitalis lanata	Acetyldigoxin	Cardiotonic
Berberis vulgaris	Berberine	Bacillary Dysentery
Camellia sinensis	Caffeine	CNS Stimulant
Papaver somniferum	Codeine	Analgesic
Colchicum atumnale	Colchicine	Anti-tumor Agent
Hydrangea macrophylla	Phyllodulcin	Sweetener
Taxus bravifolia	Taxol	Anti-tumor Agent
Camptothecaacuminata	Topotecan	Anti-cancer Agent
Catharanthus roseus	Vinblastine	Anti-leukemic Agent
Papaver somniferum	Morphine	Pain-killer
Artemesiaannua	Artemisinin	Anti-Malarial

Plant-Based Drugs or medicines are use for treatment and cure of various infectious, parasitic, oncological, neurological, pain, inflammatory, metabolic and cardiac related diseases and problems. For example, Artemisone/Artemifon is a drug for malaria, Calanolide A for HIV coumarin, Umbelliferone for hepatitis B & C. Dexanabinol is a drug used for dreadful brain injuries and also as an antioxidant, anti-inflammatory (Table 3).

For Cardiac problems, drugs like digoxin, sennosides, forskolin are used, An α-glucosidase inhibitors such as miglitol is used for diabetes mellitus (Ahmad et al., 2014). P-57 (P-57AS3) is a functional food product that helps reducing calorie intake in overweight. Flavocoxid extractis used for osteoarthritis, Grazax for hay fever, for the symptoms of Chronic Hepatitis C (CHC). Napabucasin, a naphthoquinone, as an antileukemic agent (Rao and Kingston, 1982). CA-1P (OXi4503), for the treating myeloid leukemia (Khazir et al., 2014).

Vaccines are also an important part of pharmaceutical industry. But for the production and commercialization of vaccines or any clinical drug and medicine, a complete Business plan is required. This business plan requires collaborations, a company with a proper board. After this, a proper well studied business plan is required and at last comes Financing. Financing is done in three consecutive investment stages. Initial financing most often includes money from all of the founders, investment from family and friends, research grants, and in-kind donations from an affiliated university or research institution. Then, these first stage investor seek for angel investors, who are wealthy individuals or groups who are looking for start-up investment opportunities that in-turn allows them huge profit and so the new enterprise become successful. And last third level of investment includes venture capital, partnerships, and entering into the stock market. Entry into a public stock market is a major step for a new company

(MacDonald et al., 2015). After all this, before developing a product or when it is in research phase, it is also required to check Market viability (Miralpeix et al., 2014).

FLORAL INDUSTRY

Over tha past few decades, plants have been genetically engineered and with billions of hectares cultivated, it has brought great success in Scientific, Humanitarian and Commercial sectors. Commodity crops like corn, cotton, canola, soybean, sugar beet and alfalfa etc came to light but speciality crops like fruits, nuts, vegetables and ornamental plants haven't been presented duly. Especially, the ornamental plants which have also been genetically engineered are completely ignored. Large number of laboratories all over the world arc conducting research on flowers like carnation, rose, chrysanthemum and petunia and their traits (Roh and Lawson, 1992).

Cupressus 'Goldcrest' with lemon-scented light green foliage, *Achimenes longiflora*, D.C., *Achimens*, *Achimentha* (Roh and Lawson, 1989), *Columnea* hybrids, *Nemantanthus* and *Sinningia cardinalis* are some example of ornamental plants which have been genetically engineered and grown various countries like China, Japan and some major parts of the world (Harun et al., 2015).

A recently introduced genetic engineering approach is indoor farming. Indoor farming is applied to upgrade the growth of the plant, and control flowering. This method controls the length of stem, period of flower growth which are otherwise crucial for plant factory. Different light spectrum has different effect on plant growth. In this technique, light source is artificially made as it is the most important factor for plant growth. For example, flowering in a plant is promoted by red light while stem growth is suppressed by blue light. The most important requirement in this setup is the proper intensity of light and facilitating growth environment (Harun et al., 2015; Rabara et al., 2017).

STEPS FOR LAB TO MARKET IN AGRICULTURAL BIOTECHNOLOGY

In economic growth of many countries especially developed countries, agricultural biotechnology is seen as the major pillar of growth. Various products of agricultural biotechnology such as insect resistant crops, herbicide resistant crops, biopesticides, biofertilizers, biosensors, GM crops, hybrid seeds etc. are currently available in market and nobody is aware about them. The reason behind the unawareness of the agricultural biotechnology products maybe they are expensive, and consumer awareness is less.

The seeds of agricultural biotechnology product are synthesised in laboratory and from laboratory they are transfer to market for social-economic impacts as depicted in Figure. 5. "The transfer, distribution and the flow of goods and services from laboratory to market in respect of producer to consumer is defined as marketing". The performance of business activities depends upon the marketing strategies. The efficient business step and management techniques via laboratory to market give the final consumption and benefits to the products/ seeds at industry level.

Figure 5. Schematic diagram showing lab to market steps in agriculture biotechnology

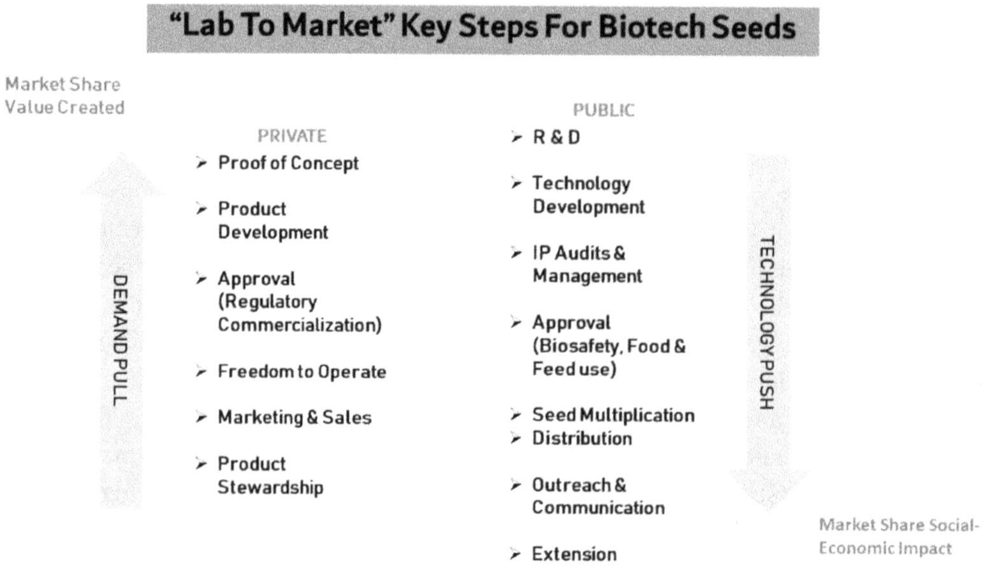

CONCLUSION

With the help of biotechnology, agriculture has moved to a different level of height and has overcome the food availability requirements in such rapidly growing population all around the world. Various modern has identified techniques like micropropagation, somatic embryogenesis is adding up to a great extent for the production of diseases free plants and also in large quantities. For improving quality of food, the crops are added with nutritious value and several genetic modifications are made for the better growth and results. The genetically modified or GM crops is one such boom for preparing food stocks for the over growing population. The plants can be made to delete or inherit any trait using gene transfer to produce better quality food, in large quantities and disease free. Use of nanoparticles also ensures the enhancement in food quality and rapidness in growth of a particular plant or species to meet the needs.

ACKNOWLEDGMENT

This study was funded by DBT BIG-BIRAC Ref No. BIRAC/CCAMP0723/BIG-13/18 and DST major project entitled "Low Cost-Renewable Energy Driven (LC-RED) Water Treatment Solution Centre" Ref No. DST/TM/WTI/WIC/2K17/124. We acknowledged Prof. Aditya Shastri for providing research amenities and bioinformatics centre for providing computational facilities.

REFERENCES

Agarwal, G., Carcache, P. J. B., Addo, E. M., & Kinghorn, A. D. (2019). Current status and contemporary approaches to the discovery of antitumor agents from higher plants. *Biotechnology Advances*, *38*, 1–27.

Ahmad, I., Husain, F. M., Maheshwari, M., & Zahin, M. (2014). Medicinal plants and phytocompounds: a potential source of novel antibiofilm agents. In *Antibiofilm agents* (pp. 205–232). Springer. doi:10.1007/978-3-642-53833-9_10

Ajila, C. M., Brar, S. K., Verma, M., Tyagi, R. D., Godbout, S., & Valéro, J. R. (2012). Bio-processing of agro-byproducts to animal feed. *Critical Reviews in Biotechnology*, *32*(4), 382–400. doi:10.3109/07388551.2012.659172

Bakshi, A. (2003). Potential adverse health effects of genetically modified crops. *Journal of Toxicology and Environmental Health. Part B*, *6*(3), 211–225.

Bouis, H. E., Hotz, C., McClafferty, B., Meenakshi, J. V., & Pfeiffer, W. H. (2011). Biofortification: A new tool to reduce micronutrient malnutrition. *Food and Nutrition Bulletin*, *32*(1), S31–S40. doi:10.1177/15648265110321S105

Camps, P., & Munoz-Torrero, D. (2002). Cholinergic drugs in pharmacotherapy of Alzheimer's disease. *Mini-Reviews in Medicinal Chemistry*, *2*(1), 11–25. doi:10.2174/1389557023406638

Carsrud, A. L., Brännback, M., & Renko, M. (2008). Strategy and strategic thinking in biotechnology entrepreneurship. In *Handbook of bioentrepreneurship* (pp. 83–103). Springer. doi:10.1007/978-0-387-48345-0_5

Chakravarty, B. (2011). Trends in mushroom cultivation and breeding. *Australian Journal of Agricultural Engineering*, *2*(4), 102.

Chen, M., Shelton, A., & Ye, G. Y. (2011). Insect-resistant genetically modified rice in China: From research to commercialization. *Annual Review of Entomology*, *56*(1), 81–101. doi:10.1146/annurev-ento-120709-144810

Chen, T. H. H., Thompson, B. G., & Gerson, D. F. (1987). In vitro production of alfalfa somatic embryos in fermentation systems. *Journal of Fermentation Technology*, *65*(3), 353–357. doi:10.1016/0385-6380(87)90100-2

Collins, J. (2009). *Good to Great-(Why Some Companies Make the Leap and others Don't)*. Academic Press.

Collonnier, C., Fock, I., Kashyap, V., Rotino, G. L., Daunay, M. C., Lian, Y., Mariska, I. K., Rajam, M. V., Servaes, A., Ducreux, G., & Sihachakr, D. (2001). Applications of biotechnology in eggplant. *Plant Cell, Tissue and Organ Culture*, *65*(2), 91–107. doi:10.1023/A:1010674425536

Conner, A. J., Glare, T. R., & Nap, J. P. (2003). The release of genetically modified crops into the environment: Part II. Overview of ecological risk assessment. *The Plant Journal*, *33*(1), 19–46. doi:10.1046/j.0960-7412.2002.001607.x

De Steur, H., Gellynck, X., Blancquaert, D., Lambert, W., Van Der Straeten, D., & Qaim, M. (2012). Potential impact and cost-effectiveness of multi-biofortified rice in China. *New Biotechnology*, *29*(3), 432–442. doi:10.1016/j.nbt.2011.11.012

De Steur, H., Gellynck, X., Storozhenko, S., Liqun, G., Lambert, W., Van Der Straeten, D., & Viaene, J. (2010). The health benefits of folate biofortified rice in China. *Nature Biotechnology*, *28*(6), 554–556. doi:10.1038/nbt0610-554

Devendra, C. (1987). *Expanding the utilisation of agro-industrial by-products and non-conventional feed resources in Asia*. Academic Press.

Ferré, J., Van Rie, J., & MacIntosh, S. C. (2008). Insecticidal genetically modified crops and insect resistance management (IRM). In *Integration of insect-resistant genetically modified crops within IPM programs* (pp. 41–85). Springer. doi:10.1007/978-1-4020-8373-0_3

Fischer, K., Ekener-Petersen, E., Rydhmer, L., & Björnberg, K. E. (2015). Social impacts of GM crops in agriculture: A systematic literature review. *Sustainability*, *7*(7), 8598–8620. doi:10.3390u7078598

Hamill, J. D., Prescott, A., & Martin, C. (1987). Assessment of the efficiency of cotransformation of the T-DNA of disarmed binary vectors derived from Agrobacterium tumefaciens and the T-DNA of A. rhizogenes. *Plant Molecular Biology*, *9*(6), 573–584. doi:10.1007/BF00020534

Harun, A. N., Ahmad, R., & Mohamed, N. (2015, May). Plant growth optimization using variable intensity and Far Red LED treatment in indoor farming. In *2015 International Conference on Smart Sensors and Application (ICSSA)* (pp. 92-97). IEEE. 10.1109/ICSSA.2015.7322517

Heinrichs, E. A. (1986). Perspectives and directions for the continued development of insect-resistant rice varieties. *Agriculture, Ecosystems & Environment*, *18*(1), 9–36. doi:10.1016/0167-8809(86)90172-6

Hellmich, R. L., Albajes, R., Bergvinson, D., Prasifka, J. R., Wang, Z. Y., & Weiss, M. J. (2008). The present and future role of insect-resistant genetically modified maize in IPM. In *Integration of insect-resistant genetically modified crops within IPM programs* (pp. 119–158). Springer. doi:10.1007/978-1-4020-8373-0_5

Hu, H., & Xiong, L. (2014). Genetic engineering and breeding of drought-resistant crops. *Annual Review of Plant Biology*, *65*(1), 715–741. doi:10.1146/annurev-arplant-050213-040000

Ismail, K., Azhar, T. T., Yong, C. Y., Aslan, A. S., Omar, W. Z., Majid, I., & Ajagbe, A. M. (2012). Problems on commercialization of genetically modified crops in Malaysia. *Procedia: Social and Behavioral Sciences*, *40*, 353–357. doi:10.1016/j.sbspro.2012.03.199

Kashman, Y., Gustafson, K. R., Fuller, R. W., Cardellina, J. H. II, McMahon, J. B., Currens, M. J., ... Boyd, M. R. (1992). The calanolides, a novel HIV-inhibitory class of coumarin derivatives from the tropical rainforest tree, Calophyllumlanigerum. *Journal of Medicinal Chemistry*, *35*(15), 2735–2743. doi:10.1021/jm00093a004

Kashyap, V., Kumar, S. V., Collonnier, C., Fusari, F., Haicour, R., Rotino, G. L., ... Rajam, M. V. (2003). Biotechnology of eggplant. *Scientia Horticulturae*, *97*(1), 1–25. doi:10.1016/S0304-4238(02)00140-1

Klaine, S. J., Alvarez, P. J., Batley, G. E., Fernandes, T. F., Handy, R. D., Lyon, D. Y., & Lead, J. R. (2008). Nanomaterials in the environment: Behavior, fate, bioavailability, and effects. *Environmental Toxicology and Chemistry: An International Journal*, *27*(9), 1825–1851. doi:10.1897/08-090.1

Leung, J., & Giraudat, J. (1998). Abscisic acid signal transduction. *Annual Review of Plant Biology, 49*(1), 199–222. doi:10.1146/annurev.arplant.49.1.199

MacDonald, J., Doshi, K., Dussault, M., Hall, J. C., Holbrook, L., Jones, G., ... McLean, M. D. (2015). Bringing plant-based veterinary vaccines to market: Managing regulatory and commercial hurdles. *Biotechnology Advances, 33*(8), 1572–1581. doi:10.1016/j.biotechadv.2015.07.007

Malone, L. A., Gatehouse, A. M., & Barratt, B. I. (2008). Beyond Bt: alternative strategies for insect-resistant genetically modified crops. In *Integration of insect-resistant genetically modified crops within IPM programs* (pp. 357–417). Springer. doi:10.1007/978-1-4020-8373-0_13

Mastronardi, E., Tsae, P., Zhang, X., Monreal, C., & DeRosa, M. C. (2015). Strategic role of nanotechnology in fertilizers: potential and limitations. In *Nanotechnologies in food and agriculture* (pp. 25–67). Springer. doi:10.1007/978-3-319-14024-7_2

Miralpeix, B., Sabalza, M., Twyman, R. M., Capell, T., & Christou, P. (2014). Strategic patent analysis in plant biotechnology: Terpenoid indole alkaloid metabolic engineering as a case study. *Plant Biotechnology Journal, 12*(2), 117–134. doi:10.1111/pbi.12134

Mitra, J. (2001). Genetics and genetic improvement of drought resistance in crop plants. *Current Science*, 758–763.

Murashige, T. (1974). Plant propagation through tissue cultures. *Annual Review of Plant Physiology, 25*(1), 135-166.

Nap, J. P., Metz, P. L., Escaler, M., & Conner, A. J. (2003). The release of genetically modified crops into the environment: Part I. Overview of current status and regulations. *The Plant Journal, 33*(1), 1–18. doi:10.1046/j.0960-7412.2003.01602.x

Nestel, P., Bouis, H. E., Meenakshi, J. V., & Pfeiffer, W. (2006). Biofortification of staple food crops. *The Journal of Nutrition, 136*(4), 1064–1067. doi:10.1093/jn/136.4.1064

Pathak, D. V., & Kumar, M. (2016). Microbial inoculants as biofertilizers and biopesticides. In *Microbial inoculants in sustainable agricultural productivity* (pp. 197–209). Springer. doi:10.1007/978-81-322-2647-5_11

Patwardhan, B., & Gautam, M. (2005). Botanical immunodrugs: Scope and opportunities. *Drug Discovery Today, 10*(7), 495–502. doi:10.1016/S1359-6446(04)03357-4

Perez-Prat, E., & van Lookeren Campagne, M. M. (2002). Hybrid seed production and the challenge of propagating male-sterile plants. *Trends in Plant Science, 7*(5), 199–203. doi:10.1016/S1360-1385(02)02252-5

Prakash, J. (1989). Large-Scale Production of Plants through Micropropagation: Problems, Prospects and Opportunities for India. In *Applications of Biotechnology in Forestry and Horticulture* (pp. 265–274). Springer. doi:10.1007/978-1-4684-1321-2_21

Qaim, M., & De Janvry, A. (2003). Genetically modified crops, corporate pricing strategies, and farmers' adoption: The case of Bt cotton in Argentina. *American Journal of Agricultural Economics, 85*(4), 814–828. doi:10.1111/1467-8276.00490

Qaim, M., & Zilberman, D. (2003). Yield effects of genetically modified crops in developing countries. *Science*, *299*(5608), 900–902. doi:10.1126cience.1080609

Rabara, R. C., Behrman, G., Timbol, T., & Rushton, P. J. (2017). Effect of spectral quality of monochromatic LED lights on the growth of artichoke seedlings. *Frontiers in Plant Science*, *8*, 190. doi:10.3389/fpls.2017.00190

Raman, C. D., & Kanmani, S. (2016). Textile dye degradation using nano zero valent iron: A review. *Journal of Environmental Management*, *177*, 341–355. doi:10.1016/j.jenvman.2016.04.034

Rao, M. M., & Kingston, D. G. (1982). Plant anticancer agents. XII. Isolation and structure elucidation of new cytotoxic quinones from Tabebuia cassinoides. *Journal of Natural Products*, *45*(5), 600–604. doi:10.1021/np50023a014

Roh, M. S., & Lawson, R. H. (1992). Propagation and transplant production technology of new floral crops. In *Transplant Production Systems* (pp. 1–20). Springer. doi:10.1007/978-94-011-2785-1_1

Sahayaraj, K. (2014). Nanotechnology and plant biopesticides: an overview. In *Advances in Plant Biopesticides* (pp. 279–293). Springer. doi:10.1007/978-81-322-2006-0_14

Sajc, L., Grubisic, D., & Vunjak-Novakovic, G. (2000). Bioreactors for plant engineering: An outlook for further research. *Biochemical Engineering Journal*, *4*(2), 89–99. doi:10.1016/S1369-703X(99)00035-2

Saklani, A., & Kutty, S. K. (2008). Plant-derived compounds in clinical trials. *Drug Discovery Today*, *13*(3-4), 161–171. doi:10.1016/j.drudis.2007.10.010

Salgaller, M. L., & Marincola, F. M. (2010). *Biotechnology entrepreneurship-where no research has gone before*. Academic Press.

Shimasaki, C. (2014). What is Biotechnology Entrepreneurship? In *Biotechnology Entrepreneurship* (pp. 45–56). Academic Press. doi:10.1016/B978-0-12-404730-3.00004-X

Terán, H., & Singh, S. P. (2002). Comparison of sources and lines selected for drought resistance in common bean. *Crop Science*, *42*(1), 64–70. doi:10.2135/cropsci2002.0064

Veeresham, C. (2012). *Natural products derived from plants as a source of drugs*. Academic Press.

Wang, S., Just, D. R., & Pinstrup-Andersen, P. (2008). Bt-cotton and secondary pests. *International Journal of Biotechnology*, *10*(2/3), 113. doi:10.1504/IJBT.2008.018348

Xia, H., Chen, L., Wang, F., & Lu, B. R. (2010). Yield benefit and underlying cost of insect-resistance transgenic rice: Implication in breeding and deploying transgenic crops. *Field Crops Research*, *118*(3), 215–220. doi:10.1016/j.fcr.2010.05.008

Yesil-Celiktas, O., Gurel, A., & Vardar-Sukan, F. (2010). Large scale cultivation of plant cell and tissue culture in bioreactors. *Transworld Research Network*, *37*(661), 2.

Chapter 12
Bioentrepreneurship in Medical Biotechnology:
Starting, Managing, and Leading Innovative Technologies

Neeti Sharma
Banasthali University, India

ABSTRACT

Being a developing sector, biotechnology combines both medical science and various facets of a sustainable environment. Scientific innovations from academics and industry contribute towards the rise of bioentrepreneurship across the world. Medical biotechnology helps the treatment and prevention of human diseases by using living cells and cell materials to research and produce pharmaceutical and diagnostic products. It requires incubation of research, product, and its yield for the improvement of humans to transform medical research into an entrepreneurial industry. Biotechnology provides an opportunity for entrepreneurs to harness the power of genomics for the development and marketing of new therapeutics. These opportunities allow entrepreneurs to visualize the creation of both disruptive business and disruptive technologies for today's business models. This chapter will summarize multiple features of entrepreneurship in the biotechnology industry in combination with other industries and will explain the significance of bio-entrepreneurship in the field of medical biotechnology.

INTRODUCTION

This chapter explains the business need of the rapidly growing area of biotechnology management. Its main emphasis is on the field of biotechnology entrepreneurship and innovation. It addresses the most important theoretical and practical facets of entrepreneurship, concentrating mainly on the innovation strategies that support the growth of new biotechnology firms (NBFs) (Hine & Kapeleris, 2006).

DOI: 10.4018/978-1-7998-7411-9.ch012

Biotechnology describes the commercial application of biological species and approaches for the production of pharmaceutical, food and consumer goods (Oakey et al., 1990). Applications for biotechnology include, but are not limited to, bulk and specialist chemicals, health care, food and beverage goods, waste or emissions control, and agriculture (Sager, 2001). On the basis of these definitions, biotechnology entrepreneurship can be described as the inspiration, expertise and behaviour needed to effectively find and leverage business opportunities for the use, production and consumption of goods and services resulting from the use of biological organisms and processes (Gurau, 2021). Biotechnology remains an integral part of our lives in multiple ways. It is now regarded as a crucial knowledge-based organization that produces goods and processes for increasing global needs. Biotechnology provides latest solutions for economic, social and environmental areas of human life. (Roming & Ghidurus, 2019).

An "Entrepreneur" is one who reorganizes and manages only high-risk businesses in particular. An entrepreneur starts his own enterprise. He recognizes the potential of an opportunity, and then employs means and methods to extract maximum benefits out of that opportunity. Entrepreneurship is defined as the potential to develop, organize and run a business enterprise, in addition to all the unpredictability so that profit can be returned in future. A well-known example of entrepreneurship is that of launching a new business. Difference between Entrepreneur and Entrepreneurship is given in Figure 1 (Surbhi, 2020).

Figure 1. Difference between entrepreneur and entrepreneurship (Surbhi, 2020)

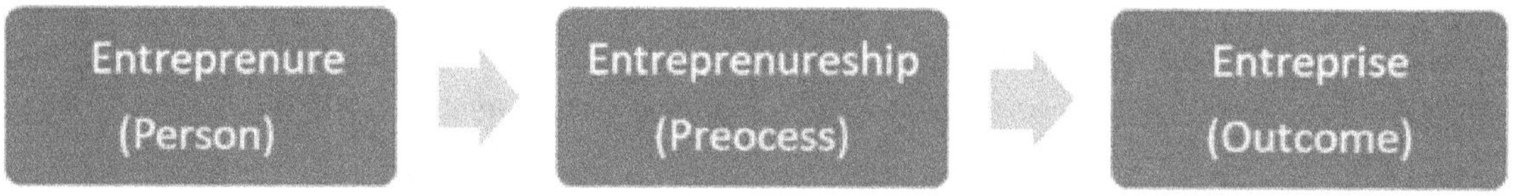

The two major factors required for the growth of biotechnology business are entrepreneurship and innovation. However, this growth is hampered due to lack of managers and researchers who have sufficient entrepreneurial and business skills in the biotechnology industry (Batterham, 2000; Sainsbury, 2002).

Entrepreneurial characteristics comprises of natural creativity, capability and desire to make decisions in the absence of solid data and a risk-taking temperament. Entrepreneurs are motivated by the desire of creating something new or building something tangible.

Process of Entrepreneurship

While companies are as different and special as the entrepreneurs who build them, most of them seem to be going through a process. The diagram given below describes the process through which most of them create their enterprise. Process of Entrepreneurship is given in Figure 2.

- The six steps of Entrepreneurship are as follows:
  - Idea Generation.
  - Developing Business Plan
  - Funding Raising
  - Promoting
  - Commencing

    - Harvesting.
- The entrepreneurial role encompasses the following responsibilities:
    - Perception of market opportunities
    - Gaining command over scarce resources
    - Purchasing inputs
    - Marketing the products
    - Dealing with bureaucrats
    - Managing human relations within the firm
    - Managing customer and supplier relations
    - Managing finance
    - Managing production
    - Acquiring and overseeing assembly of the factory
    - Industrial engineering
    - Upgrading process and product
    - Introducing new production techniques and products.

Figure 2. Process of entrepreneurship

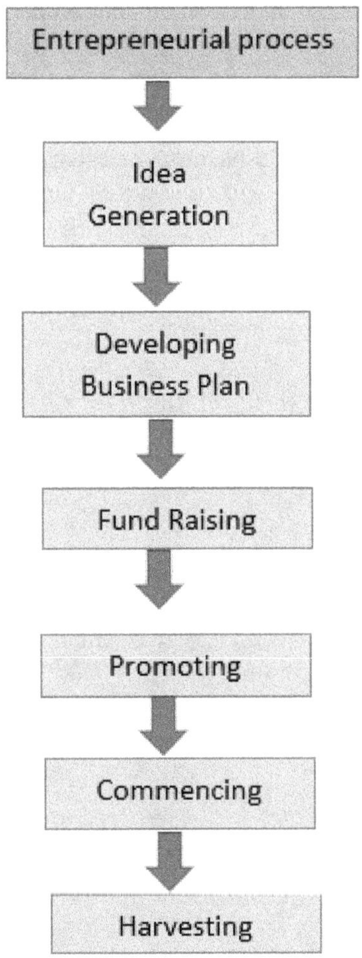

BIOENTREPRENEURSHIP

Biotechnology entrepreneurship is a combination of all the actions carried out by a group of people, working together over time, to create a business that commercialises life-changing goods through the convergence of science and corporate fields.

A biotechnology start-up or a bio start-up refers to a company manufacturing end-user product that require research and development. The majority of bio start-ups operate in different fields of healthcare technology, such as medical devices, diagnostic kits, pharmaceuticals etc. (Shahid & Azim, 2019). Entrepreneurship in biotechnology is the method of generating value through innovation in life sciences. It is known by several names such as bioscience entrepreneurship, life science entrepreneurship or bioscience enterprise (Meyers, 2008). It is primarily focussed on two distinct disciplines– Science and Business (Collins, 2009).

A single person can plan and complete a research project successfully. But developing and commercializing a biotechnology product, needs a business. Entrepreneurs in the biotechnology sector are the cornerstone of industry and the foundation of its potential innovation.

A biotechnology company cannot be visualized without the entrepreneurs. These entrepreneurs are driven by the belief that their commodity or service will positively impact the well-being of its consumers, and this belief pushes them to achieve their goals. Although all entrepreneurs possess a unique set of skills and abilities, what sets them apart is their unique perspective on the world around them. A biotechnological company is formed by integrating biology with industry, resulting in an uncertain business. This requires an entrepreneur to lead the business out of uncertainty in order to increase the company value. Therefore, a biotech pioneer must master the art of risk management. (Shimasaki,2020). Combining Biology and Business results in a business of uncertainty is given in Figure 3.

Figure 3. Combining biology and business results in a business of uncertainty. (Shimasaki,2020).

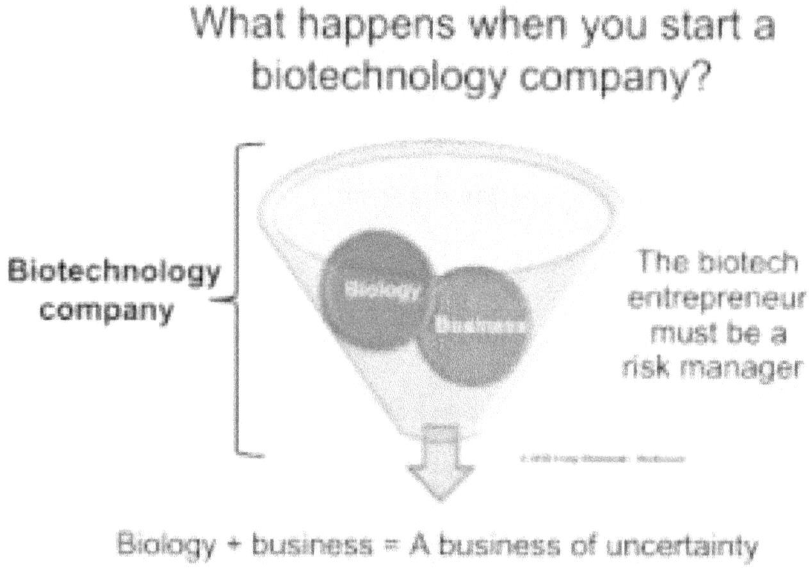

"Bioenterprise" refers to any business created from biological material and products (Shimasaki, 2014). Most medical and life-saving devices, efficient crops and advanced aircraft fuels have been developed and marketed through biotechnology companies.

From science to solutions is a realistic guide to launching and developing a life science business. as well as provides information for medical researchers who wish to make their tools accessible to as many people as possible (Salgaller, 2010). For such innovations including medical instruments or diagnostics, the risk is marginally smaller as they have shorter time spans and retail price tags. However, therapeutics are more common and their timeframe for commercialization is lengthy (usually > 5 years), but less expensive than the often-quoted $1-1.7B for a single medication from a major pharmaceutical company. (Janodia, 2007).

In contrast to the consumption of biotechnology-derived products, bioentrepreneurship is not uniformly practiced throughout the world. It is most common in the United States and Canada, with Europe narrowing the gap recently and Japan a distant third. Australia, Hong Kong, Korea, Singapore, China, and India are the next countries on the list (Persidis, 1997; Littlejohn, 2002).

MEDICAL BIOTECHNOLOGY

Medical biotechnology, also known as red biotechnology, is defined as the application of biological techniques to research and development of products in healthcare and medicine. Health practise has been influenced by the scientific advances in this and similar research fields. These advances have resulted in accurate tests for a more effective treatment of the disorder; molecular and proteomic tests for disease prevention; more reliable strategies for developing and producing medicines that are molecularly targeted and therefore practically more effective but less toxic; the ability for gene therapy to cure previously incurable diseases (Hsu et. al., 2018).

The medical aspects of biotechnology are discussed in medical biotechnology. It's commonly used in the manufacture of pharmaceuticals and other complex biological molecules that would be impossible to produce otherwise. Gene therapy, which is focused on disrupting the genetic development of living cells, is another application that has the potential to become a key tool for developing new treatments for a variety of inherited and acquired disorders in the future.

Stem cell technology is one of technology in the field of medical biotechnology; it is based on the idea of preserving genetic make-up as a whole and guiding its capacity to express itself for new therapeutic applications (EIB, 2002).

MEDICAL BIOTECHNOLOGY INNOVATION

Science based innovations in high-tech industries are growing at a rapid pace. This rate of innovation has come a long way from gradual innovations by occasional radical novelties to innovation cascades. These series of innovations are made up of a collection of intertwined progressive advances that can be monitored using scientific and technical measures such as patents and publications. Innovation cascades are important to companies, as they make the future less predictable. They are specifically interesting because these developments also make it easier to test a multitude of new business models (Niosi & McKelvey, 2018).

By 2020, the global demand is expected to be worth €513 billion. Biotechnology has grown into a promising area with new concepts, that will completely transform our view of medical care. Study of artificial intelligence (AI) data obtained from wearables and biosensors support clinicians in real-time tracking of medication outcomes and recommending changes; Antibiotics are transmitted to the precise site of inflammation by 3D bio printed nanorobots. Tissue Engineering repairs injured portions of the organs without the need for surgery; and Gene Therapy prevents many genetic diseases from even occurring.

Brief start-ups are based on innovations and provide an opportunity for employment, research and analytical progress to a nation. Innovation is a new idea that can meet all the requirements at once without any disadvantages. It is to be noted that such progress in biotechnology has benefitted multiple human studies such as Human Genome Project of 2003, which has shown that how disease related study, physiology, morphological studies become much easier (Srivastava et.al., 2016).

In the last few decades, developments in medical biotechnology have had a significant effect on millions of people's lives. Medical biotechnology has not only helped curing deadly diseases such as the Ebola outbreak in West Africa in 2014, it has also developed experimental techniques and vaccines such as comprehensive mapping of human DNA. Medical biotechnology is the study and manufacture of medicinal and diagnostic products that assist in the treatment and prevention of human diseases using living cells and cell materials. Some of the most recent fields of medical biotechnological innovation include breakthrough work in genetic testing, experimental drug delivery and artificial tissue development.

The country's dedication to health-care cost containment may interfere with its deeper commitment to medical technology innovation—drugs, medical equipment, diagnostic and therapeutic procedures, and administrative infrastructure. Medical science is related to growing health-care rates as it extends medicine's capabilities on a net basis. The opportunity to resolve the potential conflict is hindered by theoretical, methodological, structural, and political influences. These limitations must be challenged and resolved if sound policy solutions are to be formulated.

There are multiple areas of medical biotechnology innovation. Some of those are described below:

a. Biosensor
b. Three Dimensional (3-D) Bioprinting
c. Using CRISPR to Search for an HIV Cure
d. Virtual and augmented reading (VR &4AR) for surgery
e. Stem Cell Therapies
f. Human Genome Project
g. Nanotechnology
h. Targeted Cancer Therapies
i. HPV vaccine
j. Face Transplants
k. Nerve Regeneration
l. Nanozymes

a. Biosensor

A biosensor is an analytical device that transforms a biological response into an electrical signal (Mehrotra, 2016). Applications of biosensors is rising quickly in the field of medical science. There is a continuous increase in sophistication of medical technology. And biosensors will play a key role in shaping the industry over the next decade. Moreover, biosensors will transform the way we regulate our health since they can be calibrated and designed to monitor various biosignature such as blood pressure, pulse, breathing and body temperature. Biosensor is given in Figure 4.

Figure 4. Biosensor

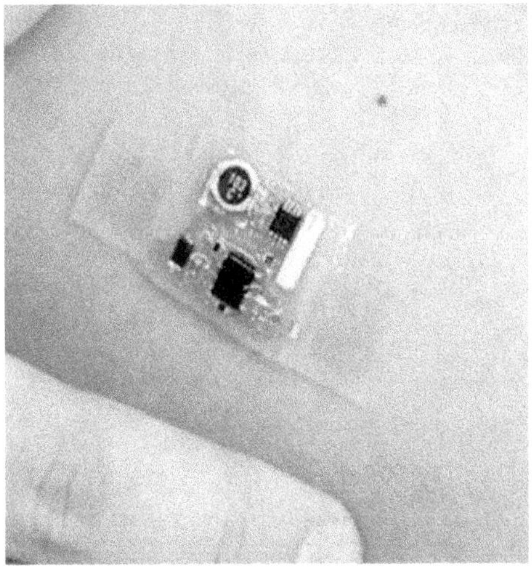

Sensible Medical is one of the leading biotech innovation company. They've designed and developed a vest monitor which helps in monitoring the amount of fluid in the lungs of patients with heart failure problem. This device will send an urgent alert to doctors at the hospital if it exceeds dangerous levels, which can save multiple lives (Milis, 2020).

b. Three Dimensional (3-D) Bioprinting

3-D bioprinting is another promising development in the field of biotech innovation. This technology can develop different human body parts such as heart valves, skin and cartilage for medical use, by using living cells. This is a promising technology which can create drugs and pills, in addition to entire organs such as hearts or livers that are grown from the body cells of a patient. The ability to print human organs will also be extended to the field of medical research and training, so that accurate samples can be provided for study and analysis. 3D Bioprinting is given in Figure 5.

c. Using CRISPR to Search for an HIV Cure

Another promising innovation in the field of medical biotechnology is Clustered Regular Interspaced Short Palindromic Repeats (CRISPR). This technology allows for genetic editing and shows the promise to cure cancer and multiple other deadly diseases. It is basically a gene editing technology which is simpler and faster than ever and has created various opportunities which go far beyond human health. For instance, in order to improve the resistance of food crops against diseases and environmental conditions, scientists are conducting various research with this technology. CRISPR Gene Editing is given in Figure 6.

Figure 5. 3D bioprinting

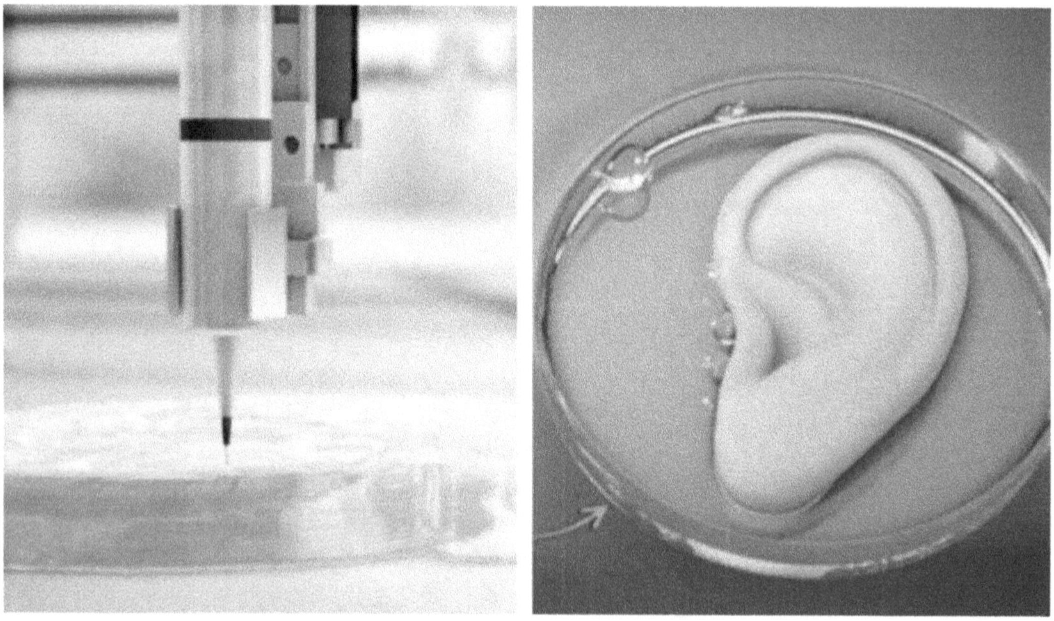

Figure 6. CRISPR gene editing

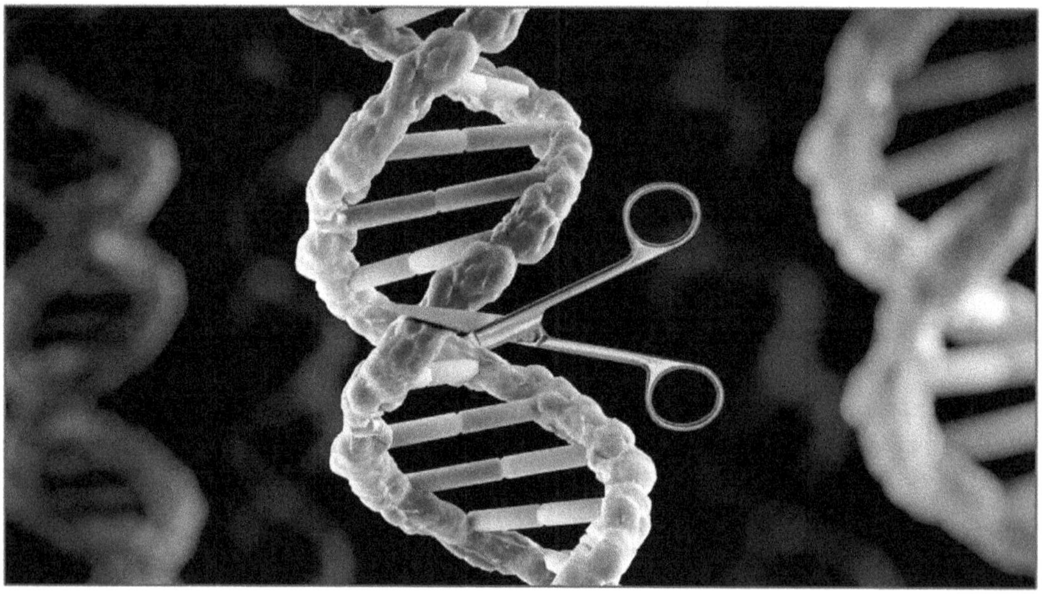

Sequencing of human genome was once a pioneering project in science. It was termed as the zenith of biological research. Now, genome sequencing has become so cheap that is has dropped from $95 million to just $950 over the course of ten years. Greater understanding of our genetics provides us with a greater potential for their manipulation. Today, gene editing stands out as the pioneering field of research in biotech industry.

In order to treat people afflicted with hereditary diseases, Swiss-based CRISPR Therapeutics is testing the potential of genetic engineering. They are using gene therapy to cure ailments and have created a platform called CRISPR/Cas9 for that purpose. Furthermore, they aim to provide pre-birth genetic disease screening services to *in-utero* and *in-vitro* patients.

d. Virtual and Augmented Reading (VR &AR) for Surgery

Surgery takes its toll on human body, and this makes a great cause for making surgical and healing process efficient through medical innovation. Using MRI and CT scans, doctors can now view an entire 3D image of the inside of patient's body. This enables the precise projection of each organ so that the surgeon can make directed incisions to minimize bodily trauma to the patient. In addition, relevant information will be directly overlaid over the relevant body parts by using AR (Dahal, 2018).

e. Stem Cell Therapies

Due to stem cells limitless self-renewal potential and differentiation capacity to produce cells and tissues of the whole human body, stem cell technology has revolutionised medical biotechnology in past decades. A great deal of work has been done to include cutting-edge stem cell treatment to restore or destroy compromised cells or tissues, aiming eventually to cure catastrophic diseases. While stem cells have made a substantial contribution to medical science, many challenges remain, including ethical and regulatory considerations, functional maturation of stem cell progenitors, strict manufacturing guidelines, immune rejection, and tumorigenicity. Moreover, biotechnological applications are still commonly used in veterinary medicine, and stem cell-based biotechnology is ushering in a new age in medical therapeutics. Scientists with a powerful entrepreneurial spirit are vital to creating economic potential in the field of medicinal biotechnology (Duelen et.al.,2019).

There is an increasing use of these cells for treatment of multiple diseases. There is a significant potential advantage of using stem cells in treatment of diseases (stem cell therapy). During an organism's early growth, stem cells have the ability to divide indefinitely and differentiate into various forms of body cells. Stem Cell Therapy is given in Figure 7.

Figure 7. Stem cell therapy

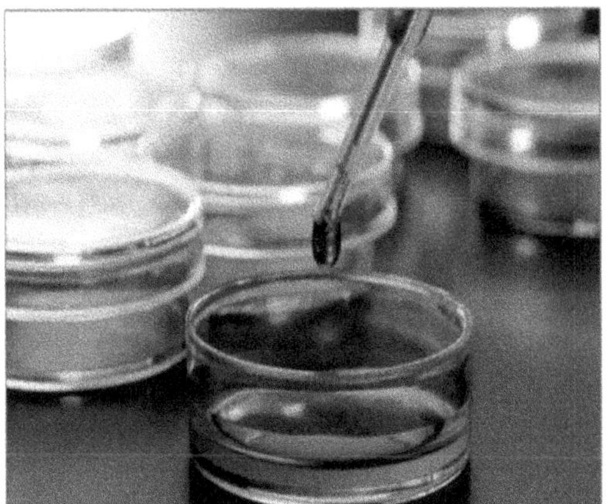

f. Human Genome Project

The Human Genome Project (HGP), coordinated by the National Institute of Health and the U.S. Department of Energy, is one of the pioneering exploration achievements in the human history. With its official launch in 1990, this project started working towards the goal of determination of sequence of nucleotide base pairs constituting human DNA. The researchers announced in April 2003, that they had completed an initial sequencing of the whole human genome. This breakthrough helped researchers to understand the blueprint for creating a person. Due to further advancement of research on functions of genes and proteins, scientists can now identify disease causing genes. Human Genome Project is given in Figure 8.

Figure 8. Human genome project

g. Nanotechnology

Nanotechnology is a field of science and technology that studies particles with sizes ranging from 1 to 100 nanometers. Nanoparticles can quickly migrate across the human body through the bloodstream due to their microscopic scale. Nanoparticles are biological nanomachines or basic substance nanostructures that have been shown to aid in the delivery of anti-cancer drugs while also reducing toxicity. This technology is progressing rapidly and researchers are now developing nanotechnology that can control when patients take their medication to encourage enhanced adherence. Nanotechnology is given in Figure 9.

Researchers are now researching nanotechnology that can track when patients take their medications in order to improve adherence. Upon ingested, the particles would transmit messages to a practitioner and the patient via a smartphone app, indicating that the drug had been taken.

h. Targeted Cancer Therapies

Leukaemia is a cancer in the tissues of blood creating cells and it can affect people of all ages- including new-born babies. Researchers have created cells using gene therapy to fight this disease. This is now a pioneering medical technology proposed for treatment of patients.

Medical experts are actively working to find solutions to the most urgent human health problems. The huge demand for innovative health solutions provide an opportunity to talented biomedical students. A brilliant mind could just find a revolutionary treatment in health care.

Figure 9. Nanotechnology

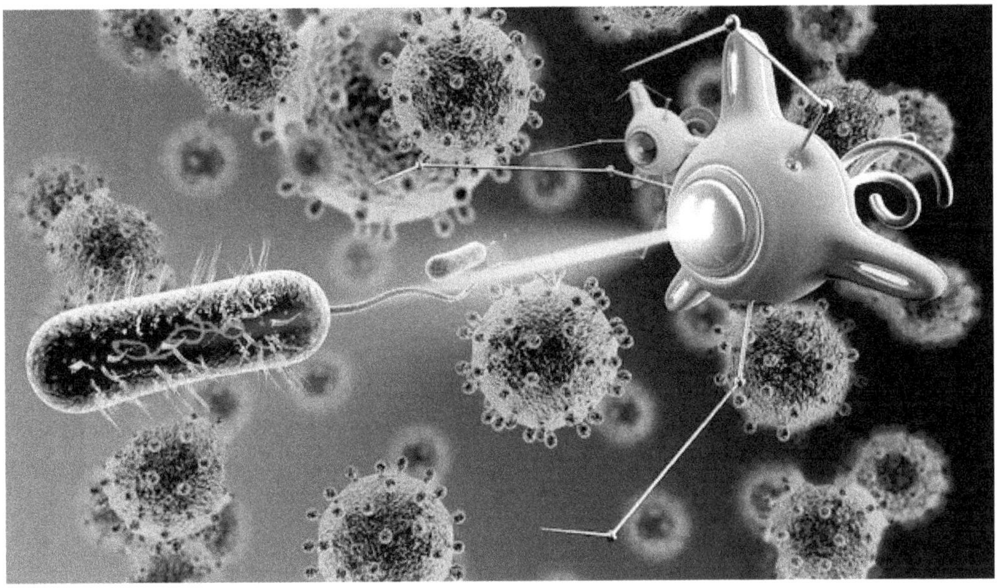

i. HPV Vaccine

Cervical cancer is caused by the Human Papilloma Virus (HPV). It is the second most deadly cancer in women after breast cancer, killing about 275,000 women worldwide each year. Successful HPV vaccination is therefore considered to be a major medical achievement. HPV vaccines such as Gardasil and Cervarix have been approved by U.S. Food and Drug Administration (FDA) for females between 9-26 years of age. HPV Vaccine is given in Figure 10.

Figure 10. HPV vaccine

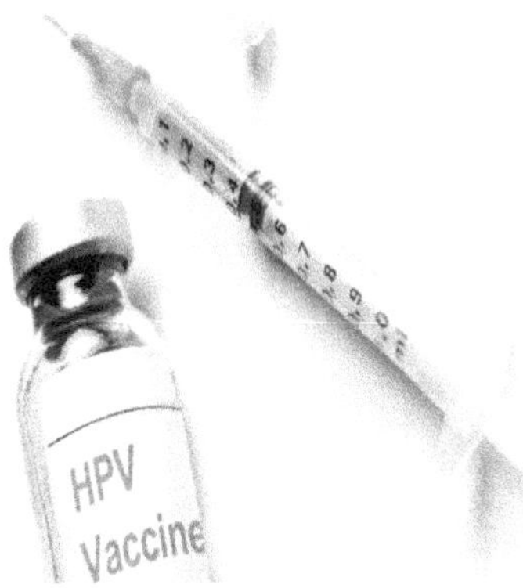

j. Face Transplants

Face transplantation is defined as the process of replacing all or a part of the patient's face with a donor's face using skin grafts. In Amiens, France, the first partial face transplant was performed in 2005. Five years later, another successful face transplant was carried out in Spain, which also happened to be first-ever full-face transplant. A transplant recipient whose face was seriously injured in an accident obtained a new nose, mouth, jaws, and cheekbones during the 24-hour surgery.

k. Nerve Regeneration

Nerve trauma caused by neurogenerative disease and spinal cord injury is generally believed to be permanent. However, researchers have made considerable progress in the synthesis of rare enzymes that facilitates the regeneration and development of damaged nerve cells. Development of neurons is assisted by proteins known as Neurotrophins. It is a series of small molecular chains with strong neurotrophic properties.

Although some of the deficiencies of protein-based agents are present in neurotrophis, researchers are exploring this as a potential route for nerve regeneration. Nerve Regeneration is given in Figure 11.

Figure 11. Nerve regeneration

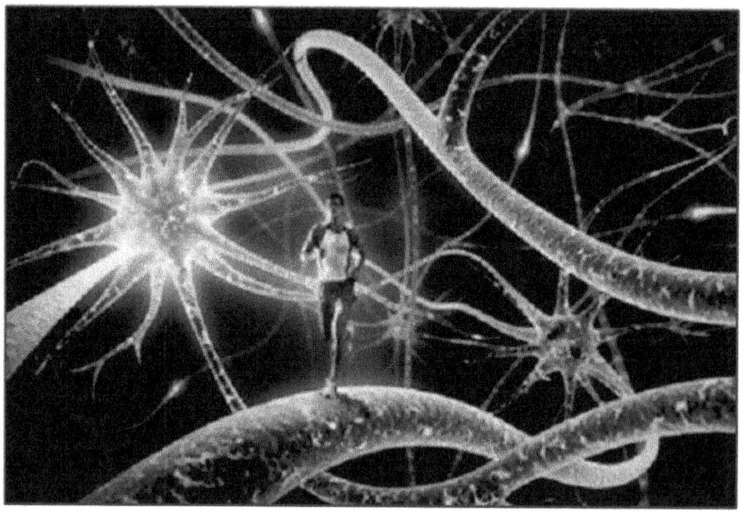

l. Nanozymes

Recent years have seen the creation of many artificial enzymes, using various materials to imitate natural enzymes in terms of their form and function. Nanozymes are nanomaterials with similar properties to natural enzymes. These have recently appeared as an important class of artificial enzymes. Nanozymes have gained tremendous interest from researchers and important advances have been made due to their special properties relative to normal enzymes and classical artificial enzymes.

Several nanomaterials have been studied in this regard to mimic various natural enzymes for a wide range of applications, including imaging, sensing, water treatment, pollutant removal, and therapeutics. Nanozymes are widely being used in biomedicine science, with multiple nanozymes being involved in diagnostic medicine and targeted cancer therapy. Such abilities allow them a feasible choice for the production of low-cost, long-term, and secure diagnostic and therapeutic agents. (Munier et.al., 2020).

ENTREPRENEURSHIP IN BIOTECH HEALTHCARE

Now, we need to focus on the contributions made by health care industries for making a healthy future. Some of the innovative fields such as invention of Monoclonal antibodies, stem cell engineering is dominating the health care industries, but in India there is a need to concentrate on more serious issues such as malnutrition, high blood pressure, diabetes etc. There are various forms of medical therapies in drug development research that can be beneficial without any side effects.

Entrepreneurship has gained little recognition in the healthcare sector, perhaps partly because of the obstacles found in the structure and culture of healthcare organisations. Eliminating obstacles can support in the promotion of entrepreneurship practises, which can lead to further growth and the discovery of new revenue streams (Phillips & German, 2006). Digital wellness goods or services, care-delivery creativity, or innovative enterprise models, services, or networks are some examples of health entrepreneurship.

INNOVATION IN HEALTH CARE

Three types of research have the potential to improve and lower the cost of health care. First one modifies the way patients purchase and use health insurance. Second one uses methods to create novel drugs and therapies or otherwise improve care. The third creates new business models, especially those involving the horizontal or vertical convergence of different health-care organisations or practises.

1. Consumer Focused.

For today's time-strapped and continually motivated health-care customers, innovations in the delivery of health care will result in more convenient, reliable, and affordable services. For example, by delivering low-cost, high-deductible benefits, a health plan will include customers in the service delivery process and allow participants more control of their personal health care expenses.

2. Technology

New medications, testing technologies, medication delivery systems, and medical equipment provide potential for safer health and care that is less expensive, invasive, and uncomfortable. For example, Implanted sensors can allow patients to track their illnesses more efficiently.IT technologies that join the many islands of knowledge in the health-care system will greatly increase both quality and performance as well as expense savings by, for instance, keeping the different providers of the patient informed and thereby reducing omission or commission mistakes.

High and raising health-care rates are a result of technological innovation along with ineffective cost-cutting strategies. It is evident from multiple studies that improved health care technologies usually raise instead of decrease spending on health care. Magnetic resonance imaging, coronary artery bypass graft, cardiac and neonatal intensive care units, computed tomography, positron emission tomography, angioplasty, and radiation oncology facilities are also correlated with higher per capita usage and expenditure on these resources as they are more widely available. Since the spread of emerging technology is largely unrestricted in the United States, many of these techniques are used to a larger degree here than in other countries. Countries with a higher level of penetration of the health sector depend on spending caps and global budgets to manage costs. While technological proliferation is slower in systems with tighter budgets, the use of advanced innovations in such systems continues to catch up over time (Bodenheimer, 2005).

3. Business Model

Health care is a remarkably fragmented sector. More than half of the doctors in the United States serve in groups of three or less. Independent hospitals account for a quarter of the country's 5,000 community hospitals and nearly half of its 17,000 nursing homes and there are thousands of small businesses in the medical device and biotechnology industries. Innovative business models, especially ones that incorporate healthcare services, will maximise productivity, optimise care and save time for customers. In addition, they reduce the risk that the individual's treatment will slip through the cracks of various medical professions.

'Reverse Innovation" is a well-known concept in the business community and it defines the flow of innovations from new to more advanced economies. Although there is a lot of interest in extending this idea to health care, yet there is no mechanism currently for defining the phases of reverse engineering or finding ways to speed up the production process. (Depasse & Lee, 2013).

Healthcare innovation is characterised as the implementation of a new concept, design, service, procedure, or product with the long-term goal of improving health, protection, outcomes, effectiveness, and costs in treatment, diagnosis, education, outreach, prevention, and analysis (Omachonu & Einspruch, 2010).

There are multiple areas of health care innovation. Some of those are described below:

a. Electronic Personal Health Record Solution (ePHR)

An electronic Personal Health Record (ePHR) allows customers to record and selectively exchange health information about themselves and their loved ones in a safe manner.

b. BSC BioNEST Bio-Incubator (BBB)

The BSC BioNEST Bio-Incubator (BBB) is the only incubator in Delhi-NCR devoted solely to 'Healthcare Innovation' (in both product & service). A perfect incubator not only assists the entrepreneur, but also raises awareness of Bio-entrepreneurship among young people.

c. Rehabilitation Therapy

There is an increasing use of robots in rehabilitation therapy of stroke victims. A team at MIT is developing robotics that can help provide treatment with reduced elbow and shoulder impairments in stroke patients (Riezenman, 2008).

d. CyberKnife Stereotactic Radiosurgery System

Physicians use the CyberKnife Stereotactic Radiosurgery System to administer heavy doses of radiation with great precision, which facilitates incision-free treatment for previously inoperable tumors. Due to this technique, exposure of healthy tissues to radiation is minimized and it allows doctors to work on several tumors at different locations.

This has reduced the time patients spend on operating table to around 30 minutes to 90 minutes (some cases may require up to five sessions), and there is no recovery time. CyberKnife Stereotactic Radiosurgery System is given in Figure 12.

Figure 12. CyberKnife stereotactic radiosurgery system

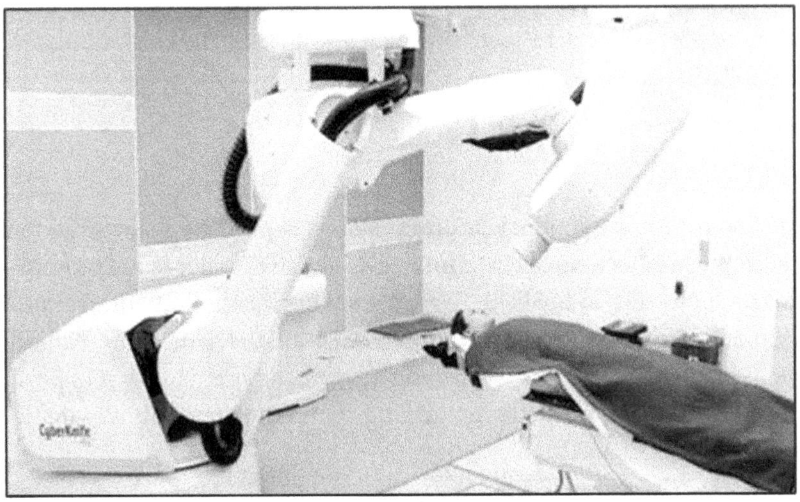

e. Synthetic 3-D Tumors

The synthetic 3D tumours provide researchers a greater understanding of how tumours function and a more precise assessment of how they react to treatment. The growth, metastasis, invasion, and treatment of cancer cells from patients can all be studied using synthetic 3D tumours. They will also use this model to assess the safety and effectiveness of experimental cancer treatments and medications.

f. Microenvironments

A chip that can simulate the microenvironment of a tumour has been created by researchers. The new device will be used to monitor the efficacy of cancer-targeting nanoparticles and medications.

g. **Advanced Instrumentation**

This is another significant factor that contributes to the pharmaceutical industry's development. Pharmaceutical research institutes are developing new and innovative tools to aid in healthcare and proper treatment of a variety of diseases (Anurag, 2018).

h. Surgeons now use high-definition tv signals in cameras (known as videoscopes) to snake into patients' bodies to scan for stomach tumours, perform colonoscopies, and help remove diseased gallbladders.

i. **Artificial Intelligence**

Researchers in the life sciences who use artificial intelligence (AI) are under more pressure than ever to invent at a faster pace. Large, multilevel, and interconnected data sets hold the promise of revealing new information and speeding up innovations. While more data is available than ever before, only a fraction is curated, integrated, interpreted and analysed. The field of artificial intelligence is concerned with how machines learn from data and imitate human thought processes.AI enhances learning ability and delivers decision support systems, by focussing on learning from data and mimicking human thought process (Sabet et.al., 2019).

j. **Biosensor**

Biosensors' enormous promise in medical diagnostics has prompted scientists to evolve biosensor technology and develop newer techniques over time. The key to the success of biosensors in the sensing of a wide variety of biomolecules in medical diagnostics is their simplicity of operation, increased sensitivity, ability to do multiplex analysis, and ability to combine the same chip with different functions. There is an enormous challenge to satisfy the criteria of performance and yet remain simple and affordable. The ultimate aim is to bring point-of-care testing to remote areas all over the world, particularly in developed countries. (Patel et.al., 2016).

THE CHALLENGE OF INNOVATING IN HEALTHCARE

Many individuals are confronted with a host of critical challenges that must be resolved if we are to innovate effectively.

1. **Budgets are tight**- To bridge the expected £22 billion revenue deficit between patient demands and available resources, the NHS must make efficiency savings.
2. **Demand is increasing**- Our society is living longer than it has ever lived before, and all of us are dealing with several comorbidities.
3. **The front line is under increasing pressure**- New methods of doing things are often the first casualties as therapeutic demands rise.
4. Demands from the public are rising.

5. **Embracing loss as a necessary part of the creative process**- Following tradition and culture has little repercussions. However, if you try to make a novel adjustment, and it fails, responsibilities for the clinician or the trust/clinical commissioning party should be considered.

ENTREPRENEURSHIP IN PHARMACEUTICAL

In the context of pharmaceuticals, Entrepreneurship is commonly associated with the start-up of a neighbourhood pharmacy and the management of a company. Entrepreneurship and related skills are, therefore, critical to the growth of a variety of health services in both the community and hospital sectors (Laverty et.al.,2015).

Since biology and technology become even more closely connected now, the use of advanced digital technologies is providing more opportunities to transform healthcare. Mentioned below are some of the considerable progress that innovation teams are making in the emerging area of digital health in pharmaceutical companies.

Entrepreneurial enterprise is increasingly becoming a key determinant for a country's growth and development. If entrepreneurial activity is efficiently channelled, it may compensate for other factors' unavoidable deficiencies. In this case, the Indian Pharmaceutical Industry is a fitting example. Against all odds, Indian pharmaceutical pioneers have turned a medicine-short economy into a nation that is self-sufficient in drugs, not just for its own citizens but also for one-fourth of the world's population. Moreover, India went from being a net importer of pharmaceutical goods to being a net exporter (Angrish & Agarwal, 2015).

Innovation in Pharma

For the pharmaceutical industry, innovation is critical, particularly when it comes to bringing new products to market (Achilladelis & Antonakis 2001; Bianchi et al., 2011). Every year, hundreds of reports on the sector are written, examining the various developments and challenges in innovation (Bianchi et al., 2011; Bierly & Chakrabarti 1996; Malerba & Orsenigo 2015; Rafols et al., 2014; Tierney et al., 2013).

The pharmaceutical industry needs to use creative technology to improve research and development, production and analytical capabilities. This will help them to discover and produce new drugs for increasingly complex diseases. This industry has made phenomenal strides in medication and pharmaceutical safety efficacy. Innovation is a major contributor to the phenomenal success of patient care. Multiple advances have regained trust in market results. Resistance to many antibiotics developed by microbes has postponed the launch of newer medications to counter resistant microbes. It is a state of war between microbes and humans. In comparison to immune strains, the use of bio-enhancers of natural origin has contributed greatly.

Nanotechnology has revolutionized drug delivery mechanisms of nanoparticle scale by improving drug solubility and permeability to allow therapeutic effectiveness in a significant range of drug therapies. This technology has opened wide-ranging perspectives on modern medication delivery technologies, a newer approach to health care, diagnostics, a chip lab to introduce superior patient care to the door with the use of IT. Regenerative medicines -referencing stem cells (Stemceuticals) have greatly improved survival rates and life span of patients over the last one and a half decades. Due to their presence in human body, a great deal of expertise has been generated in fighting some of the latest terminal cases.

It is now mandatory to follow a multidisciplinary approach in drug discovery and patient care due to innovations in biomedical sciences. Similar to other innovative technologies, professionals also need to focus their attention on risk and responsibility (Shrotriya, 2016).

Here we begin with some trending innovations that are already evolving and will make a greater contribution to the reshaping of the pharmaceutical industry.

a. Artificial intelligence and Machine learning
b. Digitization of Medicine through Healthcare Mobile Apps
c. IoT Integration
d. 3D-Printing Drugs/Tablets
e. Precision medicine
f. Organs-On-Chips
    h. Needle Free Injection Technology
    i. Robotic surgery

1. Artificial Intelligence and Machine Learning

The pharmaceutical industry's next major breakthroughs will be possible through artificial intelligence and machine learning. Data entry, clinical research analyses, data collection, review of healthcare processes to detect errors or inefficiencies, and patient consultations using AI-based applications are all examples of how AI is now being used in the healthcare industry, medication treatment under the supervision of an AI-based scheme etc. Disease prediction and detection, radiology and radiotherapy preparation, clinical trial testing, personalised medicine, rare disease identification, and new drug development are all examples of where machine learning is being used. Artificial intelligence and Machine learning are given in Figure13.

Figure 13. Artificial intelligence and machine learning

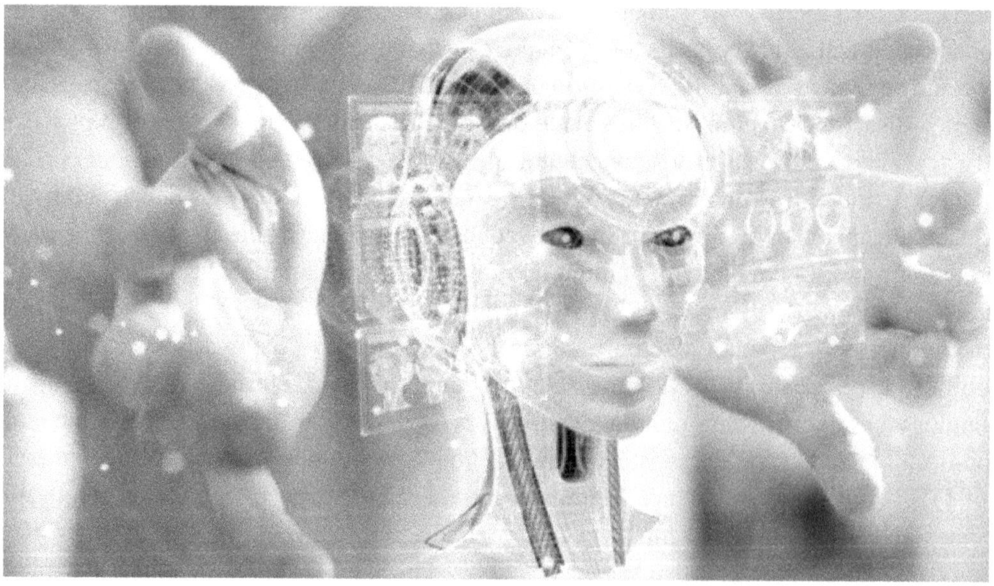

The concern now is how AI and machine learning can help the pharmaceutical industry reshape its future. In fact, since the pharmaceutical sector has so many silos of patient records, these innovations have the greatest potential to contribute in the future. Instead of taking months to see how a drug affects thousands of individuals, it would take seconds to see how a drug affects billions of models of the human body's physiology based on medical data. Artificial intelligence (AI) and machine learning (ML) are supposed to be incorporated into most, if not all, pharmaceutical R&D operations. As a result, the success rate of drug production should potentially increase, and R&D activities should be streamlined.

2. Digitization of Medicine Through Healthcare Mobile Apps

With the advent of powerful and portable computing devices in the early years of the twenty-first century, we have seen tremendous technological progress. Simultaneously, a global connectivity enabled by broadband and satellite technology has led to an increase in the number of "linked users" for knowledge sharing.

The temporal intersection of many coincidental trends has resulted in the advent of modern mobile health (mHealth) innovations. These trends include - (i) the immediate need to solve the increasing burden of chronic diseases; (ii) Moore's law—the rapid growth in processing capacity that has resulted in the production of smaller and less expensive handheld devices (Moore, 1965); and (iii) changing the healthcare paradigm to one that is more patient-centred (Topol, 2010). The practise of medicine assisted by portable medical instruments is referred to as mHealth. In our dynamic modern age, the integration of science and technology has resulted in the creation of advanced digital health devices that allow for quick and precise characterization of health and disease.

Technological advances and the miniaturisation of medical instruments to new smartphone-connected and mobile health (mHealth) applications like the iECG, portable ultrasound, and lab-on-a-chip technology have sparked a surge of interest in patient care, promising to lower healthcare costs and increased outcomes. (Bhavani et.al.,2016).

Pharma firms all over the world have recently realised that simply manufacturing and designing products is no longer sufficient. The current trend indicates that they must offer a full product in addition to the physical presentation of medicines. The "around the pill" multimedia products includes: Apps, computers, or programmes for digital wellbeing that may be prescribed by a doctor or bundled with a prescription. As a result, more digital applications are coming up with the emergence of emerging technology.

3. IoT Integration

IoT has tremendous capacity to support the pharmaceutical industry. By identifying problems and making changes until they become a challenge, introducing a network of linked devices with tracking sensors will reduce the possibility of machinery malfunctions and ensure precise efficiency.

The pharmaceutical industry's manufacturing business, such as inventory monitoring and control in the manufacturing phase of drugs, will benefit from IoT incorporation. Furthermore, IoT-enabled data-gathering systems can be used in shipping and receiving stations, where they can capture data from RFID tags and barcodes and compare data from different sites, such as manufacturing plants and warehouses, to ensure the data is accurate.

4. 3D Printed Tablets/ Drug

3D printing, also known as rapid prototyping or additive manufacturing, is a new revolutionary technique that uses computer-aided drug modelling technology to create 3D forms in a layer-by-layer process. Computer-aided drug design (CADD) is a new technology for drug discovery and testing since it lowers the time and cost of the project. To produce an object, successive layers of material are created under machine control in 3D printing. It has a high degree of stability in terms of controlling the release of a drug that is formulated in several layers of tablets. This printing was once just a science fiction idea (figure 14). 3d Printed Tablets/ Drug is given in Figure 14. However, in 2015, this idea was brought to light and introduced. Aprecia Pharmaceuticals created Zip dose, a proprietary technique for 3D printing drugs that allows high-dose prescriptions to be delivered in a quickly dissolving manner (Swati et.al.,2016).

Figure 14. 3D printed tablets/drugs

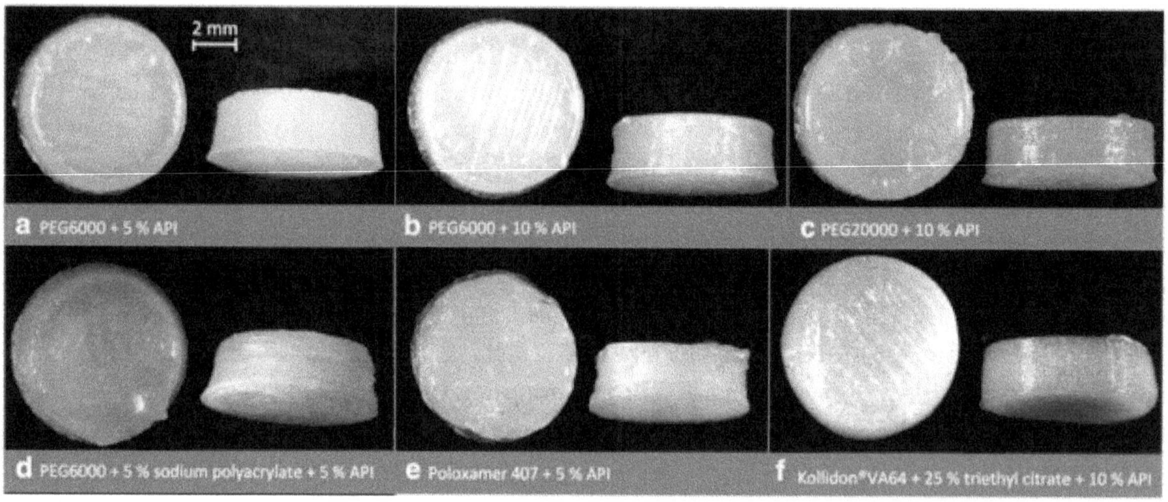

5. Precision Medicine

Precision medicine is an approach that integrates clinical and molecular information in order to understand the biological basis of the disease. This information can be obtained through genome sequencing, which is a technique to convert DNA into data. In order to determine which types of patients a medication will be most effective and who are likely to suffer significant side-effects, researchers use this information to classify particular gene abnormalities or biomarkers.

This approach potentially assists in the development of new targeted treatments and the re-design of approved drugs. Since targeted treatments are adapted to the genetic profile of particular patients, genomic testing is needed before it is performed to assess the most appropriate therapy. Precision Medicine is given in Figure 15.

This knowledge of the interaction between the medication and the human genes allows physicians to prescribe the correct drug for the right patient at the right dosage for the first time – leading to improved outcomes and fewer adverse reactions.

Figure 15. Precision medicine

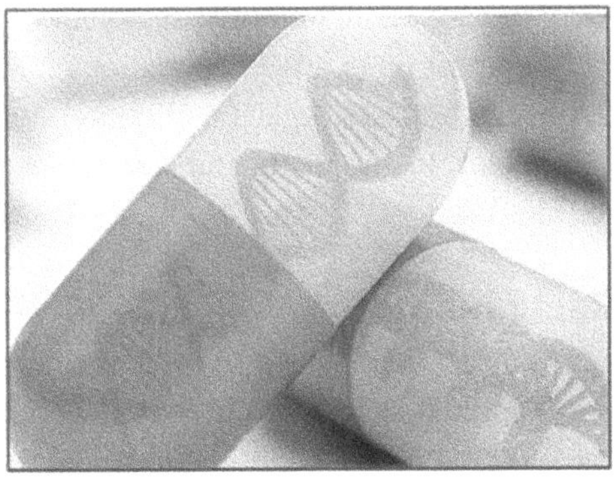

6. Organs-On-Chips

Drug testing on humans or animals in the context of expensive and time-consuming clinical trials is a thing of the past, and the "Organs on Chips" idea is the latest craze. Imagine that the characteristics of living organisms are so precisely replicated that a clinical trial can be completed in less time, with less resources, and yet produce incredible results. This approach is called the "silicon trial "Organ-on-a-chip (OOAC) is one of the top 10 new innovations and applies to a physiological biomimetic organ structure based on a microfluidic chip. The microenvironment of the chip mimics that of the organ in terms of tissue interfaces and mechanical stimulation using a mixture of cell biology, chemistry, and biomaterial technology. Organs-on-Chips is given in Figure 16.

Figure 16. Organs-on-chips

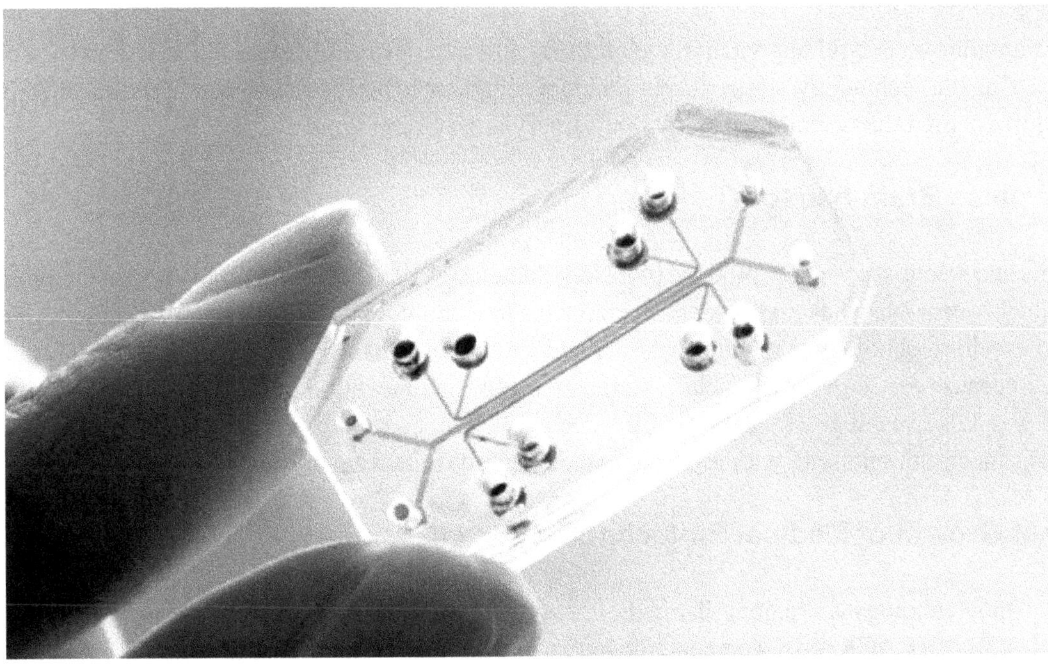

This illustrates the structural and functional properties of human tissue and can be used to determine how people will respond to a variety of factors, including drug reactions and environmental effects (Wu et.al., 2020). "HumMod" is one of the most innovative applications in this regard. It offers a top-down model of human physiology, starting with entire organs and ending with individual molecules. Body fluids, hormones, circulation, electrolytes, metabolism, and skin temperature are among the more than 1,500 calculations and 6,500 variables used.

7. Needle Free Injection Technology

In order to satisfy consumer demands, the needle-free industry now has a wide variety of outstanding technologies. The pharmaceutical and biotechnological industries are the only remaining impediment. Without generating an investment solution, the industry has invested heavily in seeking a solution to this problem. There is also strong evidence that the demand for current goods is rapidly segregated by the supply of technologies. The use of traditional vials with needles and syringes by patients and diabetics has decreased in recent years, especially outside of the United States. (Harrison, 2004). The Antrares PharmaMedi Jector vision Needle free injection device is given in Figure 17.

Figure 17. The Antrares PharmaMedi Jector vision needle free injection device (Harrison, 2004)

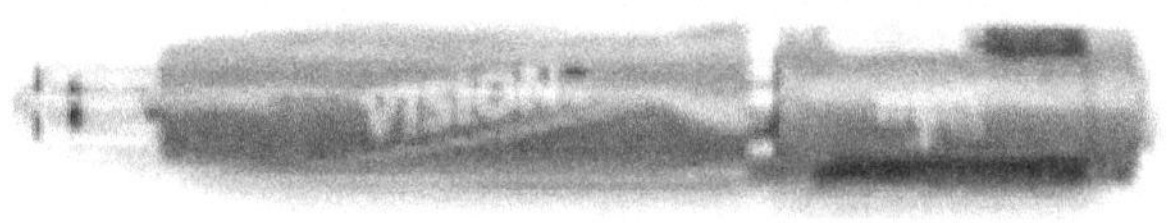

8. Robotic Surgery

This is another successful approach in the pharmaceutical industry. It's expected to rise in the coming years. Using this technology, surgeons may conduct complicated and delicate operations that are difficult to perform using other technologies. Robotic surgery is given in Figure 18.

9. Wireless Brain Sensors

Doctors and scientists can now produce bioresorbable electronics that can be implanted in the brain and then quickly dissolve when no longer needed, thanks to technological advancements. Doctors would be able to use this technology to monitor pressure and temperature in the brain. There is no need for further surgery because the sensors will melt. As a result, scientific innovation in pharmaceuticals helps to increase people's lives. It gives patients confidence to live longer. It helps to cure very complex illnesses, such as cancer, tumours, etc. with less pain and damage. Wireless brain sensors are given in Figure 19.

Market Growth of Medical Biotechnology

Medical biotechnology is a major pillar in the economic growth of many countries, especially developed countries. With a CAGR of 16.4 percent, the Indian biotechnology industry is expected to cross US$ 150 billion by 2025.The Indian biotechnology industry is projected to rise from 3% of the global biotechnology market in 2017 to 19% by 2025. In 2019, the biopharmaceutical industry is the most profitable, accounting for 62% of overall sales, led by bio-agriculture (14%), and bio-services (18%). Clinical trials, contract testing, and production operations are increasingly being conducted in India, which accounts for 16 percent of the country's biotechnology industry.

Figure 18. Robotic surgery

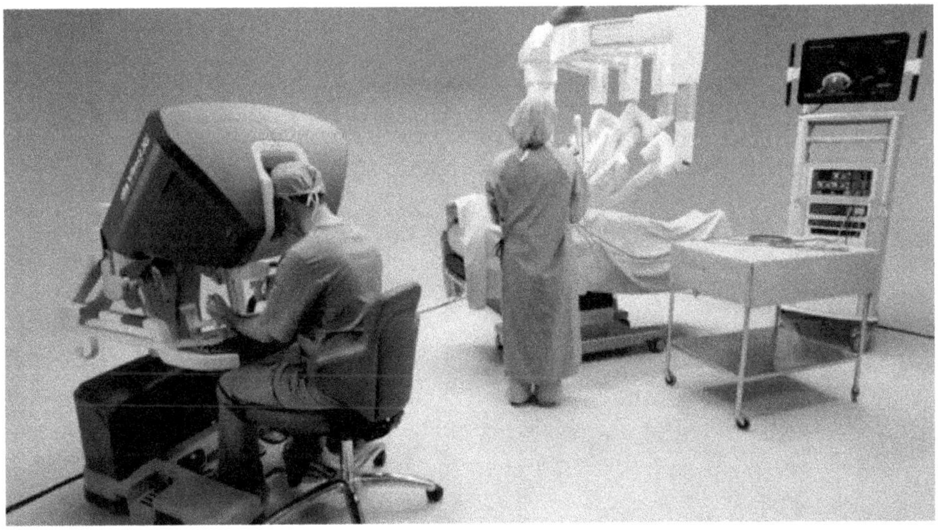

Figure 19. Wireless brain sensors

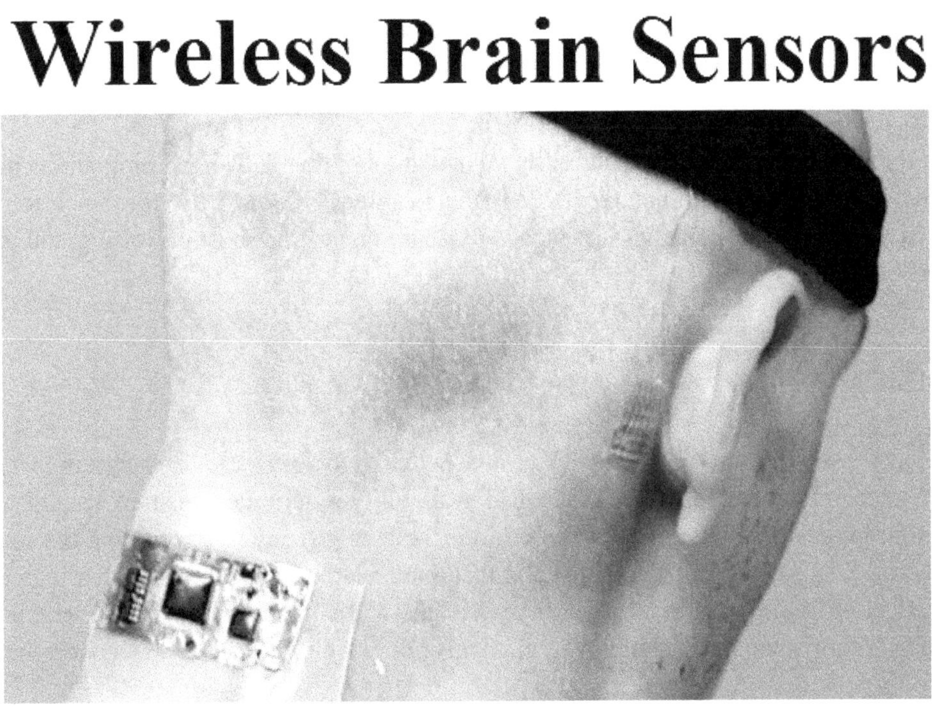

India produces the most generic medicines in the world. The Indian pharmaceutical industry provides more than 50 per cent of the global market for multiple vaccines, 40 per cent of generic demand in the US and 25 per cent of all medication in the UK. Biopharmaceuticals, bio services, bio agriculture, bio-industry, and bioinformatics are all part of India's biotechnology sector. In 2019, the Indian biotechnology sector was worth US$ 64 billion, and by 2025, it is projected to be worth US$ 150 billion. In 2019, India's domestic pharmaceutical industry turnover increased by 9.8% year on year to Rs 1.4 lakh crore (US$ 20.03 billion), up from Rs 129,015 crore (US$ 18.12 billion) in 2018. Biotechnology Market Size, Share, Trends & Analysis Report 2020-2026 is given in Figure 20.

Figure 20. Biotechnology market size, share, trends and analysis report 2020-2026

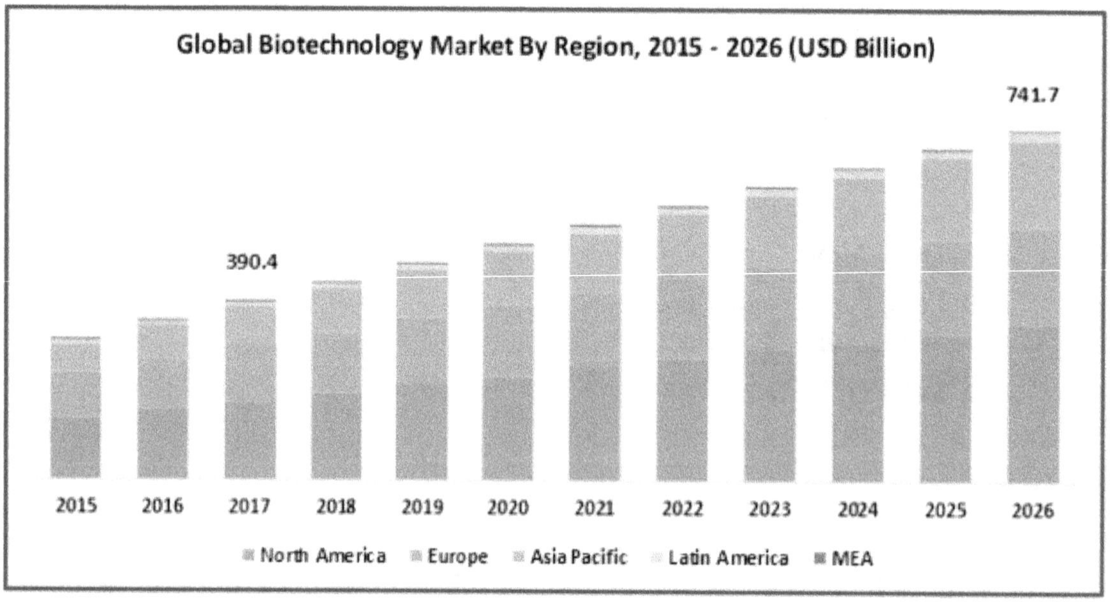

The healthcare industry in India is currently valued at more than US$ 70 billion and is projected to grow further to reach US$ 280 billion by 2020. With a healthy CAGR of 21% (for the period 2010-20), healthcare as an industry in India has emerged to become one of the most promising and progressive sectors in recent times.

CONCLUSION

Biotechnology is a rapidly growing sector. It has huge potential for innovation and entrepreneurship. Due to medical biotechnology, the problem of medical availability requirements is now diminished around the world. Entrepreneurial skills in health care are increasingly required to promote the development of new and emerging programs, technology, and therapies related to health. Biotechnology has had an incredible effect on health care in the last 30 years. This will continue into the foreseeable future, as understanding of the pathophysiology of many currently untreatable diseases grows; governments around the world continue to advance initiatives that support biotech innovation; and business practices evolve to manage the expensive, time-consuming, and risky process of product development. The result will be an ongoing influx of experimental therapies that will lead to breakthroughs in health care. Modern medical biotechnology, however, offers better healthcare for the world's aging population and impoverished, and innovative treatments for previously non- or ill-cured diseases.

REFERENCES

Achilladelis, B., & Antonakis, N. (2001). The dynamics of technological innovation: The case of the pharmaceutical Industry. *Research Policy*, *30*(4), 535–588. doi:10.1016/S0048-7333(00)00093-7

Angrish, A. K., & Aggarwal, V. (2015). *Mapping of Entrepreneurship in Pharmaceutical Sector in India*. EDII Institutional Repository.

Anurag. (2018). 16 Tech Advancements in Pharmaceuticals to Re-invent Healing. Healthcare. *Health-Tech, technology trends.*

Batterham, R. (2000). The Chance to Change, Chief Scientist of Australia. Canberra: Dept. of Industry, Science and Resources (DISR).

Bhavnani, S. P., Nirula, J., & Sengupta, P. P. (2016). Mobile technology and the digitization of healthcare. *European Heart Journal*, *37*(18), 1428–1438. doi:10.1093/eurheartj/ehv770 PMID:26873093

Bianchi, M., Cavaliere, A., Chiaroni, D., Frattini, F., & Chiesa, V. (2011). Organisational modes for Open Innovation in the bio-pharmaceutical industry: An exploratory analysis. *Technovation*, *31*(1), 22–33. doi:10.1016/j.technovation.2010.03.002

Bierly, P., & Chakrabarti, A. (1996). Generic knowledge strategies in the U.S. pharmaceutical industry. *Strategic Management Journal*, *17*(S2), 123–135. doi:10.1002mj.4250171111

Bodenheimer, T. (2005). High and Rising Health Care Costs. Part 2: Technologic Innovation. *Annals of Internal Medicine*, *142*(11), 932. doi:10.7326/0003-4819-142-11-200506070-00012 PMID:15941701

Collins, J. (2009). *Good to Great-(Why Some Companies Make the Leap and others Don't)*. Academic Press.

Dahal, S. (2018). *Recent Biotechnology advance in Medicine*. Academic Press.

Depasse, J. W., & Lee, P. T. (2013). A model for 'reverse innovation' in health care. *Globalization and Health*, *9*(1), 9–40. doi:10.1186/1744-8603-9-40 PMID:24001367

Duelen, R., Corvelyn, M., Tortorella, I., Leonardi, L., Chai, Y. C., & Sampaolesi, M. (2019). *Medicinal Biotechnology for Disease Modelling*. Clinical Therapy, and Drug Discovery and Development.

EIB – European Investment Bank. (2002). *Biotechnology: An overview*. EIB Sector Papers.

Gurau, C. (2021). *Entrepreneurship in biotechnology: World Encyclopedia of Entrepreneurship*. Edward Elgar Publishing.

Harrison, R. G. (2004). *Needle free Drug Delivery Technology*. Innovation in Pharmaceutical Technology.

Hine, D., & Kapeleris, J. (2006). *Innovation and Entrepreneurship in Biotechnology, An International Perspective- Concept, theories and cases*. Edward Elgar Publishing Limited. doi:10.4337/9781845428853

Hossain, F.R. (2019). Pharmaceutical Industry: Top 7 Technologies to Reshape the Future. *Brain Station, 23*.

Hsu, L. Y., Teo, F. S., & Chin, T. M. (2018). *Medical Biotechnology - Modern Development. Encyclopedia of Life Support Systems* (Vol. 11). EOLSS.

Janodia, D. M. (2007). Drug Development Process. *RE:view*.

Kelly, C. J., & Young, A. J. (2017). Promoting innovation in healthcare. *Future Healthcare Journal, 4*(2), 121–125. PMID:31098448

Laverty, G., Hanna, L. A., Haughey, S., & Hughes, C. (2015). Instructional Design and Assessment-Developing Entrepreneurial Skills in Pharmacy Students. *American Journal of Pharmaceutical Educationm 79*(7), 106.

Littlejohn, T. (2002). Sun baked biotechnology in Australia. *Nature Biotechnology*, *20*(September). PMID:12205502

Malerba, F., & Orsenigo, L. (2015). The evolution of the pharmaceutical industry. *Business History, 57*(5), 664–687. doi:10.1080/00076791.2014.975119

Mehrotra, P. (2016). Biosensors and their applications – A review. *Journal of Oral Biology and Craniofacial Research*, *6*(2), 153–159. doi:10.1016/j.jobcr.2015.12.002 PMID:27195214

Meyers, A. D. (2008). Enterprise for Life Scientists: Developing Innovation and Entrepreneurship in the Biosciences. *Journal of Commercial Biotechnology*, *14*(4), 355–356. doi:10.1057/jcb.2008.21

Moore, G. E. (1965). Cramming more components onto integrated circuits. *Electronics (Basel)*, *38*, 114–117.

Munier, S., Shah, A. A., Rehman, H., Bilal, M., Rajoka, M. S. R., Khan, A. A., & Khursid, M. (2020). Nanozymes for medical biotechnology and its potential applications in biosensing and nanotherapeutics. *Biotechnology Letters*, *42*(3), 357–373. doi:10.100710529-020-02795-3 PMID:31950406

Niosi, J., & McKelvey, M. (2018). Relating business model innovations and innovation cascades: The case of biotechnology. *Journal of Evolutionary Economics*, *28*(5), 1081–1109. doi:10.100700191-018-0561-9 PMID:30613125

Oakey, R., Faulkner, W., Cooper, S., & Walsh, V. (1990). *New Firms in the Biotechnology Industry*. London Printer.

Omachonu, V. K., & Einspruch, N. G. (2010). Innovation in Healthcare Delivery Systems: A Conceptual Framework. *The Innovation Journal*, *15*(1), 2.

Patel, S., Nanda, R., & Sahoo, S. (2016). Biosensors in Health Care: The Milestones Achievedin Their Development towards Lab-on-Chip-Analysis. Biochemistry Research International, 16.

Persidis, A. (1997). Bioentrepreneurship around the world; Bioentrepreneur II. *Nature Biotechnology, 16.*

Philips, F. S., & Garman, A. N. (2006). Barriers to Entrepreneurship in healthcare Organizations. *Journal of Health and Human Services Administration*, *28*(4), 472–484. PMID:16583847

Rafols, I., Hopkins, M. M., Hoekman, J., Siepel, J., O'Hare, A., Perianes-Rodríguez, A., & Nightingale, P. (2014). Big Pharma, little science? *Technological Forecasting and Social Change*, *81*, 22–38. doi:10.1016/j.techfore.2012.06.007

Riezenman, M. J. (2008). *Robots in Rehab*. p. 6 The Institute.

Roming, F. I., & Ghidurus, M. (2019). *The Potential of Biotechnology to generate Prosperity*. pp. 1-5 Springer Nature Limited.

Sabet, N. N., Zand, R., Zheng, Y., & Abedi, V. (2019). Artificial Intelligence Transforms the Future of Health Care. *The American Journal of Medicine*, *32*(7), 795–801. doi:10.1016/j.amjmed.2019.01.017 PMID:30710543

Sager, B. (2001). Scenarios on the future of Biotechnology. *Technological Forecasting and Social Change*, *68*(2), 109–129. doi:10.1016/S0040-1625(00)00107-4

Salgaller, M. (2010). *Biotechnology Entrepreneurship: From Science to Solutions*. Logo Press.

Sansbury, L. (2002). Strong Government support for UK biotech. *Biotechnology Investors Forum Worldwide*, *2*, 20–22.

Shahid, M. F., & Azim, M. K. (2019). Bio-entrepreneurship: Scenario and opportunities for developing countries. *Pakistan Journal of Biochemistry and Molecular Biology*, *52*(2), 27–33.

Shimakshi, C. D. (2020). *Biotechnology Entrepreneurship- Leading, Managing and Commercializing Innovative Technologies*. Elsevier Science Publishing.

Shimasaki, C. (2014). What is Biotechnology Entrepreneurship? In *Biotechnology Entrepreneurship* (pp. 45–56). Academic Press. doi:10.1016/B978-0-12-404730-3.00004-X

Srivastava, A., Singh, V., Srivastava, P., & Sinha, R. (2016). Innovation Incubation and Entrepreneurship in Biotechnology- Review. *International Journal of Technical Research and Applications, 4*(4), 66-71.

Surbhi, S. (2020). *Difference Between Entrepreneur and Entrepreneurship (with Comparison Chart) - Key Differences*. Academic Press.

Swati, S., Jyothi, N., & Prasanthi, N. K. (2016). A Review On 3d Printed Tablets: A Downloadable Medicine. *Asian Journal of Pharmthiaceutical Technology & Innovation*, *04*(20), 34–39.

Tierney, R., Hermina, W., & Walsh, S. (2013). The pharmaceutical technology landscape: A new form of technology road mapping. *Technological Forecasting and Social Change*, *80*(2), 194–211. doi:10.1016/j.techfore.2012.05.002

Topol, E. J. (2010). Transforming medicine via digital innovation. *Science Translational Medicine*, *2*(16), 16. doi:10.1126citranslmed.3000484 PMID:20371472

Wu, Q., Liu, J., Wang, X., Feng, L., Wu, J., Zhu, X., Wen, W., & Gong, X. (2020). Organ-on-a-chip: Recent breakthroughs and future prospects. *Biomedical Engineering Online*, *19*(1), 9. doi:10.118612938-020-0752-0 PMID:32050989

Chapter 13
Entrepreneurship in Industrial Biotechnology:
Biotech Entrepreneurship

Shaili Yadav
Janta College, Chhatrapati Shahu Ji Maharaj University, Kanpur, India

Jyoti Mathur
Banasthali University, India

ABSTRACT

In the 20th century, biotechnology has been growing quickly on industrial platforms with a vast scope for innovation and the entrepreneurial market. Entrepreneurship in biotechnology including its various sub-disciplines focuses on biotech commercial components and possible fundamental strategies combined with laboratory practical analysis and productive outcome of working biotech entrepreneurs, professionals, researchers, and scientists. Likewise, biotechnology in India has risen with the various pharma-biotechnology-based industries leading the charge. Across India, more than 350 well-capitalized companies are working in various related fields of biotechnology including biopharmaceuticals, nanotechnology, bio-services, agriculture computational biotechnology, and bioinformatics.

INTRODUCTION

Over the last few years, the industry of biotechnology has been growing successfully. Since the dawn of civilization, humans have been using products based on biotechnology. Today, these products, mainly based on our scientific research, are part of our daily life. The biotech field leads to real-outcomes that allow the production of advanced technologies and products. Also, help to preserve the environment, encounter diseases, new biomedical devices, eliminate hungry, bio-fabric and biofuel production and more.

Since the beginning of Genentech firm, the first modern biotechnology established in 1976, many thousands of innovative biotechnology projects have been started and some of these projects have been ended with successful outcome in respect of society and bio-industries. The expected business economic

DOI: 10.4018/978-1-7998-7411-9.ch013

benefit of Genentech's market was $100 billion in 2012, and the Genentech employed more than 11,000 professionalists. Also the Genentech is the first firm to produce insulin from bacterial recombinant technology to treat diabetes in human.

Another firm Amgen started in 1980 had market capitalization $53 billion in 2012 with about 17,000 employees. Similarly market capitalization of firm Biogen started in 1978 was $28 billion for 2012. Biogen employed 5000 employees for development of commercialized new technologies based on scientific research and advancements that improved and conceptualized our understanding of cellular experiments at the molecular level (Mark & Mirvis, 2001; Maurer & Ebres, 2006; Patzelt et al., 2012).

The global biotechnology industry had total profits of $200 billion in 2009 while according to new research report by Global Market Insights Inc, the significant economic impact by 2025 will be $729 Billion. Biotechnology sector has fascinated substantial attention from policy makers as well as academic researchers (Alper, 2002, Lehrer, 2007). Many studies have been probed how Government of India can set off local environment for biotechnology sector or how does government provide facilities and scopes to biotechnologists, microbiologists, environmentalists and pharmacists in regional areas for research and development (R&D). The study found that regional universities, firms, bio-laboratories, industrial enterprises related to biotechnology or pharmaceutics, projects sectioned under government schemes with financial interest can explore the biotechnology and pharmaceutical industries and networks in India (Athreye & Chaturvedi, 2007; Dodgson et al., 2008).

Indeed, advanced techniques of biotechnology have vigorously triggered the research productivity and value in many industrial firms and sectors (Catherine et al., 2004; Cohen & Levinthal, 1990). According to current industrial statistics biotechnology industry discovers double as many new quick effective drugs as the conventional back established pharmaceutical industry, but expenditure is only one quarter on drugs just like research and development (Douglas et al., 2010; Swann & Prevezer, 1998). The industrial set up and development of biotechnology requires more than $100 million and minimum 10 years of research and development asset with 5000 candidates working on drug finding and its manufacture to explore in industrial market (Evans & Varaiya, 2003). Though many biotechnological sectors fail to launch and commercialize further their technology and products due to vibrant competition that demonstrates biotechnology as a high risk sector also.

With emerging implements and government's investment in biotechnology entrepreneurs are being more aware and further focused towards Biotechnology for the sustainable profit of their business in India. Moreover understanding and working on the factors that contribute to the success of biotechnology business enterprises have been important research opportunity for researchers from the field of academics and entrepreneurship (Phillip, 2002).

To establish the Indian government's venture 'Make in India' on commercial level, the scientific academic research and its analytics require advance infrastructure, high-tech tools, scientific human resources like organization or laboratories and most importantly skilled manpower for the biotech, pharmaceutics and chemical industries (Acs & Audretsch, 1988).

Biotechnology Industry Research Assistance Council (BIRAC), a public sector venture started by Department of Biotechnology (DBT) in India encourages the entrepreneurship under collaboration of Government of India and World Bank for accelerating research and growth of Biopharmaceutical enterprises worldwide. Ministry of Science & Technology and Department of Biotechnology have launched a very appealing project called 'Innovate in India (I3)' of about $ 250 million to bring together industry and academic world to promote entrepreneurship and indigenous production in the biopharmaceutical industry.

CONCEPT OF ENTREPRENEURSHIP

Entrepreneurship is defined as a process of designing, formulating, starting and running a successful new small budget business into developed high capitalization business venture along with any of risks related to reward and profit of business (Shane & Venkataraman, 2000).

Entrepreneurship is the collaborative activity that requires the finding, the discovery, assessment and utilization of opportunities to set up new commodities products, services and technologies, approaches to organize, markets, methods and raw constructive material through organizing efforts that never worked or existed before (Shane & Venkataraman, 2001). This is the process of producing something creative and value adding in human life by merging the required time and manpower, associated finances, ethics to anticipation of consumer's behavior, likes and dislikes of consumers, taste and trend, social risks and fruitful reward and growth of enterprises (Alvarez & Busenitz, 2001; Bellu & Flume, 2004; Carrier, 1996; Hisrich et al., 2005).

Types of Entrepreneurship

On the strategic approach and theoretical viewpoint entrepreneurship is categorized differently into innovative entrepreneurship and non-entrepreneurship.

1. **Innovative Entrepreneurship** is entrepreneurial opportunities in innovative businesses, small and medium-sized enterprises (SMEs) and young and high-growth businesses that create economic growth, support global job challenges and finical overcome in society (figure 1) (Lafuente & Salas, 1989; Schumpeter, 1934).

Figure 1. The module for innovative entrepreneurship

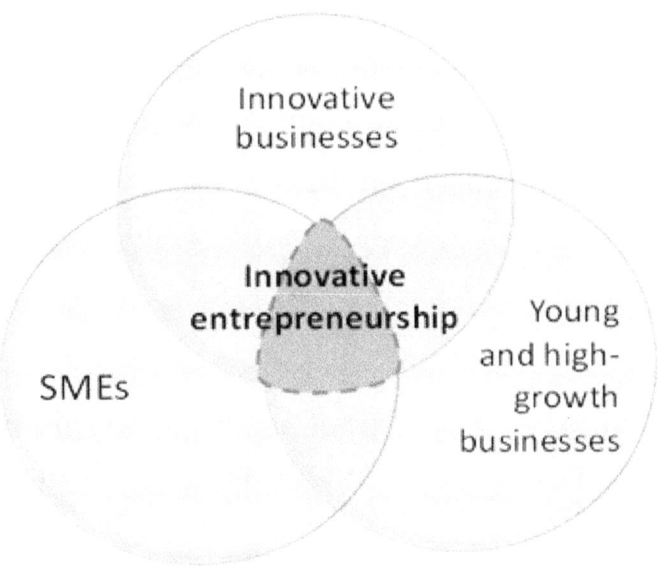

Competitiveness in businesses, lack of financial resources, unskilled manpower, improper management of information and government's guidelines reduce the growth and possibilities of industrial sectors (Hisrich, 1990). The word innovation involves a number of commercial features such as process and implementation, technology, marketing, organizational or product executive innovation.

2. **Non-Innovative Entrepreneurship** is the social opportunities that are already available and easily accessible in society to the people (Liebeskind et al., 1996; Luo et al., 2009). These opportunities are not individually created by anyone but the people identify and formulate them attentively in society to overcome the shortage and surplus of businesses (Kirzner, 1973).

THE ENTREPRENEURIAL PROCESS

Entrepreneurship, a long process of setting a business involves multiple ideas visionary mind and effective steps to be started. Setting a business always needs an idea which ends with the success of the well performed objective and building marked capitalization including recovery of the initial investment as well as obtained extra profit in firm or industry. There are many representative models and encountered theories in competitive entrepreneurial world which help to understand the strategies of business establishment and economic development (Kirzner, 1997).

- Model based on opportunities
- Model based on performance
- Model based on environmental factors
- Model based on business sustainability monitor
- Model based on administrative entrepreneurship

Model Based on Opportunities

The very first step to set a business in enterprising world is understand and grasp the opportunities at right time before it gets explored and exploited by some other entrepreneurs (Figure 2). Any idea that has capability and strength to hit the business market superiorly will counter the small business (McMullen et al., 2007).

Figure 2. Flow of opportunities based entrepreneurship

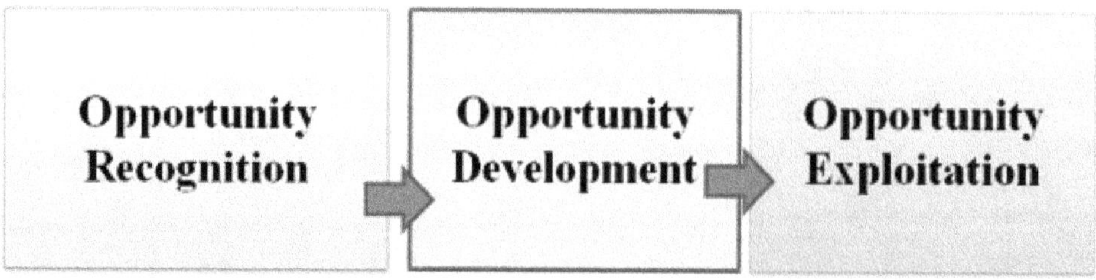

Model Based on Performance

Entrepreneurial performance is the work capability of the community who starts business with the sense of setting growing satisfactory turnover as a result of the opening of the new business (Stuart & Abetti, 1990). One way to establish the growing business is discovering the existence of opportunities and decision to develop it for profit while the other way involves arrange of required resources, learning the entrepreneurial strategies and performing the process to work on enterprising opportunity (Figure 3).

Figure 3. Performance based entrepreneurship

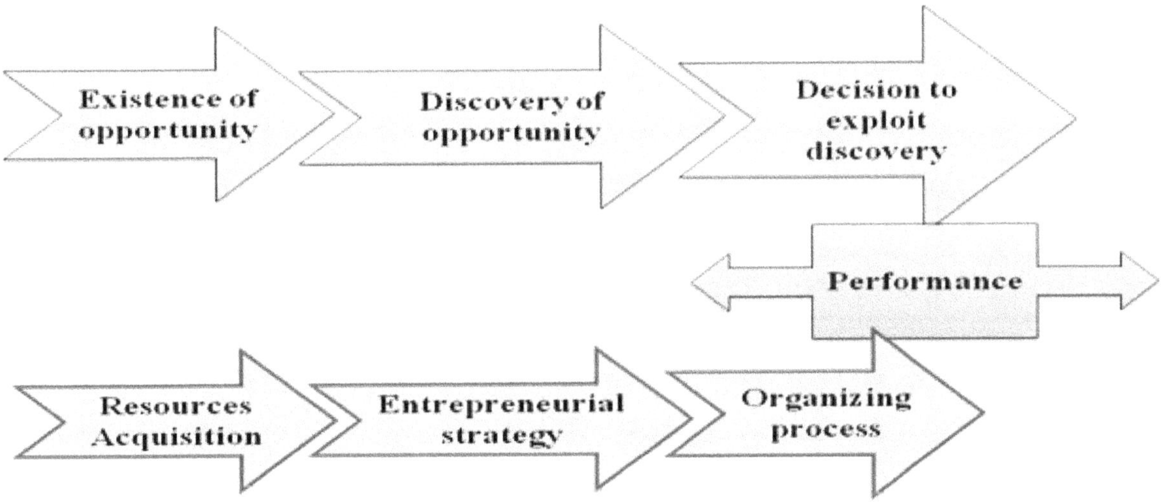

Model Based on Environmental Factors

Combination of external and internal factors that play vital role in set up and development of industrial enterprises is considered as environmental factors which include economic, social need, cultural issues, political consent related to industries and ventures.

All strategy must be following foreign exchange regulations, financial assistance, technological development and social-ecological changes in business environment (Figure 4).

Model Based on Business Sustainability Monitor

Business sustainability monitor is based on annual assessment of entrepreneurial settings, skilled manpower selection, opportunities, work verity and activities subjected to set an enterprise (Carsrud et al., 2008). Global entrepreneurship monitor (GEM) is a consortium linked with world-bank, world competitive reports, national data on venture capital investment and world carrying entrepreneurial research organizations (Figure 5). In India global entrepreneurship monitor assesses growth of entrepreneurship at provincial and state level to explore entrepreneurial and research activities in multiple dimensions.

Figure 4. Environmental based entrepreneurship

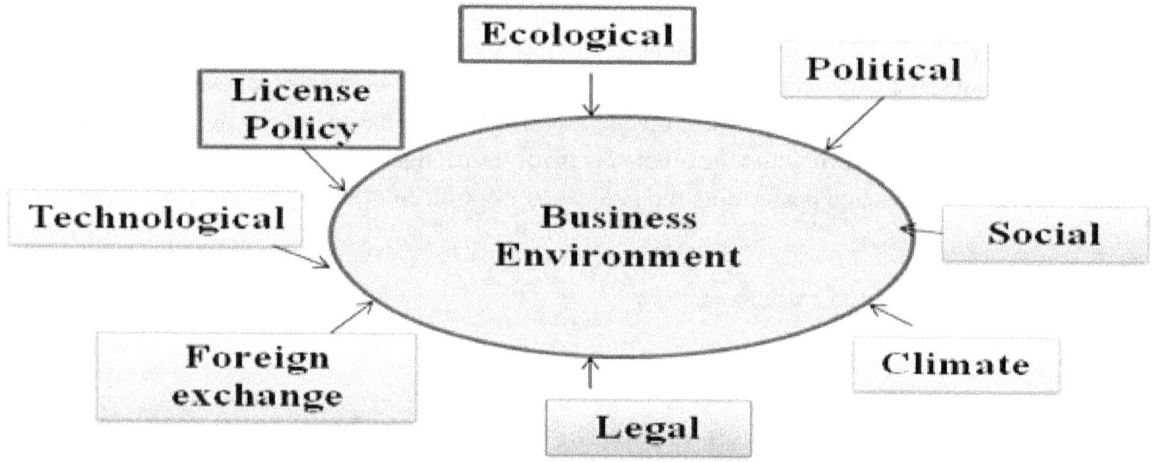

Figure 5. Global business monitor based entrepreneurship

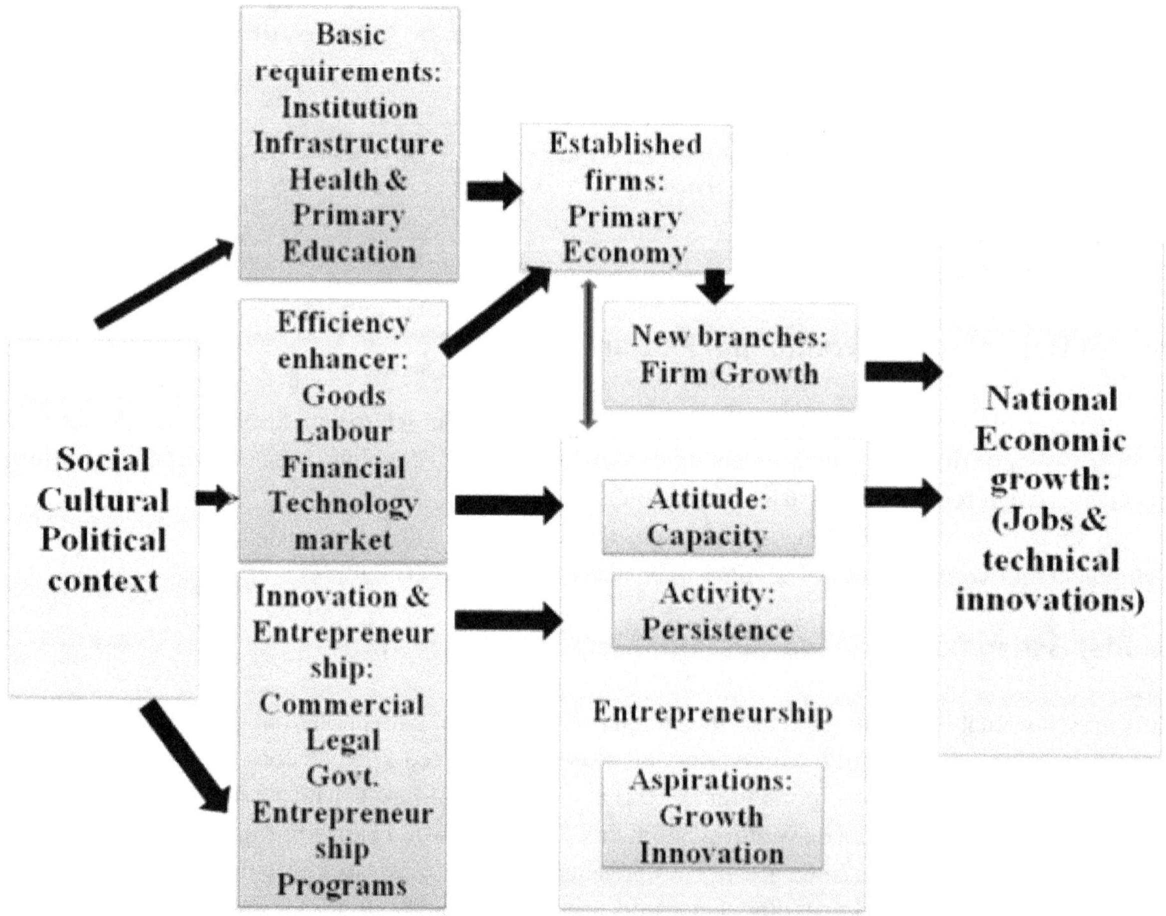

ADMINISTRATIVE ENTREPRENEURSHIP

All administrative techniques based on administration and management of business and products are subjected into administrative entrepreneurship. Administrative entrepreneurship gives ideas of managing the quality, redesigning of job, new techniques to do things and management by consensus. All these tasks of this type of entrepreneurship maximize the efficiency of an organization and nukes the achievements of the firm and sustain in the competitive marketplace (Korunka et al., 2003).

Figure 6. Administrative based entrepreneurship

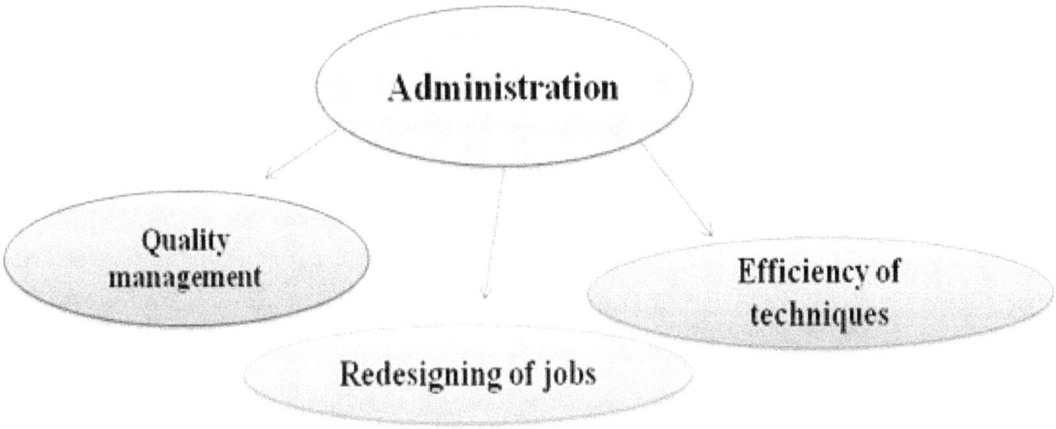

Biotechnology Entrepreneurship

Biotechnology is the key sector to solve problems or make products by using cellular and molecular processes (Zekos, 2006). Biotechnology is categorized into human health care, recombinant DNA technology, agricultural, installing advance instruments, providing lab chemical and setting the working environment. Biotechnology has materialized its role in different field of enhancing competitiveness, economic growth and environmental sustainability (DaSilva, 2004; Haeussler, 2007, 2011 a, b). Biotechnology industry needs to develop the solutions for better medical policy, agro-industry, environmental clean-up, and sustainability of aquatic and terrestrial resources (Figure 7). Bioprofessionals need to develop new strategies, instrumental and computer devices, methods, wet-labs, infrastructure for better products of high market value, diverse utility and durability at affordable cost (Gupta & Sapienza, 1992; Klein et al., 2001). These challenges in biotechnology can be centered through research and development with the excellent awareness, data and information and communication technology (Lerner & Merges, 1998; Lerner et al., 2003; Lerner & Malmendier, 2010; Levitt, 1983). Entrepreneurship of bio-sciences, biotechnology and pharmaceutics can enhance the exposure among male and female students, researchers and professionals through new approaches (Langan-Fox & Roth, 1995). Development of bio-entrepreneurial activities also can improve start-up to endorse micro small and medium enterprises. Development of computing and engineering technology for validation and delivery of products can expend the venture from ground to top level with growing economy in various fields.

Figure 7. Sub-divisions of biotechnology with some of their products, (Shaikh, 2013)

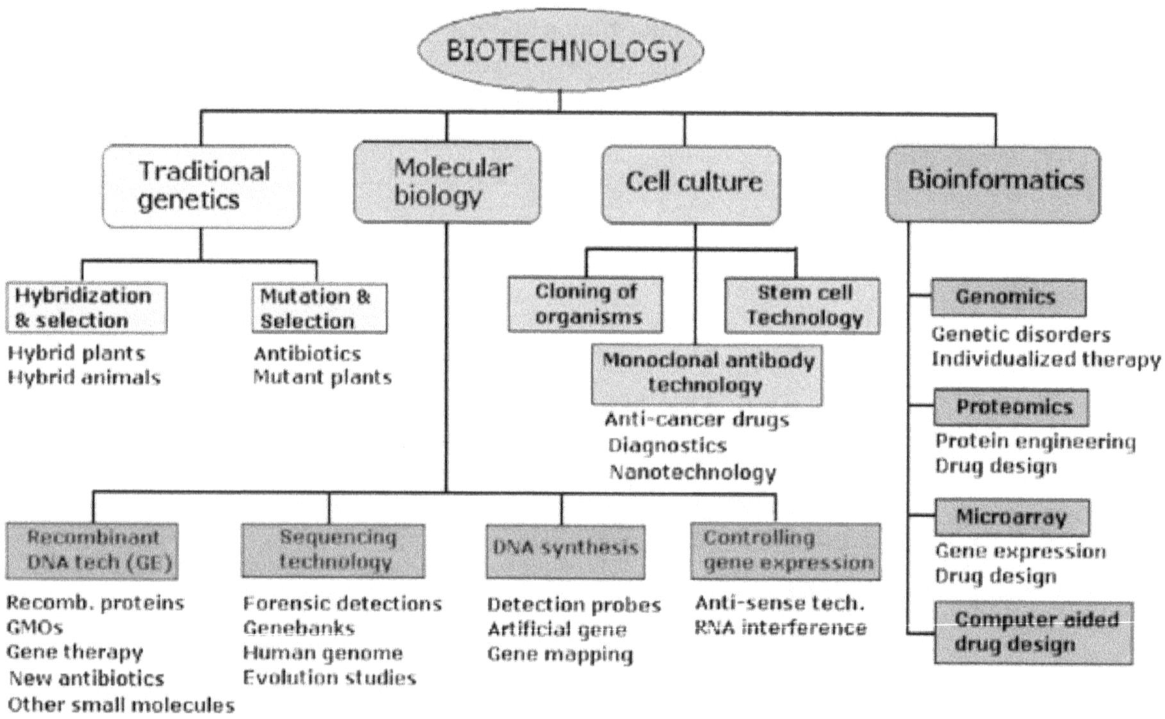

Medical Biotechnology

This deals with application of biotechnology in medical aspects to produce pharmaceutical and complex biological molecules to diagnose, prevent or cure the diseases (Shaikh, 2013). Researchers and scientist are growing forward in stem cell therapy through biotechnology (Figure 8). The Salk Research Institute, a nonprofit medical biotechnical organization, produced a new pluripotent stem cell in 2017 which developed embryo of mice to the adult stage. Also these extended pluripotent stem cell were helpful to generate muscle, blood, bone and tissue cells and placenta. Gene therapy based on intertwines of living organisms are another future of biotechnology to treat a variety of inherited and acquire diseases (Young et al., 2006).

The U.S. developed first direct administered gene therapy Luxturna targets a disease caused by mutations in a specific gene. The therapy helps to deliver a normal copy of the RPE65 gene directly into retinal cells. The retinal cells start producing enzymes that convert light into vision. Likewise medicinal proteins have been procured and evaluated in microorganism through genetic engineering in microorganisms (bacteria, fungi and virus). By recombining the human gene of beta cells of the Islets of Langerhans into bacteria biotechnologists had developed life-saving insulin protein on large level. This genetically procured insulin was given to the diabetes patients who were not able to metabolize the glucose in body. Recombinant DNA technology developed some other human serum albumin proteins, interferon signaling proteins, erythropoietin and growth hormone hormones used as vaccines to treat the diseases (Kim, 2013).

Figure 8. Biotechnology in various medical sectors

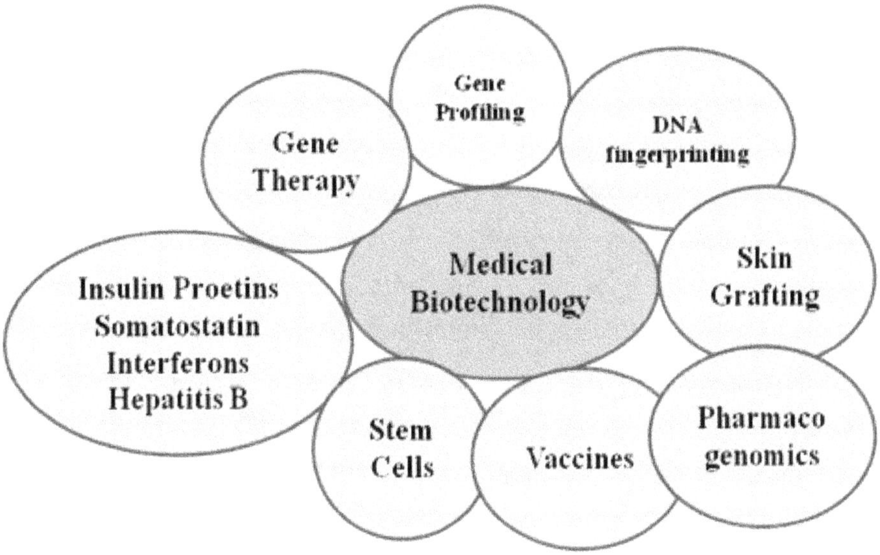

Hepatitis B, the first recombinant vaccine was developed by slipping a gene fragment into genetic machinery of yeast cell (Kniskern & Miller, 1992). Stem cells are capable to produce any kind of tissues in human and animal body to replace damaged tissue. These cells have been used in treatment of human diabetes and Alzheimer diseases (Becker et al., 1963). So that is how biotechnology is using biological systems to evolve any desirable product to gratify human need.

Agricultural Biotechnology

Biotechnology is becoming an extended field in agriculture to improve genetic variations in plant species to adopt the environment factors and demand of higher yield (Dookun, 2001, Giddings et al., 2000; Serageldin, 1999). Biotechnology allows improvement of genetic map, gene manipulation, genetic engineering in plants, animals and microorganisms to increase their important nutritional traits and life value (Figure 9.). The development of disease and pest resistant varieties of wheat has been practiced by cross-breeding in a resulting new improved variety with desirable traits (Phillips, 2002). This branch includes the genetically modified products GM foods and biotech foods produced from transgenic plants through transgenic technique of gene alteration and transform (Dookun, 2001; Gidding et al., 2000; Toenniessen et al., 2003). DNA transform, DNA transgenic technology progressed in field of recombining the DNA segment or gene of a specific characteristic in the new organism to enhance its quality in terms of life, yield and work efficiency (Paul, 2016).

Research professionals from the Cornell University and Hawaii University developed two improved papaya verities resistant to virus papaya ringspot by transferring one of the virus genes in papaya plant. These two modified verities SunUp and Rainbow were supplied to farmers under legal agreements in 1998 for papaya farming (Ferreira et al., 2002).

Figure 9. Biotechnology in various agricultural sectors

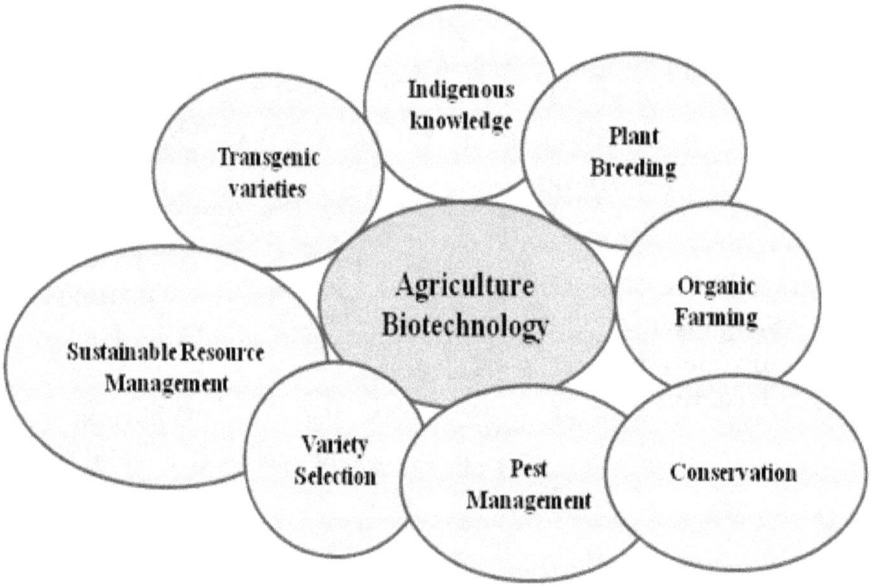

Similarly several other crops such as corn, golden rice rich in carotene and vitamin A, Bt cotton (Hu et al., 2009), and potato have been genetically engineered through genetic manipulation technique for better edible and marketing qualities. The protein isolated from the soil bacterium *Bacillus thuringiensis* has been used as effective insecticides for pest management. India also hosts the International Crops Research Institute for the Semi-Arid Tropics (ICRISAT), a Consultative Group on International Agricultural Research (CGIAR) supported center involved in agricultural research. International organizations such as United Nations Industrial Development Organization (UNIDO), World Health Organization (WHO), United States Agency for International Development (USAID) and some European agencies have been financially supporting research and development in agriculture and healthcare.

Chemical and Environmental Biotechnology

Environmental biotechnology is tool to sustain microbial interaction with environment to keep it globally ideal and naturally productive. To eliminate the negative toxic human influence and promoting the well-being and vitality of all living organisms (plants and animals) in the environment biotechnology techniques and genetic modifications are being used as major criteria for environment sustainability (Ahuja & Katila, 2001).

Red biotechnology covers the genetic modification technique to develop the drugs and vaccines in microorganisms, animal cell and in plant cells. White biotechnology encompasses the fermentation technology, produced material and chemicals such as enzymes, biofuels, alcohol bio-ethanol and bioplastics. Biotechnology has evolved its scope in in-situ bioremediation by recycling waste water and municipal sewage, industrial effluents, and solid wastes to reduce global pollution level (Figure 10).

Figure 10. Implement of biotechnology in environment

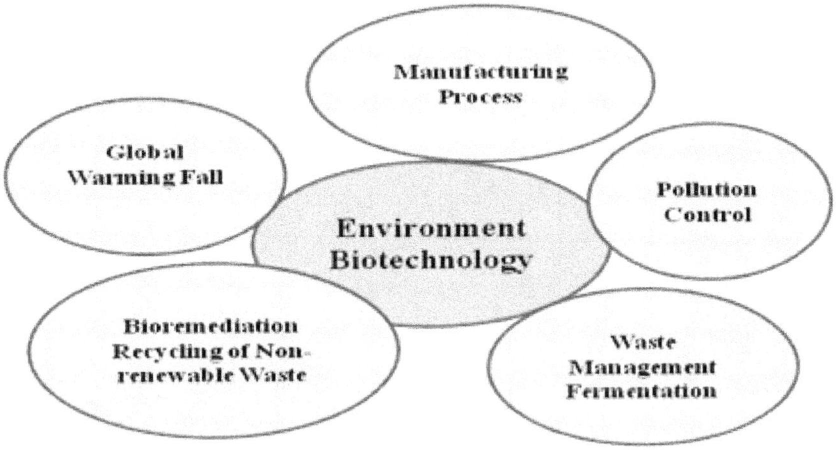

BIOTECHNOLOGY MARKET

Biotechnology is a junction of various bio-fields pharmaceutical, medical, agricultural and environmental which constitute in total biotechnology market internationally (Hauser et al., 2006; Henkel & Maurer, 2010). The world second-largest economy remodels the potential of biotechnology to endorse economic growth by transforming health, energy, agriculture, environment and more (Hagedoorn, 1993; Haleblian et al., 2006; Hambrick & Cannella, 1993).

In 2000 biopharmaceuticals market reported 25% of Europe and 16% of Japan with market capacity of about USD 17 billion (Figure 11). The section for GM crops and pesticides reported less than USD 8 billion. In cumulative estimate of USD 26 billion, biotechnology and pharmaceutics showed higher productivity than the rest of the market (EIB, 2002).

Biotechnology share in China is schemed to beat USD 60 billion by 2025 in medicinal field (Figure 12). Several investments in medicinal enterprises and healthcare transformations will overcome the drug shortage at considerable market growth. In May 2018, Illumina an American company purchased San Diego based Edico Genome company working in field of development of cutting edge solutions for next-generation sequencing (NGS). This collaborative interaction of genomic companies will improve the nucleotides sequencing, genotyping and gene expression and proteomics markets in future (Ugalmugle & Swain, 2020).

In 2018, U.S Department of Agriculture (USDA) published a report that global calculated worth of bio-economy together with industrial biotechnology, renewable chemicals, and polymers, biofuels, enzymes, and biomaterials – is $355.28 billion.

It is expecting to increase to approximately $487 billion by 2024. Between 2010 and 2015, venture capitalists invest $9.2 billion into the industrial biotechnology sector. Synthetic biology startups raised the largest share of that venture capital – $1.7 billion in 2017.

Figure 11. Biotechnology in therapeutics to explore the industrial growth of medicine and bio-pharmacy (Ugalmugle and Swain, 2020)

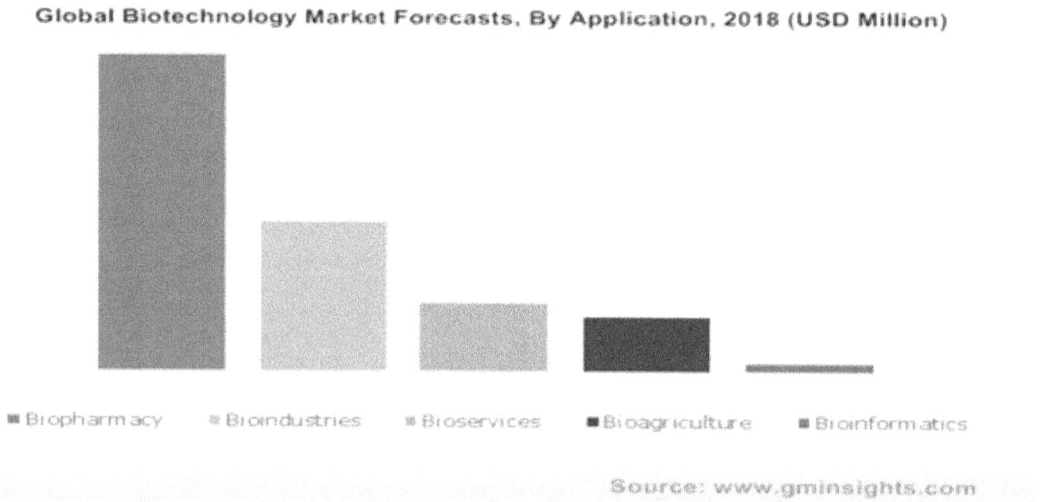

Figure 12. China: as major emerging country in field of biotechnology (Ugalmugle and Swain, 2020)

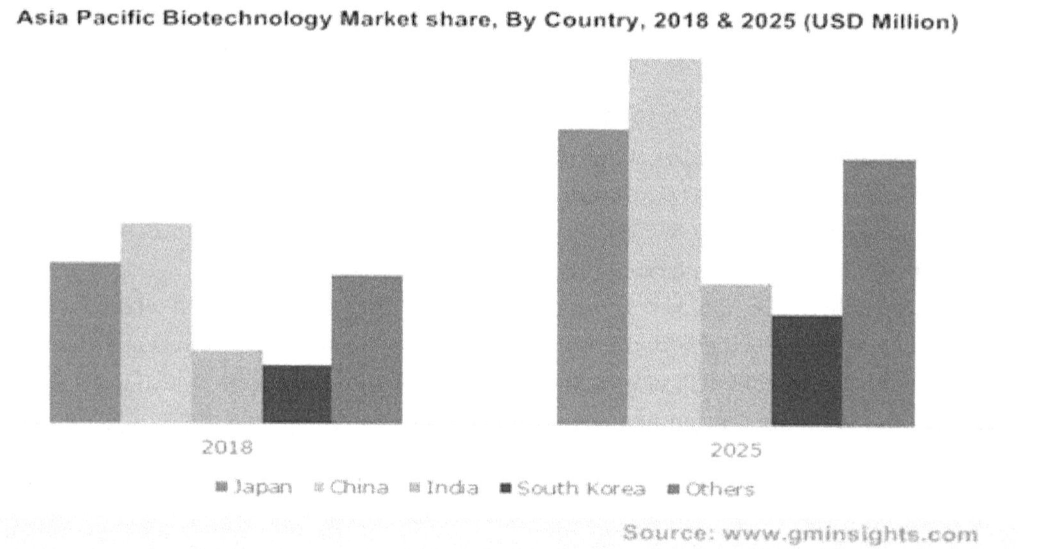

FACTORS AFFECTING THE BIOTECHNOLOGY ENTERPRISES

The survey of EuropaBio (1997) categorized some key factors that affect the investment share and strategies of companies in biotechnological market on the basis of market condition, consumer's demand and feedback (Aghmiuni et al., 2020; Persidis, 1997).

Advancement and growth in biotechnology is outcome of collaboration of fundamental analytical research of national research institutes and marketing based applied research and development firms (Table 1). Figure 13, shows how the institutional and industrial features affect the entrepreneurial explore of biotechnology in nation. Stock of experimental knowledge in research institutions, synchronization of marketing knowledge between research institutions and industry and implement of that marketing knowledge in industry are the pointing features of bio-economic analysis in any country (Hoang & Rothaermel, 2005, 2010; Hsu, 2007). These growth models and entrepreneurial knowledge of methodical research and industry create new innovative ideas and marketing bioproducts into research and development with great turnover (Huckman & Zinner, 2008; Kaiser & Prange, 2004).

Corporate in Alliance with Research and Development in India

The world is developing faster. Competition in industries is growing harder and more with many cut-off points (Alok, 2011; Fritsch & Mueller, 2007; Luo and Deng, 2009). To build the business enterprise in competitive environment, it is very important to develop the alliances with other research and development firms for fundamental knowledge and entrepreneurial set up to continue (Audretsch, 2001; Audretsch & Stephan, 1999). Alliances based on joint projects, strategic research and development, syndicate involving technology transfers, licensing agreements, management service, franchising agreements, outsourcing agreements and cross-manufacturing offer dynamic profits and challenging market coverage (Baum et al., 2000; Carayannopoulos & Auster, 2010; Lundvall, 1992). India is among the world's top 12 biotech authorities and ranked 3rd in Asia-Pacific region with the growth rate of 25% (Kumar & Srivastava, 2012). India has a good percentage of companies working in agriculture sectors with the foreign alliances (Figure 14), while about 800 companies (worth US$ 11 billion) related to biotechnology is emerging with 20% annual growth rate in different healthcare, pharmaceutics, vaccines and medicines, food production, agriculture, seed technology and environmental field (Table 2).

Table 1. Factors that affect the investment

Factor	Percentage of companies that believe factor is important
Market Opportunity	100%
Patent Protection	85%
Regulatory environment	60%
Competitor Pressure	60%
Consumer Acceptance	55%
Availability of Skilled Labor	40%
Technology Transfer Mechanisms	35%
Availability of Equity Capital	20%
Scale and Quality of Public R&D	15%
Access to Innovative Suppliers	8%

Figure 13. Flow of biotechnology on national entrepreneurial level

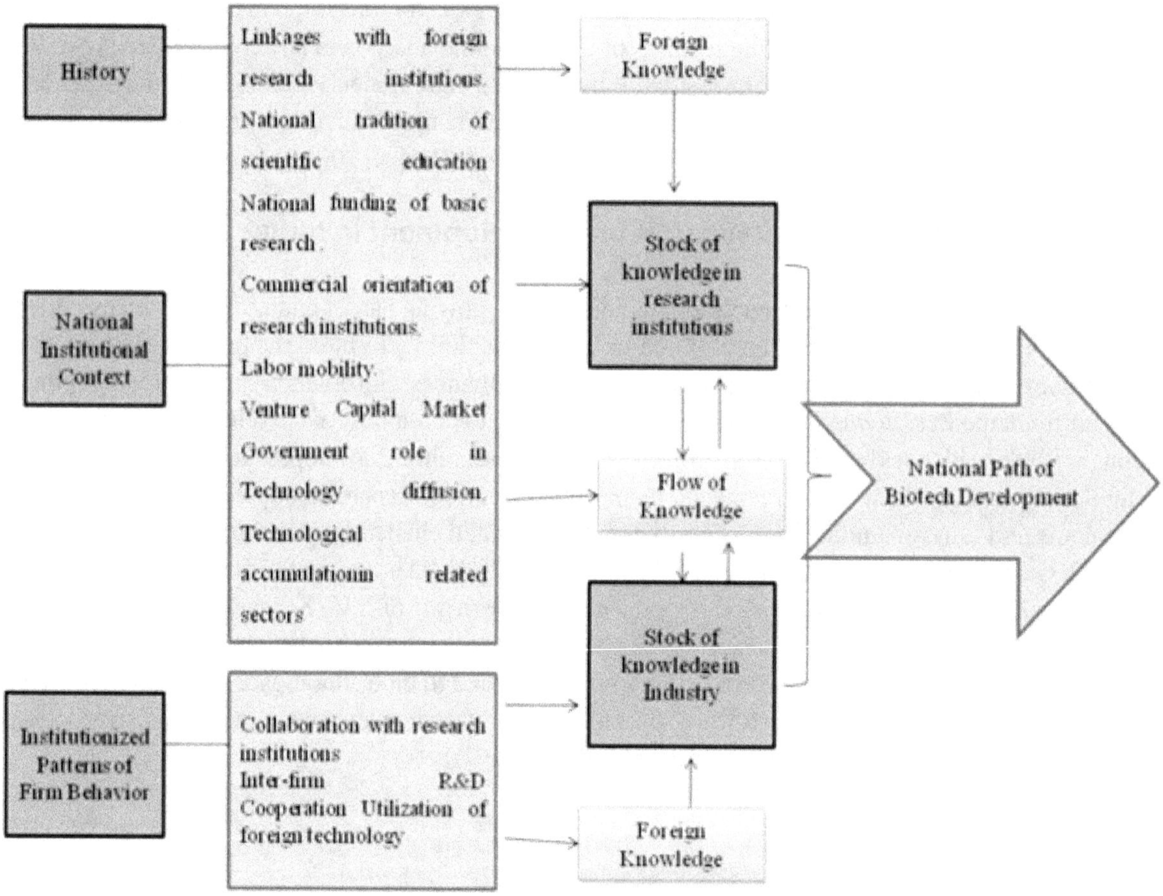

Biotech Consortium India Ltd was set up in 1990 as a public company, with the objective of providing the linkages among research institutions, industry, government and funding institutions, to facilitate accelerated commercialization of biotechnology (Kale et al., 2002, Katila & Mang, 2003; Kim & Higgins, 2007; king et al., 2008). To flourish the international research market in collaboration of Indian research and industry, Indian government has signed several bilateral agreements for executing joint ventures and human resource development programs with both developed and developing countries such as Switzerland, Sweden, Germany, United Kingdom, Japan, Taiwan, France, Israel, Sri Lanka, Myanmar successfully (Lecher, et al., 2006; Lee, 2010; Lehrer, 2007).

We are moving forward in every field of science. Soon a time will come, there will be more demand for highly effective and better medical care. Also, the production of better crops and other life-related problems will become such huge challenges (Kogut, 1988; Konde, 2009; Larsson & Finkelstein, 1999).

Biotechnology and *Synthetic Biology* based startups will be needed to come forward and tackle these changes. Till then let us see how things move forward and how things get unfold.

As per national reports on Biotechnology market in India the estimate goes between USD 1.5 to USD 2.5 billion, which comprises into agriculture sector market between USD 450 to USD 500 million and diagnostic share between USD 150 to USD 420 million (Chaturverdi, 2002). So, the industry showed revenue from USD 1.5 to USD 4.3 billion between 1999 and 2010. During the 2017-18, India estimated the raise above 5.0 billion USD in Biotechnology by the entrepreneurship of more than 500 national companies working in Biotech industry with a share of 3% in the global biotechnology market and 80-85% share of the Indian market to standardize the national biotech institutions and research centers challenging the world standards.

Figure 14. A – Sectoral breakup of biotechnology firms in India B – Foreign alliances of Indian biotechnology firms (Chaturverdi, 2002)

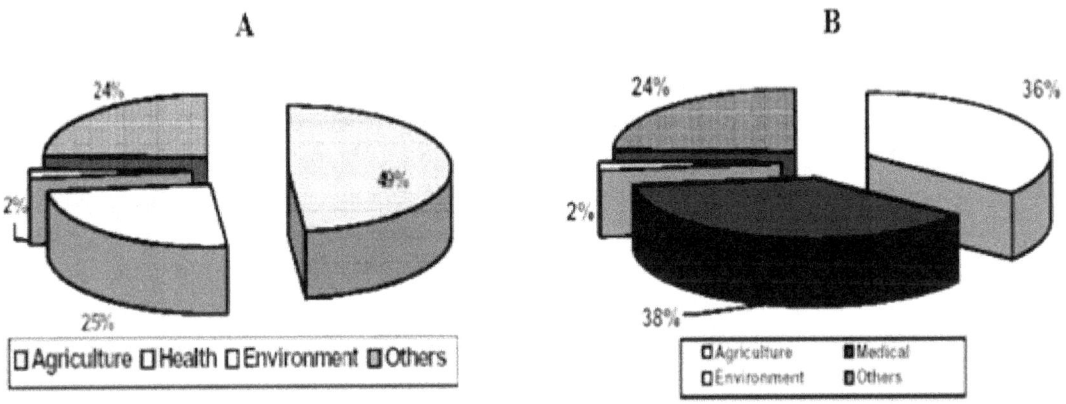

To manufacture oral polio vaccine India has collaborated with United States under Indo-US Vaccine Action Program focused on developing vaccines and diagnostics for communicable diseases. Recent in 2020 India has joined international Covax alliance program (GAVI, the vaccine alliance) directed by the World Health Organization (WHO) to develop vaccine against corona virus COVID-19 for every nation in world. The 92 countries of low and middle economy were approved by the GAVI- The Vaccine Alliance Board for accessing the COVID-19 vaccines through the COVAX AMC at low cost.

At global Vaccine summit 2020, The Indian Prime Minister Mr. have pledged USD 15-million as India's contribution to GAVI, the Vaccine Alliance.

Vivek Ramaswami, Indian (Kerala) origin based entrepreneur established the pharmaceutical companies Roivant Sciences and Axovant Sciences working on treatments for dementia, Axovant for neurology, Myovant for women's health and endocrine disease, urovant for urology and dermavant for dermatology. Ramaswamy was ranked the 24th richest American entrepreneur under 40 in 2016 with net worth at $600 million.

LOCALIZATION OF BIOTECH INDUSTRY IN INDIA

The entrepreneurs have started and developed companies in three major group across the India. The terms of income received through biotech market the western group includes Aurangabad, Mumbai, Pune and Ahmadabad cities, followed by the Hyderabad, Bangalore and Chennai as southern groups. The third northern group started biotech industrialization in Delhi, Gurgaon and Noida sectors. Bangalore,

Hyderabad (Knowledge Park, the Biotech Park, Genome Valley) and Chennai are the foremost cities in India working in cooperation with international biotech companies (Table 3). Also many cities like Coimbatore, Goa, Mysore, Kolkata, Gurgaon, Thrissur, Nagpur and Tiruchirapalli have huge prospective to focus and become developed in biotechnology area (Bagchi-Sen & Smith, 2008).

BIRAC has established many Bio-Incubators in the country for the same purpose. Top Bio-incubators are located in the Biotech Science Clusters. So far, four Bio-clusters have been established (at Faridabad, Bangalore, Kalyani and Pune) to spur innovative research and development and boost Bio-entrepreneurship. NCR Biotech Science cluster, located at Faridabad, is one of the most sought after destinations for Scientist, Innovators and Bio-entrepreneurs. It aims to provide strategic support to national & regional research organizations in creation and integration of scientific, technical & business related frameworks that would accelerate and translate discoveries and carry out validation and transfer of product technologies to enterprises.

BSC BioNEST Bio-Incubator (BBB) is one such Bio-Incubator located in NCR Biotech Science cluster. BBB is one of the largest and most advanced types of Bio-incubator in Delhi NCR. BBB is funded by BIRAC under the BioNEST (Bioincubators Nurturing Entrepreneurship for Scaling Technologies) scheme, managed and operated by Regional Centre for Biotechnology (RCB) which is recognized as an institute of national importance by the Parliament of India and is a Category II centre under the auspices of UNESCO. Presence of a world class Biotech Science Cluster facility with an access to pool of scientists from the cluster makes the journey of Bio-entrepreneurship more fulfilling & enriched in India.

UNIVERSITIES CONDUCTING BIOENTREPRENEURSHIP

Some International universities are providing bioentrepreneurship courses to the bioentrepreneurs to learn different skills in marketing allianced with science.

Karolinska Institutet
Copenhagen Business School
Enterprises University of Pretoria
Simonyi BEDC
Novo Nordisk Foundation
University of Zurich
The University of Queensland, Australia

RECOMMENDED BOOKS FOR BIOENTREPRENEURSHIP

"Handbook of Bioentrepreneurship" by Thomas Brenner & Holger Patzelt
"What's Your Bio Strategy?" By John Cumbers & Karl Schmieder
"Biology is Technology" by Robert H. Carlson
"The Industries of the Future" by Alec Ross

Table 2. Top 10 biotech companies in India

Rank	Company	Biotech turnover (Rs Crore)	Growth (% age)	Working/ Production Sector
1	Biocon	646.36	28.76	Biopharmaceutical
2	Serum Institute of India	565	2.73	Immunobiological drugs including vaccines
3	Panacea Biotech	217.29	45.83	Pharmaceutical and vaccine
4	Venkateshwara Hatcheries	188	113.64	Human and animal vaccines, pharmaceutical and healthcare
5	Mahyco Monsanto	166.4	208.15	Joint venture between US agriculture company Monsanto and Maharashtra Hybrid Seeds Company, sublicenses Bt cotton technology
6	Novo Nordisk	135	22.73	Globally working on diabetes, rare bleeding disorders, growth hormone- disorders and obesity
7	Rasi Seeds	86.87	-	Specializes in producing quality hybrid seeds
8	Aventis Pharma	84.3	15.48	Pharmaceuticals
9	Bharat Serums	81	1.66	Biological, biotech and pharmaceutical products
10	Chiron Behring Vaccines	78	16.42	Vaccines and medicines

BIOENTREPRENEURSHIP CONFERENCES/SUMMITS

SynBioBeta – A Synthetic Biology Innovation Network
Bioentrepreneurship Summit

Table 3. Miscellaneous list of companies dealing with biotech in India

Biotech Parks in India	Indian Biotech Companies	International Companies in India
Andhra Pradesh - Development and scale-up of bioprocesses and technologies	Biocon, Shantha Biotechnics, Bharat Biotech Dr. Reddy's Laboratories, Serum Institute of India	Monsanto, Pfizer, Astra Zeneca
Andhra Pradesh - Development and scale-up of bioprocesses and technologies	Zydus Cadila, Aventis Pharma Reliance Life Sciences, Panacea Biotec	Dupont, Bayer, Eli Lilly,
Karnataka - Drugs and Pharma	Ranbaxy Laboratories Ltd., Sun Pharmaceuticals Industries Ltd.	Novozymes South Asia
Punjab - Agribusiness and Certification of Export Goods	GVK Biosciences Pvt. Ltd., Nuziveedu Seeds, Rasi Seeds	Millipore,
Kerala - Traditional Medicines	Novo Nordisk,	Unilever
Himachal Pradesh - Medicinal and Aromatic Plants, Horticulture	Indian Immunologicals, Mahyco Jubilant, Themis Medicare	Hoechst Roussel Vet

REGULATIONS AND CONCLUSION

The important aspect that would support more the various industrial sectors to survive and attain long-term sustainable growth on an international scale would be innovative policy and academic research and methodical explore. Also regional universities, firms, bio-laboratories, industrial enterprises related to biotechnology or pharmaceutics, projects sectioned under government schemes with great financial interest can explore the long-term biotechnology and pharmaceutical industries and networks in India with the working skills of male and female successful entrepreneurs supervising the multidiscipline business problems and risk factors in bioindustry. Biotechnology is dealing with several aspects from agriculture to environment factors for improved genetic changes in plant species and good yield. Several reports and strategies have been brought in light to suggest that how the participation of national and international governments can facilitate the platform and one to one interaction between researchers and scientists for research and development (R&D). Biotechnology Entrepreneurship and Management supports the national and international clusters to cover different challenge of technology and methodology into a working business case by managing all the aspects of business valuation, business development, partnering, biological manufacturing, FDA approvals and regulatory requirements. Commercializing the biotechnology or pharmaceutical industry in the way of market income has many technical, analytical and scientific risks also, which control the capitalization and enhance uncertainty of return on investment for investors in any project. Early stage companies generally fail to convince big sponsors to invest money on set up of small or large scale business venture with these market risks, so as an entrepreneur one should has the stock of knowledge to clear the doubts that will encourage the shareholders to invest and will decrease the risks. Thus, the main objective of entrepreneurship is to raise awareness on the importance of marketing in pharmaceutical, medicinal and biotechnology sectors and to provide them with an entrepreneurial knowledge stock for successful business and return on invest. This way the biotechnology and pharmaceutical industries will have cumulative massive potential in the coming few years with the help of skilled graduates, post-graduates aware of marketing needs and capitalization. By 2025 the biotechnology sector in the country is likely to reach $100 billion level with the present annual growth rate of around 20 per cent and may accelerate its average growth rate to about 30 per cent. The overall share of biotechnology sector in the country is around $ 4.5 billion at the moment, of which around 60 per cent is the share of pharmaceutical industry. Gross Domestic Product (GDP) of agriculture and allied sectors in India has been growing at a compound annual growth rate (CAGR) of 3.3 per cent. Despite the focus on industrialization, agriculture remains a dominant sector of the Indian economy both in terms of contribution to GDP as well as a source of employment to millions across the country.

Pharmaceuticals and agricultural food products developed by in-vitro technology are needed to be regulated in all aspects of the life span, implement, safety, effectiveness, manufacturing quality and intellectual value in terms of its effect on human health. Regulation of biotech market involves both resource costs and delayed apply of drugs or clinical pharmaceutical products on patients. Regulation should preferably restrict pricing ethical risk while maintaining insurance for patients and incentive for research and development. This chapter depicts the growth of market in various industrial disciplines of biotechnology and its regulation across the world for welfare and finical profit and novelty in science.

Biotech field is growing enormous in India which will lead this sector one of the top techno-industries in next few years with millions of jobs in national biotech companies. Though, the concept of bioentrepreneurship is fairly emerging in India, so researchers, institutions and scientists in India need to work on commendable fundamental research and technology. Also the entrepreneurs must understand the entrepreneurial collaboration, infrastructure and commercialization capital to come up with booming alternative business venture. Governments can also regulate the system to support small biotech research and development agencies and firms, research institutions and universities by funding on innovative project proposals to be performed. Public domains and national international agencies can explore these research findings and their benefits. Also the governments need to ensure the legal validity and intellectual property rights of entrepreneurs so that the famers, common people and users of biotech products are not exploited.

REFERENCES

Acs, Z. J., & Audretsch, D. B. (1988). Innovation in large and small firms: An empirical analysis. *The American Economic Review*, *78*(4), 678–690.

Adelberger, K. E. (2000). Semi-Sovereign Leadership? *The State's Role in German Biotechnology and Venture Capital Growth in German Politics.*, *9*, 103–122.

Aghmiuni, K. S., Siyal, S., Wang, Q., & Duan, Y. (2020). Assessment of factors affecting innovation policy in biotechnology. *Journal of Innovation and Knowledge*, *5*(3), 180–190. doi:10.1016/j.jik.2019.10.002

Ahuja, G., & Katila, R. (2001). Technological acquisitions and the innovation performance of acquiring firms: A longitudinal study. *Strategic Management Journal*, *22*(3), 197–220. doi:10.1002mj.157

Alok, K. S. (2011). Biotechnology: The new horizon for Indian leadership. *VSRD Technical and Non Technical Journal.*, *2*(3), 144–159.

Alper, J. (2002). The rise of the European Bioentrepreneur. *Nature Biotechnology*, *20*(S6), 3–5. doi:10.1038/nbt0602supp-BE3 PMID:12089569

Alvarez, S. A., & Busenitz, L. W. (2001). The entrepreneurship of resource-based theory. *Journal of Management*, *27*(6), 755–775. doi:10.1177/014920630102700609

Athreye, S., & Chaturvedi, S. (2007). Industry Associations and Technology-based Growth in India. *European Journal of Development Research*, *19*(1), 156–173. doi:10.1080/09578810601144426

Audretsch, D. B. (2001). The role of small firms in US biotechnology clusters. *Small Business Economics*, *17*(1/2), 3–15. doi:10.1023/A:1011140014334

Audretsch, D. B., & Stephan, P. E. (1999). Knowledge spillovers in biotechnology: Sources and incentives. *Journal of Evolutionary Economics*, *9*(1), 97–107. doi:10.1007001910050076

Bagchi-Sen, S., & Smith, H. L. (2008). Science, institutions, and markets: Developments in the Indian biotechnology sector. *Regional Studies*, *42*(7), 961–975. doi:10.1080/00343400701652800

Baum, A., Calabrese, T., & Silverman, B. S. (2000). Don't go it alone: Alliance network composition and startup's performance in Canadian biotechnology. *Strategic Management Journal*, *21*(3), 267–294. doi:10.1002/(SICI)1097-0266(200003)21:3<267::AID-SMJ89>3.0.CO;2-8

Becker, A. J., McCulloch, E. A., & Till, J. E. (1963). Cytological de-monstration of the clonal nature of spleen colonies derived from transplanted mouse marrow cells. *Nature, 197*(4866), 452–454. doi:10.1038/197452a0 PMID:13970094

Bellu, R. R., & Flume, P. (2004). Religiosity and entrepreneurial behavior. *International Journal of Entrepreneurship and Innovation, 5*(3), 191–201. doi:10.5367/0000000041513411

Carayannopoulos, S., & Auster, E. R. (2010). External knowledge sourcing in biotechnology through acquisition versus alliance: A KBV approach. *Research Policy, 39*(2), 254–267. doi:10.1016/j.respol.2009.12.005

Carrier, C. (1996). Intrapreneurship in small businesses: An exploratory study. *Entrepreneurship Theory and Practice, 21*(1), 5–20. doi:10.1177/104225879602100101

Carsrud, A. L., Brannback, M., & Renko, M. (2008). Strategy and strategic thinking in biotechnology entrepreneurship. Handbook of Bioentrepreneurship, 81 – 101.

Catherine, D., Corolleur, F., Carrere, M., & Mangematin, V. (2004). Turning scientific and technological human capital into economic capital: The experience of biotech start-ups in France. *Research Policy, 33*(4), 631–642. doi:10.1016/j.respol.2004.01.009

Chaturvedi, S. (2002). *Measuring Developments in Biotechnology*. OECD.

Cohen, W., & Levinthal, D. (1990). Absorptive capacity: A new perspective on learning and innovation. *Administrative Science Quarterly, 35*(1), 128–152. doi:10.2307/2393553

DaSilva, J. E. (2004). The colours of biotechnology: Science, development and humankind. *Electronic Journal of Biotechnology, 7*(3).

Dodgson, M., Gann, D., & Salter, A. (2008). *The management of technological innovation: Strategy and Practice*. Oxford University Press.

Dookun, A. (2001). Agricultural biotechnology in developing countries. *Biotechnology Annual Review, 7*, 261–285. doi:10.1016/S1387-2656(01)07040-5 PMID:11686047

Douglas, F. L., Narayanan, V. K., Mitchell, L., & Litan, E. R. (2010). The case for entrepreneurship in R&D in the pharmaceutical industry. *Nature Reviews. Drug Discovery, 9*(9), 683–689. doi:10.1038/nrd3230 PMID:20725093

EIB – European Investment Bank. (2002). *Biotechnology: An overview*. EIB Sector Papers.

Evans, A. G., & Varaiya, N. (2003). Anne Evans: Assessment of a biotechnology market opportunity. *Entrepreneurship Theory and Practice, 28*(1), 87–105. doi:10.1111/1540-8520.00033

Ferreira, S. A., Pitz, K. Y., Manshardt, R., Zee, F., Fitch, M., & Gonsalves, D. (2002). Virus coat protein transgenic papaya provides practical control of Papaya ringspot virus in Hawaii. *Plant Disease, 86*(2), 101–105. doi:10.1094/PDIS.2002.86.2.101 PMID:30823304

Fritsch, M., & Mueller, P. (2007). The persistence of regional new business formation-activity over time–assessing the potential of policy promotion programs. *Journal of Evolutionary Economics, 17*(3), 299–315. doi:10.100700191-007-0056-6

Giddings, G., Allison, G., Brooks, D., & Carter, A. (2000). Transgenic plants as factories for biopharmaceuticals. *Nature Biotechnology*, *18*(11), 1151–1155. doi:10.1038/81132 PMID:11062432

Gupta, A. K., & Sapienza, H. J. (1992). 'Determinants of venturecapital firms' preference regarding the industry diversity and geo-graphic scope of their investments'. *Journal of Business Venturing*, *7*(5), 347–362. doi:10.1016/0883-9026(92)90012-G

Haeussler, C. (2007). Proactive versus reactive M&A activities in the biotechnology industry. *The Journal of High Technology Management Research*, *17*(2), 109–123. doi:10.1016/j.hitech.2006.11.001

Haeussler, C. (2011a). The determinants of commercialization strategy: Idiosyncrasies in British and German biotechnology. *Entrepreneurship Theory and Practice*, *35*(4), 653–681. doi:10.1111/j.1540-6520.2010.00385.x

Haeussler, C. (2011b). Information sharing in academia and the industry: A comparative study. *Research Policy*, *40*(1), 105–122. doi:10.1016/j.respol.2010.08.007

Hagedoorn, J. (1993). Understanding the rationale of strategic technology partnering: Inter organizational modes of cooperation and sectoral differences. *Strategic Management Journal*, *14*(5), 371–385. doi:10.1002mj.4250140505

Haleblian, J., Kim, J. Y., & Rajagopalan, N. (2006). The influence of acquisition experience and performance on acquisition behavior: Evidence from the US commercial banking industry. *Academy of Management Journal*, *49*(2), 357–370. doi:10.5465/amj.2006.20786083

Hambrick, D. C., & Cannella, A. A. (1993). Relative standing: A framework for understanding departures of acquired executives. *Academy of Management Journal*, *36*, 733–762.

Hauser, J., Tellis, G., & Griffin, A. (2006). Research on innovation: A review and Agenda for marketing science. *Marketing Science*, *25*(6), 687–717. doi:10.1287/mksc.1050.0144

Henkel, J., & Maurer, S. (2010). Network effects in biology R&D. *The American Economic Review*, *100*(2), 159–164. doi:10.1257/aer.100.2.159

Hisrich, R., Langan-Fox, J., & Grant, S. (2007). Entrepreneurship research and practice: A call to action for psychology. *The American Psychologist*, *62*(6), 575–589. doi:10.1037/0003-066X.62.6.575 PMID:17874898

Hisrich, R. D. (1990). Entrepreneurship/intrapreneurship. *The American Psychologist*, *45*(2), 209–222. doi:10.1037/0003-066X.45.2.209

Hoang, H., & Rothaermel, F. T. (2005). The effect of general and partner-specific alliance experience on joint R&D project performance. *Academy of Management Journal*, *48*(2), 332–345. doi:10.5465/amj.2005.16928417

Hoang, H., & Rothaermel, F. T. (2010). Leveraging internal and external experience: Exploration, exploitation, and R&D project performance. *Strategic Management Journal*, *31*, 734–758. doi:10.1002mj.834

Hsu, D. H. (2007). Experienced entrepreneurial founders, organizational capital, and venture capital funding. *Research Policy*, *36*(5), 722–741. doi:10.1016/j.respol.2007.02.022

Hu, R., Pray, C., Huang, J., Rozelle, S., Fan, C., & Zhang, C. (2009). Reforming intellectual property rights and the Bt cotton seed industry in China: Who benefits from policy reform. *Research Policy*, *38*(5), 793–801. doi:10.1016/j.respol.2008.12.008

Huckman, R. S., & Zinner, D. E. (2008). Does focus improve operational performance? Lessons from the management of clinical trials'. *Strategic Management Journal*, *29*(2), 173–193. doi:10.1002mj.650

Kaiser, R., & Prange, H. (2004). The reconfiguration of National Innovation Systems— The example of German biotechnology. *Research Policy*, *33*(3), 395–408. doi:10.1016/j.respol.2003.09.001

Kale, P., Dyer, J. H., & Singh, H. (2002). Alliance capability, stock market response, and long term alliance success: The role of the alliance function. *Strategic Management Journal*, *23*(8), 747–767. doi:10.1002mj.248

Katila, R., & Mang, P. Y. (2003). Exploiting technological opportunities: The timing of collaborations. *Research Policy*, *32*(2), 317–332. doi:10.1016/S0048-7333(02)00102-6

Kim, J. W., & Higgins, M. C. (2007). Where do alliances come from? The effects of upper echelons on alliance formation. *Research Policy*, *36*(4), 499–514. doi:10.1016/j.respol.2007.02.017

Kim, W. (2013). Recombinant protein polymers in biomaterials. *Frontiers in Bioscience*, *18*(1), 289–304. doi:10.2741/4100 PMID:23276922

King, D. R., Slotegraaf, R. J., & Kesner, I. (2008). Performance implications of firm resource interactions in the acquisition of R&D-intensive firms. *Organization Science*, *19*(2), 327–340. doi:10.1287/orsc.1070.0313

Kirzner, I. M. (1973). *Competition and entrepreneurship*. University of Chicago Press.

Kirzner, I. M. (1997). Entrepreneurial discovery and the competitive market process: An Austrian approach. *Journal of Economic Literature*, *35*, 60–85.

Klein, K., Conn, A., & Speer, S. A. (2001). Implementing computerized technology: An organizational analysis. *The Journal of Applied Psychology*, *86*(5), 811–829. doi:10.1037/0021-9010.86.5.811 PMID:11596799

Kniskern, P. J., & Miller, W. J. (1992). Hepatitis B vaccines: Blueprints for vaccines of the future. *Biotechnology*, *20*, 177–204. PMID:1600381

Kogut, B. (1988). Joint ventures: Theoretical and empirical perspectives. *Strategic Management Journal*, *9*(4), 319–332. doi:10.1002mj.4250090403

Konde, V. (2009). Biotechnology business models: An Indian perspective. *Journal of Commercial Biotechnology*, *15*(3), 215–226. doi:10.1057/jcb.2008.52

Korunka, C., Frank, H., Lueger, M., & Mugler, J. (2003). The entrepreneurial personality in the context of resources, environment, and the startup process: A conðgurational approach. *Entrepreneurship Theory and Practice*, *28*(1), 23–42. doi:10.1111/1540-8520.00030

Kumar, A., & Srivastava, L. (2012). Biotechnology industry in India: Opportunities or challenges. *African Journal of Business Management*, *6*(44), 10834–10839. doi:10.5897/AJBM10.1236

Lafuente, A., & Salas, V. (1989). Types of entrepreneurs and ðrms: The case of new Spanish ðrms. *Strategic Management Journal*, *10*(1), 17–30. doi:10.1002mj.4250100103

Langan-Fox, J., & Roth, S. (1995). Achievement motivation and female entrepreneurs. *Journal of Occupational and Organizational Psychology*, *68*(3), 209–218. doi:10.1111/j.2044-8325.1995.tb00582.x

Larsson, R., & Finkelstein, S. (1999). Integrating strategic, organizational, and human resource perspectives on mergers and acquisitions: A case survey of synergy realization. *Organization Science*, *10*(1), 1–26. doi:10.1287/orsc.10.1.1

Lechner, C., Dowling, M., & Welpe, I. (2006). Firm networks and firm development: The role of the relational mix'. *Journal of Business Venturing*, *21*(4), 514–540. doi:10.1016/j.jbusvent.2005.02.004

Lee, J. (2010). Heterogeneity, brokerage, and innovative performance: Endogenous formation of collaborative inventor networks. *Organization Science*, *21*(4), 804–822. doi:10.1287/orsc.1090.0488

Lehrer, M. (2007). Organizing knowledge spillovers when basic and applied research is interdependent: German biotechnology policy in historical perspective. *The Journal of Technology Transfer*, *32*(3), 277–296. doi:10.100710961-006-9017-8

Lerner, J., & Malmendier, U. (2010). Contractibility and the design of research agreements. *The American Economic Review*, *100*(1), 214–246. doi:10.1257/aer.100.1.214

Lerner, J., & Merges, R. P. (1998). The control of technology alliances: An empirical analysis of the biotechnology industry. *The Journal of Industrial Economics*, *46*(2), 125–156. doi:10.1111/1467-6451.00066

Lerner, J., Shane, H., & Tsai, A. (2003). Do equity financing cycles matter? Evidence from biotechnology alliances. *Journal of Financial Economics*, *67*(3), 411–446. doi:10.1016/S0304-405X(02)00256-8

Levitt, T. (1983). The globalisation of markets. *Harvard Business Review*, *61*, 92–102.

Liebeskind, J. P., Oliver, A. L., Zucker, L., & Brewer, M. (1996). Social networks, learning, and flexibility: Sourcing scientific knowledge innew biotechnology firms. *Organization Science*, *7*(4), 428–443. doi:10.1287/orsc.7.4.428

Lundvall, B. K. (1992). *National innovation systems towards a theory of innovation and interactive learning*. Pinter.

Luo, X. R., Koput, K. W., & Powell, W. W. (2009). Intellectual capital or signal? The effects of scientists on alliance formation in knowledge-intensive industries. *Research Policy*, *38*(8), 1313–1325. doi:10.1016/j.respol.2009.06.001

Marks, M. L., & Mirvis, P. H. (2001). Making mergers and acquisitions work: Strategic and psychological preparation. *The Academy of Management Executive*, *15*(2), 80–92. doi:10.5465/ame.2001.4614947

Maurer, I., & Ebers, M. (2006). Dynamics of social capital and their performance implications: Lessons from biotechnology start-ups. *Administrative Science Quarterly*, *51*(2), 262–292. doi:10.2189/asqu.51.2.262

McMullen, J. S., Plummer, L. A., & Acs, Z. J. (2007). What is an entrepreneurial opportunity? *Small Business Economics*, *28*(4), 273–283. doi:10.100711187-006-9040-z

Patzelt, H., Schweizer, L., & Behrens, J. (2012). Biotechnology entrepreneurship. *Foundations and Trends in Entrepreneurship, 8*(2).

Paul, V. (2016). Genetic engineering and sustainable crop disease management: Opportunities for case-by-case decision-making. *Sustainability, 8*(495), 1–22.

Persidis, A. (1997). Bioentrepreneurship around the world; Bioentrepreneur II. *Nature Biotechnology*, 16.

Phillips, P. W. (2002). Biotechnology in the global agri-food system. *Trends in Biotechnology, 20*(9), 376–381. doi:10.1016/S0167-7799(02)02039-5 PMID:12175768

Schumpeter, J. A. (1934). The theory of economic development: an inquiry into profits, capital, credit, interest and the business cycle. Harvard Economic Studies, 46.

Serageldin, I. (1999). Biotechnology and food security in the 21st century. *Science, 285*(5426), 387–389. doi:10.1126cience.285.5426.387 PMID:10411497

Shaikh, M. (2013). Medical biotechnology: Problems and prospects in Bangladesh. *Journal of Enam Medical College., 3*(1), 32–46. doi:10.3329/jemc.v3i1.13873

Shane, S., & Venkataraman, S. (2000). The promise of entrepreneurship as a field of research. *Academy of Management Review, 25*(1), 217–226. doi:10.5465/amr.2000.2791611

Shane, S., & Venkataraman, S. (2001). Entrepreneurship as a field of research: A response to Zahra and Dess, Singh, and Erikson. *Academy of Management Review, 26*(1), 13–16. doi:10.5465/amr.2001.27879269

Stuart, R. W., & Abetti, P. A. (1990). Impact of entrepreneurial and management experience on early performance. *Journal of Business Venturing, 5*(3), 151–162. doi:10.1016/0883-9026(90)90029-S

Swann, P., & Prevezer, M. (1998). A comparison of the dynamics of industrial clustering in computing and biotechnology. *Research Policy, 25*(7), 1139–1158. doi:10.1016/S0048-7333(96)00897-9

Toenniessen, G. H., O'Toole, J. C., & DeVries, J. (2003). Advances in plant biotechnology and its adoption in developing countries. *Current Opinion in Plant Biology, 6*(2), 191–198. doi:10.1016/S1369-5266(03)00002-5 PMID:12667878

Ugalmugle, S. & Swain, R. (2020). *Health Economics & Outcomes Research (HEOR) Services Market Size and Share.* Industry Report. 2020-2026.

Young, L. S., Searle, P. F., Onion, D., & Mautner, V. (2006). Viral gene therapy strategies: From basic science to clinical application. *The Journal of Pathology, 208*(2), 299–318. doi:10.1002/path.1896 PMID:16362990

Zekos, G. I. (2006). Nanotechnology and biotechnology patents. *International Journal of Law and Information Technology, 14*(3), 310–369. doi:10.1093/ijlit/eal011

Chapter 14
Bioentrepreneurship in Environmental Biotechnology

Shalini Verma
Banasthali University, India

Mohd. Bilal Khan
Bhagat Phool Singh Government Medical College, India

ABSTRACT

Bioentrepreneurship is the combination of different activities carried out by groups of people to form an enterprise that designs and commercializes great products by merging various scientific and business disciplines. In this chapter, the authors review the impact of bioentrepreneurship in the field of environmental technology. This approaches as an alternative to protect and sustain nature focusing on different aspects like nanotechnology-assisted water purification, phytoremediation of polluted environment, microbial and vermi remediation, etc. Another aspect approached is the finding and development of new plants as a biomass source for energy production, which are objectives for start-ups and have great business potential. Finally, the chapter examines the ability of the proposed theoretical framework to transcend its environmental context and provide insight into expanding the domain of the study of entrepreneurship. Simply put, economic logics embody principles of economic coordination or conventions that guide interpretation of the technology and its value.

INTRODUCTION

Today, as the world is advancing in different fields in terms of technology, knowledge etc it is also facing many consequences due to the overexploitation of the natural resources. Main concerned fields are the biodiversity loss, species extinction, soil, air and water quality deterioration (Leitao, 2016). Like pesticides, petroleum hydrocarbons, herbicides, different pharmaceutical byproducts and other heavy metal compounds causes serious damage to the environment. Various methods and projects have been proposed and implemented by the government as well as the local bodies for pollution reduction and protection of the environment from different waste produced at the industrial, agricultural and the household level. In

DOI: 10.4018/978-1-7998-7411-9.ch014

spite of all the efforts, the results are partially satisfactory (Wang et al., 2018). Remediation process at contaminated sites takes conventional approaches that are usually costly like 'excavation and removal', 'pump and treat', 'soil vapor extraction method' and various other chemical treatments. These methods are less effective, time consuming and disruptive to the environment (Elekwachi et al., 2014).

Moreover, with the terrestrial environment, the marine ecosystem is also to be taken care of as it is being rapidly polluted by the human involvement. Thus, environmental biotechnology can help by providing important tools and methods to protect various marine resources (Kalogerakis et al., 2015).

Gillespie and Philp (2013) performed a study in which according to the estimation of EEA (European Environmental Agency) in Europe there are more than 3 million areas where polluting activities occurred. It also stated that the contaminated zones can further increase to 50% by 2025 (Gillespie & Philp, 2013).

Thus, in the way of resolving these issues, environmental biotechnology plays an important role in protecting the ecosystem by providing various measures and processes to reduce the pollutants and thereby pollution (Khan, 2016). Bioremediation in this has proven to be effective, safe, ecofriendly as well as economically low. This process involves various biological methods and catabolic activity by bacteria, fungi, plants to transform dangerous pollutants into less harmful compounds such as water, CO_2, salt etc (Elekwachi et al., 2014). Phytoextraction process of desalinization of various agricultural fields is implemented in different regions of the world. Recently, microorganisms are implemented both in situ (treatment at the contaminated site level) as well as ex situ (treatment after the contaminant removal from the site) (Figure 1).

Figure 1. Different techniques of bioremediation (Azubuike et al., 2016)

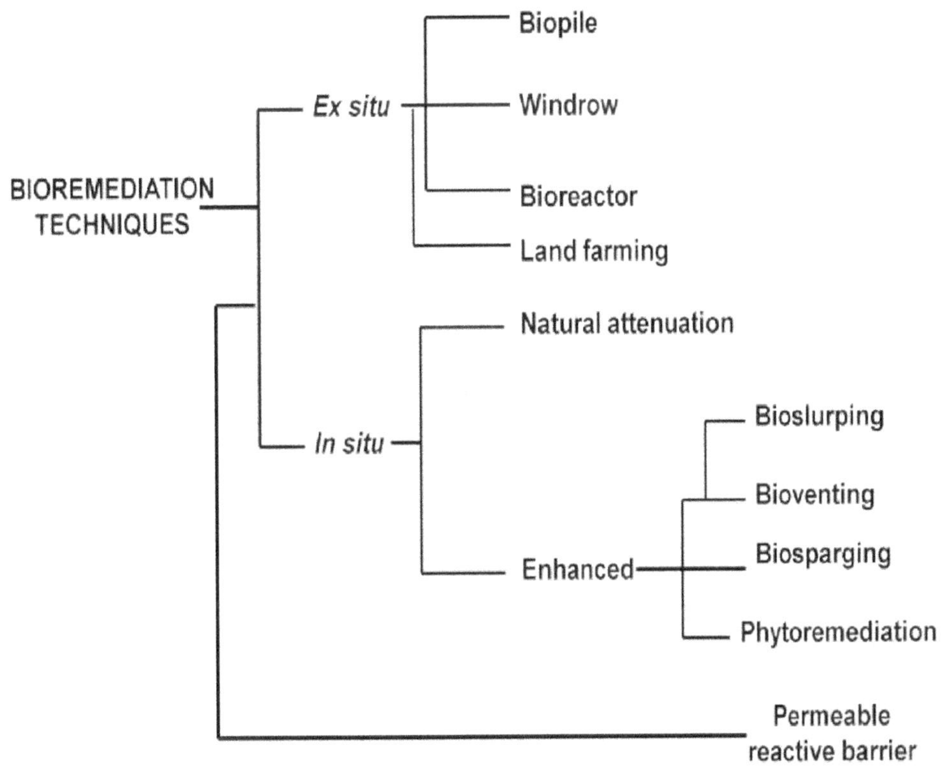

Among different techniques of bioremediation, some of the following can be mentioned:

- In situ remediation technique involves bioinventing in which microorganisms are utilized to degrade various organic compounds (Sharma, 2019). This technique increases the soil bacterial activity by enhancing aeration in the soil particles, limited nutrient quantity, thus stimulating the whole process of biodegradation (Margesin et al., 2000).
- Another is the compositing technique which stimulates the decay process of organic constituent by providing the optimum condition for the development of microorganisms involved in process. Thus resulting in high nutrient quality soil (Ross, 2018).
- Bioaugmentation method involves introduction of group of microorganisms in the contaminated/polluted area of the soil which are selected from the natural environment to increase degradation (Brown et al., 2015).
- Biostimulation method involves the introduction of limited nutrient quantity in the polluted area to speed up the development of microganism which eliminates the toxic compound commonly hydrocarbons (Sarkar et al., 2016).
- Phytoremediation involves plant in the cleansing process of the environment (Grison et al., 2015).
- Rhizofilteration technique involves absorption of the contaminant on roots of the plant from the contaminated area which are released from various industries etc. This process also decontaminates water using different plants (Abdullahi, 2015).

Elekwachi et al. (2014) conducted survey globally in which bioremediation was studied in different countries. Low cost bioremediation of in situ techniques (like 'monitored natural attenuation, biostimulation techniques and bio-augmentation methods') was mostly used in the developed countries whereas high cost ex situ techniques (like 'biorector method, compositing, landfarming, biopile') was prominent in the developing countries.

PHYTOREMEDIATION

This word phytoremediation comes from the greek with the combination of two words i.e. the first *phyto* which is plant and the other word *remedy* which means to rectify or to restore. This method involves both natural plants as well as genetically developed plants which detoxifies the contaminated area (Adriano et al., 2004; Robinson et al., 2009). Likewise, this can also be defined as the involvement of science and different techniques to study various environment issues related to the pollution/contamination and provide the result (Conesa et al., 2012). Different techniques are shown in figure 2.

Phytoremediation removes various heavy metals like Cr, Cu, Cd, Hg, Zn, Ni, As, Pd, Mo, Se (Bolan et al., 2011; Ayotamuno et al., 2009; Andreazza et al., 2013; Meeinkuirta et al., 2013), organic compounds like hydrocarbons, pesticides, fungicides (White et al., 2005; Yavari et al., 2015), radioactive isotopes like U, Cs (Yavari et al., 2015).

In comparison with the old classical method for cleaning the environment, the scientists are most focused towards the green method by utilizing plants for the decontamination. These classical methods include various chemical and thermal treatment which are expensive and detritus to the ecosystem (Wenzel et al., 2004). In the process of the plant utilization for the decontamination, proper potential of the plant in relation with the environment has to be known to rectify the problem (Andreazza et al., 2013). As the plant varies with the change in the environment as well as the contaminant constituent, these plants are found to be specific regarding the problem and therefore require specific approaches (Boros et al., 2016).

Different Techniques of Phytoremediation

- *Phytoextraction:* This process involves the plant which uptake the contaminants and accumulate it in different harvesting parts which from there can be used or can also be disposed (Trapp & Karlson, 2001). This includes different techniques like
  - Bioaugmentation phytoextraction
  - Phytomining
  - Chelated phytoextaction
- *Phytofilteration:* In this process, plant absorbs or adsorbs the toxic compound into the root from the contaminated area. This method is employed for the purification of the water from heavy metals by various aquatic plants (Trapp & Karlson, 2001; Rahman & Hasegawa, 2011). This includes:
  - Biosorption (toxic compound is absorp/adsorb in plant part)
  - Rhizofilteration (the toxic compound is adsorb/absorb in the root)
  - Blastofilteration (the pollutant is adsorb/absorb in the seedling) (Conesa et al., 2012).
- *Phytodegradation*: In this technique, plant with their metabolic activities degrades the toxic compound of the polluted area. This principle works as the defense process of plant which modifies, immobilize and degrade the toxic constituent (Rahman & Hasegawa, 2011). Similarly, Rhizodegradation is the conversion or degradation of the pollutant in the root zone of plant. This process may or may not involve the rhizophere microbes.
- *Phytovolatilization:* This process works only for the volatile compounds or those compounds that can be transformed into volatile (Trapp & Karlson, 2001). Plants in the contaminated area uptake the toxic compound and by translocation moves to the aerial region of the plant and from their by transpiration it releases into atmosphere after volatization (Conesa et al., 2012). This process is not the proper way of removal of the pollutant.
- *Phytostabilization:* This process works on the principle of precipitation in which the soluble compounds convert into non-soluble form. Therefore, the plants in the contaminated zone adsorb/absorb the pollutant compounds in the root part and further precipitation into non-soluble form of the compound (Andreazza et al., 2013). This includes:
  - Phytoexclusion
  - Assisted phytostabilization
  - Hydraulic control
  - Phytorestoration (Conesa et al., 2012).

To improve the phytoremediation process, various development and researches were conducted especially the removal of the heavy metals. These efforts include genetic modified plants, addition of hormones/ chelating compounds, mycorrhizae formation (Vamerali et al., 2010), interaction of the plant root with the rhizophere microbes, endophytic bacteria accumulates heavy metal and degradation on the pollutants (Schwitzguebel et al., 2002).

Phytoremediation process has many advantages and also disadvantages/limitations.

Figure 2. Schematic representation of phytoremediation processes (Favas et al., 2014).

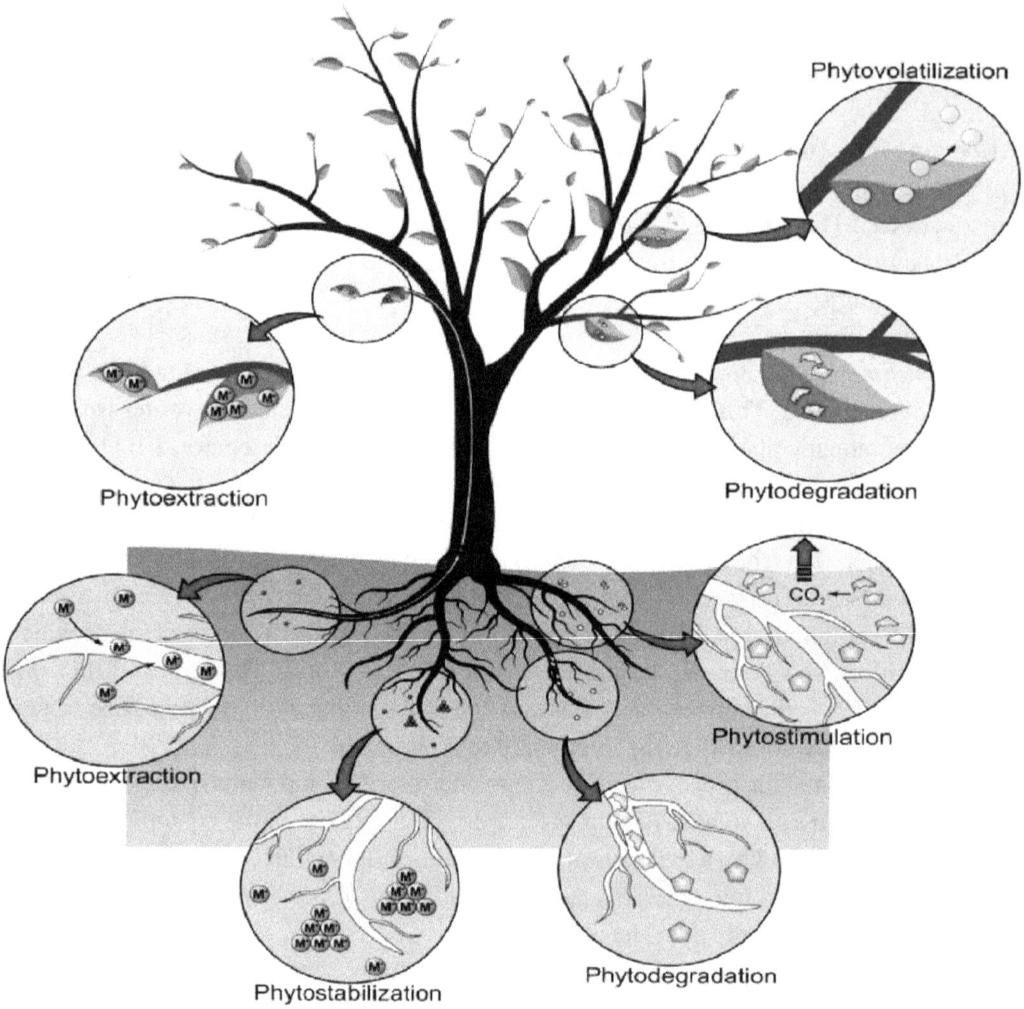

Following are the advantages of the process (Trapp & Karlson, 2001; Ekta & Modi, 2018):

- Process can be applied at both levels i.e. in situ and ex situ.
- Easy monitored technique.
- Reduces the disturbance in the soil as well as the pollutant spread in the area.
- Low cost method as it costs less than 20% of the conventional treatment.
- Environmental friendly, a green tool.
- Maintains and stimulate soil quality.
- Faster contaminant removal process
- Easy implementation technique
- Can treat wide type of pollutants from different environment conditions.

Table 1. Some plant species used in the remediation processes

PLANT SPECIES	REMEDIATION TECHNIQUE	CONTAMINANT	REFERENCES
Brassica juncea	Phytovolatilization Phytoextraction Reduction Phytoimmobilization Chelation Accumulation	Heavy metal	Bolan et al. (2011) Bolan et al. (2011) Bolan et al. (2011) Bolan et al. (2011) Duqucne et al. (2009) Sampanpanish et al. (2006)
Brassica napus L.	Chelation Phytoextraction Phytoremediation accumulation	Heavy metals	Bolan et al. (2011) Bolan et al. (2011) Shams et al. (2009) Sampanpanish et al. (2006)
Medicago sativa	Chelation Phytovolatilization Phytoremediation	Heavy metals Polychlorinated biphenyls	Lopez et al. (2005) Bolan et al. (2011) Yavari et al. (2015)
Pome fruit trees	Phosphate induced desorption	Heavy metals	Bolan et al. (2011)
Raphanus sativus	Phytoextraction	Heavy metals	Bolan et al. (2011)
Cannabis sativa	Chelation	Heavy metals	Bolan et al. (2011)
Helianthus annuus	Hyperaccumulation phytoremediation	Heavy metals	January et al. (2009) Yavari et al. (2015)
Zea Mays	Phytoextraction Phytoremediation	Heavy metals pesticide	Bolan et al. (2011) Shams et al. (2009)
Oryza sativa	Phytoextraction	Heavy metals	Bolan et al. (2011)
Glycine max	Phytoextraction	Heavy metals	Bolan et al. (2011)
Lycopersicon esculentum	Phytovolatilization	Heavy metals	Bolan et al. (2011)
Pteris vittata	Phytoremediation	Reduce As (V) into As (III)	Shoji et al. (2008)
Iris pseudacorus	Phytoremediation	Pesticide	Yavari et al. (2015)
Lemna minor	Phytoremediation	Fungicide	Yavari et al. (2015)
Tagetes patula	Phytoremediation	Textile dye	Yavari et al. (2015)

Limitations of the process (Trapp & Karlson, 2001; Ali et al., 2013; Ekta & Modi, 2018):

- This process is time consuming and also the polluted area may not be fully decontaminated.
- Process is slower in comparison with the conventional and chemical method.
- Absorption/adsorption process is limited by the root depth and also with the availability as well as with the solubility of the toxic compound in the soil.
- High pollutant content in the soil can be toxic and may be lethal to the plant.
- Toxic compounds may accumulate/ precipitate in the ground water which may not be completely removed.
- Pollutant can also be transferred from one environment to the other by different media such as by entering the food chain and due to mismanagement of the process.
- Process is applicable only in the low contaminated zone.
- Plant recovered after the remediation process require proper disposal.

- This technique is dependent on the climate as well as on the season as it regulates the plant growth which ultimately removes the toxic elements from the polluted area.

Phytoremediation depends on different factors present in the field includes temperature variation, nutrient, moisture, existence of various pathogens, type of soil, pH as well as the structure. Therefore, this pollutant remediation technique requires strong knowledge in terms of soil, plant and soil microbes (Ali et al., 2013).

In last ten years, many commercial industries using the same principle of phytoremediation technique have developed in many countries such as in USA- Phytotech, Applied Natural Sciences, Ecolotree, Earthcare, Phytoworks, Viridian Resources, Verdant technologies; Germany- Bioplanta, Piccoplant; Italy- Consulagri, Plantechno, New Zealand- Thomas Consultants; Canada- Aquaphyte Remediation (Sicuia & Babeanu, 2019).

Today, in according to the 'transparency market research' different companies in this bioremediation market are: Altogen Labs, Drylet, LLC, INsitu Remediation services limited, Probiosphere, Regenesis, Sarva Bio Remes etc

According to the global 2017 report of bioremediation techniques and the services was found to be worth of USD 32.2 billion and estimated that this value will reach to nearby USD 65.7 billion by 2025 (Arora et al., 2018).

MICROBIAL BIOREMEDIATION

In maintaining balance of the environmental quality and the restoration of the damaged environment, microbes play an important role as these have biodegradative and also the biosynthetic ability (Olaniran et al., 2013). Major application of the microorganism in the remediation process is in the creation of cleaning process in oil polluted zone, other than this can also be applied in polluted area of polychlorinated biphenyls, heavy metals, dyes, pesticides (Sharma et al. 2018). In comparison with the other techniques, biological processes using microbes are lower in maintenance as well as highly efficient.

Water Bioremediation

Another major source of pollution is the sewage water from local residence, industrial establishment, hospitals etc. Various treatment plants are established to treat the sewage water that involve at least twelve phases, this treatment also involve microorganisms performing aerobic processes (Kanu & Achi, 2011). These techniques are well established and highly applicable. Bacteria like *Pseudomonas, Bacillus, Flavobacterium, Acinetobacter, Alcaligenes* and *Zooglea* sp. are involved in many biological processes in treating municipal water waste. This treatment degrades many toxic compounds like nitrobenzene, hydrocarbons, fatty acids, textile dyes, insecticides etc (Shah, 2017).

Case study performed in China (2018) in which a microbial product named as HP-RPe-3 consist of more than hundred types of microbes isolated from snow line region of Tibetan Plateau (this includes species like nitrifying bacteria, lactic acid bacteria, yeasts, *Actinomycetes, Acetobacter, Bacillus, Micrococcus,* photosynthetic bacteria) used for the conversion/degradation of the inorganic and organic waste and other toxic compounds, sediments of the Chengnan River (Gao et al., 2018).

Table 2. Microorganisms used in the bioremediation techniques (Biswas et al. 2015)

MICROORGANISM		TOXIC COMPOUND
Bacteria	*Bacillus* spp.	Heavy metals, phenol, textile dye, oil based paints
	Pseudomonas spp.	Heavy metals, benzene, hydrocarbons
	Pseudomonas putida	Benzene, xylene
	Xanthomonas sp.	Hydrocarbons
	Nocardia sp.	Hydrocarbons
	Mycobacterium sp.	Aromatics, benzene
Fungi	*Coprinellus radians*	Heavy metal, hydrocarbons
	Aspergillus niger	Hydrocarbons
	Aspergillus versicolor	Hydrocarbons, Heavy metals
	Saccharomyces cerevisiae	Heavy metals
	Pycnoporus sanguineus	Induatrial dyes
Algae	*Chlamydomonas* sp.	Napthalene
	Dunaliella sp.	Napthalene
	Euglena gracilis	DDT, Phenol
	Chlorella sp.	Heavy metals
	Zooglea sp.	Heavy metals
	Phormidium valderium	Heavy metals
	Volvariella volvacea	Heavy metals
	Oscillatoria sp.	Heavy metals
	Spirogyra hyalina	Heavy metals

Oil Spill Bioremediation

With respect to the oil pollution, accidental oil spill by Exxon Valdez (1989) and Gulf of Mexico's BP deepwater horizon oil spill (2010) are known; in both the oil spill 0.75 & 4.9 million barrels crude oil was released respectively. This accidental oil pollution still affecting the productive and precious marine life and also have heavy impact on the terrestrial life also (Yavari et al., 2015). In situ bioremediation techniques are divided into natural attenuation, biostimulation and bioaugmentation. For the maximum activity of the microorganisms in this process, it is necessary to isolate such microbes which are highly stable, can perform even in the highest level of contamination (Dhal et al., 2013). The microbial analysis performed at the polluted area showed the presence the many heterotrphic bacteria and fungi like *Fusarium* spp., *Alcaligenes odorans, Bacillus subtilis, Bacillus cereus, Aspergillus niger, Candida glabrata, Saccharomyces cerevisiae, Pseudomonas cepacia, Citrobacter koseri.* etc. In Kuwait, oil polluted lakes identified the presence of extreme halophilic strains of bacteria belonging to *Halococcus, Halobacterium* (Yateem, 2014).

Microbes present in the toxic polluted sites are selected and isolated which can further be used in the remediation or the cleaning process of various sites polluted with heavy metals, pesticides, organic toxic compounds etc (Ojuederie & Babalola, 2017). *Pseudomonas putida* (Gram negative soil saprophytic bacteria) is highly applied in green remediation processes like the removal of aromatic hydrocarbons, chlorophenols etc. bacterial strain utilized in the remediation technique were subjected to patents for legal protection; first patent was recorded in 1974 for the strain of *P. putida* which is capable of degrading petroleum (Biswas et al., 2015).

Based on the experiments performed and the obtained results from the microbial enzymes, various useful products for different applications in oil spill remediation were developed. The US EPA defined the bioremediation agents as "microbiological cultures, enzyme additives, nutrient additives that significantly increase the rate of biodegradation to mitigate the effects of the discharge" (Venosa, 2004). Various products for the bioremediations were developed and promoted by many manufactures. The advantages of the bioremediation using microbes are related to the application of natural process that is less deleterious to the ecosystem. Microbial products are applied underground to cleanse the contaminants of the ground water and also of the soil. These bioremediation processes are of low cost and does not require any special equipment or skilled labor (Kumar et al., 2018)

In this field, many companies are established and commercialized the use of microbial product for the bioremediation processes. In according to the transparency market research performed in 2018, the market value was USD 32.2 billion in 2016 which was estimated to increase to USD 65.7 billion by 2025. Major industries established in the market are: Altogen Labs, Drylet LLC, Aquatech International LLC, Insitu Remediation Services Limited, Probiosphere Inc, Sarva Bio Remed LLC, Regenesis, Sevenson, Solutions Ltd and Xylem Inc (Venosa, 2004).

Vermiremediation

Vermiremediation is the technique in which the earthworms are utilized to convert the organic waste into compost. These processes are of low cost and dedicated to waste obtained from agriculture, city garbage, household kitchen waste etc (Khan, 2016). Different species of earthworms like *Eisenia fetida, Aporrectodea caliginosa, Lumbricus terrestris, A. nocturna, Pantoscolex, Pheretima hawayana* etc. are utilized for the removal of different contaminants like oil, pesticides, heavy metal etc (Rodriguez-Campos et al., 2014; Rorat et al., 2017). Vermiremediation process cost is bit too high as compared with the other bioremediation processes because of the conditions required to maintain for the survival, maintainance and the growth of the earthworms (Adhikary, 2013). According to the report of 2019, vermicompost manufacturers are mainly in India and the South east Asia, and the products are distributed all over the world. The main manufacturers in the vermicompost market are MyNOKE, Earthworm, Worm Farms, Wormpower, Sri Gayathri Biotech, SLO Country Worm Farm, Davo's Worm farms, SAOSIS and Suman Vermi Compost. In comparision with the report of 2014, the vermicompost market increase to 24.89% which is USD 38.09 million worth.

Microbial Biofertilizers

Biofertilizers manufactured with the help of microorganisms contain living cells of the selected microbe which is beneficial to improve the soil quality as well as also promote the growth and development of the plant by increasing the nutrient uptake (Hayat et al., 2010). Biofertilizers promote bioconversion process in the substrate and increase the availability of nutrient for the plants. This is applicable for soil, plant surface and also for the seeds.

In agriculture, biofertilizers are low cost supplements for the plant nutrition that reduces the dependency for the chemical fertilizers (Adesemoye et al., 2009). Microorganisms utilized as biofertilizers are mycorrhiza, several fungi, bacteria and few blue green algae (Santra et al., 2015). On the basis of their function, these are classified as phosphorus solubilizers, nitrogen fixers, phytohormone and others.

Nitrogen fixing microorganisms convert the available atmospheric nitrogen into organic nitrogen compound which are present for the plant utilization (Figure 3). These nitrogen fixer biofertilizers can replace the nitrogen fertilization. The microorganisms utilized for the nitrogen fixing includes some symbiotic as well as some non-symbiotic microorganisms. In the symbiotic nitrogen fixing bacteria, *Rhizobium, Bradyrhizobium, Ensifer, Azorhizobium, Sinorhizobium,* etc are utilized to fix atmospheric nitrogen. The commercialized products based on this are Rhizolife, Effect Grow, Rhizo-Enrich, Polarhizo, Biobium, Biodoz, Cell Tech, Nitragin, Nitrofix etc (Bashandy et al., 2019).

Figure 3. Nitrogen flow and utilization by legume plant (Basu & Kumar, 2020)

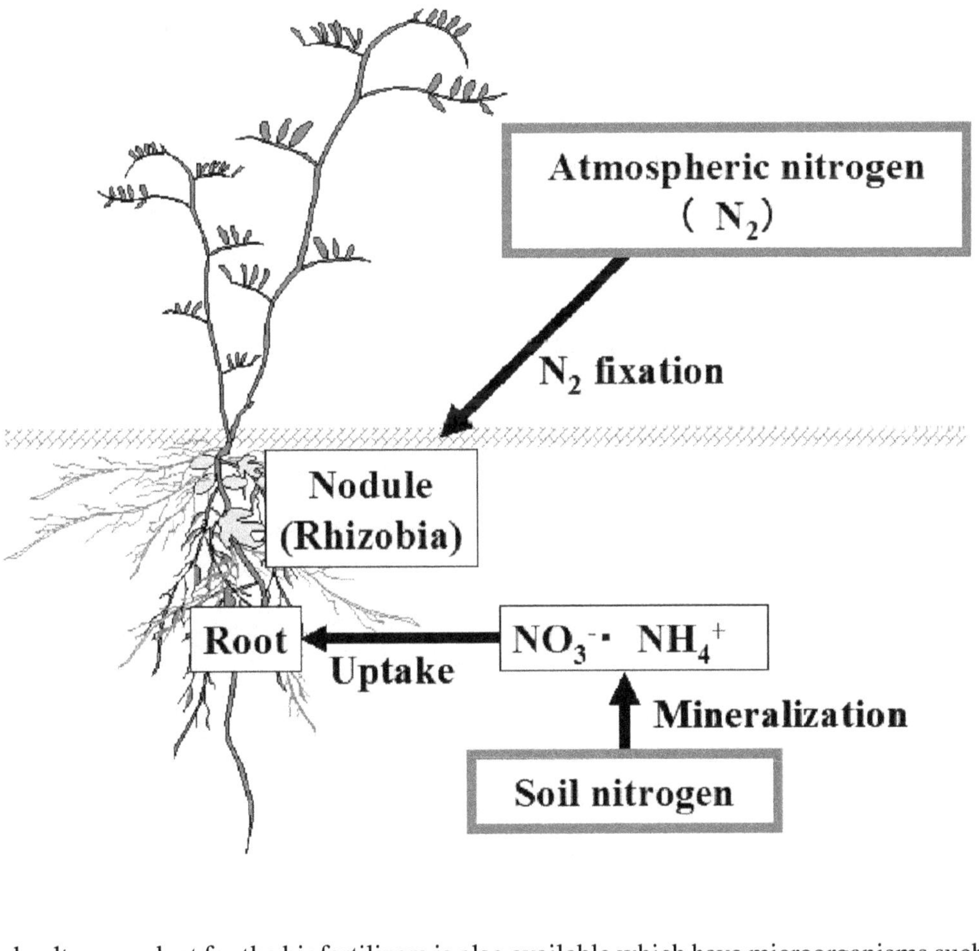

Mixed culture product for the biofertilizers is also available which have microorganisms such as Rhizodyne (containing *Acetobacter, Azotobacter, Azospirillum, Rhizobium*), Micosat (*Glomus intraradices and G. mosseae*), Bharpur and BIO-NPK (contain stains which provide balanced nitrogen, potassium and phosphorus nutrient to the plant) and TagTeam LCO (Peter et al., 2020). Some of the biofertilizers utilizes phosphorus solubilizing microbes which enhance the uptake of phosphorus from phytic acid and organic phosphorus and therefore improves the solubility of inorganic phosphorus. Commercial biofertilizers with same quality are Rich Paddy biofertilizer, Rhizocell C, VICI Routz GR soil probiotics. Other commercial biofertlizers which increase the accumulation of the potassium is Potash cure and BioPotash, solubilization of sulphur like SULF-CURE and BIOSULF, zinc solubilization like ZINC-CURE and BIOZINC (Singh & Satyanarayana, 2011).

BIOPESTICIDES

Biopesticides are the plant products which protect the plant from various pests, disease etc. Some of these products regulate the growth and influence the storage period after the harvest (Khater, 2012). These protection products contain more than one active component that could be natural or chemical. Natural components are of low risk and include various microbes, plant extract and insect pheromones (Canttrel et al., 2012). In European Union (EU), the active component of the PPPs should be by the European commission before being marketed. Today, around 25% are the natural component of the active compound which means more than 70 active component of natural quality is approved by the commission (http://ec.europa.eu). In the microbial strain which are approved as PPPs have 52.7% bactericidal and fungicidal activity, 29.1% insecticidal effects, remaining 18.2% includes nematicides, elicitors etc (Cornea et al., 2019).

Plant Pathogens Biocontrol using Microorganisms

Microorganisms utilized as biocontrol agents are of wide range. Around 22 fungal and bacterial species are approved by the commission for the protection purpose. This spectrum is much wider in China, India, USA and South America countries (Waghunde et al., 2016).

During the selection of the microbial strain which can be utilized as the biocontrol agent must some traits. Preferred microbes are spore forming fungi and bacteria resulting in high viability of the product. In microbially formulated PPPs, together with the protective efficiency, self-replicating quality of the microbes are also considered (Chattopadhyay et al., 2017). Other factors are colonization and adaptability of the microbes.

Entomopathogenic Fungi

These are highly efficient because of their spore producing quality in which they produce spores which infect the insects that induces death in around 5-10 days, depending on the strain of the fungi (Jackson, 1997). Together with this, the infecting fungi continues to grow and sporulate on the dead insect body, thus the process of biological control activity goes on in and around the area of infection. Phylum Zygomycota and Ascomycotina mainly have the entomopathogenic fungi such as *Beauveria, Lecanicillium, Isaria, Purpureocillium* and *Metarhizium* (Kim et al., 2018).

These biocontrol agents are produced on mass scale and are formulated into PPPs. Products are formed in solid-state, liquid suspension, oil dispersion, dry flowable, wetable powder (Cornea et al., 2019).

Entomopathogenic Bacteria

Entomopathogenic bacteria produce toxic compounds and other factors which causes death of the insect after ingestion. These bacteria have resistive range activity as they are specifically active against the pest species (Ruiu, 2015). *Bacillus thuringiensis (Bt)* is the most common insecticide. Several products are registered with *Bt* as the active ingredient such as *Bt* ssp. *Aizawai, kurstaki* (have efficiency against caterpillars) *israeliensis* (effective against mosquitos and flies) and *Bt* ssp. *tenebrionis* (effective against Coleoptera larvae). Other bacterial species are also identified to be effective against insects, nematodes and mites. Commercial available bacteria product include species like *Bacillus firmus* and *Pasteuria nishizawae* are effective against cyst, lesion and nematodes (Kaya et al., 2008 and Glare et al., 2017), *Clostridium bifermentans* and *Lysinibacillus sphaericus* effective against mosquito (Qureshi et al., 2014), *Saccharopolyspora spinosa* effective against spider mites (Sparks et al., 2012), *Pseudomonas alcaligenes* effective against grasshoppers (Ruffner et al., 2015). Among these, most popular and successful biopesticide product is of *Bacillus* species because of their stability nature for long period (Chattopadhyay et al., 2017).

Plant Protection Product using Plant's Extract

Plant extract, oils, decoctions and powders have found to be effective to use as PPPs and are approved as fungicides, acaricides, insecticides and repellents (Sicuia et al., 2019). Such bioproducts containing these plants extract as active ingredient are considered to be safe. For example,

- *Equistum arvense* L. is used as fungicide to protect against pathogens like *Podosphaera leucotricha* and *Venturia inaequalis* for apple trees and is used in the form of decoction]\7in water; against *Tapherina deformans*; against downy and powdery mildew in grapes; active ingredient in PPPs against *Pythium* spp., *Podosphaera xhanthii, Alternania solani* for legumes (SANCO/12386/2013-rev. 5/2014).
- Powder form of mustard seeds of varieties *Brassica alba, B. juncea* and *B. nigera* is approved as an active ingredient in PPPs against *Tilletia caries* and *T. foetida* in wheat by slurry seed treatment (SANTE/11309/2017-rev. 2/2017).
- Cortex of *Salix* spp. is prepared in form of water infusion and used as PPPs as fungicide controlling leaf curl in peaches, powdery mildew in grapes and apples (SANCO/12173/2014-rev. 4/2015).
- *Urtica dioica* and *U. urens* is used as fungicides, insecticide and acaricidal in plant protection in form of complex mixture for mulch and spray treatment applications. As fungicide, extract is used against *Alternaria* on species of Brassicaceae family and Cucurbitaceae family, black and grey mold in fruit trees, downy mildew in potato and grapes (SANTE/11809/2016-rev.0.1/2017).

CONCLUSION

Bioentrepreneurship is the blend of dissimilar actions carried out by group of peoples to form a venture that plan and commercializes great products by integration of a range of scientific and business disciplines. Present chapter summarizes the effect of bioentrepreneurship in the area of ecological knowledge. For the improvement of the phytoremediation processes, various researches were conducted especially the genetic modified plants, addition of hormones/ chelating compounds, mycorrhizae formation. Other than this, microorganisms utilized as biofertilizers are mycorrhiza, several fungi, bacteria and few blue green algae. Basically, economic logics embody principles of economic coordination that guide interpretation of the knowledge and its worth.

REFERENCES

Abdullahi, M. S. (2015). Soil contamination, remediation and plants. In Soil remediation and plants. Academic.

Adesemoye, A. O., Torbert, H. A., & Kloepper, J. W. (2009). Plant growth-promoting rhizobacteria allow reduced application rates of chemical fertilizers. *Microbial Ecology*, *58*(4), 921–929. doi:10.100700248-009-9531-y PMID:19466478

Adhikary, S. (2012). Vermicompost, the story of organic gold: A review. *Scientific Research, 3*(7), 1-13.

Adriano, D. C., Wenzel, W. W., Vangronsveld, J., & Bolan, N. S. (2004). Role of assisted natural remediation in environmental cleanup. *Geoderma*, *122*(2-4), 121–142. doi:10.1016/j.geoderma.2004.01.003

Ali, H., Khan, E., & Sajad, M. A. (2013). Phytoremediation of heavy metals—Concepts and applications. *Chemosphere*, *91*(7), 869–881. doi:10.1016/j.chemosphere.2013.01.075 PMID:23466085

Andreazza, R., Bortolon, L., Pieniz, S., Camargo, F. A., and Bortolon, E. S. O. (2013). Copper phytoextraction and phytostabilization by Brachiaria decumbens Stapf. in vineyard soils and a copper mining waste. *Open Journal of Soil Science, 3*(6), 273-282.

Arora, N. K., Fatima, T., Mishra, I., Verma, M., Mishra, J., & Mishra, V. (2018). Environmental sustainability: challenges and viable solutions. *Environmental Sustainability, 1*(4), 309-340.

Ayotamuno, J. M., Kogbara, R. B., & Agoro, O. S. (2009). Biostimulation supplemented with phytoremediation in the reclamation of a petroleum contaminated soil. *World Journal of Microbiology & Biotechnology*, *25*(9), 1567–1572. doi:10.100711274-009-0045-z

Azubuike, C. C., Chikere, C. B., & Okpokwasili, G. C. (2016). Bioremediation techniques–classification based on site of application: Principles, advantages, limitations and prospects. *World Journal of Microbiology & Biotechnology*, *32*(11), 1–18. doi:10.100711274-016-2137-x PMID:27638318

Bashandy, S. R., Abd-Alla, M. H., & Bagy, M. M. K. (2019). Biological nitrogen fixation and biofertilizers as ideal potential solutions for sustainable agriculture. *Integrating Green Chemistry and Sustainable Engineering*, *1*(1), 343-396.

Basu, S., & Kumar, G. (2020). Nitrogen fixation in a legume-rhizobium symbiosis: the roots of a success story. Plant Microbe Symbiosis, 1(1), 35-53. doi:10.1007/978-3-030-36248-5_3

Biswas, B., Sarkar, B., Rusmin, R., & Naidu, R. (2015). Bioremediation of PAHs and VOCs: Advances in clay mineral–microbial interaction. *Environment International*, *85*, 168–181. doi:10.1016/j.envint.2015.09.017 PMID:26408945

Bolan, N. S., Park, J. H., Robinson, B., Naidu, R., & Huh, K. Y. (2011). Phytostabilization: A green approach to contaminant containment. *Advances in Agronomy*, *112*, 145–204. doi:10.1016/B978-0-12-385538-1.00004-4

Boroş, M. N., Micle, V., Flămînd, L., & Sur, I. M. (2016). Phytoremediation planning in the case of former industrial sites. *Studia ubb ambientum, 61*(1-2), 5-14.

Brown, L. D., Ulrich, A. C., & Fingas, M. (2015). Bioremediation of oil spills on land. In *Oil spill science and technology*. John Wiley & Sons.

Cantrell, C. L., Dayan, F. E., & Duke, S. O. (2012). Natural products as sources for new pesticides. *Journal of Natural Products*, *75*(6), 1231–1242. doi:10.1021/np300024u PMID:22616957

Chattopadhyay, P., Banerjee, G., & Mukherjee, S. (2017). Recent trends of modern bacterial insecticides for pest control practice in integrated crop management system. *Biotech, 7*(1), 60.

Conesa, H. M., Evangelou, M. W., Robinson, B. H., & Schulin, R. (2012). A critical view of current state of phytotechnologies to remediate soils: Still a promising tool? *The Scientific World Journal*, *2012*(5), 17382. doi:10.1100/2012/173829 PMID:22272168

Cornea, C. P., Voaides, C., Sicuia, O. A. B., Matei, F., & Babeanu, N. (2019). Creating Products and Services in Environmental Biotechnology. In Introduction to biotech entrepreneurship: from idea to business. Springer. doi:10.1007/978-3-030-22141-6_4

Dhal, B., Thatoi, H. N., Das, N. N., & Pandey, B. D. (2013). Chemical and microbial remediation of hexavalent chromium from contaminated soil and mining/metallurgical solid waste: A review. *Journal of Hazardous Materials*, *250*, 272–291. doi:10.1016/j.jhazmat.2013.01.048 PMID:23467183

Ekta, P., & Modi, N. R. (2018). A review of phytoremediation. *Journal of Pharmacognosy and Phytochemistry*, *7*(4), 1485–1489.

Elekwachi, C. O., Andresen, J., & Hodgman, T. C. (2014). Global use of bioremediation technologies for decontamination of ecosystems. *Journal of Bioremediation and Biodegredation, 5*(4), 1.

Favas, P. J., Pratas, J., Varun, M., D'Souza, R., & Paul, M. S. (2014). Phytoremediation of soils contaminated with metals and metalloids at mining areas: potential of native flora. *Environmental Risk Assessment of Soil Contamination, 17*, 485-517.

Gao, H., Xie, Y., Hashim, S., Akhtar Khan, A., Wang, X., & Xu, H. (2018). Application of microbial technology used in bioremediation of urban polluted river: A case study of Chengnan River, China. *Water (Basel)*, *10*(5), 643. doi:10.3390/w10050643

Gillespie, I. M., & Philp, J. C. (2013). Bioremediation, an environmental remediation technology for the bioeconomy. *Trends in Biotechnology*, *31*(6), 329–332. doi:10.1016/j.tibtech.2013.01.015 PMID:23427900

Glare, T. R., Jurat-Fuentes, J. L., & O'callaghan, M. (2017). Basic and applied research: entomopathogenic bacteria. In Microbial control of insect and mite pests. Academic Press.

Grison, C., Escande, V., & Biton, J. (2015). Ecocatalysis: A new integrated approach to scientific ecology. Elsevier.

Hayat, R., Ali, S., Amara, U., Khalid, R., & Ahmed, I. (2010). Soil beneficial bacteria and their role in plant growth promotion: A review. *Annals of Microbiology, 60*(4), 579–598. doi:10.100713213-010-0117-1

Jackson, M. A. (1997). Optimizing nutritional conditions for the liquid culture production of effective fungal biological control agents. *Journal of Industrial Microbiology & Biotechnology, 19*(3), 180–187.

January, M. C., Cutright, T. J., Van Keulen, H., & Wei, R. (2008). Hydroponic phytoremediation of Cd, Cr, Ni, As, and Fe: Can Helianthus annuus hyperaccumulate multiple heavy metals? *Chemosphere, 70*(3), 531–537.

Kalogerakis, N., Arff, J., Banat, I. M., Broch, O. J., Daffonchio, D., Edvardsen, T., ... Fava, F. (2015). The role of environmental biotechnology in exploring, exploiting, monitoring, preserving, protecting and decontaminating the marine environment. *New Biotechnology, 32*(1), 157–167.

Kanu, I., & Achi, O. K. (2011). Industrial effluents and their impact on water quality of receiving rivers in Nigeria. *Journal of Applied Technology in Environmental Sanitation, 1*(1), 75–86.

Kaya, H. K., Klein, M. G., & Burlando, T. M. (1993). Impact of *Bacillus popilliae, Rickettsiella popilliae* and entomopathogenic nematodes on a population of the scarabaeid, Cyclocephala hirta. *Biocontrol Science and Technology, 3*(4), 443–453.

Khan, F. A. (2016). *Biotechnology fundamentals* (2nd ed.). CRC.

Khater, H. F. (2012). Prospects of botanical biopesticides in insect pest management. *Pharmacologia, 3*(12), 641–656.

Kim, J. C., Lee, M. R., Kim, S., Lee, S. J., Park, S. E., Nai, Y. S., ... Kim, J. S. (2018). Tenebrio molitor-mediated entomopathogenic fungal library construction for pest management. *Journal of Asia-Pacific Entomology, 21*(1), 196–204.

Kumar, V., Shahi, S. K., & Singh, S. (2018). Bioremediation: an eco-sustainable approach for restoration of contaminated sites. In Microbial bioprospecting for sustainable development. Springer.

Leitão, A. (2016). Bioeconomy: the challenge in the management of natural resources in the 21st century. *Open Journal of Social Sciences, 4*(11), 26-42.

Mani, D., & Kumar, C. (2014). Biotechnological advances in bioremediation of heavy metals contaminated ecosystems: An overview with special reference to phytoremediation. *International Journal of Environmental Science and Technology, 11*(3), 843–872.

Margesin, R., Zimmerbauer, A., & Schinner, F. (2000). Monitoring of bioremediation by soil biological activities. *Chemosphere, 40*(4), 339–346.

Meeinkuirt, W., Kruatrachue, M., Pichtel, J., Phusantisampan, T., & Saengwilai, P. (2016). Influence of organic amendments on phytostabilization of Cd-contaminated soil by *Eucalyptus camaldulensis. Science Asia, 42*(2), 83–91.

Ojuederie, O. B., & Babalola, O. O. (2017). Microbial and plant-assisted bioremediation of heavy metal polluted environments: A review. *International Journal of Environmental Research and Public Health, 14*(12), 1504.

Olaniran, A. O., Balgobind, A., & Pillay, B. (2013). Bioavailability of heavy metals in soil: Impact on microbial biodegradation of organic compounds and possible improvement strategies. *International Journal of Molecular Sciences*, *14*(5), 10197–10228.

Peter, A. J., Amalraj, E. L. D., & Talluri, V. R. (2020). Commercial Aspects of Biofertilizers and Biostimulants Development Utilizing Rhizosphere Microbes: Global and Indian Scenario. In Rhizosphere microbes. Springer.

Qureshi, N., Chawla, S., Likitvivatanavong, S., Lee, H. L., & Gill, S. S. (2014). The cry toxin operon of *Clostridium bifermentans* subsp. malaysia is highly toxic to Aedes larval mosquitoes. *Applied and Environmental Microbiology*, *80*(18), 5689–5697.

Rahman, M. A., & Hasegawa, H. (2011). Aquatic arsenic: Phytoremediation using floating macrophytes. *Chemosphere*, *83*(5), 633–646.

Robinson, B. H., Bañuelos, G., Conesa, H. M., Evangelou, M. W., & Schulin, R. (2009). The phytomanagement of trace elements in soil. *Critical Reviews in Plant Sciences*, *28*(4), 240–266.

Rodriguez-Campos, J., Dendooven, L., Alvarez-Bernal, D., & Contreras-Ramos, S. M. (2014). Potential of earthworms to accelerate removal of organic contaminants from soil: A review. *Applied Soil Ecology*, *79*, 10–25.

Rorat, A., Wloka, D., Grobelak, A., Grosser, A., Sosnecka, A., Milczarek, M., ... Kacprzak, M. (2017). Vermiremediation of polycyclic aromatic hydrocarbons and heavy metals in sewage sludge composting process. *Journal of Environmental Management*, *187*, 347–353.

Ross, R. (2018). The science behind composting. *REAd (Porto Alegre)*, *15*, 2020.

Ruffner, B., Péchy-Tarr, M., Höfte, M., Bloemberg, G., Grunder, J., Keel, C., & Maurhofer, M. (2015). Evolutionary patchwork of an insecticidal toxin shared between plant-associated pseudomonads and the insect pathogens Photorhabdus and Xenorhabdus. *BMC Genomics*, *16*(1), 1–14.

Ruiu, L. (2015). Insect pathogenic bacteria in integrated pest management. *Insects*, *6*(2), 352–367.

Sampanpanish, P., Pongsapich, W., Khaodhiar, S., & Khan, E. (2006). Chromium removal from soil by phytoremediation with weed plant species in Thailand. *Water Air and Soil Pollution Focus*, *6*(1-2), 191–206.

SANCO/12173/2014–rev. 4/2015. Final review report of the Standing Committee on Plants, Animals Food and Feed at its meeting on 29 May 2015 in view of the approval of Salix spp. cortex as basic substance in accordance with Regulation (EC) No 1107/2009.

SANCO/12386/2013–rev. 5/2014. Final review report of the Standing Committee on the Food Chain and Animal Health at its meeting on 20 March 2014 in view of the approval of Equisetum arvense L. as basic substance in accordance with Regulation (EC) No 1107/2009.

SANTE/11309/2017–rev. 2/2017. Final review report of the Standing Committee on Plants, Animals, Food and Feed at its meeting on 6 October 2017 in view of the approval of mustard seeds powder as basic substance in accordance with Regulation (EC) No 1107/20091.

SANTE/11809/2016–rev. 0.1/2017. Final Review report of the Standing Committee on Plants, Animals, Food and Feed at its meeting on 24 January 2017 in view of the approval of Urtica spp. as basic substance in accordance with Regulation (EC) No 1107/2009.

Santra, S. C., Mallick, A., & Samal, A. C. (2015). Biofertilizer for bioremediation. In *Recent trends in biofertilizers*. IK international publishing house Pvt. *Ltd*.

Sarkar, J., Kazy, S. K., Gupta, A., Dutta, A., Mohapatra, B., Roy, A., ... Sar, P. (2016). Biostimulation of indigenous microbial community for bioremediation of petroleum refinery sludge. *Frontiers in Microbiology*, *7*, 1407.

Schwitzguébel, J. P., van der Lelie, D., Baker, A., Glass, D. J., & Vangronsveld, J. (2002). Phytoremediation: European and American trends successes, obstacles and needs. *Journal of Soils and Sediments*, *2*(2), 91–99.

Shah, M. P. (2017). Waste water pollution. *Journal of Applied Biomaterials & Functional Materials*, *3*(1), 262–263.

Shams, K. M., Tichy, G., Fischer, A., Sager, M., Peer, T., Bashar, A., & Filip, K. (2010). Aspects of phytoremediation for chromium contaminated sites using common plants *Urtica dioica, Brassica napus and Zea mays. Plant and Soil*, *328*(1), 175–189.

Sharma, B., Dangi, A. K., & Shukla, P. (2018). Contemporary enzyme based technologies for bioremediation: A review. *Journal of Environmental Management*, *210*, 10–22.

Sharma, J. (2019). Advantages and limitations of in situ methods of bioremediation. *Recent Advances. Biology and Medicine (Aligarh)*, *5*, 10941.

Shoji, R., Yajima, R., & Yano, Y. (2008). Arsenic speciation for the phytoremediation by the Chinese brake fern, Pteris vittata. *Journal of Environmental Sciences (China)*, *20*(12), 1463–1468.

Sicuia, F. M., & Babeanu, N. (2019). Calina Petruta Cornea, Catalina Voaides, Oana Alina Boiu. *Introduction to Biotech Entrepreneurship: From Idea to Business*, *1*, 53.

Singh, B., & Satyanarayana, T. (2011). Microbial phytases in phosphorus acquisition and plant growth promotion. *Physiology and Molecular Biology of Plants*, *17*(2), 93–103.

Sparks, T. C., Dripps, J. E., Watson, G. B., & Paroonagian, D. (2012). Resistance and cross-resistance to the spinosyns–a review and analysis. *Pesticide Biochemistry and Physiology*, *102*(1), 1–10.

Trapp, S., & Karlson, U. (2001). Aspects of phytoremediation of organic pollutants. *Journal of Soils and Sediments*, *1*(1), 37–43.

Vamerali, T., Bandiera, M., & Mosca, G. (2010). Field crops for phytoremediation of metal-contaminated land. A review. *Environmental Chemistry Letters*, *8*(1), 1–17.

Venosa, A. D. (2004). *Literature review on the use of commercial bioremediation agents for cleanup of oil-contaminated estuarine environments. In National risk management research laboratory, office of research and development*. US Environmental Protection Agency.

Waghunde, R. R., Shelake, R. M., & Sabalpara, A. N. (2016). Trichoderma: A significant fungus for agriculture and environment. *African Journal of Agricultural Research*, *11*(22), 1952–1965.

Wang, R., Cao, Q., Zhao, Q., & Li, Y. (2018). Bioindustry in China: An overview and perspective. *New Biotechnology*, *40*, 46–51.

Wenzel, W. W., Lombi, E., & Adriano, D. C. (1999). Biogeochemical processes in the rhizosphere: role in phytoremediation of metal-polluted soils. In *Heavy metal stress in plants* (pp. 273–303). Springer.

White, P. M., Wolf, D. C., Thoma, G. J., & Reynolds, C. M. (2006). Phytoremediation of alkylated polycyclic aromatic hydrocarbons in a crude oil-contaminated soil. *Water, Air, and Soil Pollution*, *169*(1), 207–220.

Yateem, A. (2014). *Bioremediation strategies for the cleanup of oil contamination in an arid environment: an insight on the Kuwaiti experience. In Bioremediation: processes, challenges and future prospects.* Nova.

Yavari, S., Malakahmad, A., & Sapari, N. B. (2015). A review on phytoremediation of crude oil spills. *Water, Air, and Soil Pollution*, *226*(8), 1–18.

Chapter 15
Bioentrepreneurship Globally

Madhura N. Hegde
Sahyadri College of Engineering and Management, Mangalore, India

Jayapadmini Kanchan
Sahyadri College of Engineering and Management, Mangalore, India

Ganaraj K.
Sahyadri College of Engineering and Management, Mangalore, India

Asha B. Shetty
Sahyadri College of Engineering and Management, Mangalore, India

Rajatha
SJB Institute of Technology, Bengaluru, India

ABSTRACT

Since 1992, the biotechnology business has expanded. There is an attempt to make an educated workforce with the capacities to lead biotechnology research and to regulate bioscience advancement. Governments need to create knowledge about industries and are thus driving numerous initiatives to build and provide incentives for this nascent industry. Government financing as awards, advantages, motivators, and tax reductions is a noticeable component all through the world. Framework and groups are starting to rise, and designs are in progress to fabricate a biotechnology industry in pretty much every nation. This chapter explores bioentrepreneurship globally.

INTRODUCTION

Latest developments in the field of biotechnology have developed a need to train larger numbers of those who can meet their complex duties. After the 1992, there were more biotechnology companies, And higher work prospects. Several attempts are being made to develop a trained workforce with the capabilities to perform studies on biotechnology and to conduct Managing innovation in biosciences (Meyers et al., 2008) Effectual Management would promote the conversion of Item, process and systems

DOI: 10.4018/978-1-7998-7411-9.ch015

research to satisfy the biotechnical criteria in the medical field, Agricultural and processing industries. Many Governments implement different programmes to stimulate Innovation and entrepreneurship. In a nation or country, with a focus on high technology. This is being proven by the numerous biotechnology clusters that are self-declared Emerging in many country normally backed by Governments of the area (Back et al., 2009). Many university encourage the commercialization of study in biotechnology. Technology should be developed by universities transfer offices to deal with patenting and patenting Permission, Licensing. Logical and administrative ability, programming and money are three establishments of Bio business. As indicated by a new National Science Foundation study report, the interest for biotech labourers is outperforming. Talents are scarce and some of the time the least in most biotechnological firms. The way from R&D-headed to a market-driven culture takes an intricate collection of information, abilities and talents (Dyson et.al, 2007).

Management is the first foundation to be Safeguarded in every new biopharmaceutical company. No technology transition can still be an opportunity for product sales cannot happen if they do not have professional managerial abilities. A chief executive officer and management team to running a start-up biotechnology company by commercialization is The industry's scarcest capital (Grima et al., 2003). The Management is most weakest column in most biotechnology organizations.

One of the important drivers of economic growth is entrepreneurial activity. The legislatures of several developed and developing countries nations are considering the creation of little and medium-sized ventures (SMEs) as high-innovation endeavours for financial development, global competition and decreased economic growth Joblessness (Baumol et al., 2005). Biotechnology is one of these modern areas that has the potential for is development later on.

Biotechnology's scope of applications covers mass and specialty chemicals, health care merchandise, numerous food sources and drinks, strategies for extraction, waste and emanations agriculture and contamination treatment techniques of biotechnology. In general it incorporates the use of cutting edge fields biochemistry, cell biology, chemistry, biology, chemical engineering, computer science and process engineering (Stata et al., 2004).

During the 1980s, the development of the British biotechnology area started when the public authority expanded the subsidizing of the National Research Councils liable for Basic science, fundamentally for exploration and research in biotechnology. The public authority of the UK interfered to build the stockpile of funding for the capital market and Freshly established biotechnology firms (Nurmemmedov et al., 2004). The program 'Biotechnology Means Business' was presented in 1995 by the Department of Trade and Industry (DTI) to assist organizations with growing their connections with research focuses and are the wellsprings of Funding to turn out to be more effective in the field of applied biotechnology. In 2003, the UK biotechnology area industry included 455 organizations utilizing more than 22 000 individuals and creating creation of €5 billion (EuropaBio, 2005). Most of these organizations are little, youthful and secretly helped organizations.

Within Europe (EuropaBio, 2005) the French biotechnology sector is in third rank, with 225 biotechnology firms. French biotechnology industry was born in the 1980s, more than 80% of French biotechnology companies were founded after 1990. There has been a true explosion of biotechnology companies all over France since 1997(Haycock, P et al.,1998). In 2000, French biotechnology companies' growth rate was over 25 percent. In France, biotechnology and life sciences are funded by a significant number of major organisations like Public research centres (UK Tradeinvest, 2001): the French National Centre for ScientificResearch (CNRS); INSERM the French Institute for Scientific Research (INSERM), the French Institute for Agronomic Research (INRA), the Atomic Energy Commission (CEA), the French

Institute for Exploitation of the Sea (IFREMER). In view of the France governmental initiatives carried out in the last 10 years, the degree of State support for biotechnology is still considered inadequate, especially when biotechnology is not funded much compared to the funds paid for by the United Kingdom and the German government (Meyers et al., 2008) Recently, the French government has introduced a programme advocated by EuropaBio for encouraging entrepreneurial activity – the Young Innovative Company status, which offers important tax and social security exemptions (EuropaBio, 2003).

The German government recognized the requirement for new things in the 1990s. Government arrangements have now changed to advance models of innovative business in high-innovation areas, for example, data, pioneering plans of action Software and Biotechnology (Ernst & Young, 2004). At present Germany is one of the quickest developing biotechnology locales on the planet. 525 German biotech organizations were included in their biotechnology survey, EuropaBio. Biotechnology is considered as pivotal innovation for the 21st century. The demand for biomedical medicine Entrepreneurial talent and healthcare professionals is increased in Biomedical and wellness innovation and entrepreneurship programmes to fill the gap (Crispeels et al., 2009)

AN OVERVIEW OF BIO ENTREPRENEURSHIP IN INDIA

Biotechnology is a field that is fast-growing. For incubation, creativity and entrepreneurship, it provides vast reach. In recent years, the indigenous biotechnology sector in India has risen rapidly, with the country's biopharmaceutical industry leading the charge (Patzeltet et al., 2014). By 2020, India's industry is likely to hit $100 billion, with an annual growth rate of about 20 percent at present. More than 350 companies operate across the country in various sub-sectors of biotechnology, such as biopharmaceuticals, agronomics, etc.

The emergence of innovation-led bio-entrepreneurship across India has laid the foundations for a start-up nation of biotechnology and it is imperative to expand on this to amplify activities related to entrepreneurship (Meyers et al., 2008). BIRAC has partnered with C-CAMP to set up the BIRAC Regional Entrepreneurship Centre in order to encourage and facilitate bio-entrepreneurship, including providing bio-entrepreneurs with the requisite expertise and skills to turn creative biotech ideas into profitable and sustainable projects that generate national and global impact (Alper et al., 2002). There are many Bio entrepreneurship in India. Few of the examples will be discussed here:

Bharat Serums and Vaccines Ltd. (BSVL): The belief in 'Bringing life to life' is rooted in a passion that has helped the company to sustain, preserve and improve the quality of life. The company have been using the scientific expertise to produce a variety of biological, biotech and pharmaceutical products for over 4 decades. The affect patient outcomes in the clinical fields of Women's health and Critical Care and IUI-IVF, they have the luxury of being a partner of choice (Meyers et al, 2008).

BioCon: They are the global biopharmaceutical business company that believes that everyone has a right to quality medicines that are affordable. Generics, biosimilars, testing services and innovative biologics are included in their 4 global firms. They reflect the risk-balanced approach of Biocon, underpinned by agile network ties, a robust pipeline and a timely orientation of 'emerging markets.' To deliver size, pace and efficiency, they have leveraged India's value advantage of unparalleled scientific talent and cost-competitive manufacturing. They are working towards doing that by making medications more readily available to patients around the world (Nurmemmedov et al., 2004).

Bioprime:-bio-activators to replace chemical fertilizers: For crop improvement, nutrition, and protection, the start-up develops alternative bio-organic and sustainable solutions. With agricultural biological acting as bio-activators, the start up ensures sustainable crops despite the growing impact of climate change and crop losses (Teng et al., 2016). The bio-activators - an alternative to conventional chemical pesticides - also allow growers to maintain beneficial insect populations in their fields. The company has been awarded the Biotechnology Ignition Grant (BIG) & Seed fund from BIRAC, DBT, for developing new solutions in agriculture biotechnology (Banguero Camacho et al., 2012).

HelpUsGreen: It is the first slim alternative to the colossal question of 'temple-waste' in the world. In order to prevent the Ganges Rivers from becoming a religious sewer by up-cycling the monumental temple-waste in India, we have pioneered the 'flower cycling' technology. In Uttar Pradesh, India, HelpUsGreen collects 2.4 tonnes of floral waste daily from temples and mosques. The waste is recycled into the world's first aromatic sticks and compost for flower cycling, revolutionising the way India treats the 'Millioo' (Bolz et al., 2019)

Bio-entrepreneurship is now, because of enhanced government incubation funding, also seen as a strong career opportunity. Incubation of biotechnology is different from the other incubation, as start-ups focused on biotechnology need a wide space for wet laboratory and excellent instrumentation facilities to perform the experiments (Banguero Camacho et al., 2017). The Biotechnology Industry Research Assistance Council (BIRAC) is a state-owned, non-profit corporation under the Government of India's Department of Biotechnology (DBT) to empower emerging biotech companies strategically (Langer et al., 2017). For any bio-entrepreneur, incubation support is a must because they need laboratory infrastructure, mentoring support and high-tech instrumentation facilities to turn their ideas into prototypes. A special scheme, BioNEST (Bioincubators Nurturing Entrepreneurship for Scaling Technologies), has been launched by BIRAC to provide incubation support to startups focused on biotech / life sciences (Shukla et al., 2008). The BioNEST scheme offers resources either as a stand-alone organisation or as part of the academy to build Bio-Incubators. BIRAC has funded about fifty bio-incubators via BioNEST (Bridge, 2017).

AIC is an creative financing plan pointed toward supporting business people by taking care of their working expenses of capital which was begun in 2016 by the NITI Aayog (Bouchie, 2003). The new companies chosen will be surrendered subsidizing of toRs 10 crore over a five-year term. Understudies, specialists or recently settled associations from fields like vehicle, wellbeing, power, schooling, horticulture, water and disinfection can apply to conspire (Patzelt, 2008). The AICs might be established either in openly subsidized organizations or foundations financed by the private area, or in Public-Private Partnership (PPP) mode. Venture Capital Scheme for Agri-Business began by the Small Farmer's Agribusiness Consortium (SFAC), this plan intends to help the country's agrarian development by furnishing makers with a market and empowering ranchers and graduates in horticulture to expand their investment. People, ranchers, maker gatherings, organization/Proprietary organizations, self-improvement organization, Agripreneurs are qualified for the plan (Lawrence, 2005).

The Social Innovation Program for Products (SPARSH),the goal of this programme is to encourage technological growth. The affordable and relevant healthcare options for social welfare. It seeks to encourage the production of innovative solutions to the most pressing social challenges facing society (Jong, 2011). The framework discusses major social problems and offers innovative ideas for widespread reform. The aim of the scheme is to invest in ideas and technologies that enhance health care for all Indians and facilitate accessible social sector product growth. The initiative aims to build a pool of social innovators in biotechnology. The Financial and technical support is provided to social innovators to create market-based innovations that have the ability, in particular, to bring cost-effective health care breakthroughs to disadvantaged communities (Dorey, 2003).

Social Innovation Immersion Program, SIIP is the social innovation fellowship/award programme of BIRAC that is targeted at the development of a "Social Innovators" biotech pool that can recognise needs and needs gaps within societies and can then help bridge the gaps through either creative product or service creation (Rienhoff, 1998). The immersion programme is a unique forum for social innovation which is the potential for clinical and rural immersion and also for clinical and rural immersion Apart from the monthly fellowship, financial support for creating the prototype through a mini kick start grant to young social innovators (Fletcher & Triendl, 2003). The programme has already established nationwide clusters on the "Ageing and Health" in the three thematic areas: "Maternal and Child Health" "and "Waste to value". Many of the mentored social innovators and the programme has been active in increasing the following funds or launching its own company through the programme. The programme is introduced through BIRAC SIIP partners and is mentored through the knowledge advisor of BIRAC SIIP (Waltz, 2005).

Transforming the ecosystem of biotech innovation Founded in *1986 and among the first dedicated biotechnology departments* developed by any country, the Department of Biotechnology (DBT) in India's Ministry of Science and Technology has been a catalyst for spearheading creative solutions to developmental challenges (Howard, 2003). Today, biotechnology has played a major role in shaping food and agriculture, nutrition, healthcare, the environment and industry.

As the field has advanced, DBT has made considerable progress and has supported the country's economic and social development. From studies on the prevention and treatment of major diseases, to addressing the challenges of improving agricultural production, to creating novel solutions for national nutrition needs and a clean environment, DBT is leading the way in pioneering biotechnology research (Powell, 2004). DBT has been committed to providing solutions to societal problems with a Make in India emphasis since its inception. Today, as we are situated from discovery science to translational research, from academia to startups, from institutional cooperation to translational clusters of expertise, DBT has transformed India's scope of scientific innovation (Reid, 2003).

DBT has developed a very effective research and translation ecosystem across the nation over the last three decades and has built strong foundations, leveraging the influence of national and international partnerships (Williams & Walsh, 2004). DBT sponsors nearly 10,000 biotechnology research fellows and students annually, with over 15,000 scientists and 800 institutes and laboratories funded. World-class state-of-the-art infrastructure has been developed, which has now been made available to all researchers and startups through the DBT's SAHAJ scheme to take research and innovation across the country (Reid, 2003). Vigyan Expertise Life Science and Biotechnology Centers have helped develop a professional human resource base that is employable.

In aligning its work with the national growth agenda and designing creative solutions for the national missions of Swasth Bharat, Ayushman Bharat, Swatch Bharat, Poshaan Abhiyan, Start-up India, Make in India and Talent India, DBT has also made significant contributions (Gunn & Langer, 2017). Academic and business experts have supplied the nation successfully.

To promote and nurture a vibrant start-up and entrepreneurial ecosystem, the Biotechnology Industry Research Assistance Council (BIRAC) was created. BIRAC strives to encourage excellence while promoting bio-innovation for the good of society (Edgington, 1998). In our short history, through an exponential learning curve, we have been able to consolidate efforts in different areas of biotechnology to facilitate sustainable funding. We have found that there has been a substantial boost to discovery research and a change to product creation through various funding schemes, a field in which we want to create deeper roots so that the benefits of innovation-driven research reach everyone. BIRAC will fund more than 1,000 start-ups and entrepreneurs (Langer, 2018).

The DBT has developed an infrastructure to carry scientific research from the laboratory to the end user, enabling the seamless transfer of research from the translation process to commercialization. This has led to 16 institutions, four bioclusters, two public sector undertakings and over 5,000 extramural research ventures. Over the years, we have seen an increasing pattern of shifting from single-investigator to multi-investigator projects, from single-institute to multi-institute projects, and from academic research alone to research and translation of industry-academic innovation (Jayaraman, 2004). New institutional alliances and models of governance have arisen.

It is necessary for us not to mix a self-reliant India with a self-centered India. At the heart of self-reliance are foreign cooperation and partnership. Without a doubt, India's success would lead to global progress. By implementing several joint research and development programmes with several countries and philanthropic organisations, the DBT and BIRAC have embodied this importance (Mitchell, 2004). Our effort is to ensure that our technologies continue to concentrate on scalability, sustainability and replicability, as the world is searching for fast ways to address the enormous healthcare challenges raised by the COVID-19 pandemic. The incorporation of new and emerging technologies, linking biological science with data science, clinical research and engineering sciences, is the way forward in preparing to meet our ambitious goal of achieving a bio economy of US$150 billion by 2025 and becoming a bio manufacturing hub for India of US$100 billion.

Our task in the future is not only to improve the foundation of research and translation, but also to ensure sustainability and scalability. The DBT has continuously brought the importance of science in all walks of life to the fore and has integrated national growth with innovation (Haycock, 1998). Instead of a siloes area of work, it has encouraged science and technology as a way of thought and aims to continue to do so and be a vital part of India's growth story.

Our emphasis must be on the value of indigenous science and the advancement of impact-driven innovation as we brace ourselves for a new world. This is the secret to our march towards the Atmanirbhar Bharat.

The concept of Bio entrepreneurship basically stands upon the three basic fundamental pillars names technology, scientific and managerial skill and the money. Tragically, the stock of both scientific furthermore, administrative ability isn't meeting the request (Beylin, 2011). As per a new National Science Foundation report, the interest for biotech labourers is outperforming the rate at which US colleges are producing graduates, and in light of the fact that scholastic establishments can't fulfil the business ' s interest for new PhD graduates, drawing in and keeping labourers is turning into an inexorably genuine issue in the medication improvement measure (Kearney & Langer, 2018). Three classifications of workers are in the briefest stockpile: scholars to make disclosures, specialists to take those revelations through the confirmation of-idea stage, and individuals to design furthermore, execute clinical preliminaries (Basu, P,2003).

The interest for ability is a global issue. A new report depicting the Singapore bunch, for instance, noticed that their most serious issue is its proceeded with deficiency of enterprising researchers and administrators. While trying to distinguish those elements that pull in bioscience organizations, The New York Monetary Development Council met with in excess of 600 bioscience organizations in 18 nations. They likewise connected with the more than 100 bioscience organizations situated in New York City and worked intimately with the city's significant scholarly foundations. All through this comprehensive cycle they identified the rules utilized by organizations to make fire up or then again movement choices. Curiously, the components utilized by both new companies and prepared organizations are very comparative. Admittance to ability was second just to vicinity to a-list research focuses in their rundown (Bell, 2010).

Biotechnology and life science commercialisation endeavors have remarkable qualities that different them from other innovation based enterprises. thus, Li and Halal note that heads of such endeavors have extraordinary difficulties (Vermij, 2004). Bioentrepreneurs need to establish a climate that adjusts imaginative and imaginative opportunity with responsibility. They need to assemble an ethos of cooperation and make an informal community of researchers. At long last, they need to accentuate the estimation of science and its benefits to patients and mankind without overemphasizing the business objectives (Moran, 2010). Given these difficulties and accordingly to the requirement for appropriately prepared individuals, bio entrepreneurship instructive projects, intended to prepare pioneers and directors of new furthermore, existing life science organizations, are arising all through the world. A few projects are offered by business colleges, some as a component of a innovation improvement program in schools of designing or other specialized schools and some are affiliated with other specialist co-op or bioscience exchange affiliation elements (Basu, 2003).

A few patterns are molding the eventual fate of graduate-level training that apply to bio entrepreneurship programs:

- Worldwide rivalry for ability;
- Low investment of ladies and minorities in science, innovation, designing and math programs;
- The proceeding with battle to express the vision of graduate training as a public benefit, not just as a private decent;
- Endeavors to change the cycle and result of graduate-level projects;
- The internationalization of projects what's more, the difficulties of joint effort.

No two bio entrepreneurship projects will be the equivalent, much the same as no other expert schools will be indistinguishable whether they instruct designing, medication or law. Nor should they be. Each will reflect neighborhood culture, resources and governmental issues. In any case, like other expert schools, there should be a defined assortment of center information with learning targets that fulfill market and accreditation rules. Overseers of bio entrepreneurship projects can speed the cycle by:

- Making consortia and offer workshops and gatherings to create learning targets furthermore, a centre bio entrepreneurship schooling educational plan.
- Share instructive assets, for example, bioscience business contextual analyses.
- Distribute research on such projects.
- Share best practices and improvement systems for trading thoughts.
- Work with other industry affiliations, specialist co-ops and public labour improvement organizations to give the sort of ability the market requests.

Bio entrepreneurship schooling programs try not to must be in significant bioscience bunches like Maryland, Massachusetts or California to be effective. There are a few colleges with solid notorieties in business venture that solitary location the biotechnology field in a superficial way or don't address it all. There is space for development and advancement in business schools for people in the future of bio entrepreneurs, especially those situated in geographic closeness to arising bio clusters. Bio entrepreneurship schooling programs can possibly address an around the world market need, to add to the monetary imperativeness of a network and help professionalize the business. They will be effective in any case, just in the event that they give a quantifiable, convincing incentive that obviously satisfies a market need (Dove, 2003).

The idea of 'Bio entrepreneurship' is still genuinely new in India, however India is among the world's best 12 biotech pioneers. Our biotech area has pulled in a lot of consideration in the course of recent many years. A few global companies have forcefully held hands with Indian Companies because of India's solid conventional biotechnology potential. A fruitful biotechnology undertaking relies upon prepared experts who comprehend science as well as talented in the complexities of biotechnology commercialization. Each biotechnology entrepreneur should completely comprehend the essentials of the biotechnology area, for example, research, cooperation, foundation, and innovation and capital and think of an elective plan of action to bio farming. Consequently the program would help construct a solid establishment on bio entrepreneurship, giving an exceptional illuminating setting to the members to comprehend the whole Biotechnology venture and remarkable issues to the business (Garner, Marchington, & Pfeifer, 2007).

THE GROWTH OF BIO- ENTREPRENEURSHIP IN JAPAN

Biotechnology is maybe the most prospering regions close to the beginning of the twenty-first century. It has a verifiably huge impact on monetary areas and controls going from clinical to green nature, so much that its inevitability licenses it to be seen to go about as a representation of "universally useful innovation".

Over the last 35 years bio technology based industries has been booming. Since its inception in the form of genetech, which is often regarded as the first modern biotech firm, many thousands of biotechnology ventures have been founded and many of these have been extraordinarily successful ventures. Today, the biotech sectors have an important role in economic impact.

Genentech made the primary biotechnology drug called Humulin in 1978. Humulin was cloned from human insulin using recombinant DNA strategies. Genentech's accomplishment in Humulin just as first sale of stock (IPO) in 1980, made a model and plan for biotechnology startup's in the US to explore and abuse new progressions in biotechnology.

After twenty years, a comparable example of biotechnology bloom was seen in Japan. With the bursting of the speculative "bubble economy" and the longest downturn in Japan's post-war history that followed it, a variety of changes unfurled in Japan. These included among others, increased government budgets for R&D, reforms in legal and policy frameworks support college industry linkages; Intellectual property reforms and advancement of new companies. The Japanese government too directed biotechnology as one of its new frontier ventures. Therefore, in the most recent decade, Japan has made a plethora of biotechnology start-ups known as bio ventures.

At the point when genetic engineering had its underlying business triumphs in the mid 1980s, Japanese breweries and food organizations were the first to embrace the new innovation. These 'new members' were viable in dispatching different recombinant prescriptions, inferable from their total data on bioprocessing and key associations created with unfamiliar biotechnology fire up firms.

In any case, paying little heed to their flourishing, inferable from customary drug businesses, Japan can't be called as a pioneer in the commercialisation of biotechnology. Japan addresses the second biggest individual market for the merchandise and ventures of biotechnology, after the USA. With just 2 percent of the total populace, Japan represents 12 percent of the world's complete drug utilization. In addition, in life science research, Japan has a superb standing. It holds around 20% of biotechnology licenses, contrasted and 21 percent for Europe and 52 percent for the USA. Unendingly, enormous associations rule this zone in Japan, representing around 76 percent of all patent filings as opposed to 53% of USA. By 1996, almost 50% of all secretly held human genome licenses had a place with Japanese organizations. Details of Biotechnology IPO in Japan, US and Europe is given in table 1.

Table 1. Comparison of biotechnology ipos between Japan, US and Europe

	Japan		US		Europe	
Year	**Ave. Of IPO Funding (US$ Million)**	**#of Biotech Companies**	**Ave. Of IPO Funding (US$ Million)**	**#of Biotech Companies**	**Ave. Of IPO Funding (US$ Million)**	**#of Biotech Companies**
2004	42.27	3	51.88	8	59.99	28
2005	38.00	1	38.90	21	48.15	13
2006	28.29	2	32.76	25	47.20	20
2007	19.50	3	48.10	21	56.27	22
2008	7.42	3	37.00	3	6.00	1

Source: Ernst and Young[2005,2006,2007a,b,2008,2009] and TSE[2010]

The Japanese government has taken phenomenal measures to help biotech inside its lines. One model is the public authority financed Okinawa Health Biotechnology Research and Development Centre, which gives free investigation workplaces to qualified biotechnology associations. The mission of the center is to make new endeavours and improve made items through government-industry-the scholarly world cooperation. In 2011, Japan positioned #11 among other top countries for biotechnology, with strong scores in the quantity of licenses the nation creates just as generally advancement. For the government of Japan, the biotech-based economy/industry is an essential part of Prime Minister Abe Administration growth strategy, as caught in the "Basic Policy on Economic and Fiscal Management and Reform 2015". The Ministry of Energy Trade and Industry (METI) expects to cultivate the biotech-based economy, projected to develop as extensive as multiple times continuously 2030, through the turn of events and commercialization of the creative advancements, items and administrations, remarkably including regenerative medication.

In 2016, METI gave the record "New patterns in the field of biotechnology and its effect on society and economy: Creating Smart Cell Industry" where it was percieved that phone innovation, with its imaginative potential, will bring accomplish unprecedented changes in modern design and activity of major mechanical fields and give the reason to address worldwide difficulties. In Japan, the Science and Technology Policy is controlled by the principles set by Science and Technology Basic Plan, which is supported at regular intervals. The objective of the plan is to achieve a superior nature of science and development, to add to the headway of the economy and society of Japan (Garner, Marchington, & Pfeifer, 2007).

It incorporates a progression of measures to advance translational R&D, especially in the field of regenerative medication, where the market is required to extend from 9 billion yen (€67.5 million) in

2012 to 1 trillion yen (€7.5 billion) in 2030.Since 2014, the guidelines of the comprehensive strategy on Science, Technology and Innovation, incorporate advancement measures towards the social usage of regenerative medication: - Promotion of contiguous basic research, clinical research and practical applications of somatic stem cells, embryonic stem cells (ES cells) and induced pluripotent stem cells (iPS cells) - Establishment of infrastructure for regenerative medicine industry - Preparation of development guidelines. Several regulatory-led initiatives were designed in Japan to promote the research and development of regenerative medicine products. Tomohiro fujita, the CEO of Chitose group who is often referred as "the hub of development for Japan's biotech industry". Japanese entrepreneur and scientist is involved in everything from producing edible algae to manufacturing biopharmaceuticals (Dove, 2003).

Fujita said bio projects require ventures of in any event $100 million to get an opportunity. Japanese biotech adventures commonly figure out how to raise only one-10th of that, probably. Fujita is determined to stimulate Japan's biotech area. As an educator at Kyoto University, he controls coordinated effort between Japanese colleges and the private area. Also, he sits on a compelling government board entrusted with planning a procedure for Japan's biotech sector. Japanese biotech skill is dispersed among unique organizations. One of Fujita's qualities is his capacity to put together numerous players around a shared objective. Indeed, Chitose's primary wellspring of income is the charges it procures in co-advancement projects. It as of now works with Ajinomoto, Kyowa Kirin, Mitsui Chemicals, and Kaneka on approaches to improve mechanical maturation measures. Chitose has collaborated with the Japanese fuel and ointment maker Eneos to make green growth based stream fuel. Fujita sees the market for bio-based fly fuel growing as controllers around the planet order that biofuel be essential for the stream fuel blend. Stream fuel would be one market for the microalgae that Chitose is filling in Malaysia. In Sarawak state on the island of Borneo, the organization works an exhibit plant to show algal biomass can be mass-created to make fuel and different materials. Chitose says the office is the world's biggest in a tropical area.

Other than biofuels, Chitose is additionally looking at drugs. In Japan it built up an improved method for delivering counter acting agent drugs. Offering fast cell engendering and high immune response efficiency, the technique can reduce the expense of creation by 75%Chitose's most eager task is planning a real city for the oil-rich nation of Brunei, additionally on Borneo. There, Fujita needs to show the plausibility of a biobased economy that completely reuses all materials. Intended to be open for inhabitants in 2030, the alleged Bio Eco Town will be based on lacking area in the locale of Temburong. Chitose chose Brunei since it was simpler to get land there than in Japan. In addition, the solid Brunei sun favors making a "photosynthesis-based society.

The monetary motor of Bio Eco Town will be ease energizes, synthetics, and food from green growth, Fujita says. "We intend to extend creation of green growth utilizing the innovation we showed in Malaysia," he says, noticing that the two lipids and proteins can be extricated from a similar living being. "The world will not have the option to place green growth into useful utilize except if we plan a mechanical construction dependent on green growth."

Chitose is creating measurements to gauge the ecological manageability of the venture. Wastewater will be treated with a duckweed-based framework that is normal in Malaysian palm oil estates. Moreover, the city will oversee soil fruitfulness by diverting the solids from water treatment into fertilize.

Japan has effectively made a plenty of bio ventures. Since subsidizing from investment is especially essential for the advancement of such bio ventures, one potential arrangement is to build the measure of funding financing. As indicated by the Wall Street Journal, the Japanese Government Pension Investment is the biggest single annuity reserve in the world Increasing the measure of funding financing for biotechnology is the principal significant advance of numerous different advances expected to help the biotechnology business in Japan. That by itself is an enormous test since it requires a difference in mentality to acknowledge higher dangers and an adjustment in the old methods of working together. There will be protection from change since establishments and associations exist inside a complex, interwoven snare of associations with every framework profoundly established in its own quirks, history, culture and social examples. Anyway change is a lot of required if Japan needs to develop its bio ventures to fabricate an effective biotechnology industry.

BIO ENTREPRENEURSHIP IN EUROPE COUNTRIES

There is a widespread opinion that biotechnology organizations worldwide had the opportunity to follow plans of action started inside the US. These models, as a rule, are upheld improvement of a chose innovation stage. The common astuteness recommends this innovation are regularly sold as an apparatus or administration to drug organizations or are frequently wont to build up a lead compound which will at that point be offered to enormous pharm for R&D dollars and single-digit downstream eminences.

Biotechnology new businesses all over the place, not simply in Europe, are normally not productive in leading drug improvement. For the most part, they're disclosure centered organizations that need both the skill and accordingly the contacts in these regions to productively deal with this process. Europe and to much lesser degree Japan were developing their own biotechnology regions, yet the United States was the world head in regards to the amount of dedicated biotechnology firms, the proportion of capital they raised, and the amount of licenses and wages they delivered.

Present day biotechnological techniques and items are important for our regular day to day existence. In the market, we purchase biotechnologically designed food, for example, bug safe vegetables and organic products. We drink lager which was produced with the assistance of hereditarily designed yeast, and wine from grapes of quality-controlled plants, and we use cups of biodegradable plastics delivered by present day biotechnological measures. The garments we wear and the paper we compose on are produced by usage of biomolecules, for example, compounds picked up from hereditarily designed microorganisms. At the drug store, we buy drugs and demonstrative tests which are created, tried, and delivered by current biotechnological strategies.

Since current bio entrepreneurial adventures are portrayed by long item advancement cycles, high mechanical and market vulnerability, and a high capital power, beginning a biotechnology firm is among the most mind-boggling enterprising assignments. The disappointment pace of firms is high and it has become evident that achievement factors which are significant with regards to different enterprises are just somewhat important for youthful biotech firms in light of their particular attributes. The principle inspirations for executing this high-innovation business instruction program are the dangers presented by the low pioneering action in Belgium and by the European development Catch 22. The biotechnology program was executed to animate and show bio entrepreneurship among ace understudies in business and bioengineering at the college. The principle objective of the venture is to create and execute a bunch of incorporated, interdisciplinary courses, coordinated by various resources and went to by understudies in business and in bio-designing.

Biotech Start-Ups and Venture Capital: The financial hypothesis of mechanical change centres around the firm as the essential examination unit and analyses the microeconomic impetuses and effects of private exploration for commercialization. Advancement permits firms to create better than ever items, capital reserve funds and, on account of mechanical cycles, it brings cost decreases or quality enhancements. This clarifies why firms are the fundamental entertainers of the cycle of mechanical development. Their ability to advance is incompletely dictated by their abilities, somewhat by their ability to adjust and apply information created somewhere else (Feneuille, 1997). Recent investigations of effect of imaginative action at the firm level on the bigger economy, with center on 'endogenously' created development on macroeconomic development, exchange and mechanical area accepted that development is a discrete occasion that happens inside firms (Romer, 1990; Krugman, 1998).

Another and a significant element of BEP is to expand number of biotech new businesses and make VC accessible by means of corporate associations. In view of the way that it is the new businesses, which fill in as the information creating units in biotech work division, and which later change into different sorts of working biotech organizations, as they prove their logical and monetary base, their significance should be seen as the seeds of business biotechnology. Since BEP focuses on economical corporate relations and wellbeing, in its center falschoods productive collaboration regarding instruments that stand imperative for longterm usefulness, development and reasonability of a biotech organization.

The European biotech industry has gained traction and is now poised to take full advantage of the new decade. The following are some of the significant biotech industries in European countries:

Ynsect: The industry was started in the year 2011, located in Paris-France. Ynsect aims to provide an eco-friendly option for food and insect feed processing. The company raised a €110M Series C round in 2019 to fund the development of the largest automated insect farm in the world. The company had planned to receive EU approval in 2020 for the use of insects in chicken feed and fertilisers, and for some organisms to be used for human consumption.

Targedys: The industry was found in the year 2011, located in Paris-France. By addressing the gut microbiome, Targedys develops therapies to modulate appetite. The company expected results from a clinical trial evaluating the effect of a live bacterial therapy on the weight of overweight people at the beginning of 2020. The company had to begin funding for Series B in 2020 after a €10M Series A round in 2019.

Promethera: The industry was started in the year 2009, located in Mont-Saint-Guibert, Belgium. Promethera is developing human liver cell-based cell therapies and has earned EUR 47 million in 2019 to fund on-going clinical trials. The company expected the results of a phase IIa clinical trial testing its technology for the treatment of non-alcoholic steatohepatitis (NASH) in the first half of 2020, a liver disease with a large demand for which no approved treatment is yet available. Although some are more advanced in the NASH space, Promethera is proposing a much more imaginative approach aimed at resolving the difficulty of this condition.

Oryzon Genomics: The industry was found in the year 2000, located in Barcelona, Spain. Oryzon Genomics focuses on epigenetic drug discovery for the treatment of cancer and neurodegenerative diseases. The organisation has published promising clinical results from trials of patients with leukaemia and lung cancer, as well as Alzheimer's disease, over the course of 2019. The business will await additional phase IIa outcomes from ongoing trials through all these indications in year ahead.

Orphazyme: The industry was started in the year 2009, located in Copenhagen, Denmark. Orphazyme develops rare disease therapies that disrupt proper protein folding, and hence their work. In the further years ahead, the company will apply for the first marketing authorisation in both Europe and the US for the treatment of Niemann-Pick disease. Orphazyme also expects findings from a phase II trial of Gaucher disease to be published.

Meatable: The industry was started in the year 2018, located in Delft, Netherlands. Meatable is developing a technology to scale up lab-grown meat production. While other players in the field with more advanced programmes concentrate primarily on developing alternatives to beef, Meatable raised EUR 9M Series A in December to allow the company to develop the first prototype of lab-grown pork by the summer of 2020.

MaaTPharma: The industry was found in the year 2014, located in Lyon, France. MaaT Pharma creates treatments made from living bacteria that, by preventing the destruction of the gut microbiome, aim to improve the outcome of cancer treatments. The company expected results from two clinical trials in the previous year, a phase I trial in chemotherapy patients and a phase II trial in patients suffering complications following bone marrow transplantation.

HookipaBiotech: The industry was found in the year 2011, located in Vienna, Austria. For infectious diseases and cancer, Hookipa Biotech creates immunotherapies. The company raised about EUR 100 million from a Series D round and a Nasdaq IPO in 2019. In the nest year, Hookipa expected results from a phase II trial investigating whether its lead vaccine candidate will avoid infections and complications from cytomegalovirus-infected donors in patients receiving organ transplants. The organisation will also begin a phase I/II analysis with a treatment for cancers caused by the human papillomavirus.

GenSightBiologics: The industry was found in the year 2012, located in Paris-France. To treat hereditary variants of blindness, GenSight Biologics advances gene therapies. In 2019, despite struggling to show it was superior to placebo care in a recent phase II trial, the company announced it would be seeking regulatory approval for its lead candidate therapy. The company has compiled data supporting the fact that the results of the therapy given in one eye extend to that given by placebo. The organisation also plans next year to announce a fresh fundraising.

Genfit: The industry was started in the year 1999, located in Loos, France. For metabolic and liver disorders, Genfit creates therapies. The company expected result from a phase III trial in the first quarter of 2020 following a €120M fundraising in 2019. The trial is evaluating its lead candidate drug, elafibranor, in non-alcoholic steatohepatitis patients with chronic liver disease (NASH).

Follicum: The industry was found in the year 2011, located in Lund, Sweden. Follicum develops peptide drugs intended to treat hair loss and diabetes. The company plans to start a phase I trial with a drug that has shown potential to stimulate the secretion of insulin and delay the onset of type 1 diabetes. Follicum is also preparing for the start of a phase II trial testing its hair growth treatment.

F2G: The industry was started in the year 1998, located in Manchester, UK. F2G is an Austrian-British company which produces antifungals. A small range of antifungal groups is currently available, and the production of new solutions is urgently required to address the growing challenge of antimicrobial resistance.

CRISPR Therapeutics: The industry was found in the year 2013, located in Zug, Switzerland. CRISPR Therapeutics, leading the first wave of CRISPR/Cas9 gene editing therapies, published the first preliminary human evidence to test this technology in patients with genetic blood disorders at the end of last year, with complete findings anticipated next year. The company plans to conduct no fewer than five simultaneous clinical trials in upcoming years. In addition, the European Patent Office will hold an appeal hearing early next year on the famously contested patents of US rivals of CRISPR Therapeutics to determine the intellectual property status of CRISPR technology in Europe.

In the recent decade, plenty of biotechnology companies are being established all over the world. The rise and the improvement of bio ventures are significant in light of the fact that they are a basic wellspring of biotechnology development. There could be different hindrances to clarify the immature condition of bio ventures such as business, portability of analysts, college industry linkages and collusions. The advancement of bio ventures is compromised by the absence of a feasible arrangement of subsidizing that takes into account high danger advancements, long incubation periods and high capital power.

CONCLUSION

The quantity of bio entrepreneursand bio entrepreneurship instructive projects are developing all through the world. To start with, the convergence of new advances and disclosures in the existence sciences, designing, data innovation and materials sciences are setting out new advertisement open doors not just in biotechnology also in drug discovery, development and medical devices and modern designing and nanotechnology. A better understanding of sickness at the cell, subcellular and hereditary level has set out open doors to grow new, imaginative medication treatments. Setting up of Bio clusters in basically every state in and most created nations to quicken the commercialisation of these disclosures and receive the monetary benefits that outcome. In reaction to this stunning monetary opportunity, and understanding that positions and financing for essential scholastic exploration are declining, understudies at the undergrad and graduate level whose interest is in science, designing, innovation and science are requesting instructive projects that will furnish them with the information, abilities and perspectives needed to begin a bioscience organization , there will be remarkable development in projects, for example, MD/MBA and PhD/MBA contributions, giving bio business schooling to specialists, life researchers furthermore engineers.

REFERENCES

Alper, J. (2002). The rise of the European bioentrepreneur. *Nature Biotechnology*, *20*(6), BE3–BE5. doi:10.1038/nbt0602supp-BE3 PMID:12089569

Back, S. M. (2009). The Bioentrepreneurship MBA: Options for mid-tier business schools. *Journal of Commercial Biotechnology*, *15*(2), 183–193. doi:10.1057/jcb.2008.57

Banguero Camacho, C. V., & GiraldoDíaz, R. (2012). Bio-entrepreneurship: Productive reconfiguration of agro-ecosystems in the district of La Elvira, Santiago de Cali. *Entramado*, *8*(1), 168–175.

Basu, P. (2003). Technology transfer survey reveals disparities but growth at US universities. *Bioentrepreneur*, 1–2. doi:10.1038/bioent745

Basu, P. (2003). How the US government can fund your company. *Bioentrepreneur*, 1–4.

Baumol, W. J. (2005). Education for innovation: Entrepreneurial breakthroughs versus corporate incremental improvements. *Innovation Policy and the Economy*, *5*, 33–56. doi:10.1086/ipe.5.25056170

Bell, J. R. (2010). *Handbook of bioentrepreneurship. New England Journal of Entrepreneurship*, 13(1), 79.

Beylin, D., Chrisman, C. J., & Weingarten, M. (2011). Granting you success. *Bioentrepreneur*, 1–4. PMID:21874663

Bolz, K., & Volkmann, C. (2019). Responsible Bioentrepreneurs. *NanoEthics*, *13*(2), 147–150. doi:10.100711569-019-00342-7

Bouchie, A. (2003). Private biotech companies face new funding challenges. *Bioentrepreneur*, 1–2. doi:10.1038/bioent757

Bridge, W. (2017). The Struggle to Establish Bioentrepreneurship Education Programs: An Australian Perspective. *Technology Transfer and Entrepreneurship*, *4*(2), 107–114. doi:10.2174/2213809904666170809145045

Crispeels, T., Uecke, O., Goldchstein, M., & Schefczyk, M. (2009). Best practices for developing university bioentrepreneurship education programmes. *Journal of Commercial Biotechnology*, *15*(2), 136–150. doi:10.1057/jcb.2008.44

Dorey, E. (2003). Biotechs critique big pharma's collaboration skills. *Bioentrepreneur*, 1–2.

Dove, A. (2003). Perfecting your patent search. *Bioentrepreneur*, 1–2.

Dyson, F. (2007). Our biotech future. *The New York Review of Books*, *54*(12).

Edgington, S. M. (1998). The future belongs to the bioentrepreneur. *Nature Biotechnology*, *16*(S1), 1–1. doi:10.1038/5387 PMID:9591246

Eyers, A. (2015). Bioentrepreneurship: opportunities and challenges. In *Embracing Entrepreneurship Across Disciplines*. Edward Elgar Publishing.

Fletcher, L., & Triendl, R. (2003). Japan's first biotechnology graduate school will open in April. *Bioentrepreneur*, 1–2.

Garner, C., Marchington, T., & Pfeifer, A. (2007). Key ingredients for success in Europe. *Bioentrepreneur*, 1–4.

Grima, E. M., Belarbi, E. H., Fernández, F. A., Medina, A. R., & Chisti, Y. (2003). Recovery of microalgal biomass and metabolites: Process options and economics. *Biotechnology Advances*, *20*(7-8), 491–515.

Gunn, M., & Langer, L. J. (2017). *One Course, Two… Four Courses–A Bioentrepreneurship Concentration-Case Studies*: Johns Hopkins University and the University of San Francisco. *Technology Transfer and Entrepreneurship*, *4*(2), 115–120.

Haycock, P. (1998). Europe discovers bioentrepreneurship. *Nature Biotechnology*, *16*(1), 6–6.

Howard, K. (2003). Three US states launch biotech seed funds. *Bioentrepreneur*, 1–2.

Jayaraman, K. S. (2004). Foreign VC funds get mixed reception in India. *Bioentrepreneur*, 1–2.

Jong, S. (2011). Commercializing a disruptive technology. *Bioentrepreneur*, 1–4.

Kearney, C., & Langer, L. J. (2018). Effective Leadership through Bioentrepreneurship and Bioinnovation. *Journal of Commercial Biotechnology*, *24*(2), 3–5.

Langer, L. J. (2017). Developing Global Biotechnology Enterprise, Entrepreneurship and Regulatory Science Programs: Profile from the Center for Biotechnology Education at Johns Hopkins University. *Technology Transfer and Entrepreneurship*, *4*(2), 139–143.

Langer, R. (2018). Mastering Bioentrepreneurship. *Innovative Research in Life Sciences: Pathways to Scientific Impact, Public Health Improvement, and Economic Progress*, 291.

Lawrence, S. (2005). Looking at US versus European exit opportunities. *Bioentrepreneur*, 1–2.

Meyers, A. (2014). Bioentrepreneurship Education and Training Trends. *Journal of Commercial Biotechnology*, *20*(2).

Meyers, A. D., & Hurley, P. (2008). Bioentrepreneurship education programmes in the United States. *Journal of Commercial Biotechnology*, *14*(1), 2–12.

Meyers, A. D., McCubbrey, D. J., & Watson, R. T. (2008). Open content textbooks: Educating the next generation of bioentrepreneurs in developing economies. *Journal of Commercial Biotechnology*, *14*(4), 277–281.

Mitchell, P. (2004). The changing attitude of European VCs. *Bioentrepreneur*, 1–2.

Nurmemmedov, E. (2004). *Bioentrepreneurial Partnership-A toll for Biotechnology transfer* (Doctoral dissertation). Lund University.

Patzelt, H., & Brenner, T. (2008). Introduction to the Handbook of Bioentrepreneurship. In Handbook of Bioentrepreneurship (pp. 1-6). Springer.

Powell, K. (2004). Business model competitions catch investors' eyes. *Bioentrepreneur*, 1–3.

Reid, B. (2003). Budget shortfalls threaten US biotechnology programs. *Bioentrepreneur*, 1–2.

Rienhoff, H. Y. (1998). Becoming a bioentrepreneur. *Nature Biotechnology*, *16*(1), 37–38.

Sohl, J. (2004). The importance of angels in starting a US biotech venture. *Bioentrepreneur*, 1–3.

Stata, R. (2004). New ways to evaluate innovative ventures. *MIT Sloan Management Review*, *45*(3), 96.

Teng, P. P. (2016). *Bio-entrepreneurship in Asia: Some learnings to accelerate innovation*. ILRI.

Vermij, P. (2004). Patenting costs cast a shadow on European biotech. *Bioentrepreneur*, 1–2.

Waltz, E. (2005). Biotech entrepreneur, educate thyself! *Bioentrepreneur*, 1–2.

Williams, G., & Walsh, G. (2004). Scaling the biobusiness information mountain. *Bioentrepreneur*, 1–4.

Compilation of References

Abbott, R. B., Bader, R., Bajjali, L., ElSamen, T. A., Obeidat, T., Sboul, H., & Alabbadi, I. (2012). The price of medicines in Jordan: The cost of trade-based intellectual property. *Journal of Generic Medicines, 9*(2), 75–85. doi:10.1177/1741134312447499

Abdullahi, M. S. (2015). Soil contamination, remediation and plants. In Soil remediation and plants. Academic.

Achilladelis, B., & Antonakis, N. (2001). The dynamics of technological innovation: The case of the pharmaceutical Industry. *Research Policy, 30*(4), 535–588. doi:10.1016/S0048-7333(00)00093-7

Acres, B., Limacher, J. M., & Bonnefoy, J. (2007). Discovery and development of therapeutic cancer vaccines. *Current Opinion in Drug Discovery & Development, 10*(2), 185–192. PMID:17436554

Acs, Z. J., & Audretsch, D. B. (1988). Innovation in large and small firms: An empirical analysis. *The American Economic Review*, 678–690.

Acs, Z. J., & Audretsch, D. B. (1990). *Innovation and Small Firms.* MIT Press. doi:10.1007/978-94-015-7854-7

Acs, Z., Braunerhjelm, P., Audretsch, D. B., & Carlsson, B. (2009). The knowledge spillover theory of entrepreneurship. *Small Business Economics, 32*(1), 15–30. doi:10.100711187-008-9157-3

Adam, D. J., & Sparrow, J. C. (2008). Enterprise for Life Scientists: Developing Innovation and Entrepreneurship in the Biosciences. *Journal of Commercial Biotechnology, 14*(4), 355–356. doi:10.1057/jcb.2008.21

Adams, R., Bessant, J., & Phelps, R. (2006). Innovation Management Measurement: A Review. *International Journal of Management Reviews, 8*(1), 21–47. doi:10.1111/j.1468-2370.2006.00119.x

Adelberger, K. E. (2000). Semi-Sovereign Leadership? *The State's Role in German Biotechnology and Venture Capital Growth in German Politics., 9*, 103–122.

Adesemoye, A. O., Torbert, H. A., & Kloepper, J. W. (2009). Plant growth-promoting rhizobacteria allow reduced application rates of chemical fertilizers. *Microbial Ecology, 58*(4), 921–929. doi:10.100700248-009-9531-y PMID:19466478

Adhikary, S. (2012). Vermicompost, the story of organic gold: A review. *Scientific Research, 3*(7), 1-13.

Adlim, M., Samingan, & Rossy, A. H. (2014). Integrating entrepreneurial practice in contextual learning of biotechnology for senior high school student. *Journal of Turkish Science Education, 11*(2), 111–122.

Adriano, D. C., Wenzel, W. W., Vangronsveld, J., & Bolan, N. S. (2004). Role of assisted natural remediation in environmental cleanup. *Geoderma, 122*(2-4), 121–142. doi:10.1016/j.geoderma.2004.01.003

Afandi, M. H. (2018). What is Bioentrepreneurship? *Nculineers website.* Retrieved December 1, 2020, from https://nuclineers.com/whats-bioentrepreneurship/

Agarwal, G., Carcache, P. J. B., Addo, E. M., & Kinghorn, A. D. (2019). Current status and contemporary approaches to the discovery of antitumor agents from higher plants. *Biotechnology Advances, 38*, 1–27.

Agathangelou, A. M. (2014). Wither Anarchy? Harvesting the 'Global'Bio-tech Body, Indian Markets and Biomedical Technologies. In *The Global Politics of Science and Technology-Vol. 2* (pp. 179–204). Springer.

AgBiotechNet. (2003). *Grant Changes Monsanto Management Team*. AgBiotechNet.

Aggarwal, A. (2019). Promoting Special Economic Zones as a Strategy of Industrialization and Lessons Learned. In *A Concise Handbook of the Indian Economy in the 21st Century* (pp. 276–320). Oxford University Press. doi:10.1093/oso/9780199496464.003.0010

Aghmiuni, K. S., Siyal, S., Wang, Q., & Duan, Y. (2020). Assessment of factors affecting innovation policy in biotechnology. *Journal of Innovation and Knowledge, 5*(3), 180–190. doi:10.1016/j.jik.2019.10.002

Agricultural Biotechnology Market Size, Share & Trends Analysis Report By Application (Vaccine, Flower Culturing, Biofuels), Organism (Plants, Animals, Microbes), By Region And Segment Forecasts, 2019 - 2025. (2019). Report ID: GVR-3-68038-839-8. Retrieved December 10, 2020, from https://www.grandviewresearch.com/industry-analysis/agricultural-biotechnology-market

Ahmad, H. (2017). *Bioentrepreneurship: Beginner's guide*. Retrieved from https://techooid.com>Money

Ahmad, I., Husain, F. M., Maheshwari, M., & Zahin, M. (2014). Medicinal plants and phytocompounds: a potential source of novel antibiofilm agents. In *Antibiofilm agents* (pp. 205–232). Springer. doi:10.1007/978-3-642-53833-9_10

Ahmann, D., & Dorgan, J. R. (2007). Bioengineering for Pollution Prevention through Development of Biobased Energy and Materials State of the Science Report. Washington, DC: U.S. Environmental Protection Agency. EPA/600/R-07/028. doi:10.1089/ind.2007.3.218

Ahn, M. J., & Meeks, M. (2008). Building a conducive environment for life science based entrepreneurship and industry clusters. *Journal of Commercial Biotechnology, 14*(1), 20–30. doi:10.1057/palgrave.jcb.3050076

Ahuja, G., & Katila, R. (2001). Technological acquisitions and the innovation performance of acquiring firms: A longitudinal study. *Strategic Management Journal, 22*(3), 197–220. doi:10.1002mj.157

Ajila, C. M., Brar, S. K., Verma, M., Tyagi, R. D., Godbout, S., & Valéro, J. R. (2012). Bio-processing of agro-byproducts to animal feed. *Critical Reviews in Biotechnology, 32*(4), 382–400. doi:10.3109/07388551.2012.659172

Akgün, A. E., Byrne, J. C., Lynn, G. S., & Keskin, H. (2007). Team stressors, management support, and project and process outcomes in new product development projects. *Technovation, 27*(10), 628–639. doi:10.1016/j.technovation.2007.02.008

Alam, I., & Perry, C. (2002). A customer-oriented new service development process. *Journal of Services Marketing, 16*(6), 515–534. doi:10.1108/08876040210443391

Albaladejo, M., & Romijn, H. (2000). *Determinants of innovation capability in small UK firms: an empirical analysis*. Eindhoven Centre for Innovation Studies.

Alhabeeb, M. J. (2014). *Entrepreneurial finance: fundamentals of financial planning and management for small business*. John Wiley & Sons.

Ali, H., Khan, E., & Sajad, M. A. (2013). Phytoremediation of heavy metals—Concepts and applications. *Chemosphere, 91*(7), 869–881. doi:10.1016/j.chemosphere.2013.01.075 PMID:23466085

Alok, K. S. (2011). Biotechnology: The New Horizon for Indian Leadership. *VSRD Technical and Non Technical Journal, 2*(3), 144–159.

Alok, K. S. (2011). Biotechnology: The new horizon for Indian leadership. *VSRD Technical and Non Technical Journal.*, *2*(3), 144–159.

Alori, E. T., & Babalola, O. O. (2018). Microbial Inoculants for Improving Crop Quality and Human Health in Africa. *Frontiers in Microbiology*, *9*, 2213. doi:10.3389/fmicb.2018.02213 PMID:30283427

Alper, J. (2002). The rise of the European bioentrepreneur. *Nature Biotechnology*, *20*(6), BE3–BE5. doi:10.1038/nbt0602supp-BE3 PMID:12089569

Altman, A. (1997). *Agricultural biotechnology*. CRC Press. doi:10.1201/9781420049275

Alvarez, S. A., & Busenitz, L. W. (2001). The entrepreneurship of resource-based theory. *Journal of Management*, *27*(6), 755–775. doi:10.1177/014920630102700609

Amarakoon, I. I., Hamilton, C.-L., Mitchell, S. A., Tennant, P. F., & Roye, M. E. (2017). Biotechnology. *Pharmacognosy*, 549–563. doi:10.1016/b978-0-12-802104-0.00028-7

Anandaram, H. (2017). A Review on Application Of Biomarkers In The Field Of Bioinformatics & Nanotechnology For Individualized Cancer Treatment. *MOJ Proteomics & Bioinformatics*, *5*(6), 00179. doi:10.15406/mojpb.2017.05.00179

Andreazza, R., Bortolon, L., Pieniz, S., Camargo, F. A., and Bortolon, E. S. O. (2013). Copper phytoextraction and phytostabilization by Brachiaria decumbens Stapf. in vineyard soils and a copper mining waste. *Open Journal of Soil Science, 3*(6), 273-282.

Angrish, A. K., & Aggarwal, V. (2015). *Mapping of Entrepreneurship in Pharmaceutical Sector in India*. EDII Institutional Repository.

Anonymous. (2010a). BioPharma to grow over 10% for next 5 years. *BioSpectrum*, *8*, 36–38.

Anonymous. (2010b). Enzyme market leader. *BioSpectrum*, *8*, 70.

Ansoff, I. (1957). Strategies for Diversification. *Harvard Business Review*, *35*(5), 113–124v.

Anurag. (2018). 16 Tech Advancements in Pharmaceuticals to Re-invent Healing. Healthcare. *HealthTech, technology trends.*

Anwar, M., Supriyadi, & Sugiharto. (2012). Pengembangan Perangkat Pembelajaran Biologi Dengan Pendekatan Bio-enterpreneurship Untuk Meningkatkan Keterampilan Proses Ilmiah dan Minat Berwirausaha Siswa. *Innovative Journal of Curriculum and Educational Technology*, *1*(1), 38–44.

Armstrong, A., & Foley, P. (2003). Foundations for a learning organization: Organization learning mechanisms. *The Learning Organization*, *10*(2), 74–82. doi:10.1108/09696470910462085

Arora, N. K., Fatima, T., Mishra, I., Verma, M., Mishra, J., & Mishra, V. (2018). Environmental sustainability: challenges and viable solutions. *Environmental Sustainability, 1*(4), 309-340.

Arundel, A., & Kabla, I. (1998). What percentage of innovations are patented? Empirical estimates for European firms. *Research Policy*, *27*(2), 127–141. doi:10.1016/S0048-7333(98)00033-X

Asha, C. N., & Bhattacharya, S. (2011). Intellectual property rights: An overview and implications in pharmaceutical industry. *Journal of Advanced Pharmaceutical Technology & Research*, *2*(2), 88–93. doi:10.4103/2231-4040.82952 PMID:22171299

Ashammakhi, N., Elkhammas, E. A., & Hasan, A. (2017). Glomerulus-on-a-chip life up. *Transplantation*, *101*(11), e343–e344. doi:10.1097/TP.0000000000001896 PMID:28737605

Associate of Biotechnology led Enterprises. (n.d.). https://www.ableindia.in

AstraZeneca. (2012). *AstraZeneca: Our Leadership Team*. Author.

AstraZeneca. (2015). *AstraZeneca to present comprehensive data from its diabetes portfolio and pre-clinical research at EASD 2015*. Author.

AstraZeneca. (2019). *Key Facts: AstraZeneca*. Author.

Athreye, S., & Chaturvedi, S. (2007). Industry Associations and Technology-based Growth in India. *European Journal of Development Research*, *19*(1), 156–173. doi:10.1080/09578810601144426

Atieno, M., Herrmann, L., Nguyen, H. T., Phan, H. T., Nguyen, N. K., Srean, P., Than, M. M., Zhiyong, R., Tittabutr, P., Shutsrirung, A., Bräu, L., & Lesueur, D. (2020). Assessment of biofertilizer use for sustainable agriculture in the Great Mekong Region. *Journal of Environmental Management*, *275*, 111300. doi:10.1016/j.jenvman.2020.111300 PMID:32871522

Audretsch, D. B. (2001). The role of small firms in US biotechnology clusters. *Small Business Economics*, *17*(1/2), 3–15. doi:10.1023/A:1011140014334

Audretsch, D. B., & Stephan, P. E. (1996). Company-scientist locational links: The case of biotechnology. *The American Economic Review*, *86*(3), 641–652.

Audretsch, D. B., & Stephan, P. E. (1999). Knowledge spillovers in biotechnology: Sources and incentives. *Journal of Evolutionary Economics*, *9*(1), 97–107. doi:10.1007001910050076

Ayotamuno, J. M., Kogbara, R. B., & Agoro, O. S. (2009). Biostimulation supplemented with phytoremediation in the reclamation of a petroleum contaminated soil. *World Journal of Microbiology & Biotechnology*, *25*(9), 1567–1572. doi:10.100711274-009-0045-z

Azubuike, C. C., Chikere, C. B., & Okpokwasili, G. C. (2016). Bioremediation techniques–classification based on site of application: Principles, advantages, limitations and prospects. *World Journal of Microbiology & Biotechnology*, *32*(11), 1–18. doi:10.100711274-016-2137-x PMID:27638318

Babu, S. M. (2020). *Why 'Make in India' has failed*. Retrieved December 12, 2020, from https://www.thehindu.com/opinion/op-ed/why-make-in-india-has-failed/article30601269.ece

Back, S. M. (2009). The Bioentrepreneurship MBA: Options for mid-tier business schools. *Journal of Commercial Biotechnology*, *15*(2), 183–193. doi:10.1057/jcb.2008.57

Bagchi, N., & Chatterjee, K. (2017). Identification of gaps in performance of services provided to start-ups in high technology, low technology and social & agri-business incubation centers in India: Constraints to growth. *ASCI Journal of Management, 46*.

Bagchi, N., Roy, K., Roychowdhury, A., Subrahmanya, M. B., Chatterjee, K., Gulati, M., ... Chakravarthy, S. (2017). Science, Technology and Innovation. *Journal of Management*, *46*(1).

Bagchi-Sen, S., & Smith, H. L. (2008). Science, institutions, and markets: Developments in the Indian biotechnology sector. *Regional Studies*, *42*(7), 961–975. doi:10.1080/00343400701652800

Bagodi, V. (2021). *Unit -1: Entrepreneurship: An Introduction*. Retrieved 12 January 2021, from https://www.academia.edu/27130605/Unit_1_Entrepreneurship_An_Introduction

Bakshi, A. (2003). Potential adverse health effects of genetically modified crops. *Journal of Toxicology and Environmental Health. Part B*, *6*(3), 211–225.

BangueroCamacho, C. V., & GiraldoDíaz, R. (2012). Bio-entrepreneurship: Productive reconfiguration of agro-ecosystems in the district of La Elvira, Santiago de Cali. *Entramado, 8*(1), 168–175.

Bannerman, P. L. (2008). Risk and risk management in software projects: A reassessment. *Journal of Systems and Software, 81*(12), 2118–2133. doi:10.1016/j.jss.2008.03.059

Bannerman, P. L. (2015). A reassessment of risk management in software projects. In *Handbook on Project Management and Scheduling* (Vol. 2, pp. 1119–1134). Springer. doi:10.1007/978-3-319-05915-0_20

Baregheh, A., Rowley, J., & Sambrook, S. (2009). Towards a multidisciplinary definition of innovation. *Management Decision, 47*(8), 1323–1339. doi:10.1108/00251740910984578

Bashandy, S. R., Abd-Alla, M. H., & Bagy, M. M. K. (2019). Biological nitrogen fixation and biofertilizers as ideal potential solutions for sustainable agriculture. *Integrating Green Chemistry and Sustainable Engineering, 1*(1), 343-396.

Basu, S., & Kumar, G. (2020). Nitrogen fixation in a legume-rhizobium symbiosis: the roots of a success story. Plant Microbe Symbiosis, 1(1), 35-53. doi:10.1007/978-3-030-36248-5_3

Basu, P. (2003). How the US government can fund your company. *Bioentrepreneur*, 1–4.

Basu, P. (2003). Technology transfer survey reveals disparities but growth at US universities. *Bioentrepreneur*, 1–2. doi:10.1038/bioent745

Battelle/BIO. (2012). *State Bioscience Industry Development Report*. Author.

Batterham, R. (2000). The Chance to Change, Chief Scientist of Australia. Canberra: Dept. of Industry, Science and Resources (DISR).

Baum, A., Calabrese, T., & Silverman, B. S. (2000). Don't go it alone: Alliance network composition and startup's performance in Canadian biotechnology. *Strategic Management Journal, 21*(3), 267–294. doi:10.1002/(SICI)1097-0266(200003)21:3<267::AID-SMJ89>3.0.CO;2-8

Baumol, W. J. (2005). Education for innovation: Entrepreneurial breakthroughs versus corporate incremental improvements. *Innovation Policy and the Economy, 5*, 33–56. doi:10.1086/ipe.5.25056170

BBC. (2011). *Start-up Stories: Kiran Mazumdar-Shaw*. BBC News.

Becker, A. J., McCulloch, E. A., & Till, J. E. (1963). Cytological de-monstration of the clonal nature of spleen colonies derived from transplanted mouse marrow cells. *Nature, 197*(4866), 452–454. doi:10.1038/197452a0 PMID:13970094

Bell, J. (2010). Handbook of bioentrepreneurship. New England Journal of Entrepreneurship, 13, 79-80. doi:10.1108/NEJE-13-01-2010-B007

Bell, J. R. (2010). *Handbook of bioentrepreneurship. New England Journal of Entrepreneurship*, 13(1), 79.

Bello, G., Alabi, H. I., Ahmed, A. R., Sulaiman, M. M., Bello, Z. A., & Bello, A. A. (2020). Biology education and bioentrepreneur opportunities in Nigeria. *Nigerian Online Journal of Education Sciences and Technology, 1*(2), 1–17.

Bellu, R. R., & Flume, P. (2004). Religiosity and entrepreneurial behavior. *International Journal of Entrepreneurship and Innovation, 5*(3), 191–201. doi:10.5367/0000000041513411

Beltramino, N. S., Lema, D. G. P. D., & Juarez, L. E. V. (2020). Impact of the human capital on the performance of micro-enterprise: An empirical study in Argentina. *International Journal of Entrepreneurship and Small Business, 40*(4), 439–464. doi:10.1504/IJESB.2020.109009

Ben-David, J. (1971). *The Scientist's Role in Society: A Comparative Study*. Prentice-Hall, Inc.

Beylin, D., Chrisman, C. J., & Weingarten, M. (2011). Granting you success. *Bioentrepreneur*, 1–4. PMID:21874663

Bhattacharya, S., & Guriev, S. (2006). Patents vs. trade secrets: Knowledge licensing and spillover. *Journal of the European Economic Association*, *4*(6), 1112–1147. doi:10.1162/JEEA.2006.4.6.1112

Bhavnani, S. P., Nirula, J., & Sengupta, P. P. (2016). Mobile technology and the digitization of healthcare. *European Heart Journal*, *37*(18), 1428–1438. doi:10.1093/eurheartj/ehv770 PMID:26873093

Bianchi, M., Cavaliere, A., Chiaroni, D., Frattini, F., & Chiesa, V. (2011). Organisational modes for Open Innovation in the bio-pharmaceutical industry: An exploratory analysis. *Technovation*, *31*(1), 22–33. doi:10.1016/j.technovation.2010.03.002

Biemans, W. G. (1991). User and third-party involvement in developing medical equipment innovations. *Technovation*, *11*(3), 163–182. doi:10.1016/0166-4972(91)90032-Y

Bierly, P., & Chakrabarti, A. (1996). Generic knowledge strategies in the U.S. pharmaceutical industry. *Strategic Management Journal*, *17*(S2), 123–135. doi:10.1002mj.4250171111

Bigoniya, P. (2017). Biosimilar: Opportunity Thrusted over Indian Pharmaceutical Market. *Annals of Pharmacology and Pharmaceutics*, *2*(14), 1073.

Binod, P., Palkhiwala, P., Gaikaiwari, R., Nampoothiri, K. M., Duggal, A., Dey, K., & Pandey, A. (2013). *Industrial enzymes-present status and future perspectives for India*. Academic Press.

BioBusiness. (2004). Landmark discoveries in biotechnology. Academic Press.

BioCentury. (2005). *The Bernstein Report on BioBusiness*. Academic Press.

Biocon. (2010). *Biocon Annual Report, 2010*. Author.

Biotech Consortium India Limited (BCIL). (2018). *Bio entrepreneurship development*. Retrieved December 14, 2020, from https://www.biotech.co.in/sites/default/files/2020-01/Bioentrepreneurship Development.pdf

Biotech Consortium India Limited (BCIL). (n.d.). https://www.biotech.co.in/en

Biotechnology Innovation Organization Website. (n.d.). *The Economic Contributions of the Biotechnology Industry*. Retrieved January 1, 2021, from https://archive.bio.org/articles/economic-contributions-biotechnology-industry

Birkbeck, C. D. (2016). *The World Intellectual Property Organization (WIPO): A Reference Guide*. Edward Elgar Publishing. doi:10.4337/9781785364785

Bisman, J., & Goela, N. (2010). The Small Industries Development Bank of India: A retrospective on SME financing. *Indian Journal of Economics and Business*, *9*(4), 803.

Biswas, B., Sarkar, B., Rusmin, R., & Naidu, R. (2015). Bioremediation of PAHs and VOCs: Advances in clay mineral–microbial interaction. *Environment International*, *85*, 168–181. doi:10.1016/j.envint.2015.09.017 PMID:26408945

Björk, J., & Magnusson, M. (2009). Where do good innovation ideas come from? Exploring the influence of network connectivity on innovation idea quality. *Journal of Product Innovation Management*, *26*(6), 662–670. doi:10.1111/j.1540-5885.2009.00691.x

Blind, K. (2012). *The impact of regulation on innovation*. Nesta Working Paper 12/02.

Blind, K. (2006). A taxonomy of standards in the service sector: Theoretical discussion and empirical test. *Service Industries Journal*, *26*(4), 397–420. doi:10.1080/02642060600621597

BloombergTV. (n.d.). *Need To Change Mindset: Kiran Mazumdar Shaw*. Bloomberg TV.

Boaz, N., Murnane, J., & Nuffer, K. (2010). The basics of Business-to-business sales success. *The McKinsey Quarterly*.

Bodenheimer, T. (2005). High and Rising Health Care Costs. Part 2: Technologic Innovation. *Annals of Internal Medicine, 142*(11), 932. doi:10.7326/0003-4819-142-11-200506070-00012 PMID:15941701

Bogers, M., Bekkers, R., & Granstrand, O. (2012). Intellectual property and licensing strategies in open collaborative innovation. In Open innovation in firms and public administrations: Technologies for Value Creation (pp. 37-58). IGI Global. doi:10.4018/978-1-61350-341-6.ch003

Bolan, N. S., Park, J. H., Robinson, B., Naidu, R., & Huh, K. Y. (2011). Phytostabilization: A green approach to contaminant containment. *Advances in Agronomy, 112*, 145–204. doi:10.1016/B978-0-12-385538-1.00004-4

Bolz, K., & Volkmann, C. (2019). Responsible Bioentrepreneurs. *NanoEthics, 13*(2), 147–150. doi:10.100711569-019-00342-7

Bonnafous-Boucher, M., & Lamy, E. (2010). Hybridisation of the profiles of entrepreneurs and intrapreneurs: The case of French biotechnology SMEs. *International Journal of Entrepreneurship and Small Business, 10*(3), 410–427. doi:10.1504/IJESB.2010.033575

Boroş, M. N., Micle, V., Flămînd, L., & Sur, I. M. (2016). Phytoremediation planning in the case of former industrial sites. *Studia ubb ambientum, 61*(1-2), 5-14.

Boucher, J., & Friot, D. (2017). *Primary microplastics in the oceans: a global evaluation of sources*. IUCN. doi:10.2305/IUCN.CH.2017.01.en

Bouchie, A. (2003). Private biotech companies face new funding challenges. *Bioentrepreneur*, 1–2. doi:10.1038/bioent757

Bouis, H. E., Hotz, C., McClafferty, B., Meenakshi, J. V., & Pfeiffer, W. H. (2011). Biofortification: A new tool to reduce micronutrient malnutrition. *Food and Nutrition Bulletin, 32*(1), S31–S40. doi:10.1177/15648265110321S105

Boyer, K., & Verma, R. (2009). *Operations and supply chain management for the 21st century*. Nelson Education.

Brackley, P. (2020). *Coronavirus: AstraZeneca donates nine million face masks and steps up Covid-19 drugs research*. Cambridge Independent.

Brady, M., & Saranga, H. (2013). Innovative Business Models in Healthcare: A Comparison Between India and Ireland. *Strategic Change, 22*(5-6), 339–353. doi:10.1002/jsc.1944

Braun, A., & Schreiber, F. (2017). *The current InsurTech landscape: business models and disruptive potential* (No. 62). I. VW HSG Schriftenreihe.

Brennan, V. (2018). *Grant, other executives to leave Monsanto after Bayer acquisition closes*. St. Louis Business Journal.

Breschi, S., Lissoni, F., & Miguelez, E. (2019). *Does India gain from high-skilled migration to the US?* Ideas for India Website. Retrieved December 12, 2020, from https://www.ideasforindia.in/topics/productivity-innovation/does-india-gain-from-high-skilled-migration-to-the-us.html

Bridge, W. (2017). The Struggle to Establish Bioentrepreneurship Education Programs: An Australian Perspective. *Technology Transfer and Entrepreneurship, 4*(2), 107–114. doi:10.2174/2213809904666170809145045

Brown, L. D., Ulrich, A. C., & Fingas, M. (2015). Bioremediation of oil spills on land. In *Oil spill science and technology*. John Wiley & Sons.

Brown, D., & Wilson, S. (2007). *The black books of outsourcing: how to manage the changes, challenges, and opportunities*. John Wiley & Sons.

Brown, T. E., Davidsson, P., & Wiklund, J. (2001). An operationalization of Stevenson's conceptualization of *entrepreneurship* as opportunity-based firm behaviour. *Strategic Management Journal, 22*(10), 953–968. doi:10.1002mj.190

Bruns, B. S. (2017). Criticism of the Defend Trade Secrets Act of 2016: Failure to Preempt. *Berkeley Technology Law Journal, 32*, 469–502.

Brush, T. H., Bromiley, P., & Hendrickx, M. (1999). The relative influence of industry and corporation on business segment performance: An alternative estimate. *Strategic Management Journal, 20*(6), 519–547. doi:10.1002/(SICI)1097-0266(199906)20:6<519::AID-SMJ32>3.0.CO;2-8

Bruyat, C., & Julien, P. A. (2000). Defining the field of research in *entrepreneurship. Journal of Business Venturing, 16*(2), 165–180. doi:10.1016/S0883-9026(99)00043-9

Bull, U., & Willard, G. E. (1993). Towards a theory of Entrepreneurship. *Journal of Business Venturing, 8*, 183-195. doi: 10.1.1.458.709

Burhanuddin, H., Nurmalina, R., & Pambudy, R. (2013). Entrepreneurial Activity and Economic Growth: Learning from Indonesian Broiler Farmers. *Asia Pacific Journal of Innovation and Entrepreneurship, 7*(3), 25–51.

Business Opportunity in India: Investment Ideas. (n.d.). Industry Research, Reports IBEF. Https://www.bio.org

Bygrave, W. D., & Zacharakis, A. (2010). *The portable MBA in entrepreneurship* (4th ed.). John Wiley & Sons Inc.

Cabaleiro-Cerviño, G., & Burcharth, A. (2020). Licensing agreements as signals of innovation: When do they impact market value? *Technovation, 98*, 102175. doi:10.1016/j.technovation.2020.102175

Calantone, R. J., Harmancioglu, N., & Droge, C. (2010). Inconclusive innovation "returns": A meta-analysis of research on innovation in new product development. *Journal of Product Innovation Management, 27*(7), 1065–1081. doi:10.1111/j.1540-5885.2010.00771.x

Campart, S., & Pfister, E. (2007). Technology, cooperation and stock market value: An event study of new partnership announcements in the biotechnology and pharmaceutical industries. *Economics of Innovation and New Technology, 16*(1), 31–49. doi:10.1080/10438590600661764

Camps, P., & Munoz-Torrero, D. (2002). Cholinergic drugs in pharmacotherapy of Alzheimer's disease. *Mini-Reviews in Medicinal Chemistry, 2*(1), 11–25. doi:10.2174/1389557023406638

Cant, M. C., Strydom, J. W., Jooste, C. J., & du Plessis, P. J. (Eds.). (2009). *Marketing management*. Juta and Company Ltd.

Cantrell, C. L., Dayan, F. E., & Duke, S. O. (2012). Natural products as sources for new pesticides. *Journal of Natural Products, 75*(6), 1231–1242. doi:10.1021/np300024u PMID:22616957

Carayannopoulos, S., & Auster, E. R. (2010). External knowledge sourcing in biotechnology through acquisition versus alliance: A KBV approach. *Research Policy, 39*(2), 254–267. doi:10.1016/j.respol.2009.12.005

Carneiro, A. (2000). How does knowledge management influence innovation and competitiveness? *Journal of Knowledge Management, 4*(2), 87–98. doi:10.1108/13673270010372242

Carrier, C. (1996). Intrapreneurship in small businesses: An exploratory study. *Entrepreneurship Theory and Practice, 21*(1), 5–20. doi:10.1177/104225879602100101

Carroll, J. (2013). *UPDATED: AstraZeneca to ax 1,600, relocate thousands in global R&D reshuffle*. FierceBiotech.

Carsrud, A. L., Brännback, M., & Renko, M. (2008) Strategy and Strategic Thinking in Biotechnology Entrepreneurship. In Handbook of Bioentrepreneurship. Springer. doi:10.1007/978-0-387-48345-0_5

Carsrud, A. L., Brannback, M., & Renko, M. (2008). Strategy and strategic thinking in biotechnology entrepreneurship. Handbook of Bioentrepreneurship, 81 – 101.

Casey Jr, W. L. (2013). National investment promotion policies and foreign direct investment flows. *International Journal of Business and Economics Perspectives, 8*(1), 14-29.

Catherine, D., Corolleur, F., Carrere, M., & Mangematin, V. (2004). Turning scientific and technological human capital into economic capital: The experience of biotech start-ups in France. *Research Policy, 33*(4), 631–642. doi:10.1016/j.respol.2004.01.009

Cauchon, N., Oghamian, S., Hassanpour, S., & Abernathy, M. (2021). Innovation in Chemistry, Manufacturing, and Controls—A Regulatory Perspective From Industry. Academic Press.

Chaganti, R., & Greene, P. G. (2002). Who Are Ethnic Entrepreneurs? A Study of Entrepreneurs' Ethnic Involvement and Business Characteristics. *Journal of Small Business Management, 40*(2), 126–143. doi:10.1111/1540-627X.00045

Chakraborty, C., & Agoramoorthy, G. (2010). A special report on India's biotech scenario: Advancement in biopharmaceutical and health care sectors. *Biotechnology Advances, 28*(1), 1–6. doi:10.1016/j.biotechadv.2009.10.007 PMID:19931371

Chakravarty, B. (2011). Trends in mushroom cultivation and breeding. *Australian Journal of Agricultural Engineering, 2*(4), 102.

Chandel, A. K., Rudravaram, R., Rao, L. V., Ravindra, P., & Narasu, M. L. (2007). Industrial enzymes in bioindustrial sector development: An India perspective. *Journal of Commercial Biotechnology, 13*(4), 283–291. doi:10.1057/palgrave.jcb.3050065

Chandy, R., Hopstaken, B., Narasimhan, O., & Prabhu, J. (2006). From invention to innovation: Conversion ability in product development. *JMR, Journal of Marketing Research, 43*(3), 494–508. doi:10.1509/jmkr.43.3.494

Chattopadhyay, P., Banerjee, G., & Mukherjee, S. (2017). Recent trends of modern bacterial insecticides for pest control practice in integrated crop management system. *Biotech, 7*(1), 60.

Chaturvedi, K., & Chataway, J. (2006). Strategic integration of knowledge in Indian pharmaceutical firms: Creating competencies for innovation. *International Journal of Business Innovation and Research, 1*(1–2), 27–50. doi:10.1504/IJBIR.2006.011087

Chaturvedi, S. (2002). *Measuring Developments in Biotechnology*. OECD.

Chen, M., Shelton, A., & Ye, G. Y. (2011). Insect-resistant genetically modified rice in China: From research to commercialization. *Annual Review of Entomology, 56*(1), 81–101. doi:10.1146/annurev-ento-120709-144810

Chen, T. H. H., Thompson, B. G., & Gerson, D. F. (1987). In vitro production of alfalfa somatic embryos in fermentation systems. *Journal of Fermentation Technology, 65*(3), 353–357. doi:10.1016/0385-6380(87)90100-2

Chesbrough, H. (2007). Business model innovation: It's not just about technology anymore. *Strategy and Leadership, 35*(6), 12–17. doi:10.1108/10878570710833714

Chesbrough, H., & Rosenbloom, R. S. (2002). The Role of the Business Model in Capturing Value from Innovation: Evidence from Xerox Corporation's Technology Spin-Off Companies. *Industrial and Corporate Change, 11*(3), 529–555. doi:10.1093/icc/11.3.529

Chiesa, V., & Chiaroni, D. (2005). *Industrial Clusters in Biotechnology—Driving Forces, Development Processes and Management Practices*. Imperial College Press.

Christopher, D., & Kaur, S. (2011). Entrepreneurship in Biotechnology Sector. *IUP Journal of Entrepreneurship Development*, *8*(3), 40–59.

Cohen, W. M., Nelson, R. R., & Walsh, J. P. (2002). Links and Impacts: The influence of Public Research on Industrial R&D. *Management Science*, *48*(1), 1–23. doi:10.1287/mnsc.48.1.1.14273

Cohen, W., & Levinthal, D. (1990). Absorptive capacity: A new perspective on learning and innovation. *Administrative Science Quarterly*, *35*(1), 128–152. doi:10.2307/2393553

Collet, C., & Wyatt, D. (2005). "Bioneering"–teaching biotechnology entrepreneurship at the undergraduate level. *Education + Training*, *47*(6), 408–421. doi:10.1108/00400910510617033

Collins, J. (2009). *Good to Great-(Why Some Companies Make the Leap and others Don't)*. Academic Press.

Collonnier, C., Fock, I., Kashyap, V., Rotino, G. L., Daunay, M. C., Lian, Y., Mariska, I. K., Rajam, M. V., Servaes, A., Ducreux, G., & Sihachakr, D. (2001). Applications of biotechnology in eggplant. *Plant Cell, Tissue and Organ Culture*, *65*(2), 91–107. doi:10.1023/A:1010674425536

Conesa, H. M., Evangelou, M. W., Robinson, B. H., & Schulin, R. (2012). A critical view of current state of phytotechnologies to remediate soils: Still a promising tool? *The Scientific World Journal*, *2012*(5), 17382. doi:10.1100/2012/173829 PMID:22272168

Conner, A. J., Glare, T. R., & Nap, J. P. (2003). The release of genetically modified crops into the environment: Part II. Overview of ecological risk assessment. *The Plant Journal*, *33*(1), 19–46. doi:10.1046/j.0960-7412.2002.001607.x

Coombs, R., & Miles, I. (2000). Innovation, measurement and services: the new problematique. In *Innovation systems in the service economy* (pp. 85–103). Springer. doi:10.1007/978-1-4615-4425-8_5

Cooper, R. G. (1988). The new product process: A decision guide for management. *Journal of Marketing Management*, *3*(3), 238–255. doi:10.1080/0267257X.1988.9964044

Cooper, R. G. (1990). Stage-gate systems: A new tool for managing new products. *Business Horizons*, *33*(3), 44–54. doi:10.1016/0007-6813(90)90040-I

Cooper, R. G., & Edgett, S. J. (2009). *Generating breakthrough new product ideas: Feeding the innovation funnel*. Product Development Institute.

Cornea, C. P., Voaides, C., Sicuia, O. A. B., Matei, F., & Babeanu, N. (2019). Creating Products and Services in Environmental Biotechnology. In Introduction to biotech entrepreneurship: from idea to business. Springer. doi:10.1007/978-3-030-22141-6_4

Correa, C. M. (1997). New intellectual standards for intellectual property: Impact on technology flows and innovation in developing countries. *Science & Public Policy*, *24*(2), 79–92.

Correa, C. M. (1999). Review of the TRIPs Agreement: Fostering the transfer of technology to developing countries. *The Journal of World Intellectual Property*, *2*(6), 9–39. doi:10.1111/j.1747-1796.1999.tb00100.x

Correa, C. M. (2006). Implications of bilateral free trade agreements on access to medicines. *Bulletin of the World Health Organization*, *84*(5), 399–404. doi:10.2471/BLT.05.023432 PMID:16710551

Costa, C. (2004). *A methodological approach to the marketing process in the biotechnology based companies*. Academic Press.

Crispeels, T., Uecke, O., Goldchstein, M., & Schefczyk, M. (2009). Best practices for developing university bioentrepreneurship education programmes. *Journal of Commercial Biotechnology*, *15*(2), 136–150. doi:10.1057/jcb.2008.44

Cvele, S. (2021). *Strategic alliances, mergers and acquisitions - the influence of culture on successful cooperation*. Academic Press.

Czech, M., Kooiker, A. B., Atikeler, K., Demirtshyan, M., Gaitova, K., Voloskova, M. H., Stiolica, A. D., Kooiker, C., Piniazhko, O., Konstandyan, N., Zalis'ka, O., & Cegielska, J. S. (2020). A Review of Rare Disease Policies and Orphan Drug Reimbursement Systems in 12 Eurasian Countries. *Frontiers of Public Health*.

Dahal, S. (2018). *Recent Biotechnology advance in Medicine*. Academic Press.

Dahlman, C. J., & Utz, A. (2005). *India and the knowledge economy: leveraging strengths and opportunities*. World Bank Publications. doi:10.1596/0-8213-6207-0

Dandekar, V., & Sukumar, C. (2018). There's an explosion of data & digital opportunities in Indian healthcare: Vasant Narasimhan, CEO, Novartis. *The Economic Times*.

Das, G. (2019). *At 0.7% of GDP, India's R&D expenditure in science is less than BRIC nations*. Retrieved December 12, 2020, from https://www.businesstoday.in/current/world/india-gdp-randd-expenditure-in-science-is-less-than-bric-nations/story/390874.html

DaSilva, J. E. (2004). The colours of biotechnology: Science, development and humankind. *Electronic Journal of Biotechnology*, *7*(3).

Davenport, T. H. (1993). *Process innovation: reengineering work through information technology*. Harvard Business Press.

De Jong, J. P., & Vermeulen, P. A. (2006). Determinants of product innovation in small firms: A comparison across industries. *International Small Business Journal*, *24*(6), 587–609. doi:10.1177/0266242606069268

de Lorenzo, V., Prather, K. L., Chen, G.-Q., O'Day, E., von Kameke, C., Oyarzún, D. A., Hosta-Rigau, L., Alsafar, H., Cao, C., Ji, W., Okano, H., Roberts, R. J., Ronaghi, M., Yeung, K., Zhang, F., & Lee, S. Y. (2018). The power of synthetic biology for bioproduction, remediation and pollution control. *EMBO Reports*, *19*(4), e45658. doi:10.15252/embr.201745658 PMID:29581172

De Steur, H., Gellynck, X., Blancquaert, D., Lambert, W., Van Der Straeten, D., & Qaim, M. (2012). Potential impact and cost-effectiveness of multi-biofortified rice in China. *New Biotechnology*, *29*(3), 432–442. doi:10.1016/j.nbt.2011.11.012

De Steur, H., Gellynck, X., Storozhenko, S., Liqun, G., Lambert, W., Van Der Straeten, D., & Viaene, J. (2010). The health benefits of folate biofortified rice in China. *Nature Biotechnology*, *28*(6), 554–556. doi:10.1038/nbt0610-554

De Vita, G., & Kyaw, K. S. (2009). Growth effects of FDI and portfolio investment flows to developing countries: A disaggregated analysis by income levels. *Applied Economics Letters*, *16*(3), 277–283. doi:10.1080/13504850601018437

Deb, R., & Kaushik, V. (2013). Management of Intellectual Property Rights: A Focus on Biotechnology. *Global Journal of Management and Business Studies*, *3*(9), 1029–1034.

Defrancesco, L. (2019). Genentech trade secrets theft highlights risk for biotechs. *Nature Biotechnology*, *37*(1), 9. doi:10.1038/nbt0119-9b PMID:30605145

Department of Biotechnology, Ministry of Science and Technology. (n.d). http://www.dbtindia.nic.in/#

Depasse, J. W., & Lee, P. T. (2013). A model for 'reverse innovation' in health care. *Globalization and Health*, *9*(1), 9–40. doi:10.1186/1744-8603-9-40 PMID:24001367

Desai, R. (2013). *Biocon Foundation – Social impact through sustainable community development*. Academic Press.

Devendra, C. (1987). *Expanding the utilisation of agro-industrial by-products and non-conventional feed resources in Asia*. Academic Press.

Dewenter, K. L., & Malatesta, P. H. (2001). State-owned and privately owned firms: An empirical analysis of profitability, leverage, and labor intensity. *The American Economic Review*, *91*(1), 320–334. doi:10.1257/aer.91.1.320

Dhal, B., Thatoi, H. N., Das, N. N., & Pandey, B. D. (2013). Chemical and microbial remediation of hexavalent chromium from contaminated soil and mining/metallurgical solid waste: A review. *Journal of Hazardous Materials*, *250*, 272–291. doi:10.1016/j.jhazmat.2013.01.048 PMID:23467183

DiBella, A. J. (1997). Gearing up to become a learning organization. *Journal for Quality and Participation*, *20*(3), 12.

Didraga, O. (2013). The role and the effects of risk management in IT projects success. *Informatica Economica, 17*(1).

Digital India. (n.d.). *Ebiz*. Retrieved December 12, 2020, from https://digitalindia.gov.in/content/ebiz

DiMasi, J. A., Hansen, R. W., & Grabowski, H. G. (2003). The price of innovation: New estimates of drug development costs. *Journal of Health Economics*, *22*(2), 151–185. doi:10.1016/S0167-6296(02)00126-1 PMID:12606142

DiversityInc Staff. (2013). *Diversity Leadership: Hugh Grant, Monsanto*. DiversityInc.

Dodgson, M., Gann, D. M., & Salter, A. (2008). *The management of technological innovation: strategy and practice*. Oxford University Press.

Dodgson, M., Gann, D., & Salter, A. (2008). *The management of technological innovation: Strategy and Practice*. Oxford University Press.

Donlon, J. P. (2010). *Monsanto's Hugh Grant, CEO of the Year 2010*. Chief Executive Magazine.

Dookun, A. (2001). Agricultural biotechnology in developing countries. *Biotechnology Annual Review*, *7*, 261–285. doi:10.1016/S1387-2656(01)07040-5 PMID:11686047

Dorey, E. (2003). Biotechs critique big pharma's collaboration skills. *Bioentrepreneur*, 1–2.

Dossani, R., & Kenney, M. (2009). Service provision for the global economy: The evolving Indian experience. *The Review of Policy Research*, *26*(1-2), 77–104. doi:10.1111/j.1541-1338.2008.00370.x

Douglas, F. L., Narayanan, V. K., Mitchell, L., & Litan, E. R. (2010). The case for entrepreneurship in R&D in the pharmaceutical industry. *Nature Reviews. Drug Discovery*, *9*(9), 683–689. doi:10.1038/nrd3230 PMID:20725093

Dove, A. (2003). Perfecting your patent search. *Bioentrepreneur*, 1–2.

DST website. (n.d.). *NIDHI Entreprenuer-in-residence program. Nurturing budding entreprenuer*. Retrieved December 14, 2020, from http://www.nidhi-eir.in/about.php

Duelen, R., Corvelyn, M., Tortorella, I., Leonardi, L., Chai, Y. C., & Sampaolesi, M. (2019). *Medicinal Biotechnology for Disease Modelling*. Clinical Therapy, and Drug Discovery and Development.

Duhera, R. (2007). Destination India: Favorable policies. *Biospectrum India*, (April issue), 32–36.

Dureja, C. (2016). Economic rights of broadcasting organisation under copyright law 1957. *International Journal of Advanced Research in Management and Social Sciences*, *5*(5), 37–51.

Durmuşoğlu, S. S., & Barczak, G. (2011). The use of information technology tools in new product development phases: Analysis of effects on new product innovativeness, quality, and market performance. *Industrial Marketing Management*, *40*(2), 321–330. doi:10.1016/j.indmarman.2010.08.009

Dyson, F. (2007). Our biotech future. *The New York Review of Books, 54*(12).

Eaton, J., & Kortum, S. (1996). Trade in ideas Patenting and productivity in the OECD. *Journal of International Economics, 40*(3-4), 251–278. doi:10.1016/0022-1996(95)01407-1

Eckhardt, J. T., & Shane, S. A. (2003). Opportunities and entrepreneurship. *Journal of Management, 29*(3), 333–349. doi:10.1177/014920630302900304

Edgington, S. M. (1998). The future belongs to the bioentrepreneur. *Nature Biotechnology, 16*(S1), 1–1. doi:10.1038/5387 PMID:9591246

EIB – European Investment Bank. (2002). *Biotechnology: An overview*. EIB Sector Papers.

Ejilibe, O. C. (2012). Entrepreneurship in biology education as a means for employment. *Knowledge Review, 26*(3), 96–100.

Ekta, P., & Modi, N. R. (2018). A review of phytoremediation. *Journal of Pharmacognosy and Phytochemistry, 7*(4), 1485–1489.

Elekwachi, C. O., Andresen, J., & Hodgman, T. C. (2014). Global use of bioremediation technologies for decontamination of ecosystems. *Journal of Bioremediation and Biodegredation, 5*(4), 1.

Eliashberg, J., Lilien, G. L., & Rao, V. R. (1997). 12 Minimizing technological oversights: A marketing research perspective. *Technological innovation: Oversights and foresights, 214.*

El-Said, H., & El-Said, M. (2007). TRIPS-Plus implications for access to medicines in developing countries: Lessons from Jordan–United States Free Trade Agreement. *The Journal of World Intellectual Property, 10*(6), 438–475. doi:10.1111/j.1747-1796.2007.00330.x

Energysage. (2018). *What are the most efficient solar panels on the market? Solar panel cell efficiency explained.* Academic Press.

Entrepreneur. (2020). *AstraZeneca Claims to Have the 'Winning Formula' for Its Vaccine*. Author.

Erickson, B., & Winters, P. (2012). Perspective on opportunities in industrial biotechnology in renewable chemicals. *Biotechnology Journal, 7*(2), 176–185. doi:10.1002/biot.201100069 PMID:21932250

Ernst & Young. (1997). *European Biotech 97—A New Economy*. Ernst & Young.

Ernst & Young. (2000). *Gründerzeit - Deutscher Biotechnologie-Report*. Ernst & Young.

Ernst & Young. (2002). *Neue Chancen - Deutscher Biotechnologiereport*. Ernst & Young.

Estudio. (n.d.). *India: Biocon*. Estudio AGML.

EU Skills Panorama. (2014). *Entrepreneurial skills Analytical Highlight*. Retrieved December 01, 2020, from https://skillspanorama.cedefop.europa.eu/sites/default/files/EUSP_AH_Entrepreneurial_0.pdf

EuropaBio. (1997). *Benchmarking the Competitive–ness of Biotechnology in Europe. EuropaBio Independent Report, 1997*. EuropaBio.

EuropaBio. (2006). *The European association of bioindustries. Biotechnology in Europe: 2006 Comparative Study.* Retrieved December 28, 2020, from https://anibalcavacosilva.arquivo.presidencia.pt/archive/doc/Critical2006.pdf

Evans, A. G., & Varaiya, N. P. (2003). Assessment of a biotech market opportunity. *Entrepreneurship Theory and Practice, 28*(1), 87–105. doi:10.1111/1540-8520.00033

Evans, G. G., & Furlong, J. (2011). *Environmental biotechnology: theory and application*. John Wiley & Sons.

Eyers, A. (2015). Bioentrepreneurship: opportunities and challenges. In *Embracing Entrepreneurship Across Disciplines*. Edward Elgar Publishing.

Favas, P. J., Pratas, J., Varun, M., D'Souza, R., & Paul, M. S. (2014). Phytoremediation of soils contaminated with metals and metalloids at mining areas: potential of native flora. *Environmental Risk Assessment of Soil Contamination, 17*, 485-517.

Ferguson, S. M., & Kaundinya, U. S. (2014). Licensing the Technology: BiotechnologyCommercialization Strategies UsingUniversity and Federal Labs. In C. Shimasaki (Ed.), *Biotechnology Entrepreneurship: Starting, Managing, and Leading Biotech Companies*. Elsevier Inc. doi:10.1016/B978-0-12-404730-3.00014-2

Ferreira, J. J., Fernandes, C. I., Alves, H., & Raposo, M. L. (2015). Drivers of innovation strategies: Testing the Tidd and Bessant (2009) model. *Journal of Business Research, 68*(7), 1395–1403. doi:10.1016/j.jbusres.2015.01.021

Ferreira, S. A., Pitz, K. Y., Manshardt, R., Zee, F., Fitch, M., & Gonsalves, D. (2002). Virus coat protein transgenic papaya provides practical control of Papaya ringspot virus in Hawaii. *Plant Disease, 86*(2), 101–105. doi:10.1094/PDIS.2002.86.2.101 PMID:30823304

Ferré, J., Van Rie, J., & MacIntosh, S. C. (2008). Insecticidal genetically modified crops and insect resistance management (IRM). In *Integration of insect-resistant genetically modified crops within IPM programs* (pp. 41–85). Springer. doi:10.1007/978-1-4020-8373-0_3

Fetterhoff, T. J., & Voelkel, D. (2006). Managing open innovation in biotechnology. *Research Technology Management, 49*(3), 14–18.

Figueiredo, L. H. M., Vasconcellos, A. G., Prado, G. S., & Grossi-de-Sa, M. F. (2019). An overview of intellectual property within agricultural biotechnology in Brazil. *Biotechnology Research and Innovation, 3*(1), 69–79. doi:10.1016/j.biori.2019.04.003

Fildes, R. A. (1990). Strategic challenges in commercializing biotechnology. *California Management Review, 32*(3), 63–72. doi:10.2307/41166618

Fischer, K., Ekener-Petersen, E., Rydhmer, L., & Björnberg, K. E. (2015). Social impacts of GM crops in agriculture: A systematic literature review. *Sustainability, 7*(7), 8598–8620. doi:10.3390u7078598

Fitriah, E. (2012). Pengembangan perangkat pembelajaran bioteknologi berorientasi bioentrepreneurship untuk meningkatkan keterampilan proses sains, minat wirausaha dan hasil belajar siswa. *Scientiae Educatia: Jurnal Pendidikan Sains, 1*(1), 1–14.

Fitriah, E. (2016). Implementasi bioentrepreneurship pada pembelajaran biologi untuk meningkatkan life skills dan minat wirausaha siswa madrasah aliyah berbasis pesantren di Cirebon. *Scientiae Educatia: Jurnal Pendidikan Sains, 2*(1), 1–19.

Fletcher, L., & Triendl, R. (2003). Japan's first biotechnology graduate school will open in April. *Bioentrepreneur*, 1–2.

Fogler, H. S., & LeBlanc, S. E. (2014). *Strategies for creative problem solving*. Prentice Hall.

Forbes. (2021). Power Women #68 Kiran Mazumdar-Shaw. *Forbes*.

Fortune. (2009). *Global 500 – Pharmaceuticals*. Author.

Freel, M. S. (2000). Barriers to product innovation in small manufacturing firms. *International Small Business Journal, 18*(2), 60–80. doi:10.1177/0266242600182003

Fritsch, M., & Mueller, P. (2007). The persistence of regional new business formation-activity over time–assessing the potential of policy promotion programs. *Journal of Evolutionary Economics*, *17*(3), 299–315. doi:10.100700191-007-0056-6

Gallagher, J. (2020). *Covid-19: Oxford University vaccine is highly effective*. BBC News.

Gao, H., Xie, Y., Hashim, S., Akhtar Khan, A., Wang, X., & Xu, H. (2018). Application of microbial technology used in bioremediation of urban polluted river: A case study of Chengnan River, China. *Water (Basel)*, *10*(5), 643. doi:10.3390/w10050643

Garg, M., & Gupta, S. (2021). *Startups and the Growing Entrepreneurial Ecosystem*. Academic Press.

Gargate, G., & Momaya, K. S. (2018). Intellectual property management system: Develop and self-assess using IPM model. *World Patent Information*, *52*, 29–41. doi:10.1016/j.wpi.2018.01.005

Garg, R., & Dua, P. (2014). Foreign portfolio investment flows to India: Determinants and analysis. *World Development*, *59*, 16–28. doi:10.1016/j.worlddev.2014.01.030

Garner, C., Marchington, T., & Pfeifer, A. (2007). Key ingredients for success in Europe. *Bioentrepreneur*, 1–4.

Garnier, J. P. (2008). Rebuilding the R&D engine in big pharma. *Harvard Business Review*, *86*(5), 68–70. PMID:18543809

Gauba, R., & Dhingra, R. (2018). *Make in India-An Initiative to Change the Economic Landscape of the Country*. Academic Press.

Gaur, A. D., & Padiya, J. (2015). A Conceptual Study of "Skill India" Mission Bridge to "Make in India" Program. Editorial Advisory Board, 52.

Gaurav, J. K., Rathi, V., Burnwal, K., & Chaturvedi, A. (2019). Green startups in India: Challenges and opportunities. *Special Issue on Environment*, *235*, 234.

George, G., Zahra, S. A., Wheatley, K. K., & Khan, R. (2001). The effects of alliance portfolio characteristics and absorptive capacity on performance: A study of biotechnology firms. *The Journal of High Technology Management Research*, *12*(2), 205–226. doi:10.1016/S1047-8310(01)00037-2

Giddings, G., Allison, G., Brooks, D., & Carter, A. (2000). Transgenic plants as factories for biopharmaceuticals. *Nature Biotechnology*, *18*(11), 1151–1155. doi:10.1038/81132 PMID:11062432

Gillespie, I. M., & Philp, J. C. (2013). Bioremediation, an environmental remediation technology for the bioeconomy. *Trends in Biotechnology*, *31*(6), 329–332. doi:10.1016/j.tibtech.2013.01.015 PMID:23427900

Ginarte, J. C., & Park, W. G. (1997). Determinants of patent rights: A cross-national study. *Research Policy*, *26*(3), 283–301. doi:10.1016/S0048-7333(97)00022-X

Glare, T. R., Jurat-Fuentes, J. L., & O'callaghan, M. (2017). Basic and applied research: entomopathogenic bacteria. In Microbial control of insect and mite pests. Academic Press.

Global Market Insights. (2021). *Biotechnology Market Value Worth $729 Billion by 2025*. Global Market Insights, Inc. Retrieved 12 January 2021, from https://www.prnewswire.com/news-releases/biotechnology-market-value-worth-729-billion-by-2025-global-market-insights-inc-300969541.html

Gomez, M. I., McLaughlin, E. W., & Wittink, D. R. (2004). Customer satisfaction and retail sales performance: An empirical investigation. *Journal of Retailing*, *80*(4), 265–278. doi:10.1016/j.jretai.2004.10.003

Gotsch, M., & Hipp, C. (2012). Measurement of innovation activities in the knowledge-intensive services industry: A trademark approach. *Service Industries Journal*, *32*(13), 2167–2184. doi:10.1080/02642069.2011.574275

Government of India, Ministry of Commerce & Industry, Department for promotion of Industry and Internal Trade. (n.d.). *Problems being faced by Indian Startups*. Retrieved December 28, 2020, from https://dipp.gov.in/sites/default/files/lu2115_0.pdf

Government of India, order number F.NO. 21-10S/201S-TS.ll/TC, dated 22.12.2015. Retrieved December 24, 2020, from https://www.iitrpr.ac.in/sites/default/files/uay_guidelines.pdf

Grand View Research Website. (2015). *Bioinformatics Market Analysis By Product (Sequence Analysis, Manipulation, Alignment, Structural & Functional Analysis Platforms, Data Management, Sequencing, Data Analysis Service, Generalized, Specialized Biocontent), By Application (Genomics, Molecular Phylogenetics, Metabolomics, Proteomics, Transcriptomics, Chemoinformatics & Drug Designing) And Segment Forecasts To 2020*. Report ID: 978-1-68038-008-8. Retrieved December 14, 2020, from https://www.grandviewresearch.com/industry-analysis/bioinformatics-industry

Grant, H. (2011). *Improving Lives/Interviewer* . Leaders Magazine.

Greis, N. P., Dibner, M. D., & Bean, A. S. (1995). External partnering as a response to innovation barriers and global competition in biotechnology. *Research Policy*, *24*(4), 609–630. doi:10.1016/S0048-7333(94)00789-6

Grima, E. M., Belarbi, E. H., Fernández, F. A., Medina, A. R., & Chisti, Y. (2003). Recovery of microalgal biomass and metabolites: Process options and economics. *Biotechnology Advances*, *20*(7-8), 491–515.

Grison, C., Escande, V., & Biton, J. (2015). Ecocatalysis: A new integrated approach to scientific ecology. Elsevier.

Grossmann, M. (2003). *Entrepreneurship in Biotechnology: Managing for Growth from Start-Up to Initial Public Offering*. Springer-Verlag Berlin Heidelberg. doi:10.1007/978-3-642-57432-0

Grubel, H. G. (1968). Internationally diversified portfolios: Welfare gains and capital flows. *The American Economic Review*, 1299–1314.

Grudin, J., & Pruitt, J. (2002). Personas, participatory design and product development: An infrastructure for engagement. In *Proc. PDC* (*Vol. 2*). Academic Press.

Gunn, M., & Langer, L. J. (2017). *One Course, Two… Four Courses–A Bioentrepreneurship Concentration-Case Studies*: Johns Hopkins University and the University of San Francisco. *Technology Transfer and Entrepreneurship*, *4*(2), 115–120.

Gupta, S. (2019). *The Role of Effective Communication in Entrepreneurial Success*. Retrieved December 10, 2020, from https://www.entrepreneur.com/article/336347

Gupta, V., Sengupta, M., Prakash, J., & Tripathy, B. C. (2016). An Introduction to Biotechnology. *Basic and Applied Aspects of Biotechnology*, 1–21.

Gupta, V., Sengupta, M., Prakash, J., & Tripathy, B. C. (2016). An Introduction to Biotechnology. *Basic and Applied Aspects of Biotechnology*, 1–21. doi:10.1007/978-981-10-0875-7_1

Gupta, A. K. (2008). National Bamboo Mission: A holistic scheme for development of bamboo sector in Tripura. *Indian Forester*, *134*(3), 305.

Gupta, A. K., & Sapienza, H. J. (1992). 'Determinants of venturecapital firms' preference regarding the industry diversity and geo-graphic scope of their investments'. *Journal of Business Venturing*, *7*(5), 347–362. doi:10.1016/0883-9026(92)90012-G

Gupta, C. B., & Khanka, S. S. (2003). *Entrepreneurship and small business*. Academic Press.

Gurau, C. (2006). Bio-entrepreneurship in different economic systems: A comparative analysis of bio-entrepreneurs' profile in UK, France and Germany. *International Journal of Biotechnology*, *8*(3-4), 169–186.

Gurǎu, C. (2021). Entrepreneurship in biotechnology. In *World Encyclopedia of Entrepreneurship*. Edward Elgar Publishing. doi:10.4337/9781839104145.00031

Gurau, C. (2021). *Entrepreneurship in biotechnology: World Encyclopedia of Entrepreneurship*. Edward Elgar Publishing.

Haakonsson, S. J., & Richey, L. A. (2007). TRIPs and public health: The Doha Declaration and Africa. *Development Policy Review*, *25*(1), 71–90. doi:10.1111/j.1467-7679.2007.00360.x

Haeussler, C. (2007). 'Proactive versus reactive m&a activities in the biotechnology industry. *The Journal of High Technology Management Research*, *17*(2), 109–123.

Haeussler, C. (2007). Proactive versus reactive M&A activities in the biotechnology industry. *The Journal of High Technology Management Research*, *17*(2), 109–123. doi:10.1016/j.hitech.2006.11.001

Haeussler, C. (2011a). The determinants of commercialization strategy: Idiosyncrasies in British and German biotechnology. *Entrepreneurship Theory and Practice*, *35*(4), 653–681. doi:10.1111/j.1540-6520.2010.00385.x

Haeussler, C. (2011b). Information sharing in academia and the industry: A comparative study. *Research Policy*, *40*(1), 105–122. doi:10.1016/j.respol.2010.08.007

Hagedoorn, J. (1993). Understanding the rationale of strategic technology partnering: Inter organizational modes of cooperation and sectoral differences. *Strategic Management Journal*, *14*(5), 371–385. doi:10.1002mj.4250140505

Haleblian, J., Kim, J. Y., & Rajagopalan, N. (2006). The influence of acquisition experience and performance on acquisition behavior: Evidence from the US commercial banking industry. *Academy of Management Journal*, *49*(2), 357–370. doi:10.5465/amj.2006.20786083

Hall, B., Helmers, C., Rogers, M., & Sena, V. (2014). The choice between formal and informal intellectual property: A review. *Journal of Economic Literature*, *52*(2), 375–423. doi:10.1257/jel.52.2.375

Haman, G. (1996). Techniques and tools to generate breakthrough products. In PDMA Handbook of New Product Development. John Wiley and Sons.

Hambrick, D. C., & Cannella, A. A. (1993). Relative standing: A framework for understanding departures of acquired executives. *Academy of Management Journal*, *36*, 733–762.

Hamill, J. D., Prescott, A., & Martin, C. (1987). Assessment of the efficiency of cotransformation of the T-DNA of disarmed binary vectors derived from Agrobacterium tumefaciens and the T-DNA of A. rhizogenes. *Plant Molecular Biology*, *9*(6), 573–584. doi:10.1007/BF00020534

Handoo, S., Arora, V., Khera, D., Nandi, P. K., & Sahu, S. K. (2012). A comprehensive study on regulatory requirements for development and filing of generic drugs globally. *International Journal of Pharmaceutical Investigation*, *2*(3), 99–105. doi:10.4103/2230-973X.104392 PMID:23373001

Hanumappa, H. G., & Bhinde, M. J. (1995). Towards operationalizing Small Farmers' Agri-Business Consortium: A case of dharwad district in Karnataka. *Agricultural Economics Research Review, 8*, 59-77.

Harrison, D., & Waluszewski, A. (2008). The development of a user network as a way to re-launch an unwanted product. *Research Policy*, *37*(1), 115–130. doi:10.1016/j.respol.2007.10.001

Harrison, R. G. (2004). *Needle free Drug Delivery Technology*. Innovation in Pharmaceutical Technology.

Hart, S., Jan Hultink, E., Tzokas, N., & Commandeur, H. R. (2003). Industrial companies' evaluation criteria in new product development gates. *Journal of Product Innovation Management*, *20*(1), 22–36. doi:10.1111/1540-5885.201003

Harun, A. N., Ahmad, R., & Mohamed, N. (2015, May). Plant growth optimization using variable intensity and Far Red LED treatment in indoor farming. In *2015 International Conference on Smart Sensors and Application (ICSSA)* (pp. 92-97). IEEE. 10.1109/ICSSA.2015.7322517

Hauser, J., Tellis, G., & Griffin, A. (2006). Research on innovation: A review and Agenda for marketing science. *Marketing Science*, *25*(6), 687–717. doi:10.1287/mksc.1050.0144

Hayat, R., Ali, S., Amara, U., Khalid, R., & Ahmed, I. (2010). Soil beneficial bacteria and their role in plant growth promotion: A review. *Annals of Microbiology*, *60*(4), 579–598. doi:10.100713213-010-0117-1

Haycock, P. (1998). Europe discovers bioentrepreneurship. *Nature Biotechnology*, *16*(1), 6–6.

Hayes, A. (2020, July). *Entrepreneur*. Retrieved https://www.investopedia.com/terms/e/entrepreneur.asp

Heikkilä, J. (2019). IPR gender gaps: A first look at utility model, design right and trademark filings. *Scientometrics*, *118*(3), 869–883. doi:10.100711192-018-2979-0

Heikkinen, M. T., Mainela, T., Still, J., & Tähtinen, J. (2007). Roles for managing in mobile service development nets. *Industrial Marketing Management*, *36*(7), 909–925. doi:10.1016/j.indmarman.2007.05.014

Heinrichs, E. A. (1986). Perspectives and directions for the continued development of insect-resistant rice varieties. *Agriculture, Ecosystems & Environment*, *18*(1), 9–36. doi:10.1016/0167-8809(86)90172-6

Hellmich, R. L., Albajes, R., Bergvinson, D., Prasifka, J. R., Wang, Z. Y., & Weiss, M. J. (2008). The present and future role of insect-resistant genetically modified maize in IPM. In *Integration of insect-resistant genetically modified crops within IPM programs* (pp. 119–158). Springer. doi:10.1007/978-1-4020-8373-0_5

Henkel, J., & Maurer, S. (2010). Network effects in biology R&D. *The American Economic Review*, *100*(2), 159–164. doi:10.1257/aer.100.2.159

Henry, E., & Ponce, C. J. (2011). Waiting to imitate: On the dynamic pricing of knowledge. *Journal of Political Economy*, *119*(5), 959–981. doi:10.1086/662721

Herdt, R. W. (2006). Biotechnology in agriculture. *Annual Review of Environment and Resources*, 31.

Herz, B., & Mejer, M. (2019). Effects of the European Union trademark: Lessons for the harmonization of intellectual property systems. *Research Policy*, *48*(7), 1841–1854. doi:10.1016/j.respol.2019.04.010

Higgins, M. C. (2005). *Career Imprints: Creating Leaders Across an Industry*. Harvard Business School.

Hine, D., & Kapeleris, J. (2006). *Innovation and Entrepreneurship in Biotechnology, An International Perspective- Concept, theories and cases*. Edward Elgar Publishing Limited. doi:10.4337/9781845428853

Hisrich, R. D. (1990). Entrepreneurship/intrapreneurship. *The American Psychologist*, *45*(2), 209–222. doi:10.1037/0003-066X.45.2.209

Hisrich, R., Langan-Fox, J., & Grant, S. (2007). Entrepreneurship research and practice: A call to action for psychology. *The American Psychologist*, *62*(6), 575–589. doi:10.1037/0003-066X.62.6.575 PMID:17874898

Hoang, H., & Rothaermel, F. T. (2005). The effect of general and partner-specific alliance experience on joint R&D project performance. *Academy of Management Journal*, *48*(2), 332–345. doi:10.5465/amj.2005.16928417

Hoang, H., & Rothaermel, F. T. (2010). Leveraging internal and external experience: Exploration, exploitation, and R&D project performance. *Strategic Management Journal*, *31*, 734–758. doi:10.1002mj.834

Hogarth, S. (2017). Valley of the unicorns: Consumer genomics, venture capital and digital disruption. *New Genetics & Society*, *36*(3), 250–272. doi:10.1080/14636778.2017.1352469

Holman, C. M. (2020). GlaxoSmithKline v. Teva: Holding a Generic Liable for an artificial Act of Inducement. *Biotechnology Law Report*, *39*(6), 425–439. doi:10.1089/blr.2020.29209.cmh

Hombal, S. G., & Prasad, K. N. (2012). Digital copyright protection: Issues in the digital library environment. *DESIDOC Journal of Library and Information Technology*, *32*(3), 233–239. doi:10.14429/djlit.32.3.2380

Hooley, G. J., Lynch, J. E., & Jobber, D. (1992). Generic marketing strategies. *International Journal of Research in Marketing*, *9*(1), 75–89. doi:10.1016/0167-8116(92)90030-O

Horner, R. (2014). The impact of patents on innovation, technology transfer and health: A pre-and post-TRIPs analysis of India's pharmaceutical industry. *New Political Economy*, *19*(3), 384–406. doi:10.1080/13563467.2013.796446

Horoszowski, M. (2021). *5 Reasons Your Business Should Be Socially Responsible*. Retrieved 12 January 2021, from https://blog.movingworlds.org/5-reasons-your-business-should-be-socially-responsible/

Hossain, F.R. (2019). Pharmaceutical Industry: Top 7 Technologies to Reshape the Future. *Brain Station, 23.*

Howard, K. (2003). Three US states launch biotech seed funds. *Bioentrepreneur*, 1–2.

Hsu, D. H. (2007). Experienced entrepreneurial founders, organizational capital, and venture capital funding. *Research Policy*, *36*(5), 722–741. doi:10.1016/j.respol.2007.02.022

Hsu, L. Y., Teo, F. S., & Chin, T. M. (2018). *Medical Biotechnology - Modern Development. Encyclopedia of Life Support Systems* (Vol. 11). EOLSS.

Huckman, R. S., & Zinner, D. E. (2008). Does focus improve operational performance? Lessons from the management of clinical trials'. *Strategic Management Journal*, *29*(2), 173–193. doi:10.1002mj.650

Hu, H., & Xiong, L. (2014). Genetic engineering and breeding of drought-resistant crops. *Annual Review of Plant Biology*, *65*(1), 715–741. doi:10.1146/annurev-arplant-050213-040000

Hu, R., Pray, C., Huang, J., Rozelle, S., Fan, C., & Zhang, C. (2009). Reforming intellectual property rights and the Bt cotton seed industry in China: Who benefits from policy reform. *Research Policy*, *38*(5), 793–801. doi:10.1016/j.respol.2008.12.008

India Brand equity foundation website. (2020). *Biotechnology Industry in India*. Retrieved December 12, 2020, from https://www.ibef.org/industry/biotechnologyindia.aspx#:~:text=The%20Indian%20biotechnology%20industry%20amounted,%25%20from%203%25%20in%202017

ISAAA. (2012). *Global Status of Commercialized Biotech GM Crops*. ISAAA.

ISAAA. (2017). *Global status of commercialized biotech GM crops in 2017: biotech crop adoption surges as economic benefits accumulate in 22 years. ISAAA brief no. 53*. ISAAA.

Ismail, K., Azhar, T. T., Yong, C. Y., Aslan, A. S., Omar, W. Z., Majid, I., & Ajagbe, A. M. (2012). Problems on commercialization of genetically modified crops in Malaysia. *Procedia: Social and Behavioral Sciences*, *40*, 353–357. doi:10.1016/j.sbspro.2012.03.199

Israel-Roming, F., & Ghidurus, M. (2019). The potential of Biotechnology to generate prosperity. In F. Matei & D. Zirra (Eds.), *Introduction to Biotech Entrepreneurship: From Idea to Business. Springer Nature Switzerland AG 2019*. doi:10.1007/978-3-030-22141-6_1

Jackson, M. A. (1997). Optimizing nutritional conditions for the liquid culture production of effective fungal biological control agents. *Journal of Industrial Microbiology & Biotechnology*, *19*(3), 180–187.

Jacobs, S., De Vos, A., Stuer, D., & Van der Heijden, B. (2019). "Knowing Me, Knowing You" the Importance of Networking for Freelancers' Careers: Examining the Mediating Role of Need for Relatedness Fulfillment and Employability-Enhancing Competencies. *Frontiers in Psychology*, *10*, 2019.

Jagannathan, P. (2009). India fourth largest adopter of biotech crop in world. *ET Bureau*. http://www.biotechnitaly.com/pdfufffici/RubriaIndia.pdf

Janeitz, E. (2003). 'Biotech + medicine'. *Technology Review*, *106*(8), 72–79.

Janodia, D. M. (2007). Drug Development Process. *RE:view*.

January, M. C., Cutright, T. J., Van Keulen, H., & Wei, R. (2008). Hydroponic phytoremediation of Cd, Cr, Ni, As, and Fe: Can Helianthus annuus hyperaccumulate multiple heavy metals? *Chemosphere*, *70*(3), 531–537.

Jayaraman, K. S. (2004). Foreign VC funds get mixed reception in India. *Bioentrepreneur*, 1–2.

Jeannet, J. P., & Hennessey, H. D. (2005). *Global marketing strategies*. Dreamtech Press.

Jegannathan, K. R., Jun-Yee, L., Chan, E. S., & Ravindra, P. (2010). Production of biodiesel from palm oil using liquid core lipase encapsulated in κ-carrageenan. *Fuel*, *89*(9), 2272–2277. doi:10.1016/j.fuel.2010.03.016

Johnson, E. B. (2007). Contextual Teaching and Learning: Menjadikan Kegiatan Belajar-Mengajar Mengasyikkan dan Bermakna. In Contextual Teaching and Learning: What It Is and Why It's Here To Stay. Bandung: Penerbit MLC.

Jones Lang LaSalle. (2012). *Life Sciences Cluster Report Global*. Author.

Jong, S. (2011). Commercializing a disruptive technology. *Bioentrepreneur*, 1–4.

Kaiser, R., & Prange, H. (2004). The reconfiguration of National Innovation Systems— The example of German biotechnology. *Research Policy*, *33*(3), 395–408. doi:10.1016/j.respol.2003.09.001

Kale, P., Dyer, J. H., & Singh, H. (2002). Alliance capability, stock market response, and long term alliance success: The role of the alliance function. *Strategic Management Journal*, *23*(8), 747–767. doi:10.1002mj.248

Kalogerakis, N., Arff, J., Banat, I. M., Broch, O. J., Daffonchio, D., Edvardsen, T., ... Fava, F. (2015). The role of environmental biotechnology in exploring, exploiting, monitoring, preserving, protecting and decontaminating the marine environment. *New Biotechnology*, *32*(1), 157–167.

Kannebley, S. Jr, Porto, G. S., & Pazello, E. T. (2005). Characteristics of Brazilian innovative firms: An empirical analysis based on PINTEC—industrial research on technological innovation. *Research Policy*, *34*(6), 872–893. doi:10.1016/j.respol.2005.04.003

Kanu, I., & Achi, O. K. (2011). Industrial effluents and their impact on water quality of receiving rivers in Nigeria. *Journal of Applied Technology in Environmental Sanitation*, *1*(1), 75–86.

Kaplan, R. S., Kaplan, R. E., Norton, D. P., Davenport, T. H., & Norton, D. P. (2004). *Strategy maps: Converting intangible assets into tangible outcomes*. Harvard Business Press.

Kariyawasam, K., & Palliyaarachchi, R. (2020). The song would be nothing without someone to sing it: Copyright and performers' rights in music. *International Review of Law Computers & Technology*, 1–24. doi:10.1080/13600869.2020.1820684

Karlsson, C., & Olsson, O. (1998). Product innovation in small and large enterprises. *Small Business Economics, 10*(1), 31–46. doi:10.1023/A:1007970416484

Kashman, Y., Gustafson, K. R., Fuller, R. W., Cardellina, J. H. II, McMahon, J. B., Currens, M. J., ... Boyd, M. R. (1992). The calanolides, a novel HIV-inhibitory class of coumarin derivatives from the tropical rainforest tree, Calophyllumlanigerum. *Journal of Medicinal Chemistry, 35*(15), 2735–2743. doi:10.1021/jm00093a004

Kashyap, V., Kumar, S. V., Collonnier, C., Fusari, F., Haicour, R., Rotino, G. L., ... Rajam, M. V. (2003). Biotechnology of eggplant. *Scientia Horticulturae, 97*(1), 1–25. doi:10.1016/S0304-4238(02)00140-1

Kathuria, C. (2020). *Entrepreneurship Lessons From Kiran Mazumdar Shaw*. SheThePeople.TV.

Katila, R., & Mang, P. Y. (2003). Exploiting technological opportunities: The timing of collaborations. *Research Policy, 32*(2), 317–332. doi:10.1016/S0048-7333(02)00102-6

Kaya, H. K., Klein, M. G., & Burlando, T. M. (1993). Impact of *Bacillus popilliae, Rickettsiella popilliae* and entomopathogenic nematodes on a population of the scarabaeid, Cyclocephala hirta. *Biocontrol Science and Technology, 3*(4), 443–453.

Kearney, C. (2018). Regulation and market influences on innovation in biotechnology. *Journal of Commercial Biotechnology, 24*(3), 57–62.

Kearney, C., & Langer, L. J. (2018). Effective Leadership through Bioentrepreneurship and Bioinnovation. *Journal of Commercial Biotechnology, 24*(2), 3–5.

Kelly, C. J., & Young, A. J. (2017). Promoting innovation in healthcare. *Future Healthcare Journal, 4*(2), 121–125. PMID:31098448

Kermani, F., & Bonacossa, P. (2003). Current and future prospects for the global biotechnology industry. *Journal of Commercial Biotechnology, 10*(2), 154–161. doi:10.1057/palgrave.jcb.3040069

Kerr, S. P., & Kerr, W. R. (2020). *Immigration policy levers for us innovation and startups*. National Bureau of Economic Research Working Paper Series, (w27040).

Kerry, V. B., & Lee, K. (2007). TRIPS, the Doha declaration and paragraph 6 decision: What are the remaining steps for protecting access to medicines? *Globalization and Health, 3*(1), 1–12. doi:10.1186/1744-8603-3-3 PMID:17524147

Kettinger, W. J., Zhang, C., & Marchand, D. A. (2011). CIO and Business Executive Leadership Approaches to Establishing Company-Wide Information Orientation. *MIS Quarterly Executive, 10*(4).

Khan, F. A. (2016). *Biotechnology fundamentals* (2nd ed.). CRC.

Khater, H. F. (2012). Prospects of botanical biopesticides in insect pest management. *Pharmacologia, 3*(12), 641–656.

Khidzir, N. Z., & Ahmed, S. A. A. M. (2018). Legal Protection of Intellectual Property Rights (IPR) in Bangladesh. *International Journal of Law, Government and Communication, 3*(12), 71–89.

Khilji, S. E., Mroczkowski, T., & Bernstein, B. (2006). From invention to innovation: Toward developing an integrated innovation model for biotech firms. *Journal of Product Innovation Management, 23*(6), 528–540. doi:10.1111/j.1540-5885.2006.00222.x

Kihlstrom, R. E., & Laffont, J. J. (1979). General equilibrium entrepreneurial theory of firm formation based on risk aversion. *Journal of Political Economy, 87*(4), 719–748. doi:10.1086/260790

Kihlstrom, R., & Laffont, J. J. (2002). Entrepreneurial theory of firm formation based on risk aversion. *Entrepreneurship: Critical Perspectives on Business and Management, 1*(4), 29.

Kim, J. C., Lee, M. R., Kim, S., Lee, S. J., Park, S. E., Nai, Y. S., ... Kim, J. S. (2018). Tenebrio molitor-mediated entomopathogenic fungal library construction for pest management. *Journal of Asia-Pacific Entomology, 21*(1), 196–204.

Kim, J. W., & Higgins, M. C. (2007). Where do alliances come from? The effects of upper echelons on alliance formation. *Research Policy, 36*(4), 499–514. doi:10.1016/j.respol.2007.02.017

Kim, J., & Wilemon, D. (2002). Strategic issues in managing innovation's fuzzy front-end. *European Journal of Innovation Management, 5*(1), 27–39. doi:10.1108/14601060210415153

Kim, W. (2013). Recombinant protein polymers in biomaterials. *Frontiers in Bioscience, 18*(1), 289–304. doi:10.2741/4100 PMID:23276922

Kinch, M. (2014). The Rise and Decline of Biotechnology. *Drug Discovery Today, 19*(11), 1686–1690. doi:10.1016/j.drudis.2014.04.006 PMID:24747562

King, D. R., Slotegraaf, R. J., & Kesner, I. (2008). Performance implications of firm resource interactions in the acquisition of R&D-intensive firms. *Organization Science, 19*(2), 327–340. doi:10.1287/orsc.1070.0313

Kirner, E., Kinkel, S., & Jaeger, A. (2009). Innovation paths and the innovation performance of low-technology firms—An empirical analysis of German industry. *Research Policy, 38*(3), 447–458. doi:10.1016/j.respol.2008.10.011

Kirzner, I. M. (1973). *Competition and entrepreneurship.* University of Chicago Press.

Kirzner, I. M. (1997). Entrepreneurial discovery and the competitive market process: An Austrian approach. *Journal of Economic Literature, 35*, 60–85.

Klaine, S. J., Alvarez, P. J., Batley, G. E., Fernandes, T. F., Handy, R. D., Lyon, D. Y., & Lead, J. R. (2008). Nanomaterials in the environment: Behavior, fate, bioavailability, and effects. *Environmental Toxicology and Chemistry: An International Journal, 27*(9), 1825–1851. doi:10.1897/08-090.1

Klein, K., Conn, A., & Speer, S. A. (2001). Implementing computerized technology: An organizational analysis. *The Journal of Applied Psychology, 86*(5), 811–829. doi:10.1037/0021-9010.86.5.811 PMID:11596799

Kniskern, P. J., & Miller, W. J. (1992). Hepatitis B vaccines: Blueprints for vaccines of the future. *Biotechnology, 20*, 177–204. PMID:1600381

Kogut, B. (1988). Joint ventures: Theoretical and empirical perspectives. *Strategic Management Journal, 9*(4), 319–332. doi:10.1002mj.4250090403

Kollewe, J. (2012). AstraZeneca appoints new chief executive. *The Guardian.*

Konde, V. (2008). Biotechnology in India: Public–private partnerships. *Journal of Commercial Biotechnology, 14*(1), 43–55. doi:10.1057/palgrave.jcb.3050079

Konde, V. (2009). Biotechnology business models: An Indian perspective. *Journal of Commercial Biotechnology, 15*(3), 215–226. doi:10.1057/jcb.2008.52

Korunka, C., Frank, H., Lueger, M., & Mugler, J. (2003). The entrepreneurial personality in the context of resources, environment, and the startup process: A conðgurational approach. *Entrepreneurship Theory and Practice, 28*(1), 23–42. doi:10.1111/1540-8520.00030

Kotler, P., & Armstrong, G. (2010). *Principles of marketing.* Pearson education.

Kotler, P., & Armstrong, G. (2015). *Principles of marketing-global edition.* Pearson.

Kotler, P., Kartajaya, H., & Setiawan, I. (2010). *Marketing 3.0.* John Wiley & Sons, Inc. doi:10.1002/9781118257883

Kraus, S., Pohjola, M., & Koponen, A. (2012). Innovation in family firms: An empirical analysis linking organizational and managerial innovation to corporate success. *Review of Managerial Science, 6*(3), 265–286. doi:10.100711846-011-0065-6

Kristanti, E. A., Bintari, S. H., & Ridlo, S. (2012). Pengembangan perangkat pembelajaran bioentrepreneurship pembuatan makanan dari limbah cair pengolahan kedelai. *Journal of Innovative Science Education, 1*(2), 112–118.

Kumar, A. (2020) IILM College of engineering and Technology website. *Biotechnology entrepreneurship: An Indian perspective.* Retrieved December 14, 2020, from https://iilmcet.ac.in/blog/biotechnology-entrepreneurship-an-indian-perspective/

Kumar, V., & Sinha, K. (2015). Status and challenges of intellectual property rights in agriculture innovation in India. *Journal of Intellectual Property Rights, 20*, 288-296.

Kumar, V., Shahi, S. K., & Singh, S. (2018). Bioremediation: an eco-sustainable approach for restoration of contaminated sites. In Microbial bioprospecting for sustainable development. Springer.

Kumar, A., & Srivastava, L. (2012). Biotechnology industry in India: Opportunities or challenges. *African Journal of Business Management, 6*(44), 10834–10839. doi:10.5897/AJBM10.1236

Kumar, N. K., Quach, U., Thorsteinsdóttir, H., Somsekhar, H., Daar, A. S., & Singer, P. A. (2004). Indian biotechnology—Rapidly evolving and industry led. *Nature Biotechnology, 22*(12), DC31–DC36. doi:10.1038/nbt1204supp-DC31 PMID:15583682

Kunert, K. J., Okole, B., Vorster, B. J., Brewin, N. J., & Cullis, C. A. (2012). A general model for training the next generation of biotechnology entrepreneurs based on recent experience of USA-UK-South Africa collaborations. *Journal of Commercial Biotechnology, 18*(4), 63–66.

Lafuente, A., & Salas, V. (1989). Types of entrepreneurs and ðrms: The case of new Spanish ðrms. *Strategic Management Journal, 10*(1), 17–30. doi:10.1002mj.4250100103

Lamertz, K. P., Heugens, P. M. A. R., & Calmet, L. (2005). The configuration of organizational images among firms in the Canadian beer brewing industry. *Journal of Management Studies, 42*(4), 817–843. doi:10.1111/j.1467-6486.2005.00520.x

Langan-Fox, J., & Roth, S. (1995). Achievement motivation and female entrepreneurs. *Journal of Occupational and Organizational Psychology, 68*(3), 209–218. doi:10.1111/j.2044-8325.1995.tb00582.x

Langer, R. (2018). Mastering Bioentrepreneurship. *Innovative Research in Life Sciences: Pathways to Scientific Impact, Public Health Improvement, and Economic Progress*, 291.

Langer, L. J. (2017). Developing Global Biotechnology Enterprise, Entrepreneurship and Regulatory Science Programs: Profile from the Center for Biotechnology Education at Johns Hopkins University. *Technology Transfer and Entrepreneurship, 4*(2), 139–143.

Larsson, R., & Finkelstein, S. (1999). Integrating strategic, organizational, and human resource perspectives on mergers and acquisitions: A case survey of synergy realization. *Organization Science, 10*(1), 1–26. doi:10.1287/orsc.10.1.1

Laverty, G., Hanna, L. A., Haughey, S., & Hughes, C. (2015). Instructional Design and Assessment-Developing Entrepreneurial Skills in Pharmacy Students. *American Journal of Pharmaceutical Educationm 79*(7), 106.

Lawrence, N. W. (2000). *Social Research Methods: Qualitative and Quantitative approaches* (International Edition). Pearson New.

Lawrence, S. (2005). Looking at US versus European exit opportunities. *Bioentrepreneur*, 1–2.

Lechner, C., Dowling, M., & Welpe, I. (2006). Firm networks and firm development: The role of the relational mix'. *Journal of Business Venturing*, *21*(4), 514–540. doi:10.1016/j.jbusvent.2005.02.004

Lee, A. (2020). *10 Things You Didn't Know About Pascal Soriot*. Academic Press.

Lee, J. (2010). Heterogeneity, brokerage, and innovative performance: Endogenous formation of collaborative inventor networks. *Organization Science*, *21*(4), 804–822. doi:10.1287/orsc.1090.0488

Legal500. (2019). *GC Powerlist: Sweden Teams 2019- AstraZeneca*. Author.

Lehrer, M. (2007). Organizing knowledge spillovers when basic and applied research is interdependent: German biotechnology policy in historical perspective. *The Journal of Technology Transfer*, *32*(3), 277–296. doi:10.100710961-006-9017-8

Leitão, A. (2016). Bioeconomy: the challenge in the management of natural resources in the 21st century. *Open Journal of Social Sciences, 4*(11), 26-42.

Leitch, J. A. (2021). *10 principles of strategic leadership*. Retrieved 12 January 2021, from https://www.strategy-business.com/article/10-Principles-of-Strategic-Leadership

Leonard-Barton, D., & Pisano, G. P. (1990). Monsanto's March into Biotechnology (A). *Harvard Business Review*, 17.

Lepeley, M. T., Kuschel, K., Beutell, N., Pouw, N., & Eijdenberg, E. L. (2019). *The Wellbeing of Women in Entrepreneurship. A Global Perspective*. Routdlege. doi:10.4324/9780429279836

Lerner, J., & Malmendier, U. (2010). Contractibility and the design of research agreements. *The American Economic Review*, *100*(1), 214–246. doi:10.1257/aer.100.1.214

Lerner, J., & Merges, R. P. (1998). The control of technology alliances: An empirical analysis of the biotechnology industry. *The Journal of Industrial Economics*, *46*(2), 125–156. doi:10.1111/1467-6451.00066

Lerner, J., Shane, H., & Tsai, A. (2003). Do equity financing cycles matter? Evidence from biotechnology alliances. *Journal of Financial Economics*, *67*(3), 411–446. doi:10.1016/S0304-405X(02)00256-8

Lettice, F., Roth, N., & Forstenlechner, I. (2006). Measuring knowledge in the new product development process. *International Journal of Productivity and Performance Management*, *55*(3/4), 217–241. doi:10.1108/17410400610653200

Leung, J., & Giraudat, J. (1998). Abscisic acid signal transduction. *Annual Review of Plant Biology*, *49*(1), 199–222. doi:10.1146/annurev.arplant.49.1.199

Levitt, T. (1983). The globalisation of markets. *Harvard Business Review*, *61*, 92–102.

Levy, A. (2012). Drug Test Can one self-made woman reform health care for India, and the world? *The New Yorker*.

Lewis, K. K. (1999). Trying to explain home bias in equities and consumption. *Journal of Economic Literature*, *37*(2), 571–608. doi:10.1257/jel.37.2.571

Liebeskind, J. P., Oliver, A. L., Zucker, L., & Brewer, M. (1996). Social networks, learning, and flexibility: Sourcing scientific knowledge innew biotechnology firms. *Organization Science*, *7*(4), 428–443. doi:10.1287/orsc.7.4.428

Li, J., & Halal, W. (2002). Reinventing the biotech manager. *Nature Biotechnology*, *20*(S6), BE61–BE63. doi:10.1038/nbt0602supp-BE61 PMID:12089592

Lilien, G. L., Morrison, P. D., Searls, K., Sonnack, M., & Hippel, E. V. (2002). Performance assessment of the lead user idea-generation process for new product development. *Management Science*, *48*(8), 1042–1059. doi:10.1287/mnsc.48.8.1042.171

Littlejohn, T. (2002). Sun baked biotechnology in Australia. *Nature Biotechnology*, *20*(September). PMID:12205502

Littlejohn, T. (2002). Sunbaked biotechnology in Australia. *Nature Biotechnology*, *20*(9), 873–877.

Lonsdale, R. T., Noel, N. M., & Stasch, S. F. (1996). *Classification of sources of new product ideas*. Wiley.

Loredana, E. M. (2017). The use of Ansoff matrix in the field of business. *Annals-Economy Series*, *2*, 141–149.

Lovejoy, K. (2012). *Information, community, and action: How nonprofit organizations use social media*. Wiley Online Library.

Lundvall, B. K. (1992). *National innovation systems towards a theory of innovation and interactive learning*. Pinter.

Luoma, T., Paasi, J., & Nordlund, H. (2008, June). Managing commercialisation risks in innovation development: Linking front end and commercialisation. In *Proceedings of the XIX ISPIM Annual Conference. Open Innovation: Creating Products and Services through Collaboration. Tours, France* (*Vol. 18*). Academic Press.

Luo, X. R., Koput, K. W., & Powell, W. W. (2009). Intellectual capital or signal? The effects of scientists on alliance formation in knowledge-intensive industries. *Research Policy*, *38*(8), 1313–1325. doi:10.1016/j.respol.2009.06.001

Lynn, G. S., & Akgün, A. E. (1998). Innovation strategies under uncertainty: A contingency approach for new product development. *Engineering Management Journal*, *10*(3), 11–18. doi:10.1080/10429247.1998.11414991

Lynn, J. L. (2014). Building a curriculum for bioentrepreneurs. *Nature Biotechnology*, *32*(9), 863–865. doi:10.1038/nbt.3012 PMID:25203028

MacDonald, J., Doshi, K., Dussault, M., Hall, J. C., Holbrook, L., Jones, G., ... McLean, M. D. (2015). Bringing plant-based veterinary vaccines to market: Managing regulatory and commercial hurdles. *Biotechnology Advances*, *33*(8), 1572–1581. doi:10.1016/j.biotechadv.2015.07.007

Mahboudi, F., Hamedifar, H., & Aghajani, H. (2012). Medical biotechnology trends and achievements in Iran. *Avicenna Journal of Medical Biotechnology*, *4*(4), 200. PMID:23407888

Malerba, F., & Orsenigo, L. (2015). The evolution of the pharmaceutical industry. *Business History*, *57*(5), 664–687. doi:10.1080/00076791.2014.975119

Malhotra, B., Huddone, S., Verma, A., Chamil, A., Sanju, S., Thakur, A., Sindhu, R., Singh, Y., Patil, V. U., Siddappa, S., Gupta, R., & Pattanayak, D. (2012). Indian entrepreneurship in biotechnology comes of age. *Journal of Plant Biochemistry and Biotechnology*, *21*(1), 90–99. doi:10.100713562-012-0145-y

Malik, K. A., & Zafar, Y. (2005). Intellectual Property Rights in Plant Biotechnology: A Contribution to Crop Biosecurity. *Asian Biotechnology and Development Review*, *8*(1), 7–43.

Malone, L. A., Gatehouse, A. M., & Barratt, B. I. (2008). Beyond Bt: alternative strategies for insect-resistant genetically modified crops. In *Integration of insect-resistant genetically modified crops within IPM programs* (pp. 357–417). Springer. doi:10.1007/978-1-4020-8373-0_13

Mangold, W. G., & Faulds, D. J. (2009). Social media: The new hybrid element of the promotion mix. *Business Horizons*, *52*(4), 357–365. doi:10.1016/j.bushor.2009.03.002

Mani, D., & Kumar, C. (2014). Biotechnological advances in bioremediation of heavy metals contaminated ecosystems: An overview with special reference to phytoremediation. *International Journal of Environmental Science and Technology, 11*(3), 843–872.

Manshani, S., & Dubey, A. (2017). Startup Women in Startup India: A Study Of Women Entrepreneurs in India. *International Journal of Business and Management*, 91–100.

Marcati, A., Guido, G., & Peluso, A. M. (2008). The role of SME entrepreneurs' innovativeness and personality in the adoption of innovations. *Research Policy, 37*(9), 1579–1590. doi:10.1016/j.respol.2008.06.004

Margesin, R., Zimmerbauer, A., & Schinner, F. (2000). Monitoring of bioremediation by soil biological activities. *Chemosphere, 40*(4), 339–346.

Marks, M. L., & Mirvis, P. H. (2001). Making mergers and acquisitions work: Strategic and psychological preparation. *The Academy of Management Executive, 15*(2), 80–92. doi:10.5465/ame.2001.4614947

Marshall, C. (2000). *Enterprise modeling with UML: designing successful software through business analysis*. Addison-Wesley Professional.

Mastronardi, E., Tsae, P., Zhang, X., Monreal, C., & DeRosa, M. C. (2015). Strategic role of nanotechnology in fertilizers: potential and limitations. In *Nanotechnologies in food and agriculture* (pp. 25–67). Springer. doi:10.1007/978-3-319-14024-7_2

Mathew, J. C., & Jayakumar, P. (2020). *We need short-term launches to keep driving growth: Novartis CEO*. Business Today.

Maurer, I., & Ebers, M. (2006). Dynamics of social capital and their performance implications: Lessons from biotechnology start-ups. *Administrative Science Quarterly, 51*(2), 262–292. doi:10.2189/asqu.51.2.262

Mazumdar-Shaw, K. (2020). *The challenges and opportunities of innovating in India.Observer* Retrieved December 12, 2020, from https://www.orfonline.org/expert-speak/challenges-opportunities-innovating-india/

Mazumdar-Shaw, D. K. (2014). *Healthcare Innovation: An Interview with Dr. Kiran Mazumdar-Shaw/Interviewer: D. B. Weidmann*. Nature Education, Sitable.

Mazzarol, T., Volery, T., Doss, N., & Thein, V. (1999). Factors influencing small business startups. *International Journal of Entrepreneurial Behaviour & Research, 5*(2), 48–60. doi:10.1108/13552559910274499

McDonough III, E. F., Kahnb, K. B., & Barczaka, G. (2001). An investigation of the use of global, virtual, and colocated new product development teams. *Journal of Product Innovation Management, 18*(2), 110-120.

McKinsey. (2015). *The impact of regulation*. Author.

McKinsey. (2018). *The state of fashion 2019: An 'Urgent Awakening' for the Industry*. Author.

McMullen, J. S., Plummer, L. A., & Acs, Z. J. (2007). What is an entrepreneurial opportunity? *Small Business Economics, 28*(4), 273–283. doi:10.100711187-006-9040-z

McNally, J. (2009). Indian CROs can stay competitive. *BioSpectrum, 7*, 90–92.

Meckenna, R. (1991). Marketing is everything. *Harvard Business Review, 69*(1), 65–79. PMID:10109473

Meeinkuirt, W., Kruatrachue, M., Pichtel, J., Phusantisampan, T., & Saengwilai, P. (2016). Influence of organic amendments on phytostabilization of Cd-contaminated soil by *Eucalyptus camaldulensis*. *Science Asia, 42*(2), 83–91.

Mehrotra, P. (2016). Biosensors and their applications – A review. *Journal of Oral Biology and Craniofacial Research, 6*(2), 153–159. doi:10.1016/j.jobcr.2015.12.002 PMID:27195214

Mehta, S. (2004). Paths to entrepreneurship in thelife sciences. *Nature Biotechnology, 22*, 1609–1612. PMID:15605429

Mendoza, N., & Escamilla Silva, E. M. (2018). Introduction to phytochemicals: Secondary metabolites from plants with active principles for pharmacological importance. In T. Asao & M. Asaduzzaman (Eds.), *Phytochemicals. Source of antioxidants and role in disease prevention*. IntechOpen. doi:10.5772/intechopen.78226

Meyers, A. (2008). Enterprise for Life Scientists: Developing Innovation and Entrepreneurship in the Biosciences. *Journal of Commercial Biotechnology, 14*, 355–356.

Meyers, A. (2012). The birth of a discipline: Bioentrepreneurship. *Journal of Commercial Biotechnology, 18*(4), 3–4. doi:10.5912/jcb567

Meyers, A. (2014). Bioentrepreneurship Education and Training Trends. *Journal of Commercial Biotechnology, 20*(2).

Meyers, A. D., & Hurley, P. (2008). Bioentrepreneurship education programmes in the United States. *Journal of Commercial Biotechnology, 14*(1), 2–12.

Meyers, A. D., McCubbrey, D. J., & Watson, R. T. (2008). Open content textbooks: Educating the next generation of bioentrepreneurs in developing economies. *Journal of Commercial Biotechnology, 14*(4), 277–281.

Mikulic, M. (2020). *Number of biotechnology firms in selected European countries in 2017*. Retrieved December 25, 2020, from https://www.statista.com/statistics/439960/number-of-biotechnology-companies-europe-eu/

Miller, D. (1983). The correlates of entrepreneurship in three types of firms. *Management Science, 29*(7), 770–791. doi:10.1287/mnsc.29.7.770

Millson, M. R., & Wilemon, D. (2008). Designing strategic innovation networks to facilitate global NPD performance. *Journal of General Management, 34*(2), 39–56. doi:10.1177/030630700803400203

Miralpeix, B., Sabalza, M., Twyman, R. M., Capell, T., & Christou, P. (2014). Strategic patent analysis in plant biotechnology: Terpenoid indole alkaloid metabolic engineering as a case study. *Plant Biotechnology Journal, 12*(2), 117–134. doi:10.1111/pbi.12134

Mitchell, P. (2004). The changing attitude of European VCs. *Bioentrepreneur*, 1–2.

Mitra, R. M. (2007). *India's emergence as a global R&D center. An overview of the Indian R&D system and potential.* ITPS WorNing paper, 12.

Mitra, J. (2001). Genetics and genetic improvement of drought resistance in crop plants. *Current Science*, 758–763.

Monsanto. (n.d.). *Omega-3-Enhanced Soybean Oil*. Author.

Moore, G. E. (1965). Cramming more components onto integrated circuits. *Electronics (Basel), 38*, 114–117.

Moran, T. H. (2012). *Foreign direct investment and development*. The Wiley-Blackwell Encyclopedia of Globalization. doi:10.1002/9780470670590.wbeog217

Morris, N. (2009). *Understanding digital marketing: marketing strategies for engaging the digital generation*. Academic Press.

Motohashi, K. (2013). The role of the science park in innovation performance of start-up firms: An empirical analysis of Tsinghua Science Park in Beijing. *Asia Pacific Business Review, 19*(4), 578–599. doi:10.1080/13602381.2012.673841

Mudra Website. (n.d.). Retrieved December 14 2020 from https://www.mudra.org.in/

Mueller, J. M. (2007). Biotechnology patenting in India: will bio-generics lead a sunrise industry to bio-innovation. *UMkC l. reV., 76*, 437.

Mukherjee, A., Pal, P., Deb, S., Ray, S., & Goyal, T. M. (2016). Special SEZs for Services: India's Experiences and the Way Forward. In *Special Economic Zones in India* (pp. 117–152). Springer. doi:10.1007/978-81-322-2806-6_6

Müller, R. M., & Thoring, K. (2012). Design thinking vs. lean startup: A comparison of two user-driven innovation strategies. *Leading Through Design, 151*, 91-106.

Müller, C. (2002). Strategic Management: A Tool for Growth in the Biotechnology Sector. *Journal of Commercial Biotechnology, 8*(3), 226–234. doi:10.5912/jcb436

Muller, C., Fujiwara, T., & Herstatt, C. (2004). Sources of bioentrepreneurship: Thecase of Germany and Japan. *Journal of Small Business Management, 42*(1), 93–101. doi:10.1111/j.1540-627X.2004.00099.x

Mumford, M. D. (2000). Managing creative people: Strategies and tactics for innovation. *Human Resource Management Review, 10*(3), 313–351. doi:10.1016/S1053-4822(99)00043-1

Munier, S., Shah, A. A., Rehman, H., Bilal, M., Rajoka, M. S. R., Khan, A. A., & Khursid, M. (2020). Nanozymes for medical biotechnology and its potential applications in biosensing and nanotherapeutics. *Biotechnology Letters, 42*(3), 357–373. doi:10.100710529-020-02795-3 PMID:31950406

Murashige, T. (1974). Plant propagation through tissue cultures. *Annual Review of Plant Physiology, 25*(1), 135-166.

Naidu, N. V. R., & Rao, T. K. (2008). *Management and Entrepreneurship*. International Publishing House.

Namugenyi, C. (2019). *Shastri L Nimmagadda*. Torsten Reiners.

Namugenyi, C., Nimmagadda, S. L., & Reiners, T. (2019). Design of a SWOT Analysis Model and its Evaluation in Diverse Digital Business Ecosystem Contexts. *Procedia Computer Science, 159*, 1145–1154. doi:10.1016/j.procs.2019.09.283

Nap, J. P., Metz, P. L., Escaler, M., & Conner, A. J. (2003). The release of genetically modified crops into the environment: Part I. Overview of current status and regulations. *The Plant Journal, 33*(1), 1–18. doi:10.1046/j.0960-7412.2003.01602.x

National Dairy Development Board. (2017). *DIDF - Dairy Processing & Infrastructure Development Fund*. Retrieved December 12, 2020, from https://www.nddb.coop/didf/didf-in-brief

National Research Council of Canada. (n.d.). https://nrc.canada.ca/en

National Research Council. (2002). *Animal biotechnology: science-based concerns*. Author.

National Research Council. (2002). *Environmental effects of transgenic plants: the scope and adequacy of regulation*. Author.

Nealey, T., Daignault, R. M., & Cai, Y. (2015). Trade secrets in life science and pharmaceutical companies. *Cold Spring Harbor Perspectives in Medicine, 5*(4), a020982. doi:10.1101/cshperspect.a020982 PMID:25414378

Nestel, P., Bouis, H. E., Meenakshi, J. V., & Pfeiffer, W. (2006). Biofortification of staple food crops. *The Journal of Nutrition, 136*(4), 1064–1067. doi:10.1093/jn/136.4.1064

Newman, D. J., & Cragg, G. M. (2016). Natural products as sources of new drugs from 1981 to 2014. *Journal of Natural Products, 79*(3), 629–661. doi:10.1021/acs.jnatprod.5b01055 PMID:26852623

Nie, J., Sun, Y., Zhou, Y., Kumar, M., Usman, M., Li, J., & Tsang, D. C. (2020). Bioremediation of water containing pesticides by microalgae: Mechanisms, methods, and prospects for future research. *The Science of the Total Environment, 707*, 136080. doi:10.1016/j.scitotenv.2019.136080 PMID:31869621

Ninawe, A. S., & Indulkar, S. T. (2017). Intellectual Property Rights and Innovation in Marine Biotechnology. *Asian Biotechnology and Development Review, 19*(1).

Niosi, J., & McKelvey, M. (2018). Relating business model innovations and innovation cascades: The case of biotechnology. *Journal of Evolutionary Economics, 28*(5), 1081–1109. doi:10.100700191-018-0561-9 PMID:30613125

Nitiayog. (n.d.). *Atal Innovation Mission*. Retrieved December 14, 2020, from https://niti.gov.in/aim

Nitu, V. I. (2014). Comparative Analysis of the Community Trademark Registration Activity of Germany, the United States and China. *Procedia Economics and Finance, 15*, 603–608. doi:10.1016/S2212-5671(14)00528-0

Noble, C. H., & Mokwa, M. P. (1999). Implementing marketing strategies: Developing and testing a managerial theory. *Journal of Marketing, 63*(4), 57–73. doi:10.1177/002224299906300406

Nogrady, B. (2018). How Indian biotech is driving innovation. *Nature, 564*(7735), S53–S53. doi:10.1038/d41586-018-07671-9 PMID:30542184

Novartis.in. (2021). *Company History*. Author.

Nurmemmedov, E. (2004). *Bioentrepreneurial Partnership-A toll for Biotechnology transfer* (Doctoral dissertation). Lund University.

Nybakk, E., & Jenssen, J. I. (2012). Innovation strategy, working climate, and financial performance in traditional manufacturing firms: An empirical analysis. *International Journal of Innovation Management, 16*(02), 1250008. doi:10.1142/S1363919611003374

Oakey, R., Faulkner, W., Cooper, S., & Walsh, V. (1990). *New Firms in the Biotechnology Industry*. London Printer.

Obama Administration. (2012). *National Bioeconomy Blueprint*. Author.

Odzaly, E. E., Greer, D., & Sage, P. (2009, October). Software risk management barriers: An empirical study. In *2009 3rd International Symposium on Empirical Software Engineering and Measurement* (pp. 418-421). IEEE.

Ojone, A. S. (2017). Effects of students' awareness of bio entrepreneurship opportunities in biology education in biology education on combating economic recession in Nigeria. *International Journal of Education and Evaluation, 3*(10), 22–29.

Ojuederie, O. B., & Babalola, O. O. (2017). Microbial and plant-assisted bioremediation of heavy metal polluted environments: A review. *International Journal of Environmental Research and Public Health, 14*(12), 1504.

Olaniran, A. O., Balgobind, A., & Pillay, B. (2013). Bioavailability of heavy metals in soil: Impact on microbial biodegradation of organic compounds and possible improvement strategies. *International Journal of Molecular Sciences, 14*(5), 10197–10228.

Oliver, A. L. (2004). Biotechnology entrepreneurial scientists and their collaborations. *Research Policy, 33*(4), 583–597.

Omachonu, V. K., & Einspruch, N. G. (2010). Innovation in Healthcare Delivery Systems: A Conceptual Framework. *The Innovation Journal, 15*(1), 2.

Onuoha, G. (2007). Entrepreneurship. *AIST International Journal, 10*, 20–32.

Örnek, A. S., & Danyal, Y. (2015). Increased Importance of Entrepreneurship from Entrepreneurship to Techno-Entrepreneurship (Startup): Provided Supports and Conveniences to Techno-Entrepreneurs in Turkey. *Procedia: Social and Behavioral Sciences*, *195*, 1146–1155. https://doi.org/10.1016/j.sbspro.2015.06.164

Oyovwi, E. O. (2016). Developing entrepreneurial skills in biology education: A necessary tool for poverty alleviation. *Ibadan Journal of Educational Studies*, *16*(2), 31–42.

Pacifico, C., & Polacek, R. (1981). *New Product Development. ACS Audio Course*. American Chemical Society.

Padula, W. V., Parasrampuria, S., Socal, M. P., Conti, R. M., & Anderson, G. F. (2020). Market exclusivity for drugs with multiple orphan approvals (1983–2017) and associated budget impact in the US. *PharmacoEconomics*, *38*(10), 1115–1121. doi:10.100740273-020-00934-2 PMID:32533523

Palepu, K. G., Healy, P. M., Wright, S., Bradbury, M., & Coulton, J. (2020). *Business analysis and valuation: Using financial statements*. Cengage AU.

Palmer, M. (1971). The application of psychological testing to entrepreneurial potential. *California Management Review*, *13*(3), 32–38. doi:10.2307/41164291

Parmar, H. (2005). Biotechnology in India: Emerging opportunities. *Journal of Commercial Biotechnology*, *12*(1), 61–66. doi:10.1057/palgrave.jcb.3040150

Partanen, J., Möller, K., Westerlund, M., Rajala, R., & Rajala, A. (2008). Social capital in the growth of science-and-technology-based SMEs. *Industrial Marketing Management*, *37*(5), 513–522. doi:10.1016/j.indmarman.2007.09.012

Patel, S., Nanda, R., & Sahoo, S. (2016). Biosensors in Health Care: The Milestones Achievedin Their Development towards Lab-on-Chip-Analysis. Biochemistry Research International, 16.

Pathak, D. V., & Kumar, M. (2016). Microbial inoculants as biofertilizers and biopesticides. In *Microbial inoculants in sustainable agricultural productivity* (pp. 197–209). Springer. doi:10.1007/978-81-322-2647-5_11

Patra, S. K. (2014). Knowledge Production by Indian Biotechnology Parks. *Asian Biotechnology and Development Review*, *16*(1).

Patwardhan, B., & Gautam, M. (2005). Botanical immunodrugs: Scope and opportunities. *Drug Discovery Today*, *10*(7), 495–502. doi:10.1016/S1359-6446(04)03357-4

Patzelt, H., & Brenner, T. (2008). Introduction to the Handbook of Bioentrepreneurship. In Handbook of Bioentrepreneurship (pp. 1-6). Springer.

Patzelt, H., Schweizer, L., & Behrens, J. (2012). Biotechnology entrepreneurship. *Foundations and Trends in Entrepreneurship, 8*(2).

Paull, J. (2018). Genetically Modified Organisms (GMOs) as Invasive Species. *Journal of Environment Protection and Sustainable Development*, *4*(3), 31–37.

Paul, V. (2016). Genetic engineering and sustainable crop disease management: Opportunities for case-by-case decision-making. *Sustainability*, *8*(495), 1–22.

Pawar, R. K. (2020). Article. *International Journal of Rudiments in Pharmaceutical Sciences and Clinical Research.*, *1*(1), 14–18.

Perez-Prat, E., & van Lookeren Campagne, M. M. (2002). Hybrid seed production and the challenge of propagating male-sterile plants. *Trends in Plant Science*, *7*(5), 199–203. doi:10.1016/S1360-1385(02)02252-5

Perju-Mitran, A. (2019). Key Elements of the Biotech Market. In F. Matei & D. Zirra (Eds.), *Introduction to Biotech Entrepreneurship: From Idea to Business*. Springer. doi:10.1007/978-3-030-22141-6_11

Persidis, A. (1996). Building molecular value. *The Journal of Business Strategy*, *17*(2), 18–21. doi:10.1108/eb039765

Persidis, A. (1997). Bioentrepreneurship around the world; Bioentrepreneur II. *Nature Biotechnology*, 16.

Persidis, A. (1998). Bioentrepreneurship around the world. *Nature Biotechnology*, *16*(1), 3–4.

Peshev, M. (2017). *What Are The Most Important Skills Entrepreneurs Need?* Retrieved December 10, 2020, from https://www.forbes.com/sites/quora/2017/09/11/what-are-the-most-important-skills-entrepreneurs-need/?sh=4c867954106c

Peter, A. J., Amalraj, E. L. D., & Talluri, V. R. (2020). Commercial Aspects of Biofertilizers and Biostimulants Development Utilizing Rhizosphere Microbes: Global and Indian Scenario. In Rhizosphere microbes. Springer.

Phadnis, A. (2017). *Indian-origin Vasant Narasimhan to head $48 billion pharma giant Novartis*. Buisness Standard.

Phạm, L. (2021). *Unit-1: Introduction to Human Resource Management Structure of Unit*. Retrieved 12 January 2021, from https://www.academia.edu/11542314/Unit_1_Introduction_to_Human_Resource_Management_Structure_of_Unit

Pham, P. V. (2018). Medical biotechnology: techniques and applications. In *Omics Technologies and Bio-Engineering* (pp. 449–469). Academic Press. doi:10.1016/B978-0-12-804659-3.00019-1

Phan, Moffitt, Stokes, Liu, Young, Nie, & Wang. (2009). Convergence of biomarkers, bioinformatics and nanotechnology for individualized cancer treatment. *Trends in Biotechnology, 27*(6), 350-358. doi:10.1016/j.tibtech.2009.02.010

Pharmabiz.com. (2013). *Biocon puts the spotlight on heart disease in women via 'Queen of Heart' campaign*. Pharmabiz.com

Philips, F. S., & Garman, A. N. (2006). Barriers to Entrepreneurship in healthcare Organizations. *Journal of Health and Human Services Administration*, *28*(4), 472–484. PMID:16583847

Phillips, P. W. (2002). Biotechnology in the global agri-food system. *Trends in Biotechnology*, *20*(9), 376–381. doi:10.1016/S0167-7799(02)02039-5 PMID:12175768

Pisano, G. P. (2006). Can science be a business? Lessons from biotech. *Harvard Business Review*, *84*(10), 114–150.

Plucker, J. A., & Beghetto, R. A. (2000). Book review: Conceptual blockbusting, Creative teachers, creative students, Fundamentals of creative thinking, Creativity is forever, Serious creativity: Using the power of lateral thinking to create new ideas, The mind's best work, Understanding those who create, Creativity in the classroom: Schools of curious delight, A whack on the side of the head (Rev. ed.). Gifted Child Quarterly, 44(2), 135-138.

Poltorak, A. I., & Lerner, P. J. (2011). *Essentials of intellectual property: law, economics, and strategy*. John Wiley & Sons. doi:10.1002/9781118983805

Poon, J. P., & MacPherson, A. (2005). Innovation strategies of Asian firms in the United States. *Journal of Engineering and Technology Management*, *22*(4), 255–273. doi:10.1016/j.jengtecman.2005.09.001

Poon, P., & Liyanage, S. (2004). Commercialisation of biotechnology in newly industrialised economies. *International Journal of Biotechnology*, *6*(2-3), 243–259.

Poon, P., & Shantha, L. (2004). 'Commercialisation of biotechnology in newly industrialized economies'. *International Journal of Biotechnology*, *6*(2-3), 243–259. doi:10.1504/IJBT.2004.004812

Porter M. (1998). *Competitive strategy: Techniques for analyzing competitors*. Free Press.

Pota, V. (2010). *India Inc.: How India's Top Ten Entrepreneurs are Winning Globally*. Academic Press.

Powell, K. (2004). Business model competitions catch investors' eyes. *Bioentrepreneur*, 1–3.

Prabu, S. L., Timmadonu, N. K. S., & Thirumurugan, R. (2017). *Introductory Chapter: Intellectual Property Rights, Intellectual Property Rights*. Intech Open.

Prakash, J. (1989). Large-Scale Production of Plants through Micropropagation: Problems, Prospects and Opportunities for India. In *Applications of Biotechnology in Forestry and Horticulture* (pp. 265–274). Springer. doi:10.1007/978-1-4684-1321-2_21

Prasanna, P. L., Rao, L. S., Prasad, A. H., Waris, A., Meera, S. N., Nirmala, B., & Syamaladevi, D. P. (2020). Intellectual property rights protection for plant varieties in India: status, emerging issues, and challenges. *Agricultural Economics Research Review, 32*.

Press Information Bureau (PIB), Media Reports and Press Releases, Department of Industrial Policy and Promotion (DIPP), Department of Biotechnology. (n.d.). http://globalbusinessventures.in/biotechnology-report/

Press Information Bureau Government of India Ministry of Commerce & Industry. (n.d.). *Start-up India Scheme*. Retrieved December 12, 2020, from https://pib.gov.in/newsite/PrintRelease.aspx?relid=190914

Priapantja, P. (2000). Trade secret: how does this apply to drug registration data. In *ASEAN Workshop on the TRIPS Agreement and its Impact on Pharmaceuticals. Department of Health and World Health Organization.*

Prihatiningrum, P., Susilowati, S. M. E., & Prasetyo, A. P. B. (2020). Effect of Bioentrepreneurship on Biology Learning Achievement, Creativity, and Entrepreneurial Interest. *Journal of Innovative Science Education*, *9*(3), 250–259.

PTI. (2013). *Biocon to launch psoriasis drug novel biologic in July*. The Indian Express.

Qaim, M., & De Janvry, A. (2003). Genetically modified crops, corporate pricing strategies, and farmers' adoption: The case of Bt cotton in Argentina. *American Journal of Agricultural Economics*, *85*(4), 814–828. doi:10.1111/1467-8276.00490

Qaim, M., & Zilberman, D. (2003). Yield effects of genetically modified crops in developing countries. *Science*, *299*(5608), 900–902. doi:10.1126cience.1080609

Qureshi, N., Chawla, S., Likitvivatanavong, S., Lee, H. L., & Gill, S. S. (2014). The cry toxin operon of *Clostridium bifermentans* subsp. malaysia is highly toxic to Aedes larval mosquitoes. *Applied and Environmental Microbiology*, *80*(18), 5689–5697.

Quy Loan Duong-Saarits, D. (2012). *Establishing an oriental business in Finland: case: start-up Vietnamese handmade home-textiles company*. Academic Press.

Rabara, R. C., Behrman, G., Timbol, T., & Rushton, P. J. (2017). Effect of spectral quality of monochromatic LED lights on the growth of artichoke seedlings. *Frontiers in Plant Science*, *8*, 190. doi:10.3389/fpls.2017.00190

Rader, R. A. (2008). *Paucity of biopharma approvals raises alarm*. Academic Press.

Rafols, I., Hopkins, M. M., Hoekman, J., Siepel, J., O'Hare, A., Perianes-Rodríguez, A., & Nightingale, P. (2014). Big Pharma, little science? *Technological Forecasting and Social Change*, *81*, 22–38. doi:10.1016/j.techfore.2012.06.007

Ragatz, G. L., Handfield, R. B., & Petersen, K. J. (2002). Benefits associated with supplier integration into new product development under conditions of technology uncertainty. *Journal of Business Research*, *55*(5), 389–400. doi:10.1016/S0148-2963(00)00158-2

Raheem, A., Prinsen, P., Vuppaladadiyam, A. K., Zhao, M., & Luque, R. (2018). A review on sustainable microalgae based biofuel and bioenergy production: Recent developments. *Journal of Cleaner Production, 181*, 42–59. doi:10.1016/j.jclepro.2018.01.125

Rahman, M. A., & Hasegawa, H. (2011). Aquatic arsenic: Phytoremediation using floating macrophytes. *Chemosphere, 83*(5), 633–646.

Ramachandran, S. (1992). Agricultural research under conditions of biotic and abiotic stress and scarce resources. *Biotechnology and Crop Improvement in Asia*, 9-15.

Ramanaiah, T. V. (2002). Indian Acts, Rules, Regulations and Procedures for Handling Genetically Modified Organisms and r-DNA Products. *International Conference on Biotechnology and Development: Challenges and Opportunities for the Asian Region.*

Raman, C. D., & Kanmani, S. (2016). Textile dye degradation using nano zero valent iron: A review. *Journal of Environmental Management, 177*, 341–355. doi:10.1016/j.jenvman.2016.04.034

Rangaswamy, A., & Lilien, G. L. (1997). Software tools for new product development. *JMR, Journal of Marketing Research, 34*(1), 177–184. doi:10.1177/002224379703400115

Rani, M. A. (2017). Startup India: Opportunities & challenges "Start up India stand up India". *ACADEMICIA: An International Multidisciplinary Research Journal, 7*(1), 104–113. doi:10.5958/2249-7137.2017.00008.8

Rao, M. M., & Kingston, D. G. (1982). Plant anticancer agents. XII. Isolation and structure elucidation of new cytotoxic quinones from Tabebuia cassinoides. *Journal of Natural Products, 45*(5), 600–604. doi:10.1021/np50023a014

Rao, Y. V., & Srirekha, G. (2018). Intellectual property rights in business organizations. *International Journal of Engineering and Management Research, 8*(1), 118–124.

Ravi, I., Baunthiyal, M., & Saxena, J. (Eds.). (2014). *Advances in biotechnology.* Springer India. doi:10.1007/978-81-322-1554-7

Read, J. S., & Wiltbank, R. (2012). *How one social entrepreneur creates progress and profits.* Academic Press.

Reddy, A. C., & Anbalagan, C. (2011). Application and Analysis of Marketing and Management on Biotechnology. *International Journal of Research in Management, Science and Technology, 1*, 61–65.

Reid, B. (2003). Budget shortfalls threaten US biotechnology programs. *Bioentrepreneur*, 1–2.

Renkoski, M. A. (1997). Marketing Strategies of Biotechnology Firms: Implications for U.S. Agriculture. *Journal of Agricultural and Applied Economics, 29*(1), 123–128. doi:10.1017/S1074070800029175

Reynolds, P. D. (2005). Understanding business creation: Serendipity and scope in two decades of business creation studies. *Small Business Economics, 24*(4), 359–364. doi:10.100711187-005-0692-x

Rienhoff, H. Y. (1998). Becoming a bioentrepreneur. *Nature Biotechnology, 16*(1), 37–38.

Riezenman, M. J. (2008). *Robots in Rehab.* p. 6 The Institute.

Rifkin, J. (1999). *The biotech century.* New York, NY: Penguin Putnam. *Journal of Technology Education, 10*(2), 272.

Roberts, E. B. (2007). Managing invention and innovation. *Research Technology Management, 50*(1), 35–54. doi:10.1080/08956308.2007.11657418

Robinson, B. H., Bañuelos, G., Conesa, H. M., Evangelou, M. W., & Schulin, R. (2009). The phytomanagement of trace elements in soil. *Critical Reviews in Plant Sciences, 28*(4), 240–266.

Rodriguez-Campos, J., Dendooven, L., Alvarez-Bernal, D., & Contreras-Ramos, S. M. (2014). Potential of earthworms to accelerate removal of organic contaminants from soil: A review. *Applied Soil Ecology*, *79*, 10–25.

Rogers, M. (2000). *Understanding innovative firms: An empirical analysis of the GAPS*. Academic Press.

Roh, M. S., & Lawson, R. H. (1992). Propagation and transplant production technology of new floral crops. In *Transplant Production Systems* (pp. 1–20). Springer. doi:10.1007/978-94-011-2785-1_1

Römer, A., Pache, M., Weißhahn, G., Lindemann, U., & Hacker, W. (2001). Effort-saving product representations in design—Results of a questionnaire survey. *Design Studies*, *22*(6), 473–491. doi:10.1016/S0142-694X(01)00003-5

Roming, F. I., & Ghidurus, M. (2019). *The Potential of Biotechnology to generate Prosperity*. pp. 1-5 Springer Nature Limited.

Ronstadt, R. C. (1984). *Entrepreneurship*. Lord Publishing Corportaion.

Roper, S. (1997). Product innovation and small business growth: A comparison of the strategies of German, UK and Irish companies. *Small Business Economics*, *9*(6), 523–537. doi:10.1023/A:1007963604397

Rorat, A., Wloka, D., Grobelak, A., Grosser, A., Sosnecka, A., Milczarek, M., ... Kacprzak, M. (2017). Vermiremediation of polycyclic aromatic hydrocarbons and heavy metals in sewage sludge composting process. *Journal of Environmental Management*, *187*, 347–353.

Ross, R. (2018). The science behind composting. *REAd (Porto Alegre)*, *15*, 2020.

Ruffner, B., Péchy-Tarr, M., Höfte, M., Bloemberg, G., Grunder, J., Keel, C., & Maurhofer, M. (2015). Evolutionary patchwork of an insecticidal toxin shared between plant-associated pseudomonads and the insect pathogens Photorhabdus and Xenorhabdus. *BMC Genomics*, *16*(1), 1–14.

Ruiu, L. (2015). Insect pathogenic bacteria in integrated pest management. *Insects*, *6*(2), 352–367.

Sabet, N. N., Zand, R., Zheng, Y., & Abedi, V. (2019). Artificial Intelligence Transforms the Future of Health Care. *The American Journal of Medicine*, *32*(7), 795–801. doi:10.1016/j.amjmed.2019.01.017 PMID:30710543

Sadique, S. (2018). Bio Entrepreneurship for Future Sustainable Small Business Perspective. *International Journal of Family Business Management*, *2*(2), 1–3.

Sager, B. (2001). Scenarios on the future of Biotechnology. *Technological Forecasting and Social Change*, *68*(2), 109–129. doi:10.1016/S0040-1625(00)00107-4

Sahayaraj, K. (2014). Nanotechnology and plant biopesticides: an overview. In *Advances in Plant Biopesticides* (pp. 279–293). Springer. doi:10.1007/978-81-322-2006-0_14

Sajc, L., Grubisic, D., & Vunjak-Novakovic, G. (2000). Bioreactors for plant engineering: An outlook for further research. *Biochemical Engineering Journal*, *4*(2), 89–99. doi:10.1016/S1369-703X(99)00035-2

Saklani, A., & Kutty, S. K. (2008). Plant-derived compounds in clinical trials. *Drug Discovery Today*, *13*(3-4), 161–171. doi:10.1016/j.drudis.2007.10.010

Salgado–Banda, H. (2005). *Entrepreneurship and economic growth: An empirical analysis*. Research Paper. Banco de Mexico.

Salgaller, M. L., & Marincola, F. M. (2010). *Biotechnology entrepreneurship-where no research has gone before*. Academic Press.

Salgaller, M. (2010). *Biotechnology Entrepreneurship: From Science to Solutions*. Logo Press.

Sampanpanish, P., Pongsapich, W., Khaodhiar, S., & Khan, E. (2006). Chromium removal from soil by phytoremediation with weed plant species in Thailand. *Water Air and Soil Pollution Focus*, *6*(1-2), 191–206.

SANCO/12173/2014–rev. 4/2015. Final review report of the Standing Committee on Plants, Animals Food and Feed at its meeting on 29 May 2015 in view of the approval of Salix spp. cortex as basic substance in accordance with Regulation (EC) No 1107/2009.

SANCO/12386/2013–rev. 5/2014. Final review report of the Standing Committee on the Food Chain and Animal Health at its meeting on 20 March 2014 in view of the approval of Equisetum arvense L. as basic substance in accordance with Regulation (EC) No 1107/2009.

Sansbury, L. (2002). Strong Government support for UK biotech. *Biotechnology Investors Forum Worldwide*, *2*, 20–22.

SANTE/11309/2017–rev. 2/2017. Final review report of the Standing Committee on Plants, Animals, Food and Feed at its meeting on 6 October 2017 in view of the approval of mustard seeds powder as basic substance in accordance with Regulation (EC) No 1107/20091.

SANTE/11809/2016–rev. 0.1/2017. Final Review report of the Standing Committee on Plants, Animals, Food and Feed at its meeting on 24 January 2017 in view of the approval of Urtica spp. as basic substance in accordance with Regulation (EC) No 1107/2009.

Santra, S. C., Mallick, A., & Samal, A. C. (2015). Biofertilizer for bioremediation. In *Recent trends in biofertilizers*. IK international publishing house Pvt. *Ltd.*

Saputra, K. (2015). *Entrepreneurship Based Education.* Yogyakarta: Diva Press.

Sarah, E. F., Rahim, R., Stephen, M. S., Monali, R., Abdullah, S. D., & Peter, A. S. (2007). India's health biotech sector at a crossroads. *Nature Biotechnology*, *25*(4), 403–417. doi:10.1038/nbt0407-403 PMID:17420744

Saranraj, P., & Naidu, M. A. (2013). Hyaluronic Acid Production and its Applications: A Review. *International Journal of Pharmaceutical and Biological Archives*, *4*(5), 853–859.

Sarkar, J., Kazy, S. K., Gupta, A., Dutta, A., Mohapatra, B., Roy, A., ... Sar, P. (2016). Biostimulation of indigenous microbial community for bioremediation of petroleum refinery sludge. *Frontiers in Microbiology*, *7*, 1407.

Say, J. B. (1827). *Production, Distribution and Consumption of Wealth, John Gragg No.* North Forth Sheet.

Schmoch, U. (2003). Service marks as novel innovation indicator. *Research Evaluation*, *12*(2), 149–156. doi:10.3152/147154403781776708

Schneider, J. (2002). Intellectual property: The driving force for growth and funding. *Journal of Commercial Biotechnology*, *8*(4), 320–324.

Schoemaker, H. J., & Schoemaker, A. F. (1998). The three pillars of bioentrepreneurship. *Nature Biotechnology*, *16*(1), 13–15.

Schumpeter, J. A. (1934). The theory of economic development: an inquiry into profits, capital, credit, interest and the business cycle. Harvard Economic Studies, 46.

Schumpeter, J. A. (1982). *The theory of economic development: An inquiry into profits, capital, credit, interest, and the business cycle (1912/1934).* Transaction Publishers.

Schumpeter, J. (1952). *Can Capitalism survive*. Harper and Row.

Schumpeter, J. A., & Nichol, A. J. (1934). Robinson's economics of imperfect competition. *Journal of Political Economy*, *42*(2), 249–259. doi:10.1086/254595

Schwitzguébel, J. P., van der Lelie, D., Baker, A., Glass, D. J., & Vangronsveld, J. (2002). Phytoremediation: European and American trends successes, obstacles and needs. *Journal of Soils and Sediments*, *2*(2), 91–99.

Segal, M. N., & Johar, J. S. (1992). On improving the effectiveness of test marketing decisions. *European Journal of Marketing*, *26*(4), 21–33. doi:10.1108/03090569210012390

Selvadurai, N., & Matulionyte, R. (2020). Reconsidering creativity: Copyright protection for works generated using artificial intelligence. *Journal of Intellectual Property Law & Practice*, *15*(7), 536–543. doi:10.1093/jiplp/jpaa062

Senior, M. (2020). Europe's biotech renaissance. *Nature Biotechnology*, *38*(4), 408–415.

Serageldin, I. (1999). Biotechnology and food security in the 21st century. *Science*, *285*(5426), 387–389. doi:10.1126cience.285.5426.387 PMID:10411497

Shah, S. (2000). *Sources and patterns of innovation in a consumer products field: Innovations in sporting equipment* (Vol. 4105). Cambridge: Sloan Working Paper.

Shahid, M. F., & Azim, M. K. (2019). Bio-entrepreneurship: Scenario and opportunities for developing countries. *Pakistan Journal of Biochemistry and Molecular Biology*, *52*(2), 27–33.

Shahid, M. F., & Azim, M. K. (2019). Bio-entrepreneurship: Scenario and opportunities for developing countries. *Pakistan Journal of Biochemistry and Molecular Biology.*, *52*(2), 27–33.

Shah, M. P. (2017). Waste water pollution. *Journal of Applied Biomaterials & Functional Materials*, *3*(1), 262–263.

Shaikh, M. (2013). Medical biotechnology: Problems and prospects in Bangladesh. *Journal of Enam Medical College.*, *3*(1), 32–46. doi:10.3329/jemc.v3i1.13873

Shams, K. M., Tichy, G., Fischer, A., Sager, M., Peer, T., Bashar, A., & Filip, K. (2010). Aspects of phytoremediation for chromium contaminated sites using common plants *Urtica dioica, Brassica napus and Zea mays*. *Plant and Soil*, *328*(1), 175–189.

Shane, S., & Venkataraman, S. (2000). The promise of entrepreneurship as a field of research. *Academy of Management Review*, *25*(1), 217–226. doi:10.5465/amr.2000.2791611

Shane, S., & Venkataraman, S. (2001). Entrepreneurship as a field of research: A response to Zahra and Dess, Singh, and Erikson. *Academy of Management Review*, *26*(1), 13–16. doi:10.5465/amr.2001.27879269

Shapiro, R. J., & Mathur, A. (2014). *How India can attract more foreign direct investment, create jobs and increase GDP: the benefits of respecting the intellectual property rights of foreign pharmaceutical producers*. Georgetown McDonough School of Business Research Paper, (2540591).

Sharma, B., Dangi, A. K., & Shukla, P. (2018). Contemporary enzyme based technologies for bioremediation: A review. *Journal of Environmental Management*, *210*, 10–22.

Sharma, J. (2019). Advantages and limitations of in situ methods of bioremediation. *Recent Advances. Biology and Medicine (Aligarh)*, *5*, 10941.

Shimakshi, C. D. (2020). *Biotechnology Entrepreneurship- Leading, Managing and Commercializing Innovative Technologies*. Elsevier Science Publishing.

Shimasaki, C. (2014). Five Essential Elements for Growing Biotechnology Clusters. In Biotechnology Entrepreneurship (pp. 57-72). Academic Press.

Shimasaki, C. (2014). *Biotechnology Entrepreneurship*. Academic Press. doi:10.1016/B978-0-12-404730-3.00004-X

Shimasaki, C. (2020). What is Biotechnology Entrepreneurship. In *Biotechnology Entrepreneurship* (pp. 3–16). Academic Press. doi:10.1016/B978-0-12-815585-1.00001-2

Shoemaker, H., & Shoemaker, A. (1998). The threepillars of bioentrepreneurship. *Nature Biotechnology*, *16*(S1), 13–15. doi:10.1038/5399

Shoji, R., Yajima, R., & Yano, Y. (2008). Arsenic speciation for the phytoremediation by the Chinese brake fern, Pteris vittata. *Journal of Environmental Sciences (China)*, *20*(12), 1463–1468.

Shukla, A. C. (2020). IPR: An Overview. In *Advances in Pharmaceutical Biotechnology* (pp. 439–447). Springer. doi:10.1007/978-981-15-2195-9_28

Sibanda, M. (2021). Enabling Intellectual Property And Innovation Systems For South Africa's Development and Competitiveness. Academic Press.

Sicuia, F. M., & Babeanu, N. (2019). Calina Petruta Cornea, Catalina Voaides, Oana Alina Boiu. *Introduction to Biotech Entrepreneurship: From Idea to Business*, *1*, 53.

Singh, R., Kumar, M., & Mittal, A. (2016). Microbial enzymes: industrial progress in 21st century. *Biotech*, *3*(6), 174 doi:10.100713205-016-0485-8

Singh, V. K. (2020). *Policy and Regulatory Changes for a Successful Startup Revolution: Experiences from the Startup Action Plan in India*. Academic Press.

Singh, A., & Jaiswal, K. K. (2018). Ease of doing business in India: A vision of make in India. *Economic Affairs*, *63*(1), 129–135. doi:10.30954/0424-2513.2018.00150.16

Singh, B., & Satyanarayana, T. (2011). Microbial phytases in phosphorus acquisition and plant growth promotion. *Physiology and Molecular Biology of Plants*, *17*(2), 93–103.

Singh, K. K. (2016). Intellectual property rights in agricultural biotechnology and access to technology: A critical appraisal. *Asian Biotechnology and Development Review*, *18*(3).

Singh, R. K. (2018). *Animal biotechnology*. Oxford and IBH Publishing.

Sinha, D. K. (2020). *Main Functions of an Entrepreneur (Explained With Examples)*. Retrieved December 16, 2020, from https://www.yourarticlelibrary.com/entrepreneur/4-main-functions-of-an-entrepreneur-explained-with-examples/40646

Smale, W. (2020). *It was never my plan to be the boss of a huge company*. BBC News.

Smith, N. C. (1995). Marketing strategies for the ethics era. *Sloan Management Review*, *36*, 85–85.

Smithson, E. (2015). *What Is Branding And Why Is It Important For Your Business?* Retrieved December 12, 2020, from https://www.brandingmag.com/2015/10/14/what-is-branding-and-whyisitimportantforyourbusiness/#:~:text=Branding%2C%20by%20definition%2C%20is%20a,from%20other%20products%20and%20services

Smith, W. K., & Tushman, M. L. (2005). Managing strategic contradictions: A top management model for managing innovation streams. *Organization Science*, *16*(5), 522–536. doi:10.1287/orsc.1050.0134

Sohl, J. (2004). The importance of angels in starting a US biotech venture. *Bioentrepreneur*, 1–3.

Som, N. (2011). Cipla at the forefront of HIV battle. *BioSpectrum, 9*, 12–14.

Soriot, P. (2016). *The magic of leadership: one man's leap into the unknown*. Academic Press.

Sparks, T. C., Dripps, J. E., Watson, G. B., & Paroonagian, D. (2012). Resistance and cross-resistance to the spinosyns–a review and analysis. *Pesticide Biochemistry and Physiology, 102*(1), 1–10.

Srivastava, A., Singh, V., Srivastava, P., & Sinha, R. (2016). Innovation Incubation and Entrepreneurship in Biotechnology- Review. *International Journal of Technical Research and Applications, 4*(4), 66-71.

Srivastava, A., & Prasad, R. (2000). Triglycerides-based diesel fuels. *Renewable & Sustainable Energy Reviews, 4*(2), 111–133. doi:10.1016/S1364-0321(99)00013-1

St. Louis Business Journal. (2009). *Monsanto's Grant named among world's best CEOs. St. Louis Business Journal.*

Stamboulis, Y., & Skayannis, P. (2003). Innovation strategies and technology for experience-based tourism. *Tourism Management, 24*(1), 35–43. doi:10.1016/S0261-5177(02)00047-X

Stam, E., & van de Ven, A. (2019). Entrepreneurial ecosystem elements. *Small Business Economics*, 1–24.

StartupIndia website. (n.d.). *Aspire-A Scheme for Promotion of Innovation, Rural Industries and Entrepreneurship.* Retrieved December 12, 2020, from https://www.startupindia.gov.in/content/sih/en/government-schemes/aspire-scheme-promotion-innovation-entrepreneurship-and-agro-industry.html

Stata, R. (2004). New ways to evaluate innovative ventures. *MIT Sloan Management Review, 45*(3), 96.

Staton, T. (2012). *Joseph Jimenez - The 25 most influential people in biopharma today*. Fierce Biotech.

Stefanec, N. P. (2011). The impact of firm strategies on stock market value in the biotechnology industry. *Applied Financial Economics, 21*(5), 343–352. doi:10.1080/09603107.2010.530214

Steiner, U. (2020). Biotechnology. *FachenglischfürBioTAs und BTAs*, 1–80. doi:10.1007/978-3-662-60666-7_1

Stevenson, H. H., & Jarillo, J. C. (1990). A Paradigm of Entrepreneurship: Entrepreneurial Management. *Strategic Management Journal, 11*, 17–27.

Stevenson, H. H., & Jarillo, J. C. (2007). A paradigm of entrepreneurship: Entrepreneurial management. In *Entrepreneurship* (pp. 155–170). Springer.

Stone, B. (2012). *The Flavr Savr Arrives*. Academic Press.

Stuart, R. W., & Abetti, P. A. (1990). Impact of entrepreneurial and management experience on early performance. *Journal of Business Venturing, 5*(3), 151–162. doi:10.1016/0883-9026(90)90029-S

Subrahmanya, M. B. (2015). New generation start-ups in India: What lessons can we learn from the past? *Economic and Political Weekly*, 56–63.

Sucharitha, P., & Venkateswarlu, D. (2012). Socio-Economic Conditions of Women Micro Entrepreneurs - A Case Study of SPSR Nellore District. *Paripex - Indian Journal of Research, 3*(3), 17-19. doi:10.15373/22501991/mar2014/5

Surana, K., Singh, A., & Sagar, A. D. (2020). Strengthening science, technology, and innovation-based incubators to help achieve Sustainable Development Goals: Lessons from India. *Technological Forecasting and Social Change, 157*, 120057. doi:10.1016/j.techfore.2020.120057

Surbhi, S. (2020). *Difference Between Entrepreneur and Entrepreneurship (with Comparison Chart) - Key Differences.* Academic Press.

Suryana. (2013). *Enterpreneurship: Kiat dan Proses Menuju Sukses.* Jakarta: Salemba Empat.

Su, Y. S., & Hung, L. C. (2008). Spontaneous vs. policy-driven: The origin and evolution of the biotechnology cluster. *Technological Forecasting and Social Change, 76*(5), 608–619. doi:10.1016/j.techfore.2008.08.008

Suzuki, K. (2019). Competition, patent protection, and innovation with heterogeneous firms in an endogenous market structure. *Journal of Public Economic Theory, 22*(3), 729–750. doi:10.1111/jpet.12415

Swain, T. (2019). Biotechnopreneurship: A Resource for the Developing Countries. *Thirteenth Biennial Conference on Entrepreneursh, 120*, 1133-1141.

Swann, P., & Prevezer, M. (1998). A comparison of the dynamics of industrial clustering in computing and biotechnology. *Research Policy, 25*(7), 1139–1158. doi:10.1016/S0048-7333(96)00897-9

Swati, S., Jyothi, N., & Prasanthi, N. K. (2016). A Review On 3d Printed Tablets: A Downloadable Medicine. *Asian Journal of Pharmthiaceutical Technology & Innovation, 04*(20), 34–39.

Tajonar, A. (2014). How to start a biotech company. *Molecular Biology of the Cell, 25*(21), 3280–3283. https://doi.org/10.1091/mbc.E14-06-1162

Tang, C. M., Mahmud, M. A., Foo, F. K., Chu, S. Y., Chiu, R. I., Tanticharoen, M., Zhang, L., & Chang, T. W. (2003). Realizing potential: The state of Asian bioentrepreneurship. *Bioentrepreneur*, 1–10. doi:10.1038/bioent731 PMID:12874972

Tang, W. L., & Zhao, H. (2009). Industrial biotechnology: Tools and applications. *Biotechnology Journal: Healthcare Nutrition Technology, 4*(12), 1725–1739. doi:10.1002/biot.200900127 PMID:19844915

Teece, D. J. (2000). Strategies for managing knowledge assets: The role of firm structure and industrial context. *Long Range Planning, 33*(1), 35–54. doi:10.1016/S0024-6301(99)00117-X

Teixeira, A. A., & Ferreira, C. (2019). Intellectual property rights and the competitiveness of academic spin-offs. *Journal of Innovation & Knowledge, 4*(3), 154–161. doi:10.1016/j.jik.2018.12.002

Teller, J., & Kock, A. (2013). An empirical investigation on how portfolio risk management influences project portfolio success. *International Journal of Project Management, 31*(6), 817–829. doi:10.1016/j.ijproman.2012.11.012

Teng, P. S. (2008). Bioscience entrepreneurship in Asia: Creating value with biology. National Institute of Education Singapore.

Teng, P. P. (2012). Linking education to socially-relevant bioentrepreneurship for Sustainable Development. In *Biology Education for Social and Sustainable Development* (pp. 5–18). Brill Sense.

Teng, P. P. (2016). *Bio-entrepreneurship in Asia: Some learnings to accelerate innovation.* ILRI.

Terán, H., & Singh, S. P. (2002). Comparison of sources and lines selected for drought resistance in common bean. *Crop Science, 42*(1), 64–70. doi:10.2135/cropsci2002.0064

Thakur, S. (2012). Lipases, its sources, properties and applications: A Review. *International Journal of Scientific and Enginewering, 3*(7), 1–29.

The Seattle Times. (2018). Novartis 1Q profit jumps 12 percent as heart drug sales soar. *The Seattle Times.*

Tiago, M. T. P. M. B., & Veríssimo, J. M. C. (2014). Digital marketing and social media: Why bother? *Business Horizons, 57*(6), 703–708. doi:10.1016/j.bushor.2014.07.002

Tidd, J., & Bessant, J. (2011). *Managing innovation: Integrating technological, market and organizational change.* John Wiley & Sons.

Tierney, R., Hermina, W., & Walsh, S. (2013). The pharmaceutical technology landscape: A new form of technology road mapping. *Technological Forecasting and Social Change*, *80*(2), 194–211. doi:10.1016/j.techfore.2012.05.002

Titu, M. A. (2015). Penerapan Model Pembelajaran Project Based Learning (Pjbl) Untuk Meningkatkan Kreativitas Siswa Pada Materi Konsep Masalah Ekonomi. *Prosiding Seminar Nasional Pendidikan Ekonomi FE UNY: Profesionalisme Pendidik dalam Dinamika Kurikulum Pendidikan di Indonesia pada Era MEA. Fakultas Ekonomi UNY*, *13*(7), 176–186.

Tiwari, R., Tiwari, G., Rai, A. K., & Srivastawa, B. (2011). Management of intellectual property rights in India: An updated review. *Journal of Natural Science, Biology, and Medicine*, *2*(1), 2. doi:10.4103/0976-9668.82307 PMID:22470229

Toenniessen, G. H., O'Toole, J. C., & DeVries, J. (2003). Advances in plant biotechnology and its adoption in developing countries. *Current Opinion in Plant Biology*, *6*(2), 191–198. doi:10.1016/S1369-5266(03)00002-5 PMID:12667878

Tonukari, N. J. (2004). Fostering biotechnology entrepreneurship in developing countries. *African Journal of Biotechnology*, *3*(6), 299–301. doi:10.5897/AJB2004.000-2055

Topol, E. J. (2010). Transforming medicine via digital innovation. *Science Translational Medicine*, *2*(16), 16. doi:10.1126citranslmed.3000484 PMID:20371472

Trapp, S., & Karlson, U. (2001). Aspects of phytoremediation of organic pollutants. *Journal of Soils and Sediments*, *1*(1), 37–43.

Troshani, I., & Doolin, B. (2007). Innovation diffusion: A stakeholder and social network view. *European Journal of Innovation Management*, *10*(2), 176–200. doi:10.1108/14601060710745242

Tushman, M. L., & Anderson, P. (1986). Technological discontinuities and organizational environments. *Administrative Science Quarterly*, *31*(3), 439–465. doi:10.2307/2392832

Tyagi, P., Kumar, A., & Sengar, R. S. (2018). The opportunities to develop a successful entrepreneurship and business model in biotechnology: An overview. *Journal of Commercial Biotechnology*, *24*(3), 63–68.

Uctu, R., & Jafia, R. C. C. (2013). Bio-entrepreneurship as a bridge between science and business in a regional cluster: South Africa's first attempts. *Science & Public Policy*, *41*(2), 219–233. doi:10.1093cipolct049

Ugalmugle, S. & Swain, R. (2020). *Health Economics & Outcomes Research (HEOR) Services Market Size and Share.* Industry Report. 2020-2026.

Ullah, R., & Zohra, R. R. (2018). *The Entrepreneurial Scientists Serving Science and Society*. SATHA.

Ulrich, K. T., & Eppinger, S. D. (2011). *Product design and development*. McGraw-Hill/Irwin.

USDA. (2013). *Adoption of Genetically Engineered Crops in the U.S.* USDA.

Vamerali, T., Bandiera, M., & Mosca, G. (2010). Field crops for phytoremediation of metal-contaminated land. A review. *Environmental Chemistry Letters*, *8*(1), 1–17.

Van Lijsebettens, M., & Angenon, G. (2013). Thirty years of transgenic research in plants. *The International Journal of Developmental Biology*, *57*(6-8), 447.

van Tulder, R., & Lucht, L. (2019). Reversing Materiality: From a Reactive Matrix to a Proactive SDG Agenda. In Innovation for Sustainability (pp. 271-289). Palgrave Macmillan.

VanGundy, A. B. (1988). Techniques of Structured Problem Solving, Van Norstrand Reinhold. *Techniques, 4*(6), 4-57.

Veeresham, C. (2012). *Natural products derived from plants as a source of drugs*. Academic Press.

Venosa, A. D. (2004). *Literature review on the use of commercial bioremediation agents for cleanup of oil-contaminated estuarine environments. In National risk management research laboratory, office of research and development.* US Environmental Protection Agency.

Verma, A. S., Agrahari, S., Rastogi, S., & Singh, A. (2011). Biotechnology in the realm of history. *Journal of Pharmacy & Bioallied Sciences, 3*(3), 321–323.

Vermij, P. (2004). Patenting costs cast a shadow on European biotech. *Bioentrepreneur,* 1–2.

Vernon, J. A. (2005). Examining the link between price regulation and pharmaceutical R&D investment. *Health Economics, 14*(1), 1–16. doi:10.1002/hec.897 PMID:15386673

Veryzer Jr, R. W. (1998). Key factors affecting customer evaluation of discontinuous new products. *Journal of Product Innovation Management, 15*(2), 136-150.

Veugelers, R., & Cassiman, B. (1999). Make and buy in innovation strategies: Evidence from Belgian manufacturing firms. *Research Policy, 28*(1), 63–80. doi:10.1016/S0048-7333(98)00106-1

Vijayaraghavan, K., & Dutz, M. A. (2012). *Biotechnology innovation for inclusive growth: a study of Indian policies to foster accelerated technology adaptation for affordable development.* The World Bank.

Vishwasra, S., Mane, & Khot, N. (2020). Copyright Act, (1957): A Study with reference to selected cases in India. *Journal of Advancements in Library Science, 6*(1), 336–341.

Von Krogh, G., Nonaka, I., & Aben, M. (2001). Making the most of your company's knowledge: A strategic framework. *Long Range Planning, 34*(4), 421–439. doi:10.1016/S0024-6301(01)00059-0

Waghunde, R. R., Shelake, R. M., & Sabalpara, A. N. (2016). Trichoderma: A significant fungus for agriculture and environment. *African Journal of Agricultural Research, 11*(22), 1952–1965.

Wagner, M., Van Phu, N., Azomahou, T., & Wehrmeyer, W. (2002). The relationship between the environmental and economic performance of firms: An empirical analysis of the European paper industry. *Corporate Social Responsibility and Environmental Management, 9*(3), 133–146. doi:10.1002/csr.22

Walsh, V. (1984). Invention and Innovation in the Chemical Industry: Demand-pull or Discovery-push? *Research Policy, 13*(4), 211–234. doi:10.1016/0048-7333(84)90015-5

Walsh, V., & Green, K. (1993). Walsh, V. and Green, K. (1993) 'Demand, the public sector and innovation in biotechnology. In E. J. Blakely & K. W. Willoughby (Eds.), *The Management and Economic Potential of Biotechnology* (pp. 28–46). Special Publication of the International Journal of Technology Management.

Walton, A. (1998). Some thoughts on bioentrepreneurship. *Nature Biotechnology, 16*(1), 7–8.

Waltz, E. (2005). Biotech entrepreneur, educate thyself! *Bioentrepreneur,* 1–2.

Wang, R., Cao, Q., Zhao, Q., & Li, Y. (2018). Bioindustry in China: An overview and perspective. *New Biotechnology, 40,* 46–51. doi:10.1016/j.nbt.2017.08.002 PMID:28827157

Wang, S., Just, D. R., & Pinstrup-Andersen, P. (2008). Bt-cotton and secondary pests. *International Journal of Biotechnology, 10*(2/3), 113. doi:10.1504/IJBT.2008.018348

Watal, J. (2014). Is TRIPS a Balanced Agreement from the Perspective of Recent Free Trade Agreements? In *EU Bilateral Trade Agreements and Intellectual Property: For Better or Worse?* (pp. 41–57). Springer. doi:10.1007/978-3-642-39097-5_3

Wellington, S., & Jammu, S. (2014). Foreign direct investment in India. *International Journal Of Econometrics And Financial Management*, *2*(3), 95–101.

Wenzel, W. W., Lombi, E., & Adriano, D. C. (1999). Biogeochemical processes in the rhizosphere: role in phytoremediation of metal-polluted soils. In *Heavy metal stress in plants* (pp. 273–303). Springer.

White, P. M., Wolf, D. C., Thoma, G. J., & Reynolds, C. M. (2006). Phytoremediation of alkylated polycyclic aromatic hydrocarbons in a crude oil-contaminated soil. *Water, Air, and Soil Pollution*, *169*(1), 207–220.

Williams, G., & Walsh, G. (2004). Scaling the biobusiness information mountain. *Bioentrepreneur*, 1–4.

Wind, Y., Douglas, S. P., & Perlmutter, H. V. (1973). Guidelines for developing international marketing strategies. *Journal of Marketing*, *37*(2), 14–23. doi:10.1177/002224297303700205

WIPO website. (2020). *Global Innovation Index 2020*. Retrieved December 12, 2020, from https://www.wipo.int/global_innovation_index/en/2020/

Wise Guy Reports. (2017). *Agricultural biotechnology – global market outlook (2016–2022)*. Author.

Witholt, B. (1999). The European university as a startup generator. *Nature Biotechnology*, *17*(1), BE7–BE8.

Woiceshyn, J., & Hartel, D. (1996). Predicting value-added progress of biotechnology firms: An exploratory study. *Journal of Engineering and Technology Management*, *13*(2), 163–187. doi:10.1016/S0923-4748(96)01002-8

Wu, J. X., & Li, L. (2019). Sustainability Initiatives in the Fashion Industry. In R. Beltramo, A. Romani, & P. Cantore (Eds.), *Fashion Industry - An Itinerary Between Feelings and Technology*. IntechOpen London.

Wu, J., Li, S., & Selover, D. D. (2012). Foreign direct investment vs. foreign portfolio investment. *Management International Review*, *52*(5), 643–670. doi:10.100711575-011-0121-0

Wu, Q., Liu, J., Wang, X., Feng, L., Wu, J., Zhu, X., Wen, W., & Gong, X. (2020). Organ-on-a-chip: Recent breakthroughs and future prospects. *Biomedical Engineering Online*, *19*(1), 9. doi:10.118612938-020-0752-0 PMID:32050989

Wyse, J., & Luria, G. (2021). Trends in intellectual property rights protection for medical cannabis and related products. *Journal of Cannabis Research*, *3*(1), 1–22. doi:10.118642238-020-00057-7 PMID:33526141

Xia, H., Chen, L., Wang, F., & Lu, B. R. (2010). Yield benefit and underlying cost of insect-resistance transgenic rice: Implication in breeding and deploying transgenic crops. *Field Crops Research*, *118*(3), 215–220. doi:10.1016/j.fcr.2010.05.008

Xu, B. (2009). *R&D innovation and the value of cash in the biotech industry*. Academic Press.

Yang, G., & Maskus, K. E. (2001). Intellectual property rights and licensing: An econometric investigation. *Weltwirtschaftliches Archiv*, *137*(1), 58–79. doi:10.1007/BF02707600

Yateem, A. (2014). *Bioremediation strategies for the cleanup of oil contamination in an arid environment: an insight on the Kuwaiti experience. In Bioremediation: processes, challenges and future prospects*. Nova.

Yavari, S., Malakahmad, A., & Sapari, N. B. (2015). A review on phytoremediation of crude oil spills. *Water, Air, and Soil Pollution*, *226*(8), 1–18.

Yesil-Celiktas, O., Gurel, A., & Vardar-Sukan, F. (2010). Large scale cultivation of plant cell and tissue culture in bioreactors. *Transworld Research Network*, *37*(661), 2.

Young, L. S., Searle, P. F., Onion, D., & Mautner, V. (2006). Viral gene therapy strategies: From basic science to clinical application. *The Journal of Pathology*, *208*(2), 299–318. doi:10.1002/path.1896 PMID:16362990

Yusuf, S., & Nabeshima, K. (2005). Creative industries in east Asia. *Cities (London, England), 22*(2), 109–122. doi:10.1016/j.cities.2005.01.001

Zekos, G. I. (2006). Nanotechnology and biotechnology patents. *International Journal of Law and Information Technology, 14*(3), 310–369. doi:10.1093/ijlit/eal011

Zeljezić, D. (2004). Geneticki preinaceni organizmi u hrani—proizvodnja, detekcija i moguće opasnosti [Genetically modified organisms in food--production, detection and risks]. *Arhiv za Higijenu Rada i Toksikologiju, 55*(4), 301–312.

Zucker, L. G., & Darby, M. R. (1996). Star scientists and institutional transformation: Patterns of invention and innovation in the formation of the biotechnology industry. *Proceedings of the National Academy of Sciences of the United States of America, 93*(23), 12709–12716. doi:10.1073/pnas.93.23.12709 PMID:8917483

Zucker, L. G., Darby, M., & Armstrong, J. (2002). Commercializing knowledge: University science, knowledge capture, and firm performance in biotechnology. *Management Science, 48*(1), 138–153.

About the Contributors

Avinash Gupta has more than 14 years of rich experience in academics and industry. Dr. Gupta is an alumnus of IIM Indore. He has awarded with a Ph.D. in Project Management from the Department of Accounting & Business Statistics, University of Rajasthan, Jaipur. He has involved in Accounting, cost planning, and control management division in Aditya Birla Group, Infosys, and Polymedicure Group. Dr. Gupta has presented National & International research papers & attended conferences. He has published research papers and case studies in reputed international journals. His area of specialization is Financial Accounting, Banking, Entrepreneurship Development, and General Management.

Avni Jain is pursuing her doctorate in Biotechnology from Banasthali Vidyapith.

Ganaraj K. received the Bachelor's and Master's degree from Visvesvaraya Technological University, Belagavi in Computer Science and Engineering in 2015 and 2018, respectively. He has 7 months of Industry experience and 3 years of Teaching experience. He is currently working as Assistant Professor in Information Science & Engineering Department, Sahyadri College of Engineering and Management, Mangaluru. His current research interests include Machine Learning, Data Analytics.

Jayapadmini Kanchan is Assistant Professor of Information Science & Engineering department. She has pursued B.E from HKBKCE, Bangalore, M.Tech from SCEM, Mangaluru. Her area of interest includes Network Security, Data Analytics, and Machine Learning.

Diksha Kumar is research scholar from Banasthali vidyapith (2017-20121) and was selected for traineeship under the DBT supported Bioinformatics Centre (Sub DIC).

Pawan Kumar is an assistant professor of Botany at Kalindi College, University of Delhi, India. A strong enthusiasm in the botanical and allied fields of biology motivated him to pursue an honours course in Bachelor of Science followed by a Master's degree in Botany from University of Delhi. He has qualified National level Eligibility Test for lecturership conducted by Indian Agriculture Research Institute, New Delhi, India and has been a recipient of a prestigious Junior and Senior Research Fellowship (2013-2018) granted by University Grants Commission, (UGC), India. During his PhD research at Department of Botany, University of Delhi, he has worked extensively on molecular biology and biochemistry of proteolytic digestion of a notorious pest of crucifer unraveling the mechanisms of host-plant preference and performance. He has published his work in peer reviewed journals of international repute thereby reporting unique sequences of proteases expressed in guts of a specialist pest. He is actively involved in teaching courses at undergraduate level that are interdisciplinary in nature such as 'Biostatistics', 'Analytical techniques in plant sciences' and 'Industrial and Environmental Microbiology'. An online e-Lecture portal (available to see at www.botanypedia.com) that caters to students at different levels of their study has been created by him to provide an innovative and interactive environment for learning biology. Deriving inspiration from the life of a plant, he has co-authored a self-help book entitled, 'Garden of Life…Learning to blossom within' that follows an analogy of a life of a garden and inspires students to undertake biology and most importantly their life goals as a leader. He is greatly inspired by the revolution brought in the field of biology due to simultaneously advancements in the allied fields of system biology and aspires to bring innovation in teaching and research through academia-industry collaborations in future.

Vijay Laxmi is currently working as research scholar in department of Bioscience and Biotechnology, Banasthali Vidyapith. She is currently working in nanomaterial synthesis and characterization.

Jyoti Mathura is Associate Professor in department of Bioscience and Biotechnology at Banasthali Vidapith, Banasthali, Newai, Rajasthan, India.

Shubhita Mathur received the Bachelor's and Master's degree from Banasthali Vidyapith. She was awarded Ph.D. in Biochemistry from Delhi University, India. She has presented her research work in National and International conferences. She has also received the prestigious travel grant from Bill and Melinda Gates Foundation. She is currently employed as Assistant Professor at Jaipur National University, Jaipur, India. Her research area of interest includes Vaccine development and gut microbiome interaction.

Rajatha received her Bachelor's degree in Information science and engineering, Master of technology in Computer Science and Engineering from Visvesvaraya Technological Institute in the year 2014 and 2016 respectively. She has 3 years of teaching experience. She is currently working in the department of Computer Science and Engineering, SJB institute of Technology, Bengaluru. Her current research interests include data mining,machine learning, data science and data analytics.

Asha B. Shetty received the Bachelor's degree from Visvesvaraya Technological University, Belagavi in Computer Science and Engineering in 2015 and Master's degree from Visvesvaraya Technological University, Belagavi in Computer Network Engineering in 2017, respectively. She has got 3 years of teaching experience. She is currently working as Assistant Professor in Information Science & Engineering Department, Sahyadri College of Engineering and Management, Mangaluru. Her current research interests include Computer Networks, Data Analytics

Anjana Singh is an assistant professor of Botany at Deshbandhu College, University of Delhi, India. Formerly, she has been associated with teaching undergraduate students of Sri Venkateswara College and Kirorimal College at University of Delhi. She is a graduate in Bachelor of Science in Environmental Science and holds master degree in Sciences and philosophy in Botany from University of Delhi. She has qualified National level Eligibility Test for lecturership conducted by The Council of Scientific & Industrial Research (CSIR), University Grants Commission (UGC) & Indian Agriculture Research Institute (IARI), New Delhi, India. During her Master of Philosophy research at Department of Botany, University of Delhi, she has worked extensively on 'Studies on Accumulation of Heavy Metals in Mosses of Contrasting Habitats'. Furthermore, her research interests include the study of diversity and distribution of Bryophytes, study of growth pattern in relation to the changing climatic conditions, accumulation of metals especially the pollutants by bryophytes. She has published her work in peer reviewed journals of international repute thereby unraveling the mechanisms of heavy metal accumulation in mosses of ecological importance. She has been actively involved in teaching courses at undergraduate level.

Neha Singh is pursuing her doctorate in Biotechnology from Banasthali Vidyapith.

Dwaipayan Sinha is an Assistant Professor in Botany under West Bengal Education Service, Government of West Bengal and is presently posted in Government General Degree College, Mohanpur, Paschim Medinipur, West Bengal. He was previously posted in Department of Botany, Bidhannagar College Salt Lake. He had completed his graduation with honours in Botany from the prestigious Presidency College, Kolkata and then post graduation in Botany from University of Delhi, North Campus, Delhi. He had done his PhD from CSIR-Indian Institute of Toxicology Research and worked on antioxidant potential of Pines. He is actively involved in research and is having a number of papers in reputed peer reviewed journals. He is also author of several chapters in edited book. He is presently working on phytodiversity and medicinal plant and bioprospection of antioxidant principles from medicinal plants. He is a life member of International Academy of Science and Research and International Foundation for Environment and Ecology, Kolkata.

Jyoti Yadav is a research scholar in Department of Bioscience and Biotechnology, Banasthali Vidyapith, under the supervision of Dr. Suphiya Khan. She has an expertise in Nanoplastic pollution detection and remediation.

Shaili Yadav is assistant professor in Department of Biotechnology and Microbiology at Janta Degree College, Bakewar-Etawah affiliated to ChhatraPati Shahu ji Maharaj University, Kanpur), Uttar Pradesh, India.

Index

www.ingramcontent.com/pod-product-compliance
Lightning Source LLC
LaVergne TN
LVHW062137300926
849161LV00010B/2560